A Grammar of Bora
with
Special Attention to Tone

SIL International®
Publications in Linguistics

Publication 148

Publications in Linguistics are published by SIL International®. The series is a venue for works covering a broad range of topics in linguistics, especially the analytical treatment of minority languages from all parts of the world. While most volumes are authored by members of SIL, suitable works by others will also form part of the series.

Editor in Chief
Michael C. Cahill

Volume Editor
Mary Ruth Wise

Production Staff
Bonnie Brown, Managing Editor
Barbara Alber, Cover design
Diana Weber, Cover photograph

A Grammar of Bora
with
Special Attention to Tone

Wesley Thiesen
and
David Weber

SIL International®
Dallas, Texas

©2012 by SIL International®
Library of Congress Catalog No: 2012933805
ISBN:978-1-55671-301-9
ISSN: 1040-0850

Printed in the United States of America

All Rights Reserved

No part of this publication may be reproduced, stored in a retrieval system, or transmitted in any form or by any means—electronic, mechanical, photocopy, recording, or otherwise—without the express permission of the SIL International®. However, short passages, generally understood to be within the limits of fair use, may be quoted without written permission.

Typeset by the second author with X̅ƎTEX. The Bora texts were formatted with the interlinear text package of Kew & McConnel (1990).

Copies of this and other publications of the SIL International® may be obtained from:

SIL International Publications
7500 W. Camp Wisdom Road
Dallas, TX 75236-5629

Voice: 972-708-7404
Fax: 972-708-7363
publications_intl@sil.org
www.ethnologue.com/bookstore.asp

In memory of Eva Thiesen (1925–2009)

Contents

List of Figures — xviii

List of Tables — xxi

Preface — xxv
   Authorship — xxv
   Acknowledgments — xxvi
   Why is Bora so interesting? — xxvii

Abbreviations and Conventions — xxix
   Abbreviations — xxix
   Conventions — xxxii

1 The Bora People — 1
   1.1 Demographics and history — 1
   1.2 The future of the Bora language — 5
   1.3 Social structure — 6
      1.3.1 Festivals — 7
      1.3.2 The *patrón* system — 11
   1.4 Work — 12
      1.4.1 Agriculture and gathering — 12
      1.4.2 Food preparation — 13
      1.4.3 Hunting — 15
      1.4.4 Fishing — 15
      1.4.5 Animal husbandry — 16
      1.4.6 House construction — 16
      1.4.7 Weaving — 18
   1.5 Dress and personal adornment — 18
   1.6 Religion — 19
      1.6.1 The boa constrictor — 20
      1.6.2 Burial — 21
   1.7 Music — 21

	1.8	The Bora signal drums	21
		1.8.1	Various functions of the drums	22
		1.8.2	How the signal drums are made	23
		1.8.3	How messages are drummed	23
2	**Phonology**		**27**
	2.1	The Bora writing system	27
	2.2	Syllables	28
	2.3	Vowels	29
		2.3.1	Rules applying to vowels	30
		2.3.2	Vowel length	31
	2.4	Consonants	33
		2.4.1	The glottal stop	35
		2.4.2	Palatalization	37
		2.4.3	Preaspiration	40
	2.5	Apocope	42
	2.6	Reduplication	43
	2.7	Quantity	47
		2.7.1	The minimal word	48
		2.7.2	"Heavy" syllables	48
		2.7.3	Suffixes that add weight to a monosyllabic root	49
		2.7.4	Quantity alternations	50
			2.7.4.1 Length suppressed by -ːcu 'duIn' and -ːne 'plural'	50
			2.7.4.2 Vowel length alternating with [*] before vowel length	51
			2.7.4.3 Maintaining syllable weight in imperatives	51
			2.7.4.4 Length in pronouns	52
			2.7.4.5 Allomorphy conditioned by preceding syllable weight	52
	2.8	Unresolved issues	53
3	**Tone**		**55**
	3.1	Some basic facts and overview	56
	3.2	The tonal elements	60
	3.3	Default tones	60
		3.3.1	Final default low tone	60
		3.3.2	Default high tone	62
	3.4	The cyclical nature of suffixation	63
	3.5	Lexically marked tones	64
		3.5.1	Lexically marked low tones	65
		3.5.2	Lexically marked high tones	66

	3.5.3 Nonfinite verbs	68
3.6	The *LLX constraint	69
3.7	Phrase final tone changes	70
	3.7.1 Penultimate low tone split	70
	3.7.2 Final low tone split	73
3.8	The interaction of tone and vowel length	75
3.9	The tones of isolated words ("citation forms")	76
3.10	Tone changes caused by suffixes	76
	3.10.1 Suffixes affecting the host's final tones	77
	3.10.2 Affixes that affect the host's initial tones	78
	3.10.3 Suffixes affecting both initial and final tones	79
3.11	Tone conflicts and their resolution	79
	3.11.1 Blocking	80
	3.11.2 Delinking	82
	3.11.2.1 Delinking by the person markers	83
	3.11.2.2 Delinking by -Ⓛdi 'animate', -Ⓛke 'objAn', -Ⓛki 'purpose', -Ⓛma 'with', -Ⓛte 'go.do' and -Ⓛdu 'like'	84
	3.11.2.3 Delinking by #Ⓗ...jɨɨ(va) 'deny'	85
	3.11.2.4 Delinking by -Ⓛσ 'future'	86
	3.11.2.5 Delinking by -ro ~ -ra 'frustrative, contra-expectation'	87
	3.11.3 Bumping	88
3.12	Grammatical tone	88
	3.12.1 Tone on the verbs of subordinate clauses	89
	3.12.2 The tones of proclitics	93
	3.12.3 The default tone of nouns and classifiers	94
3.13	The rule of three and boundary marking	95
3.14	Areas for further study	96
4	**Word Formation**	**99**
4.1	Derivation with tone: nonfinite verbs	100
4.2	Compounding	103
	4.2.1 Compound nouns	103
	4.2.1.1 Headed by classifiers	103
	4.2.1.2 Headed by nouns	103
	4.2.1.3 Object incorporation	105
	4.2.2 Compound verbs	106
4.3	Affixal derivation	108
	4.3.1 Verbs derived from verbs	108
	4.3.2 Verbs derived from nouns	109
	4.3.2.1 -lle 'treat like, regard as'	109

		4.3.2.2	-nu 'do'	110

- 4.3.2.2 -nu 'do' 110
- 4.3.2.3 -ːve 'sIn' and -te 'become' 111
- 4.3.2.4 -vɑ 'have' 111
- 4.3.2.5 -jkimei 'behave like' 112
- 4.3.3 Nouns from verbs with -tɑ 'corresponding to' ... 113
- 4.3.4 Participles 113
- 4.3.5 Negative deverbal adjectives 116
- 4.3.6 Affixal "verbs" 116
  - 4.3.6.1 -pi 'excessive' 117
  - 4.3.6.2 -lle 'try' 117
  - 4.3.6.3 -pejtso 'upon encountering' 117
  - 4.3.6.4 Relocation to or from doing 118
- 4.3.7 Adverbs and adjectives 121
- 4.4 Verbs with incorporated instruments 123

5 Main Clauses and Verbs   125

- 5.1 Basic sentence structure 125
- 5.2 Subjects indicated with classifiers 127
- 5.3 Predicate complements 129
- 5.4 End of main verb markers 131
  - 5.4.1 -hi ∼ -h ⟨t⟩ 131
  - 5.4.2 -ne ⟨n⟩ 132
- 5.5 Statements of fact 133
- 5.6 The structure of the verb 135
- 5.7 Verbal categories 136
  - 5.7.1 Transitive, intransitive, stative 136
  - 5.7.2 Single or multiple action 137
  - 5.7.3 Marking multiple action with intransitive verbs .. 140
- 5.8 Valence-changing suffixes 144
  - 5.8.1 -tso 'causative' 144
  - 5.8.2 -mei 'reflexive or passive' 147
  - 5.8.3 -jcɑtsi 'reciprocal' 148
- 5.9 Tense 149
  - 5.9.1 The present-past tense 149
  - 5.9.2 The future tense 149
  - 5.9.3 Tense-marking second-position clitics 151
    - 5.9.3.1 -pe 'remote past' 152
    - 5.9.3.2 -ne ∼ -hne 'recent past' 152
    - 5.9.3.3 -i ∼ -iíkye 'projected time (PT)' 153
- 5.10 Aspect 154
  - 5.10.1 Aspect and the singular versus multiple contrast . 154
  - 5.10.2 Aspect indicated by -ʔiˣkʲʰa 'habitual' 154

		5.11 Mood 157

- 5.11 Mood . . . 157
- 5.12 Adverbs . . . 157
  - 5.12.1 Affixal adverbs . . . 157
    - 5.12.1.1 -juco (:) 'now' . . . 157
    - 5.12.1.2 -ro ~ -ra ~ -yo ~ -ya 'frustrative, contra-expectation' . . . 158
  - 5.12.2 Lexical adverbs . . . 159

6 Classifiers — 163
- 6.1 Form, distribution, tone . . . 163
  - 6.1.1 General facts about animate and inanimate classifiers . . . 163
    - 6.1.1.1 Animate classifiers . . . 163
    - 6.1.1.2 Inanimate classifiers . . . 167
  - 6.1.2 Classifiers derived from verb roots . . . 168
  - 6.1.3 Classifiers cognate with other morphemes . . . 170
  - 6.1.4 The tones of classifiers . . . 171
- 6.2 The uses of classifiers . . . 173
  - 6.2.1 Classifiers indicating the subject . . . 173
  - 6.2.2 Classifiers with adjectives . . . 174
  - 6.2.3 Classifiers with bound nouns . . . 175
  - 6.2.4 Classifiers to form qualifier phrases . . . 175
    - 6.2.4.1 Classifiers with demonstrative, indefinite, and interrogative modifiers . . . 175
    - 6.2.4.2 Classifiers with numerals and quantifiers . 176
    - 6.2.4.3 Classifiers forming connectives with a(:)- 'thematic' . . . 177
  - 6.2.5 Classifiers with nonfinite verbs . . . 177
  - 6.2.6 Classifiers as heads of relative clauses . . . 178
  - 6.2.7 The classifier -nɛ with complement clauses . . . 178
  - 6.2.8 Classifiers with free possessive pronouns . . . 179
  - 6.2.9 Classifiers to individuate collective or general nouns 179
  - 6.2.10 Multiple classifiers . . . 179
  - 6.2.11 Classifiers after -ɛ 'pertain to' or -ɛmɛ 'similar to' . 180
  - 6.2.12 Reference in discourse . . . 181
- 6.3 The structural status of classifiers . . . 182
  - 6.3.1 Some classifiers have corresponding free nouns . . 182
  - 6.3.2 Classifiers have the referential properties typical of nouns . . . 184
  - 6.3.3 Classifiers have the distribution typical of nouns . 185
  - 6.3.4 Classifiers head their phrases . . . 186

7 Nouns and Noun Phrases — 189

- 7.1 Apposition 190
- 7.2 Nouns 193
  - 7.2.1 Concrete 193
    - 7.2.1.1 Animate 193
    - 7.2.1.2 Inanimate 195
  - 7.2.2 Abstract 197
  - 7.2.3 Locative nouns 198
- 7.3 Number 200
  - 7.3.1 The singular of collective nouns 200
  - 7.3.2 Plural nouns formed with plural classifiers 200
  - 7.3.3 Pluralization with -⑴mɯ 201
  - 7.3.4 The plural suffix -nɛ 202
  - 7.3.5 The plural suffix -⁽ʔ⁾hì̀ 202
  - 7.3.6 The plural suffix -ʔaɲɛ 'various' 204
  - 7.3.7 The plural suffix -βa 205
- 7.4 Suffixes that modify nouns 206
  - 7.4.1 -coba 'augment' 206
  - 7.4.2 -wuu ~ -wu 'diminutive, small, few' 207
  - 7.4.3 -uvu 'maximal' 207
- 7.5 Quantifier phrases 208
- 7.6 Conjoining noun phrases 208
- 7.7 Numeral phrases 210
  - 7.7.1 The composition of numeral phrases 212
  - 7.7.2 Agreement with numeral phrases 218
- 7.8 Adjectives 219
  - 7.8.1 Prenominal modifiers 219
    - 7.8.1.1 ímɨa 'of good quality' 219
    - 7.8.1.2 mítyane 'much' 222
  - 7.8.2 Qualifier phrases 223
  - 7.8.3 Predicate adjectives 225
  - 7.8.4 Adjectives used as adverbs 226
  - 7.8.5 Suffixes added to adjectives 226
    - 7.8.5.1 -wuu ~ -wu 'diminutive, very' 226
    - 7.8.5.2 -icho 'somewhat' 227
    - 7.8.5.3 The co-occurrence of -kpɯ(ɯ)(:) and -itʃʰo 228
    - 7.8.5.4 -uvu 'maximal' 229

8 Pronouns — 231

- 8.1 Personal pronouns 231
  - 8.1.1 The form of personal pronouns 231
  - 8.1.2 The use of personal pronouns 234

	8.2	Inanimate anaphoric pronouns	236
	8.3	The anaphor i 'self'	237
	8.4	Demonstrative pronouns	240
	8.4.1	Animate demonstrative pronouns	240
	8.4.2	Inanimate demonstrative pronouns	241
	8.5	Indefinite pronouns	242
	8.5.1	Animate indefinite pronouns	242
	8.5.2	Inanimate indefinite pronouns	245
	8.6	Possessive pronouns	247

9 The Genitive Construction — 251
- 9.1 Genitive tone — 251
  - 9.1.1 Stem-forming suffixes — 254
  - 9.1.2 Lexically marked tones — 255
  - 9.1.3 Affixation — 258
  - 9.1.4 The possessor's penult high extension — 258
- 9.2 The uses of the genitive construction — 260

10 Case and Grammatical Relations — 267
- 10.1 Subject — 268
- 10.2 -ke ~ -ø 'object' — 273
  - 10.2.1 Object complements — 274
  - 10.2.2 The addressee — 274
  - 10.2.3 Objects as cliticized classifiers — 274
  - 10.2.4 Causee — 275
- 10.3 -vu 'goal' or 'theme' — 275
  - 10.3.1 Goal — 276
  - 10.3.2 Theme — 276
  - 10.3.3 The object of a causativized verb — 280
- 10.4 -tu 'source' (ablative) — 282
  - 10.4.1 Some matters of form — 282
  - 10.4.2 Source — 283
  - 10.4.3 Partitive — 285
  - 10.4.4 About, concerning — 286
  - 10.4.5 Site of attachment — 287
  - 10.4.6 Time after — 289
  - 10.4.7 Contrast — 290
- 10.5 -ri 'inanimate obliques' — 290
  - 10.5.1 Instrument — 290
  - 10.5.2 Cause or reason — 291
  - 10.5.3 Location — 292
  - 10.5.4 Medium — 293

10.5.5 Topic of conversation	294
10.6 -ma 'with'	294
10.6.1 Co-subject	294
10.6.2 Circumstance	296
10.6.3 Instrument	296
10.6.4 Beneficiary	297
10.7 -hlliíhye ~ -llii 'motive'	298
10.7.1 Beneficiary	298
10.7.2 Reason	298
10.8 -hdu 'comparative'	299
10.9 Vocative	302

11 Clitics 305

11.1 Evidential clitics	306
11.1.1 -hja 'nonwitnessed'	306
11.1.2 -va 'reportative'	307
11.2 Adverbial clitics	310
11.2.1 -re ~ -ye 'only'	310
11.2.2 -juco 'focus'	311
11.2.3 -uba 'probable'	312
11.2.4 -háaáca ~ -ha 'realize'	313
11.2.5 -ra ~ -ro 'frustrative, contraexpectation'	313
11.2.6 -ca 'affirm'	314
11.2.7 -haja ~ -ha 'challenge veracity'	314
11.2.8 -ami 'disgust'	315
11.2.9 -hde 'be able'	316
11.2.10 -mei 'pity'	316
11.2.11 -jtane 'exclude'	316
11.2.12 -véjɨu 'similar to'	317
11.2.13 The combination -i-ro 'contrary'	317

12 Some Minor Categories 319

12.1 Conjunctions	319
12.2 Interjections	320
12.3 Particles	320
12.4 Onomatopoeia	322

13 Negation 325

13.1 Negation with adjectives	325
13.2 Simple negation in finite clauses	326
13.3 Contrastive negation with -jɨɨva 'deny'	327
13.3.1 -jɨɨva with verbs	328

13.3.2 -jɨ́ɨ́va with nominals	329
13.4 Prohibitions	330
13.5 Negation in subordinate clauses	331

14 Imperatives 333
- 14.1 The form of imperatives ... 333
  - 14.1.1 Tone in imperatives ... 334
  - 14.1.2 Comparison of imperative and genitive pronominal proclitics ... 337
  - 14.1.3 Stem changes in imperatives ... 337
- 14.2 Modifying imperatives ... 340
  - 14.2.1 Emphatic imperatives ... 340
  - 14.2.2 -co 'implore' and -juj 'quick' with imperatives ... 341
  - 14.2.3 The adverb ɨ́ɨ́cúi 'quickly; hurry' ... 342
- 14.3 Degrees of strength of imperatives ... 344
  - 14.3.1 Explanations ... 345
  - 14.3.2 Exhortation ... 345
  - 14.3.3 Hortatives with májo and métsu 'let's go' ... 346
  - 14.3.4 Softening imperatives with kpai 'permit' ... 347

15 Question Formation 349
- 15.1 Yes/no questions ... 349
- 15.2 Content questions ... 349
  - 15.2.1 Animate interrogative pronouns ... 351
  - 15.2.2 Inanimate interrogative pronouns ... 353
- 15.3 Rhetorical questions ... 354

16 Complementation 357
- 16.1 General comments about subordination ... 357
- 16.2 Complements ... 359
  - 16.2.1 Subject complements ... 360
  - 16.2.2 Object complements ... 360
- 16.3 -ne ⟨ø⟩ versus ⟨event⟩ ... 364

17 Adverbial Clauses 369
- 17.1 Purpose clauses ... 369
- 17.2 Conditional adverbial clauses ... 371
  - 17.2.1 "Normal" conditional clauses ... 371
  - 17.2.2 Counterfactual conditional clauses ... 372
- 17.3 Temporal adverbial clauses ... 373
- 17.4 Adverbial relative clauses ... 375
  - 17.4.1 Place ... 376

	17.4.2	Causal adverbial clauses	376
	17.4.3	Comparison and manner	377

18 Relative Clauses   379
    18.1 The structure of relative clauses 380
        18.1.1 Appositive embedded clauses 381
        18.1.2 Relative clauses with an internal coreferent 387
        18.1.3 Relative clauses possessing their head 388
    18.2 Relativizing into subjects 389
    18.3 Relativizing into nonsubject positions 391

19 Some Comments on Discourse   395
    19.1 The thematic connective 395
        19.1.1 The form of connectives 395
               19.1.1.1 Pronominal connectives 396
               19.1.1.2 Adverbial connectives 397
        19.1.2 The use of thematic connectives 397
        19.1.3 Thematic connectives and subordinate clauses . . . 402
        19.1.4 Topic decay and reestablishment 404
    19.2 Co-text or context 404
    19.3 Ellipsis and gapping 405

Appendices   407

A Dialect Differences   407

B Speculations on Diachronic Processes   411

C A List of Bound Adjectival Stems   413

D Affixes   419
    D.1 Affixes without segments 420
    D.2 Suffixes with segments 421

E The Bora Classifiers   449
    E.1 Explanation and disclaimers 449
    E.2 Classifiers 450

F Bora Kinship Terminology   465
    F.1 Husband — wife relationship 468
    F.2 Sibling — sibling relationship 469
    F.3 Parent — child relationship 469

F.4	Grandparent — grandchild relationship	470
F.5	Uncle/aunt — nephew/niece relationship	470
F.6	Brother-in-law — sister-in-law relationship	471
F.7	Parents-in-law — son-/daughter-in-law relationship	471
F.8	Fathers-in-law — mothers-in-law relationship	472
F.9	Addessing persons not related by kinship	472

G Bora Texts — 473

Bibliography — 531

Index — 535

List of Figures

1.1	Where the Bora people live	2
2.1	Light and heavy syllables	28
3.1	The relationship of tone and syllabification	57
3.2	Final default low tone (FDLT)	61
3.3	Default high tone DHT	62
3.4	TD: úmehe, níívuwa, majcho	62
3.5	TD: llííñájaatéébé mujtáhi	63
3.6	TD: májchotémevaj, úmehéénehéñe, níívúwaúvuma	63
3.7	TD: ɨhvetétsotéroóbe	64
3.8	TD: úméhevu, úmɨhévu, nohcówu	65
3.9	TD: awácunu, áwacúnu	66
3.10	TD: máánimáréjuco, ámánamúréjuco	67
3.11	TD: túkévetsóhi, túkévétsoobe	69
3.12	TD: túkevétso, túkevétsohaamɨ, túkevétsoobe	69
3.13	The *LLX constraint	69
3.14	Penultimate Low Tone Split (PLTS)	70
3.15	TD: llámaára, majchóvaábe	71
3.16	The singular masculine pronoun	72
3.17	Final Low Tone Split (FLTS)	74
3.18	TD: mééníívyeébe	75
3.19	TD: awácunútéhi, úméhewáréjuco	80
3.20	TD: májchóvámejɨɨ(va)	81
3.21	TD: májchotéhi, májchojéhi, majchóvaábe	81
3.22	TD: májchotéébe, majchóváme	82
3.23	TD: dómájcotéébevaj, ɨhvetéteebévaj	82
3.24	TD: májchótsoóbe	83
3.25	TD: ímíbájchótumútsi, ímíbajchóvájúcoomútsi	84
3.26	TD: ní:vúwáwúudi, úméhéwáwúuma	84
3.27	TD: waháróuvúdu	85
3.28	TD: lléénéébejɨɨva, á:hɨvéváábejɨɨva	86

LIST OF FIGURES

3.29	TD: ó májchóteéhi	86
3.30	TD: májchótsotéjúcóóroóbe, íhvetétsojéjúcooráhi	87
3.31	TD: íhvetétsójeráhi	87
3.32	TD: úújetérólleke	89
3.33	TD: dsɨ́jɨ́vétsómeke	90
3.34	TD: ímíbájchoki, májchómeke	92
3.35	TD: dsɨ́jɨ́vétsóíyónélliíhye	93
4.1	Nonfinite tone	100
4.2	TD: wákimyéi múnáajpi	104
4.3	TD: ó cáyobávatéhi, cáyobávatétsómé	120
5.1	The verb stem	134
5.2	The verb (nonimperative)	135
5.3	The imperative verb	135
5.4	Grammatical relations: 'cause to see'	145
5.5	Grammatical relations: reflexive and causative	146
5.6	Another view of 'he allowed himself to be beaten'	146
5.7	Grammatical relations: 'cause to cut oneself'	147
5.8	TD: a:hɨ́vetéhi, a:hɨ́vétéehi	151
6.1	Classifiers derived from verb roots by length	169
6.2	TD: tsiíwa, íwaá	172
6.3	TD: tsúúcáawa, tsíeméwa	172
6.4	'A table like this one.'	186
7.1	The order of nominal suffixes	193
7.2	The grammatical relation of prenominal modifiers	219
8.1	STR: example 531	235
9.1	TD: tá ñáhbeke	256
9.2	TD: tácáraca	257
9.3	The possessor's penultimate high extension (PPHE)	259
9.4	STR: díñáhbé táábake 'your brother's wife'	259
9.5	TD: díñáhbé táábake	260
10.1	Grammatical relations: causatives	275
10.2	Grammatical relations: verbs like pícyo 'put'	277
10.3	STR: tsaalle ímujpáñeécú íhyójtsɨvu iwátájcónema	278
10.4	Inversion with watájco 'cover'	278
10.5	Animacy-motivated inversion	279
10.6	Grammatical relations: 'Put on all your little jewels.'	280

10.7 Grammatical relations: causatives of transitive verbs 281
10.8 STR: O chéméébedi góócóóbeke úhbaábe. 285

14.1 A comparison of imperative and nonfinite tone 335
14.2 TD: májchóteé 341

16.1 STR: subordinate clause verbs 357
16.2 STR: Ó aahɨveté u méénújá pañévu 359
16.3 STR: ...oohííbyé oke ɨhdoobe dsɨɨ́nene bájú pañe. 363
16.4 STR: ɨmɨáájú o úwaabómé ímí úraavyéné oke ditye úúbállé(neri) 364
16.5 TD: mecáhcújtsóne, meímíba:vyéné 366
16.6 TD: delinking by ⟨event⟩: i wá:jacújúcó:ne 366

17.1 STR: O májchóné boone o péjucóóhi. 375

18.1 STR: Ó ájtumɨ́ tsaapi Jóáa imyéme íjcyáábeke. 385
18.2 STR: Árónáa diibye oohííbyeke dsɨ́jɨ́vétsóóbeke ɨ́daatsólléme. 386
18.3 STR: Dííbyema wákímeíbyema péjúcoóbe. 391

D.1   TD: ó ca:yóbáhi 421
D.2   TD: llo:rácobámu 422
D.3   TD: cá:nídivu, ámánadítyu 424
D.4   TD: te:híubáha, wajpíubáhaáca 426
D.5   TD: bájtsóille, májchoíme, májchoóhi 430
D.6   TD: úmɨhéwuúne 437
D.7   TD: cóhpene, cóhpéneúvu 437
D.8   TD: tútávaavéne. 438
D.9   TD: wáñehjɨ́núiyáhi, wáñehjɨ́núíyólleke 439
D.10 TD: ɨhvetéráhi, ɨhvetéróne 441
D.11 TD: ɨhvetéturóne, ááhɨvetétuúbe 443
D.12 TD: újɨcoúvu, ajchúhó:uúvuréjuco 444
D.13 TD: wáñehjɨ́vaténevu 445
D.14 TD: majchóva:bévaj 446
D.15 TD: mɨamúnáájpí:vyeébe 447
D.16 TD: ámánáwuúmu, áyánéwu 448
D.17 TD: óhtsárɨ́jɨwuúmuréjuco 448

F.1   Terms of reference for kinsmen 466
F.2   Terms for addressing another person 467

List of Tables

1.1	A Bora drum message: Come to sing!	24
2.1	Vowels	30
2.2	Consonants	33
2.3	A palatalization shift	40
2.4	Palatalization with 'stretch out the leg'	40
2.5	Reduplication: nothing at the boundary	43
2.6	Reduplication: [ʔ] at the boundary	44
2.7	Reduplication: optional [ʔ] at the boundary	45
2.8	Reduplication: [ˣ] at the boundary	46
2.9	Reduplication: [ˣ] deleted at the boundary	46
2.10	Reduplication: optional [ˣ] at the boundary	47
3.1	Some simple tone examples	59
3.2	Where tone conflicts arise	79
3.3	Suffixes that follow subordinate clause verbs	91
3.4	Words with exceptional tone	96
4.1	Relocation suffixes	118
4.2	Instrumental prefixes	123
4.3	Instrumental prefixes with púju 'break something fragile'	123
4.4	Instrumental prefixes with hdahɨ 'break, sever'	124
5.1	Animate subject classifiers	128
5.2	The formation of single and multiple action verbs	138
5.3	Making the first syllable heavy with a glottal stop	140
5.4	When the first syllable of the singular is closed by a glottal stop	142
5.5	When the first syllable of the singular is closed by preaspiration	143
5.6	Adding vowel length when the second syllable begins with a glottal stop	143

5.7	Adding vowel length when the second syllable has no onset	143
6.1	Animate classifiers	164
6.2	Classifiers for which there is a corresponding root	170
6.3	The basic tone patterns of classifiers	171
7.1	Combining nouns, classifiers, and noun phrases into noun phrases	190
7.2	Nouns that form the plural by replacing the classifier	202
7.3	The Bora numeral phrase	210
7.4	The numerals 5, 10, 15, and 20	213
7.5	The numerals 1–4	214
7.6	The numerals 6–9	215
7.7	The numerals 11–14	216
7.8	The numerals 16–19	217
8.1	Personal pronouns	232
8.2	The roots of demonstrative pronouns	240
8.3	Animate demonstrative pronouns	240
8.4	Inanimate demonstrative pronouns	242
8.5	Animate indefinite pronouns: 'one'	243
8.6	Animate indefinite pronouns: 'other'	243
8.7	Composition of animate indefinite pronouns	244
8.8	Inanimate indefinite pronouns: 'one'	245
8.9	Inanimate indefinite pronouns: 'other'	245
8.10	Inanimate indefinite pronouns: 'some'	246
8.11	Possessive pronouns	247
9.1	The basic tone patterns of the genitive construction	253
10.1	Personal pronominal subject proclitics	270
11.1	The order of clitics	306
14.1	Singular imperatives: changes in the initial syllable	339
14.2	Simple imperatives and complements to íícúi 'hurry'	344
14.3	Three degrees of urgency with májo and métsu	347
15.1	The interrogative roots	350
15.2	Interrogative phrases with mu- 'WH' and ívee- 'why'	350
15.3	Animate interrogative pronouns formed with mu- 'who'	351
15.4	Animate interrogative pronouns formed with ca- 'which'	352
15.5	Inanimate interrogative pronouns formed with ke- 'which'	354

18.1 STR: relative clauses 381

19.1 Animate thematic pronouns (connectives) 396
19.2 Common adverbial connectives 397

D.1 Tone resistance by -jte ⟨AnPl⟩ 442

Preface

This book is intended as a baseline description of the the Bora language.[1] It makes both structural and functional claims. Most of the description is framed in terms of basic notions accepted across linguistic theories; occasionally we make a theory-specific excursus.

Authorship

Wesley Thiesen, who—along with his wife Eva—worked intimately with the Bora people from 1952 to 1998, drafted a grammar sketch of Bora in Spanish but for the Bora people, to be included in the Bora dictionary (Thiesen & Thiesen 1998). In response to questions from David Weber (as linguistic consultant) this sketch grew to the point that it was decided that it should be published as a separate volume (Thiesen 1996).[2]

Weber began transforming one of the intermediate Spanish versions into a more linguistically oriented English document, raising more questions, exploring deeper linguistic issues, dividing examples into morphemes and glossing them, and refining analyses. The analysis of tone was particularly difficult, but we are now satisfied that the analysis given in this volume gives reasonable coverage, although there are still a few unresolved issues.[3]

---

[1] An earlier draft of this grammar was circulated in 1998 and another in 2000. The content has not changed much since the 2000 draft. Publication has been delayed a decade for work-related reasons beyond the authors´ control.

[2] Unless otherwise indicated, references to Thiesen are to Wesley Thiesen.

[3] To study the Bora tone system, Thiesen (circa 1954) identified 18 verbs that instantiated the range of tonal behaviors. He elicited each verb in 165 frames consisting mostly of different suffix combinations. He also identified 15 animate and 15 inanimate nouns. He elicited each animate noun in 28 frames and each inanimate noun in 31 frames. Although some of the root-frame combinations were not possible, over 3850 words were elicited.

To facilitate seeing patterns of tone, he made exhaustive charts representing just tone and length, i.e., suppressing the phonological segments. For the verbs, this resulted in what

The list of classifiers in appendix E was translated from a draft of (Thiesen & Thiesen 1998). The description of Bora kinship terms in appendix F was written by Thiesen in 1964 and later published as (Thiesen 1975b). The current version was revised with Weber in 1996. The texts included in appendix G were provided by Bora individuals. Thiesen provided the glosses and translations.

Acknowledgments

We would like to acknowledge the indispensible role that various people have played in making this grammar possible:

The Bora people welcomed the Thiesens into their community; they taught the Thiesens their language; they collaborated on the preparation of educational material, on a translation of the New Testament, and on the preparation of a dictionary. The following individuals made particularly noteworthy contributions: Julia Mibeco N., Eduardo Soria P., and Zacarías Mibeco.

Throughout the years of involvement with the Bora people, Eva Thiesen constantly supported the work and was an active co-worker. In particular, she developed the series of reading instruction materials whereby hundreds of Bora people learned to read.

The support network of the Instituto Lingüístico de Verano (Summer Institute of Linguistics) in Peru: the aviation, radio and computer technicians, the doctors and nurses, the school teachers, the administrators..., all enabled living and working over a protracted period in an otherwise challenging environment.

The Ministry of Education of Peru, by granting the Summer Institute of Linguistics a contract, made research such as that reported here possible.

The backbone of financial and moral support for this effort has been provided by Christians who desire that the Bible be translated into "forgotten" languages, even endangered ones like Bora. Without their support none of this would have happened.

Steve McConnel and members of the "(La)TeX for linguists" mailing list (at ling-tex@ifi.uio.no) provided indispensible help for formatting this book with TeX, LaTeX and finally X∃TeX.

Thiesen called his "tone book." If we assume that there are seven tone marks per word (a conservative estimate), then the tone book has over 20,000 tone marks. After exhaustive study we have found only about a half dozen words in which Thiesen may have made an error.

We wish to thank the following people, who read and commented on an earlier draft or some portion thereof (ordered by surname): Willem Adelaar, Cheryl Black, Albert Bickford, John Clifton, David Coombs, Desmond Derbyshire, Tom Givón, Tom Headland, Mike Maxwell, David Odden, Steve Parker, David Payne, Doris Payne, Thomas Payne, Frank Seifart, and especially, *very* especially, Mary Ruth Wise.

Why is Bora so interesting?

The Bora phonology is rich in nonsegmental phenomena. There is an elaborate tone system, intimately tied to both the lexicon and the grammar. (An entire chapter is dedicated to tone, and it is discussed in virtually every chapter.) Various phenomena are sensitive to syllable weight, and perhaps conditioned by foot structure.

Morphologically, Bora is fairly agglutinative. There are many suffixes and few—if any—prefixes. Many apparent prefixes are proclitics.

Typologically, Bora is an OV language. Evidence for this claim is as follows:

1. Both Subject–Object–Verb and Object–Subject–Verb are common word orders. Predicate complement clauses generally have Complement–Subject–Verb order.
2. There are postpositions, e.g., in the locative construction, but no prepositions.
3. In the genitive construction the possessor precedes the possessed.
4. Adjectives may precede the nouns they modify but it is more common for the modifier to follow the head in an appositive phrase. (This is a consequence of the role played by the classifiers in forming referring expressions.)
5. Auxiliary verbs follow the semantically main verb (which is structurally subordinate to the auxiliary verb); see, for example, section 4.3.6.

Bora has a strong case system implemented by suffixes. There is an interesting animacy-controlled inversion of the direct object and recipient (goal).

Perhaps the most outstanding feature of Bora grammar is the presence of a large number of classifiers and the various ways they are exploited in carrying out reference. Strikingly, apposition—not constituency—is the primary "glue" for creating referring expressions.

In forming discourses, Bora has a remarkable system of sentential connectives, one that exploits the classifiers to provide great intersentential cohesion.

Abbreviations and Conventions

Abbreviations

⟨ ⟩ surrounds the gloss of a classifier. In appendix G the symbols "⟨" and "⟩" are also used to indicate the topicalized or thematic element fronted from within some other constituent.
+ in tone derivations: blocking (i.e., failure to dock a tone)
* ungrammatical or unacceptable
*LLX constraint against nonfinal low tone sequences
= in tone derivations: delinking a tone
.¿? final high tone of interrogative phrases
· sentence boundary (in phonemic representations)
. syllable boundary (in phonemic representations)
ː vocalic length
$^{(?)}$ optional glottal stop (?) in the syllable coda
⟨ø⟩ 'thing' or 'event' (two morphemes that differ only in tonal properties)
⟨Ø⟩ 'thing' on marked sentences having -huɨkʰo 'focus'
μ mora
◯ a placeholder corresponding to a syllable; e.g., -ⓁO nɛ indicates that a low tone is imposed on the penultimate syllable of the stem to which -nɛ is affixed
ø null, empty category (gap, trace,...) $ø_i$, $ø_j$, $ø_k$ empty category co-indexed with some other element
Ψ, Δ, Φ... variables
$Φ_i$... $Ψ_i$ the subscripts indicate that Φ and Ψ are coreferential
σ syllable
acc accusative
Adj adjective
  Adj/Adj a suffix that occurs on an adjective and results in an adjective
Adv adverb (or adverbial phrase)

xxix

AdvP adverbial phrase
Adv/Adv a suffix that occurs on an adverb, resulting in an adverb
AG agent
anim animate
AnPl animate plural
aug augment
C consonant
ⓒ the floating low tone at the juncture between a classifier and the preceding element
$\overset{c}{v}$ low tone (on a vowel) due to a following classifier
-caus causative
CF contrary-to-fact
DET determiner
DHT Default High Tone
dim diminutive
DO direct object
du dual
   DuF animate dual feminine
   duIn dual for inanimates
   DuM animate dual masculine
DVC deverbal classifier
emph emphasis
ex. exclusive (first person plural exclusive)
EXPER experiencer
FDLT Final Default Low Tone
FLTS Final Low Tone Split
frs frustrative, contraexpectation, counterfactual
fut future
Ⓖ the juncture between the modifier (possessor) and head (possessed) of a genitive construction. In some contexts Ⓖ is also used to indicate the floating low tone at this juncture.
$\overset{G}{v}$ low tone (on a vowel) due to the genitive construction
$\overset{G}{\underset{L}{v}}$ low tone (on a vowel) due to the genitive construction and also a lexically marked low tone
$\overset{G}{\underset{N}{v}}$ low tone (on a vowel) due to the genitive construction and nonfinite tone
H high tone
Ⓗ high tone imposed on a preceding syllable
$\overset{H}{v}$ lexically marked high tone (on a vowel)
(h) optional preaspiration (that occurs in the preceding syllable coda)
hab habitual
Imp imperative
$\overset{I}{v}$ low tone (on a vowel) due to the imperative
in. inclusive (first person plural inclusive)
inan inanimate
InPl inanimate plural
Inst instrument
irr irrealis
(j) optional palatalization
-KI implicit -ki 'purpose'
L low tone
Ⓛ low tone imposed on a preceding syllable
$\overset{L}{v}$ lexically marked low tone (on a vowel) or a low tone highlighted for the reader's benefit
L.H adjacent homorganic vowels with low and high tones respectively
Link sentence-initial connective

Abbreviations

lit. literally
***LLX** constraint against nonfinal low tone sequences
μ mora
max maximum, finalized
med medial
mIn multiple action, intransitive
mSt multiple action, stative
mTr multiple action, transitive
$\overset{N}{v}$ nonfinite low tone (over a vowel)
⟨**n**⟩ the negative verb-terminating classifier (used when there is a preverbal subject)
N noun
  N/N suffix that occurs on a noun and results in a noun
  N/N$_{case}$ suffix that occurs on a noun and results in a "cased" noun
  N/V suffix that occurs on a noun and results in a verb
-NE implicit -nɛ ⟨n⟩
neg negative
nwit nonwitnessed (evidential)
NP noun phrase
objAn animate object (the explicit accusative case marker)
oblIn oblique (case marker) for inanimate noun phrases
P postposition
palat palatalized
PC predicate complement
per pertain to
pl plural
  plAn plural for animates
  plIn plural for inanimates
  plQ plural for quantifiers
PLTS penultimate low tone split
PP postpositional phrase (or prepositional phrase)
PPHE possessor's penultimate high extension
PredAdj predicate adjective
prob probable
prox proximate
prtc participle
PT projected time
pur purpose
ques question (root)
rec recent past
recip reciprocal
rem remote past
res.pos resulting position
R/P reflexive or passive
rpt reportative
Result$_S$ result clause with same subject
S sentence or clause; subject
$\overset{s}{v}$ high tone on the first syllable of the verb of a subordinate clause
s-V verb with a proclitic subject
SAP speech act participant, first person plural inclusive
sg or **Sg** singular
  SgF animate singular feminine
  SgImp singular imperative
  SgM animate singular masculine
sib sibling
sim similar
sIn single action, intransitive
Site site of attachment
sou source
sSt single action, stative
sTr single action, transitive
STR structure (in figures)
su subject
sub subordinator (-h)
T tone
⟨**t**⟩ the verb-terminating classifier (used when there is a

preverbal subject)
TD tone derivation (in figures)
TBU tone bearing unit
-thm theme (grammatical relation)
thm- thematic connective
UTAH the "uniformity of theta assignment hypothesis"
V verb
v vowel
var variety, various
voc vocative
V/Adv suffix that occurs on a verb and results in an adverb
V/V suffix that occurs on a verb and results in a verb
V/V$_{subordinate}$ suffix that occurs on a verb and results in a subordinate verb
WH interrogative word
$^{(x)}$ optional preaspiration (that occurs in the preceding syllable coda)
-^{x} or -^{h} preaspiration from the following root (in genitive construction)
-x in the glosses of appendix G: preaspiration from the following root
y/n yes or no

Conventions

THE INDEX:
In the index, entries are ordered according to the English alphabet. Bora words are written according to the Bora writing system (the "practical orthography") to facilitate finding them in alphabetical order.

EXAMPLES:
Examples generally present four types of information. The position of these parts varies in the interest of saving space. (1) The Bora example is written in a phonetic or phonemic form using the International Phonetic Alphabet (IPA). (2) The example is also written in the Bora writing system, with this sort of font (sans serif). This is sometimes located above the phonetic / phonemic representation and sometimes following the phonetic / phonemic form (in parentheses). (3) A morpheme-by-morpheme gloss is given either below the Bora example or in parentheses following it. (4) A free translation follows, either on a line below the morpheme-by-morpheme text or following it at the end of the line.

BORA CITATION FORMS:
(a) Words given "in isolation" (i.e., without any preceding or following text) may meet the conditions for the application of either PLTS or FLTS. If so, the isolation form will be the output of the rule (which is how it would be pronounced in isolation). (b) Sometimes the phonetic / phonemic representation of words, roots, affixes,…make lexically

marked tones explicit, as discussed below, while omitting the tones of other syllables. (c) When verbs are cited, the phonetic / phonemic representation may make lexically marked tones explicit whereas the orthographic form gives the nonfinite form; see section 4.1, page 100, especially figure 4.1. For example, ákpak^{h}ú̱mɯ̱ (áwacúnu) 'to yawn'.

PHRASE MARKERS:
Phrase markers ("trees") with which structure is represented are intended as suggestive, neither definitive nor what would might be expected for any particular theoretic perspective. Some sentences are given with a rather flat structure. This makes it easier to deal with Bora's relatively free word order, but at the cost of sometimes obscuring subcategorization relationships. For example, see the tree given for example 662, page 277. Some affixes are treated as separate syntactic constituents; for example, case markers are treated as postpositions.

TONE DERIVATIONS:
The Bora forms in tone derivations are written as Bora people normally read and write their language. Tone derivations use the font with which this sentence is written.

LETTERS REPRESENTING USES OF TONE:
We sometimes use $\overset{H}{v}$ to highlight a high tone and $\overset{L}{v}$ to highlight a low tone. Further, to help the reader keep track of different *uses* of tone, we sometimes indicate the use by writing a small letter over the vowel. These letters are as follows:

LETTER	TONE	USE
$\overset{C}{v}$	low tone	classifier
$\overset{G}{v}$	low tone	genitive
$\overset{H}{v}$	high tone	lexically marked high tone
$\overset{HL}{vv}$	high-low tones	remote past tense
$\overset{I}{v}$	low tone	imperative^a (verb)
$\overset{L}{v}$	low tone	lexically marked low tone
$\overset{N}{v}$	low tone	nonfinite (verb)
$\overset{S}{v}$	high tone	subordinate (verb)

^{a}This low tone is the nonfinite tone; I is used to remind the reader that the nonfinite verb is used to form an imperative.

When two uses coincide on a syllable, we sometimes put two letters over the vowel. For example, $\overset{G}{\underset{}{\overset{N}{v}}}$ indicates that both the nonfinite and genitive tones fall on this syllable.

Chapter 1

The Bora People

This chapter is a brief description of the Bora people: their history, their culture, their position in the nation of Peru, and so forth. (The origin of the name "Bora" is not known.)

1.1 Demographics and history

Bora is a Witotoan language (Aschmann 1993) spoken by between 2,000 and 3,000 people, about 1,000 of whom live in northern Peru. At the time of European contact, the Bora were reported to number about 25,000 (see Steward 1948:750). However, their numbers declined radically as a result of abuses suffered during the rubber boom that started in 1886 (Ribeiro & Wise 1978:71–73). The Bora culture was first studied by anthropologists in Colombia before many Bora people migrated to Peru (see Steward 1948:751).

The Bora people of Peru live primarily along the Ampiyacu and Yaguasyacu Rivers and secondarily on the Momón (tributary to the Nanay) and Putumayo Rivers. There were about 500 living near Puerto Ancón on the Yaguasyacu River, but this community no longer exists. See figure 1.1.

In Colombia, about 150 Bora people live on the Ígara-Paraná River and about 100 on the Caquetá river at Mariápolis, Remanso, Santa Isabel, Las Palmas and living in scattered houses. This is the area from which the Bora of Peru migrated. These people are referred to by outsiders as "Miraña" but the Bora of Peru refer to them as the "down-river people,"

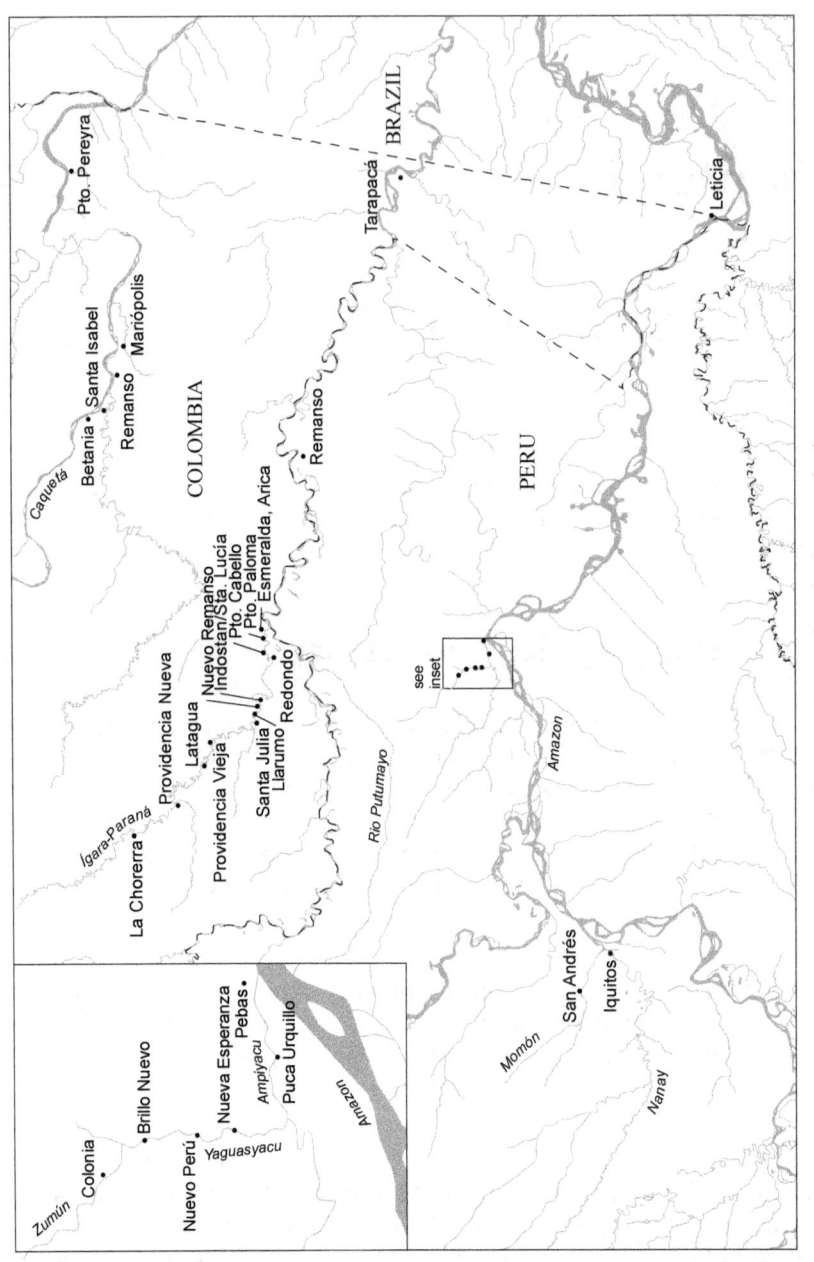

Figure 1.1 Where the Bora people live

reflecting the fact that the Bora in Peru migrated from west (upriver) of the Miraña. The speech of the Bora people in Colombia is approximately 90 percent intelligible with the Bora of Peru.[1] A closely related—but mutually unintelligible—language is Muinane (not to be confused with Muinane Huitoto, now called Nüpode Witoto). It is spoken by about 100 people on the Caquetá River, upriver from where the Miraña people live. There is also at least one Bora community in Brazil.

The Bora were alleged to be a warlike and cannibalistic people who often attacked neighboring tribes, eating the victims (Steward 1948:756–757). Thiesen was informed that they only ate certain parts of their enemies, and that they ate those to gain power. One of his sources, an elderly woman, said that she remembered how human flesh tasted. The chief who lived at Ancón and later at Brillo Nuevo also remembered. (That chief died about 1980.) To our knowledge cannibalism has not been practiced by the Bora in more than a century.

Starting in 1886, Europeans arrived in pursuit of rubber, using the native peoples to do the work in exchange for axes, machetes, beads, tin cans, mirrors, and such. The Bora were eager to obtain these things, but after a time rebelled at being enslaved by outsiders. This led to warfare and the massacre of thousands of indigenous people. Those who remained were whipped or beaten until dead, or until they were willing to penetrate the rain forest to collect rubber. Mibeco, the chief, remembered how the "Gun Men" (the Bora name for Europeans) used imported Negroes to hunt down the natives who refused to work for the rubber barons. He reported witnessing his father—along with many others—being whipped, piled on firewood, and burned to death.

The arrival of diseases to which the Bora people had no immunity (e.g., measles) further reduced their population. Their population was estimated

---

[1] One difference is that they preserve the /ai/ that accounts for /a/s in Peruvian Bora that palatalize. Also, what in Peruvian Bora is a labial-velar, in the speech of the "down-river people" is a labialized velar [k^w].

The following information was found in the archives of the Colombia Branch of the Summer Institute of Linguistics. The information—dated 1986—was provided by the New Tribes Mission:

> [It was judged that there were] some 90 speakers of Miraña scattered along the Caquetá River between La Pedrera (the downriver end, where the Caquetá enters Brazil) and Araracuara (the upriver end, approximately 72° W and about .5° S). There were perhaps 40 more who call themselves Miraña or Bora but who did not speak the language. There was definite language shift going on to Spanish. Only about 3–4 were considered to be monolingual in Miraña. Another family was reported to be some 2–3 days travel up the Cahuinarí River (a major tributary of the Caquetá coming in from the south).

We appreciate Paul Frank's help in recovering this information.

to be 12,000 in 1926 and 500 in 1940 (see Steward 1948:751). These estimates are probably conservative because many Bora people moved farther into the rain forest and away from the large rivers during this period.

About 1920 the Loayza family brought a group of Bora, Ocaina, and Witoto people from the area of the Ígara-Paraná River in Colombia to the Ampiyacu River in northeastern Peru. (The Loayza family had lumber and mineral rights to a large area on the Ampiyacu and Yaguasyacu Rivers. They claimed to own the land but did not have title to it.) The Loayzas made their home at Puca Urquillo. Some of the Witoto lived on the upstream side of the Loayza home and some of the Bora on the downstream side. Puca Urquillo is still the largest Bora settlement. The Ocaina moved upstream on the Yaguasyacu, a tributary of the Ampiyacu, to a place known as Isango. Some of the Witoto moved to Estirón, half an hour upstream from Puca Urquillo. Some of the Bora moved up to a place on the Yaguasyacu that they called Ancón and some moved farther upstream to a place they named Colonia.

Due to modern health care (particularly for infants), the population is increasing. As their population increases, they are dispersing. About 1972 some from Colonia started another town downstream from Brillo Nuevo and named it Nuevo Peru. Quite a number now live on the northern edge of Pebas. Some have settled along the Amazon upstream from Pebas. There are some in Iquitos and in the town of San Andrés about 30 minutes from Iquitos on the Momón River. Others live in Leticia (Colombia) on the Amazon River at the border with Brazil, and on the Putumayo River at Tarapacá (Colombia), at Remanso on the Peruvian side and at Arica on the Colombian side. Along the Ígara-Paraná River in Colombia there are Bora people in small groups at Esmeraldas, Redondo, Indostan, Santa Julia, Providencia and Nuevo Providencia, Latagua, and La Chorerra.

In 1975 the Bora people obtained title to 3,462.80 hectares. This was made official by Resolución Departamental 4500, *Título* 130–75 (Brack Egg & Yáñez 1997:168–169).[2]

When the Peruvian Ministry of Education, in collaboration with the Summer Institute of Linguistics, initiated bilingual education among the Bora in 1955, the people were very enthusiastic. Little by little they began moving together so their children could attend school. Because they needed more land for a larger town, the people from Ancón moved across the river and upstream to a place where there was a larger flat area. There,

---

[2]According to Brack Egg & Yáñez (1997:174–177), three other communities have land titles: (1) Betania by resolution Rd 0360–1990, *Título* 001–92, 330.46 hectares, (2) San José de Piri by Rm 0586, 1991, *Título* 022–92, 507.50 hectares, and (3) La Florida Ampliación (Bora-Ocaina) by resolution Rs 0105, *Título* 056–91, 4620.75 hectares.

starting in 1957, they built a new communal house, a school, a church, and individual homes around the plaza facing the communal house. The new town was named Brillo Nuevo.

For a time, the excitement of reading, writing, arithmetic, and classes for learning Spanish made it worthwhile to live closely together. Then they began to realize that many changes were negative. There were too many people, chickens, and dogs in one area. Women had to go farther from the town to tend their fields. Game was soon depleted, so they had to go farther away to hunt for their meat. And, while they were generally loyal to their clans, they began stealing from each other's fields.

Eventually, everyone except the chief and his family moved away from the plaza on the hill, resettling along the river front. Some built their houses farther away, yet near enough that the children could walk to school. This reduced the concentration of people and animals, but many must still go considerable distances to make their fields and to hunt. Recently, they are making fields on closer land that was farmed 20–30 years ago.

1.2 The future of the Bora language

Today there are few monolingual Bora speakers. A few elderly adults do not know Spanish well enough to be able to buy and sell. All those between 50 and 60 years of age are more or less fluent in Spanish for daily needs (although they still prefer to speak Bora). All those under 50 are quite fluent in Spanish.

All Bora children now learn Spanish. Some learn Spanish as their first language and do not go on to learn Bora as a second language, while other children do. Many Bora children still learn Bora as their first language and Spanish as a second language.

As young people move to the cities they leave Bora behind and their city-born children learn only Spanish. The Bora language may survive only a few more generations but at present there are still many of all ages speaking it.

The Bora people are interested in new ideas, anxious to learn and quick to catch on. Those who have attended schools outside their community (bilingual teacher training, Bible institutes, courses in Iquitos, and such) generally rise quickly to the top of their classes. Three who graduated in the first class from the *Instituto Superior Pedagógico Bilingüe Yarinacocha* proved to be good teachers; all were subsequently asked to teach in

future sessions of the training course.[3] There are secondary schools in Brillo Nuevo and in Puca Urquillo partially staffed by Bora people.

An initial attempt to teach Bora people to read began by teaching just the segmentals, deferring the issue of tone. This proved to be impractical, forcing the conclusion that tone should be taught first. Students listened to the tones as these were tapped on two boards having different tones and were taught to relate this to written tones. This proved successful. The booklet (written in Spanish) *El manguaré facilita la lectura del bora* (Thiesen & Thiesen 1985) follows this method. It teaches tone first and then explains the differences between Bora and Spanish segmentals. It has proven to be the case that any Bora who reads Spanish can learn to read Bora without much difficulty. Writing Bora is also taught by the same method (see Thiesen 1989).

Bora children now learn to read Spanish before learning to read Bora. There are various reasons for this, among them the following: First, there are now virtually no Bora school books in Bora communities, those used in the early years of the bilingual education program having deteriorated. Second, Bora teachers trained in bilingual education have been assigned to higher grades, to positions in educational administration, or in some cases to schools in non-Bora communities. Third, children are now exposed to considerable oral Spanish before entering school, so teaching them to read in Spanish is now feasible and strongly favored by parents. Quite a few children go on to learn to read Bora after learning to read Spanish.

In summary, the number of people who are strongly identified with the Bora language and culture is declining because of assimilation to the national culture, through contact with Spanish speakers, through the educational system, through marriage with non-Bora people, and so forth.

1.3 Social structure

The Bora people are organized into patrilineal clans, each having its own chief. Each clan speaks a slightly different dialect; see appendix A. The chief and his immediate family are in charge of the traditional dances and festivals (even in the infrequent case that it is sponsored by another individual).

---

[3]One was the director of the primary and secondary bilingual schools at Brillo Nuevo and was the director of the Instituto Superior Pedagógico Bilingüe Yarinacocha for one year. Another is the supervisor of eight or nine bilingual schools in the Pebas area. The third has been working in the Office of Bilingual Education in Iquitos.

1.3. SOCIAL STRUCTURE

When matters of discipline, festivals, fishing and hunting need to be discussed, the chief calls his council together, using the large signal drums. The council consists of all the adult men. When convened, the members sit in a circle, either around the fireplace at the center of the big house or near the signal drums. As they discuss the problem at hand, they fill their cheeks with roasted coca leaves that have been ground into a fine powder and lick a thick paste of boiled tobacco juice from a stick inserted into their small bottles.

The chieftainship is passed from father to son, but a chief's position may be revoked if the council decides that he is not capable of leading the people.[4]

As late as 1952, the Bora people were living in traditional clan units. Each clan lived in a large communal house. These were scattered with perhaps a minimum of two kilometers between them.[5] Just inside the entrance of the communal house, to the right, are the Bora signal drums. These play an important role in Bora culture; see section 1.8.

The father or grandfather was the chief of each unit. He lived in the place of honor at the back of the house (at the other end from the front door). His sons and their families lived along the sides of the house (sleeping on raised platforms that are sufficiently high so that one can work under them). This house was used for all the community activities. Also, the women did their cooking in the big house, and the men prepared their jungle salt, coca powder, and tobacco paste there.

By 1955 the system was breaking down: the sons were building individual family houses near the communal house. The men still use the big house for preparing jungle salt, coca, and tobacco paste, but increasingly the people have built their own cook houses and live as separate nuclear families. Festivals (and the preparations for them) are still held in the communal houses.

1.3.1 Festivals

Until the late 1960s, festivals were held frequently. These were central to Bora social structure. There were many different festivals, which were

---

[4]Now village authorities are appointed by outside authorities or chosen by the communities along the lines of the general pattern of village administration in Peru, with a president and a registrar (who can register births and deaths).

[5]At one point circa 1955 there were four communal houses within five kilometers of Brillo Nuevo and a fifth in an Ocaina village ten kilometers downstream from Brillo Nuevo. There was another downstream in Puca Urquillo, about fifteen kilometers direct distance but considerably farther if going by canoe.

of considerable importance because it was believed that doing them well was necessary to ensure a good life, particularly to appease supernatural spirit beings. (Generally, the Bora people did not worship any gods, but rather appeased spirits that might harm them.)

Festivals are still occasionally carried out in certain villages. When a new communal house is built a series of festivals is organized to insure protection for the house and its occupants. However, festivals today are not the grand affairs they used to be. After all, to carry out a festival takes the cooperation of all the people in a village, who must do considerable work: six or seven months in advance a big manioc field must be planted to provide food for those who attend. People are now reluctant to contribute their time for preparations.

The family that "owns" the festival provides the cassava (a form of bread made from manioc as described below), *cahuana* (an unfermented starch-based drink), fruits, and tuberous roots. Those invited are expected to bring meat. As people arrive with their meat, they exchange it for the food that is laid out for them. The chief determines how much cassava, roots, and fruit should be given in exchange for the meat, in part depending on how much of the former have been prepared. (There can be disappointments on both sides.) There is a large container on the ground made from the bark of a tree, lined with large leaves. This is filled with *cahuana*. The people at the festival drink from this throughout the festival. At the *pijuayo* festival the *cahuana* is flavored with *pijuayo*, that is, the fruit of the *pijuayo* palm (*Bactris speciosa*).[6]

A typical festival

In 1952, the senior co-author and his wife, Eva Thiesen, described a typical festival as follows:

The chief told us excitedly that he was preparing a big festival, that he remembered how his forefathers had done it, and that he was going to do the same. He wanted to make a big dance so all the people would come together, so he could talk to them.

He had been planning to make this dance for a long time, and had planted much extra food so that there would be plenty. For several weeks before the festival everybody was busy. The women prepared the food, and they weeded and swept the yard. The men worked hard weaving

---

[6]Sometimes, to have enough *pijuayo* for the festival, a considerable quantity is collected in advance and buried in the ground. It is dug up when needed. This is done because it will keep in the ground much longer than in the air.

1.3. SOCIAL STRUCTURE

leaves and repairing the roof on the big communal house. Some of them walked several days into the rain forest to gather a certain plant from which to make salt.[7]

Eight days before the festival the chief sent an invitation to the other Bora clans, as well as to the neighboring Ocaina and Witoto people. The invitation consisted of tobacco boiled to a thick syrup (like molasses). If the chief of the clan accepted, and he and his council partook of the tobacco, that meant that they would come to the festival.

However, the man communicating the invitation made a mistake: he offered the Witotos their tobacco before offering it to one of the Bora chiefs. This was an insult to the Bora chief, provoking him to refuse the tobacco. He did not come to the festival. To make amends for the insult—we were told—the chief making the festival would have to make a subsequent festival and send the slighted chief the first invitation. Until that time, they would be at enmity.

On Wednesday the clan began drumming out the bread-making song on the signal drums (which can be heard as far as twenty miles away). This drumming continued until 1:30 A.M. (Thursday while making *pijuayo* drink, they beat out the *pijuayo* song. This song continued until midnight, at which point they switched to the painting song. At this point everyone who intended to come to the festival was supposed to be painting his face and body. This song was continued all day Friday, and was accompanied by singing and dancing all through the night.)

Thursday morning the men went upriver to find a big tree. They cut it down and flattened it on one side. They brought it downriver and carried it into the large house, accompanied by much shouting. The women were not permitted to look at the log—which represented the body of their enemies—until it had been put in place. (It is believed that it would cause the death of any woman that looked at it.)[8] The two ends of the log were placed on cross logs so that when the men danced up and down on it, it hit the ground with loud thuds, according to the rhythm of the song. Once it was in place, the clan all ran to it and began to dance, the men on the log and the women on the ground facing them.

The guests began coming early Saturday morning. As they arrived, they were again given a formal invitation (consisting of a small piece of meat dipped in the tobacco syrup), after which they were taken to the communal house, clan by clan, each preceded by pairs of flute players. The Witotos

---

[7]These plants are piled on firewood and burned. The ashes are placed in a funnel and water is poured over them. Then this water is boiled until all that remains is a small amount of very strong salt.

[8]The young girls came to make sure that Eva and our daughters could not see it.

marched around the house before entering, yelling, shouting, and beating on the roof with long poles, thus staging a mock attack. Upon entering, they bargained and exchanged their meats for the other foods that were supplied by the hosts. The meat included peccaries, tapirs, monkeys, birds, and large, live grubs and worms. The food provided by the host was bread made from bitter manioc, a pure starch drink (*cahuana*), peanuts, a thick pineapple drink, and *pijuayo* drink (none of which was fermented).

One or two couples were busy all day and all night singing a song of thanksgiving for the food. The song included a line telling the people to take, eat, and drink of this food, which was their life sustenance. They sang in harmony, in a rather harsh voice, but beautifully. After each singing, the pot was refilled and passed to the next person to drink.

One reason for the festival was the name-changing ceremony. As is customary, the chieftainship is passed to the son after the death of the chief. However, long before the chief dies, a festival is carried out to pass the chief's name to his successor. In the case of this particular festival, the grandson was given the name of the father, and the father the name of the grandfather, who is still the chief.

Also, the chief's eight-year-old daughter received the name of a deceased aunt. The girl was painted black from head to foot, and wore a blue and white beaded girdle with a fringe of shells. She had rings of white cotton around her legs and arms, along with bracelets, anklets, necklaces, and earrings. The Bora ordinarily paint black around their mouths, their eyebrows, and sometimes their cheeks. For this occasion many of the girls, as well as women, had the typical Bora design painted all over their bodies; see plate 85 of Steward (1948), following page 762.

After the name-changing ceremony, which consisted of much chanting, the dancing resumed. This time the chief's family held hands and led a group that danced for a time around the women. Then they formed the front row for the completion of the dance. Some of these dancers wore nut rattles on their ankles; these greatly accentuated the rhythm.

The singing and dancing continued all day. At about 8 P.M. the singing changed to a song of insult to the chief, who—they said—had not prepared enough food. This song lasted for a couple of hours and throughout the song they were eating and drinking as much as they could to get rid of all the food.

The chief, who was sitting in a circle with his council, was merely grinning and continued chewing his coca and tobacco juice. It was apparent that this was the people's ironic way of complimenting him on a very fine festival. He seemed very pleased that everyone was having a good time.

The guests went home at 4 o'clock Sunday morning, tired but satisfied.

1.3.2 The *patrón* system

The Bora people lived for many decades under the *patrón* system whereby an outsider (and his family) exploited the labor of a group of people in exchange for assuming certain responsibilities for them. The *patrón* gave cloth, kettles, blankets, and other goods on credit. To pay for this the men were required to go into the rain forest to gather chicle, rosewood, and other raw materials. Upon paying, they were given more goods so as to keep them constantly in debt. The *patrón* kept basic medical supplies for the people. He organized soccer games for the people, but not schools. And he prohibited other outsiders from going to where the Bora people lived (on the pretext that they would "bother" them).

The Bora in Peru persisted under this system for about forty years after being brought to Peru by the Loayza family.[9]

When they learned simple mathematics, the Bora people began to question the value of the exchanges made with their *patrones* and their chiefs. Men became less willing to leave their families to work in the rain forest gathering rosewood and chicle. However, when the *patrón* would bring trade items (machetes, axes, kettles, yard goods for mosquito nets and for clothing, blankets, hair clips, and beads) they were eager to take these items on credit; they then had to go to work in the rain forest to pay for them. Working for a *patrón* was a form of security. He took care of them, provided basic medicines, and protected them from outside exploitation. Forty years after the demise of the *patrón* system many Bora people still find it difficult to be independent. They want to be in debt to someone who will provide security for them.

The *patrones* were able to keep river traders away from the people for a time, but were eventually no longer able to do so. When the traders came in, they brought liquor, which has become a disruptive factor in the communities. The people, however, discourage traders because they want everything on credit and often manage not to pay when the trader returns to collect their bananas and other products. The sale of skins of wild boar, jaguar, and ocelot are now controlled by the government, so traders can no longer count on making a profit on these. Therefore, it is now often necessary for the Bora to travel downstream to Pebas to buy supplies. The chief, the teachers, or anyone else with cash may bring back soap, kerosene, or liquor to sell in the town. At one point a store was set up in Brillo Nuevo. It prospered until the storekeeper began to sell on credit; thereafter he was soon forced out of business. The attitude of the

---

[9]We do not know how long they might have lived under the *patrón* system in Colombia before being brought to Perú.

Bora is basically that debts are to be paid off only with work, while money is to be spent on goods, not debts.

1.4 Work

The Bora people are industrious; they enjoy their work. They demonstrate a spirit of cooperation in all their activities. The principal activities are clearing and tending fields, building houses, hunting, fishing, and food preparation.

The people wake up early, eat a breakfast of má:ʔò 'cassava bread' with pʰɨmíʔtsʰò 'dip'. They then go to their fields to work and gather food. They usually return about 1 P.M.

Besides hunting and fishing and cutting down new fields, men work at house building, making canoes, and lumbering. Women are primarily involved in food preparation, childcare, agriculture, and the sewing and washing of clothes. In recent years both men and women have become increasingly dedicated to handicrafts for sale. For example, they make shoulder bags and hammocks from the fibers of the *chambira* palm, weave baskets, carve paddles, make feather headdresses, flutes, and jaguar tooth necklaces. These are generally taken to Iquitos and sold to stores that resell them to tourists.

1.4.1 Agriculture and gathering

The men cut down the trees to make a new field. The women burn it, clean it, plant it, cultivate it, and harvest the crops.

Each family owns its own field but a great part of the work is done together. One day they all work in one field, the next day in another, and so on.

Considerable manioc must be planted to keep a constant supply. As manioc is dug up, a piece of the stem is replanted for the next year. Other starches that are cultivated are: *sachapapa* (an edible tuber), arrowroot (*huitina*), sweet potato and *daledale* (*Callathea alleuia*). Peanuts are also grown in limited amounts.

There are many kinds of fruit. Some, like *cocona*, grow wild. Others are planted and tended, either in fields or near houses. These include papaya, pineapple, plantains and bananas, *uvilla*, guava, *pacae*, *anona*, *macambo*,

1.4. WORK

umarí, *aguaje*, sour sop, and *pijuayo*. When *pijuayo* or *pona* palms are cut down, the heart is eaten.

Sometimes food is found while going through the rain forest: caterpillars, honey, and so forth. The first person to see edible caterpillars carves his mark on the tree so no one else takes them before they are mature.

Suris (palm grubs) are planted in a palm log and left to grow and multiply: an *aguaje* palm tree is cut down and notches are cut in the side of the fallen trunk. A beetle then lays its eggs in these notches. These hatch and feed on the decaying pulp in the center of the tree. When the grubs are fat and juicy they are harvested and eaten.

Bora men plant coca and tobacco, both of which are important in the Bora culture, being central elements in the traditional society; see section 1.3.1.

The coca leaves are toasted. Then, using a hollow log mortar, they are pounded, along with the ashes of the burned leaves of a certain balsa tree, into a fine powder. This fine powder is sifted through a cloth bag into a large black earthenware pot. (To keep the fine powder from flying, the bag is shaken while held through a mat cover having a hole in the center.) It is stored along with a tablespoon in cans having lids (such as empty coffee cans).

Before going out to work the more traditional men fill their cheeks with this coca powder. They also do this at night when they sit around the council fire, and lick tobacco paste from small bottles. (Women never ingest coca.)

Tobacco leaves are boiled and mixed with "jungle salt" to make a thick paste. This is put in a small bottle and then licked from a short stick. When a visitor arrives, he is offered a lick of tobacco. (Tobacco is never smoked.)

1.4.2 Food preparation

The women do the cooking. Each nuclear family has its own fireplace, but often families take turns cooking for the whole household, and all eat together from one main pot.

When there is something to cook, the women cook a meal in the early afternoon. This is eaten when the children return from school. After the afternoon meal, the women work at making cassava bread, and the men process their coca and tobacco.

Most families have only a few dishes, so they eat in shifts, the men first. Alternatively, the family gathers around a shared bowl or kettle.

Manioc is the most important item in the Bora diet. It is eaten boiled or roasted. Bitter (poison) manioc is used to make cassava (bread) and *cahuana*, a starch drink. The bitter manioc must be specially prepared to destroy the poison it contains. It is difficult to distinguish from regular manioc. Several years ago a mother at Puca Urquillo, hurrying to make food for her family, cooked bitter manioc by mistake; consequently two of her children died. When in doubt a woman may take a bite and spit it out when she has determined which kind of manioc it is.

The process of making cassava takes a good deal of a woman's time. The bitter manioc must be dug in the field, carried to the house, washed, peeled, and grated. (Graters are made from tin cans opened flat, into which many holes are pounded with a nail. The under side of the can is turned up and nailed onto a board, and thus becomes a grater.)

After it is grated, the manioc must be washed many times to remove the poison. For this purpose a tripod is erected into which is mounted a large round sieve woven from reeds. A large kettle or clay pot is placed below this. The grated manioc is placed in the sieve and water poured over it. It is kneaded to get the starch to separate from the fiber. This is repeated, usually five or six times. The starch settles to the bottom of the kettle.

The water, which now contains the toxins, is poured into another kettle and boiled with fish or the meat of small animals, hot pepper (or whatever) until it becomes a black paste. (There are several regular recipes for this paste.) The boiling destroys the poisons. The resulting paste is eaten as a dip for cassava.

To remove the excess liquid from the starch, it is put into a cylindrical woven reed press called a poːahuɪ. These are stretched with weights to squeeze out the liquid. It is then gathered into a ball and placed in a basket lined with leaves and allowed to age for three days (during which the bitter flavor mellows).

To bake the má:ʔòó, some of the starch is sifted through a special sieve, one that is more loosely woven than the sieve used for washing. This sifted starch is sprinkled onto a ceramic baking plate (similar to the large, black, roasting kettle used to toast coca leaves). This has been preheated over a fire (usually made with numerous small pieces of firewood). A wooden spatula is used to shape the má:ʔòó. When one side is sufficiently cooked, it is removed from the fire and another portion is spread on the plate. Then the first portion is put on top of the second so that they become one. In this way a piece of bread may become nearly an inch thick. It is, however, sometimes made thin. In consistency, the bread is similar to a

crusty gumdrop.[10]

Some of the fiber may be mixed with the starch to stretch the starch and to give more variety. What fiber is not consumed in this way is fed to the chickens.

Cahuana, a starch drink, is a basic part of the Bora diet. It is made from manioc starch by first mixing it with cold water and then adding hot water until it becomes clear and rather thick. If pineapple, *umarí*, or *aguaje* is available, the juice is added for flavor. Anyone visiting a Bora house is offered a drink of *cahuana*.

1.4.3 Hunting

The men do the hunting. They often go hunting for several days far from the village. All hunting is now done with shotguns. (They formerly knew how to make blow guns but have not used them for at least fifty years.) The meat they get may be salted and smoked to preserve it. The men come home when they have all the meat they can carry. Meat from larger animals is shared with relatives and neighbors if they bring it in fresh, and sometimes when it is smoked. They hunt for large rodents (agouti and capybara), both for meat and to protect their crops. Monkey, deer, tapir, peccary, coati, sloth, porcupine, and birds are also eaten.

Sometimes a herd of peccaries runs near the village. When this happens most people get their own supply of meat. Several years ago a herd of peccaries crossed the river right into the village. They can be dangerous, so those who were unarmed climbed trees or ran for cover.

1.4.4 Fishing

The Bora fish with hooks, nets, spears, traps, and poison. When fishing with poison, everyone goes to help.

The children love to fish with hooks, and they prepare their fish and eat them on their own, or sell them to outsiders to buy more fish hooks and fishing line.

If a widow does not have a man to hunt for her, she relies heavily on fish. Further, all women depend heavily on fish, because they should never eat the meat of a tapir and because other meats are also taboo at various times of their lives.

---

[10]The Ocaina and Witoto also use bitter manioc but prepare it by a different method; the result is quite different.

1.4.5 Animal husbandry

Every woman has a few chickens. These are usually left to search for their own food. However some women plant corn to feed the chickens. Many baby chicks fall victim to hawks and other predators shortly after they hatch because they are not protected.

Aside from raising chickens, there is little other animal husbandry. Dogs are kept for hunting, and are valued for that purpose.

1.4.6 House construction

Two types of house are constructed, the large communal house and individual family houses. The men build the houses.

The communal house

The communal house is square, 30–40 feet on each side (depending on the number of people who will occupy it), with a sloping thatched roof and low walls of split logs. Around the sides of the house are sleeping platforms about six feet off the ground. These are large enough for mats for the whole family.

When a communal house is built, all the men of the clan, as well as others identified with the clan, participate in building it. First the four main pillars are brought from the rain forest. Each is about eight meters long and requires a solid column of men to carry it. Upon reaching the village they notch the end to support a crossbeam. Each pole is then set in a deep hole, the four holes on the corners of a square. Two crossbeams are placed on opposing sides, and then the two others over these.

Lifting these beams into place is accomplished as follows: Four strong young men are chosen. (The strongest vie for the opportunity to show their strength in doing it.) They tie two long poles against each upright such that these cross right at the top. A large vine is attached to the beam, run over the pillar, and pulled by at least a dozen people on the other side. However, these people can only support the beam, not advance it. The four men push the beam up the poles, each man on one of the four poles, each with a loop of vine around his feet to help clench the pole. They push in concert and then rest; the people pull the vine, supporting the beam while the four men rest. In this way the beam is advanced to the top and pushed over into the notch. Once erected the poles are tied in place with strong vines.

To the framework so erected are tied poles that will support the roof and sides. Panels about three meters long are prepared for the sides and roof. These consist of the leaves of the ahɨ '*carana*[11] palm' woven and attached to long strips of the outer sheath of the *pona* palm. These panels are tied to the supporting poles from the bottom to the top, each overlapping the former (as shingles do). These roofs last about four or five years, depending on how close the panels are tied one to another.

After the new house is completed, the chief calls a big festival for all of his people to inaugurate the house and to gain the blessing of the supernatural powers. It is a great day of eating, singing, and dancing.

There are five or six communal houses on the Igará-Paraná River, one on the Putumayo River, three on the Caquetá River in Colombia, and four or five on the Ampiyacu and Yaguasyacu Rivers.

Individual family houses

A nuclear family house—in contrast to the communal house—is made like those typically found along the rivers in the Amazon basin: The floor and walls are made with the flattened hard outer sheath of the *pona* palm. The floor is about a meter and a half above the ground. The roof is made of woven ahɨ palm leaves. There are one or two bedrooms and an open porch.

Off to one side, under an adjoining roof, there is a cook house. A large fire table is made with a framework of poles filled with earth; this makes a nice hard surface on which to build a fire. (Some use old sewing machine treadles and such things, propped on rocks or wood, to form a cooking surface.) A tripod made from poles serves to suspend the kettles. A hanging shelf constructed from strips of *pona* (to protect food from rats) and possibly a table complete the kitchen furniture.

Some families now have a mattress for the head of the house and some have bags, which they have sewn, filled with leaves or kapok gathered from the trees. Sometimes they make a mat from palm leaves. Most people still spread a sheet on the floor under a mosquito net. Whole families may sleep under one net. As the children grow, the family tries to buy more blankets and nets. A *lamparina*, a simple kerosene lamp, is left burning all night for protection against wild animals and the spirits. Log stairways may be pulled up or gates closed to keep dogs and animals out. Lots of people now make railings around their porches to keep small children from falling.

---

[11] This is probably not carnauba, despite the similarity of the local Spanish name.

There is no place for babies except in hammocks, so they are carried most of the time in a tò?hípà, a sling carried over one shoulder such that the child straddles the opposite hip. Traditionally this sling was made from bark cloth. Now it is usually made from any cloth.

1.4.7 Weaving

The men gather reeds and weave baskets and sieves, both for their own use and for sale. Everyone now weaves *jicras* 'shoulder bags' and hammocks to sell. These are made from the fibers of the *chambira* palm, which are twined by rolling along the thigh.

1.5 Dress and personal adornment

The Bora now wear western-style clothing. Some of this they purchase and some they sew themselves. Both the men and the women sew, either by hand or with a sewing machine. They enjoy beauty in attire as well as in ornaments such as bracelets and earrings.

In former times Bora men wore a loincloth made of bark cloth. Men (and women) used to wear sticks through their noses; some of the older people still have the holes in their noses, but no longer wear the sticks.

They used to—and to some extent still do—paint designs on their bodies. They painted their eyebrows black, as well as their lips, the area around their mouths, and a large stripe around their chins. Many still paint the typical Bora designs all over their bodies for festivals.

Until recent years, Bora men and women sewed all their own clothing. This was sewn from fabric acquired from the *patrón* or from river traders. Each household sought to acquire a sewing machine (which became a symbol of status).[12] Due to the availability of presewn clothing throughout Peru, the importance of sewing machines has greatly declined.

Women used to wash their long, straight hair in *huito*, a plant dye that would make it shiny black. Indeed, some still use this. Now, however, many women have permanents, and large, showy hair ornaments have replaced the smaller traditional hair clips.

---

[12]Whereas status was once shown by owning a sewing machine, it is now shown with radios, televisions, wrist watches, shoes for every member of the family, and gold in the teeth. For example, a lady with a toothache was once taken to a visiting dentist, who put in a white porcelain filling in the front of the woman's mouth. She was outraged. She later saved enough money to go to Pucallpa and have gold fillings put in. Sometimes Bora people have gold crowns put on the front teeth, even though these are not needed.

1.6 Religion

Relatively little is known about traditional Bora religion. The chief, Mibeco, said that the evil thunder god splits trees from top to bottom with lightning, and then plants the life of a new animal in the ground. In this way, the wild and dangerous animals of the rain forest were created. Many of these animals, especially the jaguar, were believed to have special powers, which could harm people, or which could protect a clan. If the latter, the animal in question was not killed or eaten by members of that clan, and the clan's shaman claimed that that animal gave him special power.[13] The Bora did not worship such animals but respected them for their powers. They made appeasement offerings to the spirits of some animals. (This is also true of one type of tree, for which an offering was made before it was cut down.)

The shaman still follows these beliefs and employs the teeth of the jaguar to adversely affect others: he is said to cause the swelling of knee joints, with an eventual, very painful death. Several deaths in 1953 were attributed to such shamanistic practice.

While most Bora no longer observe the practices of the traditional religion, they still have a great fear of the shaman's powers. The shaman was, perhaps, the most powerful man in Bora culture. He was feared, and was always paid for his assistance. Cultural change has diminished his power. With medicines available at the *Posta Medica* or from outsiders, the people call on the shaman less frequently.

It was the custom in the old days for the shaman to assign babies a protective totem, usually one of the following: dove, hummingbird, partridge, parrot, stork, *panguano*, partridge, paca, agouti.[14] Each person expected to receive help from his totem. This naming practice and belief has declined due to the conversion of many Bora people to Christianity.

In 1984 or 1985 a six-year-old boy was caught in the claws of a jaguar of the type known as *colorado*.[15] When the father came running with his shotgun, the jaguar was distracted, enabling the boy to get away. The father fired his only shell, but missed. The jaguar ran a short way off. After

---

[13]Several years ago a man living at the mouth of the Sumún River was reported to have claimed ownership of the *huangana*, the peccary lacking the white stripe across its shoulder. He claimed to be able to talk to them when they came to his house. He demanded that hunters pay him when they killed one, or otherwise suffer the consequences.

[14]These animals were regarded as good, while the deer, collared peccary (*sajino*), white-lipped peccary (*huangana*), tapir (*sachavaca*), owl, bat, and certain other animals were regarded as evil. The shaman also worked with the power of the evil animals.

[15]This is about two feet high, four feet long, of a reddish brown color (without spots).

getting another shell from the chief's house the father found the jaguar and killed it. He then took the boy to Thiesens for medical attention. (His wounds were many, but superficial.) Subsequently, the mother borrowed money from her friends and relatives to take the boy to the shaman, to have the boy freed from the smell of the jaguar, so that another jaguar would not come back to get him. The people of the village ate the jaguar.

A festival is performed for the white heron, the ìt͡ʃʰɯ́ɯ́ʔpà. This bird is worshipped during the festival, and it is said that it actually speaks to participants during the festival. (We know little more about this festival because the Bora people are reluctant to tell about it, and we have never been present when it was held.)

1.6.1 The boa constrictor

The Bora people have great respect for the boa constrictor. When a new communal house is dedicated, a boa is painted on one of the large horizontal logs of the framework of the house. It is believed that no one should kill a boa. If, for some reason, someone must do so, he should first locate a tall tree nearby, and wind a vine into a loop as used to support the feet when climbing a tree. Then he should go kill the boa, run to the tree, put the vine loop at the foot of the tree, and run off in the other direction. It is believed that the spirit of the boa would follow him, seeking revenge, but upon coming to the tree and seeing the vine, would deduce that he had gone up to the upper world, and thus would stop pursuing him. It is also believed that if a boa were shot with a gun, its spirit would damage the gun so that it would never shoot straight again.

Boas pose a real threat to the Bora people. Once a woman was out hunting with her husband late at night. She waited in a canoe while her husband followed the sound of an animal on the bank. He heard her scream. When he got to the canoe, she was gone. The canoe was full of water and the kerosene lamp was floating on the water. The people from the village came and searched the area thoroughly, but she was never found. She was almost certainly pulled from the canoe by a large boa. The woman's father ingested *ayahuasca* (a hallucinogenic vine) to have a vision to show him where to find her. He reported seeing her, and said that she told him to bring the church members to catch her. She was never found.

1.6.2 Burial

The bodies of deceased members of the chief's family were formerly buried in the communal house; others were buried under their individual houses. Now, however, most people are buried in the cemetery, which is a short distance from the village. A coffin is made from whatever wood is available, sometimes even the door of a house.

There is a wake where people gather to show respect to the dead and/or to his family. Usually now, the pastor leads the people in singing hymns and may preach a sermon. The family of the deceased serve coffee to all who attend the wake. The body is buried early the next morning (weather permitting). Sometimes there is a service in the home before going to the cemetery, and sometimes just a brief graveside service.

1.7 Music

Bora music is pentatonic. Each melody belongs to a certain festival. The words may be changed to fit the situation of a particular festival, but a festival's melody cannot be used in any other context. Apart from the festival songs and an occasional lullaby, there seems to be no other native Bora music.

Bora people have now adopted the eight-note scale, for example, singing hymns and choruses translated from western languages. Some have learned to play guitars. They enjoy accompanying their singing with tambourines and rattles.

1.8 The Bora signal drums

The Bora language has an elaborate tone system that, in conjunction with lexical and grammatical information, determines the pitch of each syllable. Messages can be communicated by beating the tones on suitably made drums, and this is still done in the larger villages.[16]

The Bora people use drums to communicate messages within their communities and over long distances from one community to another. Every clan has a large communal house in which there is a set of signal drums, just inside and to the right of the main door. These drums play a very

---

[16]This section was first drafted in 1955; for a published account see (Thiesen 1969). How messages are coded is described briefly in section 1.8.3.

important role in their social life. There is hardly a day when the drums are not used for some reason. Many days they are used numerous times and occasionally the sound of the drums can be heard throughout the day.

No matter where someone may be, so long as he or she is within hearing distance of the drums, the message will reach him. Early in the morning and late at night the drums can be heard as far as twenty miles away. If a message is to be sent a greater distance the next communal house relays it. In this way messages can—in a very short time—reach the whole group.

1.8.1 Various functions of the drums

The drums are used to call the people together for festivals, or to go fishing or hunting. They are used to inform the group of the arrival of visitors or to call someone back from his fields or from the rain forest, where he may be hunting.

When they prepare for a festival the drums are played to advise the people of the preparations in progress. For one festival the drums are played day and night for five days preceding the festival. There is a different message for each day that tells the people which part of the preparations is being done that day. When the festival starts, the drums are quiet. They are never used to accompany singing and dancing.

One interesting use of the drums is when they have a contest to see who can drink the most starch drink. Sitting on low stools near a large earthen vessel they dip into the liquid food pouring it down in big gulps in unbelievable quantities, until sitting becomes almost unbearable. The one who drinks the most goes over to the drums and announces his victory, giving the name of the victor and that of the loser.

Since the Bora people do not serve meals at regular hours, the drums are used to tell those at work or away from the house that dinner is ready. When a trader comes his arrival is announced on the drums. It is not necessary to send someone to advise the people. Those at greater distances hear the message as soon as those nearby, thus saving sometimes several hours. Soon the people begin coming with their produce to trade for merchandise.

The signal drums (*manguaré*) are not used to call people to school or church because—it is said—the drums belong to their traditional beliefs.[17]

---

[17]Instead, to announce school and church events, a bottle with the bottom broken out is blown like a trumpet.

1.8.2 How the signal drums are made

The drums are made in pairs from hardwood logs. Each is about five feet long; the smaller one, the "male" drum is about one and a half feet in diameter, while the larger "female" drum is about two feet in diameter; see plate 81 of Steward (1948), following page 762.

A slit is carved down the top of each drum, leaving vibrating panels on either side. One side is always made a bit wider than the other, so that the two sides yield different tones. The "mother" or "female" drum is larger than the other, so yields lower pitches. In sum, the two drums produce four distinct pitches.

It takes about a month to make each drum. After the tree has been cut down and shaped externally, a hole is started with an axe near each end of the log. Starting in these holes the log is very carefully hollowed by fire. Hardwood chips are placed in the holes and the fire is fanned with a feather fan. Every so often the charred parts are chipped out and the fire is rekindled. After the fire has penetrated the log some distance the fire is directed with a bamboo blowpipe to burn in the right places and the finished edges are protected with wet clay (that must be replaced frequently). Finally, accompanied by a special ceremony, a slit is cut to one side of center between the two holes.

Short clubs are carved and covered with latex gathered from the rain forest and cured over a fire.

The two drums are suspended parallel, the ends higher on one end than the other. As one faces the higher end, the larger drum is always on the right. The drummer stands between the drums, facing the higher end, and strikes them with the latex-covered clubs.

1.8.3 How messages are drummed

Because each drum has two pitches (one on each side of the slit) the pair of drums has four pitches. However, messages are sent using only two contrastive pitches (tones). Although all four pitches are sometimes used in the festival announcement songs, at any given time only two are contrastive.

The system of communication is based on Bora's syllable structure and tone system. Each syllable in a word has either a high or low tone and receives a corresponding high or low tone beat on the drums.[18] Thus, the

---

[18]Here, "syllable" refers to surface syllables *after* the application of rules like PLTS and FLTS; see pages 70 and 74.

order of the high and low tones is the means by which a message is sent and understood. For example, 1b is drummed as in 1a (with no extra pause at word boundaries).

(1) a. H L   H   H L L
    b. ʔí kʲʰò: kʰá ɾɛ́ tì tʃʰà   'Come here now!'
      ícyoocáré   dicha

Because many words have identical tone and syllable patterns it is necessary to have standardized phrases. A given message may have a number of different phrases; these may be repeated several times and in varying orders, but the word order within each phrase is rigid.

How someone would be called to come is illustrated in table 1.1. First, the call notice is drummed. This varies depending on whether one or more than one person is being called, and on whether the person (or persons) is instructed to come immediately or at their convenience. Second, the name of the person or persons being called is drummed, first the clan name and then the personal name (or names). Finally, the purpose for wanting the person(s) to come is drummed.

Table 1.1 A Bora drum message: Come to sing!

HL H H	LL	HL H H	LL
í kʲʰò:kʰáɾɛ́	tìtʃʰà	í kʲʰò:kʰáɾɛ́	tìtʃʰà
Ícyoocáré	dicha.	Ícyoocáré	dicha.
right.now	come.Sg	right.now	come.Sg

HL H	L H L L	L H L	L H L
í ɲèhé	tʰùɯtʰáβà:pὲ	tʃìkʲʰáʔpà	tʃìkʲʰáʔpà
Íñejé	tutávaabe	Llicyáhba	Llicyáhba.
clan.name	chief	name	name

HL H H	LL	L H H L L	L H H L L
í kʲʰò:kʰáɾɛ́	tìtʃʰà	mɛ̀máˣtsʰíβàkʰì	mɛ̀máˣtsʰíβàkʰì
Ícyoocáré	dicha	memájtsívaki	memájtsívaki.
right.now	come.Sg	for.to.sing	for.to.sing

It is particularly interesting that drum communication does not exploit the distinction between short and long vowels, or between heavy and light syllables. Although no study has been made of the effectiveness of drum communication (what range of messages can be communicated, if techniques are used to increase redundancy, how frequently "repairs" must

be made, and so forth), it is clear that some level of communication is possible. For example, Thiesen once needed his tape recorder, which was in a downriver village. Knowing that someone was travelling upriver, he had a drummer ask that the traveller bring it. Thiesen got what he had requested. On another occasion the chief from a downriver village drummed to the chief from an upriver village, asking him to send something down with Thiesen (who was travelling downriver).

Chapter 2

Phonology

This chapter deals with Bora's sound system: its phonemes, its syllables, vocalic length, and so forth. Tone is dealt with in chapter 3.

2.1 The Bora writing system

The Bora writing system uses the following letters: a for /a/; b for /p/; c (written before a, o or u) or k (written before i, ɨ or e) for /kʰ/; ch for /tʃʰ/; d for /t/; ds for /ts/; e for /ɛ/; g for /k/; h for /ʔ/; i for /i/; ɨ for /ɨ/; j for /h/ (syllable initial) or [ˣ] (syllable final); ll for /tʃ/; m for /m/; n for /n/; ñ for both /ɲ/ (a phoneme) and [ɲ] (an allophone of /n/); o for /o/; p for /pʰ/; r for /ɾ/; t for /tʰ/; ts for /tsʰ/; u for /ɯ/, v for /β/; w for /kp/; and y for either /j/ (the palatalized counterpart of /ɾ/) or the palatalization of a preceding consonant.

There are two tones: high and low. High tone is indicated by an acute accent over the vowel. Low tone is indicated by the absence of an accent. (In the phonemic representations, low tone is indicated by a grave accent.)

Vowel length is represented by doubling the vowel, e.g., aa represents /a:/ and áá represents /á:/ with a high tone. However, if the adjacent vowels bear different tones, then they represent different syllables, e.g., aá represents /a.á/ and áa represents /á.a/. (There are a few exceptions; see example 7 and discussion below.)

2.2 Syllables

The syllable is defined by the template in 2:

(2) (C) V ($\left\{\begin{array}{c}x\\ ?\\ :\end{array}\right\}$)

That is, syllables begin with an optional consonant, followed by an obligatory vowel, either short or long. A syllable may be closed by /ʔ/ (orthographic h) or /ˣ/ (orthographic j). Examples follow:

(3) a. à.mó:.pɛ̀ (amóóbe) V.CV:.CV 'fish (sg)'
b. à.mó.mɛ̀ (amóme) V.CV.CV 'fish (pl)'
c. ò:.ʔí:.pʲɛ̀ (oohííbye) V:.CV:.CV 'dog'
d. màˣ.tʃʰò (majcho) CVˣ.CV 'eat'
e. nàʔ.pɛ̀ (nahbe) CVʔ.CV 'brother'

Generally, /ʔ/ and /ˣ/ occur in the coda of a syllable only if it has a short vowel.[1] Thus, there are three ways to make a syllable heavy: /ʔ/, /ˣ/, and vowel length. (See section 2.7.2 for further discussion.) These are represented in figure 2.1, where σ represents a syllable and μ represents a mora:

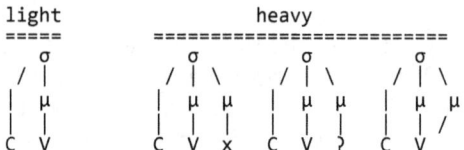

Figure 2.1 Light and heavy syllables

---

[1]The way Bora is written may mislead one to think that a word has a syllable final /ʔ/ after a long vowel, but it is not so. For example, what is written mááhdohíjcyáh is really má.á ʔ.tò.ʔɨˣ.kʲʰáʔ, in which the first syllable is (an allomorph of) the proclitic or prefix mɛ- 'SAP'. Likewise, ɨ́ɨhbotáháñeri 'with his/her coverings' is ɨ́.fʔ.pò.tʰá.ʔá.ɲɛ̀.rì by the addition of i- 'self', and dɨ́ɨhbota 'your covering' is tɨ́.fʔ.pò.tʰà by the addition of ti- 'your'.

The following have /ʔ/ after two homorganic vowels but they are not cases of a long vowel followed by /ʔ/ because the vowels bear different tones and thus form two syllables:

átsʰíʔhʲáà	(átsiíhjyáa)	V.CV.Vʔ.CV.V
ɨ́:pùrɨ́ʔháà	(ɨ́ɨbuúhjáa)	V:.CV.Vʔ.CV.V
ìmíkpùrɨ́ʔháà	(imíwuúhjáa)	V.CV.CV.Vʔ.CV.V
màáʔtótsʰòʔfˣkʲʰáítʲʰùrò	(maáhdótsohíjcyáítyuró)	CV.Vʔ.CV.CV.CVˣ.CV.V.CV.CV
mɛ̀ɛ́ʔtì:βátʃɛ̀ʔfˣkʲʰá:pɛ́	(meéhdɨɨválleh íjcyáábé)	CV.Vʔ.CV:.CV.CV.CVˣ.CV:.CV
múmàáʔháà	(múnaáhjáa)	CV.CV.Vʔ.CV.V
nɨ́pʰáˣkʰìʔtʃó	(núpájkiíhlló)	CV.CVˣ.CV.Vʔ.CV
kpápʰfjùrɨ́kʰɨ́:pɛ̀ɛ́ʔhɨ́	(wápíyuúcúúbeéhjɨ́)	CV.CV.CV.V.CV:.CV.Vʔ.CV

2.3. VOWELS

The tone system is blind to vowel length: *where* tones dock depends on *syllables*, with no regard for whether these have short or long vowels. However, there is an allophonic process that relates tone and length; see section 3.1. Adjacent homorganic vowels bearing different tones are illustrated in 4–6a and those bearing the same tone are illustrated in 4–6b. (The form between slashes indicates a more underlying form before the long vowel has been "split" by PLTS; see section 3.14.)

(4) a. tì.í.pʲɛ̀   /tìːpʲɛ̀/   (diíbye)   CV.V.CV 'he'
   b. tíː.pʲɛ̀ ɛ́ʔnɛ̀ /tíːpʲɛ̀ ɛ́ʔnɛ̀/ (diíbye éhne) CV:.CV   'his (thing)'

(5) a. taábo
      tʰà.á.pò   /tʰàːpò/   CV.V.CV   'medicine'
   b. taabóóbe
      tʰàː.póː.pɛ̀ /tʰàːpóːpɛ̀/   CV:.CV:.CV   'the doctor'
   c. tááboóbe
      tʰáː.pò.ó.pɛ̀ /tʰáːpòːpɛ̀/   CV:.CV.V.CV   'he medicates'

(6) a. cuúmu
      kʰɯ̀.ɯ́.mɯ̀   /kʰɯ̀ːmɯ̀/   CV.V.CV   'large signal drum'
   b. cúúmuba
      kʰɯ́ː.mɯ̀.pà /kʰɯ́ːmɯ̀pà/   CV:.CV.CV   'small drum'

There are a few cases where adjacent, homorganic vowels with the same tone represent different syllables. The root kpàjɛɛ- 'to rest' ends in two like vowels, each projecting a syllable. In 7, note that -Ⓛ:βɛ̀ 'sIn' lengthens only the second of the two vowels:

(7) a. ó kpájɛ́ɛ́-ːβɛ̀-tʰɛ́-ʔì   (Ó wáyééévetéhi.) 'I go to rest.'
     I rest-sIn-go.do-⟨t⟩
   b. ó kpájɛ̀ɛ̀-ːβɛ́-βá-ʔì   (Ó wáyeeevéváhi.) 'I come to rest.'
     I rest-sIn-come.do-⟨t⟩
   c. kpájɛ̀ɛ̀-ːβɛ̀   (¡Wáyeééve!)   'Rest!
     rest.imp-sIn   (sg imperative)'

Another example is kpàːkóò 'throw'. By contrast, the final /ɯ̀ɯ̀/ of ɨhɯ́ɯ̀ 'dove' is a single syllable with a long vowel, but may be followed by the classifier -ɯ ⟨round⟩ as in examples 85a and c, page 71.

2.3 Vowels

The vowels are given in table 2.1. The symbols in parentheses are those used in the Bora writing system.

Table 2.1 Vowels

	front	central	back −round	back +round
high	i (i)	ɨ (ɨ)	ɯ (u)	
mid	ɛ (e)			o (o)[a]
low		a (a)		

[a]/o/ is the only rounded vowel and is only slightly round. /ɯ/ (u), by contrast, is unrounded.

With the exception of /i/, which is tense, all the vowels are lax. /a, ɛ, i/ and /o/ are pronounced as [a], [ɛ], [ɪ] and [o] respectively. Examples follow:

(8) a. àmómè (amóme) 'fish'
  b. ò:ʔí:pʲɛ̀ (oohííbye) 'dog'
  c. kʰá:nìí (cááníí) 'father'

/ɨ/ (ɨ) is a high central unrounded vowel, as in 9:

(9) a. ṳ̀hɨ̀ (ujɨ) 'plantain'
  b. ɨ̀hṳ̀ (ɨɨju) 'horse'
  c. ɨ́hṳ̀ṳ̀ (ɨjuúu) 'dove'

/ɯ/ (u) is a high back unrounded vowel, as in 10:

(10) a. kʰṳ̀ṳ́mṳ̀ (cuúmu) 'drum'
  b. ṳ̀ṳ́ (uú) 'you'

See (Parker 2001) for a thorough discussion of the vowels.

2.3.1 Rules applying to vowels

The following rules account for certain variations in the vowels.

1. /i/ is lowered when its syllable is closed by [ˣ]. For example, ìˣkʲʰà 'to be' is pronounced [ɪˣkʲʰa]; its initial /i/ is lower than that of íhʲàá 'this house', in which the /h/ following the /i/ is the onset of the next syllable. The pronunciation of /i/ as [ɪ] is not written in the phonetic representations throughout this grammar.

/i/ becomes /ɨ/ when the following syllable has /ɨ/. For example, compare 11a and b:

2.3. VOWELS

(11) a. í-hʲàá   (íjyaá) 'this (house, clothing,...)'
       this-⟨shelter⟩
    b. í-hɨ́ɨ̯   (íjɨɨ̯) 'this (pill, country,...)'
       this-⟨disk⟩

For another example see ɨ́:tsʰɨ́:mɛ̀ 'self's children' in examples 471 and 472, page 209.

Likewise, the proclitic ti 'your' becomes tɨ immediately before a syllable containing /ɨ/; witness 12:

(12) /tì nɨ̀:tsʰɨ́ɨ̯-kpà/
     [tɨ́nɨ̀:tsʰɨ́ɨ̯kpà]
     (díniitsúwa) 'your machete'

This assimilation also occurs internal to morphemes, as in tsɨ̀:tsɨ̀ 'money'; we know of no morpheme in which /i/ precedes /ɨ/.

2. /ɛ/ is raised before /i/; for example, the /ɛ/ of kpákʰìmʲɛ̂ì 'work' is [e], whereas it is [ɛ] in úmɛ̀ʔɛ̀ 'tree'.

/ɛː/ becomes [æː] before a syllable containing /i/; for example /mɛːni/ 'pig' is pronounced [mæ̀ǽnì]. (/æː/ becomes [æ̀ǽ] by PLTS, as discussed in section 3.7.1.)

In some cases, when /ɛ/ is followed closely by /a/, it becomes /a/. For example, witness the alternation between mɛ- ~ ma- 'our' in 13:

(13) m$\begin{Bmatrix}\acute{\epsilon}\\\acute{a}\end{Bmatrix}$-àβʲɛ́hɨ̀ɨ̯-ːpɛ̀ (m$\begin{Bmatrix}\acute{e}\\\acute{a}\end{Bmatrix}$avyéjuúbe) 'our chief'

3. In a few words /a/ becomes [ɔ]; for example the /a/ of pʰámɛ̀ːrɛ̀ 'all animate' is pronounced [ɔ]: [pɔ́mæ̀ǽrɛ̀]. This seems to happen only before nasal consonants, and in relatively few words. (There is no contrast between [a] and [ɔ].)

4. A transitional [y] can sometimes be perceived between an [i] and a following [a]; for example, ìáːpɛ̀ 'animal' may be pronounced [ìyáːpɛ̀].

2.3.2 Vowel length

Bora has both short and long vowels (as amply attested throughout).

Certain suffixes lengthen the preceding vowel. For example, when -ⓁːpÈ ⟨SgM⟩ is suffixed to a stem, the stem-final vowel is lengthened, as occurs twice in 14:

(14) Oke ájcuube oohííbyedívu.
    ò-kʰɛ̀   áˣkʰɨ̀ɨ̯ːpɛ̀   òːʔíːpʲɛ̀-tí-βɨ̀ɨ̯   'He gave me a dog.'
    I-objAn give-⟨SgM⟩ dog-⟨SgM⟩-anim-thm

This long vowel may become two syllables by PLTS (discussed in section 3.7.1, as in 15:

(15) /má^xtʃʰò-ːpè/ [má^xtʃʰòópè] (májchoóbe) 'he eats'
    eat-⟨SgM⟩

Other suffixes that lengthen preceding vowels are -ːkʰɯ 'duIn', ⓛ○-ːnɛ 'plural' -ːpʰi ⟨SgM⟩, -(ː)ɾɛ 'only', in some contexts -ⓛ^(x)tʰɛ̀ ⟨AnPl⟩, and -ⓛːβɛ 'sIn'.

If the verb ends in a long vowel, such a suffix does not further lengthen it. We might posit a rule that deletes the verb's length but this is not necessary: The mora contributed by the suffix can not be syllabified because the syllable template allows only two mora; see section 2.2. Thus, it is lost by "stray erasure":

$$\begin{array}{c}\sigma\\/\;|\;\backslash\\ \mu\;\;\mu + \mu\\|\;|\;/\;\;|\\ C\;V\;\;\;\;C\end{array} \quad ==> \quad \begin{array}{c}\sigma\;\;\;\;\sigma\\/\;|\;\backslash\;\;\;/\\ \mu\;\;\mu\\|\;|\;/\;\;|\\ C\;V\;\;\;\;C\end{array}$$

For example, 16a shows that tsʰaː- 'come' has a long vowel. However, in 16b, where it is combined with -ⓛːpɛ, this remains /aː/, which becomes /àá/ by PLTS (see section 3.7.1):

(16) a. tsʰáː-mùɾtsʰì   (tsáámutsi) 'they (DuM) come'
     b. tsʰàː-ːpè   (tsaábe)   'he comes'

Examples 17a and b show that the root ends with a long vowel, while 17c shows that the addition of a suffix that ordinarily adds length does not result in three moras:

(17) a. pʰɛ̀ː-tʃɛ̀ ⟶/pʰɛ̀ːtʃɛ̀/ [pʰɛ̀ɛ́tʃɛ̀]   (peélle) 'she goes'
     b. pʰɛ̀ː-mɛ̀ ⟶/pʰɛ̀ːmɛ̀/ [pʰɛ̀ɛ́mɛ̀]   (peéme) 'they go'
     c. pʰɛ̀ː-ːpè ⟶/pʰɛ̀ːpè/ { [pʰɛ̀ɛ́pè] / *[pʰɛ̀ɛ́ːpè] } (peébe) 'he goes'

And as a final example, consider -huɨkʰo: 'initiated or very recent'. Example 18a shows only a single long vowel where three moras might be expected; examples 18b–d show that this suffix does indeed end in a long vowel:

(18) a. màˣtʃʰóhuɨkʰòópè   (majchójúcoóbe)
        /màˣtʃʰó-huɨkʰòː-ːpè/   'he has eaten'
     b. màˣtʃʰóhuɨkʰòótʃè   (majchójúcoólle)
        /màˣtʃʰó-huɨkʰòː-tʃè/   'she has eaten'
     c. màˣtʃʰóhuɨkʰóːmè   (majchójucóóme)
        /màˣtʃʰó-huɨkʰóː-mè/   'they have eaten'
     d. màˣtʃʰóhuɨkʰòːmùɾtsʰì   (majchójúcoomútsi)
        /màˣtʃʰó-huɨkʰòː-mùɾtsʰì/ 'they(DuM) have eaten'

2.4 Consonants

The consonants are given in table 2.2.

Table 2.2 Consonants

	labial	coronal			dorsal	laryngeal
obs[a] len	p (b)	t (d)		ts (ds)	k (g)	ʔ (h)
for	pʰ (p)	tʰ (t)		tsʰ (ts)	kʰ (k or c)	
len pal	pʲ (by)	tʲ (dy)		tsʲ ~ tʃ (ll)	kʲ (gy)	ʔʲ (hy)
for pal	pʲʰ (py)	tʲʰ (ty)		tsʲʰ ~ tʃʰ (ch)	kʲʰ (ky)	
lab-vel					k͡p ~ kʷ (w)	
fric plain	β (v)				x ~ h (j)	
pal	βʲ (vy)				hʲ (jy)	
nas plain	m (m)	n (n)				
pal	mʲ (my)	ɲ (ñ)				
res plain			ɾ (r)			
pal			jᵇ (y)			

[a]obs = obstruent, len = lenis, for = fortis, pal = palatal, lab-vel = labial-velar, fric = fricative, nas = nasal, res = resonant
[b]Or possibly ɾʲ.

Discussion follows. However, we will leave open various questions about the phonemic status of certain sounds: (1) Which palatalized consonants are allophones of the corresponding nonpalatalized consonant? Some instances are probably allophones while others are phonemes in their own right. (2) Is [ʔ] an allophone of /ʔ/, with which it is in complementary distribution? (3) Is [ˣ] an allophone of /h/, with which it is in complementary distribution?

/p/ (orthographic b) and /pʰ/ (orthographic p) differ by aspiration, as in the following pair:

(19) a. p̲ʰè:pè (peébe) 'he goes'
    b. p̲é:pèé (béébeé) 'the new one'

/t/ (orthographic d) and /tʰ/ (orthographic t) differ by aspiration, as in the following pair:

(20) a. t̲à:tʃʰì (daáchi) 'his son'
    b. t̲ʰà:tʃè (taálle) 'she cries'

/ts/ (orthographic ds) and /tsʰ/ (orthographic ts) differ by aspiration, as in the following pair:

(21) a. t̲sʰɨtsʰɨ̀hɨ̀ (tsɨtsɨ́jɨ) 'white button'
    b. t̲sɨ́:tsɨ̀hɨ̀ (dsɨ́ɨdsɨjɨ) 'coin'

/tʃ/ (orthographic ll) and /tʃʰ/ (orthographic ch) differ by aspiration, as in the following pairs:
   (22) a. tʃʰémè:pè (chémeébe) 'he is sick'
       b. t͡ʃéːnè:pè (llééneébe) 'he eats fruit'
   (23) a. ít͡ʃʰì: (íchii) 'here'
       b. ít͡ʃíí (íllií) 'his/her son'
/tʃʰ/ (orthographic ch) contrasts with /tʲʰ/ (orthographic ty), as in 24:
   (24) a. áàt͡ʃʰì (áachi) 'outside'
       b. àːt̪ʲʰɛ̀ (aátye) 'those'
/k/ (orthographic g) and /kʰ/ (orthographic c before a, o or u but k before e, i or ɨ) differ by aspiration, as in 25:
   (25) a. kòːkʰómɛ̀   (goocóme)   'they laugh'
       b. kʰáʔkúmùɾkʰò (cáhgúnuco) 'cahuana (starch drink)'
       c. kʰíkʰìːhʲɛ̀   (kíkiíjye) 'bat'
/kp/ (orthographic w) is a voiceless labial-velar stop, as in 26:
   (26) a. kpàʔáɾò   (waháro)   'mother'
       b. ó kpàːhákʰɯ̀-ʔì (ó waajácúhi) 'I know-⟨t⟩'
   There are interesting restrictions on /kp/ (w). First, it only occurs before /à/ or /ɯ/ (u). Second, it never undergoes palatalization (see section 2.4.2). For example, we expect palatalization after /i/ but that does not happen with /kp/: imíwu ìmíkpɯ̀ 'very good'. Third, generally neither /ʔ/ (h) nor /ˣ/ (j) (preaspiration) may precede /kp/, but a long vowel may, as in ɛ̀:-kpà (that-⟨slab⟩) and ímiá:-kpà (proper-⟨slab⟩).
/β/ (orthographic v) is a voiced labial fricative, as in 27:
   (27) a. ɾéβóːβɛ̀-ːpè (révóóveébe) 'he turns around'
       b. βàháːβɛ̀   (vajááve)   'to become punctured'
/h/ (orthographic j) may occur as the onset of a syllable, at the beginning of a word, as in 28a, or in the middle of a word, as in 28b:
   (28) a. hàá   (jaá)   'house'
       b. kpàːhákʰɯ̀ (waajácu)   'know'
/ˣ/ (orthographic j) is preaspiration. It occupies the coda of the syllable before an aspirated consonant (see section 2.4.3), as in 29a, or it may be word final as in 29b:[2]
   (29) a. màˣt͡ʃʰò   (majcho)   'food'
       b. màˣt͡ʃʰóhɯ̀ɾˣ (majchójuj) 'eat (hurriedly)'
/ˣ/ in the syllable coda is pronounced with greater friction than is /h/ in the onset.

---
[2]Since ˣ is in complementary distribution with /h/ it might be considered an allophone of /h/.

2.4. CONSONANTS

The preaspiration of the initial consonants of certain roots, when these roots head the genitive construction, are syllabified with the final syllable of the preceding word (the possessor); see section 2.4.3.

/ʔ/ (orthographic h) is discussed in 2.4.1.
/m/ (orthographic m) is a labial nasal; e.g., mé:nìmù̀ (méénimu) 'pigs'.
/n/ (orthographic n) is an alveolar nasal; e.g., mé:n̲ìmù̀ (méénimu) 'pigs'.
/ɲ/ (orthographic ñ) is an alveolar nasal with a palatal offglide; e.g., há:ʔàɲɛ̀ (jáhañe) 'various houses'. 30 shows the contrast between /n/ and /ɲ/:

(30) a. n̲àmɛ̀ (name) 'type of monkey'
    b. ɲ̲àmà (ñama) 'to bewitch'

Although /ɲ/ is a phoneme, in some contexts it might be considered an allophone of /n/.

/ɾ/ (orthographic r) is a voiced alveolar flap. The corresponding palatalized form is the palatal approximant [j] (orthographic y). It occurs in the environment of /i/ (but never of /ɨ/); for example:

(31) a. mìjímíjì   (miyímíyi) 'eyes half closed'
    b. βìjíːβʲɛ̀   (viyíívye) 'to rotate'
    c. a ʧìʔíjò   (llihíyo) 'father'
    d. ɾoːʔò ~ jòːʔò (roóho) 'mole cricket'

[j] may also be a phoneme in its own right; in the words of 32 it occurs despite not being in an environment in which /ɾ/ is palatalized:

(32) a. ájánɛ́kpù̀ (áyánéwu) 'a little'
    b. jóːʔìí (yóóhií) 'type of parrot'

In the vast majority of cases, however, orthographic y represents either (1) a palatalized /ɾ/ or (2) the palatalization of a preceding consonant [Cʲ], as discussed in section 2.4.2.

2.4.1 The glottal stop

The glottal stop /ʔ/ (orthographic h) may be the onset of a syllable, as in 33 where the syllable boundaries are indicated by a period:[3]

(33) a. ʔɛ́ː.kʰò.ó (héécoó) 'meat'
    b. ɨ́ɾ.mɨ̀.ʔɛ̀ (úmɨhe) 'planted field'

[ʔ] (also orthographic h) may also occur as the coda of a syllable, either before a consonant, as seen in 34, or word finally.

(34) a. ɨ́ʔ.ná.ʔò.ó (ɨ́hnáhoó) 'power'
    b. àʔ.tò[4] (ahdo) 'pay'

---

[3]Intervocalic /ʔ/ is always a syllable onset.

When pronounced in isolation, words that begin with a vowel are pronounced with an initial glottal stop, and words that end with a vowel are pronounced with a final glottal stop. For most words, these glottal stops disappear when the word is pronounced within a phrase.

Word initially ʔ (h) is written only in words where the glottal stop persists within a phrase. Word finally [ʔ] is never written, even those that persist in a phrase.[5] For example, what is written as 35a is pronounced as in 35b:

(35) a. Muurá tsá dibye ímílletú ipyééneé.

   b. mùːrá̰ʔ tsʰá̰ʔ tìpʲḛ̀ ímítʃè-tʰúɨ ì pʲʰɛ́ː-nɛ̀ɛ̰́ʔ
      confirm not he   want-neg   self go-⟨ø⟩
      'Well, he does not want to go.'

When a morpheme ending in [ʔ] is followed by one beginning with /ʔ/, the adjacent glottal stops are pronounced as a single one. For example, ɛʔ- 'this' followed by -ʔa:mì ⟨leaf⟩ (book, paper,...) becomes simply ɛ́ʔáːmǐ 'this leaf (book, paper, etc.)'.

Several interjections have a final glottal stop, even sentence medially;[6] for example:

(36) ànḛ́ʔ mɛ̀ɛ́nùɨ   (ané meénu)   'OK. Then do it.'
     ànḛ́ʔ kpàì mɛ̀ɛ́nùɨ (ané wai meénu) 'OK. Then you may do it.'

(37) Cána bo dipye íícúií.
     kʰánàʔ pòʔ   tì-pʲʰḛ̀   íːkʰúíí 'I encourage you to
     suggest encourage youImp-go quickly   go quickly.'

Many onomatopoeic words end with a glottal stop:

(38) Callúhcállú keeme tsáá juuváyi.
     kʰàtʃúɨʔ-kʰátʃúɨʔ kʰèːmè   tsʰáː-ʔì hùːβá-jì
     tap-tap   old.man   come-⟨t⟩ trail-oblIn
     'The old man is coming on the trail with a cane (stumbling along)'.

Some words have short forms that end in a glottal stop; e.g., tsʰá̋ʔàá ~ tsʰá̋ʔ 'no'.

---

[4]This contrasts with àtò 'drink'.
[5]This convention was established because writing these cases of h was found to be both unnecessary and confusing to Bora readers.
[6]These are generally not written.

2.4.2 Palatalization

All consonants except /kp/ (w) have palatalized counterparts:[7] Even /ʔ/ (h) may be palatalized, for example, ìʔʲà 'probably'.

Consonants are often palatalized after /i/, as in 39:

(39) a. tì-ːpʲɛ̀ (that-⟨SgM⟩ diíbye) 'he'

b. ǒːʔí-mʲɛ̀ (dog-⟨AnPl⟩ oohímye) 'dogs'

However, consonants are not always palatalized after /i/, e.g., the /m/ of ìmítʃʰò 'to encourage' is not palatalized. Likewise, in 229, page 131, neither /ʔ/ nor /m/ are palatalized after /i/ in the word ì-ʔáˣkʰí-mù̀-kʰɛ̀. See also example 404, page 194.

Consonants are also palatalized after some instances of /a/, as in 40:

(40) a. átʲʰáːpàá (átyáábaá) 'my wife'

b. àβʲɛ́nɛ̀ (avyéne) 'it hurts'

Aschmann[8] reconstructs these words as containing /*ai/, thereby accounting for why consonants following these cases of /a/ cause palatalization.[9] Consequently there are now minimal pairs that demonstrate contrast between palatalized and nonpalatalized obstruents. For example, palatalization distinguishes the conjunction in 41a from the demonstrative pronoun in 41b:

---

[7]The palatalization of a consonant is represented orthographically by a y following the consonant except in the following cases:

PLAIN		PALATALIZED	
ɾ	(r)	j	(y)
n	(n)	ɲ	(ñ)
tsʰ	(ts)	tʃʰ	(ch)
ts	(ds)	tʃ	(ll)

[8]Aschmann (1993:18, section 2.1) writes the following about /ai/:

> ...this diphthong caused the palatalization of a following alveolar consonant.... Subsequent to this process (or simultaneously), *ai was reduced to /a/ when followed by one of these palatalized alveolar consonants, thus effectively phonemicizing these consonants through the loss of the conditioning environment.

[9]In Bora there are one or two words that preserve the diphthong, for example, kpaʲtʃe 'woman'. Although the [ʲ] is pronounced in this word, it is written simply as walle.

(41) a. à-ːpè̱   tsʰáː-ˀ.   (Aabe tsáá.) (anaphoric)
       thm-⟨SgM⟩ come-⟨t⟩
    b. à-ːpʲè̱   tsʰáː-ˀ.   (Aabye tsáá.) (exophoric)
       that-⟨SgM⟩ come-⟨t⟩
    a. 'That one (aforementioned) comes.'
    b. 'That one (indicating) comes.'

Further examples of this contrast follow:

(42) a. màˣtsʰì̱   (majtsi)   'song'
        màˣʧʰì̱   (majchi)   'juice'
     b. kpàˣkʰò   (wajco)   'flower'
        kpàˣkʲʰò   (wajcyo)   'hook'
     c. kpápè̱ákʰò   (wábeáco)   'to fold (double)'
        kpápʲè̱ákʰò (wábyeáco) 'to entangle'

Because palatalized consonants have now become independent phonemes (in at least some contexts) they may now appear where no preceding vowel accounts for the palatalization; such is the case of the initial tʲʰ in tʲʰáːjàhɨ̱ (tyááyajɨ) 'peccary', and for the /ñ/ of ɲàháˀkʰò (ñajáhco) 'softness, be soft'.[10]

Bimorphemic words such as (tahjya) tʰàˀ-hʲà (my-house) 'my house' show palatalization across a morpheme boundary.[11]

Consonants directly preceding /i/ or /ɨ/ are not generally palatalized; for example, the /m/ of ìímípáˣʧʰò-kʰì̱ (iímíbájchoki) is not palatalized by the following /i/.

/ɾ/ becomes j (y) only after /i/, never after the /a/s that are reconstructable as /*ai/. Example 43 involves the suffix -ɾè̱ (-re) 'only':

(43) a. òó-ɾè̱ (oóre) 'only I'
     b. ìí-jè̱ (iíye) 'only he himself'

---

[10] See also the following entries in (Thiesen & Thiesen 1998): dyeee, dyéhpiyi, dyííyihye, dyuu, kyeehéi, kyehéjco, kyehéjkyéhe, kyéhéjkimyéi, ñáhi, ñahíñáhi, ñahíívye, ñáhiivyétso, ñahja, ñahjátso, ñahñáro, ñahóñáho, ñaj, ñáj, ñája, ñajáñája, ñama, ñámaj, ñaamáwa, ñáya, ñáyaj, ñáyájcoó, ñayáñáya, ñayááve, ñogéhñóge, ñohñócu, ñohñóro, ñohñótso, ñoohócu, ñói, ñóihjyúcu, ñojáhco, ñojáñója, ñomɨ, ñomɨ́ɨ́te, ñóñi, ñoñóñóño, ñóoo, ñóyoúúve, ñúhiúcunu, ñuhíívye, ñumɨ́ñúmɨ, tyajtya, tyekétyéke, tyocáhco, tyocáhtyóca, tyoéyeba, tyoéyeba, tyóóñojɨ, tyuuhúmɨ.

[11] tʰàˀ-hʲà 'my house' contrasts with tʰàˀhà 'to win'. Remarkably, the various allomorphs of 'my' (tʰaˀ ∼ tʰaː ∼ tʰa) do not consistently palatalize the following consonant. tʰàˀhʲà 'my house' shows that tʰaˀ causes palatalization. In i., tʰàː does not palatalize the following consonant, while tʰa- sometimes does, as in ii, and sometimes does not, as in iii:

   i.   tʰáː ⓖ kʰáːmìí   (táácáánií)   'my father'
   ii. tʰá   ɲaˀpɛ́-mù̱ⁱ (táñahbému)   'my brothers'
   iii. tʰaᴳ   mɛ́ːnì   (tamééni)   'my pig'

2.4. CONSONANTS

Example 44 involves the suffix -ɾà (-ra) 'frustrative, contraexpectation':

(44) a. ó má^xtʃʰò-ɾá-ʔì (Ó májchoráhi.) 'I ate, but not well.'
    I eat-frs-⟨t⟩
  b. ó má^xtʃʰó-ì-já-ʔì (Ó májchóiyáhi.) 'I would like to eat,
    I eat-fut-frs-⟨t⟩   but can't.'

/n/ becomes ɲ after /i/. For example, in 45 the classifier /-nè/ -⟨ø⟩ becomes [-ɲɛ]:

(45) í-ɲèɛ́ (íñeé) 'this thing'
    this-⟨ø⟩

This is a regular process only after /i/.[12]

/tsʰ/ (ts) becomes /tʃʰ/ (ch) only in some cases after /i/. For example, in the dialect of the Iñeje clan the root 'come' palatalizes; compare the unpalatalized 46a with 46b, palatalized by the /i/ of ti- (di-) 'imperative singular':

(46) a. ó tsʰá:-ʔì (Ó tsááhi.) 'I am coming.'
    b. títʃʰàá (Díchaá.) 'Come!'

However, in the other Bora clan dialects this root is invariably tʃʰa: (chaa).

Likewise, in some Bora dialects the causative suffix -tsʰo becomes -tʃʰo after /i/; e.g., àní^xtʃʰò 'to make thinner',[13] ìmítʃʰò 'to encourage'.[14]

Palatalization by /i/ or /a/ is not blocked by an intervening syllable-final /ˣ/ or /ʔ/.

(47) a. ì^xkʲʰà (ijcya) 'to be'
    b. ì^ʔtʲù (ihdyu) 'like that'
(48) a. à^xkʲʰɛ̀ (ajkye) 'get up'
    b. tʰà^ʔhʲà (tahjya) 'my house'

[ʔʲ] (orthographic hy) has two sources. It may represent either a palatalized glottal stop as in 49a or a glottal stop followed by j (palatalized ɾ) as in 49b:[15]

(49) a. íʔʲɛ́ɛ́ (íhyeé) /í-ʔè/ this-⟨tree⟩
    b. ìmíʔʲɛ̀ (imíhye) /ìmíʔ-ɾè/ good-only

---

[12] It also sometimes happens after /a/ as in aɲɯɯ 'buzzard'. This is probably due to this /a/ being a reflex of /*ai/, as discussed above.

[13] Compare àjá^xtsʰò 'to make smaller', where it does not palatalize.

[14] To this list we might add ímìpá^xtʃʰò, which historically was probably /imi-pʰai-tsʰò/ (good-become-caus) 'fix, arrange'.

[15] We are—obviously—assuming "grammatical prerequisites to phonemic analysis."

There are some mysteries regarding palatalization. For example, consider the verb 'to bag, to blister' in table 2.3. In the singular, transitive form, the root's second /p/ is palatalized, but in the other forms this palatalization shifts to following morphemes.

Table 2.3 A palatalization shift

	SINGULAR	MULTIPLE	MEANING
transitive	pàpʲáɾò (babyáro)	pàpáɲùɪ (babáñu)	'to bag'
intransitive	pàpá:βʲɛ̀ (babáávye)	pà ʔpápʲà (bahbábya)	'to blister'

Further consider the verb for 'stretch out the leg' in table 2.4:

Table 2.4 Palatalization with 'stretch out the leg'

	SINGULAR	MULTIPLE	MEANING
transitive	kʰákpà:βʲɛ́tsʰò (cáwaavyétso)	kʰáʔkpàpʲátsʰò (cáhwabyátso)	'make stretch out leg'
intransitive	kʰàkpá:βʲɛ̀ (cawáávye)	kʰàʔkpápʲà (cahwábya)	'stretch out leg'
stative	kʰákpàjɯ́kʰɯ̀nɯ̀ɪ (cáwayúcunu)		'leg stretched out'

The verb kʰàkpà- palatalizes the following consonant in all the forms except the singular stative, where instead /j/ is introduced. It is as though the palatalization must realize itself, either by palatalizing a following consonant or by the introduction of /j/.[16]

Appendix A gives comparative data for three Bora clans. Most of the differences involve palatalization.

2.4.3 Preaspiration

Generally, /ˣ/ occurs in the coda of a syllable only if the following consonant is post-aspirated (never before a nonaspirated consonant). Thus, it is perhaps best regarded as PREASPIRATION incorporated into the coda of the preceding syllable; see section 2.2.[17] There are, however, two cases of

---

[16] Assuming that historically the root-final /a/ derives from */ai/, this must be a case of */aiu/ having become /ayu/ before */ai/ became /a/.

[17] Evidence that preaspiration occupies the coda of the preceding syllable is that it is mutually exclusive with [ʔ]; see example 52.

/ˣ/ that cannot be the result of "preaspiration" because they end words. These are the suffixes -ˣ 'vocative' and -hừˣ 'quick', as in 50:

(50) Wáhaj, dichájuj.
    kpáʔà-ˣ   tì-tʃʰá-hừˣ   'Daughter, come
    daughter-voc youImp-come-quick   right now!'

Some nouns begin with an underlying /ˣCʰ/ (where Cʰ is an aspirated consonant). The /ˣ/ is realized only if the noun heads a genitive phrase[18] and /ˣ/ can be incorporated as the coda of the final syllable of the modifier (possessor), as in 51a. Note that /ˣ/ does not surface in 51b because á:nừ 'this (SgM)', a demonstrative pronoun, is the subject, not a possessor:

(51) a. á:nűˣ tsʰᴳɨ:ménè (áánúj tsɨɨméne) 'this one's child'
    b. á:nừ tsʰɨ́:mènè (áánu tsɨ́ɨmene) 'this one (SgM) is a child'

The following roots contribute aspiration to the coda of the modifier (possessor) in the genitive construction: kʰá:nìí 'father', kʰá:tʰừɾừ 'type of plant', kʰááβà 'because of', kʰòó 'firewood', kʰừpàá 'leg', kʰừ:hừkpà 'fireplace', kʰừ:hừkpàmì 'steamship', kʰừ:rừ: 'kidney', kʰừβà 'odor', kʰɛ̀ɛ́ 'voice', pʰɛ́:βɛ̀ 'free', pʰìí 'body', pʰɨ̀:ʔɨ 'near', pʰɨ́:nɛ̀ɛ́ 'middle', tʰànɛ̀ 'left behind (clitic)', tʰà:βà 'what is taken in a hunt', tʰɛ́:βɛ̀ 'by means of', tʰòó 'horn (of an animal)', tʰừʔáá 'foot'. There are other roots that begin with aspirated obstruents that do not contribute aspiration to the preceding syllable, for example, kʰà:tʰừmừɾí:ʔʲò 'pencil', pʰí:tʃʰừtʰà 'load', tʰòkpà 'sweat', and tʰừpó:kpà 'bow'.

Aspirated consonants may be preceded by /ʔ/, in which case there can be no preaspiration since the coda is already occupied by /ʔ/. Examples follow:

(52) a. kʰàʔkʰűˣtsʰò (cahcújtso) 'to believe'
    b. kʰàʔpʰíò   (cahpío)   'to pour out'
    c. pàʔtsʰíhì   (bahtsɨ́jɨ)   'type of fish'
    d. táɨ́ʔkʰòó   (dáɨhcoó)   'to be refreshing'
    e. ɨ̀ʔtʰűkʰừ   (ɨhtúcu)   'to peel'

When a suffix that begins with a preaspirated consonant (ˣCʰ) follows a stem containing a preaspirated consonant, the preaspiration in the stem is suppressed.[19] For example, the root maˣtʃʰo 'eat' has preaspiration, but when -ʔiˣkʲʰa 'always' follows, as in 53, the root's preaspiration is suppressed:

---

[18]See section 9 regarding the genitive construction.
[19]David Payne pointed out the similarity of this to Grassman's Law.

(53) mátʃʰò-ʔíˣkʲʰà-ːpè (Máchohíjcyaábe.) 'He always eats.'

This reflects a tendency to avoid sequences of heavy syllables; see in section 2.7.

2.5 Apocope

Many morphemes apocopate one or more syllables sentence medially, the full form being used sentence finally. Among these are the following: -tʃìː-(ʔʲɛ̀) 'motive' (compare 733 and 1051) with 734), -náà(ákʰà) 'while', -àˣtʃʰíː(hʲɯ̀ɾ) 'if', -hɨ́ː(βà) 'deny', and -kpɯ̀ɾ(ɯ̀ɾ) 'very'.

Some morphemes are shortened even more. For example, when not phrase final, -ʔàhà (-haja) 'challenge veracity' may apocopate to -ʔ as in 54a, -ʔàːkʰà (-haaca) 'capitulation' to -ʔ as in 54b, and so forth:

(54) a. mɯ̀ːɾá-ʔàhà (muuráhaja) ~ mɯ̀ːɾá-ʔ (muurá) } 'challenge veracity'

b. ànɛ́-ʔàːkʰà (anéhaaca) ~ ànɛ́⁽ʔ⁾ (ané) } 'concede'

c. tsʰá̰ʔàá (tsáhaá) ~ tsʰá̰ʔ (tsá) 'not'

d. pòʔò (boho) ~ pòʔ (bo) 'encouragement to do'

e. tʃìʔíjòˣ (llihíyoj) ~
tʃìʔíɯ̀ˣ (llihíuj) ~
tʃíʔìˣ (llíhij) ~
tʃì⁽ʔ⁾ (lli) } 'father/son (vocative)'

f. kpàʔáɾòˣ (wahároj) ~
kpàʔáɯ̀ˣ (waháuj) ~
kpáʔàˣ (wáhaj) ~
kpà⁽ʔ⁾ (wa) } 'mother/daughter (vocative)'

The suffix -tʰɯ 'source' is sometimes omitted following -⁽ʔ⁾ti 'animate'; see examples 651b, 674, 673, 679, 690, and 699.

The suffix -nɛ ⟨n⟩ is sometimes omitted following -tʰɯ 'negative'; see section 13.2 (especially examples 838 and 840).

The segmental portion of the suffix -Ⓛkʰi 'purpose' is sometimes omitted, as in 969, 908, 909, and 1006. In such cases the preceding two syllables usually bear high and low tones (respectively) because the low tone imposed by -Ⓛkʰi on the final syllable forces the penult to bear high tone so as to not violate the *LLX constraint *assuming the presence of syllable corresponding to* -Ⓛkʰi. However, this is not always the case for reasons discussed in chapter 3.

2.6. REDUPLICATION

The morpheme -ʔi ⟨t⟩ occurs on verbs with preverbal subjects. Utterance finally the /i/ is pronounced (and written). Utterance medially the /i/ is not pronounced (nor written), while the /ʔ/ is pronounced (but not written).[20] For example, compare 55a and b:

(55) a. ó àʔtó-ʔì   (Ó ahdóhi.)   'I paid.'
      I pay-⟨t⟩
    b. ó àʔtó-ʔ   tíːpʲɛ̀-kʰɛ̀   (Ó ahdó dííbyeke.) 'I paid him.'
      I pay-⟨t⟩ him-objAn

2.6 Reduplication

Bisyllabic onomatopoeic roots may be reduplicated. Some of these are verbal roots that—when not reduplicated—can bear verbal affixes. Others are not verbs but can replace verbs: they bear no verbal affix (although they can be the host for a clitic); the unreduplicated form refers to a single action whereas the reduplicated form refers to iterative action (corresponding to the singular versus multiple action distinction of verbs; see section 5.7.2).

The unreduplicated forms have HL tones; the reduplicated forms have LHHL tones.[21]

Either [ˣ], [ʔ], or nothing occurs at the boundary between the reduplicated parts. Since we are unable to specify the conditions under which these occur we simply give examples. In those of table 2.5 nothing intervenes:[22]

Table 2.5 Reduplication: nothing at the boundary

SIMPLE	REDUPLICATED	MEANING
áβò	àβóáβò	expresses desire to cover up
pómì	pòmípómì	side to side movement like a fish's tail
kʰáʔò	kʰàʔókʰáʔò	sound like chewing on something hard
kʰátsʰʉ̀	kʰàtsʰʉ́kʰátsʰʉ̀	expresses indecision
kʰójò	kʰòjókʰójò	sound of a stick whipped through the air
tʃʰɛ́kʰò	tʃʰɛ̀kʰótʃʰɛ́kʰò	sound like chewing something hard

continued next page

---

[20]The distinctive high tone it imposes on the verb's final syllable is sufficient evidence of its presence for Bora readers

[21]The following is exceptional in having HHHL tone: SIMPLE: íhʲò, REDUPLICATED: íhʲóʔíhʲò.

[22]The following is exceptional in that the vowel is lengthened: SIMPLE: kʰòí, REDUPLICATED: kʰòíː-kʰòíː.

continued from previous page

SIMPLE	REDUPLICATE	MEANING
kɯ́ɾʔò	kɯ̀ʔókɯ́ɾʔò	sound made by the spines of a certain fish
kʰɛ́βì	kʰɛ̀βíkʰɛ́βì	movement like that of the head of a sleeping baby
tʃó?ɨ̀	tʃò?ɨ́tʃó?ɨ̀	movement of grabbing something
pʰɨ́?pʰɨ̀	pʰɨ̀pʰɨ́pʰɨ́pʰɨ̀	sound like the flapping of wings against something
ɾíɯ̀	ɾɨ̀ɯ́ɾíɯ̀	movement of a baby scooting on its buttocks
ɾíhʲà	ɾìhʲáɾíhʲà	movement of walking
tʰɯ́ɾà	tʰɯ̀átʰɯ́ɾà	kicking the feet in the air
tsʰítʲʰɯ̀	tsʰìtʲʰɯ́ɾtsʰítʲʰɯ̀	characteristic of being brittle and breakable
βíɯ̀	βɨ̀ɯ́βíɯ̀	characteristic of being light, weightless
k͡pátʃà	k͡pàtʃák͡pátʃà	movement of lying on the back and twisting from side to side
k͡pátʰò	k͡pàtʰók͡pátʰò	movement of something snagged in the river

In the examples of table 2.6 [ʔ] intervenes between the reduplicated parts:

Table 2.6 Reduplication: [ʔ] at the boundary

SIMPLE	REDUPLICATED	MEANING
ápʲʰɯ̀	àpʲʰɯ́ʔápʲʰɯ̀	movement of a puff of dust or smoke
pótsʰɛ̀	pòtsʰɛ́ʔpótsʰɛ̀	movement of the tail of a bird walking
kʰátʃò	kʰàtʃóʔkʰátʃò	movement of one falling down head first
kʰápʰà	kʰàpʰáʔkʰápʰà	capturing a fish on a fishhook
kʰátsʰɯ̀	kʰàtsʰɯ́ʔkʰátsʰɯ̀	expresses indecision
kʰɯ́ɾtɯ̀	kʰɯ̀ɾtɯ́ʔkʰɯ́ɾtɯ̀	sound of throwing up
kʰɯ́ɾβì	kʰɯ̀ɾβíʔkʰɯ́ɾβì	manner of the walk of a man with a short leg
tʃʰíjà	tʃʰìjáʔtʃʰíjà	sound when walking in a shallow pool
tʃɛ́kʰò	tʃɛ̀kʰóʔtʃɛ́kʰò	movement like that of a wobbly building frame
máɾà	màɾáʔmáɾà	sound of gunfire
mó?à	mò?áʔmó?à	sound of a thick liquid falling into a pot
mɯ́ɾɯ̀	mɯ̀ɾɯ́ʔmɯ́ɾɯ̀	movement like the sudden disappearence of something

continued next page

2.6. REDUPLICATION

continued from previous page

SIMPLE	REDUPLICATE	MEANING
nìá	nìáↄnìá	licking of the lips
nóừ	nòừↄnóừ	gasp of breath like that caused by a scare
ɾákà	ɾàkáↄɾákà	sound of difficult breathing
ɾétsʰὲ	ɾètsʰέↄɾétsʰὲ	back and forth movement of a shaky construction
ɾúɾkừ	ɾùɾkúɾↄɾúɾkừ	twitching of a body part
tʰókʰò	tʰòkʰóↄtʰókʰò	sound of something loose inside of something else
tsʰέừ	tsʰὲύɾↄtsʰέừ	sound of cutting a plant with one slash
tsʰúmà	tsʰùmáↄtsʰúmà	jumping like a frog
βétʃʰὶ	βètʃʰίↄβétʃʰὶ	up and down movement of the end of a log in the river
βótʃʰὶ	βòtʃʰίↄβótʃʰὶ	juice squirting out of a juicy fruit
kpátừ	kpàtúɾↄkpátừ	punching holes in the ground as when planting corn
ɲájà	ɲàjáↄɲájà	sinking into the mud
ɲóὶ	ɲòíↄɲóὶ	action of a baby nursing

In the examples of table 2.7 the [ↄ] optionally intervenes between the reduplicated parts:

Table 2.7 Reduplication: optional [ↄ] at the boundary

SIMPLE	REDUPLICATED	MEANING
pínà	pìná⁽ↄ⁾pínà	movement of an object floating in the river
kʰúɾtsʰὲ	kʰùɾtsʰέ⁽ↄ⁾kʰúɾtsʰὲ	walking on the toes
tókpà	tòkpá⁽ↄ⁾tókpà	extending the hands
kóɾà	kòɾá⁽ↄ⁾kóɾà	sound of bubbling water
kúɾừ	kùɾúɾ⁽ↄ⁾kúɾừ	grunt of a pig
tʃákʰὶ	tʃàkʰί⁽ↄ⁾tʃákʰὶ	movement from side to side
tʃíkʲʰừ	tʃìkʲʰύɾ⁽ↄ⁾tʃíkʲʰừ	pulling by jerks
níhì	nìhί⁽ↄ⁾níhì	sticking out the tongue
nóhì	nòhί⁽ↄ⁾nóhì	ripples and waves on a river
ɲóɲì	ɲòɲί⁽ↄ⁾ɲóɲì	snarling of a dog
ɾépì	ɾèpί⁽ↄ⁾ɾépì	fast movement of the point of a switch
ɾúpì	ɾùpί⁽ↄ⁾ɾúpì	puffing of the smoke of a cigarette
tʰíɲì	tʰìɲί⁽ↄ⁾tʰíɲì	bouncing of a ball
tsʰúɾkừ	tsʰùɾkúɾ⁽ↄ⁾tsʰúɾkừ	sound of a hiccup

continued next page

continued from previous page

SIMPLE	REDUPLICATE	MEANING
kpámɨ̀	kpàmɨ́⁽ˀ⁾kpámɨ̀	up and down movement of the head
kpájà	kpàjá⁽ˀ⁾kpájà	side to side shaking of the head
kpúɨ̀kʰùɨ̀	kpùɨ̀kʰúɨ́⁽ˀ⁾kpúɨ̀kʰùɨ̀	sound made by hitting a hollow log

In the examples of table 2.8, the unreduplicated form ends in [ˣ], which is preserved between the reduplicated parts, but not word finally:

Table 2.8 Reduplication: [ˣ] at the boundary

SIMPLE	REDUPLICATED	MEANING
kʰópùɨ̀ˣ	kʰòpúɨ́ˣkʰópùɨ̀	sound like gurgling water in the stomach
kʰótàˣ	kʰòtáˣkʰótà	sound like swallowing water
tʃórɨ̀ˣ	tʃòrɨ́ˣtʃórɨ̀	movement like climbing up or down a tree with difficulty
mójɨ̀ˣ	mòjɨ́ˣmójɨ̀	movement like a needle point entering something soft
nóràˣ	nòráˣnórà	movement like breaking though a surface
rúɨ̀tʰùɨ̀ˣ	rùɨ̀tʰúɨ́ˣrúɨ̀tʰùɨ̀	movement like a shooting flame of fire
tʰópùɨ̀ˣ	tʰòpúɨ́ˣtʰópùɨ̀	sound like a small stone splashing into the river
βɨ́tsʰòˣ	βɨ̀tsʰóˣβɨ́tsʰò	sound like walking in very loose shoes
βíùɨ̀ˣ	βìúɨ́ˣβíùɨ̀	sound like a stick breaking
βóhòˣ	βòhóˣβóhò	movement like juice escaping from a cracked fruit
ɲáˣ	ɲààˣɲáà	sensation like getting burned

In the examples of table 2.9 the unreduplicated root ends with [ˣ] but this does not appear in the reduplication (neither at the boundary between the reduplicated parts nor at the end):

Table 2.9 Reduplication: [ˣ] deleted at the boundary

SIMPLE	REDUPLICATED	MEANING
áβɨ̀ˣ	àβɨ́áβɨ̀	sound like branches moving in a tree
pérèˣ	pèrépérè	sensation like an electric shock
kʰárùɨ̀ˣ	kʰàrúɨ́kʰárùɨ̀	movement like a head turned up looking into the sky
kʰέròˣ	kʰὲrókʰέrò	movement like submerging into something

continued next page

2.7. QUANTITY

continued from previous page

SIMPLE	REDUPLICATE	MEANING
kʰɛ́tsʰɛ̀ˣ	kʰɛ̀tsʰɛ́kʰɛ́tsʰɛ̀	movement like stetching the neck to see something
tʃɯ́hàˣ	tʃɯ̀hátʃɯ́hà	movement like something becoming smaller
mɯ́ɾtʰɯ̀ˣ	mɯ̀ɾtʰɯ́mɯ́ɾtʰɯ̀	sound like something falling from up high
βáhàˣ	βàháβáhà	characteristic like something ready to pop open

In the examples of table 2.10 [ˣ] is optionally preserved between the reduplicated parts (but not at the end):

Table 2.10 Reduplication: optional [ˣ] at the boundary

SIMPLE	REDUPLICATED	MEANING
ɾéβòˣ	ɾɛ̀βó⁽ˣ⁾ɾéβò	movement like turning around or rolling over
tʰóhɛ̀ˣ	tʰòhɛ́⁽ˣ⁾tʰóhɛ̀	movement like swimming in the river
βɯ́ɾtɯ̀ˣ	βɯ̀ɾtɯ́⁽ˣ⁾βɯ́ɾtɯ̀	sound like a liquid dripping

For many words the root may be repeated three or more times: tɯ̀ˣ 'sound like a dull thud or bump' becomes tɯ̀ˣ-tɯ̀ˣ-tɯ̀ˣ 'the sound of multiple impacts (something hitting the ground, hitting with the fist, cattle walking on hard ground,...)'; tʲɯ̀ː²³ 'the sound of a bell' becomes tʲɯ̀ː-tʲɯ̀ː-tʲɯ̀ː...'the sound of a bell ringing'; tsá:à-tsá:à-tsá:à 'the sound made by a certain hawk'; kà-kà-kà-kà 'the sound made by a chicken'; kà:-kà:-kà:-kà: 'the sound of a hammock swinging'; kpjéò:-kpjéò: 'the sound of a frog when caught by a snake'.

2.7 Quantity

This section describes phenomena that depend on quantity, that is, on syllable weight. This should not be taken as a definitive analysis; considerably more research needs to be done on this topic.

---

[23] This could also be [tʲɯ́ːː] or [tʲɛ́ː] depending on the pitch of the bell.

2.7.1 The minimal word

When a monosyllabic root is spoken in isolation, another syllable with a homorganic vowel is added, and these bear low and high tones: σ̀σ́$^{\text{L H}}$. For example, ha 'house' becomes hàá.[24] Equivalently, we might say that the minimal word is two moras. To pronounce a word with a single short vowel, the vowel would first have to be lengthened, whereupon it undergoes FLTS (see section 3.7.2).

However, monosyllabic words may occur within a sentence, as does [tsʰá?] 'not' in 56:

(56) tsʰá?(ì) ò má^{x}tʃʰò-tʰɯ́ɪ (Tsá o májchotú.) 'I did not eat'
    not   I eat-neg

2.7.2 "Heavy" syllables

What are "heavy" syllables? Generally they are syllables in which the coda is occupied by /^{x}/, /$^?$/ or /ː/ (that is, an additional mora). This allows us to state generalizations like "The first syllable of the host to which -pa 'mIn' is added is made heavy." It is normally made heavy by closing the first syllable with /$^?$/, but when the host's second syllable lacks an onset, the vowel of the first syllable is lengthened. Further, if the first syllable is already closed by preaspiration, then nothing changes. See section 5.7.3 for examples and further details. Thus, in this case /$^?$/, /^{x}/ and /ː/ all count as making the first syllable heavy.

In contrast to such cases where "heavy" unites /$^?$/, /^{x}/ and /ː/, there are others for which this characterization is too general. For example, consider the suffix -ɾiβakʰo 'resulting position'; when it is suffixed to a verb, the verb's initial vowel is lengthened as in examples 180 and 181, page 114.

The suffix -(ː)βɛ̀ 'sIn' is similar. It usually lengthens the vowel of a preceding light syllable, as in the following examples:

following a bisyllabic stem
    áí-ːβʲɛ́-nɛ̀-tʰɯ̀ɪ (áíívyénetu burn-sIn-⟨ø⟩-sou)
    kʰápʰà-ːβʲɛ́-ʔì (cápaavyéhi hook-sIn-⟨t⟩)
    kʰáɾɯ̀ː-ːβɛ́-ʔì (cáruuvéhi lift.face-sIn-⟨t⟩)
    kʰóɾɨ́-ːβɛ̀-íɲɯ́ɪ-ʔì (córɨ́ɨveíñúhi unstick-sIn-do.go-⟨t⟩)
    t-àkʰɯ́ɪ-ːβɛ́ (dacúúvé youImp-sit.down-sIn)

---

[24] ha 'house' is also lengthened when followed by a monosyllabic clitic such as -ɾɛ 'only'. The combination haː-ɾɛ undergoes PLTS to yield hàáɾɛ̀ 'only the house'.

2.7. QUANTITY

    t-èkʰɛ́-ːβɛ́ (dekéévé youImp-grab-sIn)
    ɛ́kʰɛ́-ːβɛ̀-tʃɛ̀ (ékéévelle grab-sIn-⟨SgF⟩)
    ɛ́kʰɛ́-ːβɛ́-ːpɛ̀-kʰɛ̀ (ékéévéébeke grab-sIn-⟨SgM⟩-objAn)
    úɾà-ːβʲɛ́-mɛ́ (úraavyémé follow-sIn-⟨AnPl⟩)
    úɾá-ːβʲɛ̀-ːpɛ̀ (úráávyeebe follow-sIn-⟨SgM⟩)
    úɾá-ːβʲɛ̀-ˀ íˣkʲʰà-ːpɛ̀ (úráávyeh íjcyaabe follow-sIn-sub be-⟨SgM⟩)
    úɾá-ːβʲɛ̀-KI (úráávyeki follow-sIn-pur)
    βúɾtò-ːβɛ́-ʔì (vúdoovéhi break-sIn-⟨t⟩)
    ì áɾá-ːβɛ̀-KI (i árááveki self dry.up-sIn-pur)
    ì íkʲʰá-ːβɛ́-tsʰò-KI (i ícyáávétsoki self decorate-sIn-caus-pur)
    ɨ̀ típɛ́-ːβɛ́-nɛ̀ (ɨ́ díbéévéne self put.between.lips-sIn-⟨ø⟩)

following a trisyllabic stem
    ì ípʰíjɛ́-ːβɛ́-nɛ̀ (i ípíyéévéne self become-sIn-⟨ø⟩)
    mɛ́ kpáúmì-ːβʲɛ́-ʔì (mé wáúmiivyéhi SAP repeat-sIn-⟨t⟩)

If, however, the host's penult is closed by /ˣ/, then -(ː)βɛ̀ does not lengthen the vowel of the host's final syllable:

(57) ì íˣtʃʰì-βʲɛ́-nɛ́   (iíjchivyéné self leave-sIn-⟨ø⟩)
    ì ɲúɨkʰóˣpʰɨ́-βɛ́-nɛ̀ (iñúcójpɨ́véne self shame-sIn-⟨ø⟩)

It is thus tempting to say that -(ː)βɛ̀ lengthens the preceding syllable unless this would create a sequence of heavy syllables. However, this would be incorrect because it *does* lengthen when the host's penult is closed by a glottal stop:

(58) míʔtʃʰúɨ-ːβɛ̀-kʰò (míhchúúveco close.eyesImp-sIn-implore)

Throughout this grammar we use "heavy syllable" somewhat loosely, without implying that every claim will hold for all syllables closed by /ˣ/, /ʔ/ or /ː/. We hope that further study will make it possible to make more precise claims.

2.7.3 Suffixes that add weight to a monosyllabic root

Some suffixes optionally contribute a glottal stop (ʔ) to the coda of a preceding monosyllabic root, thereby making it heavy. Among these are the following:

- -Ⓛ⁽ʔ⁾tì (-di ~ -hdi) 'negative imperative', as in pʰɛ̀-ʔtí-ɲɛ̀ (pehdíñe) 'Don't go!'
- -Ⓛ◯⁽ʔ⁾tùɾ (-du ~ -hdu) 'similarity', as in 1082 and 1085, page 424
- -⁽ʔ⁾tʃɨ̄ːʔʲɛ̀ (-lliíhye ~ -hlliíhye) 'benefactive', as in 1136, page 434
- -⁽ʔ⁾nɛ̀ (-ne ~ -hne) 'recent', as in 1154 and 1155, page 438

There are other suffixes that always make the preceding syllable heavy, regardless of the number of syllables of its host.

2.7.4 Quantity alternations

In various cases, a heavy syllable becomes light when followed in the word by a heavy syllable ($\bar{\sigma} \longrightarrow \breve{\sigma} \, / \, \_\_ \ldots \bar{\sigma}$). For example, pʰɛ: 'go' has a long vowel, as in 59a and b, but the length is suppressed when -huɪkʰo: 'now' follows, as in 59c:

(59) a. ó pʰɛ́:-ʔì   (ó pééhi)   'I go.'
     b. pʰɛ̀:-mɛ̀   (peéme)   'They go.'
     c. ò pʰɛ́-huɪkʰó:-ʔì (ó péjucóóhi)   'I am going now.'

The bound root ápʰà:- 'only' has a final long vowel, as in 60a–c, but this becomes short when, by the addition of a suffix, the following syllable has a long vowel, as in 60d:

(60) a. àpʰá:-kpá-ɾɛ̀   (apááwáre)   'the only slab'
        only-⟨slab⟩-only
     b. àpʰá:-ɲɛ́-ɾɛ̀   (apááñére)   'the only thing'
        only-⟨ø⟩-only
     c. àpʰá:-mʲɛ́-ɾɛ̀   (apáámyére)   'the only ones (AnPl)'
        only-⟨AnPl⟩-only
     d. àpʰá-ʔà:mí-ɾɛ̀   (apáhaamíre)   'the only leaf-like thing'
        only-⟨leaf⟩-only

Other cases are outlined in the following subsections.

2.7.4.1 Length suppressed by -:cu 'duIn' and -:ne 'plural'

In addition to lengthening their host's final vowel,[25] -:kʰùɪ 'duIn' and -:nɛ̀ 'plural' generally suppress the weight of any preceding syllables. For example, compare 61a and b:

(61) a. kʰá:mɛ́-ɛ̀-mì   cááméémɨ   'airplane'
        high-per-⟨canoe⟩
     b. kʰámɛ́-ɛ̀-mí-:nɛ̀   cáméemíɨne   'airplanes'
        high-per-⟨canoe⟩-plIn

In the following examples, the singulars have length but this is suppressed in the dual or plural:

---

[25]Compare 411b,c with 412b,c; we do not know why in one case the host's final vowel is lengthened while in the other it is not.

2.7. QUANTITY

MEANING	SINGULAR		DUAL OR PLURAL	
a. 'drum'	kʰɨ́ːmɨ̀ɾpà	cúúmuba	kʰɨ́mɨ̀ɾpáːnɛ̀	cúmubááne
b. 'lemon'	tʃámáːɾàpà	llámááraba	tʃámáɾàpáːnɛ̀	llámárabááne
c. 'shed'	nɨ́ɾːhɨ̀ɾkpà	núújuwa	nɨ́ɾhɨ̀ɾkpáːkʰɨ̀ɾ	nújuwáácu
			nɨ́ɾhɨ̀ɾkpáːnɛ̀	nújuwááne
d. 'auditorium'	pʰɨ̀ʔkʲʰáːβèhà pihcyááveja		pʰɨ̀ʔkʲʰáβèháːnɛ̀ pihcyávejááne	
e. 'pill'	tʰàːpóhɨ̀	taabójɨ	tʰàpóhɨ́ːkʰɨ̀ɾ	tabójɨ́ɨcu
			tʰàpóhɨ́ːnɛ̀	tabójɨ́ɨne
f. 'washboard'	nɨ̀ˣtʲʰɨ́ɾkpà	nijtyúwa	nɨ̀ˣtʲʰɨ́ɾkpáːnɛ̀	nijtyúwááne

Note that the last example begins with a syllable made heavy by /ˣ/, but that, contrary to what we might expect, -ːnɛ does not make this syllable light; that is, it seems to affect only vowel length, not syllable weight in general. See also examples 413 and 415, page 196, and example 493, page 223.

2.7.4.2 Vowel length alternating with [ˣ] before vowel length

Why does [ˣ] (preaspiration) alternate with vowel length in 62 and 63?

(62) a. ɨ́ˣ tsʰɨ́ːmɛ́nɛ̀ (ɨjtsɨ́ɨméne) 'his child'
    self child
 b. ɨ́ː tsʰɨ̀ɨmɛ̀ (ɨ́ɨtsɨɨme) 'his children'
    self children

(63) a. tʰáˣ tsʰɨ́ːmɛ́nɛ̀ (tájtsɨɨméne) my child
    my child
 b. áː tsʰɨ̀ɨmɛ̀ (áátsɨɨme) my children
    my children

Note the long vowel of the first syllable of /tsʰɨːmɛ/ 'children'. In 62a and 63a this is phonetically [ɨː]; and in these cases the possessive proclitic has [ˣ]. By contrast, in 62b and 63b, this long vowel has undergone PLTS (discussed in 3.7.1) to become two short syllables; in these cases the possessive proclitic has a long vowel. Thus, this appears to be another case where multiple long vowels are avoided within the same phonological word.

2.7.4.3 Maintaining syllable weight in imperatives

Singular imperatives sometimes change the coda of the first syllable, as discussed in section 14.1.3. Sometimes [ˣ] becomes [ː] and sometimes [ː]

becomes [ʔ]. Example 64 illustrates the latter: 64a and b show that the root has a long vowel; this alternates with a glottal stop in the imperative in 64c:

(64) a. ù:hɛ̀   (uúje)   'to see' (nonfinite tone)
       see
    b. ú:hɛ̀-tʰɛ́-ːpɛ̀   (úújetéébe) 'He went to see.'
       see-go.do-⟨SgM⟩
    c. t-ʉ́ʔhɛ̀-tʰɛ̀   (dúhjete) 'Go see it!'
       youImp-see-go.do

2.7.4.4 Length in pronouns

The pronouns (chapter 8) demonstrate many alternations between heavy and light syllables, particularly short and long vowels.[26] We will point out a few cases.

Consider examples in 532 and 533, page 236. The length of the root tʰɛ̀: 'that' surfaces when followed by a suffix consisting of a light syllable, as in 532a–c. However, when a heavy syllable follows, as in 532d and 533a–d, then the root's length is suppressed. In 532d and 533a, c, and d the weight is due to length while in 533b it is due to the coda being filled by /ʔ/.[27]

In table 8.4, page 242, consider the length of ɛ̀:- 'that (medial)'. This length is suppressed when followed by a heavy syllable, as created by -ːkʰʉ̀ 'duIn', by -⁽ʔ⁾hɨ̀ 'plural', or by a classifier bearing length such as -ʔaːmɨ 'leaf, paper,…'.

2.7.4.5 Allomorphy conditioned by preceding syllable weight

In some cases a suffix lengthens a preceding light syllable only if a heavy syllable does not precede within the word. For example, -(ː)ɾɛ̀ 'only' lengthens the preceding vowel in 65a. It does not do so in 65b because the first syllable is heavy, nor in 65c because the second syllable is heavy.

(65) a. /pʰá-nɛ̀-ːɾɛ̀/ (all-⟨ø⟩-only)   (páneére) 'all (things)'
    b. /tí-ːpʲɛ̀-ɾɛ̀/ (that-⟨SgM⟩-only) (dííbyere) 'only he'
    c. /ímíʔ-ɾɛ̀/ (good-only)   (ímíhye) 'only good'

---

[26]There seems to be a tendency to end the pronouns with a heavy syllable followed by a light syllable (σ̄σ̆).

[27]It is further interesting to compare 532a and 533a. In the former the root is long when followed by -nɛ̀ ⟨t⟩, while in the latter the length is suppressed when -nɛ̀ is followed by -(ː)kʰʉ̀ 'dual'.

2.8 Unresolved issues

Several issues beg for further study:

1. It seems that Bora does not have a stress system aside from the system of tone. We do not discount the possibility that Bora's tone system is a stress system implemented on tone. See note 8, page 98 for further discussion.
2. Throughout this grammar we make observations about quantity sensitive phenomena but we have no theory about these. We understand little about vowel length, particularly when the length of certain morphemes will surface and when not. For example, we do not know why pʰá-mè-ːɾɛ̀ (all-⟨AnPl⟩-only) 'only all of them (AnPl)' has length while pʰà-mɛ́-βá-ɾɛ̀ (all-⟨AnPl⟩-plQ-only) 'only all of them (AnPl)' does not. And we are unsure as to what constitutes a heavy versus a light syllable.
3. An attempt to define Bora foot structure has yielded no definite answers. For example, it is unclear whether the FOOT should be defined in terms of syllable weight or tone (which is not unreasonable if the tonal system were really an accentual system implemented on tone). As working hypotheses we might assume that (1) heavy syllables are those that end with ˣ, ˀ or ː, (2) the foot is a left-headed trochee, and (3) feet are assigned from left to right. (Since a phrase may begin or end with either a heavy or a light syllable, we must have degenerate feet.)
4. In one case (and only one that we know of) the case marker -tʰɯ 'source' is not aspirated, namely when it follows the classifier -tsʰi ⟨place⟩: á-tsʰì-ˀtʲɯ́-βá-à (thm-⟨place⟩-sou-rpt-rem) 'from that place (long ago, it is said)'. We do not know why.

Chapter 3

Tone

Tone plays a major role in the Bora language. (One indication of this is that messages can be communicated by beating the tones on large hollow-log drums; see section 1.8.) There are minimal pairs showing that tone may be the only difference between lexical items or grammatical constructions. For example, the only difference between 66a and b is in the tone of the first syllable. (Note: in the Bora writing system, high tone is written as an acute accent, while low tone is not written.)

(66) a. à̱:-nè má˟tʃʰò-:pɛ̀ (Aane májchoóbe.) 'He ate that.'
　　b. á̱:-nè má˟tʃʰò-:pɛ̀ (Ááne májchoóbe.) 'Then he ate.'

The only difference between 67a and b is in the tone of the second syllable:

(67) a. á:nù̱ː ò:ʔí:pʲɛ̀ (áánu oohííbye) 'This one (SgM) is a dog.'
　　b. á:nú̱ː ò:ʔí:pʲɛ̀ (áánú oohííbye) 'his dog'

Further consider ìmì 'good', cited here in the nonfinite form with two low tones. When it occurs as the head of a genitive construction, as in 68, it bears high-low tones:

(68) tí-:pʲɛ̂ᴳ　ímì̱　(dííbye ími) 'his goodness'
　　that-⟨SgM⟩ good

When it is a predicate adjective, as in 69, it bears high tone on both syllables:

(69) ímí̱　òó (Ímí oó.)　'I am good.' or
　　good I　　　　　　'I am in good health.'

When it is a verb, its tones vary depending on what suffixes follow; compare 70a and 70b:

55

(70) a. ó i̱mí-ʔi̱   (Ó imíhi.)   'I am good.' or
    I be.good-⟨t⟩   'I am in good health.'
    b. ími̱-ːpʲɛ̀   (Ímiíbye.)   'He is good.' or
    be.good-⟨SgM⟩   'He is in good health.'

Note that the penultimate vowel of 70b is given as a single long vowel in the morphemic form but as ií (bisyllabic[1]) according to the Bora writing system, which more closely represents the spoken form. The difference is due to the application of PLTS, a rule discussed in section 3.7.1. This convention is followed throughout this grammar.

Likewise, when verbs are cited, the tones of the morphemic form and the orthographic form may differ, as for example i̱ʔβɛ́tʰɛ (ɨhvéte) 'to stop doing'. The first representation shows the morphemic tone (here a single lexically marked tone on the second syllable) while the orthographic form is how the word would be pronounced in isolation (the result of imposing the nonfinite low tone on the antepenult; see section 4.1).

3.1 Some basic facts and overview

This section gives a brief overview of the Bora tone system, after which each topic will be dealt with in greater detail.

1. There are two tones, high (H) and low (L). The marked tone is low. The general default tone is high (although the default for final syllables is low).
2. A sequence of two low tones is disallowed except at the end of a word or tonal phrase. We will refer to this as the *LLX constraint.
   There is no such restriction on high tones. Any number of high tones may occur one after another.
3. Tones are placed on syllables irrespective of whether they have short or long vowels. (We can say, "Bora tone is blind to quantity.") However, there is a process that relates tone and length. At the end of a tonal phrase, a penultimate or final syllable with a long, low tone vowel (figure 3.1a) may "split" into two syllables with low-high tones (figure 3.1b). Note: adjacent homorganic vowels bearing different tones are always pronounced as two syllables.

---

[1] See section 2.2.

3.1. SOME BASIC FACTS AND OVERVIEW

Figure 3.1 The relationship of tone and syllabification

There are two environments in which this change applies: in the penultimate syllable and in the final syllable, as captured by the rules that follow. Note that the tones represented by T must be high; otherwise the changes would produce violations of the *LLX constraint.

Penultimate
Low Tone Split (PLTS):   σ̄: → σ̄σ̄   /#(...σ̄)_σ̄##[a]

Final
Low Tone Split (FLTS):   σ̄(:) → σ̄σ̄   /#((...σ̄)σ̄)_##

---
[a]# indicates word boundaries and ## phrase boundaries.

4. Morphemes may have lexically marked tones. Nouns may have lexically marked low tones or—more rarely—lexically marked high tones. Verbs may only have lexically marked low tones.
   Lexically marked tones may not occur on a stem's final syllable (presumably because such tones would be masked too much by the tones imposed by following suffixes).
5. Some suffixes bear a lexically marked low tone on one of their syllables. Many suffixes have a low tone to be docked on its host's final or penultimate syllable. A few suffixes impose a tone on the host's initial syllable.
6. As suffixes are cyclically added, their tones may come into conflict with the host's tones; that is, to dock their tone would create a sequence of nonfinal low tones violating the *LLX constraint. Such cases are resolved in two ways:
   BLOCKING: Usually the suffix's tone is simply not docked.
   DELINKING: Some suffixes have the power to delink the host's incompatible tone.
7. Verbs are made nonfinite by placing a low tone on the earliest possible syllable of the stem's last three syllables. (Any other lexically marked low tones the verb might have are delinked.)
8. Various grammatical constructions are indicated by tone:

GENITIVE: The genitive construction is formed by juxtaposing the modifier (possessor) and head (possessed) with a floating low tone, the GENITIVE TONE, at the juncture:

[tonal phrase NP$_{possessor}$ Ⓖ N$_{head}$]

When the head is mono- or bisyllabic, the genitive tone docks on the possessor's final syllable. When the head has more than two syllables, the genitive tone docks on the head's initial syllable. The combination of possessor and head forms a single tonal phrase so the *LLX constraint is respected at the juncture.

SUBORDINATE VERBS: The verb of a subordinate clause begins with a high tone.

PREDICATE ADJECTIVE: Predicate adjectives are derived from verbs by imposing high tones on their first two syllables and adding [ʔ] at the end:

$$\#[\sigma \quad \sigma \quad (X) \quad]_{StatVerb} \quad \#$$
$$\updownarrow$$
$$\#[\overset{H}{\sigma} \quad \overset{H}{\sigma} \quad (X) \quad ? \quad]_{PredAdj} \quad \#$$

In 69 above, imi 'good' is used as a predicate adjective; it has the two high tones. (The final glottal stop is not written.) Now we will consider ímìa̋ 'of good quality (proper, right, righteous, just,...)'.[2] In 71 it is a predicate adjective:

(71) ímìá? tì-ːpʲè.   (ɨ́mɨ́á díɪ́bye.)   'He is good.'
     good that-⟨SgM⟩

Here the high tones typical of predicate adjectives do not override the lexically marked tone. In light of this, we need not posit a derivational process that imposes the high tones. Rather, predicate adjectives are not marked for tone; they simply come about by default.

IMPERATIVE: The tone of imperatives is discussed in section 14.1.1.

Before entering into a more detailed discussion of these topics, let us consider some simple examples. Consider the nouns in table 3.1 and the comments that follow.[3]

---

[2]Presumably this is a cognate with imi 'good'.
[3]The labels in table 3.1 indicate the following:
lexical   the lexical form
isolation   the word as spoken alone
plural   the plural form
dim   the diminutive form
my-___   the noun in genitive construction with
                the first person possessive proclitic
my-___-pl   the noun both possessed and pluralized

3.1. SOME BASIC FACTS AND OVERVIEW

Table 3.1 Some simple tone examples

	WATCH	DEER	STORK	CHICKEN
lexical	nɯʔpa	niːβɯkpa	nòʔkʰo^L	kʰaɾakʰa^L
isolation	nɯ̀ʔpà nuhba	níːβɯ̀kpà nííνuwa	nòʔkʰò nohco	kʰáɾàkʰà cáraca
plural	nɯ́ʔpà-mɯ̀ núhbamu	níːβɯ́kpà-mɯ̀ nííνúwamu	nòʔkʰó-mɯ̀ nohcómu	kʰáɾàkʰá-mɯ̀ cáracámu
dim	nɯ́ʔpá-kpɯ̀ núhbáwu	níːβɯ́kpá-kpɯ̀ nííνúwáwu	nòʔkʰó-kpɯ̀ nohcówu	kʰáɾàkʰá-kpɯ̀ cáracáwu
my-__	tʰà nɯ́ʔpà tañúhba	tʰá nìːβɯ́kpà tániivúwa	tʰá ɲòʔkʰò táñohco	tʰá kʰáɾàkʰà tácaraca
my-__-pl	tʰá ɲɯ̀ʔpá-mɯ̀ táñuhbámu	tʰá nìːβɯ́kpà-mɯ̀ tániivúwamu	tʰá ɲòʔkʰó-mɯ̀ táñohcómu	tʰá kʰáɾàkʰá-mɯ̀ tácaracámu

1. The last two roots in table 3.1 have a lexically marked low tone on their penultimate syllable, whereas the first two have no lexically marked tone.
2. In isolation, all of these nouns end with two low tones.
3. The suffix -Ⓛmɯ 'plAn' imposes a low tone on the preceding syllable; it does so following nɯ̀ʔpà 'watch'[4] and níːβɯ̀kpà 'deer' but not following nòʔkʰò^L 'stork' and kʰàɾàkʰà^L 'chicken' because this would create a sequence of two nonfinal low tones in violation of the *LLX constraint. By default, the final syllable becomes low tone and any unmarked nonfinal syllables become high.
4. The suffix -kpɯ̀ 'diminutive' has a lexically marked low tone. The underlying form is really -kpɯ̀ɯ^L, so the preceding syllable must become high tone to avoid violating the *LLX constraint.
5. The lexically marked low tones on the penultimate syllables of nòʔkʰo^L 'stork' and kʰaɾakʰa^L 'chicken' do not conflict with the low tone of -kpɯ̀^{L} 'diminutive'.
6. The last two rows of table 3.1 illustrate the tone pattern of the genitive construction, as described above. This consists of concatenating the possessor (modifier) and the head to form a single tonal phrase, with a floating low tone between them. If the head is one or two syllables, the tone docks on the modifier's final syllable. If the head is longer, it docks on the head's initial syllable.

Consider the form for 'my stork'. Because the genitive tone should dock on the final syllable of the possessor when the head is bisyllabic, we would expect it to do so in this case. However, this tone and the noun's

---

[4]Regarding the animacy of 'watch', see the first paragraph of section 6.1.1.1, page 163.

lexically marked low tone would violate the *LLX constraint (since the possessor and head form a single tonal phrase), so the possessor bears high tone.

Consider the form for 'my chicken'. Because the genitive tone should dock on the first syllable of a trisyllabic head, we would expect it to do so in this case. However, this tone and the noun's lexically marked low tone would violate the *LLX constraint, so the possessor bears high tone.

With these comments by way of an overview, we now begin a more detailed discussion of the Bora tone system.

3.2 The tonal elements

Bora has two contrastive level tones. It has no contour tones. There are—to our knowledge—no restrictions between tones and segments: either tone may occur on any syllable.

Every syllable carries either a high or low tone. High tones may occur one after the other without limit, as in the third word of 72:

(72) Dííbyeke o ájtyúmítúrónáa ó waajácú múha teene méénune.
    tíː.pʲɛ̀.kʰɛ̀ ò áˣ.tʲʰɯ́ː.mɯ́.tʰɯ́ː.ɾó.ná.à
    him   I not.see

ó kpàː.há.kʰɯ́ mɯ́ɯ.ʔà tʰɛ̀ː.nɛ̀ mɛ́ː.nɯ̀ɯ.nɛ̀
I know   who   that   do
'Although I did not see him, I know who did it.'

A sequence of high tones rises slightly, i.e., the pitch of each syllable is slightly higher than that of the preceding syllable.

When two low tones occur at the end of a word, the second has a slightly lower pitch than the first.

3.3 Default tones

3.3.1 Final default low tone

By default the final syllable of a tonal phrase bears low tone; see figure 3.2:

3.3. DEFAULT TONES

a. σ ⟶ σ̌ / _# or _##   (any category)
b. σ ⟶ σ̌ / _σ̌##   (just nouns)

Figure 3.2 Final default low tone (FDLT)

The sentence pairs in 73–75 illustrate FDLT for verbs. In 73a, "they eat" is phrase medial and thus ends with a high tone; in 73b it is phrase final so ends with a low tone.

(73) a. Majchómé llíhyomútsi.
  màˣtʃʰó-mé̱ tʃíʔʲò-mútsʰì   MEDIAL   'Mother and
  eat-⟨AnPl⟩ mother-⟨DuM⟩   father⁵ eat.'
 b. Majchóme.
  màˣtʃʰó-mè̱   FINAL   'They eat (bread).'
  eat-⟨AnPl⟩

Examples 74 and 75 are similar:⁶

(74) a. Awákunúúbé llihíyo.
  àkpákʰùmú-ːpé̱ tʃìʔí-jò   MEDIAL   'Father yawns.'
  yawn-⟨SgM⟩   father-frs
 b. Awákunúúbe.
  àkpákʰùmú-ːpè̱   FINAL   'He yawns.'
  yawn-⟨SgM⟩

(75) a. Ícyoocáré tsaábe.
  íkʲʰòːkʰá-ɾé̱ tsʰàːpè   MEDIAL   'Only now does
  now-only   come-⟨SgM⟩   he come.'
 b. Tsaabe ícyoocáre.
  tsʰàːpè   íkʲʰòːkʰá-ɾè̱   FINAL   'Only now does
  come-⟨SgM⟩ now-only   he come.'

If the word is a noun, the final two syllables may bear low tone. For example, pronounced in isolation, the final tones of níːβùɨkpà 'deer' and pátsìˣkʰà 'female adolescents' are due simply to FDLT. By contrast, FDLT only affects the final tone of òβáʔtsʰà 'male adolescent' because the initial syllable bears a lexically marked low tone, which stops FDLT from docking a low on the penult. In other cases, like the last word of 73a, only the final syllable bears low tone.

---

⁵Parents can be referred to by the dual form of either 'mother' or 'father', depending on which parent is in focus.

⁶PLTS discussed below in section 3.7.1, does not apply in 74b because of the lexically marked low tones of ǎkpakʰǔmɨ- 'yawn'.

However, we do not fully understand the conditions for the application of FDLT. It certainly applies at the end of an utterance, as just illustrated. In figure 3.5 it does not apply to the first word because this is not phrase final, but in other cases it seems to apply word finally within a sentence. These matters merit further study.

3.3.2 Default high tone

The overall default tone is—somewhat surprisingly—the high tone. In a tone derivation, we capture this fact by positing a very late rule (applying after the previously-mentioned rule) that places high tone on any syllables that are unmarked for tone:

$$\sigma \longrightarrow \overset{H}{\sigma}$$

Figure 3.3 Default high tone DHT

This is illustrated in the tone derivations of úmɛ̀ʔɛ̀, nímɯ̀ɨkpà, and màˣt͡ʃʰò in figure 3.4:

```
umehe    tree           ni:vuwa   deer         majcho   to eat
: : :                   : : :                  L   :    nonfinite
: L L    FDLT           : L L     FDLT         :   L    FDLT
H : :    DHT            H : :     DHT          :   :
: : :                   : : :                  :   :
úmehe    'tree'         níívuwa   'deer'       majcho   'food'
```

Figure 3.4 TD: úmehe, níívuwa, majcho

The resulting words are given as the last line of each derivation, written as the Bora people would write them, except that vowel length is represented with a colon and morphemes are divided with hyphens.[7] To the right of each morpheme a gloss is given. Also at the right are the names of tone rules that apply: FDLT for the "final default low tone" rule, DHT for the "default high tone" rule, and so forth.

In tone derivations the colons are included to guide the eye to the corresponding vowel in the complete word at the bottom of the derivation. Likewise, vertical bars are used to associate tones with a vowels, but only those that are not by default. This can be seen in the tone derivation of t͡ʃíːɲáhàː-tʰɛ́-ːpɛ́ mɯ̀ˣtʰá-ʔì in figure 3.5 (from example 629). The first word does not undergo FDLT (nor PLTS discussed below) because it is not phrase final. Its final tone becomes high by DHT. (Note the use of underscores

---

[7]This works well because the writing system is quite phonemic. In some minor respects it is phonetic.

to indicate a tone imposed by a suffix on its host's final or penultimate syllable; this and "blocking" are explained below.)

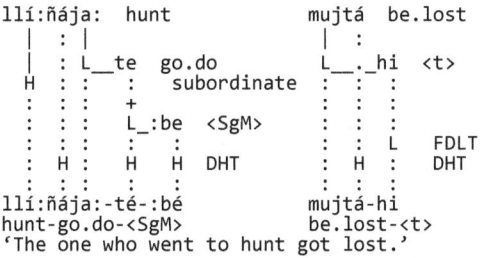

Figure 3.5 TD: llííñájaatéébé mujtáhi

3.4 The cyclical nature of suffixation

A suffix may bear a tone to be imposed on its host's penultimate or final syllable. Suffixes are attached cyclically: [[[root -suffix] -suffix] -suffix].... With the addition of each suffix, the host's tones may be modified by the suffix's tones. This is illustrated in the tone derivations of máˣtʃʰò-tʰɛ́-mɛ̀-βàˣ, úmɛ̀ʔɛ́-ːnɛ̀-ʔáɲɛ̀, and ní:βɯ́ɨkpà-ɯ́ɨβɯ̀ɨ-mà in figure 3.6. (The underscore ties a tone to the suffix that imposes it, whether on the host's final or penultimate syllable.)

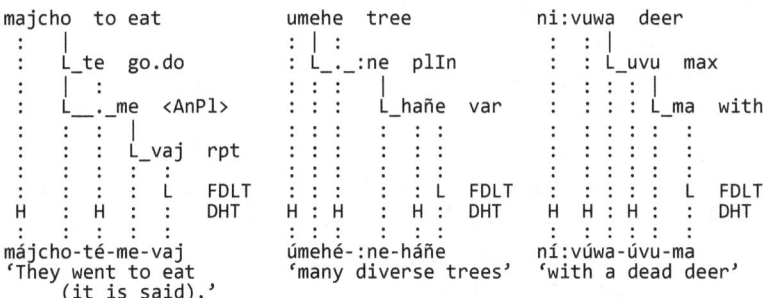

Figure 3.6 TD: májchotémevaj, úmehéénehá ñe, níívúwaúvuma

Consider the tone derivation of fʔβɛ̀tʰɛ́-tsʰò-tʰɛ́-rò-ːpɛ̀ in figure 3.7. (PLTS will be discussed below.)

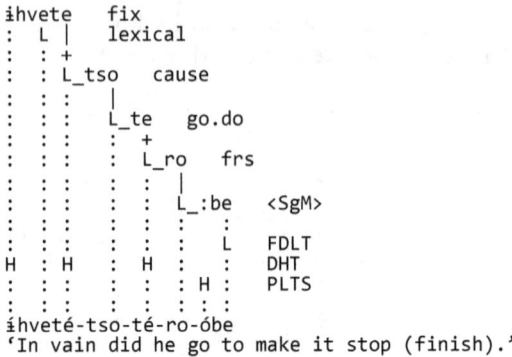

Figure 3.7 TD: íhvetétsotéroóbe

Note how the cyclical addition of suffixes affects the tone:

1. The Ⓛ of -Ⓛtsʰo (-tso) 'causative' is blocked by the root's lexically marked low tone. (In figure 3.7 the lexically marked low tone is indicated by "L" followed by "lexical." Blocking is indicated by " + " on the line connecting the root's final vowel and the L brought by -Ⓛtsʰo.)
2. The Ⓛ of -Ⓛtʰɛ 'go to do' docks on the host's final syllable. The Ⓛ of -Ⓛtsʰo does not block the Ⓛ of -Ⓛtʰɛ because the Ⓛ of -Ⓛtsʰo has not docked (as just explained).
3. The Ⓛ of -Ⓛɾo 'frustrative, contraexpectation' is blocked by the Ⓛ of -Ⓛtʰɛ.
4. The Ⓛ of -Ⓛːpɛ ⟨SgM⟩ docks. The Ⓛ of -Ⓛɾo does not block it because it is not docked.

If floating tones are not associated on the cycle in which their morpheme is attached, they are never associated.

Strong evidence for cyclical tone adjustment can be seen in the second derivation of figure 3.28, page 86: the Ⓛ of -Ⓛ○βa 'come to do' may not dock because of the root's lexically marked low on the initial syllable: àːʔɨjɛ 'visit'. However, the root's low tone is subsequently delinked by the negative suffix and ends up bearing high tone.

3.5 Lexically marked tones

Bora morphemes (prefixes, roots, suffixes, and clitics) may have lexically marked tones. These are often not the tones with which the morpheme appears; a word's surface tones are the result of a derivation that may modify these tones (as seen above).

3.5. LEXICALLY MARKED TONES

Further, a morpheme may consist in nothing more than a tone; that is, it may have no segmental material. There is considerable "grammatical" tone of this sort: notions like tense, mood, subordination, category, and even certain constructions, may be marked only by tone, as will be seen below.

Because the addition of suffixes can modify the host's tones, in some cases a stem's lexically marked tones can be determined only by seeing it with various suffix combinations.

3.5.1 Lexically marked low tones

Both roots and suffixes may have lexically marked low tones. For example, this is the case for the second syllable of the verb i̇ʔβɛ̂t̚ʰɛ (ɨhvéte) 'to stop doing', for the first syllable of the noun ó̱βaʔtsʰa (ovátsa) 'male adolescent', and for the first syllable of the suffix -kpɯ̱̀(ɯ) (-wu(u)) 'diminutive'. (The forms written according to the Bora writing system give the word as it would be spoken in isolation, with verbs given in the nonfinite form, with default tones as discussed above.)

Compare the tone derivations of úmɛ́ʔɛ̀-βɯ̀, úmɨ́ʔɛ́-βɯ̀, and nòʔkʰó-kpɯ̀ in figure 3.8:

```
umehe      tree        umɨhe      field        nohco        stork
: :  |                 : L  |     lexical      L  :         lexical
: :  |                 : :  +                  :  . _wu     dim
: :  L_vu  goal        : :  L_vu  goal         :  :  L      lexical
: :  :                 : :  :                  :  :  :
: :  :  L  FDLT        : :  :  L  FDLT         :  :  :      DHT
H H  :  :  DHT         H : H  :  DHT           :  :  :
: :  :                 : :  :                  nohcó-wu
úméhe-vu               úmɨhé-vu                'little stork'
'to the tree'          'to the field'
```

Figure 3.8 TD: úméhevu, úmɨhévu, nohcówu

The first word has no lexically marked tone whereas the second and third do. The lexically marked low in the second word blocks the docking of the suffix's Ⓛ so the final tones are different. (Blocking is discussed further in section 3.11.1.)

There is usually only one lexically marked low tone per verb root, although some verbs have two, e.g., àkpakʰɯ̱́mɯ̱ (áwacúnu[8]) 'to yawn'; see the tone derivations of àkpákʰɯ̀mɯ̀ and ákpàkʰɯ́mɯ̀ in figure 3.9:

---

[8]This orthographic form is given with nonfinite tone.

```
           awacunu    to yawn         awacunu    to yawn
           L : L :    lexical         L | L :    lexical
           : : : L    FDLT            | | | :
           : H : :    DHT             = L = :    nonfinite
           : : : :                    : : : L    FDLT
           awácunu                    H : H :    DHT
           'yawn'     (finite)        : : : :
                                      áwacúnu    'yawn'   (nonfinite)
```

Figure 3.9 TD: awácunu, áwacúnu

3.5.2 Lexically marked high tones

Nouns—but not verbs—may have lexically marked high tones.[9] For example, such is the case for the first syllable of ɯ̈mɨɯ 'side'. This tone blocks (see section 3.11.1) the genitive low tone from docking on its first syllable,[10] as seen in 76:

(76) tʰá ⓖ ɯ̈míɨ̀-rì (tá úníuri)   'at my side'
     tí-ːpʲɛ́ ⓖ ɯ̈míɨ̀-rì (dííbyé úníuri) 'at his side'

Likewise, in 77, mɯ̈maa 'countryman' has a lexically marked high tone that blocks the docking of the genitive tone, whereas it is not blocked in mɯmaa 'enemy'. (-ˣpʰi is a singular masculine classifier.)

(77) tʰá mɯ̈máà-ˣpʰì (támúnáajpi) 'my countryman'
     tʰá mɯ̈máà-ˣpʰì (támunáajpi) 'my enemy'

---

[9]There are not many of these. Some of them are: amȧna (ámánaá) 'porpoise'; aˣtʃʰɯ̇ːɯ̈ (ajchúhóóu) 'flashlight'; páːpɛ (báábeé) 'father-in-law', e.g. (ábáábeé) 'my father-in-law', (dííbyé baabe) 'his father-in-law'; paˣkʰɯ (bájcuú) 'bone'; paˣkʲʰɛ (bájkyeé) 'root'; pɛ̇pɛ (béébeé) 'new one (SgM)'; kʰȧtʰɯ (cáátuú) 'sweet potato'; kʰaːni (cáánií) 'father'; kʰȧtsʰo (cátsoó) 'grater, spices, wasp (that makes a grater-like nest)'; kʰȯːmi (cóómií) 'town'; ɛ̇pa (éébaá) 'container (drum, box,...)'; ɨ̇tsɨ (ɨdsɨɨ) 'self's daughter'; ɨkʲʰȧːβɛ̀ (ícyááveé) 'decoration'; ɨ̇ˣkʲʰo (íjcyoó) 'nest'; ɨˣtʲʰɛ (íjtyeé) 'self's ones (AnPl)'; ɨtʃi (íllií) 'self's son'; ɨːmʲɛ (íímyeé) 'self's aunt', e.g. (dííbyé iímye) 'that one's (SgM) aunt'; ɨɲɛ (íñeé) 'this (thing)'; ɨ̇kpa (íwaá) 'this slab-like thing'; ɨ̇tsɨ (ɨdsɨɨ) 'his daughter'; ɨˀtɛ (ɨhdeé) 'before, ahead of', e.g. (táɨhdye) 'before me'; maːni (máánií) 'tobacco paste'; ⁽ˣ⁾kʰȧtʰɯ ((j)cáátuú) 'writing', e.g. (dííbyéj caátu); ˀɯ̇mɨ (húmɨɨ) 'face'. There are also some pronouns that have lexically marked high tone: ȧtʃɛ (áálleé) 'that one (SgF)'; ȧmʲɛ (áámyeé) 'this one (SgF)'; ȧːti (áádií) 'that one (SgM)'; aːnɯ (áánu) 'this (SgM)'; ȧtʲʰɛ (áátyeé) 'those (few)'.

[10]That is, the genitive tone should dock on the head's first syllable because it is trisyllabic, but it can not do so because this syllable already has a tone, namely the lexically marked high tone.

3.5. LEXICALLY MARKED TONES

tʰá mǚmáà-ˣpʰì-kʲʰɛ̀ (támúnáájpikye) 'my countryman-objAn'
tʰá mǚmáà-ˣpʰì-kʲʰɛ̀ (támunáájpikye) 'my enemy-objAn'

The noun kʰá:nì 'father' has a lexically marked high tone on the first syllable.

(78) kʰá:nìí   (cááníí)   'father'
    kʰá:nímǜtsʰì (cáánímutsi) 'fathers (DuM)'

This appears to be a two syllable root but the first syllable—being both lexically marked high tone and long—counts as two syllables (moras) for determining where to dock the genitive tone. Since the root counts as three syllables (moras), the tone should dock on the first syllable of kʰá:ni, but it is blocked by the lexically marked high tone; this explains why the possessor bears high tone in example 79:[11]

(79) a. tʰá: Ⓖ kʰá:nì (táácááníí) 'my father'
     b. tí: Ⓖ kʲʰá:nì (díícyááníí) 'your father'
     c. í: Ⓖ kʲʰá:nì (íícyááníí) 'self's father'

Recall that the *LLX constraint discussed in section 3.6 prohibits adjacent low tones except at the end of a tonal phrase. Thus, a lexically marked low tone normally blocks the docking of Ⓛ on an adjacent syllable. Is this also true of a lexically marked *high* tones? Do they also block the docking of adjacent Ⓛ? The tone derivations of má:nì-má-ɾé-hùkʰò and ámánà-múɾ-ɾé-hùkʰò in figure 3.10 show that a lexically marked high tone does not block the docking of Ⓛ on an adjacent syllable.

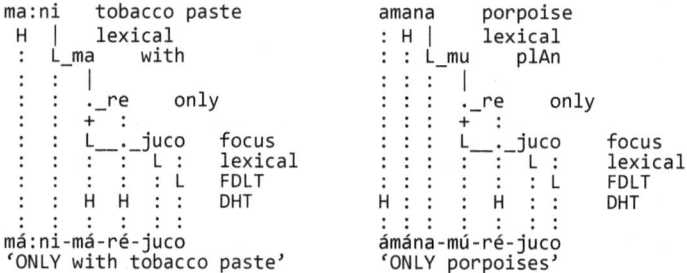

Figure 3.10 TD: mááənimáɾéjuco, ámánamúɾéjuco

---

[11]However, this is not always the case, as seen in the following example:
tí:tʃɛ́   Ⓖ ˣkʰà:nì   (díílléj caáni)   'her father'
múɾ:ʔá Ⓖ ˣkʰà:nímúɾtsʰì (múúháj caanímútsi) 'our parents'

Thus, the *LLX constraint is not about lexically marked tones per se, but only about lexically marked *low* tones. This supports seeing the *LLX constraint as a direct consequence of the Obligatory Contour Principle (OCP).

3.5.3 Nonfinite verbs

Another type of lexically marked tone is the result of a derivational process: verbs are made nonfinite by imposing a low tone according to the following rule:

$$\begin{array}{c} \sigma \quad (\sigma \quad (\sigma)) \quad]_V\# \\ \Updownarrow \\ \overset{L}{\sigma} \quad (\sigma \quad (\sigma)) \quad]_N\# \end{array}$$

That is, if the root is mono- or bisyllabic, the initial syllable bears low tone; if it is any longer, the antepenult bears low tone. This nonfinite low tone delinks any conflicting lexically marked tones the host might have (see section 3.11). Consider example 80. (N represents the nonfinite low tone and S represents the high tone of a subordinate verb.)

(80) a. Ó ájtyumɨ́ táábóóbeke.

b. Ó ájtyumɨ́ taabóóbeke.

$$\text{ó á}^x\text{t}^{jh}\text{ùmɨ́-ʔì} \quad \begin{cases} \text{a. t}^h\overset{S}{\text{a}}\text{ːpó-ːpɛ̀} \\ \text{b. t}^h\overset{N}{\text{a}}\text{ːpó-ːpɛ̀} \\ \quad \text{doctor-}\langle\text{SgM}\rangle \end{cases} \begin{matrix} \text{-k}^h\text{ɛ̀} \\ \text{-objAn} \end{matrix}$$

'I see-⟨t⟩

'I saw { a. him doctoring.' (subordinate)
        { b. the doctor.'   (nonfinite)

In 80a the Ⓛ of -Ⓛːpɛ ⟨SgM⟩ is delinked by the Ⓛ of -Ⓛkʰɛ 'objAn'. In 80b the Ⓛ of -Ⓛːpɛ ⟨SgM⟩ is blocked by the nonfinite low tone on the root's initial syllable.

Compare the tone derivations of the finite verbs tʰúɨkʰéβètsʰó-ʔì and tʰúɨkʰéβétsʰò-ːpɛ̀ in figure 3.11 with those of the nonfinite forms tʰúɨkʰèβétsʰò, tʰúɨkʰèβétsʰò-ʔàːmɨ̀, and tʰúɨkʰèβétsʰò-ːpɛ̀ in figure 3.12. Note that each verb in 3.12 is made nonfinite by putting the nonfinite low tone on the antepenult. (See section 4.1 for further discussion and examples.)

3.6. THE *LLX CONSTRAINT

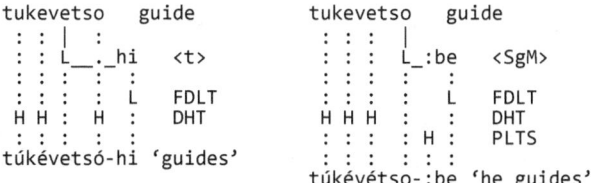

Figure 3.11 TD: túkévetsóhi, túkévétsoobe

Figure 3.12 TD: túkevétso, túkevétsohaamɨ, túkevétsoobe

3.6 The *LLX constraint

A fundamental fact about Bora tone—one that has a pervasive influence on the system—is that a sequence of low tones is not allowed except at the end of a word, where at most two low tones may occur. For example, see 81:

(81) ɯ́.mɛ̀.ʔɛ̀ (úmehe) 'tree'
ɯ́.mɛ́.ʔɛ́.kʰò.pà (úméhécoba) 'big tree'

We will refer to the constraint against a sequence of nonfinal low tones as the *LLX constraint. It can be formalized as follows:

$$*\overset{L}{\sigma}\overset{L}{\sigma}\sigma$$

Figure 3.13 The *LLX constraint

The *LLX constraint applies absolutely within a word, but also across word boundaries within a tonal phrase. This is crucial to our analysis of the tone of the genitive construction in section 9.1.

3.7 Phrase final tone changes

With rare exceptions, the final syllable of every morpheme is unspecified for tone. Whether this syllable becomes high or low tone depends on whether it occurs at the end of a tonal phrase or, if not final, on the morpheme(s) that follow(s). Thus, a word's final tones are a clue to whether the phonological phrase continues or ends.

We are not presently able to precisely characterize "phrase" or "phrase final." The end of a sentence or utterance are clearly phrase final but there are also sentence-medial cases where the "phrase final" changes apply. This subject begs for further research.

We will now discuss two rules that apply phrase finally: penultimate low tone split (PLTS) and final low tone split (FLTS).[12]

3.7.1 Penultimate low tone split

The first rule to be discussed is PENULTIMATE LOW TONE SPLIT (PLTS):

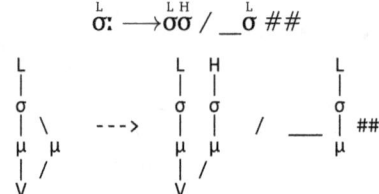

Figure 3.14 Penultimate Low Tone Split (PLTS)

There are three things to note about PLTS:
1. PLTS may never apply to a syllable that follows a low tone because the result would violate the *LLX constraint. However, this need not be stated explicitly in the PLTS rule if the *LLX constraint is understood as a general constraint on Bora phonology.
2. PLTS avoids a sequence of three moras of low tone.
3. The syllable projected from the mora (length) bears high tone. This is stipulated in figure 3.14 on the assumption that PLTS applies after DHT. However, it may be possible to reformulate the rules with PLTS preceding DHT, thus assigning high by default rather than by stipulation.

---

[12]In that the structural change of PLTS and FLTS is the same, it might be possible to capture both with a single rule, but the conditions for its application would have to be very complicated.

3.7. PHRASE FINAL TONE CHANGES

PLTS is illustrated by the tone derivations of ʧámààrà and màˣʧʰó-βà-ːpè in figure 3.15:

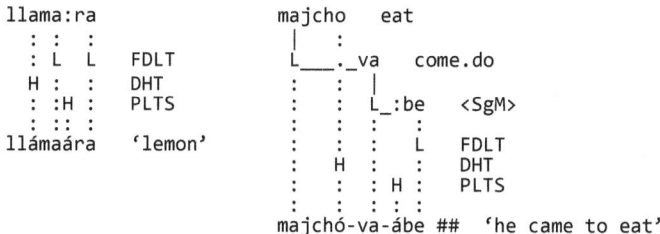

Figure 3.15 TD: llámaára, majchóvaábe

In 82a the first vowel of kʰùːmùɯ 'drum' does not split because it is not phrase final but it does split in 82b because it is at the end of the phrase:

(82) a. Cuumu ó ájtyumɨ́hi.

b. Ó ájtyumɨ́ cuúmu.

a. kʰùːmùɯ ó áˣtʲʰùmɨ́-ʔì
   drum   I saw-⟨t⟩
b. ó áˣtʲʰùmɨ́-ʔì kʰùúmùɯ
   I saw-⟨t⟩   drum
} 'I saw the drum.'

83a shows that the classifier -ʔaːmi ⟨leaf⟩ has a long vowel (one that does not split in the antepenult); however, when the long vowel occurs in the penult, as in 83b, it splits:

(83) a. tʰɛ́-ʔàːmɨ́-hɨ̀ (téhaamɨ́jɨ̀) 'those (leaves, papers, books,...)'
     b. tʰɛ́-ʔààmɨ̀   (téhaámɨ̀)   'that (leaf, paper, book,...)'

The long vowel of ɨːhɯ 'horse' splits when it is in the penult, as in 84a. It does not split in 84b,c because the long vowel is not in the penult (nor does it bear low tone):[13]

(84) a. ɨ́ɨhùɯ̀   /ɨ́ːhùɯ̀/   (ɨ́ɨju)   'horse'
     b. ɨ́ːhùɯ̀mùɯ̀ /ɨ́ːhùɯ̀-mùɯ̀/ (ɨ́ɨjumu)   'horses'
     c. ɨ́ːhúɯ̀mùɯ̀kʰɛ̀ /ɨ́ːhɯ́-mùɯ̀-kʰɛ̀/ (ɨ́ɨjúmuke) 'horses (acc)'

The long vowel of ɨhɯːɯ 'dove' splits in the penult, as in 85a–c. It does not split in 85d because the long vowel does not bear low tone, nor is it in the penult. It does not split in 85e—even though the vowel is in the penult—because the word does not end the phonological phrase.

---

[13] The high tone on the initial syllable of 84b and c comes about by default as discussed in section 3.3.2.

72   CHAPTER 3. TONE

(85) a. íˣừ:-ừɪ   (íjuú-u)   'dove'
        dove-⟨round⟩
     b. íˣừ:-mừɪ   (íjuú-mu)   'doves'
        dove-plAn
     c. íˣừ:-ừɪ-mútsʰì   (íjuú-u-mútsi)   'two doves'
        dove-⟨round⟩-DuM
     d. íˣúː-mừɪ-kʰɛ̀   (íjúúmuke)   'doves (acc)'
        dove-plAn-objAn

     e. íˣừː-mừɪ tsʰá:-ʔì (íjuumu tsááhi.) 'The doves
        dove-plAn come-⟨ø⟩   are coming.'

Consider 86 (from example 769 on page 308). In 86a, which has a direct quote, /nɛ̀-ːpɛ̀/ 'he said' ends a phonological phrase, and thus undergoes PLTS. By contrast, 86b has an indirect quote, so the phonological phrase continues after /nɛ̀-ːpɛ̀/; in this case PLTS does not apply because its conditions are not met:

(86) a. Oke ne<u>é</u>be, "Péjcore ...".
     b. Oke ne<u>e</u>be péjcore ....
     a. òkʰɛ̀ nɛ̀ɛ́pɛ̀ pʰɛ́ˣkʰòɾɛ̀   'He said to me, "Tomorrow..."'
     b. òkʰɛ̀ nɛ̀ːpɛ̀ pʰɛ́ˣkʰòɾɛ̀   'He told me that tomorrow...'

The singular masculine pronoun /tì:pʲɛ/ (diibye) is really tì- 'that' followed by -Ⓛ:pɛ ⟨SgM⟩, as in figure 3.16a. The result of this union is represented in 3.16b, where both the low tone (L) and the mora (m) have become part of the preceding syllable. This form, tì:pʲɛ̀, occurs when NOT at the end of a phrase. (The two low tones are allowed because they occur at the end of a word.) At the end of a phrase PLTS applies to produce tíípʲɛ̀ (diíbye), as in 3.16c:

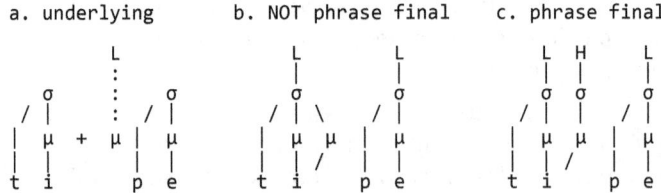

Figure 3.16 The singular masculine pronoun

Now compare 87a and b, both phrase final. In 87a, -Ⓛ:pɛ cannot dock its Ⓛ because the preceding -Ⓛtʰɛ has already docked its Ⓛ. Consequently the word does not satisfy the conditions for the application of PLTS.[14] By

---

[14]*úː:hɛ̀tʰɛ̀:pɛ̀ (úújeteébe) would violate the *LLX constraint.

3.7. PHRASE FINAL TONE CHANGES

contrast, in 87b -⓪:pɛ can dock its low tone so PLTS does apply:

(87) a. úːhɛ́-tʰɛ́-ːpɛ̀   (úújetéébe) 'he goes to inspect'
inspect-go.do-⟨SgM⟩
b. úːhɛ́-hɛ̀-ɛ́pɛ̀   (úújéjeébe) 'he returns from
inspect-do.come-⟨SgM⟩   inspecting'

Further examples follow:

(88) a. tòːpɛ̀   tʃìʔíjò (Doobe llihíyo. nonfinal) 'Father eats (meat).'
b. tòópɛ̀   (Doóbe.   final)   'He eats (meat).'

(89) a. àːʔíβɛ̀-ːpɛ̀ tʃìʔí-jò (Aahíveebe llihíyo. nonfinal) 'Father visits.'
b. àːʔíβɛ̀-ɛ́pɛ̀   (Aahíveébe.   final)   'He visits.'

GLOSS	NONFINAL		FINAL	
'thm-⟨SgM⟩'	àːpʲɛ̀	(aabye)	àápʲɛ̀	(aábye)
'grater'	kʰátsʰòːkpà	(cátsoowa)	kʰátsʰòókpà	(cátsoówa)
'river'	tʰɛ̀ːʔì	(teehi)	tʰɛ̀ɛ́ʔì	(teéhi)
'trail'	hùːɾβà	(juuva)	hùɾúβà	(juúva)

In this section, in the phonetic-phonemic form of examples we have represented the output of PLTS (ìí, ɛ̀ɛ́, àá,...). Elsewhere we generally represent the underlying form (ìː, ɛ̀ː, àː,...) counting on the reader to understand that PLTS applies, particularly since the orthographic form represents the output of PLTS.

3.7.2 Final low tone split

We now consider the second rule that applies at the end of a phrase, FINAL LOW TONE SPLIT (FLTS). This rule—which seems to be optional—"splits" a phrase-final low tone vowel into a sequence of vowels bearing low and high tone. FLTS may apply to the final syllable of (1) a monosyllabic word, (2) a bisyllabic word provided the penult bears high tone, and (3) a longer word provided the penult and antepenult bear high tone.[15]

---

[15] FLTS may also apply following nouns that have a lexically marked high tone on the penult. When such nouns are followed by suffixes, they seem to have a lexically marked high on the final syllable (although this is not without exceptions, ones we have yet to understand). Thus, FLTS may apply in some cases to *high* tones (rather than *low* ones). We must reserve judgement on this issue.

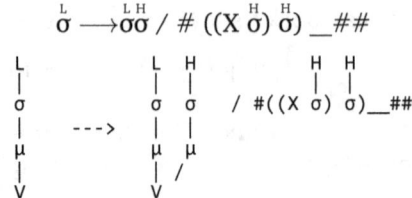

Figure 3.17 Final Low Tone Split (FLTS)

For example, in 90a "house" does not terminate the phonological phrase so FLTS does not apply, in contrast to 90b where it does apply:[16]

(90) a. Ja méénuúbe.
  b. Méénuube jaá.

  a. hà̱ mɛ́:nừ-ːpɛ̀
     house make-⟨SgM⟩
  b. mɛ́:nừ-ːpɛ̀ hà̱á̱ } 'He makes/made a house.'
     make-⟨SgM⟩ house

Further examples follow:

GLOSS	MEDIAL		FINAL	
this trail	íhʲừ̱	(íjyu)	íhʲừ̱rú̱	(íjyuú)
husband	áhʲừ̱	(ájyu)	áhʲừ̱rú̱	(ájyuú)
this.SgM	á:nừ̱	(áánu)	á:nừ̱rú̱	(áánuú)
town	kʰó:mì̱	(cóómi)	kʰó:mì̱í̱	(cóómií)
porpoise	ámánà̱	(ámána)	ámánà̱á̱	(ámánaá)
town-only	kʰó:mí-jè̱	(cóómíye)	kʰó:mí-jè̱é̱	(cóómíyeé)
salt	kʰáná:mà̱	(cánááma)	kʰáná:mà̱á̱	(cánáámaá)

In the following, compare the singulars, in which the stem final vowel splits, with the plurals, in which it does not.[17]

GLOSS	SINGULAR	PLURAL	POSSESSED PLURAL
our body	mɛ́ ˣpʰì̱í̱	mɛ́ ˣpʰí̱:-ʔɲ̀è	mừʔáˣ pʰì̱:-ʔɲ̀è
self's voice	í ˣkʲʰɛ̱̀ɛ̱́	í ˣkʲʰɛ̱́:-ʔɲ̀è	
self's speech	í ʔhʲừ̱rú̱	í ʔhʲú̱:-ʔɲ̀è	tì-:tʲʰɛ́ ì-ʔhʲú̱:-ʔɲ̀è
hunger	áhʲà̱á̱	áhʲá̱-ʔɲ̀è	
back	ʔátʃừ̱rú̱	ʔátʃú̱-ʔɲ̀è	

---

[16] In 90, the alternation between mɛ́:nừ:pɛ̀ (nonfinal) and mɛ́:nừ̱rú̱pɛ̀ (final) also illustrates PLTS.

[17] Note that in the first two examples the root of the plural ends with a long vowel whereas in the others it does not. We do not know why.
Under the right conditions the plural forms could also undergo FLTS, but are here not represented as having undergone it. Recall that FLTS is an optional rule.

3.8. THE INTERACTION OF TONE AND VOWEL LENGTH

Example 91a results from FLTS, 91b results by the addition of the classifier -Ⓛɯ ⟨spherical⟩, and 91c results by the subsequent addition of the pluralizer -ːnɛ 'plIn':

(91) a. kʰáːtʰɯ́ɾɯ́ (cáátuú) 'sweet potatoes (collective)'
 b. kʰáːtʰɯ̀ɾ-ɯ̀ (cáátuu) 'sweet potato (singular)'
 c. kʰáːtʰɯ̀ɾ-ɯ́ɾ-ːnɛ̀ (cáátuúúne) 'sweet potatoes (plural)'

3.8 The interaction of tone and vowel length

The tone bearing unit (TBU) is the syllable, not the mora. The basic tone-assignment rules are blind to vowel length; they deal with *syllables*, not *moras*:

1. They do not assign tone to a mora that is not a syllable.
2. Syllables are treated as adjacent (e.g., by the *LLX constraint) even if a mora intervenes. For example, consider the tone derivation of méːní-ːβʲɛ̀-ːpɛ̀ in figure 3.18:

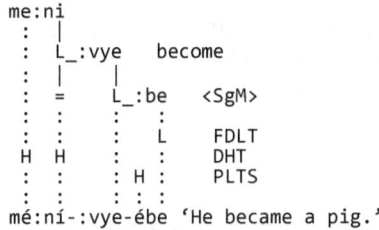

méːní-ːvye-ébe 'He became a pig.'

Figure 3.18 TD: mééníívyeébe

The Ⓛ that -Ⓛːpɛ ⟨SgM⟩ docks on the end of -Ⓛːβɛ 'become' is treated as adjacent to the Ⓛ that -Ⓛːβɛ docks on the end of mɛːni even though a mora (length) intervenes between them; this is clear because the first of these is delinked to meet the *LLX constraint. Note that in the derivation delinking is represented by "=" (equal sign). (For further discussion of delinking, see section 3.11.2.)

Likewise, see the second derivation of figure 3.28, page 86. The mora of the ⟨SgM⟩ suffix does not count as a tone bearing unit standing between the Ⓛs of the ⟨SgM⟩ and negative suffixes. That is, these two Ⓛs are adjacent.

There is one—and only one—allophonic ("implementation") rule that links vowel length and tone, namely the phenomenon captured by PLTS discussed in section 3.7.1. (FLTS is another potential candidate, but does not seem to require that the final syllable be long.)

3.9 The tones of isolated words ("citation forms")

The tones with which words are cited, that is, spoken in isolation, are often different than the tones they bear when used in a context. For example, to speak about a verb, the nonfinite form (see 4.1, page 100) must be used.

Theoretically, bisyllabic words might have the following tones: HH, HL LH, or LL. All may occur in the context of a sentence, but in isolation bisyllabic words are only LL;[18] for example, kʰùmì 'arrowroot', kpà˟pʰì 'man', tʰà˟kʰùɨ 'agouti', nò?kʰò 'stork', mà˟ʧʰò 'eat, food', tìtʲʰɛ̀ 'they (AnPl).

Theoretically, trisyllabic words might have the following tones: HHH, HHL, HLH, HLL, LHH, LHL, LLH or LLL:

1. LLL and LLH are impossible because they violate the *LLX constraint.
2. HLH, LHH, and HHH do not occur in isolation because the final syllable would become low by FDLT. The first two would become HLL and LHL, respectively. The last would become HHL, which would then become HHL.H by FLTS.
3. Words with HHL tones undergo FLTS, becoming HHL.H; for example, ámánàá 'porpoise', kʰáná:nàá 'salt'.
4. The remaining two possibilities occur: HLL (e.g., ní:βùɨkpà 'deer', úmḭ̀?ɛ̀ 'field') and LHL (e.g., kpa̋˟kʰó?ɛ̀ 'flowering plant').

3.10 Tone changes caused by suffixes

Affixes are added cyclically, possibly modifying the tones of their hosts. Thus it is necessary to understand the tonal properties of each affix, as well as any lexically marked tones borne by the root or stem.

We will illustrate this in three sections: suffixes that affect the host's final tones in 3.10.1, affixes that affect the host's initial tones in 3.10.2, and suffixes that affect initial and final tones in 3.10.3.

---

[18]Those that are HL, as by a lexically marked initial high tone, become HL.H by FLTS; for example, /kʰŏ:mi/ [kʰó:mì] (cóómíí) 'town'.

3.10.1 Suffixes affecting the host's final tones

Many suffixes affect the host's final tones. For example, -ⒽtʰE 'go to do' imposes a low tone on the preceding syllable, as in 92b and 93b.[19]

(92) a. ó màˣtʃʰó-ʔì (Ó majchóhi.) 'I eat'.
   b. ó máˣtʃʰò-tʰɛ́-ʔì (Ó májchotéhi.) 'I go to eat'.
   I eat-go.do-⟨t⟩

(93) a. ó à:ʔíβɛ́-ʔì (Ó aahívéhi.) 'I visit.
   b. ó à:ʔíβɛ̀-tʰɛ́-ʔì (Ó aahívetéhi.) 'I go to visit'.
   I visit-go.do-⟨t⟩

-ⒽΟmɛ ⟨AnPl⟩ imposes a low tone on its host's penult; for example, maˣtʃʰo 'to eat' (as in 92a) becomes màˣtʃʰó-mè 'they ate'. The stem imipaˣtʃʰo 'to fix' becomes ímípàˣtʃʰó-mè 'they fix'. In 94 the low tone of -ⒽΟmɛ coincides with that of -mɛ̀i 'reflexive'[20] and in 95 it coincides with the low tone of -Ⓗtʰɛ 'go to do'.

(94) íˣtsʰá-mɛ̀í-mʲɛ̀ (Íjtsámeímye.) 'They think.'
   think-r/p-⟨AnPl⟩

(95) à:ʔíβɛ̀-tʰɛ́-mɛ̀ (Aahívetéme.) 'They go visit.'
   visit-go.do-⟨AnPl⟩

The suffix -kpɯ̀(ɯ) (-wu(u)) 'diminutive' bears a low tone on its first syllable. This forces the host's final syllable to bear high tone to avoid violating the *LLX constraint, even when the second syllable of -kpɯ̀(ɯ) is not realized word finally, as in 96 and 97:

(96) tʃɛ́:ʔò-kpà[21] (lléehowa) 'door'
   tʃɛ́:ʔó-kpá-kpɯ̀ (lléehówáwu) 'little door'
   door-⟨slab⟩-dim

(97) kpàˣkʰó-ʔɛ̀ (wajcóhe) 'flower-bearing tree'
   kpàˣkʰó-ʔɛ́-kpɯ̀ (wajcóhéwu) 'little flower-bearing tree'
   flower-⟨tree⟩-dim

---

[19]The first syllable of the verb in 92a bears a low tone imposed by -ʔi ⟨t⟩. The first syllable of the verb in 92b bears high tone by default; if it were low, it would violate the *LLX constraint.

[20]At the end of section 5.8.2, page 148, it is suggested that -mɛ̀i 'reflexive, passive' is fused with the preceding root.

[21]The morpheme tʃɛ́:ʔò- is a bound root. It only occurs with -kpà ⟨slab⟩. The combination means 'door'.

The host's penult and preceding syllables bear high tones—by default—unless lexically marked as low. For example, the second syllable of umɨ̃ʔɛ 'planted field' bears a lexically marked low tone which, when -kpɨ̀(ɯ) 'diminutive' follows, remains low, as in 98:

(98) úmɨ̀ʔɛ́-kpɨ̀ (úmɨhéwu) 'little planted field'
    field-dim

In many cases lexically marked low tones block the docking of a suffix's tone. For example, the penult of ɨˣtsʰa-mɛ̀i (think-r/p-) 'think' bears a lexically marked low tone and this blocks the docking of the ⓛ of -ⓛtʰɛ 'go to do':

(99) ó ɨˣtsʰá-mɛ̀í-tʰɛ́-ʔì   (Ó ɨ́jtsámeítéhi.) 'I go to think.'
    I think-r/p-go.do-⟨t⟩

Likewise, consider the result of suffixing ⓛ○-βa 'have' to kʰaràkʰa 'chicken' in 100:

(100) ó kʰárákʰá-mɨ̀-βá-ʔì   (Ó cáracámuváhi.) 'I have chickens.'
    I chicken-plAn-have-⟨t⟩

The ⓛ of ⓛ○-βa may not dock because it would directly follow the root's lexically marked low tone, thus violating the *LLX constraint.

The resolution of such tone conflicts is further discussed in section 3.11.

3.10.2 Affixes that affect the host's initial tones

The suffixes -kʰa (-ca) 'counterfactual conditional', -kʰòːkʰa (-cooca) 'when', -ⓛkʰi (-ki) 'purpose', -ⓛhɨ́ːβà (-jɨ́ɨ́va) 'deny', and others, seem to impose a high tone on their host's initial syllable. For example, in 101, initial syllable of kʰɨ̀kpàkʰà 'sleep' bears a high tone on its first syllable (discounting the pronominal proclitic) because of -kʰa (-ca) 'counterfactual conditional':

(101) Ímí muha mecúwaca tsá muha mechéméturóhi.
    ímíʔ mɨ̀ʔà mè̠ kʰɨ́kpà-kʰà
    good we.ex SAP sleep-CF

    tsʰáʔ mɨ̀ʔà mè tʃʰɛ́mɛ́-tʰɨ̀-ɾó-ʔì
    not we.ex SAP be.ill-neg-frs-⟨t⟩
    'If we (ex.) had slept well, we would not have gotten sick.'

Such cases are discussed further in section 3.12.1.

3.10.3 Suffixes affecting both initial and final tones

Some suffixes affect the host's initial and final syllables. Thus, the suffix #ó̥...-⒧tʰ⁽ʲ⁾ɯ (-tu) 'negative' imposes a high tone on its host's initial syllable, as in the previous section, as well as a low tone on the syllable preceding the suffix (that is, unless the host is monosyllabic, in which case the initial high tone prevails). See chapter 13 for further discussion and examples.

The same is true for -hɨ́ːβà 'deny', as in 102. The verb ǎkpakʰɨ̆mɯ has lexically marked low tones on its first and third syllables. The high tone imposed on the first syllable overrides the lexically marked tone; the tone imposed on the host's final syllable docks on -⒧ːpɛ ⟨SgM⟩. (See also the tone derivation of figure 3.20, page 81.)

(102) ákpákʰɨ̀mɨ́-ːpɛ̌-hɨ́ːβà (áwácunúúbejɨ́ɨ́va) 'He has not yawned.'
  yawn-⟨SgM⟩-deny

3.11 Tone conflicts and their resolution

As suffixes are added one by one to a root or stem, tone conflicts arise when one low tone would be adjacent to another low tone (other than word finally). This happens in three cases:

(1) The host's final syllable has a low tone and the suffix has a low tone on its initial syllable.
(2) The host's penult has a low tone and the suffix should dock a low tone on its host's final syllable.
(3) The host's antepenult has a low tone and the suffix should dock a low tone on its host's penult.

These are represented in table 3.2:

Table 3.2 Where tone conflicts arise

The host has a low tone on the			and a suffix contributes low tone
ANTEPENULT	PENULT	FINAL	
		σ̌	-σ̌...
	σ̌	σ	-⒧σ...
σ̌	σ	σ	-⒧◯σ...

Conflicts must be resolved by BLOCKING (3.11.1) or by DELINKING (3.11.2). Blocking is the normal way tone conflicts are resolved.

Delinking—the exceptional case—applies only with certain suffixes, as discussed below.[22]

3.11.1 Blocking

One way to resolve a tone conflict is to *not* dock the suffix's low tone. We call this BLOCKING: the failure to dock the Ⓛ of a suffix because doing so would violate the *LLX constraint. In tone derivations it is represented by "+" as follows:

```
  |
  +              blocked
L__suffix
  :
  :
```

For example, -Ⓛtʰɛ or -Ⓛmuts ʰi normally docks a low tone on the host's final syllable. However, when added to àkpakʰùmuɯ 'to yawn'—which has a lexically marked low tone on the penult—the docking of the suffix's low tone is blocked; see example 103 and the tone derivation of àkpákʰùmúɯ-tʰέ-ʔì in figure 3.19:

(103) a. ó àkpákʰùmúɯ-tʰέ-ʔì   (ó awácunútéhi) 'I go to yawn.'
        I yawn-go.do-⟨t⟩
     b. àkpákʰùmúɯ-mútsʰì (awácunúmútsi) 'They (DuM) yawn.'
        yawn-⟨DuM⟩

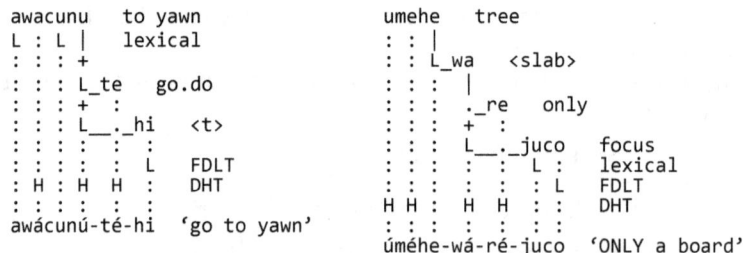

Figure 3.19 TD: awácunútéhi, úméhewáréjuco

In the tone derivation of úmέʔèkpá-ɾέ-hùɯkʰò figure 3.19 the Ⓛ of -ⓁОhùɯkʰo 'focus' is blocked by the Ⓛ of -Ⓛkpa ⟨slab⟩.

---
[22]There may be a third way to resolve conflicts, BUMPING (3.11.3); if so, it is a very restricted phenomenon that applies only to nominal roots.

3.11. TONE CONFLICTS AND THEIR RESOLUTION

In the tone derivation of máˣʧʰó-βá-mè-hɨ́ː(βà) in figure 3.20, the Ⓛ of -ⒺΟmɛ (-me) is blocked by the Ⓛ of -ⒺΟβa.[23]

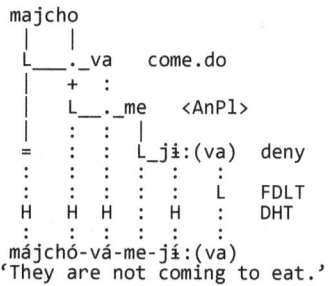

Figure 3.20 TD: májchóvámejɨ́ɨ́(va)

Compare the tone derivations of máˣʧʰò-tʰɛ́-ʔì, máˣʧʰò-hɛ́-ʔì, and máˣʧʰò-βà-ːpɛ̀ in figure 3.21, in which no blocking occurs, with those of máˣʧʰò-tʰɛ́-ːpɛ̀ and màˣʧʰó-βá-mè in figure 3.22, in which blocking does occur:

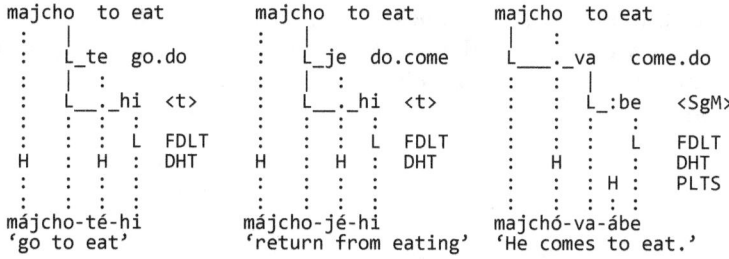

Figure 3.21 TD: májchotéhi, májchojéhi, majchóvaábe

---

[23] Also #Ⓗ...-ⒺΟhiː(βa) docks a high tone on the first syllable or, to put it another way, it delinks the Ⓛ placed on the first syllable by -ⒺΟβa, so this syllable becomes high tone by default. We return to this in section 3.11.2.3 below.

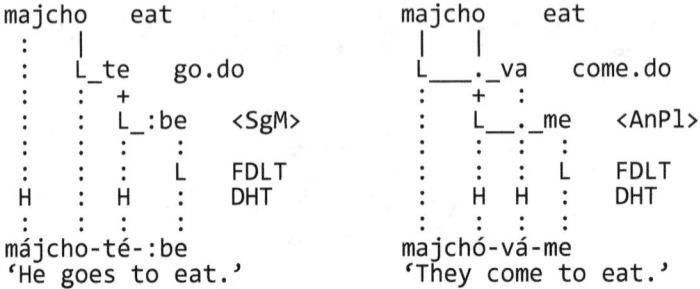

Figure 3.22 TD: májchotéébe, majchóváme

(Note that PLTS does not apply in the derivation of má^xtʃʰò-tʰɛ́-ːpɛ̀ in figure 3.22 because (1) the Ⓛ of -Ⓛtʰɛ 'go to do' blocks the docking of the Ⓛ of -Ⓛːpɛ, so (2) the penult is not low, so does not satisfy the conditions for PLTS.)

Compare the tone derivations of tómá^xkʰò-tʰɛ́-ːpɛ̀-βà^x and ɨˀβètʰɛ́-tʰɛ̀-ːpɛ́-βà^x in figure 3.23. In the first -Ⓛtʰɛ 'go to do' docks its Ⓛ and thus on the next cycle -Ⓛːpɛ ⟨SgM⟩ can not dock its Ⓛ because it would be adjacent to the previously docked low, creating a violation of the *LLX constraint. By contrast, in the second derivation the Ⓛ of -Ⓛtʰɛ does not dock because of the root's lexically marked low tone. Thus the Ⓛ of -Ⓛtʰɛ is not present to block the docking of the Ⓛ of -Ⓛːpɛ.

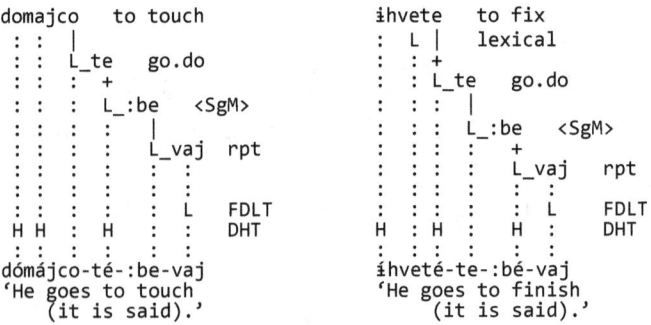

Figure 3.23 TD: dómájcotéébevaj, ɨhvetéteebévaj

3.11.2 Delinking

In addition to blocking, another way to resolve a tone conflict is to suppress the host's conflicting tone. We call this DELINKING: the delinking of a stem's low tone so that a suffix's Ⓛ can be docked without violating the

3.11. TONE CONFLICTS AND THEIR RESOLUTION

*LLX constraint.[24] In tone derivations delinking is represented by " = " as follows, where xyz represents a suffix that delinks a preceding low tone so as to dock its low tone without violating *LLX:

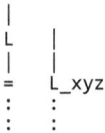

Delinking is a morphophonemic process that depends on the identity of the morphemes involved, whereas blocking is simply a phonological process driven exclusively by the *LLX constraint. We will now discuss specific cases.

3.11.2.1 Delinking by the person markers

The person markers[25] (-⓪:pɛ ⟨SgM⟩, -⓪ʧɛ ⟨SgF⟩, -⓪mɯtsʰi ⟨DuM⟩, -⓪mɯpʰi̧ ⟨DuF⟩ and -⓪○me ⟨AnPl⟩) delink conflicting tones; see the derivation of máˣʧʰó-tsʰò-:pɛ̀ in figure 3.24 and those of ímípàˣʧʰó-tʰɯ̀-mɯ́tsʰì and ímípàˣʧʰó-βá-hɯ́kʰò:-mɯ́tsʰì in figure 3.25:

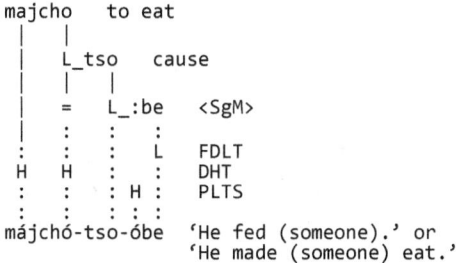

Figure 3.24 TD: májchótsoóbe

---

[24]A low tone can also be delinked by adding an affix that imposes a high tone on a low-tone-bearing syllable; see figure 3.20, page 81, and the accompanying discussion.

[25]These are classifiers so it is no surprise that their tonal behavior is like that of classifiers generally, as described in section 6.1.4.

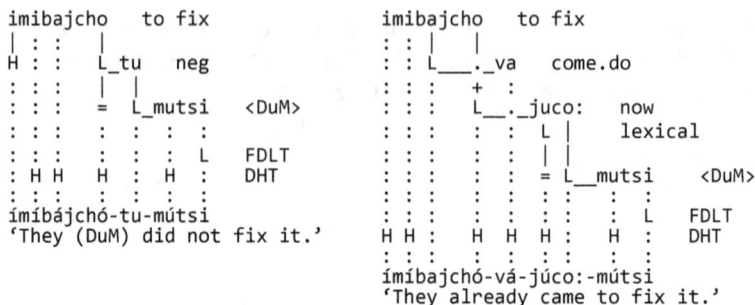

Figure 3.25 TD: ímíbájchótumútsi, ímíbajchóvájúcoomútsi

However, the Ⓛ of the person markers is blocked by—not delinked by—the Ⓛ of a relocation suffix. For example, consider the derivations of figure 3.22. The first shows the Ⓛ of -Ⓛtʰɛ 'go to do' blocking the Ⓛ of -Ⓛːpɛ ⟨SgM⟩. The second shows the Ⓛ of -ⓁО̄βa 'come to do' blocking the Ⓛ of -ⓁО̄mɛ ⟨AnPl⟩. However, contrary to this generalization, in example 104 the Ⓛ of -Ⓛhɛ 'do after coming' is delinked by the Ⓛ of -Ⓛːpɛ ⟨SgM⟩:

(104) máˣtʃʰó-h<u>ɛ̀</u>-ːpɛ̀   (Májchójeébe.) 'He returned from eating.'
      eat-do.come-⟨SgM⟩

3.11.2.2 Delinking by -Ⓛdi 'animate', -Ⓛke 'objAn', -Ⓛki 'purpose', -Ⓛma 'with', -Ⓛte 'go.do' and -Ⓛdu 'like'

The suffixes -Ⓛti 'animate', -Ⓛkʰɛ 'objAn', -Ⓛkʰi 'purpose', -Ⓛma 'with', -Ⓛtʰɛ 'go to do' and -ⓁО̄tɯ 'like' delink conflicting tones. This is illustrated by -Ⓛti and -Ⓛma in the tone derivations of níːβɯ́ɾkpá-kpɯ́ɾɯ̀-tì and ɯ́mɛ́ʔɛ́kpá-kpɯ́ɾɯ̀-mà in figure 3.26:

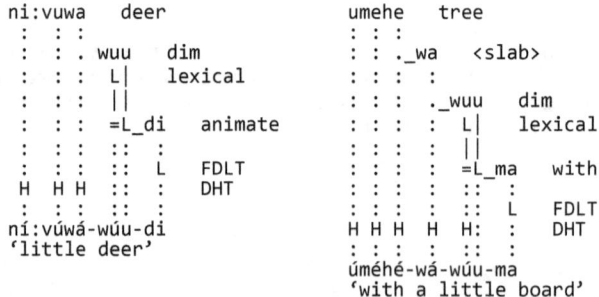

Figure 3.26 TD: níːvúwáwúudi, úméhéwáwúuma

3.11. TONE CONFLICTS AND THEIR RESOLUTION

Figure 3.32, page 89, shows that -Ⓛkʰɛ 'objAn' can delink the Ⓛ of -Ⓛtʃɛ ⟨SgF⟩. There may be a generalization: case markers can delink the tones of person markers.

We do not understand the tones of kpàʔáró-ùɨβɨ́-tùɨ 'like my deceased mother'. The derivation of figure 3.27 suggests that -tɨɨ 'like' delinks the Ⓛ of -Ⓛɨɨβɨɨ 'maximum':

```
            waharo      mother
         L :  |         lexical
         :  : L_uvu     max
         :  :  | | :
         :  : = L_._du  like
         :  :  : : :
         :  :  : : :  L    FDLT
         :  H H : H  :    DHT
         :  :  : : :
         wahárό-uvύ-du  'like my deceased mother'
```

Figure 3.27 TD: wahárόuvύdu

However, this assumes -ⓁOtɨɨ contrary to the tone we have posited for 'like' following nouns, namely -Ⓛtɨɨ, as in kʰɛ́ːmɛ̀-tùɨ 'like an old man' and the examples of 1080, page 424.

3.11.2.3 Delinking by #Ⓗ...-jɨ̈(va) 'deny'

In figure 3.20 above, we saw that #Ⓗ...-ⓁOhɨ́ː(βa) 'deny' docks a high tone on the first syllable, imposing itself where there was already a Ⓛ (in this case contributed by -ⓁOβa). This delinking differs from delinking that avoids violations of the *LLX constraint when a low tone is docked on an adjacent syllable. Although different, we treat these both as delinking because (1) both types remove a low tone and (2) both are triggered by affixes that impose tone.

#Ⓗ...-Ⓛhɨ́ː(βa) 'deny' also delinks conflicting low tones, particularly those of a preceding person classifier subject, as illustrated in the tone derivations of tʃɛ́ːnɛ́-ːpɛ̀-hɨ́ːβà and áːʔɨ́βέβá-ːpɛ̀-hɨ́ːβà in figure 3.28:

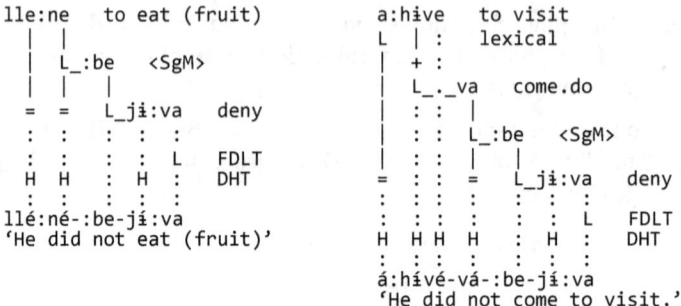

Figure 3.28 TD: lléénéébejíƚva, á:hívéváábejíƚva

Ⓗ...-Ⓛhɨː(βa) 'deny' even delinks the Ⓛ of person markers which are not adjacent to its Ⓛ. This case arises with -Ⓛmɯtsʰi ⟨DuM⟩, -Ⓛmɯpʰɨ ⟨DuF⟩ and even -ⒷⓄmɛ ⟨AnPl⟩. Such cases confirm that delinking is a morphophonemic process depending on the identity of the morphemes involved, not simply a phonological process driven by the *LLX constraint, as is the case for blocking.

3.11.2.4 Delinking by -Ⓛσ 'future'

The morpheme -Ⓛσ 'future' can delink the Ⓛ of -Ⓛtʰɛ 'go to do', as seen in the derivation of ómáˣʧʰó-tʰɛ̀-ɛ́-ʔɨ̀ in figure 3.29:[26]

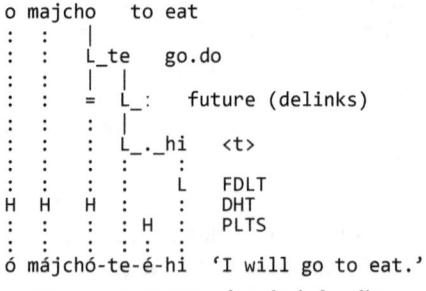

Figure 3.29 TD: ó májchóteéhi

---

[26]Frequently the tones of a person-marking proclitic and the first syllable of the following verb are either high-low or low-high. (They may not, of course, be low-low due to the *LLX constraint.) Figure 3.29 is a rare case where both tones are high.

3.11.2.5 Delinking by -ro ~ -ra 'frustrative, contraexpectation'

-Ⓛro ~ -Ⓛra (-ro ~ -ra) 'frustrative, contraexpectation' (frs) delinks the Ⓛ of the first syllable of -Ⓛ◯hùkʰo: as demonstrated by the tone derivations of máˣtʃʰó-tsʰò-tʰɛ́-hùkʰó:-rò-:pè and íʔβɛ̀tʰɛ́-tsʰò-hɛ́-húkʰò:-rá-ʔì in figure 3.30:

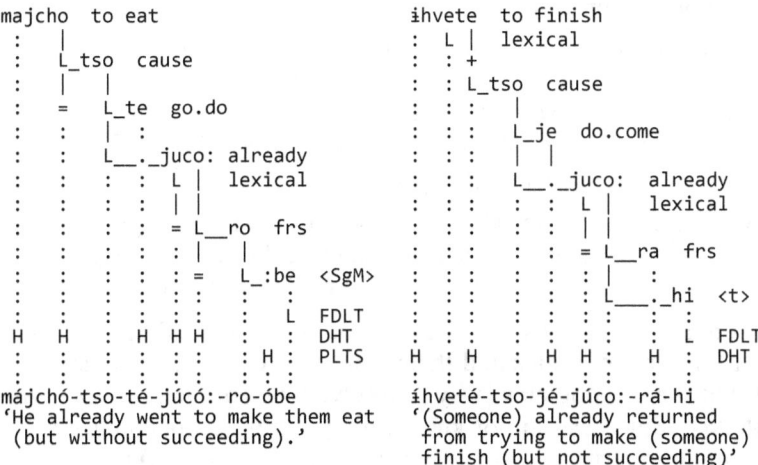

Figure 3.30 TD: májchótsotéjúcóóroóbe, íhvetétsojéjúcooráhi

In the derivation of íʔβɛ̀tʰɛ́-tsʰó-hɛ̀-rá-ʔì in figure 3.31, -Ⓛro ~ -Ⓛra 'frustrative' delinks the low tone of -Ⓛhɛ̀ 'return from doing' (do.come):

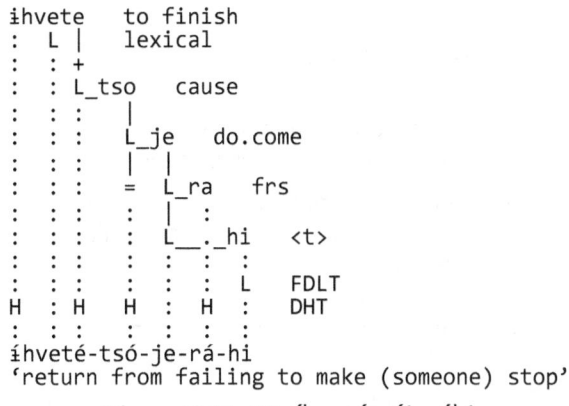

Figure 3.31 TD: íhvetétsójeráhi

3.11.3 Bumping

As discussed in section 3.5.2, nominal roots may bear lexically marked high tones. This is usually on the penult, which in most cases is also the initial syllable. Examples follow: áːnɯ 'this (SgM)', kʰáːni 'father', amána 'porpoise', kʰóːmi 'town', máːni 'tobacco paste', áˣt͡ʃʰɯʔóːɯ 'flashlight'. (For further examples see section 3.5.2, especially footnote 9.)

These nouns behave in unexpected ways when suffixes are added. The root's final syllable undergoes FLTS when utterance final, suggesting that it bears low tone. However, the addition of certain suffixes suggests that it bears a lexically marked high tone. For example, -①kʰɛ 'objAn' does not dock its ⓛ following áːnɯ 'this (SgM)' and íˣtʲʰɛ 'self's ones (AnPl)':

(105) a. á:nɯ̀   (this.SgM   áánuú) 'this one (SgM)'
   b. á:nɯ́-kʰɛ̀ (this.SgM-objAn áánúke) 'to this one (SgM)'
   c. í-ˣtʲʰɛ́-kʰɛ̀ (self-⟨AnPl⟩-objAn íjtyéke) 'to self's (AnPl)'

More research needs to be done before anything definitive can be said about this class of nouns and their tonal behaviors. Here we simply suggest that there is one more way to resolve tone conflicts, one we will call BUMPING. Since we do not know how general this phenomenon is, we will state it in terms of a single morpheme.[27] -①◯hɨ́ː(βa) normally docks a ⓛ on the penult of a nominal host. (The pattern for verbs is different.) When this ⓛ coincides with a lexically marked Ⓗ, it seems that the ⓛ is "bumped" to the following syllable. This is illustrated in kʰóːmì-hɨ́ːβà 'not a town' and kʰáːnì-hɨ́ːβà 'not a father'.

3.12 Grammatical tone

Tone plays a major role in Bora grammar. Here we mention tone patterns associated with particular grammatical structures.

1. The tone of the genitive constructions, discussed in section 9.1.
2. There are distinctive tones on imperative verbs. Two basic generalizations regarding these are:
   (a) The imperative verb—including the pronominal prefix or proclitic—bears a low tone on the second syllable.
   (b) The verb stem bears a low tone regressive to the antepenult: $...\overset{L}{\sigma}(\sigma(\sigma))\#$ (just as for nonfinite verbs). This delinks conflicting lexically marked tones.

For more details about imperatives, see section 14.1.1.

---

[27] There is some evidence that bumping also applies to -ɾɛ 'only'.

3.12. GRAMMATICAL TONE

We now discuss the tone on the verbs of subordinate clauses (3.12.1), the tone of the person marking proclitics (3.12.2), and the default tone of nouns and classifiers (3.12.3).

3.12.1 Tone on the verbs of subordinate clauses

The verb of a subordinate clause (as discussed in section 16.1 always begins with a high tone, as in 106. This high tone is represented with an s over the vowel to make the reason for this high tone more apparent.

(106) a. má˰ˣtʃʰó-ːpɛ̀-kʰɛ̀ (májchóóbeke) 'the one (SgM) who ate-objAn'
b. má˰ˣtʃʰó-tʃɛ̀-kʰɛ̀ (májchólleke) 'the one (SgF) who ate-objAn'
c. má˰ˣtʃʰó-mɛ̀-kʰɛ̀ (májchómeke) 'the ones (AnPl) who ate-objAn'

The suffix -⓪kʰɛ 'objAn' imposes a low tone on the preceding syllable, delinking the low tones docked by -⓪ːpɛ ⟨SgM⟩ in 106a and -⓪tʃɛ ⟨SgF⟩ in 106b. In 106c we expect -⓪○mɛ ⟨AnPl⟩ to impose a low tone on its host's penultimate syllable (in this case, the initial syllable). However, this is a subordinate clause, so it begins with a high tone.

In figure 3.32 úːhɛ̀tʰɛ́-ró-tʃɛ̀-kʰɛ̀ is a relative clause, with high tone on the first syllable as expected:

Figure 3.32 TD: úújetérólleke

The derivation of 107 is given in figure 3.33.

(107) dsɨ́jɨ́vétsómeke

[tsɨ̊híβɛ́-tsʰó]-mɛ̀-kʰɛ̀   'the ones who were killed-objAn'
die-caus-⟨AnPl⟩-objAn

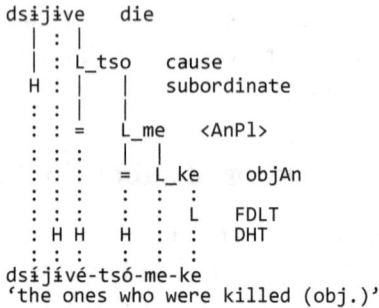

Figure 3.33 TD: dsɨ́jɨ́vétsómeke

Examples 108 and 109 contrast a sentence's main verb with the corresponding verb in a relative clause:

(108) a. màˣt͡ʃʰó-mɛ̀ (Majchóme.) 'They are eating (bread).'

b. máˣt͡ʃʰò-mɛ̀ (májchome) 'those who are eating (bread)'

(109) a. t͡ʃʰɛ́mɛ̀-ːpɛ̀ (Chémeébe.) 'He is sick.'

b. t͡ʃʰɛ́mɛ̀-ːpɛ̀ (chémeebe) 'the one (SgM) who is sick'[28]

In examples 110a, 111a, and 112a, whether the verb is used as a relative clause or as a main clause, its initial syllable bears high tone; the relative clause verbs do so because they are subordinate whereas the main clause verbs do so by default. By contrast, the verbs of 110b, 111b, and 112b bear the nonfinite low tone on their initial syllables:

(110) a. kpáˣkʰò-ʔɛ̀ (wájcohe) 'tree that is flowering' or
                                       'The tree is flowering.'

b. kpàˣkʰó-ʔɛ̀ (wajcóhe) 'a flower(ing) tree'

(111) a. ní:βà-ì (níívai) 'river that is flowing' or
                                      'The river is flowing.'

b. nì:βá-ì (niivái) 'a flowing river'

(112) a. nɛ́:βà-ʔɛ̀ (néévahe) 'tree that bears fruit' or
                                       'The tree is bearing fruit.'

b. nɛ̀:βá-ʔɛ̀ (neeváhe) 'fruit tree'

In 113 the first syllable of the verb of the relative clause has the expected high subordination tone:

(113) máˣt͡ʃʰò-ːpɛ̀ ò:mí-hùɨkʰó:-ʔì (Májchoobe oomíjucóóhi.)
     eat-⟨SgM⟩   return-now-⟨t⟩
     'The one who ate has already returned.'

---

[28]The tones of 109b are those of a non-final position in which FLTS does not apply.

3.12. GRAMMATICAL TONE

This is also true in 114a but not in 114b, which has a low tone on the first syllable. This tone is imposed by -ⓁO βa 'come to do' and—presumably—resists the imposition of the subordination tone.

(114) a. Májchotéébé oomíjucóóhi.
   b. Majchóvaabe oomíjucóóhi.

$$\begin{Bmatrix} \text{a. mă}^{x}\text{tʃ}^{h}\text{ò-t}^{h}\text{ɛ́-:pɛ́} \\ \text{eat-go.do-}\langle\text{SgM}\rangle \\ \text{b. mà}^{x}\text{tʃ}^{h}\text{ó-βà-:pɛ̀} \\ \text{eat-come.do-}\langle\text{SgM}\rangle \end{Bmatrix} \text{ò:mí-hừk}^{h}\text{ó:-ʔì} \\ \text{return-now-}\langle\text{t}\rangle$$

'The one who $\begin{Bmatrix} \text{a. went} \\ \text{b. came} \end{Bmatrix}$ to eat has already returned.'

The suffixes of table 3.3 may follow the verb of a subordinate clause, the initial syllable of which bears a high tone.[29]

Table 3.3 Suffixes that follow subordinate clause verbs

-kʰa	(-ca)	'counterfactual conditional'
-kʰǒ:kʰa	(-cooca)	'when'
-ʔǎˣtʃʰi:(hʲɯ)	(-hajchííjyu ~ -hajchí)	'if (conditional)'
-ihʲɯ	(-ijyu)	'when (at that time)'
-Ⓛkʰi	(-ki)	'purpose'
-naǎ:kʰa	(-náaáca ~ -naa)	'while'
-ne^{a}	(-ne)	⟨event⟩ or ⟨ø⟩
-Ⓛtʰ⁽ʲ⁾ɯ	(-tu)	'negative'
-Ⓛhɨ́:βà	(-jɨ́ɨva)	'deny'

^{a}Generally a case marker or -Ⓛhɨ(βa) 'deny' would follow -ne.

There are various ways the host's initial high tone might be analyzed:

1. The suffixes could be treated as discontinuous morphemes, the first part of which ensures that the host's initial tone is high. This might be implemented in one of two ways:
   (a) It could simply impose high tone on the first syllable: #Ⓗ…-suffix. This possibility, while descriptively adequate, seems stipulative and unmotivated.

---
[29]It is tempting to include -ⓁO?tɯ (-hdu) 'similar' in this list but it follows nonfinite verbs, not subordinate clauses.

(b) It could be a low tone prefix (Ⓛ-) that forces the initial syllable to bear high tone: #Ⓛ-ȯ́...-suffix. (The host's first syllable would have to bear high tone to avoid violating the *LLX constriant.)

This suggestion can be immediately rejected. Recall that o 'I', ɯ 'you', i 'self', and mɛ 'SAP' are proclitics that form a tonal phrase with the following verb. If Ⓛ occurred between the proclitic and the verb, the proclitic should necessarily bear high tone. (Otherwise it and the following Ⓛ- would violate the *LLX constraint.) However, this is not the case, as seen in mè máˣtʃʰò-kʰì (SAP eat-pur memájchoki) 'in order that we eat' and ì máˣtʃʰó-nè-mà (self eat-⟨event⟩-with imájchónema) 'after eating'.

2. The initial high tone would be imposed by an independent process of subordination, and the suffixes of table 3.3 would subcategorize for a subordinate clause. For example, the subcategorization frame of -Ⓛkʰi 'purpose' would be [[$_{S[+\text{subordinate}]}$...] __] (the verb being final within the subordinate clause). This subordination process could be implemented in either of the just-mentioned ways, namely simply imposing high tone on the verb's first syllable or by a low tone prefix.

Thus, we adopt the third possibility: (1) the suffixes of table 3.3 subcategorize for a subordinate clause, and (2) subordination is marked by docking a high tone on the verb's initial syllable. The derivations of ímípáˣtʃʰò-kʰì 'to fix' and máˣtʃʰó-mè-kʰè 'the ones (AnPl) who eat-objAn' (from example 106c) are given in figure 3.34. In the latter, -Ⓛ◯mɛ ⟨AnPl⟩ can not dock its low tone because this would displace the high tone that marks subordination.[30]

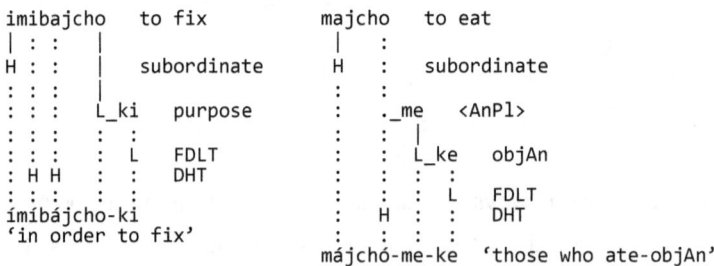

Figure 3.34 TD: ímíbájchoki, májchómeke

Finally, -nɛ ⟨event⟩—in contrast to -Ⓛ◯nɛ ⟨ø⟩ (thing) and the -nɛ ⟨n⟩ (discussed in section 13.2)—seems to delink any preceding low tones except the root's lexically marked tones; see the derivation of tsɨ́hɨ́βέ-tsʰó-í-jó-nέ-tʃiː?ʲὲ in figure 3.35:

---

[30]Alternatively, if the ⟨AnPl⟩ suffix is taken as -Ⓛmɛ, then it would be delinked by -Ⓛkʰɛ.

3.12. GRAMMATICAL TONE 93

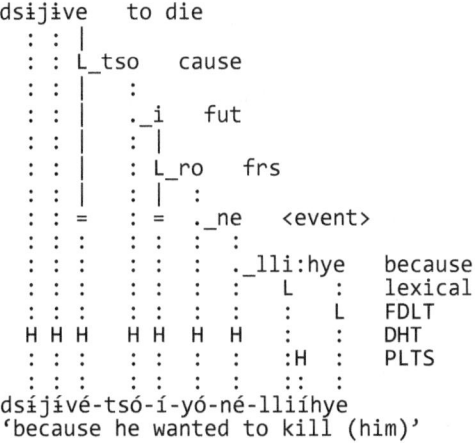

Figure 3.35 TD: dsɨ́jɨ́vétsóíyónélliíhye

3.12.2 The tones of proclitics

When the pronouns o 'I', ɯ 'you', i 'self', and mɛ 'SAP' occur before a verb, they cliticize to it. By virtue of forming phonological phrases with their host, they must bear tones that—when taken together with their host—do not violate the *LLX constraint. They are assigned tone by the following rule:

subordinate: If the verb is subordinate, the pronoun bears low tone. (This is always possible because the initial syllable of the verb bears high tone.) See example 115 below.

A clause negated by tsʰá̰ʔ 'no' behaves as though subordinate.[31] See example 116 below.

main: If the verb is not subordinate, then there are two cases:

  monosyllabic stem: If the verb stem is monosyllabic, the pronoun bears low tone. This is presumably because, to take example 117a below, -Ⓛ○ʔi ⟨t⟩ docks its Ⓛ on the proclitic. Likewise, in 117b, presumably -Ⓛ○hɯ́kʰo 'now' imposes its Ⓛ on the proclitic. (In both these cases, after a polysyllabic verb the Ⓛ would fall on the root, not on the proclitic.) For some reason, however, it is not the case when the future tense follows, as in 117c.

---

[31]This is not the only reason to regard such clauses as subordinate: they end with an explicit or implicit -nɛ ⟨ø⟩, which behaves like a subordinator.

polysyllabic root: Otherwise the pronoun bears high tone. See example 119.

Example 115 illustrates the first case (subordinate):

(115) mè kʰá⁷kʰɯ̌ˣtsʰó-nè (mecáhcújtsóne) 'after you
      SAP believe-⟨event⟩   have believed'

Example 116 further illustrates the first case showing that negations behave like subordinate clauses:

(116) Tsá o májchotétú(ne).

tsʰá⁷ ò máˣtʃʰò-tʰɛ́-tʰɯ́-(nɛ̀) 'I did not go to eat.'
no   I eat-go.do-neg-⟨n⟩

Example 117 illustrates the second case (main verb) with a monosyllabic root:

(117) a. ò̱ tó:-ʔì   (O dóóhi.)   'I eat meat.'
         I eat-⟨t⟩
      b. ò̱ pʰɛ́-hɯ̀kʰó:-ʔì (O péjucóóhi.) 'I go now.'
         I go-now-⟨t⟩
      c. ó̱ pʰɛ́-hɯ́kʰò-ó-ʔì (Ó péjúcoóhi.) 'I will go now.'
         I go-now-fut-⟨t⟩

Compare 118a and b. In 118a the Ⓛ of -Ⓛ○ʔi reaches the proclitic, whereas in 118b it can not do so because of the additional syllable added by the future.

(118) a. ǒ nɛ́:-ʔì: (O nééhií.)   'I say.'
         I say-⟨t⟩
      b. ó nɛ̌-ɛ́-ʔì   (Ó neéhi.)   'I will say.'
         I say-fut-⟨t⟩

Example 119 illustrates a main verb with a polysyllabic root; the proclitic bears high tone as expected:

(119) ó̱ máˣtʃʰò-tʰɛ́-ʔì (Ó májchotéhi.) 'I go eat'
      I eat-go.do-⟨t⟩

3.12.3 The default tone of nouns and classifiers

Ordinarily a noun—including its derivational and inflectional suffixes—ends in two low tones. (This is not true for verbs, which end in a single low tone.) For example, consider kpaˣpʰi 'man' and ni:βɯkpa 'deer' in 120:

3.13. THE RULE OF THREE AND BOUNDARY MARKING

(120) a Wajpi úmɨváhi.
   b Nííѵuwa úmɨváhi.

$\left.\begin{array}{l}\text{a. kpà}^{x}\text{p}^{h}\grave{\text{\i}}\\ \text{b. ní:}\beta\grave{\text{ɨɪ}}\text{kpà}\end{array}\right\}$ úmɨ̀βá-ʔɨ̀ 'The $\left\{\begin{array}{l}\text{a. man}\\ \text{b. deer}\end{array}\right\}$ escapes.'

A floating low tone occurs at the boundary between a classifier and its host (that is, the morpheme to which it is attached). This tone is docked by the following rule: (1) Monosyllabic classifiers dock a low tone on their host's final syllable. (2) Bisyllabic classifiers dock a low tone on the final syllable of a polysyllabic host. After a monosyllabic host, the low tone docks on the classifier's initial syllable. (3) Classifiers having more than two syllables bear the low tone on their initial syllable. See section 6.1.4 for further details.

3.13 The rule of three and boundary marking

The placement of low tone (1) in nonfinite verbs, (2) in the genitive construction, and (3) when a classifier follows are all sensitive to the number of syllables of the unit, counting from its end:

1. Verbs are made nonfinite by putting a low tone on the stem's earliest syllable not more than three syllables from the end: $\overset{\text{N}}{\sigma}(\sigma(\sigma))\#$. (It is as though the N were tethered to the end of the stem with an elastic that allowed it to stretch up to three syllables but no further.)
2. The genitive low tone (Ⓖ) docks on the modifier's final syllable unless the head is more than two syllables long, in which case it docks on the head's initial syllable. That is, when the head is short the Ⓖ can stretch back to the end of the modifier, but when the head is longer than two syllables, Ⓖ cannot stretch back across the boundary so ends up on the head's initial syllable.
3. Classifiers place a low tone (Ⓒ) on the noun's final syllable when the classifier is mono- or bisyllabic (with one exception), but when the classifier has three or more syllables, Ⓒ docks on the classifier's first syllable. That is, when the classifier (which we claim to be the head) is short, Ⓒ can stretch back to the end of the modifier, but when the classifier is longer than two syllables, Ⓒ cannot stretch that far and ends up on the classifier's initial syllable.

The last two cases—the genitive construction and the addition of classifiers—are both cases of the joining of two units into a single one, both joining a modifier and head into a single syntactic and phonological unit. The low tone at the boundary (that docks one way or the other) marks the boundary between the modifier and the head.

3.14 Areas for further study

Many issues beg for further study:

1. Some nouns have a lexically marked high tone on their initial syllable; see section 3.11.3 for examples. We understand little about the tonal behavior of such words nor, for that matter, about lexically marked high tones generally.
2. Some words (roots) simply demonstrate exceptional tonal behavior[32] (exceptional, that is, relative to our analysis). Consider the genitive constructions in table 3.4 (in which POSS'R stands for 'possessor (modifier)' and POSS'D stands for 'possessed (head)') and the discussion that follows.

Table 3.4 Words with exceptional tone

	POSS'R my H	POSS'D X HL	POSS'R his/her HL	POSS'D X HL
mother /tsʰɨːhɯ/	tʰá: tsʰɨ́ːhɯ̀		tíːpʲɛ̀ˣ tsʰɨ́ːhɯ̀	
wife /tʰaːpa/	á tʲʰáːpà		tíːpʲɛ̀ tʰáːpà	

	H	HL	HH	LL
father-in-law /paːpɛ/	á páːpɛ̀		tíːpʲɛ́ pàːpɛ̀	
father /kʰáːni/	tʰá: kʰáːnì		tíːpʲɛ́ˣ kʰàːnì	
husband /tʰahi/	á tʲʰáhì		tíːtʃɛ́ tʰàhì	

Consider the first two rows ('mother' and 'wife'). In the second column the genitive low tone docks on the possessor's final syllable as expected. In the first column, however, there is no evidence of the genitive low tone; the possessor bears high rather than low tone; compare example 573, page 253.

Consider the last three rows ('father-in-law', 'father', and 'husband'). In both columns the possessor's final syllable bears high tone rather than the expected genitive low tone; compare example 574, page 253.

Further, although there is abundant evidence that 'father' bears a lexically marked *high* tone on its first syllable (kʰáːni), in the second column it bears a low tone on its initial syllable.

---

[32] Many words with exceptional tonal behavior are common terms for humans and their relationships, e.g., kpàˣpʰì 'man', tʃìːʔíjò 'male child/parent', kpàtʃɛ̀ 'woman', kpàʔáɾò 'female child/parent'. The high frequency of such words allows them to remain exceptional, since frequent use reinforces words, making them resistent to normalization.

3.14. AREAS FOR FURTHER STUDY

3. In appendix D we list most of the suffixes, including an explicit representation of their tonal properties. These are working hypotheses: there are suffixes for which we do not fully understand their tonal properties. For example, when -ⓛtuɪ 'like' follows a monosyllabic classifier, it does not ordinarily delink the low tone imposed by that classifier on the preceding syllable; see 121a. However, if the preceding (monosyllabic) classifier's ⓛ is not docked (blocked by a preceding ⓛ), quite unexpectedly the ⓛ of -ⓛtuɪ does not dock; see 121b:

(121) a. úmɛ́ʔɛ̀-kpá-tùɪ   (úméhewádu) 'like a slab-like thing'.
      tree-⟨slab⟩-like

   b. kpáˣkʰó-ʔɛ́-tùɪ   (wɑjcóhédu) 'like a flowering tree'
      flower-⟨tree⟩-like

It is as though the classifier's ⓛ is both present (to block the ⓛ of -ⓛtuɪ) and absent.

4. Several rules (FDLT, PLTS and FLTS) are conditioned to apply only "phrase finally" but we have not adequately defined what this means. Different rules will require different broader or narrower notions of "final"; e.g., FDLT applies more generally (perhaps *word* finally) than PLTS and FLTS.

   Perhaps more seriously, we have made only feeble attempts to relate "tonal phrase" to syntactic structure; one would expect a tight relationship.

5. PLTS and the *LLX constraint both work to avoid three moras of low tone, but our analysis does not capture this commonality.

6. We note the following similarity:

   (a) The low tone that makes a verb stem nonfinite (section 4.1) or imperative (section 14.1.1) docks on the earliest of *the last three syllables, counting from its end*: …$\overset{N}{\sigma}(\sigma(\sigma))\#$.

   (b) The low "boundary" tones of the genitive construction (section 9.1) and of classifiers (section 6.1.4) reaches the final syllable of the modifier only if it is among *the last three syllables, counting from the end of the head*: $[_{\text{modifier}}…\overset{G}{\sigma}]\#[_{\text{noun stem}}\sigma(\sigma)]$.

Nothing about our analysis captures the commonality of these three cases of "a low tone regressive to the antepenult."

7. Bora's tone system seems too complex. A reader commented, "You can't be right. It is too complicated. How would children learn it?"
   We agree that our description—and the analysis implicit in it—are too complicated. Of course, the complexity of the facts themselves cannot be reduced. (Indeed, further study will undoubtedly bring to light more complexities.) The challenge, therefore, is to find analyses that reduce the complexity.
8. Bora—it seems—has no stress system aside from the system of tone: there do not seem to be stressed versus unstressed syllables, only high tone versus low tone syllables. In basic design, the Bora tone system is not unlike the accentual system of Lithuanian described by Kenstowicz (1994:584ff.). We do not discount the possibility that Bora's tone system is a stress system implemented on tone. Kenstowicz (1994) says that Milner proposes such an analysis for Winnebago; Kenstowicz writes (p. 595) "The accent is interpreted as high tone" and (p. 596) "The accent in Winnebago is apparently realized tonally (Milner 1979)". (Consult Kenstowicz (1994) for references.)
9. Bora drum communication raises various intriguing questions: Given that there is relatively little lexical tone, why is it possible at all? What is the range of messages that can be communicated? To what extent does it depend on conventional frames?
10. Across Bora clans there are small dialect differences, most prominently, with regard to palatalization. There are differences in tone. This merits further study.

    A language spoken to the north in Colombia, Muinane, is closely related to Bora. According to Mike Maxwell (personal communication) it has a pitch-accent system: very roughly, words begin with some number of high tone syllables and are thereafter followed by low tone syllables. Perhaps this is the result of the collapse of a system like that of Bora.

    Tone has not been sufficiently studied in other members of the Witotoan family such as Witoto and Ocaina.

    Aschmann (1993) has done an admirable job of reconstructing the segmental phonology of Witotoan. However, reconstructing the system of tone is an outstanding challenge.

Chapter 4

Word Formation

A Bora word is composed of a root and zero or more affixes, either suffixes, prefixes, or both. (There are more suffixes than prefixes.) As affixes are (cyclically) added, they affect the root or stem to which they are attached, particularly its tones.

There are various classes of words; these are treated in three main groups. Those that are verbal are dealt with in section 5.6. Those belonging to various minor categories are dealt with in chapter 12. Those that are nominal are dealt with in chapters 7 (nouns) and 8 (pronouns).

Inflection is discussed in other sections of this grammar (for example, section 5.2 for verbs and 7.3 for nouns). The most common notions expressed by inflection in Bora are:

NUMBER: singular, dual, plural. For example, kpàtʃɛ́:-mɯ̀ɯ̀ 'women' from kpatʃɛ 'woman' and -mɯɯ 'plural'.
GENDER: masculine, feminine. For example, má˟tʃʰò-tʃɛ̀ 'She ate.' from ma˟tʃʰo 'eat' and -Ⓛtʃɛ ⟨SgF⟩.
ANIMACY: animate, inanimate. For example, mà˟tʃʰó-mɛ̀ 'They (AnPl) ate.'

Inflectional affixes may also indicate adverbial notions, as in 122:

(122) a. îk^{jh}ŏ:kʰá-rɛ̀ (ícyoocáre) 'right now'
now-only
b. tʰá-hɯ́ɾkʰò-:pɛ̀ (Tájúcoóbe.) 'He cries now.'
cry-now-⟨SgM⟩

This chapter deals with derivation. We discuss four types: derivation by tone modification (4.1), compounding (4.2), affixal derivation (4.3), and the incorporation of instruments into verbs (4.4).

4.1 Derivation with tone: nonfinite verbs

For every verb there is (at least potentially) a nonfinite form; this may refer to objects, actions, events or states. The nonfinite form of a verb is derived by placing a low tone on a particular syllable. To make this low tone more evident we will sometimes represent it with a N over the vowel (where N stands for 'nonfinite'). For example, compare the finite verb of 123a with the nonfinite form in 123b:

(123) a. ó i˟tsʰámèí-ʔì (Ó íjtsámeíhi.) 'I think.'   (finite)
      b. i˟tsʰá̃mɛ̂ì (íjtsaméi)   'thought, thinking' (nonfinite)

The rule for deriving nonfinite verbs imposes a low tone according to the following rule: If the verb is mono- or bisyllabic, the low tone is placed on the initial syllable; if the verb is any longer, the low tone is placed on the antepenult. In a nutshell, it is "a low tone regressive to the antepenult." This rule can be formalized as follows:[1]

$$[_{\text{finite verb}} \cdots \quad \sigma\,(\sigma\,(\sigma))\,]$$
$$\Updownarrow$$
$$[_{\text{nonfinite verb}} \cdots \quad \overset{L}{\sigma}\,(\sigma\,(\sigma))\,]$$

Figure 4.1 Nonfinite tone

Nonfinite forms behave like nouns: they may take nominal affixes; they may head noun phrases; they may possess or be possessed (in the genitive construction); and so forth. They are pluralized with -ʔáɲè 'various' rather than with one of the other nominal pluralizers. For example, the nonfinite form of ma˟tʃʰo 'to eat' may refer to food or to eating, as in mã˟tʃʰóʔáɲè 'various types of food'.[2]

Additional examples follow.

(124) a. ɯ́kpá:pò-:pɛ̀   (Úwááboóbe.) 'He teaches.'
         teach-⟨SgM⟩
      b. ɯ̀kpá:pò-:pɛ̀   (uwááboóbe) 'the teacher'
         teaching-⟨SgM⟩

---

[1] This is a *lexical* rule and the nonfinite tone is lexically marked. Tentatively, the V and N subscripted to the left braces represent [+verbal, +finite, −nominal] and [−verbal, −finite, +nominal], respectively.

[2] This is written majchóháñe but is arguably a genitive construction: mã˟tʃʰó Ⓖ ʔáɲè. Its head, ʔáɲè, 'various' refers to collections and thus "pluralizes."

4.1. DERIVATION WITH TONE: NONFINITE VERBS

(125) a. kʰɯ́kpà-ːpɛ̀ (Cúwaábe.) 'He is sleeping.' (finite)
b. kʰɯ̀kpá-ːpɛ̀ (cuwáábe) 'one belonging to a
    sleep-⟨SgM⟩   clan³ (nonfinite)'

(126) a. tʰáːpòːpɛ̀ (Táábóobe.) 'He is treating.'
b. tʰàːpóːpɛ̀ (taabóóbe) 'the doctor'
    cure-⟨SgM⟩

Compare 127a, in which kʰìmóːβɛ̀ (citation form) is a verb with 127b, where it is nonfinite:

(127) a. Mítyane áátye kímoovéhi.
b. Ijcyáné kimóóvé téhulle.
a. mítʲʰà-nɛ̀ áːtʲʰɛ̀ kʰímòːβɛ́-ʔì   'Those (people) became
   much-⟨ø⟩ those be.sad-sIn-⟨t⟩   very sad.'

b. ìˣkʲʰá-né Ⓐ kʰímóːβɛ́⁴ tʰɛ́-ʔɯ̀ʧɛ̀   'There is
   be-⟨ø⟩   sadness-sIn that-⟨yonder⟩ sadness there.'

The nonfinite low tone delinks any lexically marked tones with which it conflicts. Compare àkpákʰɯ̀mɯ̀ 'to yawn', the verbal form in 128, with ákpǎkʰɯ́mɯ̀ 'a yawn', the nonfinite form in 129. In particular, note that in 129 the nonfinite tone has delinked the verb's lexically marked low tones.

(128) Áánu awácunúhi.
     áːnɯ̀ àkpákʰɯ́mɯ́-ʔì   'This (one) is yawning.'
     this yawning-⟨t⟩

(129) Keeme íhya tsájucóó áwacúnuma.
     kʰɛ̀ːmɛ̀ íʔʲà   tsʰá-hɯ̀kʰóː-ʔì ákpǎkʰɯ́mɯ̀-mà
     old.man perhaps come-now-⟨t⟩ yawn-with
     'Perhaps the old man now comes only to yawn.' (lit. '…with yawns (in the circumstance of yawning).')

The tonal difference between a finite and nonfinite verb may not be apparent in mono- and bisyllabic words; e.g., màˣʧʰò is both 'eat' (finite) and 'eating, food' (nonfinite). The difference is usually apparent in trisyllabic words, e.g., ákʰɯ̀ːβɛ̀ 'to sit down' (finite) versus àkʰɯ́ːβɛ̀ 'seat' (nonfinite). (See also example 132 below.) However the difference is not apparent

---

³We do not know how one gets from 'sleeper' to 'one belonging to a clan' but presumably it is a consequence of clans occupying a single large house (*maloca*) in which all sleep.
⁴This is appositive to the -nè subject cliticized to the verb. The sentence's structure is: Verb-⟨subject⟩ Ⓐ Subject Locative.

in some trisyllabic verbs that bear lexically marked low tones. For example, ꟲi²hʲúɪβà is both 'to talk' (finite, with lexically marked low tone on the initial syllable) and 'speaking, speech' (nonfinite).

The verbs of subordinate clauses (complements, relative clauses and adverbial clauses) bear a high tone on the first syllable; see section 3.12.1. Examples 130 and 131 contrast two constructions, the first with a possessed nonfinite form (where the nonfinite low tone is represented with N), the second with a subordinate verb (where the subordinate high tone is represented with S):

(130) Eene muurá táímibájcho.

ɛ̀:-nɛ̀   mùɪːɾá   tʰá ⓖ   ímipá×tʃʰò
that-⟨ø⟩ confirm my   fixed.one
'That is the one I fixed.' (lit. 'That is my fixed one.')

(131) Eene muurá ó ímíbajchóne.

ɛ̀:-nɛ̀   mùɪːɾá   [ó ímípàˢ×tʃʰó]-nɛ̀
that-⟨ø⟩ confirm I fix   -⟨ø⟩
'That is the one that I fixed.'

Compare also the examples of 126 with those of 80, page 68.

Example 132 illustrates the contrast between a relative clause (132a), with a high tone on the verb's first syllable, and a nonfinite verb (132b), with the nonfinite low tone on the stem's antepenult, represented by N. (See also examples 944, page 358, and 1000, page 382.)

(132) a. Túrúúvehe ííteébe.
      b. Turúúvehe ííteébe.

a. [tʰɯ̋ɾɯ́ː-ˢβɛ̀]-ʔɛ̀ ⎱ íːtʰɛ̀-ːpɛ̀
b. [tʰɯ̏ɾɯ́ː-ᴺβɛ̀]-ʔɛ̀ ⎰ look-⟨SgM⟩
   fall-sIn   -⟨tree⟩

a. 'He looks at the tree that is falling.'
b. 'He looks at the fallen tree.'

The verbs of relative clauses and nonfinite verbs also differ in the person-marking classifiers that follow, as can be seen by comparing 133a and 133b:

(133) a. ò   kpȁhʲɯ̋ˢɯ̀-mɛ̀-ˣ   (o wájyumej) 'the ones I love'
         I   love-⟨AnPl⟩-voc   (relative clause)

      b. tʰá kpȁhʲɯ́ᴳɯ̋-ˣtʰɛ̀-ˣ   (táwajyújtej) 'my loved ones'
         my beloved-⟨AnPl⟩-voc   (nonfinite)

4.2 Compounding

4.2.1 Compound nouns

Compound nouns may be headed by a classifier (4.2.1.1) or by a noun (4.2.1.2). A nonfinite verb with an incorporated object may also form a compound noun (4.2.1.3).

4.2.1.1 Headed by classifiers

The concrete noun in 134c is derived by compounding the nonfinite verb in 134a with the classifier in 134b:[5]

(134) a. kpà:hakʰɯ (waajácu) 'knowledge, know'
     b. -ʔa:mɨ (-háámɨ) '⟨leaf⟩ (paper, book,...)'
     c. kpà:hákʰɯ̀ʔá:mɨ (waajácuháámɨ) 'book'

In example 135 the second (and final) classifier is—arguably—compounded with the preceding noun phrase.

(135) tʰá ⓖ ʔoˣtsʰɨ-kpá-mɨ:ʔò[6] (táhójtsɨwámɨ́ɨho) 'my fingernail'
     my hand-⟨slab⟩-⟨sheath⟩

Regarding 135 as a compound noun is consistent with the position that classifiers are a type of bound noun.

4.2.1.2 Headed by nouns

The noun mɯ́mààa 'people, fellow countryman',[7] may be compounded with a nonfinite verb, as illustrated in 136 with kpákʰimʲɛ̀ì 'work, labor':

(136) kpákʰimʲɛ̀ì mɯ́náá-ˣpʰì (wákimyéi-múnáajpi) 'worker'
     working human-⟨SgM⟩

---

[5]In head-final (OV) languages, the second of composed elements normally heads the resulting word or phrase so its features prevail in the composition. In 134c that element is the classifier -ʔa:mɨ. Because it refers to concrete objects (as suggested by the gloss) it bears the feature [−abstract]. This feature percolates to the composed word kpà:hákʰɯ̀ʔá:mɨ (134c) so refers to something concrete and, due to 'knowledge', is understood as a book. See section 6.3.4 for further discussion.

[6]The Ⓛ of -Ⓛmɨ:ʔo is blocked by the Ⓛ of -Ⓛkpa.

[7](Thiesen & Thiesen 1998:191) gives mɯ́màà as a concrete noun occurring either without a classifier or as one of the following: mɯ́máá-ˣpʰì (masculine singular), mɯ́máá-tʃɛ̀ (feminine singular), mɯ́máá-ˣtʰɛ́tsʰì (masculine dual), mɯ́máàˣtʰɛ́pʰì (feminine dual).

The tone derivation of 136 is as follows:

```
wakimyei     work         munaa        human
: L    ::    nonfinite    : :|
: :    ::                 : :L_jpi      <SgM>
: :    ::                 : ::    :
: :    :L    FDLT         : ::    L     FDLT
: :    :     DHT          : ::    :     DHT
 H :   H:                  H H:   :
: :    ::                 : ::    :
wákimyéi                  múnáa-jpi    'worker <SgM>'
```

Figure 4.2 TD: wákimyéi múnáajpi

In 137 'judge' is the phrase ímít^{jh}úɨné^ʔhɨ ímípá^xtʃʰò-múɯná:^xpʰí, literally 'bad fixer person':

(137) Ávyéjuube cáyobáávatétsó íwákimyéi-múnáake diityéké ímítyúnéhjɨ ímíbájcho múnáájpí úmɨwávú tsane idíllóneri.

Áβʲéhùɨ-ːpè kʰájòpá-ːβà-tʰɛ́-tsʰó-ʔì
reign-⟨SgM⟩ anger-become-go.do-caus-⟨t⟩

[í   ⓖ [kpákʰɨmʲɛ̀ì múmáà]]-kʰɛ̀   tìː-tʲʰɛ́-kʰɛ́
 self   worker   human   -objAn that-⟨AnPl⟩-objAn

[[[ímí-tʲʰúɨ-né-ʔhɨ́   ímìpá^xtʃʰò] múɯná:-^xpʰí]
    good-neg-⟨ø⟩-pl   fix   human-⟨SgM⟩

úɯmɨ-kpá] -βúɨ tsʰà-nè ì tít͡ʃó-nè-rì
face-⟨slab⟩ -goal one-⟨ø⟩ self ask-⟨ø⟩-oblIn

'The chief angered his workers by asking them about something in the presence of the judge.'

(Thiesen & Thiesen 1998) gives a few dozen cases of compounds headed by múɯnàà, joining it and the preceding nonfinite verb with a hyphen.[8]

Two issues deserve further investigation. First, these compounds with múɯnàà are written with a hyphen based on the preferences of Bora literates. This may reflect an intuition that múɯnàà is neither an independent noun nor a classifier (that it has moved toward becoming a classifier but not yet arrived, so to speak). This may be because, although múɯnàà is

---

[8]See acúúve-múnaa 'person responsible for a festival', ahdó-múnáajpi 'buyer' ahdótso-múnáajpi 'money collector' aahɨve-múnaa 'visitors' állíu-múnaa 'liar', añú múnaa or añú(-)múnaa 'hunter, foreigner (lit. person who shoots)', bañú-múnáajpi 'person in whom one should not have confidence', bohdó-múnáajpi 'person who paddles', cahcújtso-múnáajpi 'believer', cóójɨ́éwa-múnaa 'column of people who sing by day in a festival', chemé-múnaa 'sick person', and so forth.

4.2. COMPOUNDING

behaving much like a classifier, there is not consistent evidence for the classifier low tone (ⓒ).

Second, it may be that múmàà is the only noun that heads this sort of compound.

4.2.1.3 Object incorporation

In 138 and 139, the first of each pair is a sentence with a finite verb, while the second is a nonfinite verb with an incorporated object.[9]

(138) a. Ɨ̀cu túkévéjtsoóbe.
  ɨ̀ːkʰɯ̀ɾ tʰɯ́ɾkʰɛ́βɛ́ˣtsʰò-ːpɛ̀ 'He directs the game.'
  game direct-⟨SgM⟩

 b. ɨ̀ɨcú-túkevéjtsoóbe
  ɨ̀ːkʰɯ́ɾ tʰɯ́ɾkʰ$\overset{N}{\epsilon}$βɛ́ˣtsʰò-ːpɛ̀ 'referee'
  game directing-⟨SgM⟩

(139) a. Obééjámuke téhmeébe.
  $\overset{L}{o}$pɛ́ːhá-mɯ̀-kʰɛ̀ tʰɛ́ʔmɛ̀-ːpɛ̀ 'He cares for the sheep.'
  sheep-plAn-objAn care-⟨SgM⟩

 b. obééjámú-tehméébe
  $\overset{L}{o}$pɛ́ːhá-mɯ́ɾ tʰ$\overset{N}{\epsilon}$ʔmɛ́-ːpɛ̀ 'shepherd'
  sheep-plAn care-⟨SgM⟩

Examples 140 and 141 are like 138b and 139b.

(140) pihcyáávé-túkevéjtsoóbe
  pʰɨ́ʔkʲʰá-ːβɛ́ tʰɯ́ɾkʰɛ̀βɛ́ˣtsʰò-ːpɛ̀ 'leader of the meeting'
  meet-sIn direct-⟨SgM⟩

(141) mɨ́ɨ́né-túkevéjtsoóbe
  mɨ́ːnɛ́ tʰɯ́ɾkʰɛ̀βɛ́ˣtsʰò-ːpɛ̀ 'pilot (of a boat)'
  boat direct-⟨SgM⟩

An alternative to 139b is 142 (which is formed as outlined in section 4.2.1.2). It would be said of someone who is professionally dedicated to caring for sheep, whereas 139b would be said about someone who is temporarily caring for sheep.

---

[9]By virtue of being incorporated, the object no longer undergoes FDLT; it could not bear two low tones without violating the *LLX constraint.

Because 'direct' in example 138b has an initial high tone, it could also be analyzed as a relative clause: [ø$_i$ ɨ̀ːkʰɯ́ɾ tʰɯ́$\overset{S}{ɯ}$kʰɛβɛ́ˣtsʰò]-ːpɛ̀$_i$. However, such an analysis is not possible for 139b because 'care' has a low tone on its initial syllable.

(142) obééjámú tehmé múnáajpi
  òpɛ́:há-mɨ́ɨ tʰɛ̰́ʔmɛ́ mɨ́ɨnáà-ˣpʰḭ̀   'shepherd'
  sheep-plAn care human-⟨SgM⟩

Example 143 is similar to 142:

(143) tsɨɨmé tehmé múnáajpi
  tsʰɨ̀ɨmɛ́ tʰɛ̰́ʔmɛ́ mɨ́ɨnáà-ˣpʰḭ̀
  children care human-⟨SgM⟩
  'one who takes care of children'

4.2.2 Compound verbs

Compound verbs are made up of two or more verbs. The first must be an active (not stative) verb. Except for any lexically marked low tones it might have, it will bear high tones.[10]

The second of compounded verbs may be either a free verb or an affix. The free verbs occur as independent verbs as well as in compounds; they are discussed in this section. The affixal verbs occur only in compounds; they are discussed in section 4.3.6.

The second of compounded verbs may be one of the following "free" verbs, which also occur as verbs outside of compounds:[11]

(-)tʰɨ̀ˣkʰénɨ̀ 'begin'. For example, tʰɨ̀ˣkʰénɨ̀ 'begin' is the second of two compounded verbs in 144, while it is an independent verb in 145:

(144) Áánéllii ihjyúvátujkénuúbe.
  á:-nɛ́-tʃì: ḭ̀ʔhʲɨ́ɨβá-tʰɨ̀ˣkʰénɨ̀-:pɛ̀
  that-⟨ø⟩-motive speak-begin-⟨SgM⟩
  'For that reason, he began to speak.'

(145) Áánéllii tujkénuube iíhjyuváne.
  á:-nɛ́-tʃì: tʰɨ̀ˣkʰénɨ̀-:pɛ̀ [ḭ̀   ḭ̀ʔhʲɨ̀βá]-nɛ̀
  that-⟨event⟩-motive begin-⟨SgM⟩   self speak   -⟨event⟩
  'For that reason, he began to speak.'

---

[10]This is simply by default: (1) none of the conditions for phrase final lowering could possibly apply, and (2) the second of compounded verbs does not impose any tones on the first.

[11]These end with what appears to have been—or might be—a suffix, either the verbalizer -nɯ 'cause to have, cause to be', that is tʰɨ̀ˣkʰɛ́-nɯ̀ (straight-do), or the verbalizer -βɛ 'become', that is, ì:hʲɛ́-βɛ̀ (bothersome-become), pʰɛ̀ˣkʰó-βɛ̀ (night-become) ⁽ˣ⁾kʰò:hí-βɛ̀ (day-become).

pʰìβʲɛ̀ 'desire' might be cognate with pʰì:βʲɛ̀ 'grow', and ultimately with the suffix -Ⓛ◯pʰi 'excessive' discussed in section 4.3.6.1.

4.2. COMPOUNDING

(-)ì:hʲéβè 'be bothersome (by doing)'

(146) Meke tááííjyévelle.
 mè-kʰè   tʰá:-í:hʲéβè-ʧè   'She bothers us (by) crying.'
 SAP-objAn cry-bother-⟨SgF⟩

(-)pʰìβʲè ~ (-)pʰìβʲénùɨ (pivye ~ pivyénu) 'desire':

(147) Ó ádópivyéhi.
 ó átó-pʰìβʲé-ʔì   'I am thirsty.'
 I drink-desire-⟨t⟩

(148) Muha mémájchópívyenúhi.
 mùɨʔà mɛ́ máˣʧʰó-pʰíβʲè-nɨ́ɨ-ʔì   'We became hungry.'
 we SAP eat-desire-do-⟨t⟩

(-)pʰèˣkʰóβè 'be tardy (by night), spend the night'

(149) Muha méihjyúvápéjcovéhi.
 mùɨʔà mɛ́ ì²hʲɨ́ɨβá-pʰéˣkʰò-βɛ́-ʔì   'We talked all night.'
 we SAP talk-night-sIn-⟨t⟩

(-)⁽ˣ⁾kʰò:híβè 'be tardy (by day), spend the day'

(150) a. Keeme cúwájcóójɨvéhi.
 b. Cóójí hajchótá keeme cuwáhi.
 a. kʰè:mè kʰɨɨkpá-ˣkʰó:hɨ̀-βɛ́-ʔì
     old.one sleep-day-sIn-⟨t⟩
 b. kʰó:hí ʔàˣʧʰó-tʰá   kʰè:mè kʰɨɨkpá-ʔì
     day duration-⟨part⟩ old.one sleep-⟨t⟩
 a. 'The old (man) sleeps all day.'
 b. 'The old (man) sleeps the length of a day.'

Although not common, three elements may be compounded:

(151) Oke tááííjyévépéjcóveébe.
 ò-kʰè   tʰá:-í:hʲé-βɛ́-pʰéˣkʰó-βɛ̀-:pè
 I-objAn cry-bother-sIn-night-sIn-⟨SgM⟩
 'He bothers me crying all night long.'

In addition to the free verbs just listed, iˣkʲʰa 'be' may follow another verb to indicate 'habitual'. We regard this as a compound tense in which the preceding verb is marked with ʔ as though it were a predicate complement. See section 5.10.

---
[11] In example 148 -nɨɨ, which is glossed as 'do', is understood as 'inchoative'.

4.3 Affixal derivation

Derivational affixes may change the category of the root (or word) to which they are attached. Examples, in which the derivational affix is underlined, are given in 152–155:[12]

(152) kʰárákʰá-mɯ̀-β̱à (cáracámuva) 'have chickens'
chicken-plAn-have

(153) mɨ́ámɯ́mààː-βɛ̀[13] (mɨamúnaááve) 'become people'
people-sIn

(154) tʰàːpá-nɯ̀[14] (taabánu) 'give a woman in marriage'
wife-do

(155) tsɨˣkʰò-hà[15] (dsɨ́jcoja) 'sewn clothing'
sew-⟨shelter⟩

4.3.1 Verbs derived from verbs

Many verb roots are followed by a "singular versus multiple action" suffix. For each verb there are potentially six forms, corresponding to the parameters transitive/intransitive/stative and singular/multiple.[16] The meaning of the singular versus multiple distinction depends on the particular verb: sometimes it is individual versus collective action, sometimes it is a single

---

[12]Note that in example 152 the derivational suffix -βa is farther removed from the root than the inflectional suffix -mɯ.

[13]The tones in isolation are: mɨ́ámɯ́màà 'people'.

[14]The tones in isolation are: /tʰàːpà/ 'wife'.

[15]The tones in isolation are tsɨˣkʰò 'sew' We will suggest below that cases like 155 can be analyzed as relative clauses modifying a classifier head.

[16]That is, each verb could have up to 6 derived forms corresponding to the cells of the following table. Rather than verbs, this table gives the abbreviations used to gloss the suffixes that indicate these contrasts:

	SINGULAR	MULTIPLE
transitive	sTr	mTr
intransitive	sIn	mIn
stative	sSt	mSt

4.3. AFFIXAL DERIVATION

action versus iteration, and so forth.[17] This is discussed in section 5.7.2.

The suffix -tʰɯ(ɯ) 'negative' may occur between the root and the singular versus multiple suffix, as in 156:

(156) kʰɛ́ʔʲɛ́-tʰɯ̀ɾɯ́-ːβɛ̀   (kéhyétuúúve) 'become listless'
      have.strength-neg-sIn

   ɯ́βá²-tʰɯ̀ɾɯ́-ːβɛ̀ (úváhtuúúve) 'be dumbfounded'
   alert(?)-neg-sIn

In this position, -tʰɯ(ɯ) 'negative' is frequently preceded by -ɾa 'frustrative, contraexpectation', as in 157, but -ɾa does not occur in this position without -tʰɯ(ɯ).

(157) tʃépò-ɾá-tʰɯ̀ɾɯ́-ːβɛ̀ (lléborátuúúve) 'become deaf'
      hear-frs-neg-sIn

   kpáhákʰɯ́-ɾá-tʰɯ̀ɾɯ́-ːβɛ̀ (wájácúrátuúúve) 'bewildered, stunned'
   know-frs-neg-sIn

4.3.2 Verbs derived from nouns

Verbs are derived from nouns by one of the following suffixes:[18] -tʃɛ 'treat like, regard as', -ⒷⓄnɯ 'do', -ːβɛ 'become', -tʰɛ 'become', -βa 'have' or -ˣkʰimɛi 'behave like'. These will be discussed in turn.

4.3.2.1   -lle 'treat like, regard as'

The suffix -ⒷⓄtʃɛ (-lle) 'treat like, regard as' and -ⒷⓄnɯ (-nu) 'cause to have, do' derive transitive verbs. With -tʃɛ (-lle) 'regard as', the referent of the direct object is compared to the referent of the host (i.e., the noun to which -tʃɛ is suffixed). For example, in 158 *he* (subject) regards *me* (object) as a *child* (host):

(158) Oke tsɨɨménélleébe.
      ò-kʰɛ̀   tsʰɨːméné-tʃɛ̀-ːpè   'He considers me to be
      I-objAn child-regard-⟨SgM⟩   like a child.'

---

[17] For this reason the Bora dictionary (Thiesen & Thiesen 1998) lists both singular and multiple forms for verbs.

[18] These might be considered noun-incorporating verbs.

4.3.2.2 -nu 'do'

The suffix -ⓁOnɯ ~ -ɲɯ (-nu) derives a verb that means 'to cause to have Φ' (where Φ is the host's referent), as illustrated in 159 with tsɨ̀:tsɨ̀ 'money':

(159) Oke dsɨɨdsɨ́nuúbe.
    ò-kʰɛ̀   tsɨ̀:tsɨ́-<u>nɯ̀</u>-:pɛ̀   'He caused me to have money.'
    I-objAn money-do-⟨SgM⟩

A verb so derived can also mean 'do something related to Φ', as illustrated with kʰɯ̀:mɯ̀ 'drum' in 160:

(160) kʰɯ̀:mɯ́-<u>nɯ̀</u>-:pɛ̀ (Cuumúnuúbe.) 'He played the drums.'
    drum-do-⟨SgM⟩

(161) àˣpʰà   (ajpa)   'a type of edible grub'
    àˣpʰá-ɲɯ̀ (ajpáñu)[19] 'make holes in palm trees for grubs'

(162) àhɨ̀   (ajɨ)   'a type of small palm'
    àhɨ́-nɯ̀ (ajɨ́nu) 'gather the leaves of this type of palm'

The verbalizer -ⓁOnɯ may be added after either a singular or a plural noun. For example, pʰákʲʰɛ́ɛ́ 'trap' is a collective noun referring to fishtraps, not to a single one. When -ⓁOnɯ follows a plural or collective noun, the resulting verb is a multiple action verb (as discussed in section 5.7.2). Thus, pʰàkʲʰɛ́:-nɯ̀ 'set traps' is a multiple action verb.

To refer to a single trap, the classifier -hɯ̀ 'long and hollow' must be added: pʰákʲʰɛ̀:-hɯ̀ 'a single trap'. The result is a single action verb: pʰákʲʰɛ̀-hɯ́ɯ:-nɯ̀ 'set a single trap'.

Although -ⓁOnɯ generally derives transitive verbs, in a few cases they are intransitive, as in 163:

(163) à:ʔɨ́-nɯ̀ (home-do aahɨ́-nu) 'to stay at home (intransitive)'
    à:ʔɨ́-βɛ̀ (home-sIn aahɨ́ve) 'to go home (intransitive)'

The suffix -ⓁOnɯ may be added to an adjective, in which case it means 'cause to be' rather than 'cause to have':

(164) tʃʰòʔhʲɯ́-nɯ̀   (chohjyúnu) 'to make smaller'
    small-do
    àjá-nɯ̀   (ayánu)   'to make smaller or fewer'
    small/few-do

---

[19] Presumably the /a/ that precedes /ɲ/ in àˣpʰá-ɲɯ̀ is a reflex of */ai/ since it palatalizes the nasal that follows; see Aschmann (1993).

4.3.2.3 -ːve 'sIn' and -te 'become'

The suffixes -ːβɛ (-ːve) 'sIn' and -tʰɛ (-te) derive verbs that mean 'to become like Φ' (where Φ is the host's referent). This is illustrated with tsʰɨ́ːmɛ̀nɛ̀ 'child' in 165 and áβʲɛhɨ̀ɨ 'reign' in 166:

(165) ó tsʰɨ́mɛ́nɛ̀-ːβɛ́ (Ó tsímɛ́neevé.) 'I became like a child.'
    I child-sIn

(166) Áátyáába ávyéjuuté ávyéjúúbé úníuri iwákímyeíñeri.[20]

á: ⓖ tʲʰáːpà áβʲɛhɨ̀ɨː-tʰɛ́-ɾì   [[áβʲɛhɨ́ɨ-ːpɛ́ ⓖ ɨ̋níɨ̀ɨ]-ɾì
my   wife   reign-become-⟨t⟩   reign-⟨SgM⟩   beside -oblIn

ì   kpȧ̊kʰímʲèí]-ɲɛ̀-ɾì
self work   -⟨ø⟩-oblIn

'My wife became important working alongside of the chief.'

The suffix -ːβɛ 'sIn' may follow the combination of the bound root pʰa- 'all' and a classifier to derive a verb that indicates becoming a complete object of the type indicated by the classifier. For example in 167 it derives a verb meaning 'to become a complete vehicle (canoe, car, airplane,…)':

(167) Tsúúca temɨ pámɨɨ́véhi.
    tsʰɨ́ɨːkʰà tʰɛ̀-mɨ̀   pʰá-mɨ̀-ːβɛ́-ʔì
    already that-⟨canoe⟩ all-⟨canoe⟩-sIn-⟨t⟩
    'That has already become a complete canoe (car, airplane, …).'

Other examples follow:

(168) Tsúúca táwajyámú pájaavéhi.
    tsʰɨ́ɨːkʰà tʰá kpaʰʲámɨ̋ɨ pʰá-hà-ːβɛ́-ʔì
    already my dress   all-⟨shelter⟩-sIn-⟨t⟩
    'My dress has already been completed.'

(169) Páábééveébe.
    pʰá-ːpɛ́-ːβɛ̀-ːpɛ̀   'He has become a mature male.'
    all-⟨SgM⟩-sIn-⟨SgM⟩

4.3.2.4 -va 'have'

The suffix -Ⓛ◯βa (-va) 'have' derives a stative verb that means 'to have Φ', where Φ is the referent of the host. This is illustrated in 170, in which

---

[20] The root aβʲɛhɨɨ refers to esteem, honor, glory, or to (the noun) reign; see (Thiesen & Thiesen 1998:45f.).

mɛ́ːnɨ̀mɨ̀ː (méénimu) 'pigs' is the host:[21]

(170) ó mɛ̀ːnímɨ̀ː-βá-ʔì (Ó meenímuvá.) 'I have pigs.'
  I pig-have-⟨t⟩

The suffix -ⓁOβa 'have' behaves like -ⓁOnɯ. For example, with pʰàːʧá 'manioc', the result, pʰàːʧá-βà 'having manioc' is a multiple action verb. However, when the noun is first made singular by the addition of -ʔò ⟨sphere⟩, the result, pʰáʧà-ʔóː-βà 'to have a single ball of grated manioc', is a single action verb.

Examples 171 and 172 show the contrast between -ⓁOβa 'have' and -ⓁOnɯ 'do':

(171) mɛ̀mɛ́-βà   (memé-va) 'to be named'
   name-have
   mɛ̀mɛ́-nɨ̀ː   (memé-nu) 'to name'
   name-do

(172) ɛ̀ʔ-nɛ́-βà   (ehnéva) 'to have things (intransitive)'
   that-⟨ø⟩-have
   ɛ̀ʔ-nɛ́-nɨ̀ː   (ehnénu) 'to cause to have things (transitive)'
   that-⟨ø⟩-do

The verbal stems derived by -ⓁOβa 'have' may be negated, as in 173:

(173) íʔhʲɨ́ɨ-βá-tʰɨ̀rɨ́ɨ-ːβɛ̀   (íhjyúvátuúúve) 'become speechless'
   mouth-have-neg-sIn

   páˣkʰɨ́ɨ-βá-tʰɨ̀rɨ́ɨ-ːβɛ̀ (bájcúvátuúúve) 'become spineless (weak)'
   bone-have-neg-sIn

   ʔáʧɨ́ɨ-βá-rá-tʰɨ̀rɨ́ɨ-ːβɛ̀ (hállúvárátuúúve) 'become blind'
   eye-have-frs-neg-sIn

4.3.2.5 -jkimei **'behave like'**

The suffix -ˣkʰimɛi (-jkimei) 'behave like' derives a verb that means 'to behave like Φ', where Φ is the host's referent. This is illustrated in 174 with tsʰɨ́ːmɛ̀nɛ̀ 'child':

(174) Ó tsɨ́ménéjkímeí.
   ó tsʰɨ́mɛ́nɛ́-ˣkʰímɛ̀í-ʔ   'I behave like a child.'
   I child-behave.like-⟨t⟩

---

[21]The tone of 170 seems inconsistent with the claim that -ⓁOβa 'have' imposes a low tone on the host's penultimate syllable.

4.3.3 Nouns derived from verbs with -tɑ 'corresponding to'

-tʰa (-tɑ) 'corresponding to (corr)' derives nouns from verbs, as in the following:

(175) níjcyotáábe
    níˣkʲʰò-tʰá-ːpɛ̀   'statue (lit. the one who is moulded)'
    mould-corr-⟨SgM⟩

(176) díájcuta
    tí   Ⓖ   áˣkʰɯ̀-tʰà   'the part given to you'
    your   give-corr

(177) díwáábyuta[22]
    tí   Ⓖ   kpáːpʲɯ̀-tʰà
    your   blame-corr
    'your share (lit. corresponding to your responsibility/fault)'

4.3.4 Participles

Participles are derived from verbs by the addition of one of the following affixes: -ʔnɛkʰɯ 'result', -ɾiβakʰo 'resulting position', -ɾatʰɯ 'not doing', or the prefix tʰɛ- 'that'. Participles indicate the state of an object resulting from a prior event, namely the event indicated by the verb from which the participle is derived. Participles are most frequently used in apposition to a noun phrase but may also be used adverbially; see example 182.

The suffix -ʔnɛkʰɯ 'result', added to an active verb, derives the adjective referring to the result of the action of that verb. For example, in 178 it is added to the verb kʰàtʃáhà- 'sprawl out':

(178) Ó áákityé callájahnécu.
    ó áːkʰìtʲʰɛ́-ʔ kʰàtʃáhà-ʔnɛ́kʰɯ̀   'I fell, landing sprawled out.'
    I fall-⟨t⟩   sprawl.out-result

The participle in 179 is derived from the verb pʰɨɾɯ- 'exhaust (some quantity)':

(179) Ó majchó pɨruhnécu.
    ó màˣtʃʰó-ʔ pʰɨ́ɾɯ̀-ʔnɛ́kʰɯ̀   'I ate everything, without
    I eat-⟨t⟩   exhaust-result   anything left over.'

---

[22] (Thiesen & Thiesen 1998:310) gives the meaning of wɑabyu (transitive verb) as 'suspect, blame, cast the blame on.'

The suffix -ɾìβakʰo 'resulting position', added to an active verb, derives the adjective referring to the position resulting from the action indicated by that verb. When -ɾìβakʰo 'resulting position' is suffixed to a verb, the verb's initial vowel is lengthened and bears low tone. For example, in 180 and 181 it is added to the verb ɨ̀βóʔò- 'to lie face down':

(180) Éhtsi tsɨɨme ɨ̈vóhóɾɨ́vaco.
 ɛ́ʔ-tsʰɨ̀   tsʰɨ́ːmɛ̀   ɨ̀ːβóʔó-ɾɨ́βàkʰò
 that-⟨place⟩ children lie.face.down-res.pos
 'There are children lying face down over there.'

(181) Ó ájtyumɨ́ tsɨ́ɨ́meke éhtsi ɨ̈vóhóɾɨ́vaco.
 ó áˣtʲʰùmɨ́-ʔì tsʰɨ́ːmɛ̀-kʰɛ̀   ɛ́ʔ-tsʰɨ̀
 I see-⟨t⟩   children-objAn that-⟨place⟩

 ɨ̀ːβóʔó-ɾɨ́βàkʰò
 lie.face.down-res.pos
 'I have seen children in that place lying face down.'

A participle derived by -ɾɨ́βàkʰò (-ɾɨ́vaco) 'resulting position' may modify the verb it follows. This reflects the fact that adjectives can be used adverbially, since participles are a type of stative deverbal adjective. For example, in 182 ɨ̀ːβóʔó-ɾɨ́βàkʰò 'lying face down' modifies kʰùɨkpà 'sleep':

(182) Tsɨɨme éhtsíi cuwá ɨ̈vóhóɾɨ́vaco.
 tsʰɨ́ːmɛ̀ ɛ́ʔ-tsʰɨ̀ɨ̀ kʰùɨkpá-ʔì ɨ̀ːβóʔó-ɾɨ́βàkʰò
 children that-⟨place⟩ sleep-⟨t⟩ lie-face.down-res.pos
 'The children over there are sleeping, lying face down.'

Another kind of participle is formed by making a stative verb nonfinite (via tone) and concatenating this with tʰɛ- 'that (aforementioned)', which provides the referential link to the noun the participle modifies. The participle must agree in number with the noun it modifies: if the noun is singular or dual, then the stative verb bears the single action suffix -ùɨkʰùmɯ 'sSt'; if the noun is plural, the stative verb must bear the multiple action suffix -ˣkʰàtʲʰɛ 'mSt'. For example, in 183 the modified noun is dual, so the participle is single action. By contrast, in 184 the modified noun is plural, so the participle is multiple action.[23] (Another example is 247, page 137.)

---

[23] Remarkably, the meaning of ɨβóʔɨˣkʰátʲʰɛ̀ (ɨ́vóhijcátye) in 184 seems to be the same as that of ɨ̀ːβóʔóɾɨ́βàkʰò (ɨ̈vóhóɾɨ́vaco) in 180 and 181.

4.3. AFFIXAL DERIVATION

(183) a. Éje, áátyétsi téɨvóhoúcunu.

b. Éje, áátyétsi cuwá téɨvóhoúcunu.

  a. ɛ́hɛ̀ , á:-tʲʰɛ́tsʰɨ̀   tʰɛ́-ɨβóʔò-úɨkʰùɨnùɨ
  b. ɛ́hɛ̀ , á:-tʲʰɛ́tsʰɨ̀ kʰùɨkpá-ʔɨ̀ tʰɛ́-ɨβóʔò-úɨkʰùɨnùɨ
    look that-⟨DuM⟩ sleep-⟨t⟩ that-lie.face.down-sSt

'Look, those (dual masculine) sleep lying face down!'

(184) Éje áátye cuwá téɨvóhojcátye.

  ɛ́hɛ̀ á:-tʲʰɛ̀ kʰùɨkpá-ʔɨ̀ tʰɛ́-ɨβóʔò-ˣkʰátʲʰɛ̀
  look that-⟨AnPl⟩ sleep-⟨t⟩ that-lie.face.down-mSt

'Look! Those sleep face down.'

Some classifiers have meanings similar to participles, i.e., indicating states that result from prior events or actions. (Many of these are derived from verbs by the suffix -ɯ.) Combinations of these classifiers with pʰa- 'all' are used as modifiers. They may be further followed by -:kʰɯ 'duIn' or -hɨ 'inanimate plural'. Examples follow.

(185) a. Ó ájtyumɨ́ tsáápikye juuváj pɨɨne páɨvóhoou íjyácunúúbeke.

b. Ó ájtyumɨ́ tsáápikye juuváyí páɨvóhoóu.

ó áˣtʲʰùɨmɨ́-ʔɨ̀ tsʰá-:pʰɨ̀-kʲʰɛ̀
I see-⟨t⟩   one-⟨SgM⟩-objAn

⎧ a. hùɨ:βáˣ pʰɨ̀:nɛ̀   pʰá-ɨβóʔò-:ɯ̀
⎪   road   middle all-lie.face.down-⟨cls⟩
⎨   íhʲá-kʰùɨnúɨ-:pɛ̀-kʰɛ̀
⎪   be-sSt-⟨SgM⟩-objAn
⎪ b. hùɨ:βá-jí   pʰá-ɨβóʔò-:ɯ̀
⎩   road-oblIn all-lie.face.down-⟨cls⟩

a. 'I saw a person (SgM) who was lying face down in the middle of the road .'

b. 'I saw a person (SgM) lying face down in the road .'

(186) Muhtsi mécuwá páɨvóhooúcu.

  mùɨʔtsʰɨ̀ mɛ́ kʰùɨkpá-ʔɨ̀ pʰá-ɨβóʔò:-úɨ-kʰùɨ
  we(DuEx) SAP sleep-⟨t⟩ all-lie.face.down-⟨cls⟩-du

'The two of us (ex.) slept face down.'

(187) Tsɨɨme cuwá páɨvóhooúji.
 tsʰɨ̀:mɛ̀ kʰɯ̀ɨkpá-ʔì pʰá-ɨβóʔò:-ɯ́ɨ-hɨ̀
 children sleep-⟨t⟩ all-lie.face.down-⟨cls⟩-InPl
 'The children sleep face down.'

Another type of deverbal adjective is described in section 4.3.6.1.

4.3.5 Negative deverbal adjectives

The suffix -tʰɯ̀ (-tu) 'negative, without doing', added to an active verb, derives the adjective referring to the state of not having done or undergone the action of that verb. It is often in apposition to another noun or pronoun, as in 188 and 189:

(188) O péé teene ímíbájchótuubére.
 ò pʰɛ́:-ʔì tʰɛ̀:-nɛ̀ ímípáˣʧʰó-tʰɯ̀-:pɛ́-rɛ̀ 'I am going without
 I go-⟨t⟩ that-⟨ø⟩ fix-neg-⟨SgM⟩-only fixing it.'

-rà 'frustrative, contraexpectation' often accompanies -tʰɯ̀ 'negative', as in the following examples. Note that in 189 the participle refers to the subject of maˣʧʰo 'eat':

(189) Májchóratú ú oomíhi.
 máˣʧʰó-rà-tʰɯ́ɨ ɯ́ɨ ò:mí-ʔì 'You are returning without
 eat-frs-neg you return-⟨t⟩ eating.'

In 190 màˣʧʰó-rà-tʰɯ̀ is used as a predicate complement:

(190) a. màˣʧʰó-rà-tʰɯ̀ tʰɛ̀:-nɛ̀   (Majchóratu teéne.)
  eat-frs-neg that-⟨ø⟩
 b. tʰɛ̀:-nɛ̀ màˣʧʰó-rà-tʰɯ̀ (Teene majchóratu.)
  that-⟨ø⟩ eat-frs-neg
 a,b. 'That has not been eaten.'

4.3.6 Affixal "verbs"

Some suffixes are like bound, complement-taking verbs. They follow a verb root or stem, heading the verb + suffix combination. These suffixes are: -tsʰo 'causative' (see section 5.8.1, page 144), -ⓁOpʰi 'do to excess, excessive' (see 4.3.6.1 below), -ʧɛ 'try to do' (4.3.6.2), -pʰɛˣtsʰo 'do upon encountering' (4.3.6.3), as well as the "relocation" suffixes discussed in section 4.3.6.4.

4.3.6.1 -pi 'excessive'

The suffix -ⓁОpʰi[24] (-pi) 'excessive' indicates that the action referred to by the host verb is or was done to excess and makes the verb stative. Forms bearing -ⓁОpʰi can be used as a verb, as in 191 and 192:

(191) Táácááni cuwápíhi.

    tʰá: Ⓖ kʰá:nì kʰɯ̀ɯ̀kpá-pʰí-ʔì   'My father sleeps excessively.'
    my   father sleep-excess-⟨t⟩

(192) Táátsɨ́ɨ́ju ihjyúvapíhi.

    tʰá: Ⓖ tsʰɨ́:hɯ̀ ìʔhʲɯ́ɯ́βà-pʰí-ʔì   'My mother talks excessively.'
    my   mother talk-excess-⟨t⟩

Forms bearing -ⓁОpʰi can also be used as predicate adjectives, as in 193 and 194. (Note that the hosts' tones are high.)

(193) máˣtʃʰó-pʰíʔ tì-ːpʲɛ̀   (Májchópí diíbye.) 'He is a glutton.'
    eat-excess   that-⟨SgM⟩

(194) Chémépí táñaálle.

    tʃʰɛ́mɛ́-pʰíʔ   tʰá Ⓖ ɲaL̀ːtʃɛ̀   'My sister is sickly.'
    be.ill-excess my   sib-⟨SgF⟩

4.3.6.2 -lle 'try'

The suffix -tʃɛ (-lle) 'try' is used as in 195:

(195) Oke méénúlleébe.

    ò-kʰɛ̀   mé:nɯ́-tʃɛ̀-ːpɛ̀   'He tried to hit me.'
    I-objAn hit-try-⟨SgM⟩

4.3.6.3 -pejtso 'upon encountering'

The suffix -pʰɛ́Lˣtsʰo (-pejtso) 'upon encountering' (meet) is exemplified in 196. It may co-occur with -tʃɛ (-lle) 'try to' as in 197.

(196) Oke méénúpéjtsoóbe.

    ò-kʰɛ̀   mé:nɯ́-pʰɛ́ˣtsʰò-ópɛ̀   'Upon encountering me,
    I-objAn hit-meet-⟨SgM⟩   he hit me.'

---

[24]In contrast to the classifier -ˣpʰì ⟨SgM⟩, the suffix -ⓁО-pʰi 'excessive' never has preaspiration.

(197) Oke méénúpéjtsólleébe.
ò-kʰɛ̀   mɛ́:nɯ́-pʰɛ́ˣtsʰó-t͡ʃɛ̀-:pɛ̀   'When he met me, he tried
I-objAn hit-meet-try-⟨SgM⟩   to hit me.'

4.3.6.4 Relocation to or from doing

The suffixes -ìɲɯ (-iñu) 'go after doing', -Ⓛtʰɛ²⁵ (-te) 'go to do', -hɛ (-je) 'come after doing', and -Ⓛ○βa²⁶ 'come to do' indicate relocation before or after the event referred to by the verb. They can be organized along two parameters: (1) whether the action is done "here" or "there" and (2) whether the movement is prior or subsequent to doing the action; see table 4.1.

Table 4.1 Relocation suffixes

	MOVE BEFORE DOING		MOVE AFTER DOING	
DO HERE	Ⓛ○-βa (-va) 'come to do' (come.do)		-iɲɯ (-iñu) 'go after doing' (do.go)	
DO THERE	Ⓛ-tʰɛ (-te) 'go to do' (go.do)		-hɛ (-je) 'come after doing' (do.come)	

Examples of the various relocational (directional) suffixes follow:

---

²⁵-Ⓛtʰɛ 'go to do' imposes a low tone on the preceding syllable, as demonstrated in the following:

ó áì̱-:βʲɛ́-ʔì̱   (Ó áiivyéhi.) 'I got burned.'
ó áí̱-:βɛ̱̌-tʰɛ́-ʔì̱   (Ó áíívetéhi.) 'I'm going to get burned.'
I burn-sIn-go.do-⟨t⟩

ó máˣt͡ʃʰò̱-tʰɛ́-ʔì̱   (Ó májchotéhi.) 'I'm going to eat.'
máˣt͡ʃʰò̱-tʰɛ́-:pɛ̀   (Májchotéébe.) 'He's going to eat.'
máˣt͡ʃʰò̱-tʰɛ́-t͡ʃɛ̀   (Májchotélle.) 'She's going to eat.'
máˣt͡ʃʰò̱-tʰɛ́-mɛ̀   (Májchotéme.) 'They are going to eat.'

²⁶-Ⓛ○βa (-va) 'come to do' imposes a low tone on its host's penult, as can be seen in the following:

ó mà̱ˣt͡ʃʰó-βá-ʔì̱   (Ó majchóváhi.) 'I'm coming to eat.'
mà̱ˣt͡ʃʰó-βà-:pɛ̀   (Majchóvaábe.) 'He's coming to eat.'
mà̱ˣt͡ʃʰó-βà-t͡ʃɛ̀   (Majchóvalle.) 'She's coming to eat.'
mà̱ˣt͡ʃʰó-βá-mɛ̀   (Majchóváme.) 'They are coming to eat.'

4.3. AFFIXAL DERIVATION

(198) a. má"tʃʰó-hɛ̀-ːpɛ̀   (Májchójeébe.) 'He came from eating.'
       eat-do.come-⟨SgM⟩
    b. má"tʃʰò-tʰɛ́-ːpɛ̀   (Májchotéébe.) 'He went to eat.'
       eat-go.do-⟨SgM⟩
    c. mà"tʃʰó-βà-ːpɛ̀   (majchóvaábe) 'He comes to eat.'
       eat-come.do-⟨SgM⟩

(199) Oke méénúɨñuúbe.
    ò-kʰɛ̀   mɛ́ːnɯ́-ɨ́ɲɯ̀ːpɛ̀   'He hit me and then left.'
    I-objAn hit-do.go-⟨SgM⟩

(200) Ó cúwaté dihjyávu.
    ó kʰɯ́ɨkpà-tʰɛ́-ʔì   tɨ̃́ʔ   hʲá-βɯ̀ː   'I am going to sleep
    I sleep-go.do-⟨t⟩ your house-goal   in your house.'

(201) Ó cúwajé dihjyári.
    ó kʰɯ́ɨkpà-hɛ́-ʔì   tɨ̃́ʔ   hʲá-rì
    I sleep-do.come-⟨t⟩ your house-sou
    'I return from sleeping in your house.'

(202) Ó cuwává dihjyávu.
    ó kʰɯ̀ɨkpá-βá-ʔì   tɨ̃́ʔ   hʲá-βɯ̀ː   'I come to sleep in
    I sleep-come.do-⟨t⟩ your house-goal   your house.'

It is possible to combine a relocation suffix with another affixal verb such as the causative, as shown in 203:

(203) Oke májchotétsoóbe.
    ò-kʰɛ̀   má"tʃʰò-tʰɛ́-tsʰò-ːpɛ̀   'He made me go to eat.'
    I-objAn eat-go.do-caus-⟨SgM⟩

The suffix -⓪tʰɛ 'go to do' and -⓪○βà 'come to do' may be followed by -⓪kʰì 'purpose' (which is otherwise used to form adverbial clauses). The combination of 'come to do' or 'go to do' and -⓪kʰì indicates that the action indicated by the host verb is the purpose for going or coming, as in 204:

(204) a. ó má"tʃʰò-tʰɛ́-kʰì (Ó májchotéki.) 'I go to eat there.'
    b. ó mà"tʃʰó-βà-kʰì (Ó majchóvaki.) 'I come to eat here.'

The suffix -⓪kʰi can be added to a main verb only if -⓪tʰɛ or -⓪○βa is first affixed to it.[27]

---

[27] In a generative framework this might be understood in terms of head-to-head movement along the following lines: 204 is derived from a structure like that in a. (below), in which an adverbial clause is within the verb phrase headed by -tʰɛ 'go to do'. First ma"tʃʰo moves

The suffix -ⓁtʰÈ 'go to do' may be used with the verbalizer -Ⓛ◯βà 'have' to indicate departure from normal state: kʰájòpá-:βà-tʰÈ 'become angry', áhʲàpá-:βà-tʰÈ 'become hungry', mèí-βà-tʰÈ 'to go crazy', tùʔkʰɯ́-βà-tʰÈ 'to become weak'.[28] The tone derivations of two affixal-verb combinations, ó kʰájò-pá-βà-tʰÉ-ʔì and kʰájò-pá-βà-tʰÉ-tsʰó-mÉ, are shown in figure 4.3:

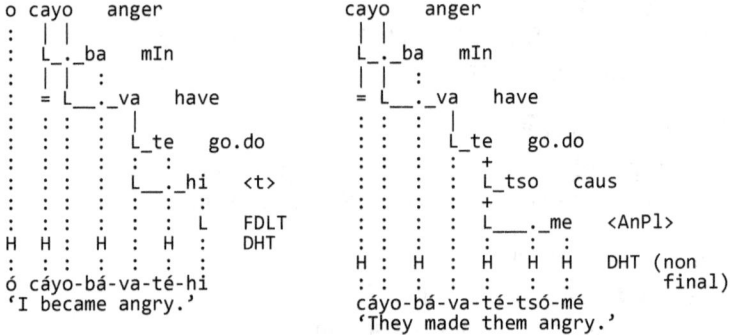

Figure 4.3 TD: ó cáyobávatéhi, cáyobávatétsómé

---

to join -tʰɛ, stranding -kʰi; see b. (below). Subsequently -kʰi cliticizes to -tʰɛ:

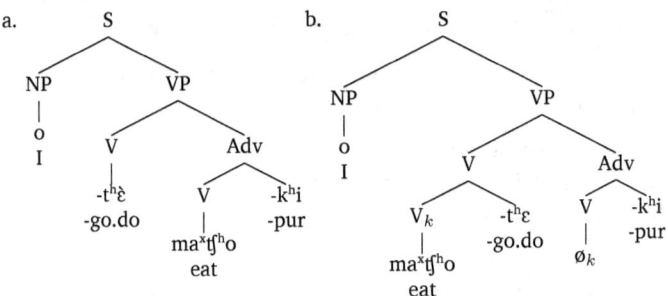

[28] Other cases of this combination indicate departure from normal state less obviously, e.g., kpáɲèʔhí-βà-tʰÈ 'to perform a festival', ápʰì:tʃʰó-βà-tʰÈ 'to hunt for the cause of illness by divination'. And some, of course, simply indicate physically going: há:ʔàɲÉ-βà-tʰÈ 'to go to visit'.

4.3.7 Adverbs and adjectives

Some words, like kpah^jɯ 'stingy', are adjectives.[29] Others are adverbs, for example, tsʰàíh^jɯ̀ 'at the same time, at the same moment'.[30] Yet others are

---

[29]See the following in (Thiesen & Thiesen 1998); these words sometimes appear within the lexical entry of the adjective's stem: ábajɨ́hco, aabópi, aabúcu, adɨ́ɨ́jɨ, adópi, aíjcyo, ajtyúva, álliu, allóócoó, ámɨ́ɨ́cuú, ámɨ́tsaráhco, ani, aapáromúva, aápi, ápííchoó, avyécu, avye, aya, baába, bahmɨ, bahri, bajtu, beréjco, bɨ́ɨ́bɨrɨ́va, bɨrɨ́hba, bɨɨ́va, bohɨ, boohówa, bolléécuú, caráhja, carájco, cááyóbaá, cáyóbanéjcu, cohpe, corɨ, cúhyumúva, cúváácuú, cuúve, cuwáácu, cuwápi, chaacháva, chéiyíva, cheme, cheméjco, cheréjco, chovájco, dáíhyañe, dáɨhcoó, daárɨ, dóllóhcoó, doópi, duhcu, duujɨnuúdu, duurúva, dsɨjɨ, dsɨɨne, dsɨnéhco, éhnííñeé, éréhcoó, ééyóií, iibórɨba, íhdyúehójtsɨ, iijyéve, illi, imye, ímídyoó, ímídyonéjcu, imíjyau, ímíjyuú, imílle, iímu, iiñúva, ɨbuúcu, ɨdáátsoó, ɨhtsu, ɨhve, ɨhvétso, ɨjca, ɨ́jɨ, ɨmɨa, ɨɨtépi, kehdóve, kehye, kyehéjco, kehju, keéme, kemu, ketúúva, kiwa, kɨ́úhcoó, llaaníva, llévanéjcu, llíɨ́hi, llijcya, lliya, llorójco, macháhco, majchi, májchíjyuú, maatyóva, méɨ́hcoó, ménunéjcu, meenúpi, meéva, mitya, mɨ́tyáhcoó, muúɨ́jyuúvu, nahtsɨ́va, najca, naníva, néhniñéjcu, nɨ́waúhco, nojco, nómiúúva, noúhco, núhnevéjco, ñajáhco, ñáyájcoó, ñojáhco, ñomɨ, oíhcyo, ókéhcoó, oonóva, oújco, oovátu, óvéheé, oyóócu, pábyanéjcu, pacyóva, pádúúcuú, pahdúva, pájúvaá, pañe, paápa, patyéhco, pavye, pecúhco, píhllóií, pívyétenéjcu, pɨ́ɨ́mɨ, pɨ́ɨ́pa, pɨrúúcuú, poáhco, pón̄óócuú, pore, pujúhco, rayúhcoó, réróhjáco, reróhco, rohdsɨ, rójɨhcoó, ruhíhcyo, ruhíhcyo, rutújco, taícho, táákívyeé, téávohjúcunu, técánohjúcunu, teéve, tɨjɨhca, toócu, tuucúva, tuhúúlle, tujpa, tújpañe, tuutáva, tútávanéjcu, tsaímijyúre, tsaɨ́ɨ́buwáre, tsápɨnéjcu, tsaráácu, tsáriñéjcu, tsijye, tsíjye, tsɨtsɨ, tsocájco, tsohco, tsuúco, tsuhjɨ́va, údíícyuú, údícyunéjcu, uhje, ujcáva, ujcútso, ujtsi, úmeco, úmuupícho, úmuupílle, úúpíyií, úraavyépi, vájɨhcoó, veúhco, viío, viújco, vúdójcoó, wahpe, waája, waajácu, wájácunéjcu, wájanéjcu, waajápi, wajyu, wáñehtsoó, wátyuáco, yaayáva.

[30]See the following entries in (Thiesen & Thiesen 1998): abájɨhnécu, abátejnécu, áábaúvúre, aaca, acádsɨhnécu, ácoóca, ácuhnécu, aacúrɨ́vaco, ahdícyane, ahdu, áhdure, áijyu, ájcoójɨ, ákyehnécu, áánáa, ááne, aanéjɨ́ɨ́va, áánélliíhye, áánema, áánetu, aanúhórɨ́vaco, apáhajchíí, apáhdyúre, ápahjɨre, apáijyúre, arónáa, ávyeta, ávohnécu, aavórɨ́vaco, bɨwáhdúre, bóóneé, bootsérɨ́vaco, botsíiíkye, caabóhjúrɨ́vaco, cábuúba, caadírɨ́vaco, caadúdárɨ́vaco, callájahnécu, callájárɨ́vaco, caallíhórɨ́vaco, caallúrɨ́jɨrɨ́vaco, caanórɨ́vaco, caapárɨ́vaco, caapátyúrɨ́vaco, caapátsɨ́rɨ́vaco, caarárɨ́jɨrɨ́vaco, caarúrɨ́vaco, caatɨ́jɨrɨ́vaco, caatórɨ́vaco, caatórórɨ́vaco, caatsóhórɨ́vaco, caatsúrɨ́vaco, caawárɨ́vaco, cójɨ́éllé(h), coomírɨ́vaco, cuujúrɨ́vaco, cúúvéhulléré, choóco, deehérɨ́vaco, dɨɨbérɨ́vaco, doobérɨ́vaco, dootóúrɨ́vaco, doovíyírɨ́vaco, ééé, ehdícyane, (ehdu, íjcyane) ehdu, éhjɨhjɨtu, éhjɨhjɨtu, éhlleé, éíjyuú, eekérɨ́vaco, élleé, hajchóta, ícyoóca, íchii, idyé, íévene, íhya, íhajchííjyu, ihdyu, íhdyure, iíjcyadúre, ijcyátúre, íjcyoójɨ, iijyócúrɨ́vaco, fijyu, iíjyu, fíjyuíɨ́jyu, íɨjyupéjco, ílleé, ílluú, íllúhwu, ílluúnéétútsihdyu, ímichi, ípyejco, ípubá, ɨ́ɨ́cuíí, ɨdsɨhɨ́vánetu, ɨhdeé, ɨhdéjuco, ɨhtsúta, ɨɨtsɨrɨ́vaco, ɨveekí, ɨɨvóhórɨ́vaco, ɨɨwárɨ́vaco, kiá, miibyérɨ́vaco, múcoóca, muhdú, múijyu, muurá(h), mútsií, nanítyari, néhijyácaá, nehíkyére, nihñe, níhñécunu, nɨɨjcáúrɨ́vaco, oobɨ́ráúrɨ́vaco, oohárɨ́vaba, oohárɨ́vaco, oohbárɨ́vaco, ojpíítyari, óuuvératu, paachíchárɨ́vaco, pahdu, paíjyuva, pane, páoohájɨ, paarúrɨ́vaco, paatúrúrɨ́vaco, paatsɨrɨ́vaco, paayúrɨ́vaco, pécóhajchóta, pécójpɨɨ́ne, peecútére, peíjuco, peíye, pejco, péjcore, péjcorétúre, pevétáre, piéhdúre, piillúrɨ́vaco, piityáhárɨ́vaco, pɨ́rune, pɨɨtórɨ́vaco, reevórɨ́vaco, rootóhórɨ́vaco, taarívájárɨ́vaco, taaróhjɨ́rɨ́vaco, téchiúcunu, tehdu, tehdújuco, téhdure, téijyu, téijyócunu, téɨ́bórɨ́baúcunu, téɨɨbúwa, téɨ́tsɨúcunu, téɨ́vóhoúcunu, téjcoojɨ́vádu, témɨ́byeúcunu, témótsiúcunu, téénélliíhye, téñáhiúcunu, tépaayúcunu, tétácúruhjúcunu, tétódsɨúcunu, téévéneúvu, teevétari, téwátyuúcunu, toodsɨrɨ́vaco, tujkénu, tsáhaá, tsahíɨ́yi,

used as both adjectives and adverbs, for example, ùɾúɾʔɨ̀ 'weak (adjective); slowly (adverb)'.³¹

Some adjectives may be used as adverbs when followed by -nɛ -⟨ø⟩. For example, in 205 mít ʲʰà-nɛ̀ (much/big-⟨ø⟩) 'much, hard' is used adverbially:

(205) mítyane wákímyeííbye
<u>mítʲʰà-nɛ̀</u>   kpákʰímʲɛ́í-ːpʲɛ̀   'He works hard' or
big-⟨ø⟩   work-⟨SgM⟩   'He works a lot.'

The word ímí-ɲɛ̀ 'well' is used as an adverb in 206:

(206) Ímiñe wákímyeííbye
<u>ímì-ɲɛ̀</u>   kpákʰímʲɛ́í-ːpʲɛ̀   'He works hard' or
good-⟨ø⟩   work-⟨SgM⟩   'He works a lot.'

Likewise, kʰóʔpʰɛ̀-nɛ̀ (hard-⟨ø⟩) 'solid, firm, hard' is used adverbially in 207:

(207) cóhpene míhchúúveco.
... kʰóʔpʰɛ̀-nɛ̀ míʔʧʰɯ́-ɯ́βɛ̀-kʰò
hard-ø   close.eyesImp-sIn-implore
'...close your eyes tight.'

When such deadjectival adverbs are followed by -Ⓛɯβɯ 'max', the low tone of -Ⓛnɛ̀ ⟨ø⟩ is delinked so that -Ⓛɯβɯ 'max' can dock its low tone; see 208:

(208) kʰóʔpʰɛ́-nɛ̀-ɯ́βɯ̀   (cóhpé-ne-úvu) 'very hard or tight'
hard-adv-max
pʰɨ́ɾɯ̀-nɛ̀-ɯ́βɯ̀   (pɨ́rú-ne-úvu)   'completely'
complete-adv-max
ímí-ɲɛ̀-ɯ́βɯ̀   (ímí-ñe-úvu)   'very well'
good-adv-max

---

tsaíjyu, tsáijyu, tsájcoójɨ, tsájcuúve, tsajɨ́jtóre, tsapéhdu, tsápehju, tsatsíhyi, tsíhyulle, tsiíñe, tsɨ́tsɨjnécu, tsúúcaja, tsuuhórɨ́vaco, uhjéta, uutsúcúrɨ́vaco, viicyórɨ́vaco, wáduhnécu, wahájchota, wahdyúre, wajácútsi, waajɨ́htárɨ́vaco, wajɨ́tahñécu, wállahnécu, waallárɨ́vaco, waapɨ́rárɨ́vaco, waaríjyárɨ́vaco, waatyóhɨ́rɨ́vaco, waatyúrɨ́vaco.

³¹See the following entries in (Thiesen & Thiesen 1998): aába, aabájke, átereé, bañu, caáme, chohju, dseréjco, íahpádyu, imi, imíchi, ímítyuú, ímiubááne, ɨ́hnáhoó, ɨ́htsútuú, keéva, kimóhcoó, lleéva, mítyane, nehni, núcojpɨ́tso, pevéne, pɨɨhɨ́re, tánéhduú, téévetúne, tuhu, tujkéve, tsahdu, tsaímíye, tsajcyu, tsajpɨ, tsari, tsatújkeve, tsaáva, tsávanéjcu, tsíhdyure, tsɨjpa, uúhɨ.

4.4 Verbs with incorporated instruments

The prefixes of table 4.2 indicate the class of the instrument used to carry out the action indicated by the verb with which they occur.[32]

Table 4.2 Instrumental prefixes

to-	(do-)	'do with the hand'
tɨ-	(dɨ-)	'do with the teeth'
tʰa-	(ta-)	'do with the foot'
kʰa-	(ca-)	'do with something pointed'
kʰi-	(ki-)	'do with some cutting tool'
pʰɨ-	(pɨ-)	'do with something like a saw'
kpa-	(wa-)	'do by a series of blows'

These are illustrated in tables 4.3 and 4.4. In table 4.3, pʰɯhɯ 'break something fragile' is followed by -ʔhákʰò 'sTr' and in table 4.4 ʔtàʔɨ́ 'break' is followed by -ɾò 'sTr'. Despite having these singular transitive suffixes, these derived verbs may be used as transitive, intransitive or stative.

Table 4.3 Instrumental prefixes with púju 'break something fragile'

tó-pʰɯ́hɯ̀-ʔhákʰò (dópújuhjáco)	'break something fragile with the hand'
tɨ́-pʰɯ́hɯ̀-ʔhákʰò (dɨ́pújuhjáco)	'break something fragile with the teeth'
tʰá-pʰɯ́hɯ̀-ʔhákʰò (tápújuhjáco)	'break something fragile with the foot'
kʰá-pʰɯ́hɯ̀-ʔhákʰò (cápújuhjáco)	'break something fragile with something pointed'
kpá-pʰɯ́hɯ̀-ʔhákʰò (wápújuhjáco)	'break something fragile with a series of blows'

---

[32]These are not productive prefixes. They are—presumably—the result of an earlier process of incorporation. Evidence for earlier incorporation is that, for some of these prefixes, there are cognate classifiers (see section 6.1.3); both the prefixes and cognate classifiers must have derived from what was once a free-standing noun.

Table 4.4 Instrumental prefixes with hdahɨ 'break, sever'

tó-ʔtàʔɨ-ɾò (dóhdahɨro)	'break something into pieces with the hand'
tɨ́-ʔtàʔɨ-ɾò (dɨ́hdahɨro)	'break something into pieces with the teeth'
tʰá-ʔtàʔɨ-ɾò (táhdahɨro)	'break something with the foot'
kʰɨ́-ʔtʲàʔɨ-ɾò (kɨ́hdyahɨro)	'sever something with a cutting tool'
pʰɨ́-ʔtàʔɨ-ɾò (pɨ́hdahɨro)	'sever with something like a saw'
kpá-ʔtàʔɨ-ɾò (wáhdahɨro)	'cut or sever by a series of blows with some tool'

Chapter 5

Main Clauses and Verbs

Clauses are either main or subordinate. Main clauses are described here. Subordinate clauses are described in chapters 16–18.

A complete sentence has at least one main clause with a subject and predicate. The subject may be either a postverbal classifier or it may be preverbal, in which case the verb is followed by either -ʔi (-hi) ⟨t⟩ or -nɛ (-ne) ⟨n⟩, as described in section 5.4. A preverbal subject may be a noun phrase or it may be a proclitic. The tone of proclitic subjects is discussed in section 3.12.2, page 93.

The predicate may be a verb or verb phrase, as discussed in sections 5.1, 5.2, and chapter 14, or it may be a noun or adjective phrase, as discussed in section 5.3. Verb phrases are conjoined by simple juxtaposition.

How sentences are conjoined to form discourses is explained in section 19.1, page 395.

5.1 Basic sentence structure

The basic clause has a subject and a predicate, and the subject precedes the predicate. For example, in 209 the subject is the noun phrase ò:ʔí:pʲɛ̀ 'dog' and the predicate is the verb tsɨ̀:nɛ̀ 'run':

(209) ò:ʔí-:pʲɛ̀   tsɨ̀:nɛ́-ʔì (Oohííbyé dsɨ̈nɛ́hi.) 'The dog runs.'
     dog-⟨SgM⟩ run-⟨t⟩

The subject may be a free, preverbal pronoun, as in 210:

(210) á:nùù ʧʰɛ̀mɛ́-ʔì (Áánu cheméhi.) 'This one (SgM) is sick.'
    this be.ill-⟨t⟩

A clause may contain many other phrases, the order of which may vary considerably. (This word-order flexibility is undoubtedly due to Bora's healthy case system.)

When the subject is an overt, preverbal pronoun, if it is either first or second person and either dual or plural, then the verb bears the proclitic mɛ ~ ma[1] 'nonsingular speech-act participants', which will be glossed SAP. For example, in 211 the subject is first person plural exclusive (that is, it does not include the hearer); in both the conditional and the main clause the verb bears mɛ 'SAP':

(211) Ímí muha mecúwaca tsá muha mechéméturóhi.

   ímíʔ   mùɨʔà mɛ̀   kʰɯ̃́ᔆkpà-kʰà
   good   we.ex SAP   sleep-CF

   tsʰã́ʔᴴ mùɨʔà mɛ̀   ʧʰɛ́mɛ́-tʰɨ̀ɨ-ɾó-ʔì
   not   we.ex SAP   be.ill-neg-frs-⟨t⟩
   'If we (ex.) had slept well, we would not have gotten sick.'

In 212 the subject is second person plural:

(212) Ímí ámuha mecúwáhajchíí tsá ámuha mechéméítyuróhi.

   ímíʔ   ámùɨʔà mɛ̀   kʰɯ̃́ᔆkpá-ʔàˣʧʰí:
   good   you.pl SAP   sleep-if

   tsʰã́ʔᴴ ámùɨʔà mɛ̀   ʧʰɛ́mɛ́-í-tʲʰɨ̀ɨ-ɾó-ʔì
   not   you   SAP   be.ill-fut-neg-frs-⟨t⟩
   'If you (pl) sleep well, you are not likely to get sick.'

Of course, mɛ ~ ma- 'SAP' is not used when the subject is third person; compare 213 with 211–212:

(213) Ímí ditye cúwáhajchíí tsá ditye chéméítyuróhi.

   ímíʔ   tì-tʲʰɛ̀   __   kʰɯ̃́ᔆkpá-ʔàˣʧʰí:
   good   that-⟨AnPl⟩   sleep-if

   tsʰã́ʔᴴ tì-tʲʰɛ̀   __   ʧʰɛ́mɛ́-í-tʲʰɨ̀ɨ-ɾó-ʔì
   not   that-⟨AnPl⟩   be.ill-fut-neg-frs-⟨t⟩
   'If they sleep well, they are not likely to get sick.'

---

[1] /ma/ occurs before /a/.

In examples 211 and 212 mɛ ~ ma 'SAP' is preceded by an overt pronoun. When a pronoun does not precede mɛ ~ ma, the subject is impersonal, as illustrated in 214:[2]

(214) Ímí mecúwáhajchíí tsá mechéméityuróhi.

ímí? __ mɛ̀ kʰɯ̃kpá-ʔàˣʧʰí: tsʰá̌? __ mɛ̀ ʧʰɛ́mɛ́-ì-tʲʰɯ̀-ɾó-ʔì
good   SAP sleep-if   not   SAP be.ill-fut-neg-frs-⟨t⟩

a. 'If we (incl.) sleep well, we are not likely to get sick.'
b. 'Whoever sleeps well is not likely to get sick.'

Perhaps the impersonal nature of the subject is even clearer in 215:

(215) má àʧɛ́-ʔì   (Máalléhi.) 'It is raining.' (lit. 'We are raining.')
      SAP rain-⟨t⟩

5.2 Subjects indicated with classifiers

When a main clause has a preverbal subject, the verb ends with -ʔì (-hi) ⟨t⟩, as in the column labeled PREVERBAL SUBJECT in 216, or—if negative—with -nɛ̀ (-ne) ⟨n⟩. This is discussed further in section 5.4.

(216)   PREVERBAL SUBJECT   POSTVERBAL SUBJECT
    a. Ó   majchóhi.
       ó   màˣʧʰó-ʔì   —   'I eat.'
       I   eat-⟨t⟩
    b. Dipye   majchóhi.   Májchoóbe.
       tì-pʲʰɛ̀   màˣʧʰó-ʔì   máˣʧʰò-ːpɛ̀   'He eats.'
       that-⟨SgM⟩ eat-⟨t⟩   eat-⟨SgM⟩
    c. Dille   majchóhi.   Májcholle.
       tì-ʧɛ̀   màˣʧʰó-ʔì   máˣʧʰò-ʧɛ̀   'She eats.'
       that-⟨SgF⟩ eat-⟨t⟩   eat-⟨SgF⟩
    d. Ditye   majchóhi.   Majchóme.
       tì-tʲʰɛ̀   màˣʧʰó-ʔì   màˣʧʰó-mɛ̀   'They eat.'
       that-⟨AnPl⟩ eat-⟨t⟩   eat-⟨AnPl⟩

Instead of a preverbal subject, a third person subject may be indicated by a classifier suffixed (or cliticized) to the verb, as in the column labeled POSTVERBAL SUBJECT in 216.[3] These will be referred to as CLASSIFIER SUBJECTS.

---

[2] The literal meaning of 214 is as given in 214a, but it is construed as in 214b.

[3] Note that there are two forms of the animate plural classifier. See section 6.1.1, especially table 6.1 on page 164, regarding such differences the distribution of different forms of the animate classifiers.

If the subject is animate, one of a very small set of animate classifiers is used, the majority of which are given in table 5.1.[4] Although these are most frequently used as third person, they sometimes occur in apposition to a first or second person subject; see, for example, 642, page 271.

Table 5.1 Animate subject classifiers

-ːpɛ	(-ːbe)	⟨SgM⟩
-tʃɛ	(-lle)	⟨SgF⟩
-mɯtsʰi	(-mutsi)	⟨DuM⟩
-mɯpʰɨ	(-mupɨ)	⟨DuF⟩
-mɛ	(-me)	⟨AnPl⟩
-tsʰɨ	(-tsɨ)	⟨child⟩

Whenever there is no preverbal subject *there must be a classifier subject*, using the classifier that corresponds to (the referent of) the subject; this is further illustrated in 217:

(217) a. ákʰɯːβɛ̀-ːpɛ̀   (Ácúúveébe.)   'He sat down.'   (SgM)
   b. ákʰɯːβɛ̀-tʃɛ̀   (Ácúúvelle.)   'She sat down.'   (SgF)
   c. ákʰɯːβɛ̀-mɯ́tsʰɨ̀ (Ácúúvemútsi.) 'They sat down.' (DuM)
   d. ákʰɯːβɛ̀-mɯ́pʰɨ̀ (Ácúúvemúpɨ.) 'They sat down.' (DuF)
   e. ákʰɯ̀ːβɛ́-mɛ̀   (Ácuuvéme.)   'They sat down.' (AnPl)

This is true of inanimate subjects as well. For example, one could report that a book is burning with 218 because 'book' corresponds to the class of -ʔaːmɨ ⟨leaf⟩.

(218) áíːβʲɛ́-ʔáːmɨ̀ (Áíívyéháámɨ.) 'The leaf (paper, book,...)
   burn-⟨leaf⟩   is burning.'

There are several hundred classifiers that can be used as classifier subjects; see appendix E for a fairly comprehensive list. There is even a semantically least-specified classifier, -nɛ̀ ⟨ø⟩, which may be used when no more-specific classifier is appropriate, as in 219:[5]

(219) àtʃé-nɛ̀ (Alléne.) 'It is raining.'
   rain-⟨ø⟩

A plural marker may follow the inanimate classifier subject, either -ːkʰɯ 'duIn' or -⁽ˀ⁾hɨ 'plural', as in 220:

---

[4]Although -mɯ-tsʰi ⟨DuM⟩ and -mɯ-pʰɨ ⟨DuF⟩ are bimorphemic, for convenience we write them as single morphemes throughout this grammar.
[5]This can also be expressed using an impersonal subject; compare 219 to 215.

(220) áí:βʲɛ́-ʔà:mɨ́-kʰɯ̀ɯ̀ (Áíívyéhaamɨ́cu.) '(The two books)
burn-⟨leaf⟩-duIn   are burning.'

(221) áí:βʲɛ́-ʔà:mɨ́-hɨ̀ (Áíívyéhaamɨ́jɨ.) '(The books
burn-⟨leaf⟩-⟨pl⟩   are burning.)'

A preverbal subject noun phrase and a classifier subject are mutually exclusive, i.e., either one or the other may occur, but not both. We will call this the PREVERBAL SUBJECT CONSTRAINT.

When the subject is indicated by both a classifier suffixed to the verb and an overt phrase, then the phrase must follow the verb and is in apposition to the classifier subject. For example, in 222 the verb is followed by the classifier subject and then a noun (phrase) in apposition to the classifier subject:

(222) Tsájúcoobe oohííbye.

tsʰá-hɯ́ɯ́kʰò-:pɛ̀ Ⓐ ò:ʔí-:pʲɛ̀   'The dog already came.'
come-now-⟨SgM⟩   dog-⟨SgM⟩

In 223, which might initiate a text, the verb is followed by the classifier subject and then by a pronominal phrase and a relative clause, both of which are in apposition to the classifier subject:

(223) Íjcyaabée tsaapi Jóáa imyéme íjcyaábe.

ɨ́ˣkʲʰà-:pɛ̌-ɛ́ Ⓐ tsʰà-:pʰì Ⓐ [hóáà [ì mʲɛ́mɛ̀] ɨ́ˣkʲʰà]-:pɛ̀⁶
be-⟨SgM⟩-rem   one-⟨SgM⟩   John self name   be   -⟨SgM⟩
'There was a man whose name was John.'

From a cross-linguistic perspective it is not unusual to have a postverbal subject in an "existential presentative" such as 223. In Bora, aside from existential presentatives, an overt postverbal subject generally serves to clarify the identity of the subject in contexts where the classifier is not sufficiently specific.

5.3 Predicate complements

The predicate complement sentence is formed by a predicate complement (a noun or adjective phrase), a subject and an (explicit or implicit) copular verb ɨˣkʲʰà 'be'. For example, consider the relative clause in 223 above; the predicate complement is hóáà 'John', the subject is ì mʲɛ́mɛ̀ 'self's name', and the copula is ɨˣkʲʰà 'be'.

---

[6]The final appositional phrase of 223 is a noun phrase headed by -:pɛ ⟨SgM⟩ and modified by a prenominal relative clause.

The subject sometimes precedes the predicate complement, and the copula is frequently absent, as will be seen below.

The predicate complement may be a noun or adjective phrase. If it is an adjective (phrase), it characterizes the subject. For example, in 224 the subject is characterized as good (and the copula is implicit):

(224) ímíʔ tì-ːpʲɛ̀   (Ímí diíbye.) 'He is good.'
      good that-⟨SgM⟩

When the predicate complement is a noun (phrase), the referents of the subject and of the complement are understood to be one and the same. For example, in 225 the referent of the subject, 'that one (singular masculine)' and the complement 'my father' are understood to be one and the same. Note that the subject and predicate complement may be in either order.[7]

(225) ⎧ a. tì-ːpʲɛ̀   tʰáː kʰáːnìí   (Diibye táácááníí.) ⎫ 'He is
      ⎨   that-⟨SgM⟩ my father   ⎬ my father.'
      ⎩ b. tʰáː kʰáːnì tì-ːpʲɛ̀   (Táácááni diíbye.) ⎭
           my father that-⟨SgM⟩

The predicate complement may be a noun (phrase) that refers to a location. For example, in 226 the predicate is aːʔɨ.

(226) àːʔɨ̀ tìːpʲɛ̀   (Aahɨ diíbye.) 'He is at home.'
      home that-⟨SgM⟩

In 227 and 228 the predicate complement is a genitive phrase headed by a locative noun; see 7.2.3. (The subject of 227 is the classifier -nɛ ⟨ø⟩.)

(227) [háʰ(ː) ⓖ pʰàɲɛ̀] ìˣkʲʰá-nɛ̀ (Já pañe ijcyáne.) 'It is in
       house   inside   be-⟨ø⟩   the house.'

(228) Méétsá lliiñe oohííbye.
      PREDICATE COMPLEMENT   SUBJECT
      [mɛ́ːtsʰá ⓖ t͡ʃìːɲɛ̀]   òːʔɨ-ːpʲɛ̀   'The dog is under
       table   under   dog-⟨SgM⟩   the table.'

The suffix -ʔiˣkʲʰa 'habitual action or characteristic' is an affixal form of iˣkʲʰa 'be'; see section 5.10.2 for discussion.

---

[7]The initial syllable of many pronouns shortens when the pronoun is the subject of the sentence. For example, in tìpʲɛ̀ pʰɛ́-hʉ̀kʰóː-ʔì 'He went', the first syllable of tìːpʲɛ̀ (diibye) is short. Contrary to what one would expect, however, the subject of a predicate complement clause never suppresses the length. For example, in 225 the subject is tìːpʲɛ̀ (nonfinal) or tíípʲɛ̀ (final).

5.4 End of main verb markers

When a main clause has a preverbal subject, the verb is followed by -ⓁO?i ⟨t⟩ (5.4.1) or -ⓁOnɛ ⟨n⟩ (5.4.2).[8]

5.4.1 -hi ~ -h ⟨t⟩

The morpheme -ⓁO?(i) ⟨t⟩ is suffixed to the verb of the main clause, as in 229:

(229) Ávyéjuube ihájkímuke néé ditye ihjya iímíbájchoki.

áβʲɛ́hɯ̀ːpɛ̀ ɨ̋ ʔáˣkʰí-mɯ̀-kʰɛ̀   nɛ́ː-ʔ(i̋) tɨ̀-tʲʰɛ̀
chief-⟨SgM⟩ self folk-plAn-objAn say-⟨t⟩ that-⟨AnPl⟩

ɨ̋ʔ hʲà ì ı̋mípáˣʧʰò-kʰì̋
self house self fix-pur
'The chief told his people to fix his[9] house.'

This suffix occurs only with explicit preverbal subjects, as in 230a. It does not co-occur with a classifier subject, as in the first alternative in 230b:

(230) a. ɨ̀ːhɯ̀ ɯ́mɨ̀βá-ʔì̀ (Ɨɨju úmɨvá.) 'The horse escaped.'
        horse escape-⟨t⟩

b. ⎧ *ɯ́mɨ́βà-ːpɛ́-ʔì̀   ⎫
   ⎪ escape-⟨SgM⟩-⟨t⟩   ⎪ (Úmɨvaábe.) 'He escaped.'
   ⎨ ɯ́mɨ́βà-ːpɛ̀   ⎬
   ⎩ escape-⟨SgM⟩   ⎭

Nor does it occur in negative clauses; such cases are discussed in the next section.

The suffix -ⓁO?(i) ⟨t⟩ imposes a low tone on its host's penult:

(231) a. ó ʧɛ̌ːnɛ́-ʔì̀ (ó lleenéhi) 'I eat (fruit).'

b. ó f̃ʔβɛ̌tʰɛ́-ʔì̀ (ó fhvetéhi) 'I stop.'

---

[8]A theory that entertains some notion of movement might consider ⟨t⟩ and ⟨n⟩ to be "traces" of subjects that have been moved to a preverbal position. This could be motivated by the following distributional facts: (1) ⟨t⟩ and ⟨n⟩ never co-occur with a classifier subject, presumably because they occupy the position of classifier subjects, and (2) ⟨t⟩ and ⟨n⟩ occur if and only if there is an overt preverbal subject (pronoun, name, or noun phrase).

[9]This could also refer to "their" house, i.e., it could be bound by the indirect object rather than the subject of the higher clause. The interpretation given in 229 is preferred because 'house' is singular. If, however, the object were plural, that is ì ʔhʲá ʔáɲɛ̀ (self house various) 'his/their various houses', then the favored interpretation would be 'their houses'.

(232) a. Ó ímíbajchóhi.
   ó ímípá⁽ᴸ⁾ˣtʃʰó-ʔì   'I fix.'
   I fix-⟨t⟩
b. Ó ímíbájchotéjucóóhi.
   ó ímípáˣtʃʰò-tʰɛ́-huɨ⁽ᴸ⁾kʰó:-ʔì   'Now I go to fix (it).'
   I fix-go.do-now-⟨t⟩

However this may be blocked by other lexically marked low tones. For example, in 233 the verb stems have a lexically marked low tone on the antepenult, so -ⓁO?(i) ⟨t⟩ cannot dock its Ⓛ on the penult:

(233) a. ó a⁽ᴸ⁾:ʔíβɛ́-ʔì   (ó aahívéhi)   'I visit.'
b. ó ámápuɨ⁽ᴸ⁾kʰúɨ-ʔì (ó ámabúcúhi) 'I hug.'

Sentence finally, the segments of -ⓁO?(i) ⟨t⟩ are both spoken and written, as in 234a; sentence medially, the /?/ is spoken but not written, whereas the /i/ is neither spoken nor written, as in 234b.[10]

(234) a. ó à²tó-ʔì   (Ó ahdóhi.)   'I paid.'
   I pay-⟨t⟩
b. ó à²tó-ʔ__ tí-:pʼɛ̀-kʰɛ̀   (Ó ahdó dííbyeke.) 'I paid him.'
   I pay-⟨t⟩ that-⟨SgM⟩-objAn

5.4.2 -ne ⟨n⟩

The morpheme -ⓁOnɛ̀ ⟨n⟩ is suffixed to the verbs of negative sentences, whether declarative or imperative. It occupies the position -ⓁO?i ⟨t⟩ occupies in a nonnegative sentence. However, unlike -ⓁO?i ⟨t⟩, an explicit preverbal subject is not required, as shown by 235:

(235) máˣtʃʰò-tí-(ɲɛ̀) (¡Májchodí(ñe)!) 'Do not eat!'
   eat-neg-⟨n⟩

Following -tʰɯ 'negative', -ⓁOnɛ ⟨n⟩ is optional:

(236) tsʰá⁽ᴴ⁾ʔ ò máˣtʃʰò-tʰúɨ-(nɛ̀) (Tsá o májchotú(ne).) 'I did not eat it.'
   not I eat-neg-⟨n⟩

In a prohibition, if -nɛ does not follow the verb, then a glottal stop does,[11] as in 237 (in which the glottal stop is not written):

---

[10] There is some variation, with younger speakers pronouncing less of the segmental material of this suffix than older speakers.
[11] This may reflect the presence of -ⓁO?ì ⟨t⟩.

5.5. STATEMENTS OF FACT

(237) a. $\begin{Bmatrix} \text{Pehdíñe} \\ \text{Pehdí} \end{Bmatrix}$ téhullévu.

b. Téullévú $\begin{Bmatrix} \text{pehdíñe.} \\ \text{pehdí.} \end{Bmatrix}$ 'Do not go (over there).'

a. $\begin{Bmatrix} \text{pʰɛ̀-ʔtí-ɲɛ̀} \\ \text{pʰɛ̀-ʔtí-ʔ} \\ \text{go-neg-}\langle n\rangle \end{Bmatrix}$ tʰɛ́-ʔùʧɛ́-βùɪ that-⟨yonder⟩-goal

b. tʰɛ́-ùʧɛ́-βúɪ that-⟨yonder⟩-goal $\begin{Bmatrix} \text{pʰɛ̀-ʔtí-ɲɛ̀} \\ \text{pʰɛ̀-ʔtí-ʔ} \\ \text{go-neg-}\langle n\rangle \end{Bmatrix}$

The -ⓁOnɛ̀, which has been glossed ⟨n⟩ is probably the same suffix as the one glossed ⟨ø⟩. This would be the case if negative clauses were complements to a negative verb (one which time has robbed of most verbal responsibilities and privileges). This would not only explain the presence of -nɛ, but also the fact that the initial syllable of the verb of negative clauses bears high tone. For example, 236 above would structurally be the following:

(238) [$_V$tsʰá̰ʔ] [$_{NP}$ [$_S$ ò má˟ʧʰò-tʰúɪ] nɛ̀] 'I did not eat it.'
      deny   I eat-neg   ⟨ø⟩

5.5 Statements of fact

Another sort of sentence, one used to state a fact, consists simply of a subordinate clause terminated with -ⓁOnɛ ⟨ø⟩. Presumably this clause is the predicate complement of an implicit verb *be*, the implicit subject of which is something like *fact*. The first sentence of 239 illustrates this type of sentence:

(239) Ó májchoróne. Árónáa tsá o óóvetúne.

ó má˟ʧʰò-ɾó-nè. Á-ɾó-náà   tsʰá̰ʔ ò òːβɛ̀-tʰúɪ-nè.
I eat-frs-⟨ø⟩   thm-frs-while not   I be.full-neg-⟨n⟩
'(It is a fact) that I ate. However, I am not full.'

This has the same feel as English *It is a fact that I ate*. Other examples are 816 and 817 on page 317.

VERB ROOT[a]	FRS[b] -ɾa	NEG -tʰɯɯ	SG/MUL[d]	AFXVRB[e]	(do.go)[f] -iɲɯ	CAUS[g] -tsʰo	R/P[h]	CAUS -tsʰo	RELOC[i]
			-ɾò	-kʰoβiβɛ		-xkʰatsʰi	-mɛi		-tʰɛ
			-ʔhàkʰo	-pʰɛxtsʰo		(recip)	-pʰi		-βa
			-xkʰò	-pʰɛxkʰoːβɛ					-hɛ
VRBLZR[c]			-nɯ̀	-tʰɯxkʰɛnɯ					
-βa			-ːβɛ̀	-pʰiːβʲɛ					
-nɯ			-pà	-tʃɛ					
NOUN ROOT -βɛ			-ɯ̀kʰɯ̀nɯ̀						
-tʃɛ			-xkʰàtʲʰɛ̀						
-xkʰimɛi									

[a] The verb root may also be preceded by an incorporated instrument as described in section 4.4.
[b] textscfrs frustrative, contraexpectation
[c] VRBLZR verbalizer
[d] SG/MUL singular or multiple
[e] AFXVRB affixal verb
[f] 'do after going'
[g] CAUS causative
[h] R/P reflexive or passive
[i] RELOC relocation

Figure 5.1 The verb stem

5.6 The structure of the verb

Verb stems are formed from verb roots by the addition of derivational affixes as indicated in figure 5.1, page 134.

Two types of verbal words are formed from verb stems. First, nonimperative verbs are formed as indicated in figure 5.2:

$$\text{VERB STEM} \begin{Bmatrix} \text{-huɨk}^h\text{o} \\ \text{focus} \\ \text{-ʔi}^x\text{k}^{jh}\text{a} \\ \text{be} \end{Bmatrix} \begin{Bmatrix} \text{FUT}^a & \text{NEG}^b & \text{FRS}^c \\ \text{-ì} & \text{-t}^h\text{ɯ} & \text{-ɾa} \end{Bmatrix} \begin{Bmatrix} \text{-ʔi} \\ \text{-nɛ (after -t}^h\text{ɯ)} \end{Bmatrix} \text{with a preverbal subject} \\ \begin{Bmatrix} \text{ANIM. CLS.}^d \text{ (-ːpɛ,...)} \\ \text{INAN. CLS.}^e \text{ (-nɛ,...)} \end{Bmatrix} \text{with a classifier subject}$$

---

^{a}FUT future
^{b}NEG negative
^{c}FRS frustrative, contraexpectation
^{d}ANIM. CLS. animate classifier
^{e}INAN. CLS. inanimate classifier

Figure 5.2 The verb (nonimperative)

When heading an adverbial clause, verbs so formed may be followed by an adverbial suffix, and when heading a relative clause or nominal complement, they may be followed by a case marker; see figure 16.1, page 357. In all cases clitics may follow.

Second, imperative verbs are formed as indicated in figure 5.3.

$$\begin{Bmatrix} \text{PERSON} \\ \text{mɛ-} \\ \text{ti-} \end{Bmatrix} \text{VERB STEM} \begin{Bmatrix} \text{ADVERB} \\ \text{-hɯ}^x \\ \text{-k}^h\text{o} \end{Bmatrix} \begin{Bmatrix} \text{NEG} & \langle\text{n}\rangle \\ \text{-ti} & \text{-ɲɛ} \end{Bmatrix} \text{-CLITIC}$$

Figure 5.3 The imperative verb

There are distinct types of verbs, as discussed in section 5.7.

Tense (locating an event relative to the time of speaking) is discussed in section 5.9.

Aspect (the nature of the event's unfolding in time, i.e., whether it is presented as occurring in an instant, as ongoing, as a persistent state,...) is inherent in verb stems. Verb roots are frequently followed by a "single versus multiple action" suffix that—to some extent—defines the verb's aspect; see section 5.7.2.

Mood (how the hearer should take the content of the utterance relative to his beliefs or behavior) is indicated in various ways. Imperatives are discussed in chapter 14. Interrogatives are discussed in chapter 15.

Evidentiality (i.e., the basis on which one knows the information being communicated) is indicated by clitics; see section 11.1.

Verbs can be modified by adverbs, which may be verbal suffixes (5.12.1) or independent words (5.12.2).

5.7 Verbal categories

Verbs express actions, events, or states. They may be transitive, intransitive, or stative (5.7.1). Some verbs are free, that is, they can occur without a following suffix. Others are bound, requiring a suffix that indicates whether the verb is transitive, intransitive, or stative and whether it is "singular" or "multiple" (5.7.2).

5.7.1 Transitive, intransitive, stative

The principle subclasses of verbs are: transitive, intransitive, and stative.

In 240 the verb à^{x}t^{jh}ùmɨ̀ is transitive, the dog being the direct object. The direct object need not be explicit. For example, when it is clear that one is speaking about a dog, one could simply say 241:

(240) Ó ájtyumɨ́ oohííbyeke.
    ó á^{x}t^{jh}ùmɨ́-ʔì ò:ʔí-:pʲɛ̀-k^{h}ɛ̀   'I saw the dog.'
    I saw-⟨t⟩   dog-⟨SgM⟩-objAn

(241) ó á^{x}t^{jh}ùmɨ́-ʔì (Ó ájtyumɨ́hi) 'I saw (it).'
    I see-⟨t⟩

Intransitive verbs are illustrated in 242 and 243:

(242) ó ák^{h}ù̀-:βɛ́-ʔì   (Ó ácuuvéhi.) 'I sat down.'
    I sit.down-sIn-⟨t⟩

(243) Ó dsɨ̵ɨ̵né (tahjyávu).
    ó tsɨ̀:nɛ́-ʔì (t^{h}ǎ^{G}ʔ hʲá-βù̀)   'I ran (to my house).'
    I run-⟨t⟩   my ⟨shelter⟩-goal

The verb aβʲɛ 'to hurt' may function both as transitive, as in 244a, or as intransitive, as in 244b. In 244c the intransitive verb is made transitive

5.7. VERBAL CATEGORIES

by the addition of the causative suffix. Without the causative, such verbs are used as transitive (as in 244a) only if the subject is inanimate.

(244) a. ò-kʰɛ̀   àβʲɛ́-nɛ̀   (Oke avyéne.)   'It hurts me.'
         I-objAn hurt-⟨ø⟩
     b. ò   áβʲɛ́-ʔì   (O ávyéhi.)   'I hurt.'
        I   hurt-⟨t⟩
     c. ò-kʰɛ̀   áβʲɛ́-tsʰò-ːpɛ̀   (Oke ávyétsoóbe.) 'He hurt me.'
        I-objAn hurt-caus-⟨SgM⟩

Some verbs are inherently stative, indicating a condition or quality, as in 245:

(245) ó tʃʰɛmɛ́-ʔì (Ó cheméhi.) 'I am sick.'
      ó àβʲɛ́-ʔì   (Ó avyéhi.)   'I am in pain.'
      ó ìmí-ʔì   (Ó imíhi.)   'I am good/healthy.'

Inherently active verbs can be made stative—to indicate the result of some action—by the addition of a suffix, as in 246:

(246) ó ákʰù̀-ú̀kʰù̀mú̀-ʔì (Ó ácuúcunúhi) 'I am seated'.
      I sit-sSt-⟨t⟩

Participles can be formed from this (second) type of stative verb by prefixing tʰɛ- 'prtc', followed by either the single action or multiple action suffix. The participles so formed indicate that what they modify is in a state that resulted from the action of the verb. For example, the participle in 247 is formed from the infinitive ákʰù̀-ˣkʰátʲʰɛ̀ (sit-mSt) 'seat':

(247) Ó ájtyumɨ́ mɨ́amúnáakye teácujcátye.

      ó áˣtʲʰùmɨ́-ʔ mɨ́ámúmáà-kʲʰɛ̀ tʰɛ́-ákʰù̀-ˣkʰátʲʰɛ̀
      I see-⟨t⟩   people-objAn   prtc-sit-mSt
      'I see people seated.'

The verbs tʃʰɛmɛ 'to be sick', aβʲɛ 'to hurt' and imi 'to be good' do not form participles, presumably because they become adjectives when they bear two high tones and are followed by an (unwritten) glottal stop.

5.7.2 Single or multiple action

Many verb stems have two forms: SINGLE ACTION verbs indicate an action performed only once or performed just a little. MULTIPLE ACTION verbs indicate that an action is performed multiple times.

To some degree the distinction is aspectual (like punctual versus iterative); in some cases it is like a single action versus an activity distributed

in a population; in some cases it is like a single event versus multiple ones.

BOUND verb roots require a suffix indicating either single or multiple action. For example, akʰɯ- 'to sit' may not occur by itself, but occurs as àkʰɯ́-:βɛ̀ (single action) or as à⁷kʰɯ́-pà (multiple action). FREE roots, like pʰɛː 'go', tsʰa: 'come' and maˣtʃʰo 'eat' do not take a single or multiple action suffix.[12]

The principle suffixes by which single and multiple action verbs are formed are listed in table 5.2. Generally a given root or stem will use one of the pairs listed to form the transitive forms, as well as the pairs for intransitive and stative forms.

Table 5.2 The formation of single and multiple action verbs

	SINGULAR		MULTIPLE	
transi-tive	-Ⓛˣkʰáɾo	(-jcáro)	-Ⓛˣkʰo	(-jco)
	-Ⓛ⁷hákʰo	(-hjáco)	-Ⓛ⁷kʰo	(-hco)
	-Ⓛ○ɾo	(-ɾo)	-Ⓛnɯ	(-nu)
	-Ⓛ○ɾo	(-ɾo)	-ø[a]	
	-Ⓛɯ́kʰɯ	(-úcu)	-Ⓛˣkʰɯ	(-jcu)
	-Ⓛákʰo	(-áco)	-Ⓛjco	(-jco)
	-Ⓛ⁷hʲɯ́kʰɯ	(-hjyúcu)	-Ⓛ⁽⁷⁾kʲʰo	(-hcyo ~ -cyo)
	-Ⓛ○kʰɯ	(-cu)	-Ⓛ○kʰɯ̀mɯ	(-cunu)[b]
	-Ⓛ○kʰɯ	(-cu)	-ø[c]	
intransi-tive	-:βɛ	(-:ve)	-pa	(-ba)[d]
	-ø		-Ⓛ○kʰɯ̀mɯ	(-cunu)
stative	-Ⓛɯkʰɯ̀mɯ	(-ucunu)	-Ⓛˣkʰatʲʰɛ	(-jcatye)

[a] For example itʃaː-jo 'strike-sTr'; compare itʃo 'to cut down (mTr)'.

[b] For example, a̋tɯ-kʰɯ 'drink-sTr'; compare a̋tɯ-kʰɯ̋mɯ 'drink-mTr'.

[c] For example mɛ⁷tɯ-kʰɯ 'drink-sTr'; compare mɛ⁷tɯ 'drink(mTr)'.

[d] The first syllable of the verb to which -pa 'mIn' is suffixed is made heavy by either vowel length, preaspiration, or a glottal stop as in 248b; see section 5.7.3.

Of the various possibilities for transitives, only -Ⓛ○kʰɯ 'sTr' and -Ⓛ○kʰɯ̀mɯ̀ 'mTr' are used with free verbs; the others are used only with bound verb roots. The intransitives with -:βɛ 'sIn' and -pa 'mIn' are formed only from bound verb roots, while -Ⓛ○kʰɯ̀mɯ̀ 'mIn' is used with free verb roots. The statives with -Ⓛɯ̀kʰⓁɯmɯ 'sSt' and -Ⓛˣkʰatʲʰɛ 'mSt' are only formed from bound verb roots.

---

[12] It may be that bound roots lack inherent aspect and thus require a single or multiple action suffix to provide it, whereas free roots have inherent aspect that cannot be overridden by a single or multiple action suffix.

5.7. VERBAL CATEGORIES

Some multiple action verbs require a plural subject. This depends on the nature of the action it indicates: if one person could perform the action indicated by the verb, then the subject may be singular or plural.

For many verbs, the difference between singular and multiple forms is made by both adding a suffix and changing the root. For example, note the glottal stop added to the first syllable of the verb of 248b:

(248) a. Áánu ácuuvéhi.
    á:nùɨ   ák^{h}ùɨ-:βέ-ʔì   'This one sat down.'
    this.SgM   sit-sIn-⟨t⟩
  b. Áátye áhcubáhi.
    á:-t^{jh}ὲ   á^{ʔ}k^{h}ùɨ-pá-ʔì   'Those sat down all at once.'
    that-⟨AnPl⟩ sit-mIn-⟨t⟩

It is also possible to say 249:

(249) á:-t^{jh}ὲ   ák^{h}ùɨ-:βέ-ʔì (Áátye ácuuvéhi.) 'Those sat down.'
    that-⟨AnPl⟩ sit-sIn-⟨t⟩

Unlike 248b, example 249 does not indicate how they sat down, i.e., individually or all together. The singular versus multiple action distinction does not correspond generally to individual versus collective action, but to one instance of an action versus multiple instances of that action.

Some verbs are inherently multiple action, with the single action form marked by the addition of -k^{h}ɯ 'sTr'. For example, as shown in 250a, mɛ^{ʔ}to 'swallow' indicates multiple action (or to put it another way, Bora 'swallow' is inherently iterative). The corresponding single action form in 250b is formed by the addition of -k^{h}ɯ 'single action':

(250) a. Ó mehdó tabójɨ́ɨ́ne.
   b. Ó mehdúcú taabójɨ.
   a. ó <u>mὲ^{ʔ}tó-ʔì</u>   t^{h}àpó-hɨ́:-nὲ   'I swallow pills.'
       I swallow(mTr)-⟨t⟩ cure-⟨disk⟩-pl
   b. ó <u>mὲ^{ʔ}tɨ́ɨ-k^{h}ɨ́-ʔì</u>[13]   t^{h}à:pó-hɨ̀   'I swallow a pill
       I swallow-sTr-⟨t⟩   cure-⟨disk⟩   (in a single gulp).'

With some verbs the single action form indicates doing the action to a small degree, e.g., átɨ́ɨ-k^{h}ùɨ 'to drink a little' and má^{x}tʃ^{h}ó-k^{h}ùɨ 'to eat a small amount':

---

[13] Note that the verb root's final vowel becomes /ɯ/ before /ɯ/.

(251) Ovíí ó majchócú ɨɨ́cúi mepéékií.
   òβíː ó má˟ʧʰó-kʰɯ́ɯ ɨːkʰɯ́ɯ̀ mè pʰɛ́ː-kʰìí.
   wait I eat-sTr   quick SAP go-pur
   'Wait, I'll eat just a little so we can go right away.'

For other verbs, the simple form indicates a single action and the multiple action form is derived from it by the addition of -kʰɯmɯ 'multiple action' (mTr or mIn). For example, in 252a tsɨ̀ːnɛ 'run' is a single action verb. The multiple action form bearing -kʰɯmɯ 'mIn' is seen in 252b:

(252) a. Áátye dsɨɨné mújcojúvu.
   b. Áátye dsɨɨnécunú mújcojúvu.

áː-tʲʰɛ̀   ⎧ a. tsɨ̀ːnɛ́-ˀ   ⎫ mɯ́ɾˣkʰòhɯ́ɯ-βɯ̀ɯ
that-⟨AnPl⟩ ⎨   run(sIn)-⟨t⟩   ⎬ port-goal
             ⎩ b. tsɨ̀ːné-kʰɯ̀mɯ́ɯ-ˀ ⎭
                run-mIn-⟨t⟩

   a. 'They run to the port (all together, as a single group).'
   b. 'They run to the port (one after the other, not as a group).'

5.7.3 Marking multiple action with intransitive verbs

As seen in table 5.2 above, the major pattern for indicating singular versus multiple with intransitive verbs is that the singular form bears -⓪○ːβɛ while the corresponding multiple form bears -⓪○pa.

In addition to the suffix, the first syllable of the multiple form is made heavy. Tables 5.3–5.7 document the various possibilities for making the first syllable heavy.

When the verb begins (C)VCV, i.e., the first syllable is open and the second syllable begins with a consonant, then the first syllable of the multiple form is closed with a glottal stop. See table 5.3.

Table 5.3 Making the first syllable heavy with a glottal stop

SINGLE ACTION		MULTIPLE ACTION		MEANING
àβóːβɛ̀	avóóve	àˀβópà	ahvóba	'cover oneself'
páhɯ̀ɯ́ːβʲɛ̀	bájuíívye	páˀhɯ̀ɯ́pà	báhjuíba	'turn one's back on'
kʰàmáːβɛ̀	camááve	kʰàˀmápà	cahmába	'put together'
kʰàɾɯ́ːβɛ̀	carúúve	kʰàˀɾɯ́ˀpà	cahrúhba	'look up'

continued next page

5.7. VERBAL CATEGORIES

continued from previous page

SINGLE ACTION		MULTIPLE ACTION		MEANING
tʃʰàhá:βɛ̀	chajááve	tʃʰàʔhápà	chahjába	'rot, decompose'
kʰòmí:βʲɛ̀	comíívye	kʰòʔmípà	cohmíba	'double over'
kʰɯ̀hɯ́:βɛ̀	cujúúve	kʰɯ̀ʔhɯ́pà	cuhjúba	'stretch out the hand'
kʰátʃʰìjá:βɛ̀	cáchiyááve	kʰáʔtʃʰìjápà	cáhchiyába	'squirt out liqiud'
kʰákʰòɾó:βɛ̀	cácoróóve	kʰáʔkʰòɾópà	cáhcoróba	'become slack or untied'
kʰápʰàtʲʰɯ́ː:βɛ̀	cápatyúúve	kʰáʔpʰàtʲʰɯ́pà	cáhpatyúba	'stab through'
kʰátsʰòtsʰó:βɛ̀	cátsotsóóve	kʰáʔtsʰòtsʰópà	cáhtsotsóba	'become overfull'
kʰáβàhá:βɛ̀	cávajááve	kʰáʔβàhápà	cáhvajába	'become punctured'
kʰáɲájàhí:βɛ̀	cáñáyajɨ́ɨ́ve	kʰáʔɲájàhípà	cáhñáyajɨ́ba	'rest on one knee'
tòtí:βʲɛ̀	dodíívye	tòʔtípà	dohdíba	'become scratched'
tɯ̀hɯ́:βɛ̀	dujúúve	tɯ̀ʔhɯ́pà	duhjúba	'double over'
tópʰòá:βɛ̀	dópoááve	tóʔpʰòápà	dóhpoába	'become unstuck'
tókpáɾàhí:βɛ̀	dówárajɨ́ɨ́ve	tóʔkpáɾàhípà	dóhwárajɨ́ba	'extend arms with open hands'
ɨɾó:βɛ̀	ɨɾóóve	ɨʔɾópà	ɨhɾóba	'become flexible'
ɨkpá:βɛ̀	ɨwááve	ɨʔkpápà	ɨhwába	'open the mouth'
kʰɛ̀ɾó:βɛ̀	keɾóóve	kʰɛ̀ʔɾópà	kehɾóba	'become visible'
mìhʲó:βɛ̀	mijyóóve	mìʔhʲópà	mihjyóba	'make a detour'
mòjí:βʲɛ̀	moyíívye	mòʔjípà	mohyíba	'penetrate a solid'
nɛ̀ɾí:βʲɛ̀	neɾíívye	nɛ̀ʔɾípà	nehɾíba	'climb up'
pʰàpɛ́:βɛ̀	pabééve	pʰàʔpɛ́pà	pahbéba	'squeeze under the arm'
ɾìhʲá:βɛ̀	rijyááve	ɾìʔhʲápà	rihjyába	'take steps'
tʰòhá:βɛ̀	tojááve	tʰòʔhápà	tohjába	'be stuck by needle'

continued next page

continued from previous page

SINGLE ACTION		MULTIPLE ACTION		MEANING
tsʰɨ̀ɨhá:βɛ̀	tsujááve	tsʰɨ̀ɨ̰hápà	tsuhjába	'disperse'
tʰɨ̀ɨrɨ́ɨ:βɛ̀	turúúve	tʰɨ̀ɨ̰rɨ́ɨpà	tuhrúba	'fall over'
tʰákʰòrɨ́:βɛ̀	tácorɨ́ɨve	tʰá̰kʰòrɨ́pà	táhcorɨ́ba	'undress'
ɨ̀ɨmɨ́ɨ:βɛ̀	umúúve	ɨ̀ɨ̰mɨ́ɨpà	uhmúba	'close the lips'
ɨ́ɨkɨ́ɨrɨ̀ɨnɨ́ɨ:βɛ̀	úgúruúúve	ɨ́ɨ̰kɨ́ɨrɨ̀ɨnɨ́ɨpà	úhgúruúba	'shrink'
ɨ́ɨtsʰɨ̀ɨkʰɨ́ɨ:βɛ̀	útsucúúve	ɨ́ɨ̰tsʰɨ̀ɨkʰɨ́ɨpà	úhtsucúba	'get stuck between'
βìkʲʰó:βɛ̀	vicyóóve	βḭ̀kʲʰópà	vihcyóba	'lie down in hammock'
βɨ̀ɨtó:βɛ̀	vudóóve	βɨ̀ɨ̰tópà	vuhdóba	'become torn apart'
kpàpé:βɛ̀	wabééve	kpà̰pépà	wahbéba	'get entangled'
kpàhɨ́:βɛ̀	wajɨ́ɨve	kpà̰hɨ́pà	wahjɨ́ba	'be put beside'
kpákʰòrɨ́:βɛ̀	wácorɨ́ɨve	kpá̰kʰòrɨ́pà	wáhcorɨ́ba	'become scraped'
kpákòó:βɛ̀	wágoóóve	kpá̰kòópà	wáhgoóba	'be tossed out'
kpárì ʔjó:βɛ̀	wárihyóóve	kpá̰rìʔjópà	wáhrihyóba	'become separated by space'
kpáβàhá:βɛ̀	wávajááve	kpá̰βàhápà	wáhvajába	'become torn apart'

If the first syllable of the singular is already heavy, then the multiple form does not add ʔ. The first syllable might be heavy by being closed by ʔ, as in the examples in table 5.4:

Table 5.4 When the first syllable of the singular is closed by a glottal stop

SINGLE ACTION		MULTIPLE ACTION		MEANING
kʰɨ́ɨʔtsʰìɨ̀ɨ:βɛ̀	cúhtsiúúve	kʰɨ́ɨʔtsʰìɨ́ɨpà	cúhtsiúba	'lie down on the side'
íʔhʲòkʰɨ́ɨ:βɛ̀	íhjyocúúve	íʔhʲòkʰɨ́ɨpà	íhjyocúba	'stand up'
pʰìʔtʃʰɨ́ɨ:βɛ̀	pihchúúve	pʰìʔtʃʰɨ́ɨpà	pihchúba	'mount upon'
kpáʔtàʔɨ́:βɛ̀	wáhdahɨ́ɨve	kpáʔtàʔɨ́pà	wáhdahɨ́ba	'be cut apart'

5.7. VERBAL CATEGORIES

Or it might be heavy by being closed by ˣj, as the examples in table 5.5:

Table 5.5 When the first syllable of the singular is closed by preaspiration

SINGLE ACTION		MULTIPLE ACTION		MEANING
kpáˣpʰòtʃá:βɛ̀	wájpollááve	kpáˣpʰòtʃápà	wájpollába	'roll over'
kpáˣtʲʰɯ̀ʔí:β̲ʲ̲ɛ̲̀	wájtyuhíívye	kpáˣtʲʰɯ̀ʔípà	wájtyuhíba	'become tightly knotted'

The first syllable is made heavy by lengthening the vowel in two cases. First, this is done when the onset of the second syllable is /ʔ/,[14] as in the examples in table 5.6. Second, the first syllable is made heavy by lengthening the vowel when the word begins with (C)V.V, that is, the second syllable lacks an onset,[15] as in the examples in table 5.7.

Table 5.6 Adding vowel length when the second syllable begins with a glottal stop

SINGLE ACTION		MULTIPLE ACTION		MEANING
pàʔʲá:βɛ̀	bahyááve	pà:ʔʲápà	baahyába	'be stacked up'
kʰɛ̀ʔí:βɛ̀	kehíɨve	kʰɛ̀:ʔípà	keehíba	'become visible'
tʃòʔí:β̲ʲ̲ɛ̲̀	llohíívye	tʃò:ʔípà	lloohíba	'surround something'
ɲàʔí:β̲ʲ̲ɛ̲̀	ñahíívye	ɲà:ʔípà	ñaahíba	'become dented'
tsʰɯ̀ʔó:βɛ̀	tsuhóóve	tsʰɯ̀:ʔópà	tsuuhóba	'fold oneself up'
tʰáìʔʲá:βɛ̀	táihyááve	tʰá:ìʔʲápà	tááihyába	'break into'
kpáʔɛ̀hɯ́:βɛ̀	wáhejúúve	kpá:ʔɛ̀hɯ́pà	wááhejúba	'develop a big hole'

Table 5.7 Adding vowel length when the second syllable has no onset

SINGLE ACTION		MULTIPLE ACTION		MEANING
àí:β̲ʲ̲ɛ̲̀	aíívye	à:ípà	aaíba	'burn up'
pɯ̀ɯ́:βɛ̀	buúúve	pɯ̀ɯ́:pà	buuúba	'submerge'
tóɯ̀ʔá:β̲ʲ̲ɛ̲̀	dóuháávye	tó:ɯ̀ʔápà	dóóuhába	'have piece broken off'
pʰòá:βɛ̀	poááve	pʰò:ápà	pooába	'pop open'
pʰíɯ̀mí:β̲ʲ̲ɛ̲̀	píumíívye	pʰí:ɯ̀mípà	píiumíba	'become folded over'

continued next page

---

[14] The first syllable could not be closed by ʔ in this case because the two glottal stops would coalesce, failing to make the first syllable heavy.

[15] The first syllable could not be made heavy by adding ʔ or ˣ because this would be syllabified as the onset of the second syllable.

continued from previous page

SINGLE ACTION		MULTIPLE ACTION		MEANING
tsʰòɨ́ː$\underline{\beta}$ɛ̀	tsoúúve	tsʰòːɨ́ɨpà	tsooúba	'drop off'
βìɨ́ː$\underline{\beta}$ɛ̀	viúúve	βìːɨ́ɨpà	viiúba	'break into'
kpáìʔʲá:$\underline{\beta}$ɛ̀	wáihyááve	kpáːìʔʲápà	wááihyába	'become fractured'

5.8 Valence-changing suffixes

This section describes the valence-increasing suffix -tsʰo 'causative' (5.8.1) and the valence-decreasing suffixes -mɛ̌i 'reflexive or passive' (5.8.2) and -ˣkʰatsʰi 'reciprocal' (5.8.3).

5.8.1 -tso 'causative'

The suffix -tsʰo 'causative (cause or allow)' increases its host's valence. It makes an intransitive verb transitive, the direct object of which is the CAUSEE; see section 10.2.4. For example, the subject of the intransitive clause in 253a is the first person. This becomes the causee—the direct object—of the corresponding transitive in 253b:

(253) a. Ó dsɨ̵ɨ́néhi.
    b. Oohííbyé oke dsɨ́ɨ́netsóhi.
    a.   ó   tsɨ̀ːnɛ́-ʔì   'I ran.'
                   I   run-⟨t⟩   (intransitive)
    b. òːʔí-ːpʲɛ́   ò-$\underline{kʰ}$ɛ̀   tsɨ́ːnɛ̀-tsʰó-ʔì   'The dog made me run.'
        dog-⟨SgM⟩ I-objAn run-caus-⟨t⟩ (transitive)

(254) a. Dsɨ́jɨ́veébe.
    b. Dííbyeke dsɨ́jɨ́vétsoóbe.
    a.   tsɨ́híβɛ̀-ːpɛ̀   'He died.'
                     die-⟨SgM⟩   (intransitive)
    b. tí-ːpʲɛ̀-$\underline{kʰ}$ɛ̀   tsɨ́híβɛ́-tsʰò-ːpɛ̀   'He killed him.'
        that-⟨SgM⟩-objAn die-caus-⟨SgM⟩ (transitive)

When a transitive verb is made causative, its direct object is marked with -βɯ 'goal' and the causee is marked as the direct object, as in 255.[16] The grammatical relations of 255 are shown in figure 5.4.

---

[16]Compare example 671, page 282, ('He showed us his ugly moral character.') in which there are two objects, the inanimate ìɲɛ́ʔnì 'ugly moral character' and the animate mè-kʰɛ̀ 'us'.

5.8. VALENCE-CHANGING SUFFIXES

(255) Dííbyedívú oke íítetsoóbe.
 tí-ːpʲè-tí-βɯ́ ò-kʰɛ̀ íːtʰɛ̀-tsʰò-ːpʲè
 that-⟨SgM⟩-anim-goal I-objAn see-cause-⟨SgM⟩
 'He showed me him (lit. He caused me to see him).'

Figure 5.4 Grammatical relations: 'cause to see'

The grammatical relations of causatives are further discussed in section 10.3.3.

Adding -mɛi 'reflexive or passive' after -tsʰo 'causative' yields only the passive interpretation in which the subject (of the whole) is the causative agent (the one who caused the action):

(256) Íñáhbedívú méénútsámeííbye.
 í ⓖ ɲáʔpɛ̀-tí-βɯ́ mɛ́ːnɯ́-tsʰá-mɛ̀í-ːpʲè
 self brother-anim-goal hit-caus-r/p-⟨SgM⟩
 'He$_i$ provoked his$_i$ brothers to beat him$_i$ up.' (lit. 'He$_i$ allowed himself$_i$ to be beaten up by his$_i$ brothers.')

If we assume that (1) when a transitive verb is made causative, its direct object is marked with -βɯ 'goal' and the causee is marked as the direct object, and (2) reflexivization identifies the direct object with the subject, then example 256 is problematic. We assume that the agent of HIT is the subject and the patient is the direct object, as consistent with UTAH, the "uniformity of theta assignment hypothesis" (Baker 1988:46f).

- If, on the one hand, we first apply causativization and then reflexivization, as in the first diagram in figure 5.5, the order of verbal suffixes is correct but the subject of the whole is incorrectly identified as the agent of HIT.
- If, on the other hand, we apply reflexivization before causativization, as in the second diagram in figure 5.5, the verbal suffixes are incorrectly ordered. Further, the patient of HIT ends up as the direct object rather than the goal, so would incorrectly bear -kʰɛ (-ke) rather than -βɯ (-vu) (as in 256).

```
              AG   PAT  HIT                      AG   PAT  HIT
              |    |    |          UTAH          |    |    |          UTAH
              [SU  DO   HIT]                     [SU  DO   HIT]
         AG   |    |               CAUSE         |   /                REFL/PASS
         |    |    |                             | /
         [SU  DO   GOAL HIT-CAUS]                [SU       HIT-R/P]
         |   /     |               REFL/PASS  AG |                    CAUSE
         |  /      |                             |
         SU        GOAL HIT-CAUS-R/P             SU   DO   HIT-R/P-CAUS
```

Figure 5.5 Grammatical relations: reflexive and causative

Neither ordering of reflexivization and causativization yields a satisfactory result. Figure 5.6 seems correct but is inconsistent with the generalization that, when transitive verbs are causativized, the subject (causee) becomes the direct object and the direct object becomes a goal.

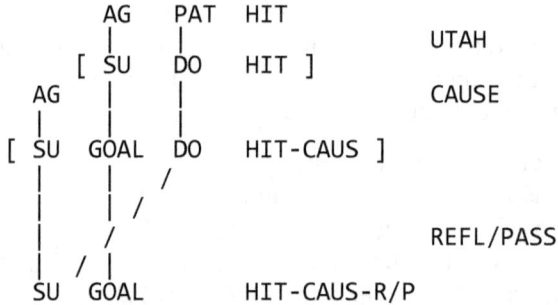

Figure 5.6 Another view of 'he allowed himself to be beaten'

We leave this question unresolved. Other examples of this type follow:

(257) Ó wáhdáhɨnútsámeíhi.
    ó kpá'tá'ínúɨ-tsʰá-mèí-ʔì[17]   'I caused myself to be cut.'
    I cut-caus-r/p-⟨t⟩

(258) Ó táábótsámeítyé.
    ó tʰá:pó-tsʰá-mèí-tʲʰɛ́   'I am going to have myself treated.'
    I cure-caus-r/p-go.do

Likewise, when -ˣkʰatsʰi 'reciprocal' follows -tsʰo 'causative', it is understood that the referents of the subject caused each other to do the action indicated by the verb; for example:

---

[17] In many cases the causative suffix has /o/, whereas in 263 and 257 it has /a/. This reflects the fact that most speakers of the Iñeje dialect apply a rule whereby -tsʰo becomes -tsʰa before -mèi.

5.8. VALENCE-CHANGING SUFFIXES

(259) Tájtsɨɨménemútsí táátsójcatsíhi.

tʰá ˣtsʰɨ́ːméne̖-mútsʰí tʰáː-<u>tsʰó-ˣkʰàtsʰí</u>-ʔì
my child-⟨DuM⟩   cry-caus-recip-⟨t⟩
'My children made each other cry.'

On the other hand, -tsʰo 'causative' *after* -mɛ́i 'reflexive or passive' yields only the reflexive interpretation in which the subject is understood as making the causee do the action to himself; for example:

(260) Oke wáhdáhɨnúmeíchoóbe.

ò-kʰɛ̀   kpáʔtáʔí-nɨ́ɨ-mèí-tʃʰò¹⁸-ópɛ̀   { a. 'He made me cut myself.'
I-objAn cut-mTr-r/p-caus-⟨SgM⟩   { b. *'He made someone cut me.'

The changes in grammatical relations can be understood as in figure 5.7:

```
        AG  PAT   CUT
         |   |     |               UTAH
      [ SU  DO   CUT ]
         | /                      REFLEXIVE/PASSIVE
      [ SU        CUT-R/P ]
   AG    |                         CAUSE
    |    |
    SU   DO     CUT-R/P-CAUSE
```

Figure 5.7 Grammatical relations: 'cause to cut oneself'

Likewise, -tsʰo 'causative' after -ˣkʰatsʰi 'reciprocal' indicates that the subject causes the referents of the direct object to do the action indicated by the verb to each other; for example:

(261) Múhtsikye méénújcatsíchoóbe.

mɨ́ɨʔtsʰì-kʲʰɛ̀   méːnɨ́ɨ-ˣkʰàtsʰí-tʃʰòː-pɛ̀   'He made us (dual)
we(DuM)-objAn hit-recip-caus-⟨SgM⟩   hit each other.'

5.8.2 -mei 'reflexive or passive'

When -mɛi 'reflexive or passive' is attached to a transitive verb, the combination is an intransitive verb indicating that the subject (rather than some other object) was affected by the verb's action. The agent of that action can be understood as the subject himself, that is, "reflexively," as in 262a, or as some other person, that is, "passively," as in 262b:

---

[18]In example 260 the causative suffix could also be -tsʰo.

(262) Ó wáhdáhɨnúmeí.

ó ƙpá⁷tá?ɨ-nú-<u>mèí</u>   { a. 'I cut myself.'
I cut-mTr-r/p   { b. 'I have been cut (by someone).'

Whether a reflexive or a passive interpretation is appropriate requires a context. For example, without a context one would not know whether 263 referred to someone who had been assassinated or to someone who had committed suicide:

(263) Juuvárí íjcyaabe tsaapi dsɨ́jɨvétsámeííbye.

hùːβá-ɾí   íˣkʲʰà-ːpè Ⓐ [tsʰà-ːpʰì   tsɨ́hɨ̀βɛ́-tsʰá-mèí]-ːpʲɛ̀
road-oblIn be-⟨SgM⟩   one-⟨SgM⟩   die-caus-r/p   -⟨SgM⟩

'In the road there is a person who { was killed   },'
                                    { killed himself }

See section 5.8.1 regarding the interaction of -mɛi 'reflexive or passive' and -tsʰo 'causative'.

Some verbs appear to be the fusion of a root and the reflexive suffix. For example, ƙpakʰimʲɛ̌i 'work' was undoubtedly ƙpakʰi-mʲɛ̌i (work-r/p) but is now co-lexicalized as a single morpheme. (Note that it preserves the lexically marked tone of the reflexive suffix.) The same is true for íˣtsʰamɛ̌i 'think', presumably from íˣtsʰa-mɛ̌i (think-r/p).

5.8.3 -jcatsi 'reciprocal'

A reciprocal verb indicates that the referents of the subject (which must be dual or plural) act on one another. Reciprocal verbs are formed by adding -ˣkʰatsʰi 'reciprocal' to the verb. For example, in 264 the brothers hit each other:

(264) Táñáhbemútsí méénújcatsíhi.

tʰá Ⓖ ɲá-⁷pè-mútsʰí   méːnɯ́-ˣkʰàtsʰí-?ì
my   sib-⟨SgM⟩-⟨DuM⟩ hit-recip-⟨t⟩

'My two brothers are hitting each other (fighting).'

(265) Muhtsi méihjyúvájcatsí.

mùɾ⁷tsʰì mɛ́ ìʔhʲɯ́βá-ˣkʰàtsʰí-?(ì)   'We two are speaking
we(Du) SAP speak-recip-⟨t⟩   to each other.'

5.9 Tense

Bora verbs distinguish present-past versus future tense. Tense is further marked by second-position clitics, as discussed more completely below. We begin by making some comments about the unmarked present-past tense (5.9.1). We then turn to the future tense (5.9.2). Finally we describe the second position clitics (5.9.3).

5.9.1 The present-past tense

The unmarked tense of Bora verbs is present-past (realis). These do not distinguish past (prior) events from present ones, that is events happening at the time of speaking. Whether past or present is intended be inferred from context. For example, in answer to "What is your brother doing?" 266 would be understood as 'He is working' but in answer to "What did your brother do yesterday?" it would be understood as 'He worked':

(266) kpák^hím^jèí-:p^jè   (Wákímyeííbye.) { a. 'He is working.'
      work-⟨SgM⟩   { b. 'He worked.'

Of course, the time reference may be made explicit by a time adverb, such as ì:h^jù̀ 'yesterday' in 267:

(267) Táñahbe wákímyeí iíjyu.
      t^há ⓖ ɲà^ʔpè   kpák^hím^jèí-^ʔ ì:h^jù̀   'My brother worked
      my   brother   work-⟨t⟩   yesterday   yesterday.'

5.9.2 The future tense

The future tense indicates that the action, event or state indicated by the verb will happen subsequent to the time of speaking. Future tense is marked by the addition of the future morpheme at the position indicated in figure 5.2, page 135. This morpheme has two forms, which are briefly described and illustrated here; for further discussion see appendix D, page 429, item 1110.

First, when a suffix *other than* -ⓛ◯ʔi ⟨t⟩ follows, the future morpheme is -i.[19] For example, consider 268b (in which -ⓛʧɛ̀ ⟨SgF⟩ follows the future suffix):

---

[19] This morpheme and the "projected time" clitic discussed in section 5.9.3.3 may be one and the same morpheme but we treat them separately because -i 'future' occurs only on verbs (a distributional difference) and never has the additional syllable /:k^{jh}è/ as does the "projected time" clitic (a formal difference).

(268) Íwajyámú { a. níjtyulle.
               { b. níjtyúille.

í kpah̬ʲámúɨ { a. níˣtʲʰùɨ-tʃɛ̀   'She washes/washed
self clothes {   wash-⟨SgF⟩   her clothes'
             { b. níˣtʲʰúɨ-ì-tʃɛ̀   'She will wash
             {   wash-fut-⟨SgF⟩   her clothes.'

The tone of -i 'future' depends on the suffix that follows. In 268b it bears low tone because of -⓪tʃɛ ⟨SgF⟩, but when followed by -⓪○mɛ ⟨AnPl⟩, it bears high tone: níˣtʲʰùɨ-í-mʲɛ̀ 'they will wash'. This is further illustrated with -⓪tʰɯ 'negative' in example 269b:

(269) a. Nɨ́jtyúille íwajyámu.
      b. Tsá dille níjtyúityú(ne) íwajyámu.

a.   níˣtʲʰúɨ-ì-tʃɛ̀   ⎫
           wash-fut-⟨SgF⟩   ⎪ í kpah̬ʲámùɨ
b. tsʰá? tì-tʃɛ̀   níˣtʲʰúɨ-ì-tʲʰúɨ-(nɛ̀) ⎬ self clothes
   not that-⟨SgF⟩ wash-fut-neg-⟨n⟩   ⎭

a. 'She will wash her clothes.'
b. 'She will not wash her clothes.'

Second, when the future tense suffix is followed by -⓪○ʔi ⟨t⟩, the future is indicated by -⓪ː, that is, a low tone on host's final syllable with the lengthening of that vowel. The verb so formed generally occurs phrase finally, so it undergoes PLTS, resulting in adjacent homorganic vowels, the first bearing low tone, the second bearing high tone. For example, compare the (unmarked) present-past tense with the future tense in 270a and b, as well as in 271a and b.

(270) a. ò pʰɛ́ː-ʔì   (o pééhi) 'I go.'
         I go-⟨t⟩
      b. ó pʰɛ̀ː-ʔì   (ó peéhi) 'I will go.'
         I go-fut-⟨t⟩

(271) a. ó àːʔɨ́βɛ̀-tʰɛ́-ʔì   (Ó aahɨvetéhi.) 'I go to visit.'
         I visit-go.do-⟨t⟩
      b. ó àːʔɨ́βɛ́-tʰɛ̀ː-ʔì   (Ó aahɨvéteéhi.) 'I will go to visit.'
         I visit-go.do-fut-⟨t⟩

The tone derivations of the verbs in 271 are given in figure 5.8. See also examples 272–274 and 1111, page 430.

5.9. TENSE

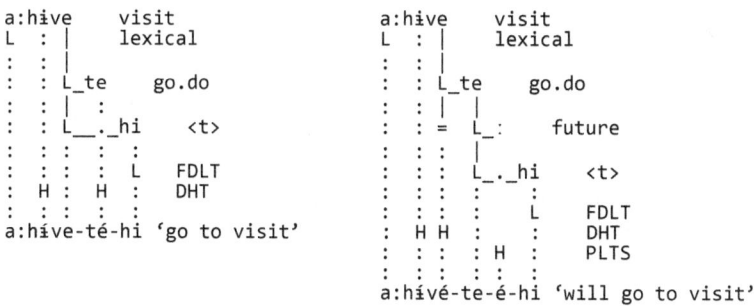

Figure 5.8 TD: a:hɨ́vetéhi, a:hɨ́véteéhi

(272) a. Ó nijtyú táwajyámu.

b. Ó níjtyuú táwajyámu.

a. ó nìˣtʲʰɨ́ɨ-ʔ   tʰá ḳpah̊ʲámɨ̀ɨ   'I wash(ed) my clothes.'
   I wash-⟨t⟩   my clothes

b. ó nɨ́ˣtʲʰɨ̀ɨ-ɨ́ɨ-ʔ   tʰá ḳpah̊ʲámɨ̀ɨ   'I will wash my clothes.'
   I wash-fut-⟨t⟩ my clothes

(273) a. ó màˣtʃʰó-ʔì   (Ó majchóhi.) 'I eat.'
   I eat-⟨t⟩

b. ó máˣtʃʰò-ó-ʔì (Ó májchoóhi.) 'I will eat.'
   I eat-fut-⟨t⟩

(274) a. ó máˣtʃʰò-tʰɛ́-ʔì   (Ó májchotéhi.) 'I go to eat.'
   I eat-go.do-⟨t⟩

b. ó máˣtʃʰó-tʰɛ̀-ɛ́-ʔì   (Ó májchóteéhi.) 'I will go to eat.'
   I eat-go.do-fut-⟨t⟩

5.9.3 Tense-marking second-position clitics

The tense may be further specified by a clitic at the end of the sentence's first constituent: word, phrase, subordinate clause, or in some cases the first constituent of a subordinate clause. There are three such clitics: -Ⓛ○pʰɛ ~ -Ⓗṍ, 'remote past', -⁽ʔ⁾nɛ 'recent past', and -i(íkʲʰɛ) 'projected time'.

The recent and remote past tense clitics require a present-past verb; they do not co-occur with a verb marked for future tense. The projected time clitic may co-occur with a present-past verb (as in 285a) or a future verb (as in 284b).

5.9.3.1 -pe 'remote past'

The clitic -pʰɛ (-pe) ~ -Ⓗŏ̱ 'remote past (rem)' indicates that the event happened a long time ago (at least some months ago). The -pʰɛ form is illustrated in 275a and 276a. The -Ⓗŏ̱ form (1) imposes a high tone on the preceeding syllable and (2) forms an additional syllable that bears low tone, the vowel of which is the same as the preceding vowel; see examples 275b and 276b:

(275) a. Táñahbépe meenú ihjya.
     b. Táñahbée meenú ihjya.

    a. tʰá Ⓖ ɲa̱-ˀpɛ́-p̲ʰ̲ɛ̲̀   ⎫
    b. tʰá Ⓖ ɲa̱-ˀp̲ɛ̲́-̲ɛ̲̀   ⎬ mɛ̀ːnɯ́-ʔì ì͡ʔ hʲà
       my   sib-⟨SgM⟩-rem ⎭ make-⟨t⟩ self house
'My brother made his house (some time ago).'

(276) a. Aanéhjápe úmɨvaábe.
     b. Aanéhjáa úmɨvaábe.

    a. àːnɛ́-ˀhá-p̲ʰ̲ɛ̲̀   ⎫
    b. àːnɛ́-ˀh̲á̲-̲à̲   ⎬ úmɨβàːpɛ̀ a,b. 'Then he escaped
       thm-⟨ø⟩-nwit-rem ⎭ escape-⟨SgM⟩   (some time ago).'

The following could be single word answers to the question *Who did that?*:

(277) tì-ːpʲɛ́-p̲ʰ̲ɛ̲̀ɛ̲́   (Diibyépeé.) 'He (some time ago).'
     that-⟨SgM⟩-rem-emph

(278) òː-p̲ʰ̲ɛ̲̀ (Oópe.) 'I (some time ago)'
     I-rem

5.9.3.2 -ne ~ -hne 'recent past'

The clitic -⁽ʔ⁾nɛ (-ne ~ -hne) 'recent past' (rec) indicates that the event happened recently, as illustrated in 279–283:

(279) Táñahbéne meenú ihjya.

     tʰá Ⓖ ɲa̱-ˀpɛ́-n̲ɛ̲̀   mɛ̀ːnɯ́-ʔì ì͡ʔ hʲà
     my   sib-⟨SgM⟩-rec make-⟨t⟩ self house
     'My brother recently made his house.'

(280) tì-ːpʲɛ́-n̲ɛ̲̀   mɛ̀ːnɯ́-ʔì (Diibyéne meenúhi.) 'He recently
     that-⟨SgM⟩-rec make-⟨t⟩   made it.'

(281) ò-ʔné ó mè:núɨ-ʔì (Ohné ó meenúhi.) 'I recently did it.'
 I-rec I make-⟨t⟩

The single words of 282 and 283 could be used to answer the questions *Who did that?*

(282) tì-:pʲɛ́-nèɛ́-ˣ   (Diibyéneéj.) 'He (recently).'
 that-⟨SgM⟩-rec-voc

(283) ò-ʔnɛ̀-ˣ   (Ohnej.) 'I (recently).'
 I-rec-voc

(See section 10.9 regarding the [ˣ] (j) glossed 'vocative'.)

5.9.3.3 -ì ∼ -iíkye 'projected time (PT)'

The clitic -ì[20] (-i) ∼ -ì:kʲʰɛ̀ (-iíkye) 'projected time' may indicate that an event is about to happen, as in 284:

(284) tʰá Ⓖ ɲa̋-ʔpɛ́-ì { a. pʰɛ́-hùɨkʰó:-ʔì (Táñahbéi péjucóóhi.)
   my   sib-⟨SgM⟩-PT   go-now-⟨t⟩
                          b. pʰɛ́-húɨkʰò-ó-ʔì (Táñahbéi péjúcoóhi.)
                             go-now-fut-⟨t⟩
 a. 'My brother is about to go.'
 b. 'My brother will go soon.'

This clitic may provoke the doubling of a pronoun. For example, compare 285a and b:

(285) a. ò pʰɛ́-hùɨkʰó:-ʔì (O péjucóóhi.) 'I am going now.'
    I go-now-⟨t⟩

 b. ó-ì ò pʰɛ́-hùɨkʰó:-ʔì (Ói o péjucóóhi.) 'I am now
    I-PT I go-now-⟨t⟩   about to go.'

The clitic -ì ∼ -ì:kʲʰɛ̀ 'projected time' may also indicate that the situation (or event) indicated by the verb persists despite our expectations or desires.

(286) Tsáhái dibye májchotú(ne)
 tsʰá̋ʔá-ì tì-pʲɛ̀   máˣtʃʰò-tʰúɨ-(nɛ̀)
 not-PT that-⟨SgM⟩ eat-neg-⟨n⟩
 'He has not eaten yet.' or 'He still has not eaten.'

This clitic often accompanies a future verb, as in 287:

---
[20] See footnote 19.

(287) Diibyéi méénuúhi.
   tì-:pʲɛ́-ɩ̀²¹   mɛ́:nɨ̀ɾ-ɨ́ɾ-ʔì   'He still expects to do it.'
   that-⟨SgM⟩-PT do-fut-⟨t⟩

The clitic -ɩ̀:kʲʰɛ̀ 'PT' may be used for single-word replies to questions:

(288) ó(:)-ɩ̀:kʲʰɛ̀ (óiíkye or óóiíkye) 'I (projected time).'
   I-PT

(289) tsʰá̋ʔá-ɩ̀:kʲʰɛ̀ (tsáháiíkye) 'not yet'
   not-PT

5.10 Aspect

Aspect is indicated by the system of singular versus multiple action verbs and by -ʔiˣkʲʰa 'imperfective, habitual'.

5.10.1 Aspect and the singular versus multiple contrast

A system of verbal contrasts involving singular versus multiple action is discussed in section 5.7.2. This system implements two aspectual contrasts: active versus stative and iterative versus noniterative. Depending on the verb, the singular versus multiple contrast may also distinguish perfective versus imperfective and telic versus atelic. See section 5.7.2 for details.

5.10.2 Aspect indicated by -ʔiˣkʲʰa 'habitual'

The verb iˣkʲʰa (ijcya) 'be' has an affixal form -ʔiˣkʲʰa (-hijcya) that, with some exceptions, occurs as a second-position clitic, where it frequently follows demonstrative pronouns. It indicates habitual or characteristic action, and will be glossed 'habitual' (hab). For example, in 290 and 291 it follows the subject phrase of a predicate complement construction indicating a characteristic of the subject:

---

[21] Note that the pronoun does not begin with a short vowel despite its being the subject. This must be due to the intervention of -i 'PT' between the pronoun and the verb. The same is true when other clitics intervene; witness:

   tí-:pʲɛ̀-ɾɛ̀   pʰɛ́hɨ̀ɾkʰó:ʔì.   'Only he is going.'
   that-⟨SgM⟩-only go-now-⟨t⟩

5.10. ASPECT

(290) Dííbyéhijcya majchópíwu.

tí-ːpʲɛ́-ʔìˣkʲʰà̰   màˣʧʰó-pʰí-kpɯ   'He is a glutton'
that-⟨SgM⟩-hab eat-excess-aug

(291) Dííbyéhijcya ávyeta ími.

tí-ːpʲɛ́-ʔìˣkʲʰà̰   áβʲɛ̀tʰà ímḭ   'He is always very good.'
that-⟨SgM⟩-hab very   good

In 292a -ʔiˣkʲʰa occurs on the predicate complement rather than the subject. (292b and c are given for comparison.)

(292) a. Ehdúhijcya dííbye.

b. Ehdu íjcyaábye.

c. Ehdu dííbye íjcya.

a. è-ʔtɯ́-ʔìˣkʲʰà̰   tí-ːpʲɛ̀   'That's how he is.'
that-⟨like⟩-hab that-⟨SgM⟩

b. è-ʔtɯ̀   íˣkʲʰà̰-ːpʲɛ̀   'He is like that.'
that-⟨like⟩ be-⟨SgM⟩

c. è-ʔtɯ̀   [tí-ːpʲɛ̀ᴳ   íˣkʲʰà̰]   'His life (existence)
that-⟨like⟩ that-⟨SgM⟩ existence   is like that.'

In 293 -ʔiˣkʲʰa occurs on the direct object, but note that the apparent main clause is really a subordinate clause (as indicated by the classifier and by the verb's initial high tone):

(293) Okéhijcya ditye ájcune.

ò-kʰɛ́ᵢ-ʔìˣkʲʰà̰   [tì-tʲʰɛ̀   ∅ᵢ áˣkʰɯ̀]-nɛ̀
I-objAn-hab that-⟨AnPl⟩ give -⟨∅⟩

'They always give to me.' (lit. 'It is to me that they give it.')

Quite transparently, -ʔiˣkʲʰa is the verb iˣkʲʰa 'be' preceded by a complement-terminating -ʔ (the same ʔ that terminates predicate adjectives, as discussed in section 7.8.3). This analysis is reflected in 294:

(294) Ó pehíjcyá mújcojúvu.

ó pʰɛ̀-ʔ   íˣkʲʰá-ʔ mɯ́ˣkʰòhɯ́-βɯ̀
I go-PredAdj be-⟨t⟩ port-goal

'I habitually go to the port.'

Although this analysis is undoubtedly correct for some diachronic stage or some synchronic level, there are some good reasons for considering it to be a suffix:

1. -ʔ iˣkʲʰa and the word that precedes it belong to the same tonal phrase (respecting the *LLX constraint at the boundary between them).
2. -ʔ iˣkʲʰa may suppress preaspiration in the verb to which it is suffixed. Such is the case in 295, where in each example the second instance of iˣkʲʰa 'be' suppresses the preaspiration of the first:

(295) méícyahíjcyáhi
    mé íkʲʰà-ʔ   íˣkʲʰá-ʔì   'we are continually being…'
    SAP be-PredAdj be-⟨t⟩

    ícyahíjcyátsihdyu
    íkʲʰà-ʔ   íˣkʲʰá-tsʰì-ʔtʲùɨ   'upon that having been done'
    be-PredAdj be-⟨place⟩-sou

3. Nothing can intervene between -ʔ and iˣkʲʰa. For example, if a subject marking proclitic occurs, it must precede the verb that -ʔ iˣkʲʰa follows, as in 296:

(296) Táiiñújɨvu o pécooca ó ávúhcúhíjcyaá paíjyuváré tééhí pañétu.
    tʰá i:ɲúɨhì-βùɨ ò pʰɛ́-kʰò:kʰà ó áβúɨʔkʰúɨ-ʔ   íˣkʲʰà-:-ʔ
    my land-goal I go-when I bathe-PredAdj be-fut-⟨t⟩

    pʰà-íhʲùɨ-βá-ɾɛ́   tʰɛ́:ʔí Ⓖ pʰaɲɛ́-tʰùɨ
    all-⟨time⟩-pl-only river inside-sou
    'When I go to my land, I will bathe every day in the river.'

For these reasons we will generally treat the combination of -ʔ and -iˣkʲʰa as a single suffix. And this is consistent with the Bora writing system, in which it is written as a suffix: -hijcya. Other examples are given in 297 and 298:

(297) Paíjyuváré ó pehíjcyá mújcojúvu.
    pʰà-íhʲùɨ-βá-ɾɛ́ ó pʰɛ̀-ʔíˣkʲʰá-ʔì múɨˣkʰòhúɨ-βùɨ
    all-⟨time⟩-pl-only I go-hab-⟨t⟩ port-goal
    'I go to the port every day.'

(298) Cóómívu ipyéécooca wákímyeíhíjcyáiíbye.
    kʰó:mí-βùɨ ì pʲʰɛ́:-kʰò:kʰà kpákʰímʲèí-ʔíˣkʲʰá-ì-:pʲɛ̀
    town-goal self go-when work-hab-fut-⟨SgM⟩
    'When he goes to town, he will work regularly.'

In most of these examples the meaning is habitual; however in 1151, page 436, it seems to be more generally imperfective than specifically habitual.

5.11 Mood

Mood indicates the speaker's attitude regarding the content of a sentence: affirming it, denying it, asking about it, ordering another to do it, and so forth. The unmarked mood is declarative. Imperatives are discussed in chapter 14, and interrogatives are discussed in chapter 15.

5.12 Adverbs

Affixal adverbs are discussed in 5.12.1 and lexical adverbs in 5.12.2.

5.12.1 Affixal adverbs

Some suffixes (or clitics) modify verbs in ways that seem adverbial (going beyond matters like tense, aspect, and argument structure). In this section we will describe two of these.

5.12.1.1 -juco (ː) 'now'

The verbal suffix -ⓁOhǔkʰoː 'now' is obviously related to the clitic -ⓁOhǔkʰo 'focus' discussed in section 11.2.2. The difference is that the verbal suffix is a temporal pointer, translated 'now', 'already', 'still' or 'yet', whereas the clitic marks information as focal.

In some cases the event indicated by the verb to which -hǔkʰoː is suffixed happens at the time of speaking, so is translated 'now'. See examples 285a and b, page 153; 543, page 241; 738, page 299; and 1062, page 405.

In other cases the event indicated by the verb happened before the time of speaking, as in 299 (where -hǔkʰoː is translated 'already') and the negative, as in 300 (where it is translated 'yet'). See also 222, page 129, and 761, page 306.

(299) màˣtʃʰó-hǔkʰòːpè (Majchójúcoóbe.) 'He has already eaten.'
　　　eat-now-⟨SgM⟩

(300) máˣtʃʰó-hǔkʰó-ːpè-híːβà (Májchójucóóbejɨ́ɨva.)
　　　eat-now-⟨SgM⟩-neg
　　　'He has not yet eaten.'

5.12.1.2   -ro ~ -ra ~ -yo ~ -ya 'frustrative, contraexpectation'

The suffix -ɾo ~ -ɾa ~ -jo ~ -ja 'frustrative, contraexpectation,' indicates that the action referred to by the verb does not fulfill its purpose, does not turn out well, or was done in vain. When -ʔì ⟨t⟩ follows, -ɾà ~ -jà is used, as in 301 and 302:

(301) Ó májchoráhi.
    ó má˟tʃʰò-ɾá-ʔì   'I have eaten (but not satisfactorily).'
    I eat-frs-⟨t⟩

(302) Ó májchóiyáhi.
    ó má˟tʃʰó-ì-já-ʔì   'I want to eat (but
    I eat-fut-frs-⟨t⟩   there is nothing to eat).'

Otherwise, that is when -ʔì ⟨t⟩ does not follow, -ɾo ~ -jo is used, as in 303 and 304:

(303) má˟tʃʰò-ɾó-mɛ̀ (Májchoróme.) 'They eat (but want more).'
    eat-frs-⟨AnPl⟩

(304) Májchóiyóme.
    má˟tʃʰó-ì-jó-mɛ̀   'They would like to eat
    eat-fut-frs-⟨AnPl⟩   (but there isn't anything).'

The suffix -ɾa ~ -ɾo 'frustrative, contraexpectation' may also express an unfulfilled desire (somewhat like a subjunctive):

(305) Úúma o pééiyáhi.
    ɯ́ː-mà ò pʰɛ́ː-ì-já-ʔì   'I would like to go with you
    you-with I go-fut-frs-⟨t⟩ (but I am not able).'

In example 306 the subject is a relative clause containing -ɾo 'frustrative, contraexpectation':

(306) Chéméroobe wákímyeítyéhi.
    tʃʰɛ́mɛ́-ɾò-ːpè kpákʰímʲɛ̀í-tʲʰɛ́-ʔì
    sick-frs-⟨SgM⟩ work-go.do-⟨t⟩
    'Even though he was sick, he went to work.'

Section 11.2.5 has further examples with the 'contraexpectation' meaning. Compare the preceding example (306) with 790.

5.12.2 Lexical adverbs

Bora has few lexical adverbs but words of other categories, especially adjectives, may be used as adverbial modifiers. (There is also a mechanism for deriving adverbs from adjectives; see section 4.3.7.) Whether lexical, derived, or a word of another category, an "adverbs' may indicate manner, time, place, duration, distance, quantity, or reason, (among other possibilities), as now illustrated.

An adverb may indicate *how* an action is carried out:

(307) ímí͡ʔ   kpák^hím^jɛ̂ì-ːp^jɛ̀ (Ímí wákímyéííbye.) 'He works well.'
      good work-⟨SgM⟩

(308) ɨ̵ːk^hɯ́ɯ̀ʔ tsʰàː-ːpɛ̀   (Ɨ̵́ɨ̵cúi tsaábe.) 'He came quickly.'
      quick come-⟨SgM⟩

(309) ɨ̵ːk^hɯ́ɯ̀ mɛ̀ áʔtò (Ɨ̵́ɨ̵cúi meáhdo.) 'Hurry and pay.'
      quick SAP pay

An adverb may indicate *when* the event took place:

(310) Péjcore eene méénúiíbye.

   p^hɛ́^xkʰòrɛ̀ [22] ɛ̀ː-nɛ̀   méːnɯ́-ì-ːp^jɛ̀   'He will make that (me-
   tomorrow   that-⟨ø⟩ make-fut-⟨SgM⟩   dial) thing tomorrow.'

Time adverbs may be restricted as to the tense with which they co-occur. For example, ìːh^jɯ́-ìh^jɯ̀ 'yesterday' may not co-occur with the future (311b) and pʰɛ́^xkʰòrò 'tomorrow' may not co-occur with the present-past (311d), as shown in 311:

(311) ìːh^jɯ́-ìh^jɯ̀ ò { pʰɛ́ː-ʔì ; go-⟨t⟩ ; *pʰɛ̀-ɛ́-ʔì ; go-fut-⟨t⟩ } Iijyúijyu o { a. péé 'I went ; b. *peé yesterday.' }
      yesterday I

      pʰɛ́^xkʰòrò ó { *pʰɛ́ː-ʔì ; go-⟨t⟩ ; pʰɛ̀-ɛ́-ʔì ; go-fut-⟨t⟩ } Péjcoro ó { c. *péé 'I will go ; d. peé tomorrow.' }
      tomorrow I

An adverb may indicate *how long* the event persisted, as in 312:

(312) Tsúúcaja íjcyaabe aáhɨ.

   tsʰɯ́ːkʰàhà ɨ́^xk^{jh}àː-ːpɛ̀ àːʔì   'He was at home a long time.'
   long.time   be-⟨SgM⟩   home

An adverb may indicate *where* the event took place, as in 313:

---
[22] pʰɛ́^xkʰòrɛ̀ 'tomorrow' may derive from pʰɛ́^xkʰo 'night' and -rɛ 'only'.

(313) Tsá dibye téhulle íjcyatú.

tsʰá²ᴴ tì-pʲè   tʰɛ́-ʔùtʃɛ̀   íˣkʲʰà-tʰúɨ   'He is not there.'
not that-⟨SgM⟩ that-⟨place⟩ be-neg

An adverb may indicate *how far* from the place of speaking the event takes place:

(314) Tsíhulle wákímyeííbye.

tsʰí-ʔùtʃɛ̀   kpákʰímʲèí-:pʲè   'He is working far off.'
other-⟨yonder⟩ work-⟨SgM⟩

An adverb may indicate *how many times* the event happened:

(315) Tsáijyúré peebe téhullévu.

tsʰá-ìhʲúɨ-ɾɛ́   pʰɛ̀-:pè   tʰɛ́-ʔùtʃɛ́-βùɨ
one-time-only go-⟨SgM⟩ that-yonder-goal
'He went over there only once.'

An adverb may indicate *why* something happened:

(316) Téénéllii tsá tsíímene májchotú.

tʰɛ́:-nɛ́-tʃì: tsʰá²ᴴ tsʰí:mènè máˣtʃʰò-tʰúɨ
that-⟨ø⟩-motive not child eat-neg
'For that reason the child does not eat.'

An adverb may be interrogative, asking about an event's manner, time, place, reason, and so forth. For example, in 317 the adverb asks about the time:

(317) ¿Múijyú tsááíbye díícyáánií?

múɨ̀ɨ̀hʲúɨ tsʰá:-ì-:pʲè   tí: ⓒ kʲʰá:nìí
when come-fut-⟨SgM⟩ your father
'When does your father come?'

The degree adverb áβʲètʰà 'very (much)' may modify a verb, an adverb, an adjective or a noun. In 318 it modifies the verb, in 319 it modifies the adjective imi 'good' used as an adverb, in 320 it modifies the adjective imi 'good' used as a predicate, and in 321 it modifies the noun ìá:pè 'animal'.

(318) áβʲètʰà   kpákʰímèí-:pʲè (Ávyeta wákímeííbye.) 'He works
very.much work-⟨SgM⟩   hard.'

(319) áβʲètʰà   ímí² kpákʰímèí-:pʲè (Ávyeta ímí wákímeííbye.)
very.much good work-⟨SgM⟩
'He works very well.'

5.12. ADVERBS

(320) áβʲètʰà   ímíʔ tì-ːpʲè   (Ávyeta ímí diíbye.) 'He (is)
very.much good that-⟨SgM⟩   very good.'

(321) áβʲétʰá   ìá-ːpè   (Ávyétá iáábe.) 'He (is) a brute.'
very.much animal-⟨SgM⟩

In 322 áβʲètʰà 'very (much)' works together with -hɨɨkʰo 'focus' to indicate the sentence's veracity. Both modify the predicate, which is the noun tì-ːpʲè 'he':

(322) Ávyeta diibyéjuco.
   áβʲètʰà   tì-ːpʲé-hɨɨkʰò   'It is really HE.'
   very.much that-⟨SgM⟩-focus

Onomatopoeic expressions can also be used to modify verbs, as in 323, and verbs may be reduplicated to indicate frequency or repetition, as in 324:

(323) Ávyeta 'ejéhéjé' ó úllehíjcyáhi.
    áβʲètʰà   èhέʔ-éhέʔ   ó ɨ́tʃè-ʔ   íˣkʲʰá-ʔì
    very.much cough–cough I walk-PredAdj be-⟨t⟩
    'I am walking, coughing a lot.'

(324) 'Machóhmáchó' diíbye.
     màtʃʰóʔ-mátʃʰóʔ tì-ːpʲè   'He eats frequently.'
     eat–eat   that-⟨SgM⟩

Chapter 6

Classifiers

Perhaps the most distinctive and structurally remarkable feature of Bora grammar is its CLASSIFIERS, suffixes that refer to classes of beings, objects, patterns, configurations, and so forth. A simple indication of their importance is that, in the texts in appendix G, four out of every ten words has a classifier!

The classifiers are discussed in three sections: their form, morphosyntactic distribution, and tone in 6.1, their use in 6.2, and their categorial and structural status in 6.3. A fairly complete list of classifiers is given in appendix E.

6.1 Classifiers: Form, distribution, tone

General facts about animate and inanimate classifiers are presented in section 6.1.1. We then discuss classifiers that are derived from verb roots in 6.1.2, and classifiers that are cognate with incorporated instruments in 6.1.3.

6.1.1 General facts about animate and inanimate classifiers

6.1.1.1 Animate classifiers

With few exceptions, animate classifiers refer to classes of persons and animals. The criterion for animacy may be the capacity for auto-locomotion,

i.e., the ability to move without an apparent external force. For example, the sun and a clock (or watch) are animate, while trees are inanimate.

The animate classifiers distinguish number (singular, dual, plural) and gender (masculine, feminine). There are three classes, given in table 6.1:[1]

Table 6.1 Animate classifiers

	1 classifier subject, relative clause	2 pronoun, adjective, nonfinite verb	3 numeral phrase, quantifier
SgM	-Ⓛ:pʰɛ (-:be)		-ˣpʰi (-jpi)
SgF	-tʃɛ (-lle)		-ˣpʰi-tʃɛ (-jpille)
DuM	-mɨ́-tsʰi (-mútsi)	-⁽ˣ⁾tʰɛ́-tsʰi (-jtétsi)	
DuF	-mɨ́-pʰɨ (-múpɨ)	-⁽ˣ⁾tʰɛ́-pʰɨ (-jtépɨ)	
AnPl	-Ⓛ◯mɛ (-me)	-⁽ˣ⁾tʰɛ (-jte)	-mɛ (-me)

1. By "postverbal subject" we mean the classifiers affixed to the verb as in example 222, page 129. (We do not mean a free noun phrase following a verb, in apposition to a classifier subject.)
2. With the exception of -Ⓛ◯mɛ ⟨AnPl⟩, these morphemes dock a low tone according to the rule for classifiers given in section 6.1.4, page 171. The low tone falls on the host's final syllable except when a bisyllabic classifier follows a monosyllabic host, in which case the low tone docks on the classifier's first syllable.
3. It is tempting to equate -Ⓛ:pʰɛ̀ ⟨SgM⟩ with 'he' (third person singular) but its use is not restricted to the third person. For example, in 1046, page 399, it refers to a first person and in 852, page 329, it may refer to a second person.[2]
4. In addition to the classifiers of table 6.1, there are a few others that are animate:

   -tsʰɨ ⟨baby⟩, e.g., tʰɛ̀-tsʰɨ 'that baby';

   -o:ʔi ⟨jaguar⟩, e.g., tʰɛ́-ò:ʔì 'that jaguar (or dog)';

   -kʰɛ:mɛ ⟨old man⟩, e.g., tʰɛ́-ˣkʰɛ̀:mɛ̀ 'that old man';

   -kʰo ⟨squirrel⟩, e.g., nɛ́:pʰi-kʲʰò 'squirrel';

   and perhaps a few other animals. All other classifiers are inanimate.

---

[1]Table 7.1 of (Seifart 2002:97) is very similar to table 6.1. Clearly, Seifart followed the 2000 draft of this grammar rather than table 9 of (Thiesen 1996:102).

[2]We hedge because example 852 may mean something like 'You are going like someone who has not eaten?!' If this is the case, then -Ⓛ:pʰɛ̀ ⟨SgM⟩ does not refer directly to the addressee.

6.1. FORM, DISTRIBUTION, TONE

The classifiers of column 1 of table 6.1 are used to mark postverbal subjects; for example:

(325) tʰá:pò-:pɛ̀   (tááboóbe)   'He cures.'
    tʰá:pò-tʃɛ̀   (táábolle)   'She cures.'
    tʰá:pò-mɯ́tsʰɨ̀ (táábomútsi) 'They (DuM) cure.'
    tʰá:pò-mɯ́pʰɨ̀ (táábomúpɨ) 'They (DuF) cure.'
    tʰà:pó-mɛ̀   (taabóme)   'They (AnPl) cure.'

(326) a. ímípà-:βʲɛ́-mɛ̀   (Ímíbaavyéme.) 'They are fixed.'
        fix-sIn-⟨AnPl⟩
     b. tʃʰɛ̀mɛ́-mɛ̀   (Cheméme.)   'They are sick.'
        be.sick-⟨AnPl⟩

The classifiers of column 1 are also used to head relative clauses, as illustrated by -:pɛ ⟨SgM⟩ in 327 and -Ⓛ◯mɛ ⟨AnPl⟩ in 328. (Note: the verb of the relative clause bears the initial high tone characteristic of subordinate clauses, here represented by s.) See also example 331a below.

(327) O úwááboobe diityéké o nééhíí...
    [ò$_i$ ɯ̋kpá:pò]-:pɛ̀$_i$ tì-:tʲʰɛ́-kʰɛ́   ò nɛ́:-ʔìí...
    I teach   -⟨SgM⟩ that-⟨AnPl⟩-objAn I say-⟨t⟩
    'I who teach (them) say to them...'

(328) a. ȉmìpá-:βʲɛ̀-mɛ̀ (ímibáávyeme)
     b. tʃʰɛ̏mɛ̀-mɛ̀ (chémeme)

    a. 'the ones (AnPl) that are fixed'
    b. 'the ones (AnPl) who are sick'

The classifiers of column 2 of table 6.1 are used with nonfinite verbs. Compare tʰa:po 'treat, medicine' with the words in 329 (in which the nominalization low tone is represented with N):

(329) a. tʰȁ:pó:pɛ̀   (taabóóbe)   'doctor (SgM)'
     b. tʰȁ:pótʃɛ̀   (taabólle)   'doctor (SgF)'
     c. tʰȁ:póˣtʰɛ́-tsʰɨ̀ (taabójtétsi) 'doctors (DuM)'
     d. tʰȁ:póˣtʰɛ́-pʰɨ̀ (taabójtépɨ) 'doctors (DuF)'
     e. tʰȁ:póˣtʰɛ̀   (taabójte)   'doctors'

In 329 the classifier's low tone is blocked by the nonfinite low tone on the host's first syllable. By contrast, in 330, where the nonfinite tone is on the antepenult, the classifier's low tone docks on the host's final syllable:

(330) ím^{N}ipáˣʧʰò-ˣtʰɛ̀ (ímibájchojte) 'fixers'
fixing-⟨AnPl⟩
^{N}ɯ̀kpá:pò-ˣtʰɛ̀ (uwáábojte) 'teachers'
teaching-⟨AnPl⟩

In 331a, -ˣtʰɛ ⟨AnPl⟩ heads a relative clause. The initial syllable of the verb of this relative clause bears the high tone characteristic of subordinate clauses (S). By contrast, in 331b -ˣtʰɛ follows a nonfinite verb, which bears the nonfinite low tone (N). (This falls on the initial syllable because the verb is bisyllabic.)

(331) a. Ámúhakye o wájyumej, méucááve.
b. Méucááve, táwajyújtej.
a. [ámɯ́ʔà-kʲʰɛ̀ ò k^{S}pahʲɯ̀ɾ]-mɛ̀-ˣ , mɛ́ ɯ̀kʰá:βɛ̀ (relative clause)
youPl-objAn I esteem-⟨AnPl⟩-voc SAP enter

b. mɛ́ ɯ̀kʰá:βɛ̀ , tʰá k^{N}pahʲɯ́-ˣtʰɛ̀-ˣ (nonfinite verb)
SAP enter my esteem-⟨AnPl⟩-voc

a. 'You (pl) whom I esteem, enter!'
b. 'Enter, my esteemed ones!'

The classifiers of column 2 are also used with bound adjectival stems to form animate plural pronouns, as described in section 7.8.2. See example 332:[3]

(332) a.	tì-:tʲʰɛ̀	(that-⟨AnPl⟩ diítye)	'they'
b.	í-ˣtʲʰɛ̀ɛ́	(self-⟨AnPl⟩ íjtyeé)	'these/those (AnPl)'
c.	à:-:tʲʰɛ̀	(thm-⟨AnPl⟩ aátye)	'those (aforementioned AnPl)'
d.	kʰà-:tʲʰɛ́	(which⟨AnPl⟩ caatyé)	'which (AnPl)'
e.	tʰàˀɲɛ́-ˣtʰɛ̀	(mine-⟨AnPl⟩ tahñéjte)	'my (people or animals)'
f.	tsʰà-:tʰɛ̀	(some-⟨AnPl⟩ tsaáte)	'some (people or animals)'

And they are used with (bound or free) adjectives and nouns, as illustrated with -ˣtʰɛ ⟨AnPl⟩ in the following:

ɨm^{L}ɨá-ˣtʰɛ̀ (ɨ́mɨájte) 'kind people, good people or animals' from ɨmɨ̀à 'truth, goodness'
í-pàˀɾí-ˣtʰɛ̀ (íbahríjte) 'the short ones of a group' from pàˀɾì 'short'
átʰɛ́ɾɛ́ɛ̀-ˣtʰɛ̀ (átéréejte) 'ones (AnPl) having no value' from átʰɛ́ɾɛ́ɛ̀ 'without value, despicable'

[3]Note that the [ˣ] of -ˣtʰɛ remains in 332b and e, but becomes vowel length in the others. We do not know why.

6.1. FORM, DISTRIBUTION, TONE

The classifiers of column 3 of table 6.1 are used following numeral phrases:

(333) tsʰà-ːpʰɨ̀ (tsaápi) 'one (masc.)'
tsʰá-ːpʰɨ̀tʃɛ̀ (tsáápille) 'one (fem.)'

(334) pʰápʰɨ̀ʔtʃʰɨ́ːː-mɛ̀-βà (pápihchúúmeva) 'three (live beings)'
three-⟨AnPl⟩-plQ
pʰɨ́ːnɛ́ɛ̀ʔóˣtsʰɨ́-mɛ̀-βà (pɨ́ɨ́néehójtsɨ́meva) 'four (live beings)'
four-⟨AnPl⟩-plQ

For other examples, consider the following:
In 479, page 218, -tʲʰɛpʰɨ ⟨DuF⟩ is used on the number mɨ́ː 'two' and -mɯpʰɨ ⟨DuF⟩ occurs on the noun kpátʃɛ 'woman'.
In 480, page 218, -mɛ 'AnPl' follows the numeral phrase …pʰápʰɨ̀ʔtʃʰɨ́ːː while -mɯ occurs on the noun kpátʃɛ 'woman'.
In 392, page 191, -mɛ follows the numeral phrase tsʰá-ʔòˣtsʰɨ́ while -mɯ follows the noun kpàˣpʰɨ́ː 'man'.

The classifiers of column 3 are also used on quantifiers, for example:

(335) mítʲʰà-mɛ̀   (many-⟨AnPl⟩   mítyame)   'many (live)'
pʰá-mɛ̀-ːɾɛ̀   (all-⟨AnPl⟩-only   pámeére)   'everyone, all (living)'
àpʰáː-mʲɛ́-ɾɛ̀ (many-⟨AnPl⟩-only   apáámyére) 'only them'
ájà-mɛ̀   (few-⟨AnPl⟩   áyame)   'few'
ɯ̀ʔhɛ́-mɛ̀   (few-⟨AnPl⟩   uhjéme)   'few'
pʰɨ́βá-mɛ̀-βà (many-⟨AnPl⟩-plQ   pívámeva) 'numerous'

Pronominal roots like ti- 'that' generally take the classifiers of column 2. However, aː- 'aforementioned' and tsʰi- 'other' may take those of column 3 (classifiers typically used with quantifiers and numerals):

(336) àː-mɛ̀ (thm-⟨AnPl⟩ aame) 'those (aforementioned)'

(337) tsʰɨ̀-ˣpʰɨ̀ (other-⟨SgM⟩ tsijpi) 'other male'
tsʰɨ́-ˣpʰɨ̀tʃɛ̀ (other-⟨SgF⟩ tsɨ́jpille 'other female'

6.1.1.2 Inanimate classifiers

Inanimate classifiers—of which there are several hundred—refer to classes of physical things and abstract concepts. (See appendix E for a list.) Most refer to physical form, e.g., shape, like those in 338:

(338) -ʔɛ(ː)   (-he)   ⟨tree⟩
      -kʰo(ː) (-co)   ⟨stick⟩   (stick-like thing)
      -ʔaːmɨ (-haamɨ)   ⟨leaf⟩   (leaf-like thing such as paper, book,...)
      -kpa   (-wa)   ⟨slab⟩   (slab-like thing such as tables, doors,...)
      -pa   (-ba)   ⟨box⟩   (things that are like a box)
      -hɨ   (-jɨ)   ⟨disk⟩   (flat, thin disk-like things, such as pills, fields,...)
      -mɨ(ː) (-mɨɨ ~ -mɨ) ⟨canoe⟩   (canoe or other means of transportation),
      -iːʔʲo (-iihyo)   ⟨stick⟩   (something long and slender)

A particularly important inanimate classifier is -nɛ ⟨ø⟩. It may refer to anything other than an animate being. It may refer to physical objects, to events or to situations. Indeed, we might say that it means nothing more than 'not animate'.

6.1.2 Classifiers derived from verb roots

Some Bora classifiers are derived from verbs. While at first blush deverbal classifiers seem remarkable, their existence is unsurprising given our claim (argued in section 6.3) that Bora classifiers are nouns.

There are two forms of derivation, one by the addition of a suffix, the other by lengthening the verb's first vowel. These are now discussed in turn.

Some classifiers are derived by the addition of -ɯ 'deverbal classifier' (glossed 'DVC') to the verb root. For example, consider the bound root ɨβoʔo- in ɨβòʔó-ːβɛ̀ (lie.face.down-sIn) 'lie face down'. To this root we can add -ːɯ 'DVC' to form the classifier -ɨβoʔo-ːɯ 'something tipped upside down'. This classifier could then be used to form a noun phrase like tʰέ-ɨβóʔò-ːɯ 'that face-down thing'. Other examples: -àβóʔò-ːɯ 'something covered', as in í-àβóʔòː-ɯ̀ (íavóhoóu) 'this covered thing';[4] -kʰàtsɨ́ɨtsɨ̀-ːɯ 'something shrunk', as in έ-kʰàtsɨ́ɨtsɨ̀-ːɯ̀ (écadsúdsuúu) 'that shrunken thing'.[5]

A sentence illustrating the use of a classifier derived with -ːɯ 'DVC' is given in 361, page 176. Note that the appositive modifier formed by a quantifier and deverbal classifier is much like a participle, that is, a deverbal adjective that indicates a state resulting from a previous event.

---

[4]Compare áβòʔó-ːβɛ̀ (ávohóóve) 'be covered (sIn)'.
[5]Compare kʰátsɨ̀ɨtsɨ́-ːβɛ̀ (cádsudsúúve) 'shrink (sIn)'.

6.1. FORM, DISTRIBUTION, TONE

In a few cases a classifier is derived from a verb by the addition of a classifier. For example, the classifier -kʰà̰ʔmá-ḭ 'stack of (people, animals or things)' is derived by means of the classifier -i ⟨stick⟩; compare the verb in 339a with the classifier in 339b:

(339) a. kʰà̰ʔmá-ːβɛ̀   (cahmááve) 'become close together'
       stack-sIn
    b. pʰá-kʰà̰ʔmá-ì   (pácahmái) 'stack of something'
       all-⟨stack-⟨stick⟩⟩

Some deverbal classifiers do not add a segmental classifier, but rather lengthen the root's first vowel, as formalized in figure 6.1:

$$\begin{array}{ccc} \# & [_V & \sigma(X)] \\ & \Updownarrow & \\ \# & [_{\text{classifier}} & \sigma{:}(X)] \end{array}$$

Figure 6.1 Classifiers derived from verb roots by length

For example, consider the verb tʃʰɛ̀ɾɛ́-ːβɛ̀ 'split (sIn)', the root of which is tʃʰɛɾɛ-. The classifier is derived by lengthening the first vowel: /-tʃʰɛːɾɛ/ ⟨crack⟩ (a split or crack); for example, í-tʃʰɛ̀ːɾɛ̀ 'this crack'. Other examples follow:

-tʃʰaːha 'something rotten' from tʃʰaha- 'to rot'; e.g., í-tʃʰàːhà (íchaája) 'this rot'.

-tsɛːɾɛ 'sharp sound' from tsɛɾɛ- 'to sound sharp and penetrating', as in 340:

(340) ¿Á ú lleebó tédseére?
      á   ɯ́   tʃɛ̀ːpó-ʔ tʰɛ́-tsɛ̀ːɾɛ̀
      ques you hear-⟨t⟩ that-⟨sharp.sound⟩
      'Did you hear that sharp sound?'

-noːɾa 'hole made by penetrating the surface' from noɾa- 'to break through', as in 341:

(341) Ó ájtyumɨ́ ténoora juuváyí ɨ̵ju nóraavéne.
      ó áˣtʲʰɯ̀mɨ́-ʔ tʰɛ́-nòːɾà   Ⓐ [hɯ̀ːβá-jí ɨ̀ːhɯ̀
      I see-⟨t⟩   that-⟨hole⟩   trail-oblIn horse
      nǒɾà-ːβɛ́-nɛ̀]
      penetrate-sIn-⟨ø⟩
      'I saw the hole the horse made on the trail (sinking a foot through the surface).'

Deriving a classifier from a verb—whether by adding -ɯ 'DVC', by adding a classifier, or by lengthening the root's first vowel—is not a pro-

ductive derivational process. One can not simply take an arbitrary verb and derive a classifier.

6.1.3 Classifiers cognate with other morphemes

Classifiers cognate with incorporated instruments

Some of the incorporated instruments (discussed in section 4.4) are cognate with classifiers and nouns. For example, compare the following incorporated instruments with the nouns and classifiers that follow:

ti- 'do with the teeth':
  -tìpé:ùɯ 'something held in a vise or between the lips or teeth'
  -tìmúɯmùɯ:ùɯ '...as when the upper teeth bite the lower lip'

tʰà- 'do with the foot'
  -tʰàríhʲà:ùɯ 'standing with the legs apart'
  -tʰàˣkʰîùɯ ~ -tʰàˣkʰípà 'a person or animal with very thick legs'
  See also the noun tʰáˣkʰì: (tájkii) 'leg'.

kʰi- 'do with some cutting tool'
  -kʰì:tʲʰúɾùɯhɨ 'a flat cut all around something round'
  -kʰì?tʲá?ɨ:ùɯ 'shaped like a very staight-cut board'
  -kʰì:tʲʰúɾùɯ 'a notched-cut all around something round (e.g., a tree)'
  -kʰì?βúɯhɨ 'a ladies short haircut'
  See also the noun kʰí?tʲà?ínùɯhɨ (kíhdyahɨnujɨ) 'saw'.

Classifiers cognate with derived nouns

The classifiers in table 6.2 have cognate nouns with some additional material, in most cases quite transparently a classifier:

Table 6.2 Classifiers for which there is a corresponding root

CLASSIFIER		ROOT		GLOSS
-hɯ	(-ju)	/hùɯ:βà/	(juúva)	'trail'
-tsʰɨ	(-tsɨ)	/tsʰɨ:mè/	(tsɨɨ́me)	'children'
-mo	(mo)	/mó:à/	(móóaá)	'big river'
-mɨ	(mɨ)	/mɨ:nè/	(mɨɨ́ne)	'canoe'
-po	(bo)	/pó:à/	(bóóaá)	'boa'

6.1.4 The tones of classifiers

A floating low tone occurs at the boundary between a classifier and what precedes it (its "host"). We represent it by C below. It is docked (with a few exceptions) by the following rules:

1. ...σ́-σ## Monosyllabic classifiers place a low tone on their host's final syllable.
2. Bisyllabic classifiers:
   a. ##σ-σ́σ## After a monosyllabic host a bisyllabic classifier bears a low tone on its initial syllable.
   b. ...σσ́-σσ## After a polysyllabic host a bisyllabic classifier imposes a low tone on the host's final syllable.
3. ...σ-σ́σσ... Longer classifiers (three or more syllables) bear a low tone on their initial syllable.

The results are charted in table 6.3:

Table 6.3 The basic tone patterns of classifiers

HOST (modifier)	CLASSIFIER (head)		
	σ#	σσ#	σσσ(...)
#σ	σ́ᶜ · σ	σ́ ·σ́ᶜ σ	σ́ ·σ́ᶜ σ́ σ(...)
#σσ	σ́ σ́ᶜ · σ	σ́ σ́ᶜ · σ́ σ	σ σ́ ·σ́ᶜ σ́ σ(...)
(...)σσσ	(...)σ σ́ σ́ᶜ · σ	(...)σ σ́ σ́ᶜ · σ́ σ	(...)σ σ σ́ ·σ́ᶜ σ́ σ(...)

A monosyllabic classifier (case 1) is illustrated in 342:

(342) a. tsʰǐ:-kpà (tsiíwa) 'other slab'
   b. í-kpà (íwaá) 'that slab'
   c. tsʰúr:kʰá-à-kpà (tsúúcáawa) 'old slab'
   d. tsʰíɛ̀mé-kpà (tsíeméwa) 'some kind of slab'

In 342a and 342c, Ⓒ dock's on the host's final syllable. In 342b Ⓒ is blocked by the host's lexically marked high tone, and in 342d Ⓒ is blocked by the host's lexically marked low tone. The tone derivations of tsʰì:-kpà and í-kpàá are given in figure 6.2 and those of tsʰúr:kʰá-à-kpà and tsʰíɛ̀mé-kpà in 6.3:

```
     tsi:   other                 i     that
      |                           H     lexical
     L__wa    <slab>              +
     :   :                        L_wa      <slab>
     :   L       FDLT             :   :
     :H  :       PLTS             :   L     FDLT
     ::  :                        :   :H    FLTS
     tsií-wa  'other slab'        :   ::
                                  í-waá    'that slab'
```
Figure 6.2 TD: tsiíwa, íwaá

```
 tsu:ca     earlier time       tsíemé       some kind
  :  :                          :L  |        lexical
  :  ._e    pertain             ::  +
  :  : |                        ::  L_wa    <slab>
  :  : L_wa   <slab>            ::  :   :
  :  : :  :                     ::  :   L    FDLT
  :  : :  L     FDLT            H:  H   :    DHT
  H  H :  :     DHT             ::  :   :
  :  : :  :                     tsíemé-wa
 tsúúcá-a-wa  'old slab'        'some kind of slab'
```
Figure 6.3 TD: tsúúcáawa, tsíeméwa

A bisyllabic classifier (case 2) is illustrated in 343. In 343a and 343b, ⓒ is on the classifier's initial syllable as expected (case 2a). In 343c ⓒ dock's on the host's final syllable as expected (case 2b). In 343d ⓒ is blocked by the host's lexically marked low tone and is thus not docked.

(343) a. tsʰí-ʔá:mɨ̀   (tsíhaámɨ)   'other leaf'
      b. í-ʔá:mɨ̀   (íhaámɨ)   'that leaf'
      c. tsʰúːkʰá-a-ʔá:mɨ̀   (tsúúcáaháámɨ)   'old leaf'
      d. tsʰíɛ́mé-ʔá:mɨ̀   (tsíeméháámɨ)   'some kind of leaf'

A polysyllabic classifier (case 3) is illustrated in 344:

(344) a. tsʰí-à:máì   (tsíaamái)   'other row'
      b. í-à:máì   (íaamái)   'that row'
      c. tsʰúːkʰá-á-à:máì   (tsúúcááamái)   'old row'
      d. tsʰíɛ́mé-à:máì   (tsíeméaamái)   'some kind of row'

When a noun bears more than one classifier, generally the low tone imposed by the first classifier prevails. For example, in 345 the ⓒ of -ʔɛ̀ ⟨tree⟩ docks on the host's final syllable and blocks the ⓒ of -ʔà:mɨ̀.

(345) ʧámá:ra-ʔɛ́-ʔá:mɨ̀   (llámáárahéháámɨ) 'leaf of a lemon tree'
      lemon-⟨tree⟩-⟨leaf⟩

Classifier-terminated phrases are remarkably like genitive constructions:

1. In section 6.3 we argue that classifiers head their phrases. On this view they are structurally parallel to the genitive construction; both are instances of [$_{NP}$ NP$_{modifier}$ N$_{head}$].
2. In both cases the two parts (modifier and head) form a single tonal phrase within which the *LLX constraint may not be violated.
3. Both have a floating low tone at the boundary between the two parts.
4. With the single exception of case 2a (page 171), the rule for WHERE to dock the floating low tone is the same: on the modifier's final syllable if the head is one or two syllables; on the head's initial syllable if it is longer.

6.2 The uses of classifiers

This section surveys the various ways classifiers are used. Classifiers may follow finite verbs to indicate the subject (6.2.1). Aside from this case, what precedes the classifier modifies the classifier. This may be a simple adjective (6.2.2). It may be a bound noun (6.2.3) or a bound stem such as demonstrative, indefinite, and interrogative modifiers (6.2.4.1), numerals and quantifiers (6.2.4.2) or a(ː)- 'thematic' to form connectives (6.2.4.3). What precedes a classifier may be a nonfinite verb which, with the classifier, forms a derived noun, e.g., 'doctor' from 'treat' (6.2.5). Classifiers may head relative clauses (6.2.6) or perhaps, in the case of -nɛ ⟨ø⟩, function like a subordinator (6.2.7). What precedes the classifier may be a free possessive pronoun (6.2.8) or a collective or general noun, in which case the classifier "individuates" it (6.2.9). Classifiers may occur multiple times in a word (6.2.10). Classifiers may follow -ɛ 'pertain to' or -ɛmɛ 'similar to' (6.2.11). And classifiers play a vital referential role in discourse (6.2.12).

6.2.1 Classifiers indicating the subject

Classifiers may be suffixed to a verb to indicate its subject, as in 346 with -Ⓛːpɛ ⟨SgM⟩, -Ⓛtʃɛ̀ ⟨SgF⟩, and -ⓁOmɛ ⟨AnPl⟩:

(346) a. tʰáːpò-ːpɛ̀ (Tááboóbe.) 'He treats (medically).'
   b. tʰáːpò-tʃɛ̀ (Tááboʆe.) 'She treats (medically).'
   c. tʰàːpó-mɛ̀ (Taabóme.) 'They treat (medically).'

(Compare these to the nonfinite verb + classifier combinations in 329.)

Inanimate classifiers may also be used as subjects as in 347–350; in 347 and 348 the classsifer is in -⒧◯nɛ

(347) àʧɛ́-nɛ̀   (Alléne.) 'It is raining.'
    rain-⟨ø⟩

(348) àβʲɛ́-nɛ̀   (Avyéne.) 'It hurts.'
    suffer.pain-⟨ø⟩

(349) áí:βʲɛ̀-ʔɛ̀   (Áíívyehe.) 'The tree is burning.'
    burn-⟨tree⟩

(350) Ímíívyémeíja.
    ímí-:βʲɛ́-mɛ́í-hà̱   'The shelter (clothes,…)
    finish-sIn-ɽ/p-⟨shelter⟩   is finished.'

6.2.2 Classifiers with adjectives

A classifier may combine with an adjective to form a noun phrase referring to an object of the type denoted by the classifier. For example, consider the noun phrases in 351 having the adjective mìtʲʰà 'big':

(351) a. mítʲʰà-ʔɛ̀   (mítyahe)   'big tree'
        big-⟨tree⟩
   b. mítʲʰà-kpà   (mítyawa)   'big slab (plank, table,
        big-⟨slab⟩   machete,…)'
   c. mítʲʰà-ʔá:mì̱ (mítyaháámɨ) 'big leaf (paper,
        big-⟨leaf⟩   book,…)'

(352) pʰáɲɛ́tʰúɛ̀-ʔá:mì̱ (páñétúeháámɨ)   'main leaf (paper, book,
    main-⟨leaf⟩   letter,…)'

(353) átʰɛ́ɾɛ́ɛ̀-kpà   (átéréewa)   'worthless slab (plank,
    worthless-⟨slab⟩   bench,…)'

A noun phrase consisting of an adjective and a classifier may be appositive to another noun phrase of the same class, either a simple noun or a noun phrase terminated by the same classifier[6] as in the second word of 354:

(354) úméhewa átéréewa
    úmɛ́-ʔɛ̀-kpà   Ⓐ átʰɛ́ɾɛ́ɛ̀-kpà   'a worthless
    tree-⟨tree⟩-⟨slab⟩   worthless-⟨slab⟩   plank'

---

[6]Schematically: [$_{NP}$ X-classifier]$_i$ Ⓐ [$_{NP}$ Y$_{Adj}$-classifier]$_i$

6.2. THE USES OF CLASSIFIERS

Indeed, this is one of the most significant functions of classifiers: they are the main mechanism for uniting various referring expressions (determiners, modifiers, nouns) into a single phrase; see section 7.1.

6.2.3 Classifiers with bound nouns

Some nouns form referring expressions only when combined with a following classifier. For example, úmè-, ínà- and mínè- never occur except when followed by a classifier, as in úmè-ʔɛ̀ 'tree', ínà-ʔáːmì 'leaf', and mínè-ˣtʰɛ̀ 'peccary'.

Other bound nouns are: pòʔtʰá- 'dish', kʰànɛ́- 'cup', tɛ̀íhʲùɪ- 'spoon', ìˣtʲʰá- 'starch', ìjá- 'animal', hʲɛ́ː- 'pet', móːʔó- 'vine', níːkpá- 'head', núɪ- 'water', òːʔí- 'jaguar', pʰɪ̀ːhʲúɪ- 'hook', ɾáːtʰá- 'can', tʰòˣpʰá- 'partridge', tʰɛ́ː- 'river', tʲʰúɪhúɪ- 'nose', tʰúɪ- 'blood', kpàà- 'mosquito', íˣtʲʰá- 'starch'.

6.2.4 Classifiers to form qualifier phrases

Classifiers are also required to form qualifier phrases from bound roots; see section 7.8.2. The various types of qualifier will be surveyed in sections 6.2.4.1–6.2.4.3.

6.2.4.1 Classifiers with demonstrative, indefinite, and interrogative modifiers

Classifiers combine with (bound) demonstrative modifiers, as in 355:

(355) a. í-ʔʲɛ̀ɛ́   (íhyeé) 'this tree'
      this-⟨tree⟩
  b. í-kpàá   (íwaá) 'this slab (bench, table,...)'
      this-⟨slab⟩

Classifiers combine with (bound) indefinite modifiers, as in 356:

(356) tsʰí-ʔʲàːmì   (tsíhyaámɨ) 'other leaf (paper, book,...)'
      other-⟨leaf⟩

Classifiers combine with (bound) interrogative modifiers, as in 357:

(357) kʰɛ́-ɪ̀ːʔʲò   (kéiíhyo) 'which pencil (pen,...)?'
      which-⟨stick⟩

6.2.4.2 Classifiers with numerals and quantifiers

Classifiers combine with (bound) numerals like tsʰa- 'one', as in 358, and with (bound) quantifiers like pʰa- 'all, completely', as in 359.

(358) a. tsʰà-ʔɛ̀   (tsahe)   'one (tree, bush, plant, etc.)'
         one-⟨tree⟩
     b. tsʰà-kpà   (tsawa)   'one slab (plank, machete,...)'
         one-⟨slab⟩
     c. tsʰá-ʔà:mɨ̀ (tsáhaámɨ) 'one (leaf, paper, book,...)'
         one-⟨leaf⟩

(359) pʰà-nɛ̀   (pane) 'all things'
       all-⟨ø⟩
       pʰà-kpà   (pawa) 'all slab-like things'
       all-⟨slab⟩
       pʰà-:pɛ̀   (paábe) 'all of him (SgM)'
       all-⟨SgM⟩)

The resulting phrase is normally used in apposition to another noun phrase. For example, in 360 mɨ́ámúmàà 'people' is modified by pʰáà:mái 'all like sticks in a row':

(360) Mɨ́amúnaa juuváyí péé páaamái.

mɨ́ámúmàà   hùː:βá-jí   pʰɛ́:-ˀ pʰá-à:má-ì
people   path-oblIn go-⟨t⟩ all-⟨in.row⟩-⟨stick⟩
'People go on the path in a column, i.e., one behind another.'

Deverbal classifiers (as discussed in 6.1.2) may also be used this way. For example, in 361 the classifier -ɨβóʔò:-ɯ̀ is derived from the verb ɨβoʔo- 'lie face down' by the addition of -ɯ 'DVC'. This is combined with pʰa- 'all' to form a noun phrase that is appositive to -mɨ̀, the classifier subject on the main verb:

(361) Teehí úníuri íjcyamɨ, mɨɨne páɨvóhoóu.

[tʰɛ̀:ʔí ǘníừ̀]-rì   íˣkʲʰà-mɨ̀ Ⓐ [mɨ̀:-nɛ̀
river beside -oblIn be-⟨canoe⟩   transport-⟨ø⟩

pʰá-ɨβóʔò:-ɯ̀]
all-overturn-DVC
'Alongside the river there is an overturned canoe.'

6.2. THE USES OF CLASSIFIERS

6.2.4.3 Classifiers forming connectives with a(:)- 'thematic'

A classifier may combine with the bound, anaphoric modifier a(:)- 'thematic' to form a sentential connective. For example, the phrases in 362 refer to a person, animal or thing mentioned in the previous sentence. For further discussion see section 19.1.

(362) a. à:-tʃɛ̀   (aalle)   'she'
          thm-⟨SgF⟩
      b. à:-mì̠   (aamɨ)   'that canoe (boat, car,...)'
          thm-⟨canoe⟩
      c. á-ʔà:mì̠   (áhaamɨ)   'that leaf (paper, book,...)'
          thm-⟨leaf⟩
      d. à:-ʔɛ̀   (aahe)   'that tree (plant,...)'
          thm-⟨tree⟩

6.2.5 Classifiers with nonfinite verbs

A verb is made nonfinite by adding a low tone regressive to the antepenult. (The nonfinite low tone is indicated by N in the examples below. For further details about the tonal modification, see figure 4.1, page 100.) A nonfinite verb may be combined with a classifier to refer to an object (of the type indicated by the classifier) associated with the event indicated by the verb.

The examples of 329, page 165, are like agentive nominalizations. Note that in 329e -ˣtʰɛ ⟨AnPl⟩ is used with a nonfinite verb, whereas in 346c above -ⓛ◯mɛ ⟨AnPl⟩ is used (to indicate the subject) following finite verbs.

In the following examples the classifier refers to an object other than the subject (agent) of the nonfinite verb:

(363) kpà:ᴺhák^hù̠-ʔá:mì̠ (waajácuhaámɨ) 'book'
      knowing-⟨leaf⟩
      ək̀ʰú:βɛ̀-kpà (acúúvewa)   'bench'
      sitting-⟨slab⟩
      kʰà:ᴺtʰúmù̠-í:ʔʲò (caatúnuííhyo) 'pencil (pen,....)'
      writing-⟨stick⟩

6.2.6 Classifiers as heads of relative clauses

A classifier may head a relative clause, either restrictive or nonrestrictive. The initial syllable of the relative clause's verb bears high tone, as characteristic of subordinate clauses. Examples follow:

(364) Ó ájtyumɨ́ teemɨ ímibájchóóbeke.

ó á^xt^{jh}ùmɨ́-ˀ [t^hὲ:-mɨ̀   ⁵imìpá^xtʃʰó]-:pὲ-k^hὲ
I see-⟨t⟩   that-⟨canoe⟩ fix   -⟨SgM⟩-objAn
'I saw the one (SgM) who fixed the canoe (launch, car,...).'

(365) Ó ájtyumɨ́ teemɨ dibye ímíbájchomɨ.

ó á^xt^{jh}ùmɨ́-ˀ t^hὲ:-mɨ̀   [tì-p^jὲ   ⁵imípá^xtʃʰò]-mɨ̀
I see-⟨t⟩   that-⟨canoe⟩ that-⟨SgM⟩ fix   -⟨canoe⟩
'I saw the canoe (launch, car,...) that he fixed.'

(366) Ópée o dsɨ́jcoja tsúúca nójcanúhi.

[ó-p^hὲὲ[7] ò ts⁵ɨ^xk^hò]-hà̱   ts^hʉ́:k^hà no^{xH}k^hànʉ́-ˀì
I-rem   I sew   -⟨shelter⟩ already deteriorate-⟨t⟩
'The clothes that I sewed are now deteriorated.'

As with adjective + classifier combinations, relative clauses headed by a classifier may be appositive to a noun phrase, thereby modifying it; see example 391, page 190. For further discussion and examples see chapter 18.

6.2.7 The classifier -nɛ with complement clauses

The classifier -nɛ may terminate a complement, attaching itself to the clause-final verb. It seems to nominalize the clause so that it can be used as the argument of a higher verb, much like the classifiers that terminate relative clauses discussed in the previous section. For example, 367 has a direct object complement to a phasal verb.

(367) Áánéllii tujkénuube iíhjyúváne.

á:-né-tʃì: t^hʉ̀^xk^hénʉ̀-:pὲ [ì   ⁵ˀi^ˀh^jɨ́ɨβá]-nὲ
that-⟨ø⟩-motive begin-⟨SgM⟩   self speak   -⟨event⟩
'For that reason, he began to speak.'

Example 958, page 362 has a sensory verb complement. It is similar to 367 in that -nɛ seems to do duty as a nominalizer.

---

[7]Note that in 366 the second-position clitic is inside the relative clause, which is the first constituent.

6.2.8 Classifiers with free possessive pronouns

Classifiers do not combine freely with the bound possessive pronouns. However, the possessive pronoun may first be combined with -nɛ ⟨ø⟩ to form a free possessive pronoun, e.g., tʰà̰ʔ-ɲɛ̀ (my-⟨ø⟩) 'mine' or tḭʔ-ɲɛ̀ (your-⟨ø⟩) 'your', and then a classifier may be added:

(368) a. tʰà̰ʔ-ɲɛ́-kpà   (tahñéwa)   'my slab (bench,
     mine-⟨ø⟩-⟨slab⟩   table,...)'
  b. tʰà̰ʔ-ɲɛ́-kpá-ʔhɨ̀   (tahñéwáhjɨ) 'my slabs (benches,
     mine-⟨ø⟩-⟨slab⟩-pl   tables,...)'
  c. tḭʔ-ɲɛ́-ʔá:mɨ̀   (dihñéháámɨ) 'your leaf (letter,
     your-⟨ø⟩-⟨leaf⟩   book,...)'

Even -nɛ ⟨ø⟩ may follow a free possessive pronoun:

(369) tʰà̰ʔ-ɲɛ́-nɛ́-ʔhɨ̀   (tahñénéhjɨ) 'my things'
   mine-⟨ø⟩-⟨ø⟩-pl

6.2.9 Classifiers to individuate collective or general nouns

COLLECTIVE nouns denote collections; they do not refer to an individual except as combined with a classifier. Other nouns denote a GENERAL concept. For example, mútsʰɨ́:tsʰɨ̀ (mútsɨ́ɨtsɨ) denotes a pear apple tree generally, including its roots, its trunk, its branches, its leaves, its fruit, its flowers, a grove of such trees, and so forth. To refer to a specific part, a classifier is used, as in 370:

(370) a. mútsʰɨ́:tsʰɨ̀-pà   (mútsɨ́ɨtsɨba) 'pear apple fruit'
  b. mútsʰɨ́:tsʰɨ̀-ʔɛ̀   (mútsɨ́ɨtsɨhe) 'pear apple tree'
  c. mútsʰɨ́:tsʰɨ̀-páhùɨ   (mútsɨ́ɨtsɨbáju) 'pear apple grove'

Note that the denotation of such expressions is an object of the type referred to by the classifier. This is evidence that the classifier heads the noun phrase.

6.2.10 Multiple classifiers

Multiple classifiers are sometimes used. Note that 371a refers to a leaf, 371b to a plank, and 371c to a pole. None refers to a tree. The final classifier always sets the semantic domain within which the referent is to be found. (This is further evidence that the final classifier heads the phrase.)

(371) a. mútsʰɨ:tsʰɨ-ʔɛ̀-ʔá:mɨ̀   (mútsɨ́ɨtsɨ́hehááamɨ) 'leaf of a pear
         pear.apple-⟨tree⟩-⟨leaf⟩   apple tree'
    b. úmɛ́-ʔɛ̀-kpà   (úméhewa)   'plank'
         tree-⟨tree⟩-⟨slab⟩
    c. úmɛ́-ʔɛ̀-kʰò   (úméheco)   'pole'
         tree-⟨tree⟩-⟨pole⟩

6.2.11 Classifiers after -ɛ 'pertain to' or -ɛmɛ 'similar to'

Classifiers may be used after -ɛ- (-e-) 'pertain to (per)' or -ɛmɛ- (-eme-) 'similar to (sim)' in the following construction:[8]

$$\text{NOUN PHRASE-}\begin{Bmatrix}\text{e}\\\text{eme}\end{Bmatrix}\text{-CLASSIFIER}$$

Examples of -ɛ- 'pertain to' follow:

(372) tʃí:ɲɛ́-ɛ̀-mɨ́ˣkʰò   (llííñéemɨ́jco) 'fence (corral,...)
        below-per-enclosure   that belongs below'
(373) tʰúɾˣkʰɛ́núɨ-ɛ̀-kpà (tújkénúewa) 'slab (table,...)
        front-per-⟨slab⟩   that belongs in front'
(374) ʔátʃúɨ-ɛ̀-kpà   (hállúewa) 'slab (bench, machete,...)
        top-per-⟨slab⟩   that pertains to the upper part'

374 might be used as in 375. Note that in 375 there is only one instance of -βɯ 'theme', one that has scope over (i.e., c-commands) the noun phrase. Within that noun phrase ɛ̀:-kpà and ʔátʃúɨ-ɛ́-kpà (hállú-é-wa) are appositive.

(375) Oke daacu eewa hállúéwavu.
      ò-kʰɛ̀   tà:kʰùɨ [ɛ̀:-kpà   Ⓐ ʔátʃúɨ-ɛ́-kpà   ]-βɯ̀
      I-objAn give   that-⟨slab⟩ above-per-⟨slab⟩   -thm
      'Give me that slab (table, machete,...) which is above.'

In 376a and b, note that the first classifier belongs to class 2 of table 6.1, while the second belongs to class 3. (In 376b the group could be one's family, clan, team, and so forth.)

(376) a. tí-:pʲɛ́-ɛ̀-ˣpʰì   (dííbyéejpi) 'a member (SgM) of
         being-⟨SgM⟩-per-⟨SgM⟩   his (SgM) group'
     b. tì:-tʲʰɛ́-ɛ̀-ˣpʰì   (diityéejpi) 'a member (SgM) of
         being-⟨AnPl⟩-per-⟨SgM⟩   their (AnPl) group'

---

[8]An English parallel is the -o- in *speedometer*, which not too long ago was written *speed-o-meter*.

Examples of -ɛmɛ- 'similar to, like' follow:

(377) tí-:pʲɛ́-ɛ̀mɛ́-ˣpʰɨ̀   (dííbyéeméjpi)
    being-⟨SgM⟩-sim-⟨SgM⟩
    'one (SgM) similar to him (SgM)' or 'He is like the other.'

(378) tʰɛ́:-né-ɛ̀mɛ́-nɛ̀   (téénéeméne) 'one similar to that (thing)'
    that-⟨ø⟩-sim-⟨ø⟩

(379) í-kpá-ɛ̀mɛ́-kpà   (íwáeméwa) 'a slab (table,...)
    this-⟨slab⟩-sim-⟨slab⟩   similar to this one'

(380) tí-:ɛ̀-tʃɛ́-ɛ̀mɛ́-tʃɛ̀   'one (SgF) like your relative (SgF)'
    you-per-⟨SgF⟩-sim-⟨SgF⟩

6.2.12 Reference in discourse

To talk about a plank, it would first be introduced into the universe of discourse with a noun phrase like

(381) úmɛ́-ʔɛ̀-kpà   (úméhewa)
    tree-⟨tree⟩-⟨slab⟩

Subsequently it could be referred to with a phrase headed by -kpa -⟨slab⟩ like those in 382:

(382) tʰɛ̀:-kpà (teéwa) 'that (aforementioned) slab-like thing'
    í-kpàá   (íwaá) 'this slab-like thing'
    ɛ́ʔ-kpàá   (éhwaá) 'that slab-like thing'
    tsʰɨ̀-kpà (tsiwa) 'another slab-like thing'
    tsʰà-kpà (tsawa) 'one slab-like thing'

Likewise, to introduce a machete into the universe of discourse we would first refer to it as nɨ̀:tsʰɨ́-kpà (cut-⟨slab⟩). Subsequently it could be referred to (in that universe of discourse) with tʰɛ̀:-kpà (teéwa) 'that (aforementioned) slab-like thing', í-kpàá (íwaá) 'this slab-like thing', and so forth.

This parallels the use of English nouns that have very general meanings, such as *thing*. In a context in which a plank is prominent (active), we can refer to a plank with *this thing*, *that thing*, and so forth. However, if a machete were more prominent (active) in the universe of discourse, *this thing* or *that thing* would refer to the machete rather than the plank.

Bora differs from English principally in three ways:

1. Whereas English has few nouns like *thing*, Bora has several hundred classifiers. Thus Bora reference with an expression like ɛʔ-kpa (that-⟨slab⟩) is much less ambiguous than English *that thing*.

2. Since this way of referring is so powerful in Bora, it has become the normal way to refer to objects in Bora discourse, the exceptional case being the use of a full noun to introduce a referent into the universe of discourse or to re-activate one that has "decayed."
3. The classifier is also used in the noun phrases that introduce objects into the universe of discourse, so classifiers occur in most referential expressions. (This is not the case for proper names.) By contrast, English *thing* is ordinarily used only to refer to things already present in the universe of discourse (the context).

6.3 The structural status of classifiers

In this section we argue that Bora classifiers are nouns.[9] We claim that a word like áth́ɛ́ɾɛ̀ɛ̀-kpà (worthless-⟨slab⟩ átéréewa) 'worthless slab (plank, table, bench, machete,...)' has the following structure:

[NP [Adj áth́ɛ́ɾɛ̀ɛ̀-   ]   [N -kpà   ]]
         worthless   ⟨slab⟩

Classifiers differ from noun roots in that they are suffixes, and thus bound. That they are bound should be clear from the abundant examples in this grammar: each classifier is attached to a verb, a noun, an adjective, and so forth, as outlined in section 6.2. By contrast, noun roots may be free or bound (requiring a following classifier). For a few classifiers there are corresponding free noun roots, as discussed in section 6.3.1.

Four reasons for believing that Bora classifiers are nouns are presented here: Some classifiers have corresponding free nouns (6.3.1), classifiers have referential properties typical of nouns (6.3.2), classifiers have the distribution typical of nouns (6.3.3), and classifiers head their phrases (6.3.4).

6.3.1 Some classifiers have corresponding free nouns

For some classifiers there are corresponding nouns. For example, corresponding to the classifier -ò:ʔì ⟨jaguar⟩, as in 383a, is the noun o:ʔi 'jaguar, dog', as in 383b and c:

---

[9]This is argued further in Weber (2006), based on *La categoría estructural de los clasificadores bora*, presented at the 51st International Congress of Americanists, Santiago, Chile, 2003.

6.3. THE STRUCTURAL STATUS OF CLASSIFIERS

(383) a. tsʰá-ò:ʔì̠ (tsáoóhi) 'one (jaguar)'
b. ò:ʔí-:pʲè̠ (oohííbye) 'jaguar (SgM)'
c. ò:ʔí-mʲè̠ (oohímye) 'jaguars (AnPl)'

The significance of such cases is this: If Bora classifiers are themselves nouns, then it is not surprising that some may also be used as independent nouns. Indeed, it is what one would expect.

This is not to suggest that the independent noun and the cognate classifier have identical meanings. For example, the classifier -ha ⟨shelter⟩ refers to something with an interior that can serve as a covering, e.g., a house, a pair of pants, a shirt, and so forth. However, the independent noun hà: refers to a house—and only to a house.

Other classifiers that are also used as nouns are (-)ʔóˣtsʰì̠ 'hand', (-)ˣtʰɯ̀ʔà 'foot', and the following:[10]

(384) í-pʲʰèˣkʰò 'this night' cf. pʰèˣkʰò 'night'
tʰɛ́-ˣkʰò:hì̠ 'that day' cf. kʰò:hì̠ 'day'
tʰɛ́-ˣkʰɛ̀:mè̠ 'that old man' cf. kʰɛ̀:mè̠ 'old man'
tsʰá-nɯ̀ʔpà 'one month' cf. nɯ̀ʔpà 'moon, sun'

The classifier -mɨ ⟨canoe⟩ refers to the class of objects that can transport people. Following different modifiers it may refer to canoes, cars, airplanes, and so forth; for example:

(385) kʰɯ̀:hɯ́kpà-mɨ̀ (cuujúwamɨ) 'launch' (i.e., a boat
 fire.burning-transport with an onboard motor)
 íˣtʃʰí-è-mɨ̀ (íjchíemɨ) 'car, truck'
 upland-per-transport
 kʰá:mɛ́-è-mɨ̀ (cáaméemɨ)) 'airplane'
 high-per-transport

When any of these is present in the universe of discourse, it could be referred to with tʰɛ̀:-mɨ̀ 'that transportation device', ɨ̀-mɨ̀ 'this transportation device', and so forth. The cognate noun mɨ̀:-nè̠ (transport-⟨ø⟩) refers to a canoe. Why does it refer specifically to a canoe? Certainly this reflects the fact that canoes are the cultural norm for transportation.

It is tempting to characterize the relationship between the referent of a classifier, a class, and the referent of that classifier followed by -nè̠ ⟨ø⟩, in terms of "prototypicality." However, it is not clear that the culturally normal object to which the latter refers is characterizable in terms of fea-

---

[10]Some of these bear an initial [ˣ] when used as a classifier. This property may be shared with the root; for example, kʰɛ̀:mè̠ 'old man' places a [ˣ] on the end of a preceding modifier: tʰáˣ̱ kʰɛ̀:mè̠ 'my old man'.

tures in the way that a sparrow would be characterizable (as opposed to a penguin) in terms of the features of a bird.

On the other hand, it may be that we simply do not understand the features associated with each class. Consider, for example, the following. The Bora terms for certain animals native to the region have been extended to animals that have been more recently introduced: okʰahi 'tapir, cow'; mɛːni 'peccary, domestic pig'; óːʔi-ːpʲɛ 'jaguar, dog', iːhɯ 'anteater, horse'. In the cases of the cow and of the domestic pig, it is easy to see why the same term would be used. Dogs are probably identified with jaguars because of their size and general shape. What is the perceived similarity between a horse and an anteater? Is it because both have long noses? Perhaps what is most distinctive for the Bora about the anteater is not that it eats ants, but that it has a long nose.

These matters merit considerably more research.

6.3.2 Classifiers have the referential properties typical of nouns

Classifiers are like typical nominal elements in denoting classes of objects, that is, referring to objects that prototypically can be localized in space and persist over time. For example, -mɨ ⟨canoe⟩ denotes the class of objects that can transport people: canoes, cars, airplanes, and so forth.

Generally, *noun roots* have rather specific meanings while *classifiers* have less specific meanings. We now consider various cases:

1. Some classifiers denote large classes of objects that share one or more properties; e.g., -iːʔʲo ⟨stick⟩ denotes the class of things that are relatively long and slender, roughly cylindrical, and have an orientation toward one end; -hi ⟨disk⟩ denotes the class of things that are disk-like, which includes pills, fields,...and even nations.
2. Some classifiers denote classes of objects defined rather narrowly; e.g., -tsʰɨ ⟨child⟩, -óːʔi ⟨jaguar⟩, -ʔɛ ⟨tree⟩, and -pa ⟨box⟩.
3. Some classifiers are like pronouns in denoting small, deictically determined classes, often singletons; e.g., -Ⓛtʃɛ̀ ⟨SgF⟩, -mɯtsʰi ⟨DuM⟩, -ⓁО mɛ ⟨AnPl⟩, and so forth.

    Note that in 386, -mɛ ⟨AnPl⟩ binds the anaphor i 'self'. See also 963c, page 366.

    (386) Imíllémé imájchone.
         ìmítʃɛ́-mɛ́   ì   máˣtʃʰòː-nè   'They want to eat.'
         want-⟨AnPl⟩ self eat-⟨ø⟩

Whether broad or narrow, whether deictically determined or not, classifiers are never used to *attribute* their properties to some other referring expresssion (as adjectives do); they are only used to *refer* to an object that has these properties.

6.3.3 Classifiers have the distribution typical of nouns

Morphologically, classifiers are like nouns in bearing inflection for number and case; e.g., ʧʰɛ́mɛ̀-mɛ́-ʔhɨ̀-kʰɛ̀ (be.ill-⟨AnPl⟩-pl-objAn) 'to the sick people'.

Functionally, classifiers are like nouns in that they may indicate a sentence's subject (see 6.2.1), as illustrated with -ːpʰɛ ⟨SgM⟩, -ʔɛ ⟨tree⟩ and -ha ⟨shelter⟩ in 387:

(387) tʰáːpòː-ːpɛ̀ (Táábo óbe.) 'He treats (medically).'

    áíːβʲɛ̀-ʔɛ̀ (Áíívyehe.) 'The tree is burning.'

    ímíːβʲɛ̀-hà (Ímíívyeja.) 'The house (clothes,...) is finished.'

Significantly, preverbal overt subjects do NOT co-occur with classifier subjects. This is because the classifier IS the subject—not simply an agreement marker.

A subject indicated by a classifier following the verb may be followed by an overt subject noun phrase, but this is appositive to the classifier subject:

(388) [predicate...verb] [subject -classifier$_i$] Ⓐ (NP$_i$)

Like nouns, classifiers may head relative clauses; see examples 364–366 and discussion in section 6.2.6.

And, like nouns, classifiers may have adpositional complements as, for example, English *(a) table like this one*. In Bora, this is í-kpá-ɛ̀mɛ́-kpà 'a slab (plank, table, machete,...) like this one', in which -ɛmɛ- 'similar to' is a postposition. Compare the structures in figure 6.4:

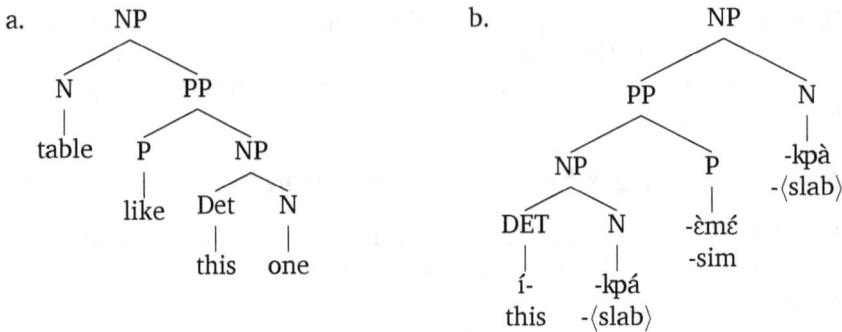

Figure 6.4 'A table like this one.'

In both cases there are two noun phrases. The lower refers to the object of comparison while the higher refers to the object being likened to it. In Bora both of these noun phrases are headed by an instance of -kpa ⟨slab⟩.

Finally, as discussed in section 6.3.4, classifiers play a role within noun phrases typical of nouns, that is, they head the noun phrase.

6.3.4 Classifiers head their phrases

In Bora the syntax of noun phrase formation is played out *internal* to the word. Indeed, the syntax of noun phrases *external* to the word amounts to little more than apposition; see section 7.1 for further discussion.

We claim that—with the exception of classifiers used as (post-verbal) subjects[11]—classifiers are the structural heads of their phrases. Given that classifiers are nouns, what is projected from them is a noun phrase. What precedes (nonfinite verb, subordinate verb, demonstrative, numeral, quantifier, adjective, and such) is a modifier.

We now present various arguments:

1. The head of a phrase is what gives the phrase its character. Formally, a head's features are shared by the phrase projected from it. For example, assuming that *dog* is [+animate] and *brown* is [+color], the phrase *the brown dog* is [+animate] because its head, *dog*, is [+animate]. It is not [+color] because *brown* is a modifier, not the phrase's head. (The phrase *very brown* is [+color] because its head, *brown*, is [+color].)
   In Bora, kpaːhakʰɯ 'know' is a verb having features like [+verbal, +cognitive], which it shares with its nonfinite form kpá̌ːhakʰɯ 'knowing'. Suppose this is combined with with -ʔaːmɨ ⟨leaf⟩ (paper, book,...),

---

[11] It might be possible to extend the claim to these cases on an analysis that projects sentences from their inflection, but we do not pursue that possibility here.

6.3. THE STRUCTURAL STATUS OF CLASSIFIERS

which has features like [+nominal, −verbal, −abstract, −animate]. Which features prevail, those of the nonfinite verb or those of the classifier? Because kpà:hák^{h}ù̀-ʔá:mɨ̀ means 'book', clearly the features of the classifier prevail, not those of the nonfinite verb. The noun phrase would, like its head, be [+nominal, −verbal, −abstract, −animate].

2. That the classifier heads the noun phrase is quite clear when we consider mit^{jh}a, which is ambiguous between 'many' [+plural] and 'big' [−plural], as in 389:

(389) a. mít^{jh}à-:pɛ̀   (mítyaábe) 'big man (or male animal)'
      many/big-⟨SgM⟩   *'many SgM'
    b. mít^{jh}à-mɛ̀   (mítyame) 'many men (or animals)'
      many/big-⟨AnPl⟩   or 'big ones (AnPl)'

The ambiguity of mit^{jh}a is blocked in 389a because the classifier -:pɛ̀ ⟨SgM⟩ is [−plural], and this feature prevails in giving the noun phrase its character. Formally, [−plural] percolates to the phrase first, blocking the percolation of [+plural] from mit^{jh}a, which may therefore not mean 'many'. Thus, the only interpretation possible for mit^{jh}a in 389a is 'big'. By contrast, the ambiguity IS possible in 389b, where the head is -mɛ ⟨AnPl⟩, because its feature [+plural] does not conflict with either interpetation of mit^{jh}a.

3. Consider now the issue of headedness in phrases that have multiple classifiers, as, for example, in mú̀ts^{h}ɨ́:ts^{h}ɨ́-ʔɛ̀-ʔá:mɨ̀ (pear.apple-⟨tree⟩-⟨leaf⟩) 'leaf of a pear apple tree'. Here -ʔɛ ⟨tree⟩ heads [[mú̀ts^{h}ɨ́:ts^{h}ɨ́] -ʔɛ̀], which denotes a pear apple tree. -ʔa:mɨ heads [[[mú̀ts^{h}ɨ́:ts^{h}ɨ́] -ʔɛ̀] -ʔá:mɨ̀], which denotes a leaf. At both levels the expression refers to a thing of the type indicated by the classifier *because it heads the phrase*.

4. It is important to understand that heads are not necessarily the *semantically* most significant part of a phrase. For example, consider English *one* in *Give me the big one*. It makes little semantic contribution to the phrase, but heads the phrase (witness **Give me the big*).

There are parallel cases in Bora with the classifier -nɛ ⟨ø⟩, which means nothing more than 'not animate'. One case would be the formation of free possessive pronouns from bound possessive pronouns by the addition of -nɛ̀ ⟨ø⟩, as discussed in 6.2.8. Indeed, in many cases the expression that -nɛ heads would not refer except as the presence of the head makes it a referring expression.

Another case is that of mɨ̀-nè transport-⟨ø⟩ 'canoe'. By itself, the root mɨ̀- does not refer to a canoe; rather, it means quite generally 'transportation'. However, it does refer to a canoe when combined with -nè ⟨ø⟩, which (1) satisfies the structural requirement for a head, and (2) denotes a class of objects, thus enabling the phrase to refer.[12]

5. It might be possible to formulate an argument against the claim that classifiers head their phrases based on the remarkable behavior of classifiers with numeral phrases.

   When a numeral phrase is used to quantify a noun, that noun must agree in animacy, gender and number. For example, consider 478, page 218. The phrase that means 'six' ends with an animate, singular, masculine classifier because 'six' is literally 'one from this hand'. When this phrase quantifies a noun (phrase), it must agree in animacy, number and gender. Thus, in 'six dogs'—contrary to what one might expect—'dogs' is marked as singular and masculine. See section 7.7.2 for further discussion. However, this lends further support for the claim that classifiers head their phrases. What matters are the features of the the numeral phrase and the noun, which are precisely the features of the classifiers with which each ends. That is, the classifiers determine the features of their phrase, even though these features do not reflect the semantics of the expression.

To conclude this section (6.3), it should be clear that Bora classifiers are eminently nominal. Here we have made a stronger claim: that Bora classifiers are nouns. By doing so, it follows that Bora classifiers should share the major properties of nouns: the types of meanings they encode, the grammatical functions they may have, their distribution/use, and so forth. Indeed, they do except that they have a more restricted distribution than other nouns. And this restricted distribution is due to a simple property: that they are bound.

Based on the claim that Bora classifiers are nouns, it seems reasonable to think that what have been called "classifiers" in Bora are not really such, but simply a subclass of nouns. We will not try to resolve this issue here because the answer depends on whether one believes in universal category definitions or that ultimately each category must be defined for each language.

---

[12]The root mɨ̀- is undoubtedly cognate with the classifier -mɨ̀, used for means of transportation (canoes, boats, cars, airplanes,...). The classifier denotes the class of objects that are means of transportation and as such may refer to a canoe, a boat, a car, and so forth. The root *attributes*; the classifier *refers*.

Chapter 7

Nouns and Noun Phrases

Noun phrases refer to persons, animals, things and abstract ideas (actions, events, states). They are formed from nouns, pronouns, numbers, nonfinite verbs, and classifiers.

To join elements with a noun or noun phrase to form referring expressions, generally languages make liberal use of constituency, conjunction, and compounding. Bora, by contrast, favors other mechanisms because it has an ample set of classifiers. These play a major role in the formation of noun phrases, arguably heading them. For example, in tʰɛ-tsʰɨ 'that baby', the head is the classifier -tsʰɨ ⟨baby⟩ and this is modified by the demonstrative "adjective" tʰɛ(ː)- 'that'. See chapter 6 for a detailed discussion of classifiers.

Various mechanisms for forming referring expressions are given in table 7.1 roughly in the order of their frequency of use.[1] The significance of this table should become clear as this chapter is read.

---

[1] In table 7.1 "NP" should not be understood strictly as a phrase projected from a noun, but loosely as a set of elements (morphemes, words, phrases, not necessarily contiguous) that cooperate in forming a referential expression.

Table 7.1 Combining nouns, classifiers, and noun phrases into noun phrases

MECHANISM	STRUCTURE	FREQUENCY
bound noun-classifier	[$_N$ N$_{bound}$-⟨classifier⟩]	very many
apposition	[$_{NP}$NP Ⓐ NP]	very many
genitive construction	[$_{NP}$NP Ⓖ N]	many
noun-e-classifier	[$_{NP}$N-ɛ-⟨classifier⟩]	many
free noun-classifier	[$_N$ N$_{free}$-⟨classifier⟩]	some
noun-eme-classifier	[$_N$ N-ɛmɛ-⟨classifier⟩]	some
compounding	[$_N$ NN]	few[a]
conjunction	?[$_{NP}$NP Conjunction NP]	very limited
phrasal constituency	*[$_{NP}$NP N]	none

[a]This judgement assumes that the second noun is not a classifier.

7.1 Apposition

The primary mechanism for combining various nominal words into a noun phrase is apposition, not—as in most languages—constituency.[2] Patterns like those in 390 are frequent (and in some cases the appositive parts are discontinuous).

(390) a. NP$_i$ Ⓐ NP$_i$ Ⓐ NP$_i$...
    b. verb-⟨classifier⟩$_i$ Ⓐ NP$_i$ Ⓐ NP$_i$...

The classifiers play an important role in linking the various parts of a phrase. Consider 391 for example:

(391) Diibye wajpi cáracádívú ó ájcuube péjucóóhi.

tì-:p<u>ʲè</u>   Ⓐ kpà^{x}pʰì Ⓐ [kʰárǎkʰá-tí-βɯ́
that-⟨SgM⟩   man   chicken-anim-thm

ó ø$_i$ a̋^{x}kʰɯ̀ɯ]-:pè$_i$ pʰɛ́-hɯ̀ɯ̀kʰó:-ʔì
I   give   -⟨SgM⟩ go-now-⟨t⟩
'The man to whom I gave the chicken left.'

The first noun phrase, tì-:pʲè 'that (SgM)' is a determiner-based pronoun; the second, kpà^{x}pʰì 'man' is a noun; and the third, kʰárǎkʰátíβɯ́ ó á^{x}kʰɯ̀ːpè 'the one (SgM) to whom I gave the chicken' is a relative clause. kpà^{x}pʰì

---

[2]By apposition we mean the use of two or more referring expressions, possibly discontinuous, interpreted as having the same referent, but lacking a syntactic relationship. Apposition depends on an interpretive link in a way that constituency does not.

7.1. APPOSITION

'man' is inherently animate, singular and masculine. The other noun phrases share those features by virtue of the classifier -ːpɛ̀ ⟨SgM⟩.

Numeral phrases and other quantifying phrases work the same way. For example, in 392 the numeral phrase tsʰá?òˣtsʰɨ́ 'five' combines with the classifier -mɛ ⟨AnPl⟩; this combination is followed by the appositive noun (the animate plural suffixes providing the referential linkage):

(392) Tsáhojtsɨ́meva wajpíímú tsááhi.

 tsʰá-?òˣtsʰɨ́-mɛ̀-βà   kpàˣpʰɨ́ː-mɨ́ɨ tsʰáː-?ì   'Five men
 one-⟨hand⟩-⟨AnPl⟩-plQ man-plAn   come-⟨t⟩   come.'

A subject noun phrase may be appositive to a postverbal subject classifier:

(393) nè-ːpɛ́-βa̋-à   Ⓐ [í̋   Ⓖ tʃìː] (neebévááa íllií) 'said his son'
 say-⟨SgM⟩-rpt-rem   self   son

A noun may be in apposition to a pronoun. For example, in 394 tʰáː kʰáːnì 'my father' is in apposition to the pronoun áːnɨ̀ 'this (SgM)':

(394) Áánu táácááni tsááhi.

 áːnɨ̀   Ⓐ tʰá: Ⓖ kʰáːnì tsʰáː-?ì   'This, my father, comes.'
 this(SgM)   my   father comes-⟨t⟩

A demonstrative adjective is made a demonstrative pronoun by the addition of a classifier. The noun it modifies is structurally appositive to it.

(395) tìː-pʲɛ̀   Ⓐ pɨ̀ːɾɨ́mɨ̀ɨ-hɨ̀ (diibye bɨɨrúmujɨ) 'that (SgM) agouti'
 that-⟨SgM⟩   agouti-sg

(396) tʰɛ́ː-nè-ɾì   Ⓐ tsʰà?ɾópà-ɾì (tééneri tsahróbari) 'in that
 that-⟨ø⟩-oblIn   basket-oblIn   basket'

A classifier often provides the referential linkage that unites the parts, as in 397:

(397) téniihyo méwánííhyoke

 tʰɛ́-nìː?ʲò   Ⓐ mékpá-níː?ʲò-kʰɛ̀   'that wife-objAn'
 that-⟨mother⟩   wife-⟨mother⟩-objAn

Example 398 has both a demonstrative and quantifier:

(398) ...íɲe páneere dɨ́ɨtsɨ́ɨju bájtsoháñé...

 í-ɲɛ̀   Ⓐ pʰá-nè-ːɾɛ̀   Ⓐ [tɨ́ː   Ⓖ -tsʰɨ́ːhɨ̋ɨ páˣtsʰő ?áɲɛ́]
 this-⟨ø⟩   all-⟨ø⟩-only   your   mother planting set
 'all of this your mother's plantings'

A relative clause can be appositive to the noun it modifies. In 391 above the relative clause is appositive to the subject of the clause (the man); in 399 it is appositive to the direct object (the squirrel) of the verb (not given here); in 400, to the goal of motion, and so forth:

(399) ...nééepicyókeváa ávyéjuube áñúúbeke...

nɛ́:pʰɨ́kʲʰó-kʰɛ̀-βa-a ⒶL [áβʲɛ́hɯ̀-:pɛ̀ aɲɯ́-:pɛ̀]-kʰɛ̀
squirrel-objAn-rpt-rem kingdom-⟨SgM⟩ shoot-⟨SgM⟩ -objAn
'...the squirrel the chief shot...'

(400) ...wañéhjɨvu, iyámé wañéhjɨ́ ɨ́jcyanévu...

kpàɲɛ́ʔhɨ̀-βɯ̀, Ⓐ [ìjá-mɛ́   kpàɲɛ́ʔhɨ́ ɨ́ˣkʲʰà-nɛ́]-βɯ̀
festival-goal   animal-⟨AnPl⟩ festival be-⟨ø⟩-goal
'...to a festival, to where there was an animal festival...'

The phrases in apposition may be noncontiguous, as in 401, where máˣtʃʰó-:pɛ̀-kʰɛ́-hɨ́:βà is in apposition to tí-:pʲɛ̀-kʰɛ̀. (See also 807, page 316.)

(401) ¿ɨ́veekí dííbyeke ú tsajtyé májchóóbekéjɨ́ɨ́va?
ɨ́βɛ̀:-kʰɨ́ tí-:pʲɛ̀-kʰɛ̀   ɯ́   tsʰàˣtʲʰɛ́-?
why-pur that-⟨SgM⟩-objAn you take-⟨t⟩

Ⓐ máˣtʃʰó-:pɛ̀-kʰɛ́-hɨ́:βà
eat-⟨SgM⟩-objAn-deny
'Why do you take him who has not yet eaten?'

A negative deverbal adjective may be appositive to a noun or pronoun, as in 188 (page 116) and 189.

A few words,[3] among them mítʲʰà-nɛ̀ 'many', function like prenominal adjectives, as in 402:

(402) mítʲʰà-nɛ̀ kpà:-mʲɯ̀   (mítyane waámyu) 'many mosquitos'
much-⟨ø⟩ mosquito-pl

However, because these require the classifier -nɛ ⟨ø⟩, the modifier and head are arguably related by apposition rather than constituency; for further discussion see section 7.8.1.2.

---

[3]Others are: àjà 'little, few', tʃʰòʔʲɯ̀ 'little, few', ɯ̀ʔhɛ̀ 'little, few', pʰɨ́βá- 'numerous', pʰà- 'all'.

7.2 Nouns

Nouns may be animate or inanimate. They may be singular, dual or plural. Animate singular and dual nouns are either masculine or feminine.[4]

The order of suffixes following a noun stem is given in figure 7.1.

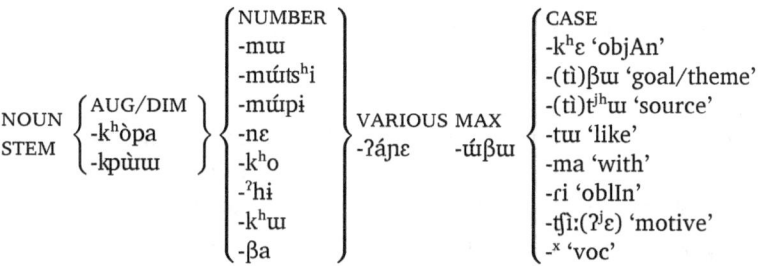

Figure 7.1 The order of nominal suffixes

There are three classes of nouns: concrete (7.2.1), abstract (7.2.2), and locative nouns (7.2.3).

7.2.1 Concrete

Concrete nouns are either animate (i.e., living beings) or inanimate.

7.2.1.1 Animate

An animate noun may be inherently masculine, feminine, or unspecified for gender. The plural and dual are formed with the following suffix combinations:

(403) -mɨ+tsʰi (-mutsi) ⟨DuM⟩
      -mɨ+pʰɨ (-mupɨ) ⟨DuF⟩
      -mɨ   (-mu)   'plAn'

The basic form of an animate noun may be singular or collective.

---

[4]The basic system of contrasts is as follows (in which [−masculine] is *feminine* and [−dual] is *plural*):

	item:	±animate,±plural
	−plural:	±dual
	+animate,−plural:	±masculine

Singular in the basic form. SINGULAR animate nouns form the dual and plural with the suffixes of 403, as in 404:

(404) a. mɛ̀ːnì (meéni) 'pig (AnSg)'
 b. mɛ́ːnì-mɯ́ɾtsʰɨ̀ (méénimútsi) 'pigs (DuM)'
 c. mɛ́ːnì-mɯ́ɾpʰɨ̀ (méénimúpɨ) 'pigs (DuF)'
 d. mɛ́ːnì-mɯ̀ɾ (méénimu) 'pigs (AnPl)'

Some words that we might regard as inanimate are animate in Bora; for example:

(405) a. nɯ̀ɾˀpà (nuhba) 'sun, moon, watch'
 b. nɯ́ɾˀpà-mɯ́ɾtsʰɨ̀ (núhbamútsi) 'the sun and the moon, two watches'
 c. nɯ́ɾˀpà-mɯ̀ɾ (núhbamu) 'watches (AnPl)'

Other words of this sort (which undoubtedly reflect something of Bora cosmology) are: mɨ́ːkʰɯ̀ɾɯ̀ 'stars', t͡ʃʰɨ̌ˣt͡ʃʰɨ̀ 'thunder', and tʰɯ̀ːʔì 'rainbow'.

Nouns referring to an individual may be followed by -mɯtsʰi to refer to that individual and his or her associate. For example, a set of parents can be referred to either as kʰáːní-mɯ̀ɾtsʰɨ̀ (father-⟨DuM⟩) or tsʰɨ́ːhɯ̀-mɯ́ɾtsʰɨ̀ (mother-⟨DuM⟩).

Collective nouns. The basic form of a COLLECTIVE animate noun refers to a collection rather than to a single entity. These form the singular and dual by adding a singular or dual classifier, or by adding a suffix following the classifier. Duals are formed with the following suffixes:

(406) -mɯtsʰi (-mútsi) ⟨DuM⟩
 -mɯpʰɨ (-múpɨ) ⟨DuF⟩

In 407 the noun íːʔʲɯ̀hɛ̀ 'curuhuinse (a type of leaf-cutter ant)' is collective. This is made singular in 407b,c by the classifier -ɯ ⟨singular⟩. In 407c it is further made dual and masculine:

(407) a. íːʔʲɯ̀hɛ̀ (ííhyuje) 'leaf-cutter ants' (collective)
 b. íːʔʲɯ̀hɛ́-ɯ̀ (ííhyujéu) 'leaf-cutter ant (sg)'
 c. íːʔʲɯ̀hɛ́-ɯ̀-mɯ́ɾtsʰɨ̀ (ííhyujéumútsi) 'two leaf-cutter ants (DuM)'

Example 408, where kʰàː refers to a type of small, stinging ant, is similar except that the classifier is -ˀpa:

(408) a. kʰàː (caá) 'ants (collective)'
 b. kʰà-ˀpà (cahba) 'ant (sg)'
 c. kʰá-ˀpà-mɯ́ɾtsʰɨ̀ (cáhbamútsi) 'two ants (DuM)'

7.2. NOUNS

The noun mɨ́:kʰɯ̀ɾɯ̀ 'stars' is inanimate and collective. The singular is formed by the addition of a classifier (as in 409b) and the dual is formed by further adding -mɯ́tsʰɨ 'DuM' (as in 409c). (Although the collective form is inanimate, individual *named* stars may be animate and the dual form is always animate.)

(409) a. mɨ́:kʰɯ̀ɾɯ̀ (mɨ́ɨcuru) 'stars (collective)'
   b. mɨ́:kʰɯ́ɾɯ̀-kpà (mɨ́ɨcúruwa) 'star (sg)'
   c. mɨ́:kʰɯ́ɾɯ̀-kpá-mɯ́tsʰɨ̀ (mɨ́ɨcúruwámútsi) 'stars (DuM)'

The animate collective nouns may be followed by one of the following classifiers: -ˣpʰi 'singular masculine', -tʃɛ 'singular feminine', -ˣtʰɛtsʰi 'dual masculine', -ˣtʰɛpʰɨ 'dual feminine'. Examples follow:

(410) a. mɨ́ámɯ́ɰ̀náà (mɨ́amúnaa) 'people (collective)'
   b. mɨ́ámɯ́ɰ̀náá-ˣpʰɨ̀ (mɨ́amúnáajpi) 'person (SgM)'
   c. mɨ́ámɯ́ɰ̀náá-tʃɛ̀ (mɨ́amúnáalle) 'person (SgF)'
   d. mɨ́ámɯ́ɰ̀náá-ˣtʰɛ́tsʰɨ̀ (mɨ́amúnáajtétsi) 'two persons (DuM)'
   e. mɨ́ámɯ́ɰ̀náá-ˣtʰɛ́pʰɨ̀ (mɨ́amúnáajtépɨ) 'two persons (DuF)'

7.2.1.2 Inanimate

Inanimate nouns are of two types: those whose basic form is singular and those whose basic form is collective (plural).

Singular in the basic form. SINGULAR inanimate nouns form the dual with -(:)kʰɯ 'duIn' and the plural with -(:)nɛ 'plIn'. For example:

(411) a. úmɨ́ʔɛ̀ (úmɨhe) 'field (sg)'
   b. úmɨ́ʔɛ́-kʰɯ̀ (úmɨhécu) 'two fields'
   c. úmɨ́ʔɛ́-nɛ̀ (úmɨhéne) 'fields (pl)'

In 412, the vowel length of -(:)kʰɯ and -(:)nɛ surfaces (following the classifier -ʔɛ 'tree'). Compare 411b and c with 412b and c; we do not know why in one case the vowel is lengthened while in the other case it is not.[5]

(412) a. úmɛ̀-ʔɛ̀ (úmehe) 'tree (sg)'
   b. úmɛ̀-ʔɛ́-:kʰɯ̀ (úmehéécu) 'two trees'
   c. úmɛ̀-ʔɛ́-:nɛ̀ (úmehééne) 'trees (pl)'

---

[5] It probably has nothing to do with the lexically marked low tone of úmɨ́ʔɛ̀.

-(:)kʰɯ 'duIn' and -(:)nɛ 'plIn' suppress the length of preceding syllables, as discussed in section 2.7.4.1. This can be seen in the following data, in which the root's length shows up in both singular forms but in neither plural form:

	'river'		'little river'	
singular	tʰɛ̀:ʔì	(teéhi)	tʰɛ́:ʔí-kpɯ̀ɨ	(tééhíwu)
plural	tʰɛ́ʔì-ɲɛ̀	(téhiñe)	tʰɛ́ʔí-kpɯ̀ɨ-:nɛ̀	(téhíwuúne)

	'trail'		'little trail'	
singular	hɯ̀ɨ:βà	(juúva)	hɯ̀ɨ:βá-kpɯ̀ɨ	(juuváwu)
plural	hɯ́ɨβà-ɲɛ̀	(júvañe)	hɯ́ɨβá-kpɯ̀ɨ-:nɛ̀	(júváwuúne)

Note that, in the nondiminutive plural forms /tʰɛ́ʔìɲɛ̀/ and /hɯ́ɨβàɲɛ̀/, the length of -(:)ɲɛ̀ 'plural' does not appear. In the case of /hɯ́ɨβàɲɛ̀/ perhaps this is because the preceding vowel was historically /*aʲ/, with the palatal semivowel filling the syllable coda. In the case of /tʰɛ́ʔìɲɛ̀/, it may be that the length of the preceding /i/ is absorbed into the palatalization of the nasal.

Collective nouns. Inanimate collective nouns, which have generic meanings, form the singular by adding a classifier, one that characterizes the referent. The dual or plural can be formed by adding -:kʰɯ 'duIn' or -:nɛ 'plIn' after the classifier, as illustrated below. These suffixes contribute length to the preceding vowel and cause the length of the root to be suppressed. Compare 413c and d to 413a and b, and 414b and c to 414a. See also 415c.

(413) a. mɯ́tsʰɨ́:tsʰɨ̀   (mútsɨ́ɨtsɨ)   'pear apple'
b. mɯ́tsʰɨ́:tsʰɨ̀-pà   (mútsɨ́ɨtsɨba)   'pear apple (sg)'
c. mɯ́tsʰɨ́tsʰɨ̀-pá-:kʰɯ̀ɨ (mútsɨ́tsɨbáácu)   'two pear apples (du)'
d. mɯ́tsʰɨ́tsʰɨ̀-pá-:nɛ̀   (mútsɨ́tsɨbááne)   'pear apples (pl)'

(414) a. mɯ́tsʰɨ́:tsʰɨ̀-ʔɛ̀   (mútsɨ́ɨtsɨhe)   'pear apple tree' (sg)
b. mɯ́tsʰɨ́tsʰɨ̀-ʔɛ́-:kʰɯ̀ɨ (mútsɨ́tsɨhéécu)   'two pear apple trees (du)'
c. mɯ́tsʰɨ́tsʰɨ̀-ʔɛ́-:nɛ̀ (mútsɨ́tsɨhééne)   'pear apple trees (pl)'

tsʰɨ̀:mɛ̀ 'offspring (either children or the offspring of animals)' is unique in adding nɛ to form the singular from an animate collective noun; compare 415a and 415b. Further, the dual is formed with -kʰɯ 'inanimate dual', which ordinarily only follows inanimate nouns; see 415c. However, the duals are also formed with -mɯtsʰi ⟨DuM⟩ and -mɯpʰɨ ⟨DuF⟩, which are used only with animate nouns; see 415d and 415e.

(415) a. tsʰɨ̀:mɛ̀   (tsɨ́ɨme)   'young (collective)'
     b. tsʰɨ́:mɛ̀nɛ̀   (tsɨ́ɨmene)   'young (sg)'
     c. tsʰɨ́mɛ̀nɛ́-:kʰɯ̀   (tsɨ́menéécu)   'two young (inan.)'
     d. tsʰɨ́:mɛ́nɛ̀-mɯ́tsʰɨ̀ (tsɨ́ɨménemútsi) 'two young (masc.)'
     e. tsʰɨ́:mɛ́nɛ̀-mɯ́ɨpʰɨ̀ (tsɨ́ɨménemúpɨ) 'two young (fem.)'

Despite this curious pattern, the words in 415 are all treated in the syntax as animate. For example, when used as a direct object they would be followed by -Ⓛkʰɛ 'objAn'.

7.2.2 Abstract

Verb stems can be made nonfinite by imposing a low tone regressive to the antepenult; see figure 4.1, page 100. These nonfinite verbs may refer to collections of things like food, fruit, meat, and such. For example, má^{N}ˣʧʰò 'food'. They may also refer to actions, events or states; for example, in 129, page 101, the nonfinite form of 'to yawn' is 'yawn(s)'; in 130 the nonfinite form of 'fix' is 'the one fixed'; in 127 the nonfinite form of 'to become sad' is 'sadness'.

Abstract nouns are pluralized by putting them in a genitive construction headed by ʔaɲɛ 'various (set)'.[6] Examples follow, first of collections of physical things like food, people and dogs, and then of more abstract things like actions, events, and states:

(416) a. má^{N}ˣʧʰó Ⓖ ʔáɲɛ̀ (majchóháñe)   'various foods,
         food   var   various types of food'

     b. mɨ́ámɯ́ɯ̀aà Ⓖ ʔáɲɛ̀ (mɨamúnaaháñe)   '(a variety of) peoples'

     c. ò:ʔímʲɛ̀ Ⓖ ʔáɲɛ̀ (oohímyeháñe)   '(a variety of) dogs'

     d. ímɨpá^{N}ˣʧʰó Ⓖ ʔáɲɛ̀ (ímibájchohañe) 'various instances
         fixing   var   of fixing'

     e. kʰáβáá^{N}ˣkʰó Ⓖ ʔáɲɛ̀-mà (cávaájcoháñema) 'with various
         poke.hole var-with   pokers'

(417) Mítyane kimóóveháñé téhulle.
      mítʲʰà-nɛ̀ kʰɨmó-:β Ⓖ ɛ̀ ʔáɲé tʰɛ́-ʔɯ̀rʧɛ̀
      large-plIn sadness-sIn various that-⟨location⟩
      'There is much sadness there.'

---

[6]This resembles the English use of the genitive as in *a lot of food, a variety of foods, a collection of dolls*, and so forth.

Abstract nouns that refer to states or qualities may be used—with tone modifications—as adjectives (see 418) and adverbs (see 421). For example, consider nɛʔni 'be ugly'. In 418a it is a verb. (The initial low tone is imposed by -⒧○ʔi ⟨t⟩.) In 418b it is a predicate adjective with high tones. In 418c,d it is a possessed nonfinite form (the genitive low tone docking on the modifier's final syllable because the head is bisyllabic).

(418) a. ó nɛ̀ʔní-ʔì   (ó nehníhi) 'I am ugly.' (finite verb)
     I be.ugly-⟨t⟩

   b. nɛ́ʔní^ʔ òó (Néhní oó.) 'I am ugly.' (adjective)
     ugly I

   c. t^hǎ^G nɛ́ʔnì   (tanéhni) 'my ugliness' (nonfinite verb)
     my ugliness

   d. Dííbye néhní bóhówaavéhi.
     [tíːpʲɛ̌^G   nɛ́ʔní]   póʔókpàː-βɛ́-ʔì
     that-⟨SgM⟩ ugliness visible-sIn-⟨t⟩
     'He manifests his meanness. (lit. His ugliness shows.)'

For example, consider imit^{jh}ɯ 'be bad'. In 419 it is a verb; in 420, a predicate adjective; in 421, an adverb:

(419) a. ímí-t^{jh}ɯ̀ː-ːpɛ̀   (Ímítyuúbe.) 'He is bad.'
     be.good-neg-⟨SgM⟩
   b. ó ìmí-t^{jh}ɯ́-ʔì   (Ó imítyúhi.) 'I am bad.'
     I be.good-neg-⟨t⟩

(420) Ímítyú dííbye wákimyéi.
     ímí-t^{jh}ɯ́^ʔ tíːpʲɛ̌^G   kpák^hǐm^{jN}ɛ́ì 'His work is bad.'
     good-neg that-⟨SgM⟩ work   (predicate adjective)

(421) Ímítyú wákímyeííbye.
     ímí-t^{jh}ɯ́^ʔ kpák^hím^jɛ̌ì-ːpʲɛ̀ 'He works bad(ly).' (adverb)
     good-neg work-⟨SgM⟩

7.2.3 Locative nouns

LOCATIVE NOUNS (sometimes referred to as "spatial relators") indicate location or position relative to someone or something. In Bora these frequently head a genitive construction, with the modifier indicating the being or thing relative to which location is indicated. For example, in 422

pʰáɲɛ heads a genitive construction; the modifier (íʔ-hʲa 'his house') is the object relative to which position is indicated. Other examples follow:

pʰáɲɛ (pañe) 'interior, inside':

(422) Íhjyá pañe íjcyaábe.
[[íʔ ⓖ hʲá] ⓖ pʰáɲɛ̀] íˣkʲʰà-ːpɛ̀   'He is in his house.'
self house inside be-⟨SgM⟩

paː (baa) 'below':

(423) pàː-tʰùɨ   tsʰá-ːpɛ̀ɛ́   (Baatu tsáábeé.) 'He comes
below-sou come-⟨SgM⟩   from below.'

tʃíːɲɛ (lliiñe) 'lower part':

(424) Táñahbe úcaavé já lliiñévu.
tʰá ⓖ ɲá-ʔpɛ̀   úɨkʰà-ːβɛ́-ʔ   há   ⓖ tʃíːɲɛ́-βùɨ
my   sib-⟨SgM⟩ enter-sIn-⟨t⟩ house   under-goal
'My brother went in under the house.'

kʰaːmɛ (caáme) 'above':

(425) kʰàːmɛ̀ íˣkʲʰà-ːpɛ̀ (Caame íjcyaábe.) 'He is above.'
above be-⟨SgM⟩

(426) kʰáːmɛ́-βùɨ nɛ́ɾíːβʲɛ̀-ːpɛ̀   (Cáámevu néríívyeébe.)
above-goal ascend-⟨SgM⟩
'He ascended to (the place) above.'

ɨ́ɨniɨ (úniu) 'along side of, beside'; e.g., tʰá ⓖ ɨ́ɨníɨ-ɾì (my beside-oblIn) 'at my side'

The locative noun aːʔɨ 'at home' is of a somewhat different sort. Generally it is used as a locative adverb, without a following case marker, as in example 427:

(427) àːʔɨ̀   tì-ːpʲɛ̀   (Aahɨ diíbye.) 'He is at home.'
at.home that-⟨SgM⟩

Locative nouns are rarely pluralized. If so, they usually bear -ʔaɲɛ 'various' (used typically to pluralize abstract nouns). However, ɨ́ɨniɨ 'along side of' is pluralized with -ːkʰùɨ 'duIn' or -ːnɛ̀ 'plIn':

(428) a. ɨ́ɨnìɨ́-ːkʰùɨ (úniúúcu) 'sides (du)'
b. ɨ́ɨnìɨ́-ːnɛ̀ (úniúúne) 'sides (pl)'

7.3 Number

This section discusses the number (singular, dual, plural) of nouns. The singular of some collective nouns is formed by the addition of a classifier; see section 7.3.1. Some animate nouns are plural by virtue of bearing a plural classifier; see section 7.3.2. A noun may be pluralized with one of five pluralizers: -mɯ, -nɛ, -ʔhɨ, -ʔɲ́ɛ, and -βa; see sections 7.3.3–7.3.7.

7.3.1 The singular of collective nouns

As discussed in section 7.2.1, collective nouns, i.e., ones that refer to collections, form singulars by the addition of a classifier. For example:

(429) tsɨ̀ːtsɨ̀   (money   dsɨ́ɨ́dsɨ́)   'money'
      tsɨ́ːtsɨ̀-hɨ̀   (money-⟨disk⟩ dsɨ́ɨ́dsɨjɨ̀)   'coin'
      tsɨ́ːtsɨ̀-ʔáːmɨ̀ (money-⟨leaf⟩ dsɨ́ɨ́dsɨháámɨ) 'bill'

(430) ʧámàːɾà   (lemon   llámaára)   'lemons'
      ʧámáːɾà-pà   (lemon-⟨sphere⟩ llámááraba)   'one lemon'
      ʧámáːɾà-ʔɛ̀   (lemon-⟨tree⟩   llámáárahe)   'lemon tree'
      ʧámáːɾà-páhɯ̀ː (lemon-⟨grove⟩ llámáárabáju)   'lemon grove'

7.3.2 Plural nouns formed with plural classifiers

As discussed in section 7.2.1, some animate nouns are plural by virtue of bearing a plural classifier. The animate nominal roots for 'jaguar', 'fish' and 'animals' are bound in the sense that they must occur with a classifier. The noun's number is determined by the number of the classifier; -ⓁOmɛ̀ ⟨AnPl⟩ is used for the plural, as in 431–433:

(431) ò:ʔí-:pʲɛ̀ (jaguar-⟨SgM⟩ oohííbye) 'jaguar (SgM)'
      ò:ʔí-mʲɛ̀ (jaguar-⟨AnPl⟩ oohímye) 'jaguars (AnPl)'

(432) àmó-:pɛ̀ (fish-⟨SgM⟩ amóóbe) 'fish (sg)'
      àmó-mɛ̀ (fish-⟨AnPl⟩ amóme) 'fish (pl)'

(433) ìjá-:pɛ̀ (animal-⟨SgM⟩ iyáábe) 'animal'
      ìjá-mɛ̀ (animal-⟨AnPl⟩ iyáme) 'animals'

The bound root mìnɛ- 'peccary' is like these except it forms the plural with -ˣtʰɛ̀ ⟨AnPl⟩. To our knowledge, this is the only root that does this.

(434) mínɛ̀-:pɛ̀ (peccary-⟨SgM⟩ míneébe) 'peccary'
      mínɛ̀-ˣtʰɛ̀ (peccary-⟨AnPl⟩ mínejte) 'peccaries'

7.3. NUMBER

The duals are formed by adding -mɯtsʰɨ ⟨DuM⟩ or -mɯpʰɨ ⟨DuF⟩ following the singular classifier. (See table 7.2 for additional examples.)

(435) o̲:ʔí-:pʲè-mɯ́-pʰɨ̀   (oohííbyemúpɨ) 'jaguars (DuF)'
    dog-⟨SgM⟩-DuM

    o̲:ʔí-:pʲè-mɯ́tsʰɨ̀   (oohííbyemútsi) 'jaguars (DuM)'
    dog-⟨SgM⟩-DuM

    mɨ́né-:pè-mɯ́tsʰɨ̀   (mɨnéébemútsi) 'peccaries (DuM)'
    peccary-⟨SgM⟩-DuM

7.3.3 Pluralization with -Ⓛmɯ

Generally, animate nouns are pluralized by suffixing -Ⓛmɯ (-mu) 'plAn', as in 436a and b. -Ⓛmɯ supplants a singular classifier with some animate nouns, as in 436c,d, or with some inanimate nouns, as in e:

(436)   SINGULAR   PLURAL
   a. anteater, horse ɨ̀:hɯ̀ (ɨ́ɨ́ju)   ɨ̀:hɯ̀-mɯ̀ (ɨ́ɨ́jumu)
   b. buzzard   àɲɯ̀   (añu)   áɲɯ̀-mɯ̀ (áñumu)
   c. rat   kʰɯ̀:βɛ́-pà (cuuvéba) kʰɯ̀:βɛ́-mɯ̀ (cuuvému)
   d. dove   ɨ́hɯ̀:-ɯ̀ (ɨ́juúu)   ɨ́hɯ̀:-mɯ̀ (ɨ́juúmu)
   e. plate   pòʔtʰá-hɨ̀ (bohtájɨ) pòʔtʰá-mɯ̀ (bohtámu)

(437) ókʰáhì-<u>mɯ́tsʰɨ̀</u> (ócájimútsi) 'tapirs (DuM)'
    ókʰáhì-<u>mɯ́pʰɨ̀</u> (ócájimúpɨ) 'tapirs (DuF)'
    ókʰáhì-<u>mɯ̀</u>   (ócájimu)   'tapirs (more than two)'.

The noun òβáʔtsʰà 'male adolescent' is singular; the plural is formed with -Ⓛmɯ̀. By contrast, pátsɨˣkʰà 'female adolescent' is plural (collective); the singular is formed with -hà:

	MALE ADOLESCENT	FEMALE ADOLESCENT
SINGULAR	òβáʔtsʰà (ováhtsa)	pátsɨˣkʰà-hà (bádsɨjcaja)
PLURAL	òβáʔtsʰà-mɯ̀ (ováhtsamu)	pátsɨˣkʰà (bádsɨjca)

Some animate nouns derive the dual by adding -mɯtsʰɨ or -mɯpʰɨ after the singular classifier, but form the plural by substituting -mɯ for the classifier. A few inanimate nouns form the plural by replacing the classifier with -mɯ, but form the dual with the -:kʰɯ 'InPl'. See table 7.2.

Table 7.2 Nouns that form the plural by replacing the classifier

ANIMATE	SINGULAR	DUAL MASCULINE	PLURAL
'toad'	àʔkʰó-kpà (ahcówa)	àʔkʰó-kpà-<u>mɨ́ɨts</u>ʰɨ̀ (ahcówamútsi)	àʔkʰó-mɨ̀ɨ (ahcómu)
'bird'	kʰò:mɨ́-kʰò (coomɨ́co)	kʰò:mɨ́-kʰò-<u>mɨ́ɨts</u>ʰɨ̀ (coomɨ́comútsi)	kʰò:mɨ́-mɨ̀ɨ (coomɨ́mu)
'turtle'	kʰúɨ:mùɨ-hɨ̀ (cúúmujɨ)	kʰúɨ:múɨ-hɨ̀-<u>mɨ́ɨts</u>ʰɨ̀ (cúúmújɨmútsi)	kʰúɨ:mùɨ-mùɨ (cúúmumu)
'cricket'	tʃʰákʰàtʃʰí-ùɨ (chácachíu)	tʃʰákʰàtʃʰí-ùɨ-<u>mɨ́ɨts</u>ʰɨ̀ (chácachíumútsi)	tʃʰákʰàtʃʰí-mùɨ (chácachímu)
'parrot'	tʃʰàʔtʃʰá-ɨ̀ (chahchái)	tʃʰàʔtʃʰá-ɨ̀-<u>mɨ́ɨts</u>ʰɨ̀ (chahcháimútsi)	tʃʰàʔtʃʰá-mùɨ (chahchámu)
INANIMATE	SINGULAR	DUAL	PLURAL
'plate'	pòʔtʰá-hɨ̀ (bohtájɨ)	pòʔtʰá-hɨ́-:<u>kʰùɨ</u> (bohtájɨ́ɨcu)	pòʔtʰá-mùɨ (bohtámu)
'scissors'	màˣtʃʰó-kpà (majchówa)	màˣtʃʰó-kpá-:<u>kʰùɨ</u> (majchówáácu)	màˣtʃʰó-mùɨ (majchómu)
'room'	mɨ́ˣkʰò-ʔò (mɨ́jcoho)	mɨ́ˣkʰò-ʔó-:<u>kʰùɨ</u> (mɨ́jcohóócu)	mɨ́ˣkʰò-mùɨ (mɨ́jcomu)

7.3.4 The plural suffix -nɛ

The pluralizer -:nɛ (-:ne) ~ -:ɲɛ (-:ñe) 'plIn' is added to singular inanimate nouns to form the corresponding plural, as in the following:

* úmɨ̀ʔɛ́-<u>nɛ̀</u>[7] (úmɨheńe) 'fields'; cf. úmɨ̀ʔɛ̀ 'field'
* kʰámɛ́ɛ̀-mɨ́-:<u>nɛ̀</u> (cámeemɨ́ɨne) 'airplanes'; cf. kʰá:mɛ̀ɛmɨ̀ 'airplane'
* úmɛ̀-ʔɛ́-:<u>nɛ̀</u> (úmeheéne) 'trees'; cf. úmɛ̀-ʔɛ̀ 'tree'

7.3.5 The plural suffix -⁽ʔ⁾hɨ̀

The pluralizer -⁽ʔ⁾hɨ̀ (-hjɨ) follows pronoun + classifier expressions, as in the following:

* tʰɛ́-ʔɛ̀-<u>ʔhɨ̀</u> (téhehjɨ) 'those trees (plants,...)'; cf. tʰɛ̀:ʔɛ̀ (teéhe) 'that tree (plant,...)'
* í-kpà-<u>ʔhɨ̀</u> (íwahjɨ) 'these slabs (planks, benches, machetes,...)'; cf. í-kpàá (íwaá) 'this slab (plank,...)'

---

[7] We do not know why -:nɛ fails to produce a long vowel in this case.

7.3. NUMBER

- kʰɛ́-hà-ʔhɨ́ (kéjahjɨ́) 'which houses (shirts, pants,...)'; cf. kʰɛ̀ː-há (keejá) 'which house (shirt,...)'
- tʰàʔɲɛ́-ʔàːmɨ́-hɨ̀ (tahñéhaamɨ́jɨ) 'my papers (books, notebooks,...)'; cf. tʰàʔɲɛ́-ʔáːmɨ̀ (tahñéháámɨ) 'my paper (book,...)'
- tsʰɨ́-mɨ̀-ʔhɨ̀ (tsɨ́mɨhjɨ) 'other canoes (cars, airplanes,...)'; cf. tsʰɨ̀ː-mɨ̀ (tsɨ́ɨ́mɨ) 'other canoe, (car,...)'
- á-ʔàːmɨ́-hɨ̀ (áhaamɨ́jɨ) 'those aforementioned papers (books, notebooks,...)'; cf. á-ʔàːmɨ̀ (áhaamɨ) 'that aforementioned paper (book,...)'
- á-ʔɛ̀-ʔhɨ̀ (áhehjɨ) 'those aforementioned trees (plants,...)'; cf. àː-ʔɛ̀ (aahe) 'that aforementioned tree, (plant,...)'

Likewise, it is used with bound inanimate modifiers, as in the following:

- átʰɛ́ɾɛ̀ɛ̀-mɨ́-hɨ̀ (átéréemɨ́jɨ) 'worthless canoes (cars, airplanes,...)'; cf. átʰɛ́ɾɛ̀ɛ̀-mɨ̀ (átéréemɨ) 'worthless canoe, (car,...)'
- àíːβʲɛ̀-há-ʔhɨ̀ (aíívyejáhjɨ) 'burned houses (shirts,...)' cf. àíːβʲɛ̀-hà (aíívyeja) 'burned house (shirt...)'

(438) Íwahjɨ muurá nɨtsúwááné oke u ájcuwáhjɨ.

ɨ́-kpà-ʔhɨ̀   mùːɾá   nɨ̀tsʰɨ́ɨ̀-kpá-ːnɛ́
this-⟨slab⟩-pl confirm knife-⟨slab⟩-pl

Ⓐ [ò-kʰɛ̀   ɨ̀ɨ̀   áˣkʰɨ̀ɨ̀]-kpá-ʔhɨ̀
I-objAn you give   -⟨slab⟩-pl

'Look, these are the machetes that you gave me.'

Finally, -⁽ʔ⁾hɨ̀ (-hjɨ) may pluralize an animate noun to indicate a large quantity or exhaustiveness, as in the following:

- tɨ̀ːtʲʰɛ́-ʔhɨ̀ (diityéhjɨ) 'all of them'; cf. tɨ̀ːtʲʰɛ̀ (díítye) 'they'
- ɨ́-ˣtʲʰɛ̀-ʔhɨ̀ (íjtyehjɨ) 'all of these' cf. ɨ́-ˣtʲʰɛ̀ɛ̀ (íjtyeé) 'these'
- pʰá-mɛ̀-ʔhɨ́-ɾɛ̀ (pámehjɨ́re) 'all (AnPl, lacking none)'; cf. pʰá-mɛ̀-ːɾɛ̀ (pámeére) 'all (AnPl)'

(439) Ɨ́mɨájtéhjɨubá diítye.

ɨ́mɨá-ˣtʰɛ́-ʔhɨ́-ɨ̀pá   tɨ̀ːtʲʰɛ̀   'All of them may be good.'
proper-⟨AnPl⟩-pl-prob that-⟨AnPl⟩

(440) Taabóóbée mítyane chémeméhjɨke taabó cóómíyií.

tʰàːpó-ːpɛ́ɛ̀   mítʲʰà-nɛ̀   ʧʰémɛ̀-mɛ́-ʔhɨ̀-kʰɛ̀
doctor-⟨SgM⟩ all-⟨ø⟩   be.ill-⟨AnPl⟩-pl-objAn

tʰàːpó-ʔ   kʰóːmí-jìí
cure-⟨t⟩ town-oblIn

'The doctor treated all the sick people in the town.'

In 441a pʰɛˣkʰo 'night' is a noun, so is pluralized with -ːnɛ. By contrast, in 441b pʰɛˣkʰo ⟨night⟩ is a classifier that, when combined with tʰɛ- 'that', forms a qualifier phrase (as explained in section 7.8.2); therefore it is pluralized with -ʔhɨ.

(441) a. pʰɛ́ˣkʰò-<u>nɛ̀</u>   (péjcone)   'nights'
       night-pl

   b. tʰɛ́-pʰɛ̀ˣkʰó-<u>ʔhɨ̀</u> (tépejcóhjɨ) 'those nights'
       that-⟨night⟩-pl

Likewise, in 442a tʰuutʰakʰo 'contents of a pot' is a noun, so is pluralized with -ːnɛ. By contrast, in 442b ɲɛ̀ʔní-ɲɛ (bad-⟨ø⟩) 'dirty one' is a qualifier phrase so is pluralized with -ʔhɨ.

(442) a. tʰúɨtʰákʰó-ìʔtʃó-<u>nɛ̀</u> (tútácóihllóne) 'cooking pots'
       cook-⟨pot⟩-pl

   b. í   ⒼⁿL ɲɛ̀ʔní-ɲɛ́-<u>ʔhɨ̀</u>   'the dirty ones (from among them)'
      self   bad-⟨ø⟩-pl

7.3.6 The plural suffix -ʔaɲɛ 'various'

The pluralizer -ʔaɲɛ (-hañe) 'various' indicates variety. It can be used with concrete nouns, as in example 443; with nonfinite verbs, as in 416 (above) and 444; and with locations, as in 445 and 446:

(443) háː-<u>ʔàɲɛ̀</u>   (jááhañe) 'various houses'
       shelter-var

(444) tʃʰɛ̀mɛ́-<u>ʔáɲɛ̀</u> (cheméháñe) 'various sicknesses'
       sickness-var

(445) kʰáːmɛ̀-<u>ʔáɲɛ̀</u> (cáámeháñe) 'above (in various places)'
       above-var

(446) Diityé úníuháñerícya diícya.

   tìːtʲʰɛ́   Ⓖ ǘmíùɨ-ʔáɲɛ̀-rí-kʲʰà   tɨ̀ːkʲʰà
   that-⟨AnPl⟩   beside-var-oblIn-doubt youImp-be
   'Remain beside them.'

Finally, -ʔáɲɛ̀ 'various' is used with plural nouns to indicate diversity:

(447) ìjá-mɛ̀-<u>ʔáɲɛ̀</u>   (iyámeháñe) 'varieties of animals'
       animal-⟨AnPl⟩-var

(448) mɨ́ámúnáà-<u>ʔáɲɛ̀</u> (mɨamúnáaháñe) 'types of people'
       people-var

(449) pʰíː-mʲɛ̀-ʔáɲɛ̀   (píímyeháñe) 'types of ants'
ant-⟨AnPl⟩-var

7.3.7 The plural suffix -βa

The pluralizer -βa (-va) 'plQ' is used only with numeral phrases and other expressions referring to quantities (such as those described in section 7.5). Examples follow:

(450) mítʲʰá-mɛ̀-βà   (mítyámeva) 'many beings (AnPl)'
big/many-⟨AnPl⟩-plQ

(451) pʰíβá-mɛ̀-βà   (pívámeva) 'numerous beings (AnPl)'
numerous-⟨AnPl⟩-plQ

(452) pʰà-mɛ́-βá-ɾɛ̀   (paméváre) 'all types of beings (AnPl)'
all-⟨AnPl⟩-plQ-only

(453) mɨ́ɨ-ʔtɨ́ɨ-mɛ̀-βá   (¿Múhdúmevá?) 'How many
how.many-⟨like⟩-⟨AnPl⟩-plQ   (AnPl)?'

(454) a. tʰɛ́-ʔtɨ́ɨ-mɛ̀-βà   (téhdúmeva) 'that many (AnPl)'
that-⟨like⟩-⟨AnPl⟩-plQ
b. tʰɛ́-ʔtɨ́ɨ-kpà-βà   (téhdúwava) 'that many slabs
that-⟨like⟩-⟨slab⟩-plQ   (planks, tables,...)

For the numbers 3, 4, 5, 8, 9, 10, 13, 14, 15, 18, 19 and 20, -βà 'plQ' follows the classifier.[8] Examples follow:

(455) pʰá-pʰɨ̀ʔʧʰɨ́ɨː-ʔàːmɨ́-βà   (pápihchúúhaamíva) 'three papers
all-pile.up-⟨leaf⟩-pl   (leaves,...)'
pʰɨ́ːnɛ́-ɛ̀-ʔóˣtsʰɨ́-mɛ̀-βà   (pɨ́ɨ́néehójtsɨ́meva)   'four people
half-per-⟨hand⟩-⟨AnPl⟩-pl   (or animals)'
tsʰá-ʔòˣtsʰɨ́-nɛ̀-βà   (tsáhojtsɨ́neva)   'five things'
one-⟨hand⟩-⟨ø⟩-pl

---

[8]Because of how numeral phrases are formed, as explained in section 7.7.1, the numeral phrases for these numbers are plural as opposed to singular or dual. This is easier to visualize when charted as follows:

singular	dual	plural		
1	2	3	4	5
6	7	8	9	10
11	12	13	14	15
16	17	18	19	20

7.4 Suffixes that modify nouns

Three suffixes modify noun phrases (including simple nouns, pronouns, numeral phrases, and qualifier phrases): -kʰópa (-coba) 'augment', -ⓁOkpúɯ (-wuu) 'diminutive', and -Ⓛɯβɯ (-uvu) 'maximal'.

7.4.1 -coba 'augment'

Suffixed to a noun phrase, -kʰópa (-coba) 'augment' indicates that its referent is large. The host's final syllable must bear high tone to avoid violating the *LLX constraint; see section 3.10.

(456) a. úmɛ́-ʔɛ́-kʰòpà   (úméhécoba)   'big tree'
        tree-⟨tree⟩-aug
    b. úmɛ́-ʔɛ́-kʰòpá-nɛ̀ (úméhécobáne) 'big trees'
        tree-⟨tree⟩-aug-pl

Note that -kʰópa directly follows and modifies the noun phrase referring to a type of tree. Further note that, in 456b, the pluralizer follows -kʰópa.

However, -kʰópa may follow the pluralizer, in which case it enhances the plurality of the referent:[9]

(457) a. úmɛ̀-ʔɛ́ː-né-kʰòpà (úmehéénécoba) 'many trees'
        tree-⟨tree⟩-pl-aug
    b. kpàˣpʰíː-mɯ́-kʰòpà (wajpíímúcoba) 'many men
        men-⟨AnPl⟩-aug   (or male animals)'

Note the alternate orders of -kʰópa 'augment' and -mɯ 'plAn' in 458 (where the G over the vowel indicates the genitive low tone):[10]

(458) a. tʰȧ́ mɛ́ːní-kʲʰópá-mɯ̀ɩ (taméénícyobámu) 'my big pigs'
        my pig-aug-plAn
    b. tʰá mɛ̇́ːní-mɯ́-kʰópà (támeenímúcoba) 'my very many
        my pig-plAn-aug   pigs'

---

[9] Perhaps the structure of 456b is [[[úmɛ́-ʔɛ́] -kʰòpá] -nɛ̀] while that of 457a is [[úmɛ̀-ʔɛ́ː] [-né-kʰòpà]].

[10] In 458a -kʰópa 'augment' is not part of the stem so the genitive tone Ⓖ docks on the modifier. By contrast, in 458b -mɯ̀ɩ 'plAn' is part of the stem so Ⓖ docks on the head's initial syllable.

7.4.2 -wuu ∼ -wu 'diminutive, small, few'

Suffixed to a noun phrase, -kpɯ̀(σ) (-wuu ∼ -wu) 'diminutive' indicates that its referent is small. The first of its vowels always bears low tone. When the second vowel is followed by another suffix, it always projects a syllable bearing high tone. When this suffix is word final, the second vowel is dropped. Examples follow:

(459) a. úmɛ́-ʔɛ́-kpɯ̀[11]   (úméhéwu)   'small tree'
         tree-⟨tree⟩-dim

   b. úmɛ́-ʔɛ́-kpɯ̀ɯ́-nɛ̀ (úméhéwuúne) 'small trees'
      tree-⟨tree⟩-dim-pl

(460) tí-ːpʲɛ́-kpɯ̀   (dííbyéwu) 'he (who is) small'
      that-⟨SgM⟩-dim

(461) mɛ́ːní-kpɯ̀ɯ́-rɛ́-hɯ̀ɯkʰò (mééníwuúréjuco) 'ONLY the little pigs'
      pig-dim-only-focus

As explained above for -kʰópa 'augment', -kpɯ̀(σ) 'diminutive' may follow the pluralizer, in which case it diminishes the plurality of the referent:

(462) a. úmɛ̀-ʔɛ́-ːnɛ́-kpɯ̀   (úmehéénéwu) 'few trees'
         tree-⟨tree⟩-pl-dim
   b. ɯ̀ʔhɛ́-mɛ́-kpɯ̀   (uhjéméwu)   'few (AnPl)'
      few-⟨AnPl⟩-dim

7.4.3 -uvu 'maximal'

Suffixed to a noun phrase, -Ⓛɯβɯ (-uvu) 'max' indicates that the host's referent is in some maximal, exhorbitant, finalized, or surprising state. In 463 it indicates that the host's referent no longer exists.[12]

(463) a. niːβɯkpá-ɯβɯ (níívúwaúvu) 'dead deer'
         deer-max

   b. tʰá: Ⓖ kʰàːní-ɯ̀βɯ̀ (táácááníuvu) 'my deceased father'
      my   father-max

---

[11] This does not undergo FLTS, probably because the final /ɯ/ is lexically marked as low.

[12] -Ⓛɯβɯ 'max' generally imposes low tone on the preceding syllable, as in 463a; in 463b and 464 it fails to do so because of the exceptional tonal character of the root.

In 464 it indicates that the host's referent has not appeared for a considerable length of time:

(464) ¿Kiátú áánúuvu tsááhi?
    kʰiá-tʰɯ́   á:nɯ́-ɯ̀βɯ̀   tsʰá:-ʔì
    where-sou this(SgM)-max come-⟨t⟩
    'From whence does this one (SgM proximate) come (after such a long time)?'

-①ɯβɯ (-uvu) 'max' may also occur on a qualifier (i.e., an adjective followed by a classifier); see examples 519 and 520, page 229.

7.5 Quantifier phrases

A QUANTIFIER is formed by adding a classifier to one of the following roots:[13] mitʲʰa 'many, much, big', aja 'little, few', tʃʰóʔʲɯ 'little, few', ɯ̀ʔhɛ 'little, few', pʰiβa- 'numerous', or pʰa- 'all, complete'. (The last two are bound roots.)

(465) ɯ̀ʔhɛ́-mɛ̀-βà   (uhjémeva) 'few'
    few-⟨AnPl⟩-plQ
    ɯ̀ʔhɛ́-mɛ̀   (Uhjéme.) 'They are few.'
    few-⟨AnPl⟩

In many cases the classifier is -nɛ̀ ⟨ø⟩, as in 466:

(466) mítʲʰà-nɛ̀ (many-⟨ø⟩   mítyane) 'many (things)'
    pʰá-nɛ̀-ːɾɛ̀ (all-⟨ø⟩-only páneére) 'all (things)'

7.6 Conjoining noun phrases

There are two ways to conjoin noun phrases (including proper nouns and pronouns). First, -ma 'with' can be added to the second of two phrases. In this case the first generally bears a pluralizer corresponding to the total number of referents of the entire phrase. For example, in 467 hóáà 'John' bears -ma 'with' and pʰɛ́:tòɾò 'Peter' bears -mɯtsʰsi ⟨DuM⟩:

(467) Péédorómútsí Jóááma péé téhullévu.
    pʰɛ́:tòɾó-mɯ́tsʰí hóá:-<u>mà</u>   pʰɛ́:-ʔ   tʰɛ́-ʔɯ̀tʃɛ́-βɯ̀
    Peter-⟨DuM⟩   John-with go-⟨t⟩ that-⟨yonder⟩-goal
    'Peter and John went over yonder.'

---

[13]The inanimate indefinite pronouns formed from tsʰa(:)- 'one' or tsʰi(:)- 'some, other' described in section 8.5.2 are not quantifiers.

7.6. CONJOINING NOUN PHRASES

That the first of conjoined elements bears the number and gender marking for the whole phrase suggests that the first heads the phrase. This is confirmed by case marking: the first member bears the object case marker. For example, in 468 -kʰɛ 'objAn' occurs on pʰɛ́:tòrò but not on hóáà:

(468) Péédorómútsikye Jóááma ájtyúmɨɨbe.

pʰɛ́:tòró-múɨtsʰì-kʲʰɛ̀ hóá:-<u>mà</u> áˣtʲʰúmì-:pɛ̀ 'He saw Peter
Peter-⟨DuM⟩-objAn John-with see-⟨SgM⟩ and John.'

The second way to conjoin noun phrases is by listing items, adding a mora to each, and following the list with one of the following "summation" words:

(469) ɛ́-ʔtùɨ-mɛ̀-(ʔhɨ̀)   (éhdumehjɨ ~ éhdume) 'that many
    that-like-⟨AnPl⟩-(pl)   (animate)'
    ɛ́-ʔtùɨ-nɛ̀-(ʔhɨ̀)   (éhdunehjɨ ~ éhdune) 'that many
    that-like-⟨ø⟩-(pl)   (inanimate)'
    íˣkʲʰà-mɛ̀-(ʔhɨ̀)   (íjcyámehjɨ ~ íjcyáme) 'these
    be-⟨AnPl⟩-(pl)   (animate)'
    íˣkʲʰà-nɛ̀-(ʔhɨ̀)   (íjcyánehjɨ ~ íjcyáne) 'these
    be-⟨ø⟩-(pl)   (inanimate)'

In the following examples the summation word bears case marking appropriate to the grammatical relation of the noun phrases being conjoined—nominative in 470 and accusative in 471 and 472:

(470) Péédoroo Jóááá Perípee éhdume péé téhullévu.

pʰɛ́:tòrò-: hóáà-á̱¹⁴ pʰɛ̀rípʰɛ̀-: ɛ́-ʔtùɨ-mɛ̀ pʰɛ́:-ʔ
Peter-and John-and Philip-and that-⟨like⟩-⟨AnPl⟩ go-⟨t⟩

tʰɛ́-ʔùɨtʃɛ́-βùɨ
that-⟨yonder⟩-goal
'Peter, John, and Philip went over yonder.'

Compare examples 471 and 472. Some speakers prefer -kʰɛ 'objAn' on each member, as in 471, while others prefer that it not to be there, as in 472:

(471) Íñáhbekee íñáállekee ɨ́ɨtsɨ́ɨmekee íjcyámeke tsajtyéébe téhullévu.

[í ⒼⒿ ɲá-ʔpɛ̀]-kʰɛ̀-: [í ⒼⒿ ɲá:-tʃɛ̀]-kʰɛ̀-:
self   sib-⟨SgM⟩ -objAn-and self   sib-⟨SgF⟩ -objAn-and

[ɨ́: ⒼⒿ tsʰɨ́:mɛ̀]-kʰɛ̀-: [íˣkʲʰá]-mɛ̀-kʰɛ̀
self   children   -objAn-and be   -⟨AnPl⟩-objAn

---

¹⁴In the case of pʰɛ́:tòrò and pʰɛ̀rípʰɛ̀ the addition of a mora simply lengthens the final vowel. However, with hóá:, the additional mora is a low following two high tones, so undergoes FLTS.

tsʰàˣtʲʰɛ́-ːpè tʰɛ́-ʔɯ̀tʃɛ́-βɯ̀ɪ
take-⟨SgM⟩ that-⟨yonder⟩-goal
'He took his brother, his sister, and his children yonder.'

(472) Íñáhbee íñaállee ίίtsiίmee íjcyámeke tsajtyéébe téhullévu.

[[í Ⓖ ɲá-ʔpè]-ː [í Ⓖ ɲa̋-tʃè]-ː
   self sib-⟨SgM⟩ -and self sib-⟨SgF⟩ -and

 [ίː Ⓖ tsʰìːmè]-ː íˣkʲʰá]-mè-kʰḛ̀   tsʰàˣtʲʰɛ́-ːpè
   self children -and be   -⟨AnPl⟩-objAn take-⟨SgM⟩

tʰɛ́-ʔɯ̀tʃɛ́-βɯ̀ɪ
that-⟨yonder⟩-goal
'He took his brother, his sister, and his children yonder.'

In 472, the object is a single relative clause in which each conjunct is a complement of íˣkʲʰa 'be', while in 471 each conjunct is an object of tsʰaˣtʲʰɛ 'take'.

7.7 Numeral phrases

Table 7.3 lists Bora numeral phrases from one to twenty. The inanimate ones bear the classifier -nɛ ⟨ø⟩ but this could be replaced by another inanimate classifier. Section 7.7.1 deals with how these numeral phrases are formed, and section 7.7.2 explains a rather remarkable fact about how nouns agree with a numeral phrase.

Table 7.3 The Bora numeral phrase

NUM	ANIM	GEN	BORA PHRASE
1	inan		tsane
			tsʰà-nè
	anim	masc	tsaápi
			tsʰàː-pʰḭ̀
	anim	fem	tsáápille
			tsʰáː-pʰìtʃè
2	inan		míñéécuú
			mí-ɲɛ́-ːkʰɯ̀ɯ́
	anim	masc	míítyétsií
			míː-tʲʰɛ́tsʰìí
	anim	fem	míítyépɨɨ́
			míː-tʲʰɛ́pʰɨ́ɨ́
3	inan		pápihchúúneva
			pʰápʰḭ̀ʔtʃʰɯ́ːnè-βà
	anim		pápihchúúmeva
			pʰápʰḭ̀ʔtʃʰɯ́ːmè-βà

continued next page

7.7. NUMERAL PHRASES

continued from previous page

NUM	ANIM	GEN	BORA PHRASE
4	inan		pɨ́ɨ́néehójtsɨ́neva
			pʰɨ́ːnɛ́-ɛ̀-ʔóˣtsʰɨ́-nɛ̀-βà
	anim		pɨ́ɨ́néehójtsɨ́meva
			pʰɨ́ːnɛ́-ɛ̀-ʔóˣtsʰɨ́-mɛ̀-βà
5	inan		tsáhojtsɨ́neva
			tsʰá-ʔòˣtsʰɨ́-nɛ̀-βà
	anim		tsáhojtsɨ́meva
			tsʰá-ʔòˣtsʰɨ́-mɛ̀-βà
6	inan		íñejcúéhójtsɨtu tsane
			í-ɲɛ̀ˣkʰɯ́-ɛ́-ʔóˣtsʰɨ̀-tʰɯ̀ tsʰà̰-nɛ̀
	anim	masc	íñejcúéhójtsɨtu tsaápi
			í-ɲɛ̀ˣkʰɯ́-ɛ́-ʔóˣtsʰɨ̀-tʰɯ̀ tsʰà̰ː-pʰɨ̰
	anim	fem	íñejcúéhójtsɨtu tsáápille
			í-ɲɛ̀ˣkʰɯ́-ɛ́-ʔóˣtsʰɨ̀-tʰɯ̀ tsʰá̰ː-pʰɨ̰tʃɛ̀
7	inan		íñejcúéhójtsɨtu míñéécuú
			í-ɲɛ̀ˣkʰɯ́-ɛ́-ʔóˣtsʰɨ̀-tʰɯ̀ mɨ́-ɲɛ́-ːkʰɯ̀ɾɯ́
	anim	masc	íñejcúéhójtsɨtu míítyétsií
			í-ɲɛ̀ˣkʰɯ́-ɛ́-ʔóˣtsʰɨ̀-tʰɯ̀ mɨ́ː-tʲʰɛ́tsʰɨ̰í
	anim	fem	íñejcúéhójtsɨtu míítyépɨɨ́
			í-ɲɛ̀ˣkʰɯ́-ɛ́-ʔóˣtsʰɨ̀-tʰɯ̀ mɨ́ː-tʲʰɛ́pʰɨ̰ɨ́
8	inan		íñejcúéhójtsɨtu pápihchúúneva
			í-ɲɛ̀ˣkʰɯ́-ɛ́-ʔóˣtsʰɨ̀-tʰɯ̀ pʰápʰɨ̰ʔtʃʰɯ́ː-nɛ̀-βà
	anim		íñejcúéhójtsɨtu pápihchúúmeva
			í-ɲɛ̀ˣkʰɯ́-ɛ́-ʔóˣtsʰɨ̀-tʰɯ̀ pʰápʰɨ̰ʔtʃʰɯ́ː-mɛ̀-βà
9	inan		íñejcúéhójtsɨtu pɨ́ɨ́néehójtsɨ́neva
			í-ɲɛ̀ˣkʰɯ́-ɛ́-ʔóˣtsʰɨ̀-tʰɯ̀ pʰɨ́ːnɛ́-ɛ̀-ʔóˣtsʰɨ́-nɛ̀-βà
	anim		íñejcúéhójtsɨtu pɨ́ɨ́néehójtsɨ́meva
			í-ɲɛ̀ˣkʰɯ́-ɛ́-ʔóˣtsʰɨ̀-tʰɯ̀ pʰɨ́ːnɛ́-ɛ̀-ʔóˣtsʰɨ́-mɛ̀-βà
10	inan		tsáhojtsɨ́cúneva
			tsʰá-ʔòˣtsʰɨ́-kʰɯ́-nɛ̀-βà
	anim		tsáhojtsɨ́cúmeva
			tsʰá-ʔòˣtsʰɨ́-kʰɯ́-mɛ̀-βà
11	inan		méjtúhatyu tsane
			mɛ́-ˣtʰɯ́ɾʔà-tʲʰɯ̀ tsʰà̰-nɛ̀
	anim	masc	méjtúhatyu tsaápi
			mɛ́-ˣtʰɯ́ɾʔà-tʲʰɯ̀ tsʰà̰ː-pʰɨ̰
	anim	fem	méjtúhatyu tsáápille
			mɛ́-ˣtʰɯ́ɾʔà-tʲʰɯ̀ tsʰá̰ː-pʰɨ̰tʃɛ̀
12	inan		méjtúhatyu míñéécuú
			mɛ́-ˣtʰɯ́ɾʔà-tʲʰɯ̀ mɨ́-ɲɛ́-ːkʰɯ̀ɾɯ́
	anim	masc	méjtúhatyu míítyétsií
			mɛ́-ˣtʰɯ́ɾʔà-tʲʰɯ̀ mɨ́ː-tʲʰɛ́tsʰɨ̰í
	anim	fem	méjtúhatyu míítyépɨɨ́
			mɛ́-ˣtʰɯ́ɾʔà-tʲʰɯ̀ mɨ́ː-tʲʰɛ́pʰɨ̰ɨ́
13	inan		méjtúhatyu pápihchúúneva
			mɛ́-ˣtʰɯ́ɾʔà-tʲʰɯ̀ pʰápʰɨ̰ʔtʃʰɯ́ː-nɛ̀-βà
	anim		méjtúhatyu pápihchúúmeva
			mɛ́-ˣtʰɯ́ɾʔà-tʲʰɯ̀ pʰápʰɨ̰ʔtʃʰɯ́ː-mɛ̀-βà
14	inan		méjtúhatyu pɨ́ɨ́néehójtsɨ́neva
			mɛ́-ˣtʰɯ́ɾʔà-tʲʰɯ̀ pʰɨ́ːnɛ́-ɛ̀-ʔóˣtsʰɨ́-nɛ̀-βà

continued next page

continued from previous page

NUM	ANIM	GEN	BORA PHRASE
	anim		méjtúhatyu píínéehójtsímeva
			mɛ́-ˣtʰɨ́ɨ́ʔà-tʲʰɨ̀ɨ pʰí:nɛ́-ɛ̀-ʔóˣtsʰí-mɛ̀-βà
15	inan		tsahójtsícuma tsájtuháneva
			tsʰà-ʔóˣtsʰí-kʰɨ̀ɨ-mà tsʰá-ˣtʰɨ̀ɨʔá-nɛ̀-βà
	anim		tsahójtsícuma tsajtúháácyúmeva
			tsʰà-ʔóˣtsʰí-kʰɨ̀ɨ-mà tsʰà-ˣtʰɨ́ɨ́ʔá-:kʲʰɨ́ɨ́-mɛ̀-βà
16	inan		íñejcúéjtúhatyu tsane
			í-ɲɛˣkʰɨ́ɨ́-ɛ́-ˣtʰɨ́ɨ́ʔà-tʲʰɨ̀ɨ tsʰà-nɛ̀
	anim	masc	íñejcúéjtúhatyu tsaápi
			í-ɲɛˣkʰɨ́ɨ́-ɛ́-ˣtʰɨ́ɨ́ʔà-tʲʰɨ̀ɨ tsʰà:-pʰì
	anim	fem	íñejcúéjtúhatyu tsáápille
			í-ɲɛˣkʰɨ́ɨ́-ɛ́-ˣtʰɨ́ɨ́ʔà-tʲʰɨ̀ɨ tsʰá:-pʰìʧɛ̀
17	inan		íñejcúéjtúhatyu míñéécuú
			í-ɲɛˣkʰɨ́ɨ́-ɛ́-ˣtʰɨ́ɨ́ʔà-tʲʰɨ̀ɨ mí-ɲɛ́-:kʰɨ̀ɨɨ́
	anim	masc	íñejcúéjtúhatyu míítyétsií
			í-ɲɛˣkʰɨ́ɨ́-ɛ́-ˣtʰɨ́ɨ́ʔà-tʲʰɨ̀ɨ mí:-tʲʰɛ́tsʰìí
	anim	fem	íñejcúéjtúhatyu míítyépɨ́ɨ
			í-ɲɛˣkʰɨ́ɨ́-ɛ́-ˣtʰɨ́ɨ́ʔà-tʲʰɨ̀ɨ mí:-tʲʰɛ́pʰɨ̀ɨ́
18	inan		íñejcúéjtúhatyu pápihchúúneva
			í-ɲɛˣkʰɨ́ɨ́-ɛ́-ˣtʰɨ́ɨ́ʔà-tʲʰɨ̀ɨ pʰápʰì²ʧʰɨ́ɨ:-nɛ̀-βà
	anim		íñejcúéjtúhatyu pápihchúúmeva
			í-ɲɛˣkʰɨ́ɨ́-ɛ́-ˣtʰɨ́ɨ́ʔà-tʲʰɨ̀ɨ pʰápʰì²ʧʰɨ́ɨ:-mɛ̀-βà
19	inan		íñejcúejtúhatyu píínéehójtsíneva
			í-ɲɛˣkʰɨ́ɨ́-ɛ́-ˣtʰɨ́ɨ́ʔà-tʲʰɨ̀ɨ pʰí:nɛ́-ɛ̀-ʔóˣtsʰí-nɛ̀-βà
	anim		íñejcúéjtúhatyu píínéehójtsímeva
			í-ɲɛˣkʰɨ́ɨ́-ɛ́-ˣtʰɨ́ɨ́ʔà-tʲʰɨ̀ɨ pʰí:nɛ́-ɛ̀-ʔóˣtsʰí-mɛ̀-βà
20	inan		tsahójtsícuma tsajtúháácyúneva
			tsʰà-ʔóˣtsʰí-kʰɨ̀ɨ-mà tsʰà-ˣtʰɨ́ɨ́ʔá-:kʲʰɨ́ɨ́-nɛ̀-βà
	anim		tsahójtsícuma tsajtúháácyúmeva
			tsʰà-ʔóˣtsʰí-kʰɨ̀ɨ-mà tsʰà-ˣtʰɨ́ɨ́ʔá-:kʲʰɨ́ɨ́-mɛ̀-βà

7.7.1 The composition of numeral phrases

Numeral phrases are headed by a classifier (underlined in the examples in the tables 7.4–7.8). The inanimates will be illustrated using -nɛ (-ne) ⟨ø⟩. The animates use one of the classifiers appearing in the third column of table 6.1, page 164.

The numeral phrases are based on a metaphor of fingers, hands, and feet. This is very evident in the numerals for five, ten, fifteen, and twenty; see table 7.4.

7.7. NUMERAL PHRASES

Table 7.4 The numerals 5, 10, 15, and 20

5	inan	tsáhojtsíneva
		tsʰá-ʔòˣtsʰɨ́-nè̱-βà
		one-⟨hand⟩-⟨ø⟩-plQ
	anim	tsáhojtsɨ́meva
		tsʰá-ʔòˣtsʰɨ́-mè̱-βà
		'one hand of'
10	inan	tsáhojtsɨ́cúneva
		tsʰá-ʔòˣtsʰɨ́-kʰɨ́ɨ-nè̱-βà
		one-⟨hand⟩-du-⟨ø⟩-plQ
	anim	tsáhojtsɨ́cúmeva
		tsʰá-ʔòˣtsʰɨ́-kʰɨ́ɨ-mè̱-βà
		'two hands of'
15	inan	tsahójtsɨ́cuma tsájtuháneva
		tsʰà-ʔóˣtsʰɨ́-kʰɨ̀ɨ-mà tsʰá-ˣtʰɨ̀ɨʔá-nè̱-βà
		one-⟨hand⟩-du-with one-⟨foot⟩-⟨ø⟩-plQ
	anim	tsahójtsɨ́cuma tsajtúháácyúmeva
		tsʰà-ʔóˣtsʰɨ́-kʰɨ̀ɨ-mà tsʰà-ˣtʰɨ́ɨʔá-:kʲʰɨ́ɨ-mè̱-βà
		'along with two hands, a foot of'
20	inan	tsahójtsɨ́cuma tsajtúháácyúneva
		tsʰà-ʔóˣtsʰɨ́-kʰɨ̀ɨ-mà tsʰà-ˣtʰɨ́ɨʔá-:kʲʰɨ́ɨ-nè̱-βà
		one-⟨hand⟩-du-with one-⟨foot⟩-du-⟨ø⟩-plQ
	anim	tsahójtsɨ́cuma tsajtúháácyúmeva
		tsʰà-ʔóˣtsʰɨ́-kʰɨ̀ɨ-mà tsʰà-ˣtʰɨ́ɨʔá-kʲʰɨ́ɨ-mè̱-βà
		'along with two hands, two feet of'

pʰà- 'all' may be used instead of tsʰà- 'one' in expressing the numbers for ten, fifteen and twenty:

(473) a. páhojtsɨ́cúmeva
 b. pahójtsɨ́cuma tsájtyuháwava
 c. pahójtsɨ́cume tsajtyúháácyúneva

a. pʰáʔòˣtsʰɨ́kʰɨ́mè̱βà   'ten beings (AnPl)'
b. pʰàʔóˣtsʰɨ́kʰɨ̀mà tsʰáˣtʲʰɨ̀ɨʔákpàβà   'fifteen slabs, tables,…'
c. pʰàʔóˣtsʰɨ́kʰɨ̀mè̱ tsʰàˣtʲʰɨ́ɨʔá:kʲʰɨ́mè̱βà   'twenty things'

The numeral phrases for one through four are illustrated in table 7.5.

Table 7.5 The numerals 1–4

1	inan		tsane
			tsʰà-**nè**
			one-⟨ø⟩
	anim	masc	tsaápi
			tsʰà:-**pʰì**
	anim	fem	tsáápille
			tsʰá:-**pʰì**-tʃè
			'one'
2	inan		míñéécuú
			mí-ɲɛ́-:kʰʉ́ɾʉ́
			two-⟨ø⟩-du
	anim	masc	míítyétsií
			mí:-tʲʰɛ́tsʰìí
	anim	fem	míítyépɨ́ɨ́
			mí:-tʲʰɛ́pʰɨ́ɨ́
			'two'
3	inan		pápihchúúneva
			pʰá-pʰìʔtʃʰʉ́:-**nè**-βà
			all-piled.up-⟨ø⟩-plQ
	anim		pápihchúúmeva
			pʰápʰìʔtʃʰʉ́:-**mè**-βà
			'piled up'
4	inan		pɨ́ɨ́néehójtsɨ́neva
			pʰɨ́:nɛ́-è-ʔóˣtsʰɨ́-**nè**-βà
			half-per-⟨hand⟩-⟨ø⟩-plQ
	anim		pɨ́ɨ́néehójtsɨ́meva
			pʰɨ́:nɛ́-è-ʔóˣtsʰɨ́-**mè**-βà
			'half a hand of'

Some speakers express 'three' as a combination of the numeral phrases for 'two' and 'one', as in the following:

(474) a. mí:-tʲʰɛ́tsʰìí tsʰà:-pʰì: (míítyétsií tsaápii) 'three (SgM)'
    two-⟨DuM⟩ one-⟨SgM⟩
  b. mí:-tʲʰɛ́pʰɨ́ɨ́ tsʰá:-pʰìtʃè: (míítyépɨ́ɨ́ tsáápillee) 'three (SgF)'
    two-⟨DuF⟩ one-⟨SgF⟩
  c. mí:-ɲɛ́-kʰʉ́ɾʉ́ tsʰà-nè (mííñécuú tsane) 'three things'
    two-⟨ø⟩-du one-⟨ø⟩

7.7. NUMERAL PHRASES

The base for the numerals from six to nine is íɲèˣkʰɨ́ɨ̀ɛ̀ʔóˣtsʰɨ̀tʰɨ̀ɨ 'from the hand on this side'. To this are added the phrases for the digits given above in table 7.5; see table 7.6.

Table 7.6 The numerals 6–9

6	inan		íñejcúehójts<del>i</del>tu tsane	
			í-ɲèˣkʰɨ́ɨ̀-ɛ̀-ʔóˣtsʰɨ̀-tʰɨ̀ɨ	tsʰà-<u>nè</u>
			this-side-per-⟨hand⟩-sou	one-⟨ø⟩
	anim	masc	íñejcúehójts<del>i</del>tu tsaápi	
			í-ɲèˣkʰɨ́ɨ̀-ɛ̀-ʔóˣtsʰɨ̀-tʰɨ̀ɨ	tsʰàː-<u>pʰì</u>
		fem	íñejcúehójts<del>i</del>tu tsáápille	
			í-ɲèˣkʰɨ́ɨ̀-ɛ̀-ʔóˣtsʰɨ̀-tʰɨ̀ɨ	tsʰáː-<u>pʰì</u>-t͡ʃɛ̀
				'one from the hand on this side'
7	inan		íñejcúehójts<del>i</del>tu míñéécuú	
			í-ɲèˣkʰɨ́ɨ̀-ɛ̀-ʔóˣtsʰɨ̀-tʰɨ̀ɨ	mí-ɲɛ́-ːkʰɨ̀ɨ́ɨ̀
			this-side-per-⟨hand⟩-sou	two-⟨ø⟩-du
	anim	masc	íñejcúehójts<del>i</del>tu míítyétsií	
			í-ɲèˣkʰɨ́ɨ̀-ɛ̀-ʔóˣtsʰɨ̀-tʰɨ̀ɨ	míː-<u>tʲʰɛ́tsʰɨ̀í</u>
		fem	íñejcúehójts<del>i</del>tu míítyépi<del>i</del>	
			í-ɲèˣkʰɨ́ɨ̀-ɛ̀-ʔóˣtsʰɨ̀-tʰɨ̀ɨ	míː-<u>tʲʰɛ́pʰɨ̀í</u>
				'two from the hand on this side'
8	inan		íñejcúehójts<del>i</del>tu pápichúúneva	
			í-ɲèˣkʰɨ́ɨ̀-ɛ̀-ʔóˣtsʰɨ̀-tʰɨ̀ɨ	pʰápʰìt͡ʃʰɨ́ːː-<u>nè</u>-βà
			this-side-per-⟨hand⟩-sou	piled.up-⟨ø⟩-plQ
	anim		íñejcúehójts<del>i</del>tu pápichúúmeva	
			í-ɲèˣkʰɨ́ɨ̀-ɛ̀-ʔóˣtsʰɨ̀-tʰɨ̀ɨ	pʰápʰìt͡ʃʰɨ́ːː-<u>mè</u>-βà
				'piled up from the hand on this side'
9	inan		íñejcúehójts<del>i</del>tu p<del>íí</del>néhojts<del>í</del>neva	
			í-ɲèˣkʰɨ́ɨ̀-ɛ̀-ʔóˣtsʰɨ̀-tʰɨ̀ɨ	pʰɨ́ːnɛ́-ʔòˣtsʰɨ́-<u>nè</u>-βà
			this-side-per-⟨hand⟩-sou	half-⟨hand⟩-⟨ø⟩-plQ
	anim		íñejcúehójts<del>i</del>tu p<del>íí</del>néhojts<del>í</del>meva	
			í-ɲèˣkʰɨ́ɨ̀-ɛ̀-ʔóˣtsʰɨ̀-tʰɨ̀ɨ	pʰɨ́ːnɛ́-ʔòˣtsʰɨ́-<u>mè</u>-βà
				'half a hand from the hand on this side'

The base for the numerals from eleven to fourteen is mé^{x}t^{h}ɯ́ʔàt^{jh}ɯ̀ 'from our foot'. To this are added the phrases for the digits given above in table 7.5, as seen in table 7.7.

Table 7.7 The numerals 11–14

11	inan		méjtúhatyu tsane
			mé ^{x}t^{h}ɯ́ʔà-t^{jh}ɯ̀ tsʰà-<u>nè</u>
			SAP foot-sou one-⟨ø⟩
	anim	masc	méjtúhatyu tsa:pi
			mé ^{x}t^{h}ɯ́ʔà-t^{jh}ɯ̀ tsʰà:-<u>pʰì</u>
		fem	méjtúhatyu tsáápille
			mé ^{x}t^{h}ɯ́ʔà-t^{jh}ɯ̀ tsʰá:-<u>pʰì</u>-tʃè
			'one from our (SAP's) foot'
12	inan		méjtúhatyu míñéécuú
			mé ^{x}t^{h}ɯ́ʔà-t^{jh}ɯ̀ mí-ɲé-:kʰɯ̀ɯ́
			SAP foot-sou two-⟨ø⟩-du
	anim	masc	méjtúhatyu míítyétsií
			mé ^{x}t^{h}ɯ́ʔà-t^{jh}ɯ̀ mí:-t^{jh}étsʰìí
		fem	méjtúhatyu míítyépíí
			mé ^{x}t^{h}ɯ́ʔà-t^{jh}ɯ̀ mí:-t^{jh}épʰɨ́ɨ́
			'two from our foot'
13	inan		méjtúhatyu pápihchúúneva
			mé ^{x}t^{h}ɯ́ʔà-t^{jh}ɯ̀ pʰápʰì?tʃʰɯ́:-<u>nè</u>-βà
			SAP foot-sou piled.up-⟨ø⟩-plQ
	anim		méjtúhatyu pápihchúúmeva
			mé ^{x}t^{h}ɯ́ʔà-t^{jh}ɯ̀ pʰápʰì?tʃʰɯ́:-<u>mè</u>-βà
			'piled up from our foot'
14	inan		méjtúhatyu pɨ́ɨ́néehójtsɨ́neva
			mé ^{x}t^{h}ɯ́ʔà-t^{jh}ɯ̀ pʰɨ́:né-è-?ó^{x}tsʰɨ́-<u>nè</u>-βà
			SAP foot-sou half-per-⟨hand⟩-⟨ø⟩-plQ
	anim		méjtúhatyu pɨ́ɨ́néehójtsɨ́meva
			mé ^{x}t^{h}ɯ́ʔà-t^{jh}ɯ̀ pʰɨ́:né-è-?ó^{x}tsʰɨ́-<u>mè</u>-βà
			'half a hand from our foot'

7.7. NUMERAL PHRASES

The base for the numerals from sixteen to nineteen is íɲèˣkʰúɛ̀ˣtʰúɾʔà-tʲʰù̀ 'from the foot on this side'. To this is added the phrases for the digits given above in table 7.5; see table 7.8.

Table 7.8 The numerals 16–19

16	inan		íñejcúéjtúhatyu tsane	
			í-ɲèˣkʰúɾ-ɛ́-ˣtʰúɾʔà-tʲʰù̀	tsʰà-n̲è̲
			this-side-per-⟨foot⟩-sou	one-⟨ø⟩
	anim	masc	íñejcúéjtúhatyu tsaápi	
			í-ɲèˣkʰúɾ-ɛ́-ˣtʰúɾʔà-tʲʰù̀	tsʰà:-p̲ʰ̲ì̲
		fem	íñejcúéjtúhatyu tsáápille	
			í-ɲèˣkʰúɾ-ɛ́-ˣtʰúɾʔà-tʲʰù̀	tsʰá:-p̲ʰ̲ì̲-t̲ʃ̲è̲
			'one from the foot on this side'	
17	inan		íñejcúéjtúhatyu míñéécuú	
			í-ɲèˣkʰúɾ-ɛ́-ˣtʰúɾʔà-tʲʰù̀	mí-ɲɛ́-:kʰù̀ɾú̀
			this-side-per-⟨foot⟩-sou	two-⟨ø⟩-du
	anim	masc	íñejcúéjtúhatyu míítyétsií	
			í-ɲèˣkʰúɾ-ɛ́-ˣtʰúɾʔà-tʲʰù̀	mí:-t̲ʲ̲ʰ̲ɛ̲̲́t̲s̲ʰ̲í̲í̲
		fem	íñejcúéjtúhatyu míítyépɨɨ	
			í-ɲèˣkʰúɾ-ɛ́-ˣtʰúɾʔà-tʲʰù̀	mí:-t̲ʲ̲ʰ̲ɛ̲̲́p̲ʰ̲ɨ̲ɨ̲
			'two from the foot on this side'	
18	inan		íñejcúéjtúhatyu pápihchúúneva	
			í-ɲèˣkʰúɾ-ɛ́-ˣtʰúɾʔà-tʲʰù̀	pʰápʰìʔtʃʰúɾ:-n̲è̲-βà
			this-side-per-⟨foot⟩-sou	piled.up-⟨ø⟩-plQ
	anim		íñejcúéjtúhatyu pápihchúúmeva	
			í-ɲèˣkʰúɾ-ɛ́-ˣtʰúɾʔà-tʲʰù̀	pʰápʰìʔtʃʰúɾ:-m̲è̲-βà
			'piled up from the foot on this side'	
19	inan		íñejcúéjtúhatyu pɨɨnéehójtsɨneva	
			í-ɲèˣkʰúɾ-ɛ́-ˣtʰúɾʔà-tʲʰù̀	pʰɨ:nɛ́-è-ʔóˣtsʰɨ-n̲è̲-βà
			this-side-per-⟨foot⟩-sou	half-per-⟨hand⟩-⟨ø⟩-plQ
	anim		íñejcúéjtúhatyu pɨɨnéehójtsɨmeva	
			í-ɲèˣkʰúɾ-ɛ́-ˣtʰúɾʔà-tʲʰù̀	pʰɨ:nɛ́-è-ʔóˣtsʰɨ-m̲è̲-βà
			'half a hand from the foot on this side'	

The numeral phrases given above are the standard forms used by the Iñeje clan,[15] but they do shorten them in certain contexts, when the meaning is clear.

It is possible to form numeral phrases that refer to numbers larger than twenty, but these are long and complicated. For that reason many speakers use numbers borrowed from Spanish, adding to these the classifier of the referent. With the exception of *uno* '1', the Spanish numbers are all treated

---

[15]Other clans use somewhat different forms, but form the numeral phrases in the same way.

as plural. Examples follow, written in a highly assimilated form. (Most Bora speakers would now say them much as pronounced in Spanish.)

(475) dyetsitsééneva
 tʲètsʰìtsʰɛ́ː-nè̱-βà¹⁶ '16 things'

(476) wareetatséétéjava
 kpàrɛ̀ːtʰàtsʰɛ́ːtʰɛ́-hà̱-βà¹⁷ '47 houses (pants, shirts,...)'

(477) tsiéétó terééta tsééheva
 tsʰìɛ́ːtʰó tʰɛ̀rɛ́ːtʰà tsʰɛ́ː-ʔè̱-βà¹⁸ '136 trees (plants)'

The pluralizer -βà 'plQ' is used only with numeral phrases and other expressions referring to quantities, as discussed in section 7.3.7.

7.7.2 Agreement with numeral phrases

The last word of a numeral phrase bears a classifier. This classifier heads the numeral phrase. The phrase's animacy, gender, and number are those of the final word.

When the numeral phrase quantifies another noun phrase, that phrase must agree in animacy, gender and number. For example, in 478 the numeral phrase (bracketed) ends with tsʰà-ːpʰì (one-⟨SgM⟩) 'one', which is animate, singular and masculine. Thus the noun phrase quantified by this numeral phrase must be animate, singular and masculine, so bears -ːpʲɛ ⟨SgM⟩, although one would expect 'dog' to be plural:

(478) íñejcúehójtsɨtu tsaapi oohííbye
 [í-ɲèˣkʰɯ́ɯ-è-ʔóˣtsʰɨ-tʰɯ̀ɯ tsʰà-ːpʰì] òːʔí-ːpʲɛ̀ 'six dogs'
 this-side-per-⟨hand⟩-sou one-⟨SgM⟩ dog-⟨SgM⟩

Likewise, in 479, the final word of the numeral phrase, míːtʲʰɛ́pʰɨ́, is animate dual feminine, so the quantified noun phrase bears -mɯ́pʰɨ ⟨DuF⟩:

(479) íñejcúehójtsɨtu míítyépɨ wállemúpɨ
 [íɲèˣkʰɯ́ɯ-è-ʔóˣtsʰɨ-tʰɯ̀ɯ míː-tʲʰɛ́pʰɨ] kpátʃè-mɯ́pʰɨ
 this-side-per-⟨hand⟩-sou two-⟨DuF⟩ woman-⟨DuF⟩
 'seven women'

In 480, the final word of the numeral phrase is animate plural (unspecified for gender) and so the quantified noun phrase bears -mɛ 'plAn':

---

[16] In Spanish, sixteen is approximately [dʲe.si.sé ʲs].
[17] In Spanish, forty-seven is approximately [kʷa.ren.taʲ.sʲé.te].
[18] In Spanish, one hundred thirty-six is approximately [sʲén.to treʲn.taʲ.séʲs].

(480) íñejcúehójtsɨtu pápihchúúmeva walléému
 [í-ɲɛ̀ˣkʰɯ́-ɛ̀-ʔóˣtsʰɨ̀-tʰɯ̀ɯ   pʰápʰì̓ʔʧʰɯ́ː-mɛ̀-βà]   kpàʧɛ́ː-mɯ̀ɯ
 this-side-per-⟨hand⟩-sou piled.up-⟨AnPl⟩-plQ woman-⟨AnPl⟩
 'eight women'

7.8 Adjectives

Adjectives may be derived from verbs as discussed in section 4.3.4. In this section we discuss adjectives as prenominal modifiers (7.8.1), qualifier phrases, i.e., adjectives combined with classifiers (7.8.2), predicate adjectives (7.8.3), adjectives used as adverbs (7.8.4), and suffixes added to adjectives (7.8.5).

7.8.1 Prenominal modifiers

There seem to be no cases of an adjective modifying a noun in which these are related simply by constituency, as represented in 7.2a. We will discuss three apparent counter-examples: a modifier followed by a classifier, as in 7.2b; a modifier in a genitive relationship to the modified NP, as in 7.2c; and a modifier in apposition to a preceding NP, as in 7.2d.

> a. NP ⟶ Adj NP
> b. NP Ⓒ NP
> c. NP Ⓖ NP
> d. NP Ⓐ NP

Figure 7.2 The grammatical relation of prenominal modifiers

We begin in section 7.8.1.1 by illustrating 7.2b and c, using the modifier imɨa 'proper, of good quality'.
ᴸ

7.8.1.1 ɨmɨa 'of good quality'

In many cases a root or stem modifies a classifier. In this case the classifier heads the word or phrase, which is a single phonological phrase that respects the *LLX constraint. We will illustrate this using imɨa (ɨmɨa) 'proper (of good quality, right, righteous, just)' as the modifier. The examples below conform to the tone patterns of classifiers discussed in section 6.1.4, although this is not readily apparent because the lexically marked low tone

of ímɨ́a stops the classifer tone from docking on the its final syllable. For example, in 481 the classifier is monosyllabic so the classifier tone should dock on the modifier's final syllable, but this is blocked by the lexically marked low tone of ímɨ́a.

(481) a. ímɨ́ájaa méénuúbe.

b. ímɨ́ácoo tsívaábe.

   a. ímɨ́á   ⓒ hà: mɛ́:nù-:pɛ̀   'He made a good house.'
       proper   house

   b. ímɨ́á   ⓒ kʰò:[19]   tsʰíβà-:pɛ̀   'He brought good firewood.'
       proper   firewood

In other cases the modifying phrase stands in a genitive relationship to the noun (phrase) that it modifies (much like English *of good quality* stands in relation to *product* in *a product of good quality*). The genitive tone pattern (as given in table 9.1) is followed although, just as for the classifier tone pattern, this is not readily apparent because the lexically marked low tone of ímɨ́a blocks the genitive tone from docking on the final syllable.

As a first example, consider 482:

(482) ímɨ̀áˣ   ⓒ kʰò: (ímɨ́áj coó) 'good firewood'
       proper   firewood

Note that the head's preaspiration surfaces in the coda of the modifier's final syllable. This happens with certain nouns when they head a genitive construction, as discussed in section 2.4.3.

In 483 and 484 the heads are bisyllabic and—conforming to the pattern of table 9.1—bear high tone on the first syllable:[20]

(483) ímɨ́á   máˣtʃʰò (ímɨ́á májcho) 'good food'
      proper eat

      ímɨ́á   átò   (ímɨ́á ádo) 'good drink'
      proper drink

(484) ímɨ́á wájyú teene íjcyatúne.

     [ímɨ́á   ƙpáhʲɯ́ɨ] tʰɛ̀:-nɛ̀ íˣkʲʰà-tʰɯ́ɨ-nɛ̀ 'That is not real love.'
     proper love   that-⟨ø⟩ be-neg-⟨n⟩

---

[20]This presents an interesting wrinkle. Because the heads are nonfinite verbs, we expect the nonfinite low tone to occur on their initial syllables. This is not the case, presumably because the genitive tone pattern behaves *as though there were* a low tone on the modifier's final syllable, by virtue of which the head's initial syllable must bear high tone.

7.8. ADJECTIVES

In 485, which are possessed nouns, and 486, which are possessed nonfinite verbs, the head is trisyllabic and bears the genitive low tone on the first syllable:

(485) a. ímɨ́á nɯ̈-ˣpʰákʲʰò   (ɨ́mɨ́á nujpácyo) 'good water'
proper water-⟨liquid⟩

 b. ímɨ́á kpáhʲámɯ̀-mà (ɨ́mɨ́á wajyámu-ma) 'with good clothes'
proper clothes-with

 c. ímɨ́á ámó-mè-kʰɛ̀   (ɨ́mɨ́á amómeke) 'good fish
proper fish-⟨AnPl⟩-objAn   (AnPl, acc)'

(486) d. ímɨ́á áβʲɛ́hɯ̀-ːpɛ̀ (ɨ́mɨ́á avyéjuúbe) 'good chief'
proper reign-⟨SgM⟩

 e. ímɨ́á ɯ̈ːpátʃɛ̀ (ɨ́mɨ́á uubálle) 'good news'
proper tell

 f. ímɨ́á kʰáʔkʰɯ́ˣtsʰò (ɨ́mɨ́á cahcújtso) 'good beliefs'
proper believe

 g. ímɨ́á ɯ̈kpáːpò-hɯ̀ (ɨ́mɨ́á uwááboju) 'good teaching'
proper teach-⟨mouth⟩

 h. ímɨ́á ɯ̈kpáːpò-ˣtʰɛ́-kʰɛ̀ (ɨ́mɨ́á uwáábojtéke) 'good teach-
proper teach-⟨AnPl⟩-objAn   ers (acc)'

In 487 the head has four syllables. It bears the genitive low tone on the first syllable:

(487) ímɨ́á nɨ̀ːβɯ́kpà-mɯ̀ (ɨ́mɨ́á niivúwamu) 'good deer (plural)'
proper deer-plAn

In 488 the head is a nonfinite verb. The nonfinite low tone (represented by N) blocks the possessive tone from docking on the head's first syllable.

(488) ímɨ́á íˣtsʰᴺámɛ̂ì (ɨ́mɨ́á íjtsaméi) 'good thought'
proper think

 ímɨ́á kpákʰᴺímʲɛ̂ì (ɨ́mɨ́á wákimyéi) 'good work'
proper work

Because ímɨ́á 'proper' and the following head conform to the tone patterns of the genitive construction, we assume that it *is* a genitive construction, and thus that ímɨ́á and what it modifies are not related by constituency per se, but stand in a genitive relationship (possessor-possessed).

Although ímɨ́á 'proper' stands in a genitive relationship with the noun it modifies, the same is not true of other "adjectives." For example, compare 485a with the ungrammatical phrase in 489.[21]

(489) *ímí nɯ̀-ˣpʰákʲʰò̖ (ímí nujpácyo) 'good water'
good water-⟨liquid⟩

7.8.1.2 mítyane 'much'

We now come to the third apparent counter-example, that of figure 7.2d. The modifier mítʲʰànɛ̀ (mítyane) 'much' precedes the noun (phrase) it modifies, as in 490a where it appears to modify mɨ́ámɯ́nàà 'people'. However, we claim that the two words are not in a modifier-head relationship, but appositive, just as (more obviously) when the first word is headed by -mɛ ⟨AnPl⟩, as in 490b.[22]

(490) a. mítyane mɨamúnaa
b. mítyame mɨamúnaa

mítʲʰà - $\begin{cases} \text{a. -nɛ̀ ⟨ø⟩} \\ \text{b. -mɛ̀ ⟨AnPl⟩} \end{cases}$ Ⓐ mɨ́á mɯ́nàà 'many people'
many   SAP people

We understand this as follows. In 490b mítʲʰàmɛ would usually suffice to refer to "many people" because people are generally more topical than other collections of animate beings. Therefore 490b is a rather strange way to refer to "many people" (perhaps being reserved for cases of repair, where midstream the speaker realizes that the hearer needs clarification, so adds mɨ́ámɯ́nàà 'people').

By contrast, in 490a the notions of "many" and "people" are spread over two words, each of which is really a noun phrase in its own right. The first refers to "many" objects from the maximally unconstrained set established by -nɛ ⟨ø⟩; the second word is required to refer to "people". The point is that the notions of "many" and "people" are linked only through the structural mechanism of apposition, where -nɛ ⟨ø⟩ plays a semantically vacuous but structurally crucial role.[23]

---

[21] One may say the following, using apposition as described in section 7.8.1.2:
ímí-ɲɛ́   Ⓐ nɯ̀-ˣpʰákʲʰò̖   'good water'
good-⟨ø⟩   water-⟨liquid⟩

Or one may say the following, using a predicate adjective construction:
ímí nɯ́ɯ̀-ˣpʰàkʲʰò̖   'The water is good.'
good water-⟨liquid⟩

[22] 490a is more common than 490b. It may initiate a sentence whereas 490b may not.

[23] A further example from the translation of the New Testament into Bora follows:

The following example illustrates the same phenomenon but with pʰèβɛ́-nɛ̀ 'ordinary':

(491) Pevéne majchóré majchóme.

pʰèβɛ́-nɛ̀	màˣtʃʰó-ɾɛ́	màˣtʃʰó-mɛ̀	'They eat only
ordinary-⟨ø⟩	food-only	eat-⟨AnPl⟩	ordinary food.'

7.8.2 Qualifier phrases

Bound adjectival stems combine with classifiers to form:

- pronouns (see chapter 8),
- numeral phrases (see section 7.7),
- sentence-initial thematic connectives (see section 19.1), and
- qualifier phrases, now to be discussed.

Qualifier phrases characterize persons, animals, or things. They are formed by combining an adjectival root (either free or bound) with a classifier, and are animate or inanimate according to the classifier used. Because the classifier heads the phrase, these are actually noun phrases; we will nonetheless refer to them as "qualifiers" or "adjectives". Qualifier phrases may occur with or without an accompanying noun.

The form of qualifier phrases

Animate qualifier phrases are formed using the animate classifiers of column 2 of table 6.1, page 164. For example, ímɨ́á 'just, good' is an independent adjective; from it qualifier phrases can be formed as in 492:

(492) a. ímɨ́á-ːpɛ̀ (ímɨáábe) 'good (SgM)'
 b. ímɨ́á-ˣtʰɛ́pʰɨ̀ (ímɨájtépɨ) 'good (DuF)'
 c. ímɨ́á-ˣtʰɛ̀ (ímɨájte) 'good (AnPl)'

Inanimate qualifier phrases are formed by adding classifiers referring to the shape (or physical form) of the object being characterized. The classifier may be followed by -ːkʰɯ 'duIn' or -⁽ʔ⁾hɨ 'plural'; for example, ímɨ́à 'proper (of good quality, right, righteous, just)' and -ʔɛ 'tree, plant' can be combined to make the qualifier phrase ímɨ́à:-ʔɛ̀ 'good tree (plant,...)'. Examples follow for -kpa ⟨slab⟩ in 493 and -mɨ ⟨canoe⟩ in 494:

mítʰà-mɛ̀ pʰàɾìtsʰɛ́ó ¹ᴳ mʲɛ́mɛ́ fˣkʰá-ʔà múɨ̀nàà
much-⟨AnPl⟩ Pharisee self name be-⟨group⟩ people
'many of the group who were called Pharisees'

(493) a. ímɨ̱́á:-kpà   (ɨmɨ́ááwa)   'good slab (plank,...)'
     b. ímɨ̱́á-kpá-:kʰɨ̀ɨ̀ (ɨmɨ́áwáácu) 'two good slabs (tables,...)'
     c. ímɨ̱́á-kpá-ʔhɨ̀   (ɨmɨ́áwáhjɨ) 'good slabs (tables,...)'

(494) a. átʰɛ́ɾɛ́-ɛ̀-mɨ̀   (átéréemɨ)   'worthless canoe (ship, car,...)'
     b. p átʰɛ́ɾɛ́-ɛ̀-mɨ́-kʰɨ̀ɨ̀ (átéréemɨ́cu) 'two worthless canoes (ships, cars,...)'
     c. átʰɛ́ɾɛ́-ɛ̀-mɨ́-hɨ̀   (átéréemɨ́jɨ) 'worthless canoes ships, cars,...)'

Additional examples follow:

(495) Táñáhbé hajchóóbe.

[tʰá ⓖ ɲáʔpɛ́] ʔáˣt͡ʃʰó-:pɛ̀   'He is the same height
 my   brother   same.size-⟨SgM⟩   as my brother.'

(496) Ó imíllé tsaaja jaa óóma u méénune íjyá hajchója.

ó ìmít͡ʃɛ́-ʔì tsʰà:-hà   hà: ó:-mà ɨ̀ɨ̀ mɛ̀nɨ̀ɨ̀-nɛ̀
I want-⟨t⟩   one-⟨house⟩   house I-with you make-⟨ø⟩

í-hʲá   ʔáˣt͡ʃʰó-hà
that-⟨house⟩   same.size-⟨house⟩

'I want you to make me a house the same size as that house.'

A fairly complete list of bound adjectival stems is given in appendix C, page 413.

The use of qualifier phrases

Qualifier phrases can be used like other noun phrases to refer to persons, animals, or things. They are not used to introduce a new participant; they are only used when the context provides a referent. With sufficient context "one" could be the subject, as in 497:

(497) ímɨ̱́á-:pɛ́   tsʰá:-ʔì   (Ɨmɨáábé tsááhi.) 'One who is
      proper-⟨SgM⟩   come-⟨t⟩   good comes.'

Or they can be the direct object:

(498) mítʲʰà-nɛ̀ màˣt͡ʃʰó-mɛ̀ (Mítyane majchóme.) 'They ate a lot.'
      much-⟨ø⟩   eat-⟨AnPl⟩

In most languages an adjective modifies a noun by means of constituency: [NP Adjective Noun]. However, in Bora adjectives are made

into qualifier phrases and the nouns they modify are in apposition. For example, consider 499 in which kpà˟pʰì 'man' is in apposition to ímiá-ːpɛ́ 'good one':

(499) Ímɨ́áábé wɑjpi tsááhi.

    ímiá-ːpɛ́   Ⓐ kpà˟pʰì tsʰá:-ʔì   'A good man comes.'
    proper-⟨SgM⟩   man come-⟨t⟩

And this is the general case: qualifier phrases "modify" by the mechanism of apposition: QualifierP Ⓐ NP. Classifiers play the crucial roles of (1) heading the qualifier phrase[24] and (2) linking them referentially. For further discussion see section 7.1.

7.8.3 Predicate adjectives

An adjective may be the predicate of a clause, stating that the subject has whatever characteristic is indicated by the adjective. Predicate adjectives precede the subject. For example, imi 'good' is the predicate of 500:

(500) ímíʔ   o: (Ímí oó.)   { 'I am good.'
    good I   'I am in good health.'

Predicate adjectives have high tones on all syllables unless followed by -ⒺⒸkpɯ́(ɯ̀) 'diminutive', as in example 510.

Predicate adjectives end with a glottal stop,[25] as in 501a and b:

(501) a. ímíʔ   tì-ːpʲɛ̀   (Ímí diíbye.)   'He is good.'
        good-⟨t⟩ that-⟨SgM⟩
   b. ímíʔ-jɛ́   tì-ːpʲɛ̀   (Ímíhyé diíbye.) 'He is only good.'
        good-only that-⟨SgM⟩

When the clitic -ɾɛ̀ ~ -jɛ̀ follows, the glottal stop remains:

(502) ímíʔ-jɛ́-ʔ   tì-ːpʲɛ̀   (Ímíhyé diíbye.) 'He is healthy.'
    good-only-⟨t⟩ that-⟨SgM⟩

However, if -kpɯ 'diminutive' follows, the glottal stop is dropped:

(503) ìmí-kpɯ́ɯ̀   tì-ːpʲɛ̀   (Imíwú diíbye.) 'He is really
    good-dim that-⟨SgM⟩   good (beautiful).'

With monosyllabic roots, the /i/ of -ⒺⒸʔi ⟨t⟩ may undergo FLTS:

(504) ó tó:-ʔíí (Ó dóóhií.) 'I eat (meat).'

---

[24] A classifier may also head the noun phrase being qualified.
[25] This /ʔ/ may be cognate with -ʔì ⟨t⟩.

7.8.4 Adjectives used as adverbs

Some adjectives may be used adverbially. For example, in 505a imi (imi) 'good' is a predicate adjective modifying the subject kʰárakʰà 'chicken' but in 505b it modifies the verb màˣtʃʰóʔì 'eat':

(505) a. Ímí cáraca.
　　　b. Ímí cáraca majchóhi.

　　a. ímíˀ　kʰárák̰ʰà　　　　　　　'It is a good chicken.'
　　　　good chicken

　　b. ímíˀ　kʰárák̰ʰà màˣtʃʰó-ʔì　'The chicken eats well.'
　　　　good chicken　eat-⟨t⟩

The word order in 505b is interesting: it is as though the adverb is predicated of "the chicken eats." To characterize the chicken as good—without "good" being interpreted as an adverb, as in 505b—it is necessary to combine imi 'good' with a classifier and make "chicken" appositive to the combination, as in 506:

(506) Ímiibye cáraca majchóhi.

　　ímì-ːpʲɛ̀　　Ⓐ　kʰáràkʰà màˣtʃʰó-ʔì　'The good chicken eats.'
　　good-⟨SgM⟩　　chicken　eat-⟨t⟩

Another example of an adjective used adverbially follows:

(507) Mítyane ímíjyuuvéme.

　　mítʲʰà-nè　ímíhʲùː-ːβɛ́-mè　'They became very happy.'
　　much-⟨ø⟩　happy-sIn-⟨AnPl⟩

7.8.5 Suffixes added to adjectives

There are three suffixes that can be added to an adjective: -kpɯ(ː) (wuu ~ wu) 'diminutive' (7.8.5.1), -itʃʰo (icho) 'somewhat' (7.8.5.2) (the co-occurrence of these is discussed in section 7.8.5.3), and -Ⓛɯβɯ (-uvu) 'max' (7.8.5.4).

7.8.5.1 -wuu ~ -wu 'diminutive, very'

The suffix -kpɯ́ɯ (-wuu) 'dim' is used to enhance the meaning of its host. -kpɯ̀ is used word finally and -kpɯ́ɯ is used when some suffix follows; compare mɛ́ːní-kpɯ̀ 'little pig' with mɛ́ːní-kpɯ́ɯ́-mɯ̀ /mɛ́ːní-kpɯ̀ː-mɯ̀/ 'little pigs'.

When -k͡pṹ(ɯ) 'dim' follows a noun, both the noun's final and penultimate syllables generally bear high tone, as in the examples just given. Following an adjective the form is generally #⑬...-k͡pṹ(ɯ̀), that is, it imposes a low tone on the adjective's initial syllable, as in 508–509:

(508) ájá-k͡pɯ̀   ɯ̀nɯ́ (Ayáwu uú.) 'You are very tiny.'
      small-dim you

(509) ìmí-k͡pɯ̀ tì:-tʃɛ̀   (Imíwu díílle.) 'She is beautiful.'
      good-dim that-⟨SgF⟩

When #⑬...-k͡pṹ(σ) 'dim' follows a scalar adjective, it indicates an extreme degree on the (implied) scale, as illustrated in 510:

(510) Imíwu dɨ́jtsɨ+méne.

   ìmí-k͡pɯ̀ tɨ́   ˣtsʰɨ̀:mɛ́nɛ̀   'Your baby is very
   good-dim your child   good (or pretty).'

Because ìmí-k͡pɯ̀ 'very good' is the predicate in 510, we might expect it to bear all high tones, but -k͡pɯ̀ imposes a low tone on its host's initial syllable. For additional examples, compare the a and b sentences in 511 and 512:

(511) a. Chémépí dííbye.
      b. Chemépíwu dííbye.
      a. tʃʰɛ́mɛ́-pʰí⁽ʔ⁾[26]   tì-:pʲɛ̀   'He is sickly'
         sick-excess   that-⟨SgM⟩
      b. tʃʰɛ́mɛ́-pʰí-k͡pɯ̀ tì-:pʲɛ̀   'He is very sickly'
         sick-excess-dim that-⟨SgM⟩

(512) a. Wákímyéípí dííbye.
      b. Wakímyéípíwu dííbye.
      a. k͡pákʰímʲɛ́í-pʰí⁽ʔ⁾   tì-:pʲɛ̀   'He is a hard worker.'
         work-excess   that-⟨SgM⟩
      b. k͡pákʰímʲɛ́í-pʰí-k͡pɯ̀ tì-:pʲɛ̀   'He is a very
         work-excess-dim   that-⟨SgM⟩   hard worker.'

7.8.5.2 -icho 'somewhat'

The suffix -itʃʰo (-icho) 'somewhat' is used with scalar adjectives to indicate a moderate degree along the (implied) scale; e.g., with *big* it means

---

[26] -⑬○pʰi 'excessive' derives stative verbs (adjectives) from verbs; see also examples 193 and 194, page 117.

somewhat big, with *small* it means *somewhat small*, and so forth. Examples follow. Note that -itʃʰo 'somewhat' may follow a predicate adjective with a following subject, as in 513b, or with a following subject classifier, as in 513c:

(513) a. ájá⁽ʔ⁾   tì-ːpʲɛ̀   (Áyá diíbye.)
     small   that-⟨SgM⟩
   b. ájá-ítʃʰóʔ   tì-ːpʲɛ̀   (Áyáichó diíbye.)
     small-ish   that-⟨SgM⟩
   c. ájá-ítʃʰò-ːpɛ̀   (Áyáichoóbe.)
     small-ish-⟨SgM⟩

a. 'He is small.'
b,c. 'He is somewhat small (medium sized, not very small).'

(514) mítʲʰá-ítʃʰóʔ tì-ːpʲɛ̀   (Mítyáichó diíbye.) 'He is rather big.'
     big-ish   that-⟨SgM⟩

(515) a. Kéémú diílle.
    b. Kéémúíchó diílle.

   a. kʰɛ́ːmɯ́ɯ   a. 'She is big.'
   b. kʰɛ́ːmɯ́ɯ-ítʃʰó } tìː-tʃɛ̀   { b. 'She is medium
     big-ish   that-⟨SgF⟩   sized (not very big).'

(516) a. Í mityáíchóóbeke tsiva
   b. Í ayáíchóóbeke tsiva
   c. Í ayáíchóóbéwuúke tsiva

   a. í   mìtʲʰá-ítʃʰó-ːpɛ̀-kʰɛ̀
      self large-ish-⟨SgM⟩-objAn
   b. í   àjá-ítʃʰó-ːpɛ̀-kʰɛ̀
      self small-ish-⟨SgM⟩-objAn
   c. í   àjá-ítʃʰó-ːpé-kpɯ̰́ɯ́-kʰɛ̀
      self small-ish-⟨SgM⟩-aug-objAn

tsʰìβà
bringImp

'Bring me one of them that is { a. somewhat large.'
                                       b. somewhat small.'
                                       c. very small.'

7.8.5.3 The co-occurrence of -kpɯ(ɯ)(ː) and -itʃʰo

The suffixes -kpɯ(ɯ)(ː) (-wuu) 'diminutive' and -itʃʰo (-icho) 'somewhat' may co-occur in the same word, as in 516c, 517, and 518:

7.8. ADJECTIVES

(517) Áyáichówú cahgúnuco mewájtúíyoki.
ájá-ìtʃhó-kpɨ́ɨ̀ kʰàʔkɨ́mɨ̀ɨ-kʰò mɛ̀ kpáˣtʰɨ́ɨ-í-jò-kʰì
small-ish-dim manioc.drink-⟨cls⟩ SAP serve-fut-frs-pur
'There is too little manioc drink for us to serve.'

(518) Cáracáwu dsɨ́jɨvé íñehnííchóóbéwuúvu.
kʰáràkʰá-kpɨ̀ɨ tsɨ́hɨ̀βέ-ʔ í ɲɛ̀ʔní-ːtʃhó-ːpɛ́-kpɨ́ɨ́ɨ́-βɨ̀ɨ
chicken-dim die-⟨t⟩ self ugly-ish-⟨SgM⟩-dim-sou
'The chick died, the rather ugly one (of them).'

7.8.5.4 -uvu 'maximal'

-Ⓛɯβɯ (-uvu) 'maximal' can be added to an adjective to indicate its maximum degree, as in 519 and 520:

(519) àˣtʲʰɨ́βá-nɛ̀-ɨ́βɯ (ajtyúváneúvu) 'the most brilliant
     green-⟨ø⟩-max   green (or blue) thing'

(520) ímí-ɲɛ̀-ɨ́βɨ́ɨ mɛ́ːnɨ̀ɨ-kʰò (Ímíñeúvú méénuco.) 'Do it as well
     good-⟨ø⟩-max do-dim   as possible.'

Compare these examples to those of section 7.4.3.

Chapter 8

Pronouns

Pronouns are noun phrases: they have the distribution of noun phrases and, in Bora, are constructed like noun phrases, being headed by a classifier. They differ from nouns in that they take different pluralizers and they may not introduce a participant into the universe of discourse.

There are various classes of pronouns: personal pronouns (8.1), inanimate anaphoric pronouns (8.2), the anaphor i 'self' (8.3), demonstrative pronouns (8.4), indefinite pronouns (8.5), and possessive pronouns (8.6). For many of these it is convenient to subdivide the discussion based on animacy. Further, interrogative pronouns are discussed in chapter 15, in sections 15.2.1 and 15.2.2.

8.1 Personal pronouns

8.1.1 The form of personal pronouns

Personal pronouns are masculine, feminine, or unspecified for gender; they may be first, second, or third person; they may be singular, dual, or plural. First person dual and plural may be either inclusive (in.) or exclusive (ex.).[1] See table 8.1.

---

[1]These forms involve the following systems of features: item: ±SAP, ±singular; +SAP: ±1person; −singular: ±dual; +dual: ±masc; −SAP, +singular: ±masc.

The morphemes from which these words are formed are: o [+1person, +singular], ɯ [−1person, +singular], mɯɨʔ- ~ mɯː- [+SAP, −singular], ti(ː)- [−SAP], tsʰi- [+masc], -ʔpʰi̢ [−masc], a- [−1person, −singular:], -tʲʰɛ [−SAP, −singular], mɛ [+1person, −exclusive], -ːpɛ [+SAP, +singular, +masc], -tʃɛ [+SAP, +singular, −masc], -ʔa [+SAP, −dual]

Table 8.1 Personal pronouns

	singular		dual		plural
	masculine	feminine	masculine	feminine	
1	o		mɨ̀ɹʔ-tshɨ̀	mɨ̀ɹʔ-phɨ̵	mɨ̀ɹː-ʔæ̀[a]
	oó		muhtsi	muhpɨ̵	muúha
2	ɯ[b]		á-mɨ̀ɹʔ-tshɨ̀	á-mɨ̀ɹʔ-phɨ̵	á-mɨ̀ɹː-ʔæ̀
	uú		ámuhtsi	ámuhpɨ̵	ámuúha
3	tìː-ːpʲɛ̀	tìː-tʃɛ̀	tìː-tʲhɛ́tshɨ̀	tìː-tʲhɛ́phɨ̵	tìːL-tʲhɛ̀[c]
	diíbye	diílle	diityétsi	diityépɨ̵	diítye

[a] This is the first person plural *exclusive* form. The corresponding *inclusive* form is mɛ 'SAP'. See example 524.

[b] In example 1182 ɯ 'you' followed by -ma 'with' at the end of a phrase becomes ɯ́ː-màá 'with you'. We do not know why the vowel of the pronoun is lengthened in this case.

[c] This has a lexically marked low tone on the first syllable. This low tone blocks the low of -Ⓛkhɛ 'objAn': tìː-tʲhɛ́-khɛ̀ 'to those (AnPl)'. Other pronouns formed with -thɛ̀ may have a lexically marked low tone, but it seems that this is not the case for all of them.

In addition to these there is (1) the first person inclusive form mɛ 'SAP', and (2) combinations of tìː- 'that' and an animate classifier like -tshɨ̀ 'child'.

Note that the second person dual and plural forms are like the corresponding first person forms except that the second person forms begin with á-.

When a personal pronoun is a preverbal subject, if it has a long vowel, this is shortened. For example, tìːpʲɛ̀ 'he (SgM)' changes to tìpʲɛ̀, as in 521:

(521) Tsá dibye péeityú.

tsʰáH? tì-pʲɛ̀   pʰɛ́ː-ì-tʲʰɯ́ː   'He will not go.'
not that-⟨SgM⟩ go-fut-neg

A monosyllabic pronoun cliticizes to a following verb. Consequently the pronoun and the first syllable of the verb may not both bear low tones as these would violate the *LLX constraint. Examples abound for the first and second person singular; mɛ 'SAP' occurs in 522 where the verb is phonetically [mɛ́pʰɛ̀ɛ́ʔ]:

(522) mɛ́   pʰɛ̀-ɛ́-ʔì   (Mépeéhi.) 'Let's (in.) go.'
     SAP go-fut-⟨t⟩

When the subject is a first or second person dual or plural pronoun, mɛ is "echoed" on the verb. For example, in 523a the subject is first person plural exclusive and in 523b it is second person dual masculine:

8.1. PERSONAL PRONOUNS

(523) a. Muha mepéjucóóhi.
    b. ¿A ámuhtsi metsááhi?

   a.   mùɨ̀ʔà   <u>mè</u>   pʰɛ́-hùɨkʰó:-ʔì   'We (ex.)
        we   SAP go-now-⟨t⟩   are going now.'
   b. à   ámùɨ²tsʰì <u>mè</u> tsʰá:-ʔì   'Are you (DuM)
       ques you(DuM) SAP come-⟨t⟩   coming?'

Note the following contrast:

(524) a. Teene újcuube memájchoki.
    b. Teene újcuube muha memájchoki.

tʰɛ̀:-nɛ̀ ɨ́ɾˣkʰɨ̀ɨ-ːpɛ̀ { a. ø / b. mùɨ̀ʔà we } mè máˣtʃʰò-kʰì
that-⟨ø⟩ get-⟨SgM⟩   SAP eat-pur

'He got that in order that we ({ a. inclusive / b. exclusive }) eat it.'

The personal pronouns may occur with case markers. When they are direct objects, they bear -①kʰɛ 'objAn', as in 525 and 526:[2]

(525) ó áˣtʲʰùɨmɨ́-² tí-ːpʲɛ̀-<u>kʰɛ̀</u>   (Ó ájtyumɨ́ dííbyeke.) 'I saw
      I see-⟨t⟩   that-⟨SgM⟩-objAn   him.'

(526) Ó ájtyumɨ́ ámúhpɨke.
     ó áˣtʲʰùɨmɨ́-² ámúɨ-²pʰɨ-<u>kʰɛ̀</u> 'I saw you two (DuF).'
     I see-⟨t⟩   you-DuF-objAn

When they are goals, they take -⁽ʔ⁾ti 'animate' along with -βɨ̀ɨ 'goal, theme', as in 527:[3]

(527) Oke daacu tétsɨdívu.
    ò-kʰɛ̀ tà:kʰɨɨ tʰɛ́-tsʰɨ̀-tí-βɨ̀ɨ   'Give me that baby.'
    I-objAn give that-⟨baby⟩-anim-thm

When o, ɯ, and mɛ are used as direct objects (followed, of course, by -kʰɛ 'objAn') they have a single vowel, as in 528 and 529:

(528) ò-kʰɛ̀   ɨ́:tʰɛ̀-ːpɛ̀   (Oke ɨ́ɨteébe.) 'He looks at me.'
    I-objAn look-⟨SgM⟩

(529) <u>mè</u>-kʰɛ̀ ɨ́:tʰɛ̀-tʃɛ̀ (Meke ɨ́ɨtelle.) 'She looks at us (in.).'
    SAP-objAn look-⟨SgF⟩

---

[2] Another example is ò-kʰɛ̀ 'I-objAn' in 527; see the following footnote.

[3] The first person pronoun is marked as a direct object due to the animacy-motivated inversion discussed on page 662, while tʰɛ-tsʰɨ 'that-⟨child⟩' (a personal pronoun, as stated just after table 8.1) is marked as goal or theme.

However, in single word responses to questions the vowel is long, as in 530:

(530) a. ò:-kʰɛ̀ (Oóke.) 'To me.'
b. mɛ̀:-kʰɛ̀ (Meéke.) 'To us (in.).'

8.1.2 The use of personal pronouns

First and second person pronouns are used to refer to the speaker(s) and hearer(s) as needed. Third person pronouns are used either to "point" to a referent in the external context or to establish coreference with another referring expression, usually one that has been previously established. This latter use of pronouns competes with two alternatives: (1) with the anaphor i 'self', and (2) with the use of a classifier subject to refer to the subject. We comment briefly on these in turn.

First, i 'self' is an anaphor, so must be bound within a very local domain (as discussed further in section 8.3) while the personal pronouns must not be bound within that domain. For example, consider 531, the structure of which is represented in figure 8.1. The possessor in the subordinate clause is tí-ːpʲɛ̀ (that-⟨SgM⟩) and it is bound from outside of the subordinate clause. (It could refer to the speaker's brother or any other male other than the speaker himself.) If instead it were i 'self', as in 1157, page 439, it would be bound by the subject of its clause and thus refer to "me" rather than to John.[4]

(531) Táñahbe oke úhbápejtsó dííbye jávu o péébeke.

tʰá ⓖ ɲa̋-ʔpɛ̀   ò$_i$-kʰɛ̀   űʔpá-pʰɛ̀ˣtsʰó-ʔ
my   sib-⟨SgM⟩ I-objAn upbraid-meet-⟨t⟩

Ⓐ [[tí-ːpʲɛ̀   há   ]-βùɪ   ò$_i$ pʰɛ̀]-ːpɛ̀$_i$-kʰɛ̀
    that-⟨SgM⟩ house -goal I   go   -⟨SgM⟩-objAn

'My brother bawled me out right when I arrived at his house.'

---

[4]Note further that what is interpreted as a time adverbial is structurally a postpositional phrase in apposition to the direct object.

8.1. PERSONAL PRONOUNS

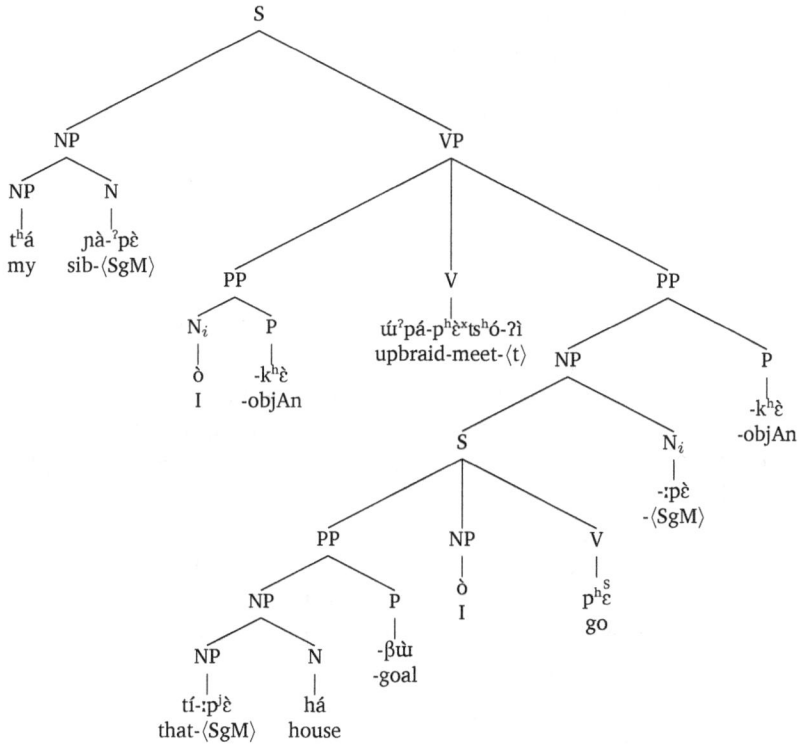

Figure 8.1 STR: example 531

Thus, the choice between a personal pronoun and the anaphor may be determined by the (structural) distance to the pronoun's coreferent: a pronoun if sufficiently far, the anaphor if sufficiently close.

Second, in some cases the choice between indicating a sentence's subject with an overt personal pronoun, as opposed to using a classifier on the verb, is determined by structural factors. For example, when a sentence is negated with tsʰá?(a)^H and -tʰɯ 'neg' an overt pronoun (or noun phrase) is required, but if it is negated (contrastively) with -hiː(βa) 'deny', a classifier subject is used; see section 13.3, particularly examples 850 and 851.

However, more generally the choice is determined by the issue of topic continuity:

continuity: A classifier subject on the verb is generally used when the subject remains the same, as in the second and third sentences of 1043, page 398. Continuity can also be maintained by making the subject a thematic connective, as in 1041, page 398.

discontinuity: Shifting the subject from the currently most topical referent to another possible referent generally requires using an overt pronoun or noun phrase. See, for example, the set in 1054–1056, page 401. A special case of this is to reestablish a topic that was earlier put aside; see section 19.1.4.

Continuity is generally more frequent than discontinuity, so subjects are more frequently indicated with a classifier than with an overt pronoun.

8.2 Inanimate anaphoric pronouns

An anaphoric pronoun refers to something previously mentioned.[5] Bora inanimate anaphoric pronouns are formed by adding a classifier to $t^h ɛ$:- 'aforementioned (that)'; they are third person, and may be singular, dual, or plural. For example:[6]

(532) a. $t^h ɛ̀ː$-nɛ̀   (teéne)   'that thing (in general)'
  b. $t^h ɛ̀ː$-kpà   (teéwa)   'that slab (plank, table, etc.)'
  c. $t^h ɛ̀ː$-mɨ̀   (teémɨ)   'that canoe (airplane, car,...)'
  d. $t^h ɛ́$-ʔàːmɨ̀ (téhaámɨ)   'that leaf (paper, book,...)'

The dual is formed by adding -ːkʰɯ̀ 'duIn' and the plural is formed by adding -⁽ʔ⁾hɨ 'plural'. Examples are given in 533:[7]

(533) a. $t^h ɛ́$-nɛ̀-ːkʰɯ̀   (téneécu)   'those two things (in general)'
  b. $t^h ɛ́$-kpà-ʔhɨ̀   (téwahjɨ)   'those slabs (benches,...)'
  c. $t^h ɛ́$-ʔàːmɨ́-kʰɯ̀ (téhaamɨ́cu)   'those two books (leaves,...)'
  d. $t^h ɛ́$-ʔàːmɨ́-hɨ̀   (téhaamɨ́jɨ)   'those leaves (papers,...)'

When an inanimate anaphoric pronoun is used as the subject of a clause, if it has a long vowel, then this shortens, as in 534:[8]

(534) tsʰá^{Hʔ} $t^h ɛ̀$-nɛ̀   ímì-tʲʰɯ́-(nɛ̀)   (Tsá tene ímityú(ne).) 'That is bad.'
  not   that-⟨ø⟩   good-neg-⟨n⟩

---

[5]Here we use *anaphoric* in its broader, traditional sense in which it contrasts with *cataphoric* 'forward-referring' and *exophoric* 'referring to something outside of the text'. Below we use *anaphor* in the narrower (more modern) sense of a pronoun that must be bound within a very local domain.

[6]In example 532a–c the root has a long vowel whereas in 532d the length is suppressed, presumably because the following suffix has a long vowel.

[7]By contrast to 532a–c (but like 532d), in 533 the length of $t^h ɛ$:- 'aforementioned (that)' is suppressed in all cases. This is presumably because—in every case—the following syllable is heavy. Further note that the length of -ːkʰɯ̀ 'duIn' is suppressed in 533c, presumably because of the length in the *preceding* syllable.

[8]Perhaps they are lengthened (or otherwise made heavy) when followed by a light syllable.

8.3. THE ANAPHOR I 'SELF'

Because these pronouns are inanimate, when occurring as the direct object they do not take -⒧kʰɛ 'objAn'; see 535. Nor do they take -ʔti 'animate' with -βùɨ 'goal, theme'; see 536.

(535) Ó ájtyumɨ́ teéwa.
  ó á˟tʲʰùɨmɨ́-ʔ tʰɛ̀ː-kpà   'I saw that slab (plank, table,...)'
  I see-⟨t⟩   that-⟨slab⟩

(536) Oke daacu téewavu.
  ò-kʰɛ̀   tàːkʰùɨ   tʰɛ́ː-kpà-βùɨ   'Give me that slab (bench,
  I-objAn give   that-⟨slab⟩-thm   table,...)'

8.3 The anaphor i 'self'

The morpheme i (i-) 'self' is an anaphor, a type of pronoun that must be bound in a very local domain. That is, an anaphor must be coreferential with an element that occupies a structurally more prominent position, but one that is not too far away. Generally it must not be farther away than the structurally closest subject (but not one that is structurally "lower" than the anaphor).[9] It may indicate the subject of a subordinate clause that is bound by the subject of the next higher verb, as shown in the following discussion and examples:

ADVERBIAL CLAUSES:

In example 537a the subject of the adverbial clause is indicated by the anaphor i 'self', which is bound by the subject of the main clause (indicated by the classifier on the main verb). By contrast, the overt pronoun in 537b must not be bound by the subject of the main clause, so necessarily refers to someone other than the subject of the main clause. Further examples: 863, page 331; 982, page 374; and 1059, page 403.

(537) a. Teene újcuube imájchoki.
   b. Teene újcuube dibye májchoki.

tʰɛ̀ː-nɛ̀   úɨ˟kʰùɨːpɛ̀   { a. ì self   }   má˟ʧʰò-kʰì
that-⟨ø⟩ get-⟨SgM⟩   { b. tì-pʲɛ̀ that-⟨SgM⟩ }   eat-pur

---

[9]Technically, an anaphor must be coindexed with a c-commanding noun phrase within the domain of the closest accessible subject.

a. He got that in order to eat it.
b. He$_i$ got that in order that he$_j$ eat it.

COMPLEMENT CLAUSES:

In 538 ì má^{x}tʃʰò-nὲ (self eat-⟨n⟩) is the complement of the ímítʃɛ- 'to want'. In 538a the subject of the complement is i 'self', which is bound by the subject of the higher verb. By contrast, the overt pronoun in 538b must not be bound by the subject of the main clause, so necessarily refers to someone other than the subject of the main clause:

(538) a. Imíllémé imájchone.

b. Imíllémé dibye májchone.

$$\text{ìmítʃé-mé} \atop \text{want-⟨AnPl⟩} \quad \begin{Bmatrix} \text{a. ì} \\ \text{self} \\ \text{b. tì-p}^j\text{ὲ} \\ \text{that-⟨SgM⟩} \end{Bmatrix} \quad \text{má}^x\text{tʃʰò-nὲ} \atop \text{eat-⟨ø⟩}$$

a. They want to eat.
b. They want him to eat.

Likewise, in 851b, page 328, the anaphoric subject of the complement is bound by the subject of 'to want' (whether indicated by a classifier as in 851a or by an overt personal pronoun as in 851b).

RELATIVE CLAUSES:

In 1030, page 392, the subject of the relative clause, indicated by i 'self', is coreferential with the subject of the main clause.

In 539, the three cases of i 'self' refer to the subject of the main clause. The two that are underlined indicate the subjects of subordinate clauses; the other (in the first word) is part of a possessive pronoun:

(539) Ihñe imújtátsóne imílleebe dihñe iújcune.

[ì^ʔ-ɲὲ   ì   mű^{x}tʰá-tsʰó]-nὲ   ìmítʃὲ-ːpὲ
self-⟨ø⟩ self lose-cause   -⟨event⟩ want-⟨SgM⟩

[tì^ʔ-ɲὲ ì ú^{x}kʰù̀]-nὲ   your-⟨ø⟩ self obtain -⟨ø⟩
'Having caused the loss of his own, he wants to get yours.'

We now turn to cases in which the anaphor is the modifier (possessor) in a genitive construction. In 540a the anaphor i 'self' modifies (possesses)

8.3. THE ANAPHOR I 'SELF'

'house' and refers to the sentence's subject (John). By contrast, in 540b the personal pronoun ti-:pʲɛ must refer to someone outside of this domain, that is, someone other than John:

(540) a. Jóáa péé ihjyávu.

b. Jóáa péé dííbye jávu.

hóáà pʰɛ́:-ʔì
John go-⟨t⟩
{
a. í̃ʔ   hʲá-βùɨ
   self   house-goal
b. tí-:pʲɛ̃   há-βùɨ
   that-⟨SgM⟩ house-goal
}

a. 'John$_i$ went to his$_i$ house.'
b. 'John$_i$ went to his$_j$ house. ($i \neq j$)'

And i 'self' behaves as an anaphor when it is part of a free possessive pronoun. For example, iʔɲɛ 'self's (thing)' must refer to something possessed by the referent of a nearby expression, one close enough to bind the anaphor. In 564, page 248, it refers to the sentence's subject.

Although i 'self' behaves like a typical anaphor in the majority of cases, some cases are unexpected. For example, in 541 it refers to the subject of the sentence, but that subject is outside of the immediate clause of the anaphor:

(541) Jóáa waajácú íoohííbye dsɨ́jɨvéne.

hóáà$_i$ kpà:hákʰúɨ-ʔ [í$_i$ Ⓖ o:ʔí-:pʲɛ̃   tsɨ́hɨ̀βɛ́]-nɛ̀
John know-⟨t⟩   self   dog-⟨SgM⟩ die   -⟨ø⟩
'John$_i$ knows that his$_i$ dog died.'

Example 542 is perhaps even more problematic. Generally anaphors must be coreferential to a noun phrase that is in a structurally more prominent position. However, in 542 i refers from within the subject to the direct object, which presumably is not more prominent:

(542) Íoohííbye Jóááke ɨhdóhi.

í   Ⓖ o:ʔí-:pʲɛ̃   hóá:-kʰɛ̀   íʔtó-ʔì   'John$_i$'s dog bit him$_i$.'
self dog-⟨SgM⟩ John-objAn bite-⟨t⟩

Technically, the binding expression should c-command the anaphor. Further, subjects generally c-command objects, but objects do not c-command subjects. This may be evidence that Bora has a "flat" structure, one lacking a verb phrase. However, this raises other questions beyond the scope of this grammar. We leave the question as an outstanding research issue.

8.4 Demonstrative pronouns

Demonstrative pronouns refer to a person or object, indicating the relative distance between it and the speaker: PROXIMATE refers to something close to the speaker; DISTAL refers to something far from the speaker; MEDIAL refers to something neither close to nor far from the speaker. The pronouns are formed from the roots listed in table 8.2:

Table 8.2 The roots of demonstrative pronouns

	PROXIMATE	MEDIAL	DISTAL
animate	í-	à:-	á:-
inanimate	í-	è:-	ɛ́ʔ-

Whether a demonstrative pronoun is animate or inanimate depends on the classifier that follows.

8.4.1 Animate demonstrative pronouns

Animate demonstrative pronouns are either masculine, feminine, or unspecified for gender. They are third person and either singular, dual, or plural. The proximate pronouns are formed with í- 'proximate' except in the singular, which forms are exceptional. The medial pronouns are formed with à:- 'medial'. The distal pronouns are formed with á:- 'distal'. See table 8.3.

Table 8.3 Animate demonstrative pronouns

		proximate (í-)	medial (à:-)	distal (á:-)
singular	masculine	á:nùɪ̀ áánuú	à:-pʲɛ̀ aábye	á:-tì (áádií)
	feminine	á:mʲɛ̀ áámyeé	à:-tʃɛ̀ aálle	á:-tʃɛ̀ (áálleé)
dual	masculine	í-ˣtʲʰɛ̀-tsʰì̠ íjtyetsi	à:-tʲʰɛ́-tsʰì̠ aatyétsi	á:-tʲʰɛ́-tsʰì̠ áátyétsií
	feminine	í-ˣtʲʰɛ̀-pʰì̠ íjtyepɨ	à:-tʲʰɛ́-pʰì̠ aatyépɨ	á:-tʲʰɛ́-pʰì̠ áátyépɨɨ́
plural		í-ˣtʲʰɛ̀ íjtyeé	à:-tʲʰɛ̀ aátye	á:-tʲʰɛ̀ áátyeé

Note that the medial and distal differ by the tone of the first syllable: low for medial and high for distal.[10]

The animate demonstrative pronouns are generally used to refer to beings (people or animals) that are within view, as in 543:

(543) á:nù̱ː   tsʰá-hù̱ɯkʰó:-ʔì̱   (Áánu tsájucóóhi.) 'This one (SgM)
      this.SgM come-now-⟨t⟩   has now come.'

They may also be used to answer a question. For example, the question in 544a could be answered by 544b:

(544) a. kʰìá   tì-:pʲɛ̀   (¿Kiá diíbye?) 'Where is he?'
         where that-⟨SgM⟩   (lit. 'Where he?')

    b. á:nù̱ː   (Áánuú.) 'He is here.'
       this.SgM

8.4.2 Inanimate demonstrative pronouns

Inanimate demonstrative pronouns are not specified for gender; they are third person and may be singular, dual or plural. These are formed by adding a classifier to í- 'demonstrative proximate' ɛ(:)- 'medial' and ɛ́ʔ- 'distal'. For example, see ɛ́-ˣpʰì in 545 and ɛ́ʔ-kpà: in 546:

(545) tsʰí-ˣpʰì   ɛ́-ˣpʰì   (tsíjpi éjpi) 'another's person
      other-⟨SgM⟩ that-⟨SgM⟩   (or animal)'

(546) ...dihñéwaa Moitsée éhwaa, Ería éhwaa...
      [tìʔɲɛ́-kpà:] [mòìtsʰɛ́ɛ́ᴳ ɛ́ʔ-kpà:]   [ɛ̀ríaᴳ ɛ́ʔ-kpà:]
      your-⟨slab⟩ Moses   that-⟨slab⟩   Elijah that-⟨shelter⟩
      '...your shelter, Moses' shelter, Elijah's shelter...'

Any of the classifiers can be used in this way. Table 8.4 illustrates this for -nɛ̀ ~ -ɲɛ̀ 'thing', -kpa 'slab, plank, table, bench, machete, knife and similar things', and -ʔa:mɨ 'leaf, paper, book, bill, and similar things'. The proximate, medial, and distal demonstratives are given as singular, dual (with -:kʰɯ 'duIn'), and plural (with -⁽ʔ⁾hɨ 'plural'). Note that, with perhaps a few exceptions, the medial and distal differ by the tone of the second syllable: low for medial and high for distal.

---

[10]Also note that in two places the first consonant is not palatalized by the preceding a:-, namely the singular masculine proximate and distal forms. In á:-tì: the palatalization may simply be masked by the following /i/. It may be that in á:-nù̱ː 'this (SgM)' palatalization is blocked to avoid confusion with à̱ɲù̱ː 'buzzard'; witness á:nù̱ː-kʰɛ̀ 'to him' versus áɲù̱ː-kʰɛ̀ 'to the buzzard'.

Table 8.4 Inanimate demonstrative pronouns

		singular	dual	plural
proximate (í-)	thing	í-ɲɛ̀ íñeé	í-ɲɛ̀-:kʰɯ̀ɪ íñeécu	í-ɲɛ̀-ʔhɪ̀ íñehjɨ
	slab	í-kpà íwaá	í-kpà-:kʰɯ̀ɪ íwaácu	í-kpà-ʔhɪ̀ íwahjɨ
	leaf	í-ʔʲà:mɨ̀ íhyaámɨ	í-ʔʲà:mɨ́-kʰɯ̀ɪ íhyaamɨ́cu	í-ʔʲà:mɨ́-hɪ̀ íhyaamɨ́jɨ
	...	...	...	...
medial (ɛ́:ŏ̄-)	thing	ɛ̀:-nɛ̀ eéne	ɛ́-nɛ̀-:kʰɯ̀ɪ éneécu	ɛ́-nɛ̀-ʔhɪ̀ énehjɨ
	slab	ɛ̀:-kpà eéwa	ɛ́-kpà-:kʰɯ̀ɪ éwaácu	ɛ́-kpà-ʔhɪ̀ éwahjɨ
	leaf	ɛ́-ʔà:mɨ̀ éhaámɨ	ɛ́-ʔà:mɨ́-kʰɯ̀ɪ éhaamɨ́cu	ɛ́-ʔà:mɨ́-hɪ̀ éhaamɨ́jɨ
	...	...	...	...
distal (ɛ́ʔŏ̄-)	thing	ɛ́ʔ-nɛ̀ (éhneé)	ɛ́ʔ-né-:kʰɯ̀ɪ éhnéécuú	ɛ́ʔ-né-ʔhɪ̀ éhnéhjɨɨ́
	slab	ɛ́ʔ-kpà éhwaá	ɛ́ʔ-kpá-:kʰɯ̀ɪ éhwáácuú	ɛ́ʔ-kpá-ʔhɪ̀ éhwáhjɨɨ́
	leaf	ɛ́ʔ-ʔá:mɨ̀ éháámɨɨ́	ɛ́ʔ-ʔá:mɨ́-kʰɯ̀ɪ éháámɨ́cuú	ɛ́ʔ-ʔá:mɨ́-hɪ̀ éháámɨ́jɨɨ́
	...	...	...	...

The combination of ɛʔ- 'that' and -nɛ ⟨ø⟩ forms a general demonstrative pronoun that can be used to point to any object (exophoric), but is most often used as the head of genitive construction, as in 547:

(547) tí-:pʲɛ̀ᴳ   ɛ́ʔ-nɛ̀   (dííbye éhne) 'that thing belonging
      that-⟨SgM⟩ that-⟨ø⟩   to him'

8.5 Indefinite pronouns

Indefinite pronouns may be animate (8.5.1) or inanimate (8.5.2).

8.5.1 Animate indefinite pronouns

The animate indefinite pronouns are all third person, and may be singular, dual, or plural. The singulars and duals may be masculine or feminine.

8.5. INDEFINITE PRONOUNS

Those in table 8.5 are derived from the root tsʰàː-ᴸ 'one, each' (also used in numeral phrases) and refer to indefinite persons or or animals. Those in table 8.6 are derived from the root tsʰi- 'other' and refer to some "other(s)".

Table 8.5 Animate indefinite pronouns: 'one'

	singular	dual	plural
masculine	tsʰàː-ːpʰì̧ tsaápi	tsʰà-ːtʰɛ́-tsʰì̧ tsaatétsi	tsʰà-ːtʰɛ̀ tsaáte
feminine	tsʰá-ːpʰì̧-tʃɛ̀ tsáápille	tsʰà-ːtʰɛ́-pʰɨ̧ tsaatépɨ	

The root tsʰaː- 'one, each' only occurs followed by a classifier; thus, "one man" or "one woman" is said as in 548:

(548) a. Tsaapi (wajpi) tsááhií.
  b. Tsaapille (walle) tsááhií.
  a. tsʰàː-ːpʰì̧   (kpà-ˣpʰì̧)
      one-⟨SgM⟩ person-⟨SgM⟩   tsʰáː-ʔìː   'One man came.'
  b. tsʰàː-ːpʰìtʃɛ̀ (kpà-tʃɛ̀)   come-⟨t⟩   'One woman came.'
      one-⟨SgF⟩   person-⟨SgF⟩

Table 8.6 Animate indefinite pronouns: 'other'

	singular	dual	plural
masculine	tsʰì̧-ˣpʰì̧ tsíjpi	tsʰí̧-ˣtʲʰɛ̀-tsʰì̧ tsíjtyetsi	tsʰì̧-ˣtʲʰɛ̀ tsijtye
feminine	tsʰí̧-ˣpʰì̧-tʃɛ̀ tsíjpille	tsʰí̧-ˣtʲʰɛ̀-pʰɨ̧ tsíjtyepɨ	

The pronouns in tables 8.5 and 8.6 result from combining morphemes from three sets; see table 8.7:[11]

---

[11] There is no masculine singular suffix; if there is no indication to the contrary, a singular is interpreted as masculine.

Table 8.7 Composition of animate indefinite pronouns

DETERMINER		NUMBER		NUMBER-GENDER	
tsʰaː-	'one'	-ˣpʰi[a]	'singular'	-tʃɛ	⟨SgF⟩
tsʰiː-	'other'	-ˣtʰɛ	'nonsingular'	-tsʰi	⟨DuM⟩
				-pʰɨ	⟨DuF⟩

[a] -ˣpʰi means 'body' but there is no simple gloss for -ˣtʰɛ.

Other animate indefinite pronouns are now illustrated. Those in 549 have tsʰaː- 'one, each (indefinite)', those of 550 have tsʰi- 'other'.

(549) a. ts<u>ʰá</u>ː-pʰìː-tsʰà   (tsáápiítsa) 'each one (SgM)'
         one-⟨SgM⟩-one
     b. ts<u>ʰá</u>ː-pʰìtʃé-tsʰà (tsáápillétsa) 'each one (SgF)'
         one-⟨SgF⟩-one
     c. ts<u>ʰà</u>-mútsʰì̀   (tsamútsi)   'both (DuM)'
         one-⟨DuM⟩
     d. ts<u>ʰà</u>-múɨpʰɨ̀   (tsamúpɨ)   'both (DuF)'
         one-⟨DuF⟩
     e. ts<u>ʰà</u>-mɛ́-ːɾɛ̀   (tsaméére)   'all of a group (AnPl)'
         one-⟨AnPl⟩-only

(550) a. ts<u>ʰí</u>-ɛ̀mɛ́-ˣpʰì   (tsíeméjpi)   'another one (SgM)'
         other-sim-sg
     b. ts<u>ʰí</u>-ɛ̀mɛ́-ˣtʰɛ̀   (tsíeméjte)   'other ones (AnPl)'
         other-sim-⟨AnPl⟩

Another animate indefinite pronoun is pʰá-mè-ːɾɛ̀ 'all (AnPl)' (formed from pʰà- 'all'); see 551 and 552:

(551) pʰá-mè-ːɾɛ̀   tsʰáː-ʔìː   (Pámeere tsááhií.) 'Everyone came.'
      all-⟨AnPl⟩-only come-⟨t⟩

(552) pʰá-mè-βá-ɾɛ̀[12]   tsʰáː-ʔìː   (Pámeváre tsááhi.) 'All kinds (AnPl)
      all-⟨AnPl⟩-pl-only come-⟨t⟩   came.'

---

[12]We do not know why -ːɾɛ̀ 'only' makes the preceding vowel long in 551 but not in 552.

8.5.2 Inanimate indefinite pronouns

The inanimate indefinite pronouns are third person and may be singular, dual or plural. They are formed by combining a classifier with a morpheme like tsʰa(:)- 'one', tsʰi- 'some, other' or tsʰí-ɛ̀mɛ́- 'something similar', (among other possibilities). The only difference between these and the animate indefinite pronouns is that these have inanimate classifiers whereas the former have animate ones.

A pluralizer may follow the classifier -ːkʰɯ 'duIn' or -⁽ʔ⁾hɨ 'plural'. These are illustrated in tables 8.8–8.10 with the classifiers -nɛ ⟨ø⟩, -ʔɛ 'tree, plant', and -⁽ʔ⁾pa 'soft fruits, thick drinks, and such'. (Note the quantity shifts.)

Table 8.8 Inanimate indefinite pronouns: 'one'

	singular	dual	plural
	one	both	some
thing	tsʰà-nɛ̀ tsane	tsʰá-nɛ̀-ːkʰɯ̀ tsáneécu	tsʰá-nɛ̀-ʔhɨ̀ tsánehjɨ
tree	tsʰà-ʔɛ̀ tsahe	tsʰá-ʔɛ̀-ːkʰɯ̀ tsáheécu	tsʰá-ʔɛ̀-ʔhɨ̀ tsáhehjɨ
fruit	tsʰà-ʔpà tsahba	tsʰá-pà-ːkʰɯ̀ tsábaácu	tsʰá-pà-ʔhɨ̀ tsábahjɨ
…	…	…	…

Table 8.9 Inanimate indefinite pronouns: 'other'

	singular	dual	plural
	another	two others	others (various)
thing	tsʰì-ːɲɛ̀ tsiíñe	tsʰí-ɲɛ̀-ːkʰɯ̀ tsíñeécu	tsʰí-ɲɛ̀-ʔhɨ̀ tsíñehjɨ
tree	tsʰì-ːʔɛ̀ tsiíhe	tsʰí-ʔɛ̀-ːkʰɯ̀ tsíheécu	tsʰí-ʔʲɛ̀-ʔhɨ̀ tsíhyehjɨ
fruit	tsʰì-ʔpà tsihba	tsʰí-pà-ːkʰɯ̀ tsíbaácu	tsʰí-pà-ʔhɨ̀ tsíbahjɨ
…	…	…	…

Table 8.10 Inanimate indefinite pronouns: 'some'

	singular	dual	plural
	some (one)	some (two)	some (various)
thing	tsʰí-èmɛ́-nè tsíemɛ́ne	tsʰí-èmɛ́-nɛ́-ːkʰùɪ tsíemɛ́néécu	tsʰí-èmɛ́-nɛ́-ʔhɨ̀ tsíemɛ́nɛ́hjɨ
tree	tsʰí-èmɛ́-ʔè tsíemɛ́he	tsʰí-èmɛ́-ʔɛ́-ːkʰùɪ tsíemɛ́héécu	tsʰí-èmɛ́-ʔɛ́-ʔhɨ̀ tsíemɛ́héhjɨ
fruit	tsʰí-èmɛ́-pà tsíemɛ́ba	tsʰí-èmɛ́-pá-ːkʰùɪ tsíemɛ́báácu	tsʰí-èmɛ́-pá-ʔhɨ̀ tsíemɛ́báhjɨ
...	...	...	...

Other inanimate indefinite pronouns are now illustrated. Those in 553 have the suffix -ːtsʰa 'each'.

(553) a. tsʰá-nè-ːtsʰà (tsáneétsa) 'each thing (one after the other)'
b. tsʰá-ʔè-ːtsʰà (tsáheétsa) 'each tree (one after the other)'
c. tsʰá-pà-ːtsʰà (tsábaátsa) 'each fruit (one after the other)'

(554) pʰá-nè-ːɾè   (páneére) 'all (things)'[13]
    all-⟨ø⟩-only

(555) mítʲʰà-nè   (mítyane) 'many (things)'
    big/many-⟨ø⟩

---
[13] Compare the animate in example 552.

8.6 Possessive pronouns

The POSSESSIVE PRONOUNS are given in table 8.11.

Table 8.11 Possessive pronouns

BOUND POSSESSIVE PRONOUNS			FREE POSSESSIVE PRONOUNS		
tʰa	(ta-)	'my'	tʰa-ʔɲɛ	(tahñe)	'mine'
ti	(di-)	'your'	ti-ʔɲɛ	(dihñe)	'yours'
mɛ	(me-)	'our (in.)'	mɛ-ʔnɛ	(mehne)	'ours (in.)'
mɯ	(mu-)	'of whom'	mɯ-ʔnɛ[a]	(muhne)	'whose?'
i[b]	(i-)	'self's'	i-ʔɲɛ	(ihñe)	'self's'[c]

[a]The final /e/ of mɯ̀ʔnɛ́ 'whose' becomes /a/ word finally.
[b]Strictly speaking, this is an anaphor, not a pronoun; see section 8.3.
[c]This is like English *his, hers, its, theirs*.

When a bound possessive pronoun tʰa-, ti-, mɛ- or i- possesses a monosyllabic noun, it is made heavy by the addition of a glottal stop. For example, compare the anaphoric pronoun in 556a with the possessive pronoun in 556b:

(556) a. /í-hà/   [íhʲà:] (íjyaá) 'this house'
      this-⟨shelter⟩
   b. /îʔ hà/   [îʔhʲà] (ihjya) 'self's house'
      self house

This is also evident in the free possessive pronouns of table 8.11.

The bound possessive pronouns are used as the modifier (possessor) in a genitive construction,[14] as discussed in chapter 9. They function much like the bound adjectival stems listed in appendix C but have a slightly different distribution.

FREE POSSESSIVE PRONOUNS are derived by adding the null classifier -nɛ ⟨ø⟩ to a bound possessive pronoun; these now function as a single

---

[14]In the following possessed forms of tsʰɨ:mɛ 'child' there are two curious alternations:

	SELF'S		MY	
CHILD	íˣtsʰɨ́:ménè	'self's child'	tʰáˣtsʰɨ́:ménè	'my child'
CHILDREN	í:tsʰɨ́:mè	'self's children'	á:tsʰɨ́:mè	'my children'

(1) The initial syllable of each *singular* form ends with ˣ whereas that of each *plural* form ends in vowel length. (2) For 'my' (in the second column), the singular form begins with /tʰ/ but this is absent in the plural form. We have no explanation for these alternations.

unit.[15] They are written as though a single morpheme throughout this grammar.

The free possessive pronouns are never used as the modifier (possessor) in a genitive construction; as stated above, this is done with bound possessive pronouns.

A free possessive pronoun may be followed by a classifier, forming a noun phrase headed by that classifier:[16]

(557) tʰàʔɲɛ́-ˣpʰɪ̀   (tahñéjpi) 'my person or animal (SgM)'
      mine-⟨SgM⟩

(558) mɯ̀ʔnɛ́-ʧɛ̀   (muhnélle) 'whose person or animal (SgF)?'
      whose-⟨SgF⟩

(559) mɛ̀ʔnɛ́-ˣtʰɛ̀   (mehnéjte) 'our (in.) persons or animals'
      our-pl

(560) páneere ihñénéhj+ma
      pʰá-nɛ-ːɾɛ̀ ìʔɲɛ́-nɛ́-ʔhɨ̀-mà   'with all the things
      all-⟨ø⟩-only self's-⟨ø⟩-pl-with   that belong to him'

(561) a. tìʔɲɛ́-ʔáːmɨ̀   (dihñéháám+)   'your leaf (paper,
         your-⟨leaf⟩   book,...)'
      b. tʰàʔɲɛ́-kpá-ːkʰɯ̀ɪ   (tahñéwáácu)   'my two slabs (planks,
         my-⟨slab⟩-du   machetes,...)'
      c. mɛ̀ʔnɛ́-ʔàːmɨ́-hɨ̀   (mehnéhaamɨ́jɨ) 'our leaves (papers,
         our(in.)-⟨leaf⟩-pl   books,...)'

(562) ìʔɲɛ́-kpà   (ihñéwa) 'his (self's) slab (table, machete,...)'
      self's-⟨slab⟩

(563) ìʔɲɛ́-íʔʧó   ⓖ pʰáɲɛ̀ (ihñéíhlló pañe)   'inside his (self's)
      self's-⟨pot⟩   inside   cooking pot'

The free possessive pronoun may itself be used as a noun phrase:

(564) ìᵢ-ʔɲɛ̀   tsʰíβàːpɛ̀ᵢ   (Ihñe tsívaábe.) 'Heᵢ brought hisᵢ own.'
      self-⟨ø⟩ bring-⟨SgM⟩

---

[15]Evidence for this claim is that a classifier may follow, as in 560, even the classifier -nɛ ⟨ø⟩, as in example 560.

[16]By contrast, the *bound* possessive pronouns are never followed directly by a classifier other than -nɛ̀ ⟨ø⟩. Thus, in 556b, ha is the noun 'house' and not the classifier -ha ⟨shelter⟩.

8.6. POSSESSIVE PRONOUNS

(565) a. Oke daaca dihñévu.
b. Oke daaca tsane dihñétu.

ò-kʰɛ̀ t-à:kʰà
i-objAn youImp-give

{ a. tì?ɲɛ́-βɯ̀ɪ
    your-thm
  b. [tsʰà-nɛ̀ Ⓐ tì?ɲɛ́]-tʰɯ̀ɪ
     one-⟨ø⟩   your -sou }

a. 'Give me yours.'
b. 'Give me some of yours.'

In example 565b the free possessive pronoun is appositive to tsʰà-nɛ̀ within the scope of the case marker. Free possessive pronouns may also be followed by one or more appositive noun phrases, as in 566. See also example 539.

(566) Oke daaca dihñéhaamɨ́vu díwaajácúhaamɨ́vu.

ò-kʰɛ̀ tà:kʰà tì?ɲɛ́-ʔà:mɨ́-βɯ̀ɪ Ⓐ tí k͡pà:hákʰɯ́ɪ-ʔà:mɨ́-βɯ̀ɪ
I-objAn give your-⟨leaf⟩-thm   your knowledge-⟨leaf⟩-thm

'Give me your book (lit. your leaf-like thing, your knowledge leaf-like thing.'

Free possessive pronouns may be used as predicate complements (which, recall, generally precede the subject in Bora) as in 567. (The final high tone in 567a and b is because they are questions.)

(567) a. mɯ̀?ná   ɛ̀:-nɛ̀   (¿Muhná eéne?) 'Whose is that?'
         whose   that-⟨ø⟩
      b. mɯ̀?nɛ́-ɾɛ́ ɛ̀:-nɛ̀   (¿Muhnéré eéne?) 'To whom only does
         whose-only that-⟨ø⟩   that belong?'
      c. tʰà?ɲɛ̀   ɛ̀:-nɛ̀   (Tahñe eéne.)   'That is mine.'
         mine   that-⟨ø⟩

Chapter 9
The Genitive Construction

The genitive construction joins two nouns or noun phrases into a single noun phrase.

[$_{NP}$ NP$_{modifier}$ N$_{head}$]

The meaning is generally that of "possession," in which the first noun (phrase) "possesses" the second. (We often refer to the modifier as the POSSESSOR and the head as the POSSESSED. The modifier (possessor) precedes the head (possessed) with the tones described in section 9.1. The modifier may cliticize to the head or it may be a separate word (or phrase).

9.1 Genitive tone

The genitive construction joins the modifier (possessor) and head (possessed) into a single phonological word. Evidence for this claim is as follows:

1. When the head begins with an aspirated stop, its preaspiration is syllabified with the modifier's final syllable. For example, in 579a (below) the final [ˣ] of the modifier is "launched by" the root ˣtsʰɨːmɛ̀ 'children'.[1]
2. When the possessor ends in /i/, it may palatalize the consonant of the following possessed noun. For example áːtí Ⓖ ɲàʔpɛ̀ /áːtí nàʔpɛ̀/ 'that (distant) person's brother'.

---
[1] When ˣtsʰɨːmɛ begins a phonological phrase, no preaspiration is possible because there is no preceding syllable coda with which it can be linked. Preaspiration is also blocked when the coda of the preceding syllable is already heavy, i.e., ends with a glottal stop or a long vowel.

251

3. Vowel harmony operates across the boundary; witness ì 'self' becoming
   ɨ̀ in 568 and 569. See also 620 below.
   (568) [ɨ̀   nɨ:tsʰɨ́-kpà   ]-rɨ̀   (ɨ́nɨɨtsúwari) 'with his machete'
         self machete-⟨slab⟩   -oblIn

   (569) [ɨ̀   ˣtsʰɨ́:ménè]-kʰɛ̀   (ɨ́jtsɨɨméneke) 'my child (acc)'
         self child   -objAn
4. Monosyllabic modifiers normally cliticize to the head. This is the case
   for the bound possessive pronouns listed in the first column of table
   8.11, page 247.
5. Because the modifier and head form a single phonological word, the
   *LLX constraint may not be violated therein. In particular, it must not
   be violated at the boundary between the modifier and head. (This is
   crucial to the analysis given below.)

In forming the genitive construction, there is a floating low tone between the modifier (possessor) and the head. We call this the GENITIVE TONE and represent it as Ⓖ:

MODIFIER Ⓖ HEAD

Ordinarily, if the head is mono- or bisyllabic (as in the first two columns of table 9.1), Ⓖ docks on the modifier's final syllable. Otherwise, that is, when the head has three or more syllables, Ⓖ docks on the head's initial syllable:

MODIFIER	HEAD
(POSSESSOR)	(POSSESSED)
(...σ)σ́ᴳ ·	σ(σ)#
(...σ) σ ·	σ́σσ(σ...)

The other tones in the word are either lexically marked or come about largely by default: The syllable preceding the one on which the genitive tone docks must bear high tone to avoid violating the *LLX constraint. At the end, unmarked syllables become low, while other unmarked syllables become high. Apparent exceptions to the defaults are due to lexically marked tones, as discussed in section 9.1.2.

If Ⓖ docks on the modifier's final syllable, then the modifier's penult (if present) must bear high tone to avoid violating the *LLX constraint. This pattern is carried through to the cases in which Ⓖ docks on the head:[2]

---

[2]We might understand this as follows. Suppose that the process of assigning tone in the genitive construction proceeds from left to right with only three syllable look-ahead. At the

9.1. GENITIVE TONE

$$((\ldots\sigma)\overset{H}{\sigma})\overset{G}{\sigma} \quad \cdot \quad \sigma(\sigma)\#$$
$$((\ldots\sigma)\overset{H}{\sigma}) \; \sigma \quad \cdot \quad \overset{G}{\sigma}\sigma\sigma(\sigma\ldots)$$

MODIFIER   HEAD

The possibilities are charted in table 9.1. The numbers in brackets refer to examples; in these, the genitive low tone is indicated by a G over the vowel.

Table 9.1 The basic tone patterns of the genitive construction

MODIFIER (POSS'R)	HEAD (POSS'D)		
	σ#	σσ#	σσσ(...)
#σ	ó· σ [570]	ó· ó σ [573]	ó·ó ó σ(...) [576]
#σσ	ó ó· σ [571]	ó ó· ó σ [574]	ó ó·ó ó σ(...) [577]
(...)σσσ	(...σ) ó ó· σ [572]	(...σ) ó ó· ó σ [575]	(...)σ ó ó·ó ó σ(...) [578]

(570) tʰǎʔ hʲà   (tahjya) 'my house'
     my house

(571) tí-ːpʲɛ̌   hà   (dííbye ja) 'his house'
     that-⟨SgM⟩ house

(572) a. mɛ́ːní-mɯ̌ hà   (méénímu ja) 'pigs' house'
       pig-pl house

     b. kpàʔáɾǒ   hà   (waháro ja) 'mother's house'
       mother

(573) a. tʰǎ máˣtʃʰò   (tamájcho) 'my food'
       my food

     b. tʰǎ mɛ́ːnì   (tamééni) 'my pig'
       my pig

     c. ǐʔ mɨ́ː-nɛ̀   (ɨhmɨ́ɨne) 'his canoe'
       self transport-⟨ø⟩

(574) a. tí-ːpʲɛ̌   máˣtʃʰò   (dííbye májcho) 'his food'
       that-⟨SgM⟩ food

     b. tí-ːpʲɛ̌   ɛ́ʔ-hà   (dííbye éhja) 'his house
       that-⟨SgM⟩ thm-⟨shelter⟩   (clothes,...)'

---

point it assigns tone to the modifier's penult it can only "see" the next three syllables, i.e., the modifier's final syllable and the head's first two. Thus, it cannot know whether Ⓖ will dock on the next syllable—in which case it would have to assign high tone—or on the head's initial syllable. The only possibility that will always avoid violating *LLX is to assign high tone to the modifier's penult.

(575) mɛ́ːní-mɯ̀ɯ̀ má*tʃʰò (méénímu májcho) 'pigs' food'
pig-pl   food

(576) a. tʰá mɛ́ːní-mɯ̀ɯ̀ (támeenímu) 'my pigs'
my pigs-plAn

b. tʰá òːʔí-ːpʲʰɛ̀ (táoohíípye) 'my dog'
my dog-⟨SgM⟩

(577) tíː-ːpʲɛ́   nìːβɯ́ɯ̀kpà (dííbyé niivúwa) 'his deer'
that-⟨SgM⟩ deer

(578) a. wahárɔ́ oohííbye
b. wahárɔ́ meenímu
c. wahárɔmútsí meenímu ja

a. kpàʔáɾó   òːʔí-ːpʲɛ̀   '(my) mother's dog'
   mother   dog-⟨SgM⟩

b. kpàʔáɾó   mɛ́ːní-mɯ̀ɯ̀   '(my) mother's pigs'
   mother   pig-plAn

c. [kpàʔárò-mútsʰí mɛ́ːní-mɯ̀ɯ̀] ⓖ hà   '(my) parents' pigs'
   mother-⟨DuF⟩   pig-plAn   house house'

Three factors obscure the basic tone patterns presented above:

1. Stem-forming suffixes must be counted in determining the number of syllables of the head (9.1.1).
2. Some roots have lexically-specified tones that resist the normal pattern (9.1.2).
3. Suffixes that affect their host's tones may be attached after the genitive construction is formed (9.1.3).

9.1.1 Stem-forming suffixes

Suffixes like -mɯɯ 'plural' and classifiers (like -Ⓛːpɛ ⟨SgM⟩) form part of the noun stem.[3] When such a stem is possessed, the rule for docking the genitive tone must take into account the entire stem. This is also true of the nɛ added to 'children' to make 'child', as in 579a. For example, the roots in 579 are bisyllabic, but each is followed by a stem-forming affix that makes the stem trisyllabic. Thus, the genitive tone docks on the root's initial syllable.

---

[3]This may strike us as strange since meanings like 'plural' and 'singular masculine' are usually inflectional and thus not part of the stem. Nonetheless, the rules that dock tones include these suffixes, counting syllables back from where they end.

9.1. GENITIVE TONE

(579) a. ní:βɯ́ɪkpá˟ tsʰɨ́:mɛ́-nɛ̀ (níívúwáj tsɨɨméne) 'deer's child'
    b. tʰá   mɛ̀:ní-mɯ̀ɪ (támeenímu)   'my pigs'
    c. á:nɯ́ɪ   o:ʔí-:pʲɛ̀ (áánú oohííbye)   'his dog'

Further examples follow:

(580) í kpáhʲá-mɯ̀ɪ (self clothing-pl) íwajyámu 'his clothes'
    í nɨ̀:tsʰɯ́ɪ-kpà (self cut-⟨slab⟩) ɨ́nɨɨtsúwa 'his machete'
    í má˟tʃʰó-kpà (self eat-⟨slab⟩) ímajchówa 'his scissors'
    í ákʰɯ́ɪ-:βɛ̀-kpà (self sit-sIn-⟨slab⟩) íacúúvewa 'his seat'

(581) í í˟tʃʰí-ɛ̀-mɨ̀   íijchíemɨ 'his car'
    self upland-per-⟨canoe⟩

9.1.2 Lexically marked tones

Some apparent exceptions are due to the head bearing a lexically marked low tone that blocks the docking of Ⓖ. For example, the first syllable of ɲáʔpɛ̀ (nahbe) 'brother' bears a lexically marked low tone so Ⓖ cannot dock on the modifier's final syllable as this would violate the *LLX constraint:

(582) a. tʰá   Ⓖ ɲáʔpɛ̀ (táñahbe)   'my brother'
    b. mɯ́ɪ:ʔá   Ⓖ ɲáʔpɛ̀ (múúhá nahbe)   'our brother'
    c. kpàʔáɾó   Ⓖ ɲáʔpɛ̀ (waháró nahbe) 'my mother's brother'

The addition of a suffix like -Ⓛkʰɛ̀ 'objAn' or -Ⓛmà 'with' may cause the first tone of ɲáʔpɛ̀ 'brother' to become high. However, since this suffix is added after the formation of the genitive phrase, the modifier's final tone remains high.

(583) a. táñáhbeke
    b. ámúhá ñáhbeke
    c. táñáhbema

    a. tʰá   Ⓖ ɲáʔpɛ̀-kʰɛ̀   'my brother (object)'
        my   brother-objAn
    b. ámɯ́ɪʔá   Ⓖ ɲáʔpɛ̀-kʰɛ̀   'your (pl) brothers (object)'
        your   brother-objAn
    c. tʰá   Ⓖ ɲáʔpɛ̀-mà   'with my brother'
        my   brother-with

256   CHAPTER 9. THE GENITIVE CONSTRUCTION

We take the structure of 583a to be as follows, with the noun phrase formed before the addition of the case marker.

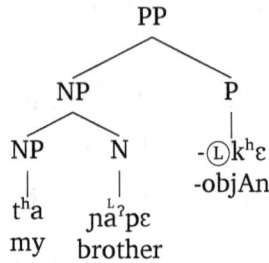

How can we understand this? Recall that ɲáʔpɛ has a lexically marked low tone. This Ⓛ blocks the genitive from docking on the possessor's final syllable. Subsequently -Ⓛkʰɛ 'objAn' delinks this Ⓛ. This analysis depends on a cyclic application of tone modifications, one when the possessor and noun are joined in the genitive construction, the other when the case marker is added. The derivation of tʰá ɲáʔpɛ̀-kʰɛ̀ is as follows:

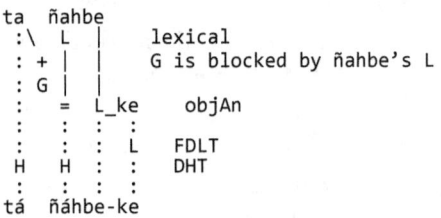

Figure 9.1 TD: tá ñáhbeke

Another situation in which the genitive tone cannot dock is when the second syllable of a trisyllabic head bears a lexically marked low tone. Such is the case for kʰaɾak̆ʰa 'chicken' in 584:

(584) a. tʰá   Ⓖ kʰáɾak̆ʰà (tácáraca)   'my chicken'
     b. mṹːʔá   Ⓖ kʰáɾak̆ʰà (múúhá cáraca) 'our chicken'
     c. kpàʔáɾó Ⓖ kʰáɾak̆ʰà (waháró cáraca) '(my) mother's chicken'

The tone derivation for tʰá kʰáɾàkʰà in 584a is as follows:

9.1. GENITIVE TONE

```
         ta  caraca
          :  /: L  :        lexical
          :  + : :  :       G is blocked by caraca's L.
          :  G : :  :
          :    : : L        FDLT
          H  H : :  :       DHT
          :    : :  :
         tá  cáraca
```

Figure 9.2 TD: tácáraca

Or, the lexically marked tone may stop the Ⓖ from docking on the possessor. Compare 585a, where it can dock, with 585b, where it cannot:

(585) a. níːβúɨkpá̇ máˣtʃʰò   (nííbvúwa májcho) 'deer's food'

  b. kʰárȧkʰá Ⓖ máˣtʃʰò   (cáracá májcho) 'chicken's food'

Some nominal roots bear lexically marked high tones. These behave differently in the genitive construction. For example, the locative noun ǔmíùr 'beside' bears a lexically marked high tone on its initial syllable. (Recall that, as discussed in section 7.2.3, these nouns may head genitive constructions to express spatial relations.) In 586, this lexically marked tone blocks[4] the docking of Ⓖ, which would otherwise dock on the initial syllable of ǔmíùr because it is trisyllabic:

(586) Diityé úníuháñerícya diícya.

  Dìːtʲʰɛ́ Ⓖ ǔmíùr ʔáɲè-rí-kʲʰà   tìː-kʲʰà.   'Stay beside
  they   beside var-oblIn-affirm you-be   them.'

The noun kʰáːnì 'father' may be a further case. It bears a lexically marked high on its initial syllable. If we assume that it is trisyllabic, we could claim that the lexically marked high blocks the docking of Ⓖ in 587b, thereby explaining why Ⓖ does not dock on the possessive pronoun:

(587) a.   kʰǎːnì: (cáánií)   'father' (citation form)

  b. tí: Ⓖ kʲʰǎːnì: (díícyáánií) 'your (sg) father'

However, in 588a–c, Ⓖ does dock on the head's initial syllable, delinking its lexically marked high tone.

(588) a. tíːpʲɛ́ ˣkʰánì (dííbyéj caáni) 'his father'

  b. ámúɨʔá ˣkʰánì (ámúháj caáni) 'your (pl) father'

  c. tíːpʲɛ́ ˣkʰáːnîi (dííbyéj caaníi) 'his father (past tense)'

This difference may hinge on whether kʰáːnì 'father' is interpreted as bi- or trisyllabic: The additional syllable in the citation form (587a) may be due

---

[4]This "blocking" is not motivated by the *LLX constraint as in other cases.

to FLTS. If so, the root is simply bisyllabic and we have no explanation for the initial tone of 587b. Note that in 588a and b kʰáːnì becomes trisyllabic by the application of PLTS. In 588c the additional syllable is the past tense suffix; see section 5.9.3.1, page 152.

9.1.3 Affixation

The tones of the head of a genitive construction may be affected by the addition of suffixes. Consider the final syllable of mɛːni 'pig' in 589. In 589a it bears low tone because of FDLT. In 589b it must become high tone because of the lexically marked low tone of -kʰópa 'augment'. In 589c it bears the low tone imposed by -ⓁOhùkʰo 'focus'.

(589) a. tʰá͡ᴳ mɛ́ːnì (tamééni) 'my pig'
       my pig

    b. tʰá͡ᴳ mɛ́ːní-kʰópà (tamééńícoba) 'my big pig'
       my pig-aug

    c. tʰá͡ᴳ mɛ́ːnì-ɾɛ́-hùɾkʰò (tamééniyéjuco) 'now only my pig'
       my pig-only-focus

9.1.4 The possessor's penult high extension

If Ⓖ docks on the modifier's final syllable (as in figure 9.3a), the modifier's penult—when present—must bear high tone to avoid violating the *LLX constraint. Surprisingly, this pattern—high tone on the modifier's penult—is carried through to the cases in which Ⓖ docks on the head, as represented in figure 9.3b. We will refer to this as the possessor's penultimate high extension (PPHE).[5]

---

[5]The PPHE is not motivated by any factor discussed to this point. We suggest the following (somewhat teleological) motivation: Suppose that the process of assigning tone in the genitive construction proceeds from left to right with only three syllable look-ahead. At the point it assigns tone to the modifier's penult it can only "see" the next three syllables, i.e., the modifier's final syllable and the head's first two. Thus it cannot know whether Ⓖ will dock on the next syllable—in which case it would have to assign high tone—or on the head's initial syllable. The only possibility that will always avoid violating the *LLX constraint is to assign high tone to the modifier's penult.

9.1. GENITIVE TONE

	MODIFIER	HEAD
a.	((...σ)σ̇̄)σ̄ ·	σ(σ)#
b.	((...σ)σ̣̇)σ̇ ·	σ̄σσ(σ...)

Figure 9.3 The possessor's penultimate high extension (PPHE)

The PPHE is illustrated in example 590.

(590) díñáhbé táábake
    tí   ɲáʔpɛ́   tʰáːpà-kʰɛ̀   'your brother's wife (object)'
    your brother wife-objAn

Note that the first syllable of náʔpɛ 'brother' ends up with high tone. How do we explain this? First, we assume that the structure of 590 is as given in figure 9.4, where there are two instances of genitive composition, the first joining 'your' and 'brother', the second joining 'your brother' and 'wife'.

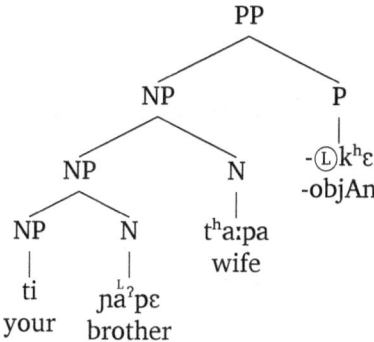

Figure 9.4 STR: díñáhbé táábake 'your brother's wife'

The tone derivation of tí ɲáʔpɛ́ tʰáːpà-kʰɛ̀ in figure 9.5 proceeds as follows. First, when 'your' is joined to 'brother' Ⓖ should dock on ti 'your' but the lexically marked low tone of náʔpɛ 'brother' blocks it from doing so. Second, when 'your brother' is joined to 'wife', Ⓖ should dock on the final syllable of náʔpɛ but its lexically marked low tone blocks this. By the PPHE the penultimate syllable of náʔpɛ should bear high tone; this—it seems—does indeed override the lexically marked low tone, producing the high tone. Examples 591 and 592 are similar.

```
        di    ñahbe         brother
        :\  L  :\           lexical
        : + |  : |          G is blocked by ñahbe's L.
        : G |  : |
        :   |  : +          G is blocked by ñahbe's L.
        :   H  : G ta:ba    wife (PPHE, GEN)
        :   :  : :  |
        :   :  : :  L_ke    objAn
        :   :  : :  :
        :   :  : :  L       FDLT
        H   :  H  H :  :    DHT
        :   :  :  : :  :
        dí  ñáhbé  tá:ba-ke
```

Figure 9.5 TD: díñáhbé táábake

(591) táñáhbéj ts<del>i</del>+méne

    [[tʰá ⓖ ɲá-ʔpɛ́]ˣ tsʰɨ́ːménɛ̀]   'my brother's child'
    my sib-⟨SgM⟩ child

(592) técoomí avyéjúúbé ajyúwa

    [[tʰɛ́-kʰòːmí⁶ àβʲɛ́húː:pɛ́] àhʲɨ́ɨ́kpà]   'the daughter of the
    that-⟨town⟩ reign-⟨SgM⟩ daughter   town's chief'

9.2 The uses of the genitive construction

The genitive construction is used to indicate various relationships between the referents of the modifier and head. The following list is not necessarily exhaustive and—as is often the case for functional taxonomies—the categories are not necessarily distinct.

OWNERSHIP:

    The referent of the modifier (possessor) owns the referent of the head (possessed):

(593) tʰáʔ míːnɛ̀ (tahmɨ́ɨ́ne)   'my canoe'

    tíːpʲɛ́ máˣtʃʰò (dííbye májcho) 'his food'

    tíːpʲɛ́ òːʔíːpʲɛ̀ (dííbyé oohííbye) 'his dog'

(594) a. áβʲɛ́húːpɛ̀ máˣtʃʰò   (ávyéjúúbe májcho)   'the chief's food'

    b. áβʲɛ́húːpɛ́ nɨ̀ːtsʰɨ́ɨ́-kpà (ávyéjúúbé nɨɨtsúwa) 'the chief's machete'

---

⁶The low tone of tʰɛ́-kʰòːmí is due to the rule that, following a monosyllabic host, a bisyllabic classifier bears a low tone on its first syllable; see the introduction to the classifier list given in chapter E.

9.2. THE USES OF THE GENITIVE CONSTRUCTION

KINSHIP:

The referent of the head bears a kinship (father, mother,...) or social relationship to the referent of the modifier:

(595) tʰá ⓖ ɲä̰ʔpɛ̀ (táñahbe) 'my brother'
tíːpʲɛ́ ⓖ nä̰ʔpɛ̀ (dííbyé nahbe) 'his brother'
tíːpʲɛ́ˣ tsʰɨ́ːmɛ̀ (dííbyej tsɨ́ɨ́me) 'his children'

PART-WHOLE:

The referent of the head is part of the referent of the modifier:

(596) tʰá̰ ʔóˣtsʰɨ̀ (tahójtsɨ) 'my hand'

THE ARGUMENT OF A NONFINITE VERB:

The modifier is the argument of a nonfinite verb. Its thematic role may be agent, i.e., the referent of the possessor does the action indicated by the head, as in 597 and 598. The low tone on the head is the nonfinite tone, indicated by N.

(597) tíːpʲɛ́ ɯ̀kpáːpò (dííbyé uwáábo) 'his teaching'
tíːpʲɛ́ ⓖ kpákʰìmʲɛ̂ì (dííbyé wákimyéi) 'his work'

Example 598 does not mean 'their' in the sense of ownership, but that 'they' are participants:[7]

(598) diityé pihcyááveja

tìː-tʲʰɛ́   pʰḭʔkʲʰáː-βɛ̀-hà
that-⟨AnPl⟩ gather-sIn-⟨shelter⟩
'the house where they gather (lit. their gathering house)'

(599) táwajyújte

tʰá kpa̰ʰʲɯ́ː-ˣtʰɛ̀   'the ones I love (lit. my loved ones)'
my love-⟨AnPl⟩

---

[7] The initial syllable of pʰḭʔkʲʰáː-βɛ̀ bears low tone both because it is the antepenult of a nonfinite verb (N) and because it is the head of a genitive construction with more than two syllables (G). The initial low tone of tìː-tʲʰɛ́ is docked by -ⓒtʰe ⟨AnPl⟩.

(600) Taabóóbej tééveri tsúúca bohɨ́júcoóbe.

[tʰà:pó-:pɛ̃̀ ˣtʰɛ́:βɛ̀]-rì̀ tsʰúɨ:kʰà pò?ɨ-húɨkʰò-:pɛ̀
cure-⟨SgM⟩ influence-oblIn already be.alive-now-⟨SgM⟩
'By the doctor's influence, he is now better.'

The modifier may also indicate the patient (or theme), i.e., the person or thing to which the verb's action is done. Such is the case in 601 where the genitive phrase means 'the one who teaches them':

(601) Díítyé uwááboobe waajácú páneére.

[tí-:tʲʰɛ́ ɯ̃kpá:pò]-:pɛ̀ kpà:hákʰúɨ-? pʰá-nɛ̀-:rɛ̀
that-⟨AnPl⟩ teach   -⟨SgM⟩ know-⟨t⟩   much-⟨ø⟩-only
'Their teacher knows everything.'

LOCATION:

Sometimes location is indicated in relation to the referent of the modifier (above it, below it,…). In this use, the head must be one of the following LOCATIONAL NOUNS: áàtʃʰì 'outside', à:?ɨ 'home', pà 'below', kʰà:mɛ̀ 'above', téhùɨ 'behind', ɛ̀?ní:ɲɛ̀ 'beyond', étʃɛ̀ 'yonder', ?àtʃùɨ 'top', ɨ́ tɛ̀ 'before', tʃì:ɲɛ̀ 'underneath', nɨˣkʰàùɨ 'end' pʰáɲɛ̀ 'inside', pʰɨ:?ɨ 'near', pʰɨ́:nɛ̀ 'middle', ?ɯ̃mɨ̀ 'in front of', ɯ̃mìùɨ 'beside'. Note that several of these have lexically marked tones.

For example, ?àtʃɯ indicates being on top of the referent of the modifier, as in 602 and 603:

(602) tí:pʲɛ́ ⓖ ?àtʃùɨ (dííbyé hallu) 'on top of him'

(603) Oke daacu éhwá hallúewávu.

ò-kʰɛ̀   t-à:kʰùɨ   [ɛ́?-kpá   ⓖ ?àtʃúɨ-ɛ̀]-kpá-βùɨ
I-objAn youImp-give that-⟨slab⟩ above-per -⟨slab⟩-goal
'Give me the plank that is on top (of the other plank).'

Generally ɛtʃɛ (élle) 'yonder' indicates a location at some distance from the referent of the modifier. Thus, in 604 should be understood as going to the vicinity of the referent of tí-:pʲɛ̀ that-⟨SgM⟩:

(604) O péé dííbye éllevu.

ò pʰɛ́:-? [tí-:pʲɛ̃́ étʃɛ̀]-βùɨ
I go-⟨t⟩ that-⟨SgM⟩ yonder -goal
'I go to where he is (lit. to his yonder).'

9.2. THE USES OF THE GENITIVE CONSTRUCTION

In considering the examples of 605, note that téhɯ̀ː 'under' has no lexically marked tone, t͡ʃíːɲɛ̀ 'underneath' has a lexically marked low tone, and ɯ̋mìɯ̀ 'beside' has a lexically marked high tone.

(605) a. tíːpʲɛ̀ téhɯ̀ː (dííbye déjuú) 'behind him'
  b. tíːpʲɛ́ t͡ʃíːɲɛ̀ (dííbyé lliiñe) 'beneath him'
  c. tíːpʲɛ́ ɯ̋mìɯ̀ (dííbyé úniu) 'beside him'

In 605a the head is bisyllabic so the genitive tone docks on the modifier's final syllable as expected. In 605b the head's lexically marked low tone blocks the docking of the genitive tone on the modifier's final syllable (since this would violate the *LLX constraint); therefore the modifier's final syllable bears a high tone. In 605c the head is trisyllablic so the genitive tone should dock on its first syllable, but this is blocked by the lexically marked high tone (so the genitive tone does not dock). This is summarized as follows:

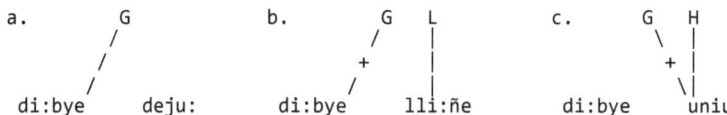

Further examples follow.

(606) tʰá ⓖ ɯ̋míɯ̀-ɾì (táúníuri)   'at my side'
  tíːpʲɛ́ ⓖ ɯ̋míɯ̀-ɾì (dííbyé úníuri) 'at his side'

(607) Táoohíbyé imíllé táúníuri icyúwane.

  tʰá òːʔí-pʲɛ́ ìmít͡ʃɛ́-ʔ [tʰá ⓖ ɯ̋míɯ̀-ɾì ì kʲʰɯ́ɾ̀kpà]-nɛ̀
  my dog-⟨SgM⟩ want-⟨t⟩ my side-oblIn self sleep -⟨ø⟩
  'My dog wants to sleep by my side.'

The locational noun pʰáɲɛ (pañe) 'inside' has a lexically marked low tone on its first syllable so ⓖ may not dock on the modifier's final syllable; see examples 608 and 609:

(608) há ⓖ pʰáɲɛ̀ (já pañe) 'inside the house'

(609) Tééhí pañe ó ájtumí amóóbeke.

  tʰɛ́ːʔí ⓖ pʰáɲɛ̀ ó áˣtʰùmí-ʔ àmóːpɛ̀-kʰɛ̀
  river inside I saw-⟨t⟩ fish-⟨SgM⟩-objAn
  'I saw a fish in the river.'

The relationship indicated by the locational noun need not be interpreted strictly as a physical relationship. For example, in 610 ɛ̀ʔníːɲɛ̀

'beyond' follows the standard of comparison to indicate that someone's stength is "beyond" that of the referent of the modifier:

(610) Dííbyé ehnííñe tsɨ́jpaábe.

 tí-ːpʲɛ́   ɛ́ʔníːɲɛ̀ tsʰɨ́ˣpʰàːpɛ̀   'He is stronger
 that-⟨SgM⟩ beyond be.strong-⟨SgM⟩   than him.'

TIME:

A period of time (i.e., before or after) is indicated in relation to the modifier's referent, as in 611 and 612:

(611) tíːpʲɛ́ Ⓖ pò̄nɛ̀   (dííbyé boóne)   'after him'

 tíːpʲɛ́ Ⓖ pò̄ːnɛ́ːpɛ̀ (dííbyé boonéébe) 'the one after him'

(612) tí-ːpʲɛ́   Ⓖ ɨ̄ʔtɛ̀   (dííbyé ɨhde) 'before him'
 that-⟨SgM⟩   before

Note that both pò̄ːnɛ 'after' and ɨ̄ʔtɛ 'before (in time or space)' have lexically marked low tones.

In a very different way, the modifier may indicate the length of time of the referent of the head, as in 613:

(613) tsʰá-ˣkʰòòhɨ́ kpákʰìmɛ̀ɨ (tsájcoojɨ́ wákiméi) 'one day's work'
 one-day   work

CHARACTERISTIC OR STATE:

The head may refer to a characteristic or the state of the referent of the modifier, as in 614. See also example 671, page 282.

(614) tʰá̄   ímì   (taími)   'my goodness'
 tʰá   ʔá̄ˣtʃʰótʰà (táhajchóta)   'my height'
 tíːpʲɛ́ ʔá̄ˣtʃʰótʰà (dííbyé hajchóta) 'his size'
 tíːpʲɛ́ tsʰɨ́ˣpʰà (dííbye tsɨ́jpa) 'his strength'
 tíːpʲɛ́ tʃʰémɛ̀ (dííbye chéme) 'his sickness'

DESCRIPTION:

The modifier may describe the head's referent, as in 615 and 616.

(615) pʰàˣtʲʰɛ́tʰɛ́ kpa̰ɲɛ́ʔhɨ̀ (pajtyété wañéhjɨ) 'salvation feast (Easter)'
 save   feast

(616) mɛ́ːnṵ̀-ˣkʰátsʰɨ́ mútnàà (méénujcátsi múnaa) 'soldiers'
 beat-recip   people

9.2. THE USES OF THE GENITIVE CONSTRUCTION

SPHERE OF EXISTENCE:

The modifier indicates the place in which the head's referent resides.

(617) [[tʰá ị̃ːɲɯ́-hɨ̃] mɯ́nàà] (táiiñújɨ múnaa) 'my country's people'
my dirt-⟨disk⟩ people

(618) tʰɛ́-kʰòːmí ã̆βʲɛ́hɯ̰ː-ːpɛ̀ (técoomí avyéjuúbe) 'that town's chief'
that⟨town⟩ reign-⟨SgM⟩

SET MEMBERSHIP:

The head's referent is a member of the set indicated by the modifier. In example 619 i 'self' refers to a collection of objects from which some are identified as dirty:

(619) íñehníñéhjɨ

í ɲɛ̃́ʔní-ɲɛ́-ʔhɨ̀ 'the dirty ones (from among them)'
self bad-⟨ø⟩-pl

In 620 i 'self' refers to the laundry, identifying the subset consisting of the white pieces:

(620) ...ménijtyú teene ɨtsɨtsɨ́ɨne...

mɛ́ nìˣtʲʰɯ́-ʔ tʰɛ̀ː-nɛ̀ Ⓐ ɨ́ tsʰɨ̃́tsʰɨ́ː-nɛ̀
SAP wash-⟨t⟩ that-⟨ø⟩ self white-⟨ø⟩
'...we wash the white ones (from among them)...'

In example 518, page 229, i 'self' refers to the set of chicks from which one is identified as rather ugly. See also example 516, page 228.

ONOMASTIC:

The head may refer to the name borne by the referent of the modifier, as in 621 and 622:

(621) Cááni mémeri teene újcuúbe.

[kʰáːnĩ́ mɛ́mɛ̀]-rì̃ tʰɛ̀ː-nɛ̀ ɯ́ˣkʰɯ̀-ːpɛ̀
father name -oblIn that-⟨ø⟩ receive-⟨SgM⟩
'He received it in his father's name.'

(622) Dííbye méme Jóááá.

[tíː-pʲɛ̃́ mɛ́mɛ̀] hóáàá 'His name is John.'
that-⟨SgM⟩ name John

RELATIVE CLAUSE:

A relative clause and the head that it modifies may be joined by the genitive, with the relative clause as the possessor and the modified noun as the possessed. In 623 and 624 the genitive tone is indicated by G over the vowel. See also section 18.1.3.

(623) dille tsɨɨ́mávátuné hajchóta
    [tì-tʃɛ̀   tsʰɨ́ːmá-βá-tʰɨ̀ː-nɛ́]⁸   ʔáˣ$\overset{G}{\text{a}}$ˣtʃʰótʰà
    that-⟨SgF⟩ children-have-neg-⟨n⟩ length.of.time
    'during the time she had not given birth'

(624) wájpiike úújétúné badsɨ́jcaja
    [kpáˣpʰìː-kʰɛ̀ úːhɛ́-tʰɨ́ː-nɛ́] $\overset{G}{\text{p}}$àtsɨ́ˣkʰà-hà
    man-objAn arrive-neg-⟨n⟩ adolescentF-sg
    'young woman who has not been with a man'

---

[8] tsʰìːma- 'children' is tsʰìːmɛ- with the /e/ assimilated to the /a/ of the following suffix.

Chapter 10

Case and Grammatical Relations

Case marking suffixes indicate the role of a noun phrase (or subordinate clause) with respect to the clause within which it occurs. Bora has the following case markers: –ø 'nominative' for subjects (10.1), -kʰɛ ~ ø (with animate and inanimate phrases, respectively) 'direct object' (10.2), -βɯ 'goal' or 'theme' (10.3), -tʰɯ 'source' (10.4), -ɾi 'inanimate obliques' (10.5), -ma 'with' (10.6), and -tʃì:ʔɛ̀ 'motive' (10.7). In addition to these, there are two "pseudo-cases": -ʔtɯ̀ 'comparative' (10.8) and -ˣ 'vocative' (10.9).

Some of the case-marking alternatives are illustrated in 625. 625a has a singular transitive verb whereas 625b–d have an intransitive verb.

(625) a. Oke ihjyúnuúbe.

  b. Óhditu ihjyúvaábe.

  c. Óóma ihjyúvaábe.

  d. Táhallúrí ihjyúvaábe.

  a. ò-<u>kʰɛ̀</u>   ìʔhʲɯ́ɪ-nɯ̀ɪ-ːpɛ̀
   I-objAn   mouth-do-⟨SgM⟩
  b. ó-ʔtì-(tʰɯ̀ɪ)
   I-anim-sou
  c. ó:-<u>mà</u>   ìʔhʲɯ́ɪ-βà-ːpɛ̀
   I-with   mouth-have-⟨SgM⟩
  d. tʰá ⓖ ʔátʃɯ́ɪ-<u>ɾí</u>
   my   top-oblIn

267

'He talks
$\begin{cases} \text{a. to (at) me.'} & \text{(object)} \\ \text{b. about me.'} & \text{(source)} \\ \text{c. with me.'} & \text{(co-subject)} \\ \text{d. in my favor.'} & \text{(inanimate oblique)} \end{cases}$

10.1 Subject

Subjects are not marked for case; that is, the nominative is unmarked. (An exception is discussed below.) Subjects are recognized by the absence of another case marker, by their position in the sentence, or by the classifier suffixed to the verb.

There are three possible patterns for the subject and predicate, as represented in 626a, b, and d:

(626) a. (NP$_{subject}$) [$_{predicate}$ ...verb-$\left\{\begin{array}{l}\langle t\rangle \\ \langle n\rangle\end{array}\right\}$]

b. [$_{predicate}$ ...verb]-classifier$_{subject}$ (Ⓐ NP$_{subject}$)

c. *NP$_{subject}$ [$_{predicate}$ ...verb]-[classifier$_{subject}$]

d. [$_{predicate\ complement}$ $\left\{\begin{array}{l}\text{NP} \\ \text{AP}\end{array}\right\}$] NP$_{subject}$ (V$_{copular}$)

First, as represented in 626a, the subject may be a noun phrase preceding the verb, as in as in 627–629. In this case the verb is followed by -Ⓛ◯ʔi ⟨t⟩ or, when negative, by -Ⓛ◯nɛ ⟨n⟩ as in 837, page 326. This order is the one most commonly used to introduce a referent into the discourse.

(627) Ávyéjuube Ilííñájatéhi.

áβʲéhù-ːpè ʧíːɲáhà-tʰɛ́-ʔì   'A/The chief went to hunt.'
reign-⟨SgM⟩ hunt-go.do-⟨t⟩

(628) Mítyane míamúnaa tsááhi.

mítʲʰà-nɛ̀ míámúmàà tsʰáː-ʔì   'Many people come.'
many-⟨ø⟩ people   come-⟨t⟩

In 629 the subject is a relative clause headed by the classifier -Ⓛ:pɛ ⟨SgM⟩:

(629) Llííñájaatéébé mujtáhi.

[$_{NP}$ ø$_i$ ʧíːɲáhàː-tʰɛ́]-ːpɛ́$_i$ mùˣtʰá-ʔì
hunt-go.do   -⟨SgM⟩ be.lost-⟨t⟩
'The one who went to hunt got lost.'

Second, as represented in 626b, a third person subject may be indicated by a classifier suffixed to the verb. This order is generally used if the

10.1. SUBJECT

subject has been previously introduced into the discourse. For example, in 630 the subject is the classifier -⒧:pɛ (-:be) ⟨SgM⟩:[1]

(630) ʧíːɲáhàː-tʰɛ́-ɛ́pɛ̀   (Llííñájaatéébe.) 'He went to hunt.'
     hunt-go.do-⟨SgM⟩

A classifier subject may be followed by an appositive subject noun phrase, as in 631:

(631) "Juúju" neebévá́a íllií.
    "hùːhùː" nɛ̀-ːpɛ́-β̃a-a̋   Ⓐ íʧií   ' "OK," said his son.'
    OK   say-⟨SgM⟩-rpt-rem   his.son

Every clause must have a subject. If there is no classifier on the verb, there must be a preverbal subject.[2] Further, as in 626c, preverbal subjects do not co-occur with classifier subjects;[3] see the preverbal subject constraint discussed on page 129.

Third, as represented in 626d, if the predicate is a noun or adjective phrase, the subject usually follows the predicate, as in 632:

(632) nɛ́ʔní⁽ʔ⁾ hùːβà (...néhní juúva) '...it is a bad trail.'
     bad   trail

We mentioned above that there was one exception to the claim that the nominative case is unmarked. As stated in section 8.1, when a personal pronoun is used as a preverbal subject, if it has a long vowel, this is shortened. For example, tìː-pʲɛ̀ tìpʲɛ̀, as in 633:

(633) Tsá dibye pééityú.
    tsʰá̋ʔ tì-pʲɛ̀   pʰɛ́ː-ì-tʲʰɯ́ɯ   'He does not go.'
    not   that-⟨SgM⟩ go-fut-neg

This also applies in subordinate clauses, as in 634. (See also 864, page 332.)

(634) Dille téhullévú péhajchíí ó imíllé dííllema o pééneé.
    [tì-ʧɛ̀   tʰɛ́-ʔɯ̀ʧɛ́-βɯ́   pʰɛ́-ʔàˣʧʰíː]
    that-⟨SgF⟩ that-⟨place⟩-goal go-if

    ó ìmíʧɛ́-ʔ   [tíː-ʧɛ̀-mà   ò pʰɛ́ː-nɛ̀ɛ́]
    I want-⟨t⟩   that-⟨SgF⟩-with I go-⟨n⟩
    'If she goes over there, I want to go with her.'

---

[1] The tone of -⒧:pɛ̀ ⟨SgM⟩ is blocked by the low imposed by -⒧tʰɛ 'go to do'.

[2] This is true in both main and subordinate clauses, although it may be that in cases of relativization into the subject, like example 629, the subject is not overt in the modifying clause.

[3] We mean, of course, except for -ʔì ⟨t⟩ or -nɛ ⟨n⟩ filling the postverbal subject position when there is a preverbal subject.

However, if the pronominal subject is followed by an appositive phrase, the length is retained, as in 635:

(635) Aanéváa diibye bɨɨrúmujɨ úújetétsó wañéhjɨvu...

a:-né-βa-a   tì:-pʲɛ̀   Ⓐ pɨ̀:rúmùɨ-hɨ̀
thm-⟨ø⟩-rpt-rem   that-⟨SgM⟩   agouti-sg

úɨ:hɛ̀-tʰɛ́-tsʰó-ʔ   kpàɲɛ́ʔhɨ̀-βùɨ
arrive-go.do.cause-⟨t⟩   festival-goal

'...he, the agouti, caused her to arrive to a party,...'

Consider example 636. In 636a the subject tì:pʲɛ̀ 'he' is followed by the appositive noun phrase tʰá: kʰá:nì: 'my father', so retains the length. By contrast, in 636b, where the appositive noun phrase does not directly follow tì-pʲɛ̀, the length is suppressed.[4]

(636) a. Diibye táácááni cheméhi.
      b. Dibye chemé táácáánií.

a. tì-:pʲɛ̀   Ⓐ tʰá: Ⓖ kʰá:nì   tʃʰɛ̀mɛ́-ʔì   'He, my father,
   that-⟨SgM⟩   my   father   be.ill-⟨t⟩   is sick.'

b. tì-pʲɛ̀   tʃʰɛ̀mɛ́-ʔ   tʰá: Ⓖ kʰá:nì: 'He is sick, my
   that-⟨SgM⟩   be.ill-⟨t⟩   my   father   father.'

We now consider the personal pronominal clitics in table 10.1.[5]

Table 10.1 Personal pronominal subject proclitics

o	(o)	'I'
ɯ	(u)	'you'
ti	(di-)	'you (imperative)'
mɛ	(me-)	'SAP'
i[6]	(i-)	'self'

The pronouns of table 10.1 indicate the subject, cliticizing to a following verb. The close relationship between the proclitic and the following verb root is evident in the following:

1. Nothing can intervene between the proclitic and the following verb. If the proclitic bears a suffix, it is "doubled," as discussed below.

---

[4]Compare 636b, which has a preverbal subject, with 645, in which the subject follows the verb.

[5]Note the similarity to the bound possessive pronouns of table 8.11, page 247.

[6]Strictly speaking, this is an anaphor, not a pronoun; see section 8.3.

10.1. SUBJECT

2. The proclitic and the verb root's initial syllable may not both bear low tones because these form a single tonal phrase which must respect the *LLX constraint.
3. tì 'you (imperative)' and ì 'self' cause a following consonant to be palatalized. (Palatalization applies across word boundaries only if the words belong to the same phonological phrase.)
Further, t(ì) 'you (imperative)' may be tì, t, or ø (nothing) depending on the number of syllables of the root and whether it begins with a consonant or a vowel.

If o 'I', ɯ 'you', or mɛ 'SAP' is used as the subject and bears any suffix, then it is repeated, procliticized to the verb. We will call this PRONOUN DOUBLING. For example, in 637 o 'I' is followed by -i 'projected time', so the pronoun is repeated:

(637) ó-ì   ò pʰɛ́-hɯ̀kʰó:-ʔì (Ói o péjucóóhi.) 'I am now about to go.'
     I-PT I go-now-⟨t⟩

In 638 ɯ 'you' is doubled:

(638) ɯ̀:-βà   ɯ́ pʰɛ̀-ɛ́-ʔì   (Uuva ú peéhi.) 'They say that
     you-rpt you go-fut-⟨t⟩   you will go.'

In 639 mɛ 'SAP' is doubled; the second cliticizes to the verb:

(639) Metsu meere mepéékií.
     mɛ̀tsʰɯ̀ mɛ̀-:ɾɛ̀   mɛ̀ pʰɛ́:-kʰì: 'Let's go alone.'
     let.us SAP-only SAP go-pur

When mɛ 'SAP' is the subject, it can be preceded by mɯ̀ʔà 'we (ex.)', mɯ̀ʔtsʰɨ 'we (DuM)', or mɯ̀ʔpʰɨ 'we (DuF)'. A word may intervene between the free pronoun and the pronominal clitic, for example, tí:pʲɛ̀kʰɛ̀ in 640:

(640) Muha dííbyeke méájtyumɨhi.
     mɯ̀ʔà tí-:pʲɛ̀-kʰɛ̀   mɛ́ áˣtʲʰɯ̀mɨ́-ʔì 'We saw him.'
     we   that-⟨SgM⟩-objAn SAP see-⟨t⟩

A preverbal subject noun phrase referring to a speech act participant (i.e., not third person) will always be accompanied by an appositive pronominal subject proclitic, as in 641 and 642:

(641) O íjcyároobe ó cheméhi.
     [ò íˣkʲʰá-ɾò]-:pɛ̀   Ⓐ ó tʃʰɛ̀mɛ́-ʔì
     I be-frs   -⟨SgM⟩   I be.ill-⟨t⟩
     'Even I am sick.' (lit. 'Even being me, I was sick.')

(642) Cóómíyi o íjcyaabe ó ájtyumɨ dííbyeke.
     [NP[skʰó:mí-jì   ò íˣkʲʰà]-:pɛ̀]   Ⓐ ó áˣtʲʰɯ̀mɨ́-ʔ
         town-oblIn I be   -⟨SgM⟩   I see-⟨t⟩

tí-:pʲɛ̀-kʰɛ̀
that-⟨SgM⟩-objAn
'When I was in town I saw him (lit. Being in town, I saw him).'

Adverbs (and other constituents, e.g., direct objects as in 640) may intervene between the subject noun phrase or free pronoun and the subject agreement proclitic. Examples follow:

(643) Ói ɨ́ɨ́cúi o péjucóóhi.
    ó-ì   ɨ́:kʰɨ́ɨ̀   ò pʰɛ́-hùkʰó:-ʔì   'I'm now about to go quickly.'
    I-PT quickly I go-now-⟨t⟩

(644) Cóómíyi o íjcyaabe tsíhullétú dííbyeke ó ájtyumɨ́hi.
    [_NP_kʰó:mí-jì   ò íˣkʲʰà]-:pɛ̀]
        town-oblIn I be   -⟨SgM⟩

    tsʰí-ʔùʧɛ́-tʰɨ́ɨ̀   tí-:pʲɛ̀-kʰɛ̀   ó áˣtʲʰùmí-ʔì
    other-⟨yonder⟩-sou that-⟨SgM⟩-objAn I see-⟨t⟩
    'When I was in town, I saw him from afar.'

Whether the subject is an overt pronoun or a classifier suffixed to the verb, another noun phrase may be appositive to it. The appositive noun phrase may follow the pronoun, the verb, or the classifier. In 645 the noun phrase is appositive to the classifier -:pɛ ⟨SgM⟩. Compare this with 636a and b, in which the noun phrase is appositive to a free pronoun.

(645) Chémeebe táácáánií.
    ʧʰɛ́mɛ̀-:pɛ̀   Ⓐ [tʰá: Ⓖ kʰá:nì:]   'He, my father, is sick.'
    be.ill-⟨SgM⟩   my   father

The appositional phrase may be a relative clause. For example, in 646 tʰá ɲàʔpɛ̀ 'my brother' is followed by ʧʰɛ́mɛ́ɾò:pɛ̀ 'the one who is sick':

(646) Táñahbe chéméroobe wákímyeítyéjucóóhi.
    [tʰá Ⓖ ɲǎ-ʔpɛ̀]   Ⓐ [ʧʰɛ́mɛ́-ɾò]-:pɛ̀
    my   sib-⟨SgM⟩   be.ill-frs   -⟨SgM⟩

    kpákʰímʲɛ̀í-tʲʰɛ́-hùkʰó:-ʔì
    work-go.do-now-⟨t⟩
    'My brother, sick though he be, has now gone to work.'

In 647 the noun phrase tsʰí:ɲɛ́ ì:ɲɨ́ɨ̀hì mɨ́mááˣpʰì 'a person from a foreign country' is appositive to á:nɨ̀ 'this (SgM)':

(647) Áánu tsííñé iiñújɨ múnáajpi cheméhi.

    á:nɨ̀ɨ   Ⓐ [NP [NPtsʰí:ɲé   í:ɲɨ́ɨ-hɨ̀]   Ⓖ mǘnáà-ˣpʰì̃] tʃʰɛ̀mɛ́-ʔɨ̀
    this.SgM   another dirt-⟨disk⟩   human-⟨SgM⟩ be.ill-⟨t⟩
    'This one, a man from another country, is sick.'

10.2   -ke ~ -ø 'object'

Inanimate direct objects are unmarked. Animate direct objects are marked by -Ⓛkʰ⁽ʲ⁾ɛ (-ke) 'objAn'.

The direct object may be a pronoun, a noun phrase, or a nominalized clause. For example, in 648 it is the pronoun o 'I'. Since this is animate, it bears -Ⓛkʰɛ 'objAn':

(648) <u>ò-kʰɛ̀</u>   í:tʰɛ̀-:pɛ̀   (Oke ɨ́ɨteébe.) 'He looks at me.'
    I-objAn look-⟨SgM⟩

In 649 the direct object is úmɛ̀ʔɛ̀ 'tree'; since it is inanimate it does not bear case marking:

(649) <u>úmɛ̀-ʔɛ̀</u>   í:tʰɛ̀-:pɛ̀   (Úmehe ɨ́ɨteébe) 'He looks at the tree.'
    tree-⟨tree⟩ look-⟨SgM⟩

In 650 the direct object is (when present) ò-kʰɛ̀ (I-objAn), followed by the appositive relative clause ò tʰá:pɛ̀ '(the one) that was crying':

(650) Oke o táábeke ɨ́ɨteébe.
    ò-<u>kʰɛ̀</u>   Ⓐ [NP [sò tʰá]-:pɛ̀   ]-<u>kʰɛ̀</u>   í:tʰɛ̀-:pɛ̀
    I-objAn   I cry -⟨SgM⟩ -objAn look-⟨SgM⟩
    'He watches me crying.' (i.e., as I cry)

Example 651 illustrates the universal tendency for objects to be more affected than phrases with other grammatical relations:[7]

(651) a. Dííbyeke ɨ́dáátsólleébe.
     b. Dííbyedi(tu) ɨ́dáátsóveébe

    a. tí-:pʲɛ̀-<u>kʰɛ̀</u>   ɨ́tá:tsʰó-tʃɛ̀-:pɛ̀
       that-⟨SgM⟩-objAn   pity-sTr-⟨SgM⟩
    b. tí-:pʲɛ̀-tì-(tʰɨ̀ɨ)   ɨ́tá:tsʰó-βɛ̀-:pɛ̀
       that-⟨SgM⟩-anim-sou pity-sIn-⟨SgM⟩

---

[7] Recall the celebrated example *He loaded the truck with hay* versus *He loaded hay onto the truck*; the former, in which the truck is the direct object, suggests that the truck is more greatly affected than the latter, in which the truck is in an oblique relation.

a. 'He takes pity on him (and does something about it).'
b. 'He feels sorry for him (but does nothing about it).'

In the next subsections we will treat object complements, objects that are addressees, and objects that cliticize to the verb.

10.2.1 Object complements

The direct object may be an object complement, as in 652 and 653, in which -nɛ ⟨ø⟩ heads the structure: [_NP_ [_S_ ...][_N_-ne]] (See section 16.2.2 for further discussion of such object complements.)

(652) ó ìmítʃɛ́-ˀ [ò má^xtʃʰò]-nɛ̀ (Ó imíllé o májchone.) 'I want
    I want-⟨t⟩   I eat   -⟨ø⟩   to eat.'

(653) Ó ájtyumɨ u áákityéne.
    ó á^xtʲʰùmɨ́-ˀ [ùɯ á:kʰìtʲʰɛ́]-nɛ̀   'I saw you fall.'
    I see-⟨t⟩   you fall   -⟨ø⟩

10.2.2 The addressee

A noun phrase indicating the addressee (the person to whom speech is directed) is marked with -Ⓛkʰɛ (-ke) 'objAn'. Since the adressee is virtually always animate, this use of -kʰɛ is natural in light of (1) the case marking pattern of a^xkʰɯ 'give' that marks the recipient with -kʰɛ, and (2) the apparent preference for treating animate goals or recipients as direct objects. For examples, see 826 and 959.

10.2.3 Objects as cliticized classifiers

When a clause has a preverbal subject, the direct object may occur as a classifier cliticized to the verb, displacing the -Ⓛ◯ˀi ⟨t⟩ that normally follows when there is a preverbal subject.

(654) a. Tsúúca ó májchone.
     b. Tsúúca ó ímíbájchoja.
     a. tsʰúːkʰà ó má^xtʃʰò-<u>nɛ̀</u>   'I have already eaten it.'
        already I eat-⟨ø⟩
     b. tsʰúːkʰà ó ímípá^xtʃʰò-<u>hà</u> 'I have already fixed the house.'
        already I fix-⟨shelter⟩

This is only possible in contexts in which the direct object is highly topical (thematic), as when responding to a question about the object. Perhaps these are not sentences, but relative clauses (in elliptical responses). As such, the high tone on the first syllable of each verb marks the clause as subordinate.

10.2.4 Causee

A CAUSEE is the subject of a clause that has been made causative (not to be confused with the CAUSER, the one who does the causing). As in many languages, in Bora, the causee becomes the direct object, as represented schematically in figure 10.1:

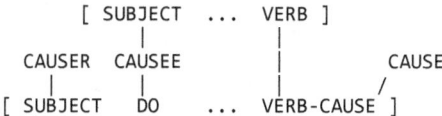

Figure 10.1 Grammatical relations: causatives

For example, the subject of 655a is ó 'I'; when this clause is made causative as in 655b, the subject becomes the causee and is marked as a direct object:

(655) a. Ó dsɨɨnéhi.
    b. Oohííbyé oke dsíínetsóhi.

a.		SUBJECT	VERB		
		ó	tsɨ̀:nɛ́-ʔì		'I ran.'
		I	run-⟨t⟩		
b.	CAUSER	CAUSEE	VERB + CAUSE		
	ò:ʔí-:pʲɛ́	ò-kʰɛ̀	tsɨ́:nɛ̀-tsʰó-ʔì		'The dog made me run.'
	dog-⟨SgM⟩	I-objAn	run-caus-⟨t⟩		

Even when a transitive verb is causativized, the causee is marked as a direct object; see examples 255, page 144, and 669–671, page 281. Causatives are discussed further in sections 10.3.3 and 5.8.1.

10.3 -vu 'goal' or 'theme'

The suffix -βɨ̀ɨ (-vu) 'goal, theme' marks a goal, i.e., the end point of a trajectory (10.3.1). With certain verbs it marks the theme (10.3.2). It also marks the direct object of a causativized transitive verb (10.3.3).

When -βɯ follow an animate phrase, that phrase must first bear -⁽ʔ⁾ti 'animate', as in 656:

(656) Ó úújeté dííbyedívu.
    ó ɯ́ːhɛ̀-tʰɛ́-ʔ   tí-ːpʲɛ̀-tí-βɯ̀   'I caught
    I arrive-go.do-⟨t⟩ that-⟨SgM⟩-anim-goal up to him.'

The glottal stop of -⁽ʔ⁾ti 'animate' occurs only after the monomoraic morphemes o, ɯ, and mɛ; see, for example, 659.

10.3.1 Goal

When a clause refers to some trajectory through space, the GOAL (i.e., the end point of the trajectory) may be indicated by a noun phrase bearing -β⁽ʲ⁾ɯ 'goal', as in 657 and 658, as well as 782, page 312.

(657) ò pʰɛ́ː-ʔ   tʰɛ́-ʔɯ̀ʧɛ́-βɯ̀   (O péé téhullévu.) 'I go over there.'
    I go-⟨t⟩ that-⟨yonder⟩-goal

(658) Táñaalle ácuuvé ácúúveíhcyú hallúvu.
    tʰá ⓖ ɲǎː-ʧɛ̀   ákʰɯ̀ː-ːβɛ́-ʔ [ákʰɯ́ː-ːβɛ̀-íʔkʲʰɯ́ ⓖ ʔǎʧɯ́]-βɯ̀
    my sib-⟨SgF⟩ sit-sIn-⟨t⟩ sit-sIn-⟨frame⟩   top -goal
    'My sister sat down on top of the chair.'

The notion of a physical path (trajectory) has metaphorical extensions, as seen in 659:

(659) Múu óhdivu cátsɨpááve.
    mɯ̌ːɯ̀ ó-ʔtì-βɯ̀   kʰátsʰɨpʰá-ːβɛ̀   'You should trust in me.'
    SAP.sg I-anim-goal dependImp-sIn

Ordinarily -β⁽ʲ⁾ɯ 'goal' and -tʰɯ 'source' are not used in the directional sense directly following an animate noun. Instead of saying, for example, *to him,* one would normally say *to the place where he is,* using a locative noun in the genitive construction:

(660) tí-ːpʲɛ̀   ɛ́ʧɛ̀-βɯ̀   (dííbye éllevu) 'to the place where he is'
    that-⟨SgM⟩ place-goal

10.3.2 Theme

There are two cases in which -βɯ marks "objects". One is with aˣkʰɯ 'give' (and perhaps a few other verbs). The other is with causatives. We will gloss these two uses 'theme'.

10.3. -VU 'GOAL' OR 'THEME'

Verbs like pʰíkʲʰò 'put', like English *put*, subcategorize for a goal (the end point of the trajectory along which the patient/theme moves). For these verbs, the patient/theme becomes the direct object, marked with -kʰɛ (-ke) and the goal is marked with -βɯ (-vu) 'goal', as represented in figure 10.2 and illustrated in 661.

```
AGENT      PATIENT/THEME    GOAL
  |              |            |
SUBJECT      DIRECT OBJECT   GOAL
  |              |            |
(nominative)    -ke          -vu
```

Figure 10.2 Grammatical relations: verbs like pícyo 'put'

(661) Ááwavúváa pícyoíñuube téniihyo méwánííhyo]ke...

á:-kpà-βúɯ-βá-á   pʰíkʲʰò-íɲùɯ-:pɛ̀
thm-⟨slab⟩-goal-rpt-rem put-do.go-⟨SgM⟩

[tʰɛ́-nì:ʔʲò   Ⓐ mɛ́kpá-ní:ʔʲò]-kʰɛ̀
 that-⟨mother⟩   wife-⟨mother⟩-objAn

'He put his wife into the shelter....'

However, with some verbs, the theme (the thing that moves) is marked with -βùɯ. For example, in 662, the hands are the things that are moved, and are marked with -βùɯ 'theme'; the structure of 662 is given in figure 10.3.

(662) ...tsaalle ímujpáñéécú íhyójtsɨvu iwátájcónema.

tsʰà:-tʃɛ̀   [í   mṹxpʰáɲɛ́-:kʰúɯ í   Ⓖ ʔʲóxtsʰɨ-βùɯ
come-⟨SgF⟩   self breast-dual   self hand-thm

ì   kpátʰá-xkʰó]-nɛ̀-mà
self cover-mTr   -⟨event⟩-with

'Therefore she came covering her breasts with her hands.'

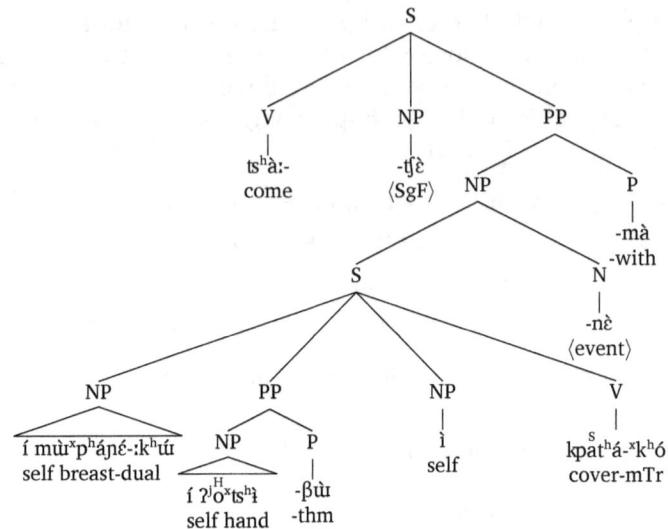

Figure 10.3 STR: tsaalle ímujpáñéécú íhyójtsɨvu iwátájcónema

There are two ways we might think of this. On the one hand, we might regard ḳpàtʰáˣkʰò 'cover' as a transitive verb that subcategorizes for a direct object, the object covered. On this view, ʔjóˣtsʰɨ 'hand' would be regarded as an adjunct that bears -βùɨ (-vu) 'theme' because it is the thing that moves. This is the first alternative presented in figure 10.4. On the other hand, we might regard ḳpàtʰáˣkʰò 'cover' as subcategorizing for both a theme and a goal. If one expects the goal to be marked with -βùɨ (-vu) 'goal' and the theme as a direct object, then the actual case marking would require inversion, as represented in the second alternative of figure 10.4.

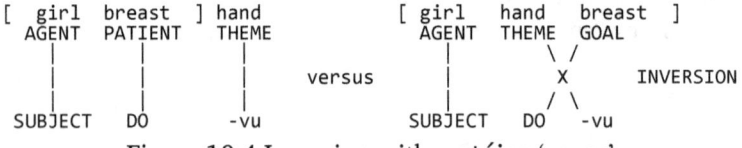

Figure 10.4 Inversion with watájco 'cover'

We withhold judgement on this case. However, there is a case where an inversion analysis is motivated for Bora.[8] The verb àˣkʰùɨ (ajcu) 'give' (and perhaps a few other verbs) presents the recipient (goal) as the direct object and marks the theme (that which passes from the giver to the recipient) with -βùɨ (-vu) 'goal/theme'; this is represented in figure 10.5:

---

[8]This inversion is similar to a phenomena described for Seri by Marlett (1993).

10.3. -VU 'GOAL' OR 'THEME'

Figure 10.5 Animacy-motivated inversion

For example, in 663 the baby is the goal or recipient but marked as a direct object, while the food, the thing given, is marked with -βɨ̀ɨ 'goal/theme':

(663) Tsɨ̵ɨju íjtsɨ̵ɨméneke ajcú majchóvu.

	RECIPIENT	THEME
tsʰɨ̀ːhɨ̀ɨ í	ˣtsʰɨ̵ːméne̋-kʰɛ̀	áˣkʰɨ́ɨ-ʔì màˣʧʰó-βɨ̀ɨ
CORRECTED mother self	child-objAn	give-⟨t⟩ food-thm

'The mother gave food to her baby.'

Further examples follow:

(664) Íllíkyeváa ájcuube íañújuvu.

RECIPIENT		THEME	
íʧí-kʲʰɛ̀-βá-à	áˣkʰɨ̀ɨːpɛ̀	[í áɲɨ́ɨ-hɨ̀ɨ]-βɨ̀ɨ	
his.son-objAn-rpt-rem	give-⟨SgM⟩	self shoot-⟨gun⟩ -thm	

'He gave his gun to his son.'

(665) Oke ájcuube cáracádívu.

RECIPIENT	THEME	
ò-kʰɛ̀	áˣkʰɨ̀ɨːpɛ̀ kʰárákʰá-tí-βɨ̀ɨ	'He gave me
I-objAn	give-⟨SgM⟩ chicken-anim-thm	a chicken.'

The theme may be left implicit, as in 666:

(666) ò-kʰɛ̀   t-àːkʰɨ̀ɨ   (¡Oke daácu!) 'Give (it) to me!'
     I-objAn youImp-give

Significantly, with aˣkʰɯ 'give' the recipient must be animate. (In Bora it is not possible to say, for example, *He gave the village a boat.*) Thus, the inversion is motivated as a process to promote an animate recipient to direct object, where its animacy is made explicit by -Ⓛkʰɛ 'objAn', with the theme becoming an oblique marked by -βɨ̀ɨ 'goal/theme'. For aˣkʰɯ 'give', this inversion is obligatory.

Are there other verbs that behave this way? Above, in connection with example 662, we mentioned this possibility for kpàtʰáˣkʰò 'cover' but came to no conclusion. Note that its goal is not animate (all body parts being inanimate) so would not result from an animacy-motivated inversion.

Example 667 suggests more strongly that a clause with pʰìkʲʰò 'put' can undergo inversion:

(667) Ané(h), wa(h) pícyaméí dípamɨ́jɨ́wuúnevuj.

àné⁷, kpà⁷ pʰíkʲʰà-méí tí   pʰǎ-mí-hí-kpɯ́ɯ́-nè-βɯ̀-ˣ
then sis putImp-r/p your all-⟨ornament⟩-pl-dim-thm-voc
'Then, sis, put on all your little jewels.'

The goal is the girl and theme is the ornaments. A possible analysis is that—by inversion—the goal becomes the direct object and the theme becomes an oblique. However, the goal-become-object does not surface because of reflexivization. This is represented in 10.6:

Figure 10.6 Grammatical relations: 'Put on all your little jewels.'

Consider example 668. Understood as 'The mother put jackets on the children...' it seems like a convincing case of inversion. However, this is not so because ɯˣkʰo does not mean 'put on' but 'insert into', so it is natural to treat the children as the direct object and the jackets as the goal.

(668) Tsɨ́ɨ́meke tsɨ̀ɨ̀ju tsucójaanévú ujcó tsúcó teene néénélliíhye.

tsʰɨ́:mè-kʰè̀   tsʰɨ̀:hɯ̀ tsʰɯ̀kʰó-hà:-né-βɯ́   ɯ̀ˣkʰó-ʔ
children-objAn mother cold-⟨shelter⟩-pl-goal insert-⟨t⟩

[tsʰɯ́ɯkʰó⁽ʔ⁾ tʰè̀:-nè né:]-né-tʃì:ʔʲè̀
cold   that-⟨ø⟩ say -⟨ø⟩-motive
'The mother inserted the children into the jackets because it was cold.'

10.3.3 The object of a causativized verb

When a causative is formed from a transitive verb, the object of that verb is generally marked with -βɯ, (-vu), as represented in figure 10.7:

10.3. -VU 'GOAL' OR 'THEME'

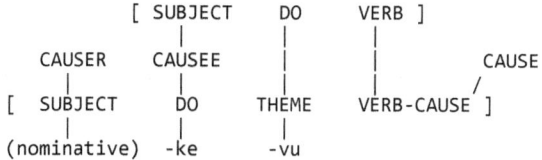

Figure 10.7 Grammatical relations: causatives of transitive verbs

For example, compare the simple transitive in 669a with the corresponding causative in 669b. (See also 670.)

(669) a. Ó tsajtyé cáracáke.
   b. Oke tsajtyétsoobe cáracádívu.

   a. SUBJECT   DIRECT OBJECT
      ó   tsʰàˣtʲʰɛ́-ʔ   kʰáɾàkʰá-<u>kʰɛ̀</u>
      I   take-⟨t⟩   chicken-objAn

   b. CAUSEE   THEME
      ò-kʰɛ̀   tsʰàˣtʲʰɛ́-tsʰò-ːpɛ̀   kʰáɾàkʰá-tí-<u>βùɯ</u>
      I-objAn   take-caus-⟨SgM⟩   chicken-anim-thm

   a. 'I took the chicken.'
   b. 'He made me take the chicken.'

Why is -βùɯ (-vu) 'goal/theme' the case marker of choice in 670?

(670) Cána bo oke duhyétsó díhjya náávevu.
   kʰánà⁽ʔ⁾ pò⁽ʔ⁾ ò-kʰɛ̀ t-ùɯʔʲɛ́-tsʰó
   suggest urge I-objAn youImp-see-caus

   [[tíʔ ⒼhʲGa] ná:βɛ̀]-βùɯ
     your house   picture -thm
   'I urge you to show me a picture of your house.'

There are two possible explanations. First, for many verbs the direct object is a theme (in the semantic sense), so -βɯ 'theme' may be used to preserve the mapping between the semantic role and the form that generally marks it.

Second, there may be reason to posit a grammatical relation of OBLIQUE OBJECT which would subsume GOAL and be marked by -βɯ. This would follow direct object on the following hierarchy of grammatical relations:

SUBJECT ≻ DIRECT OBJECT ≻ OBLIQUE OBJECT ≻ other OBLIQUES

282   CHAPTER 10. CASE AND GRAMMATICAL RELATIONS

The direct object of a causative verb would be marked with -βɯ because its prior grammatical relation, direct object, is usurped by the CAUSEE; to have a distinct case marking it takes the next relation in the hierarchy, the oblique object.

While the object of a transitive is generally marked with -βɯ 'thm' when causativized, this is not always the case. In 671 it is treated as an inanimate object and thus has no explicit case marking. We do not know why.

(671) Iñéhni meke úújétsoóbe.
$\overset{G}{\text{i}}$ ɲéʔnì mè-kʰɛ̀   úːhɛ́-tsʰò-ːpɛ̀
self bad   SAP-objAn see-cause-⟨SgM⟩
'He showed us his ugly moral character.'

10.4 -tu 'source' (ablative)

This section deals with -tʰɯ (-tu) 'source', 'location', and so forth, which in traditional terminology might be called an "ablative." The discussion is divided into the following topics: some matters of form (10.4.1), source (10.4.2), partitive (10.4.3), about or concerning (10.4.4), site of attachment (10.4.5), time after (10.4.6), and contrast (10.4.7).

10.4.1 Some matters of form

When -tʰɯ follows an animate phrase, it must first bear -⁽ʔ⁾ti 'animate', as in 672:

(672) Íñáálledítyú tsaábe.
í   ⓖ ɲáː-tʃɛ̀-tí-tʲʰɯ́   tsʰàːpɛ̀   'He came
self   sib-⟨SgF⟩-anim-sou come-⟨SgM⟩ from his sister.'

The glottal stop of -⁽ʔ⁾tì 'animate' occurs only after the mono-moraic morphemes o 'I', ɯ 'you', and mɛ 'SAP'. See example 673:

(673) Óhdi(tyu) ihjyúvalle.
ó-ʔtì-(tʲʰɯ̀r) ìʔhʲɯ́βà-tʃɛ̀ 'She talks about me.'
I-anim-sou talk-⟨SgF⟩

After -⁽ʔ⁾ti 'animate', -tʰɯ 'source' is often left implicit. For example, it need not be explicit in 674. (See also examples 673 and 682.)

10.4. -TU 'SOURCE' (ABLATIVE)

(674) Dííbyedi(tyu) ídáátsóveébe.

tí-ːpʲè-tì̀-(tʲʰù̀ɯ)   ítáːtsʰóβèːpè   'He has compassion for him.'
that-⟨SgM⟩-anim-sou pity-⟨SgM⟩

After -tsʰiʔ ⟨place⟩, -tʰ⁽ʲ⁾ɯ 'source' is not aspirated; it becomes -ʔtʲɯ, as in 675:

(675) Tétsihdyu tsaábe.

tʰɛ́-tsʰì̀-ʔtʲù̀ɯ   tsʰàːpɛ̀   'He comes from that place.'
other-⟨place⟩-sou come-⟨SgM⟩

10.4.2 Source

A SOURCE, that is, a location from which something is said to move, the initial point of a trajectory, is indicated by a noun phrase bearing -tʰɯ 'source'. Examples follow:

(676) ò tsʰáː-ʔ   tʰɛ́-ʔùɾtʃɛ́-tʰù̀ɯ   (O tsáá téhullétu.) 'I come from
I come-⟨t⟩ that-⟨yonder⟩-sou   yonder.'

(677) Ávyéjuube tsáá ihjyátu.

áβʲɛ́hù̀ɯːpɛ̀ tsʰáː-ʔ ⁱ̂ʔ hʲá-tʰù̀ɯ   'The chief comes
reign-⟨SgM⟩ come-⟨t⟩ self house-sou   from his house.'

(678) Óómille ihjyátu.

óːmì̀-tʃɛ̀   ⁱ̂ʔ hʲá-tʰù̀ɯ   'She returned from her house.'
return-⟨SgF⟩ self house-sou

The source need not be a physical location; there are metaphorical extensions, as in 679:

(679) Óhdi(tyu) ijyácunúúbe.

ó-ʔtì̀-(tʲʰù̀ɯ) ìhʲá-kʰù̀mú̀ɯːpɛ̀   'He is depending on me.'
I-anim-sou depend-mSt-⟨SgM⟩

Further, 680 speaks of the source of knowledge:

(680) ...íñe táñuubúmuba llíjcyanúnetúré ú waajácuú...

...[í-ɲɛ̀   Ⓐ   tʰá   ɲú̀ːpú̀mù̀-pà
   this-⟨ø⟩   my medicinal.plant-sg

tʃíˣkʲʰà-nú̀ɯ   ]-nɛ̀-tʰú̀ɯ-ɾɛ́   ú̀ɯ   kpàːhákʰù̀ɯ-ú̀ɯ-ʔ...
yellow-become -⟨ø⟩-sou-only   you   know-fut-⟨t⟩

'...you will know from the yellowing of my medicine plant...'

In 681 the source is human; note the use of the genitive construction headed by ˀᴸatʃɯ 'top':[9]

(681) Áádí hallútú meke uhbáme.
[á:tí Ⓖ ˀᴸatʃɯ́]-tʰɯ́ mɛ̀-kʰɛ̀ ɯ̀ˀpá-mɛ̀
he top -sou SAP-objAn rail-⟨AnPl⟩
'They railed against us because of him.'

In 682 the source indicates the motive for laughing; this is presumably an extension of source as the initial point of a trajectory through space. (Note that -tʰɯ is implicit, as indicated by the small line following -tì.) The structure of 682 is given in 10.8.

(682) O chéméébedi góócóóbeke úhbaábe.
[NP[[[NPò tʃʰɛ́mɛ́]-:pɛ̀]-t̲ì̲-__ kó:kʰó]-:pɛ̀]-kʰɛ̀
I sick -⟨SgM⟩ -anim laugh -⟨SgM⟩ -objAn

ɯ́ˀpà-:pɛ̀
upbraid-⟨SgM⟩
'He upbraided the one who laughed at me because/when I was sick.'

[9]The example that follows is like 681 in using the genitive construction to explicate the relationship (here "reason") but does not use -tʰɯ̀ 'source':

Tééjá wáábyuta tsíbaábe.

[tʰɛ́:-há Ⓖ k͡pá:pʲɯ̀ᴸtʰà tsʰípà-:pɛ̀ 'He brought it for
that-⟨shelter⟩ benefit bring-⟨SgM⟩ the house's benefit.'

The second syllable of k͡pá:pʲɯ̀tʰà has a lexically marked low tone so the preceding syllable does not have the expected genitive low tone.

10.4. -TU 'SOURCE' (ABLATIVE)

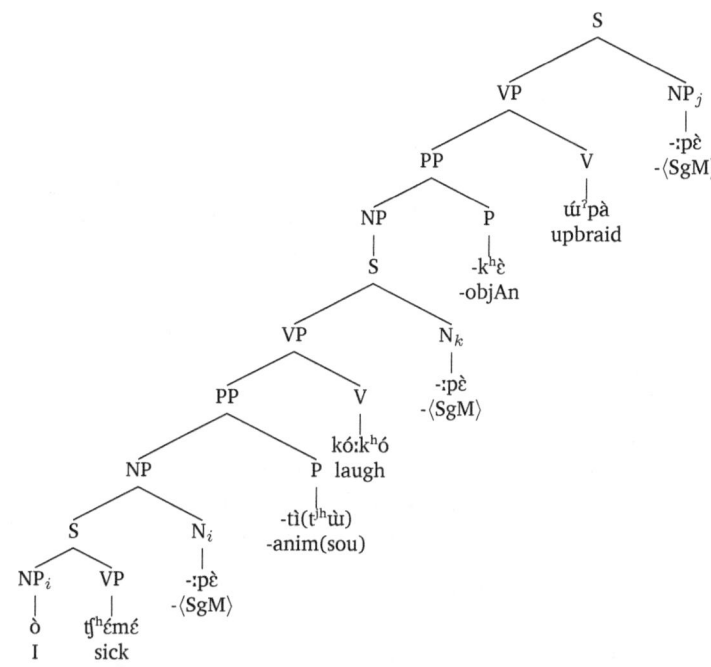

Figure 10.8 STR: O chéméébedi góócóóbeke úhbaábe.

(This is structurally like the mirror image of 'He$_j$ upbraided [$_{NP}$ the one who$_k$ [$_S$ ∅$_k$ laughed at [$_{NP}$ me who$_i$ [$_S$ ∅$_i$ was sick]]]].')

10.4.3 Partitive

The suffix -t^{h}ù 'source' may mark a partitive noun phrase, i.e., one referring to a collection (or whole) from which a subset (or part) is identified. For example, in 683, -t^{h}ù 'source' follows anomɛ 'fish', which indicates the collection from which one member should be taken:

(683) Ámómedítyú tsáápidívú oke daácu.
 ámómè-tí-t^{jh}ù tsʰá-:pʰì-tí-βúɪ   ò-kʰɛ̀   t-à:kʰù
 fish-anim-sou one-⟨SgM⟩-anim-thm I-objAn youImp-give
 'Give me one of the fish.'

(684) Tsáápidívú oke daacu diityédítyu.
 tsʰá:-pʰì-tí-βúɪ   ò-kʰɛ̀   t-à:kʰù
 one-⟨SgM⟩-anim-thm I-objAn youImp-give

tɨ̀ː-tʲʰɛ́-tí-tʲʰɯ̀ɾ
that-⟨AnPl⟩-anim-sou
'Give me one of them.'

(685) Oke ájcuube tsáneevu ityáávánetu.

ò-kʰɛ̀   áˣkʰɯ̀ɾ-ːpɛ̀   tsʰá-nɛ̀ː-βɯ̀ɾ¹⁰ [ḭ́ᴳ   tʲʰáːβá   ]-nɛ̀-tʰɯ̀ɾ
I-objAn give-⟨SgM⟩ one-⟨ø⟩-thm   self acquire.meat -⟨ø⟩-sou
'He gave me a part of what he hunted.'

Examples 683–685 have explicit direct objects (in each case tsʰa- 'one' followed by a classifier and -βɯ̀ɾ 'theme'). However a partitive phrase does not have to be accompanied by an explicit direct object, as shown by examples 686–688:

(686) ...u tsácooca cúdsɨtu tsívaco...

ɯ̀ɾ   tsʰá-kʰòːkʰà kʰɯ́ɾtsɨ̀-tʰɯ̀ɾ   tsʰíβà-kʰò
you come-when pineapples-sou bringImp-implore
'...when you come, bring some pineapple...'

(687) ...dóuháyojé mááhójɨtu.

tóɯ̀ɾʔá-jò-hɛ́-ʔ   máːʔó-hɨ̀-tʰɯ̀ɾ
break-sTr-do.come-⟨t⟩ cassava-⟨disk⟩-sou
'...he went and broke off a piece of cassava.'

(688) Ehdúváa néellere tsehdí íjcyujúwá llíjyutu.

[ɛ̀ʔ-tɯ́ɾ-β̇a-a̋   nɛ̋ː] -t͡ʃɛ̀-ɾɛ̀
that-⟨like⟩-rpt-rem say -⟨SgF⟩-only

tsʰɛ̀ʔtí-ʔì ḭ́   ˣkʲʰɯ̋ɾ̇hɯ́ɾkpá t͡ʃíhʲɯ̀ɾ-tʰɯ̀ɾ.
dig-⟨t⟩   self fire   ashes-sou
'Thus saying she dug up some ashes from her fireplace.'

10.4.4 About, concerning

A noun phrase bearing -tʰɯɾ 'source' may indicate the topic about which one is speaking, as in 689:

(689) Ehdúváa neebe dibye péénetu.

ɛ̀ʔ-tɯ́ɾ-β̇a-a̋   nɛ̀ː-pɛ̀   tɨ̀-pʲɛ̀   pʰɛ̋ː-nɛ̀-tʰɯ̀ɾ
that-⟨like⟩-rpt-rem say-⟨SgM⟩ that-⟨SgM⟩ go-⟨ø⟩-sou
'That is what he said about his going.'

---

¹⁰We do not know why tsʰá-nɛ̀ː-βɯ̀ɾ in 685 has a long vowel.

Or it may indicate the topic of a thought or attitude, as in 690. (As discussed in section 10.4.1, -tʰɯ may be left implicit.)

(690) Óhdi(tyu) ɨ́dáátsóvelle.
    ó-ʔtì-(tʲʰɯ̀ɨ) ɨ́táːtsʰó-βɛ̀-tʃɛ̀   'She has compassion for me.'
    I-anim-sou pity-sIn-⟨SgF⟩

10.4.5 Site of attachment

English treats something that is attached as directed to or against the site of attachment. For example, when we say *He tied the rope to the tree* or *The rope is tied to the tree*, we think of the rope as directed *to* (or *toward*) the tree.[11] Even when we say *The horse is tied to the tree*, in our mind's eye we see a rope running *from* the horse *to* the tree.

In Bora, the conceptual directionality of attachment is the other way around: something attached is generally conceptualized as being directed *away from* the site at which it is attached. For example, in 691 the word that indicates the site at which the rope is attached bears -tʰɯ 'source'. (See also the examples that follow 691.)

(691) Ócájikye dohjɨ́nuube úméhetu.
    ókʰáhì-kʲʰɛ̀ tòʔhí-nɯ̀ɨ-ːpɛ̀ ɯ́mɛ́-ʔɛ̀-tʰɯ̀ɨ   'He tied the cow to
    cow-objAn tie-do-⟨SgM⟩ tree-⟨tree⟩-sou   (lit. from) the tree.'

(692) Aawáváa iújcúne wájcátu pícyoólle.
    àː-kpá-βa-a̋   ì   ɯ̋ˣkʰɯ́-nɛ̀ kpáˣkʰá-tʰɯ̀ɨ pʰíkʲʰòː-tʃɛ̀
    thm-⟨slab⟩-rpt-rem self get-⟨event⟩ branch-sou put-⟨SgF⟩
    'Grabbing that hook she put it on (lit. from) a branch.'

(693) ...ɨhdééuúvutu ɨ́piijyúwá dóhjɨnúne.
    ɨ́ʔté-ɛ́-ɯ̀ɨ-ɯ̋βɯ̀ɨ-tʰɯ̀ɨ   ɨ́   pʰɨ́ːhʲɯ́-kpá tóʔhì-nɯ́-nɛ̀
    earlier-per-⟨string⟩-max-sou self hook-⟨slab⟩ tie-do-⟨ø⟩
    '...tied their hook onto (lit. from) a very old line.'

(694) ...íchihdyu dekéévé uke muhtsi mepájtyétsoki.
    í-tʃʰì-ʔtʲɯ̀ɨ   t-ɛ̀kʰɛ́-ːβɛ́   ɯ̀ɨ-kʰɛ̀
    this-⟨place⟩-sou youImp-grab-sIn you-objAn

    mɯ̀ɨʔtsʰɨ̀ mɛ̀ pʰáˣtʲʰɛ́-tsʰò-kʰɨ̀
    we.DuM SAP pass-cause-pur
    '...grab hold here (lit. from this place) so that we can pass you across.'

---

[11] See (Jackendoff 1991:112f).

(695) téénetu idyómaúcunúne

tʰɛ́:-nɛ̀-tʰɯ̀ɹ ì   tʲòmà-ɯ́kʰɯ̀mɯ́ɹ-nɛ̀   'having been touching
that-⟨ø⟩-sou self touch-sSt-⟨ø⟩   that (lit. from that)'

(696) Ípiijyúwaváa dibye wááone díílle nííwácotu cápaavyéhi.

[í   pʰì:hʲɯ́ɹ-kpà-βà-à   tì-pʲɛ̀   kpà:ò]-nɛ̀
self hook-⟨slab⟩-rpt-rem that-⟨SgM⟩ throw-⟨ø⟩

[tí:-tʃɛ́   ⓖ ní:kpá-kʰò   ]-tʰɯ̀ɹ kʰápʰà-:βʲɛ́-ʔì
that-⟨SgF⟩   head-⟨hair⟩   -sou hook-sIn-⟨t⟩

'That hook of his that he threw hooked her hair (lit. from her hair).'

-tʰɯ 'source' is used in combination with téhɯ̀ 'behind' to indicate motion toward something that is moving away, as in 697:[12]

(697) Áju, májo díítsííjúmu déjutu.

áhɯ̀ɹ⁽ʔ⁾ , máhò   [tí: ⓖ tsʰí:hɯ́ɹ-mɯ̀ɹ   téhɯ̀ɹ]-tʰɯ̀ɹ
ready let's.go your   mother-plAn behind-sou

'...OK now, let's go in pursuit of (lit. from behind) your parents.'

The use of -tʰɯ 'source' in 697 contrasts with -βɯ 'goal' to indicate motion toward a static location. Example 698 makes this clearer. In 698a the brother follows his sister, who is understood as moving away from him.[13] By contrast, in 698b the brother is moving toward the place where his sister is, that is, to a static location:[14]

(698) a. Íñáálle déjutu peébe.

b. Íñáálle éllevu peébe.

í   ⓖ ɲá:-tʃɛ́   [a. téhɯ̀ɹ-tʰɯ̀ɹ / behind-sou ; b. étʃɛ̀-βɯ̀ɹ / place-goal]   pʰɛ̀-:pɛ̀ .
self   sib-⟨SgF⟩   go-⟨SgM⟩

a. 'He follows his sister.'
b. 'He goes to where his sister is.'

The conceptual direction of attachment can help us understand 699 (in which -tʰɯ 'source' may be left implicit):

(699) ó-ʔtì-(tʰɯ̀ɹ) ìˣkʲʰá-nɛ̀ (Óhdi(tu) ijcyáne.) 'I have it.'
     I-anim-sou be-⟨ø⟩

---

[12] This can be understood in terms of the conceptual directionality of attachment, something like "going attached to a place behind the parents."

[13] This does not imply that the brother intends to catch up to her, although that might be the case.

[14] It is interesting to compare these with example 1078, page 423.

10.4. -TU 'SOURCE' (ABLATIVE)

Given the conceptual direction of attachment, 699 indicates that I am the site at which the subject (the referent of -nɛ ⟨ø⟩) is located ("attached"). And this is what it means to "have": for the owner to exert ownership "against" something.

At first blush, the instances of -tʰɯ̀ in 700 seem to indicate location:

(700) a. ¿Mútsihdyú Lli uke diíbye?
b. Íchihdyu tábooráyutu
a. mɯ́ɯ-tsʰì-ʔt̪ɯ́ɯ   tʃì⁽ʔ⁾   ɯ̀ɯ-kʰɛ̀   tì-ːpʲɛ̀
which-⟨place⟩-sou father you-objAn that-⟨SgM⟩
'Where on you, Father, is it?'

b. í-tʃʰì-ʔt̪ɯ̀ɯ   Ⓐ tʰá pòːɾ́ájɯ̀ɯ-tʰɯ̀ɯ
this-⟨place⟩-sou Ⓐ my heel-sou
'Here on my heel.'

However, given that 700 refers to an insect that burrows *into* the skin, it seems quite clear that -tʰɯ̀ is used to indicate the site at which the insect has attached itself.

10.4.6 Time after

-tʰɯ 'source' may follow a phrase that refers to time in order to indicate some subsequent time. In 701 it follows a simple noun phrase:

(701) Aabéváa cúúvénetúré iájkyéne mɨ́ɨcúmɨri ɨ́ɨtémeíhi....
àː-pɛ́-βa̋-à̏   kʰɯ́ɯːβɛ́-nɛ̀-t̪ʰɯ́ɯ-ɾɛ́   ì   a̋ˣkʲʰɛ́-nɛ̀
thm-⟨SgM⟩-rpt-rem dark-⟨time⟩-sou-only self awake-⟨ø⟩

mɨ́ːkʰɯ́ɯmɨ̀-ɾì ɨ́ːtʰɛ́-mɛ̀í-ʔì
mirror-oblIn look-r/p-⟨t⟩
'Early in the morning, having awakened, he looked at himself in the mirror....'

In 702 it follows a subordinate clause:

(702) Aanéváa áíívyénetu teene dóótou neebó "tóó".
àː-nɛ́-βa̋-à̏   a̋í-ːβʲɛ́-nɛ̀-t̪ʰɯ̀ɯ   tʰɛ̀ː-nɛ̀
thm-⟨ø⟩-rpt-rem burn-sIn-⟨event⟩-sou that-⟨ø⟩

Ⓐ tóːtʰò-ɯ̀ɯ   nɛ̀ːpó-ʔ   "tʰóː"
squash-⟨sphere⟩ pop.open-⟨t⟩ "bang"
'After it heated up, that squash popped open with a bang.'

10.4.7 Contrast

-tʰɯ 'source' may mark the noun phrase indicating something with which another is contrasted. With à:-nè (theme-⟨ø⟩) it forms a sentence-initial link indicating contrast, as at the beginning of 703b, where clothes such as socks and underwear are contrasted with single-piece clothing like dresses. (The other three instances of -tʰɯ can be understood in terms of the conceptual direction of attachment: "hang *from* hangers," "hang *from* a clothes line," "*from* where we attach the clothes pins.")

(703) a. Paja nééja páihcyútú mépicyóóhi.

b. Áánetu tsíhdyure ɨ́ɨvajáhjɨ́ mépicyóóhi; móóhóutu méɨ́hdotsó úméhewáánetu.

a. pʰà-hà   nɛ́:-hà   pʰá-ɨ́ʔkʲʰɯ̀-tʰɯ́ɯ̀ mɛ́ pʰɨ̀kʲʰó:-ʔɨ̀
all-⟨clothes⟩ say-⟨clothes⟩ all-⟨frame⟩-sou SAP put-⟨t⟩

b. á:-nè-tʰɯ̀ɯ̀ tsʰɨ́-ʔtʲùɯ̀-rɛ̀   ɨ:βà-há-ʔhɨ́
thm-⟨ø⟩-sou other-⟨like⟩-only different-⟨clothes⟩-pl

mɛ́ pʰɨ̀kʲʰó:-ʔɨ̀ mó:ʔó-ùɯ̀-tʰɯ̀ɯ̀
SAP put-⟨t⟩   vine-⟨vine⟩-sou

[mɛ́ ɨ́ʔtò-tsʰó-ʔ   úmɛ́-ʔɛ̀-kpá-:nè   ]-tʰɯ̀ɯ̀
SAP bite-cause-⟨t⟩ tree-⟨tree⟩-⟨slab⟩-plIn -sou

a. 'We put all the one-piece clothes onto hangers.'

b. 'By contrast, the other kinds of clothes we hang on the clothes line, pinning them on with clothes pins.'

10.5 -ri 'inanimate obliques'

-Ⓛrì (-ri) is used to mark various inanimate obliques; it is only used on inanimate noun phrases and nominalized clauses. -Ⓛrì is often used to mark instruments (10.5.1). Other uses include: cause (10.5.2), location (10.5.3), medium (10.5.4), and topic of conversation (10.5.5).

10.5.1 Instrument

-ri ~ -ji 'inanimate obliques' is used to mark an instrument, i.e., an object with which an action is performed. For example, in 704 the instrument is nɨ̀:tsʰɯ́kpà 'machete'. (See also 781, page 311.)

(704) Ínɨɨtsúwari wákímyeííbye.
   í   nɨ:tsʰúɨ-kpà-ɾì   kpákʰímʲèí-:pʲɛ̀
   self machete-⟨slab⟩-oblIn work-⟨SgM⟩
   'He works with his slab-like thing (machete).'

(705) Tééwari wákímyeííbye.
   tʰɛ́:-kpà-ɾì   kpákʰímʲèí-:pʲɛ̀
   that-⟨slab⟩-oblIn work-⟨SgM⟩
   'He worked with that slab-like thing (machete).'

(706) Aabéváa ... mɨ́ɨcúmɨri ɨ́ɨtémeíhi...
   à:-pɛ́-βa-a   ... mɨ́:kʰúɨmɨ̀-ɾì ɨ́:tʰɛ́-mèí-ʔì
   thm-⟨SgM⟩-rpt-rem   mirror-oblIn look-r/p-⟨t⟩
   'He ... looked at himself in the mirror...'

(707) Cááni mémeri teene újcuúbe.
   [kʰá:ni mɛ́mɛ̀]-ɾì   tʰɛ̀-:nɛ̀ úɾˣkʰùɨ-:pɛ̀
    father name   -oblIn that-⟨ø⟩ get-⟨SgM⟩
   'He got it by using his father's name.'

10.5.2 Cause or reason

-ɾì 'inanimate obliques' can mark a noun phrase or nominalized clause as the cause or reason for the event indicated by the main clause. Examples follow:

(708) Tééneri chémeébe.
   tʰɛ́:-nɛ̀-ɾì   tʃʰɛ́mɛ̀-:pɛ̀   'That was the cause
   that-⟨ø⟩-oblIn sick-⟨SgM⟩   of his being sick.'

(709) Taabóóbej tééveri tsúúca bohɨ́júcoóbe.
   [tʰà:pó-:pɛˣ tʰɛ́:βɛ̀]-ɾì   tsʰúɾ:kʰà pòʔɨ́-húɨkʰò-:pɛ̀
    cure-⟨SgM⟩ influence-oblIn already be.alive-now-⟨SgM⟩
   'By the influence of the doctor, he is now better.'

(710) Mítyane imájchóneri chémeébe.
   [mítʲʰà-nɛ̀ ì máˣtʃʰó]-nɛ̀-ɾì   tʃʰɛ́mɛ̀-:pɛ̀
    much-⟨ø⟩ self eat   -⟨ø⟩-oblIn be.ill-⟨SgM⟩
   'He got sick by eating a lot.' (or '...because he ate a lot.')

(711) Íñáállekéváa iéévátsóneri iñúcójpɨ́véne péjúcoóbe.
   í   ⓖ ɲá:-tʃɛ̀-kʰɛ́-βa-a
   self   sib-⟨SgF⟩-objAn-rpt-rem

ì ɛ̀ːβá-tsʰó-nɛ̀-ɾ̀ì
self pregnant-cause-⟨event⟩-oblIn

ì ɲúɨkʰóˣpʰɨ́-βɛ́-nɛ̀ pʰɛ́-húɨkʰòː pɛ̀
self shame-sIn-⟨event⟩ go-now-⟨SgM⟩

'He is going now because he is ashamed of having caused his sister to be pregnant.'

10.5.3 Location

-ɾi 'inanimate obliques' can mark a noun phrase or nominalized clause as the location of the event indicated by the main clause, as in 712,[15] 713, and 783, page 312.

(712) Juuváyiváa ávyéjuube méénikye iájtyúmɨ́ɨbeke añúhi.

hùːβá-jì-βa-a áβʲɛ́hùːpɛ̀ mɛ́ːnì-kʲʰɛ̀
trail-oblIn-rpt-rem reign-⟨SgM⟩ peccary-objAn

Ⓐ [ì áˣtʲʰúmí]-ːpɛ̀-kʰɛ̀ àɲúɨ-ʔì
self see   -⟨SgM⟩-objAn shoot-⟨t⟩

'The chief, seeing a peccary on the trail, shot it.'

(713) Tééjari diíbye.

tʰɛ́ː-hà-ɾ̀ì   tìː pʲɛ̀   'He is in that
that-⟨shelter⟩-oblIn that-⟨SgM⟩   shelter (house).'

-ɾi 'inanimate obliques' is frequently used with genitive constructions headed by a locative noun like ǘmiuɨ, as in example 714:

(714) Táúníuri diíbye.

tʰá Ⓖ ǘmíùɨ-ɾ̀ì tìː pʲɛ̀   'He is at my side.'
my side-oblIn that-⟨SgM⟩

See also tʰɛ̀ːʔí ǘmíùɨ-ɾi 'alongside the river' in 361, page 176, as well as 956, page 361.

Compare 715 and 716. In 715 the location of a static event is indicated with -ɾi. In 716 (and 658, page 276) the goal of a dynamic event is indicated with -βuɨ (-vu) 'goal':

---

[15]Example 712 is presented as having iáˣtʲʰúmíːpɛ̀kʰɛ̀ 'the one that he saw' in apposition to mɛ́ːnìkʲʰɛ̀ 'peccary'. An alternative is to take mɛ́ːnìkʲʰɛ̀ as the direct object of aˣtʲʰúmí 'see' in the relative clause.

10.5. -RI 'INANIMATE OBLIQUES'

(715) Táñaalle ácuúcunú ácúúveíhcyú hallúri.

tʰá ⒼɲǎL:-tʃɛ̀   ákʰɯ̀-ɯ́kʰɯ̀mɯ́-ʔ
my sib-⟨SgF⟩ sit-sSt-⟨t⟩

[ákʰɯ́ː-βɛ̀-íʔkʲʰɯ́ɯ́ ʔGátʃɯ́L]-ɾɨ̀
sit-sIn-⟨frame⟩ top -oblIn

'My sister is sitting on top of the chair.'

(716) Táñaalle ácujcáró íjtsɨɨméneke ácúúveíhcyú hallúvu.

tʰá ⒼɲǎL:-tʃɛ̀   ákʰɯ̀-ˣkʰáɾó-ʔ í   Ⓖ ˣtsʰɨ́Gːménɛ̀-kʰɛ̀
my sib-⟨SgF⟩ sit-sIn-⟨t⟩   self   child-objAn

[ákʰɯ́ː-βɛ̀-íʔkʲʰɯ́ɯ́ ʔGátʃɯ́L]-βɯ̀
sit-sIn-⟨frame⟩ top -goal

'My sister sat her child down on top of the chair.'

-ɾi is not used following a locational phrase headed by pʰáɲɛL 'inside'; for example, 717a is correct but 717b is ungrammatical:[16]

(717) Táñaalle ácuúcunú ihjyá pañe { a. ø / b. *-ri }.

tʰá ⒼɲǎL:-tʃɛ̀   ákʰɯ̀-ɯ́kʰɯ̀mɯ́-ʔ
my sib-⟨SgF⟩ sit-sSt-⟨t⟩

[[ɨ̌Gʔ hʲá] Ⓖ pʰáɲɛ̀L] { a. ø / b. *-ri }
   self house   inside

'My sister is sitting in her house.'

10.5.4 Medium

A noun phrase marked with -ɾì 'inanimate oblique' may refer to that along which something moves or to a medium of conveyance. See the following examples:

---

[16]pʰáɲɛL 'inside' may be followed by a case marker, e.g., -βɯ̀ 'goal' in the following:

tʰá ⒼɲǎL:-tʃɛ̀   pʰɛ́ː-ʔ [[ɨ̌Gʔ hʲá] Ⓖ pʰáɲɛ́L]-βɯ̀ (Táñaalle péé ihjyá pañévu.)
my sib-⟨SgF⟩ go-⟨t⟩   self house   inside -goal

'My sister goes into her house.'

(718) Tééjuri peébe.
  tʰɛ́:-hɨ̀ɨ-ɾì   pʰɛ̀-:pɛ̀   'He went along that trail
  that-⟨stick⟩-oblIn go-⟨SgM⟩   (road,...).'

(719) Téémɨri peébe.
  tʰɛ́:-mɨ̀-ɾì   pʰɛ̀-:pɛ̀   'He went in that car (boat,
  that-⟨canoe⟩-oblIn go-⟨SgM⟩   airplane,...).'

(720) Tééjuri ihjyúvaábe.
  tʰɛ́:-hɨ̀ɨ-ɾì   ìʔhʲɨ́βà-:pɛ̀   'He spoke in
  that-⟨mouth⟩-oblIn speak-⟨SgM⟩   that language.'

10.5.5 Topic of conversation

-ɾì 'inanimate obliques' may be used on a noun phrase that indicates the topic of conversation:

(721) Tééneri ihjyúvaábe.
  tʰɛ́:-nè-ɾì   ìʔhʲɨ́βà-:pɛ̀   'He talked about that.'
  that-⟨ø⟩-oblIn talk-⟨SgM⟩

(722) Árónáacáváa diibye Píívyéébe hájkímú tééneri ihjyúvahíjcyáhi.
  á-ɾó-náàkʰá-βa̋-a̋   [[tì-:pʲɛ̀   Ⓐ pʰí:βʲɛ́-:pɛ̋]
  thm-frs-while-rpt-rem   that-⟨SgM⟩   create-⟨SgM⟩

  ʔáˣkʰí-mɨ́ɨ]   tʰɛ́:-nè-ɾì   ìʔhʲɨ́βà-ʔ íˣkʲʰá-ʔì
  relative-plAn that-⟨ø⟩-oblIn talk-sub be-⟨t⟩
  'However, the Creator's relatives were talking about it.'

10.6   -ma 'with'

-mà (-ma) 'with' is used for co-subjects (10.6.1), circumstances (10.6.2), instruments (10.6.3), and benefits (10.6.4).

10.6.1   Co-subject

-ma 'with' is used to mark a co-subject, that is, a noun phrase indicating a person, animal or thing that accompanies the referent of the subject (in the event indicated by the verb). Examples follow:

10.6. -MA 'WITH'

(723) Tsaapíváa péé méwáníího̱ma bájú pañévu.

tsʰà-ːpʰí-βa̋-a̋   pʰɛ́ː-ʔ mɛ́kpá-níːʔʲò-mà
one-⟨SgM⟩-rpt-rem go-⟨t⟩ wife-⟨mother⟩-with

páhúɨ pʰa̱ɲɛ́-βùɨ
jungle inside-goal

'A man went with his wife into the jungle.'

(724) a. Táñáhbema o pééhi.
     b. Táñáhbema muhtsi mepééhi.

$$\left. \begin{array}{l} t^h\acute{a} \ \textcircled{G} \ \text{ɲá-}\text{ʔpɛ̀-mà} \\ \text{my \ sib-}\langle\text{SgM}\rangle\text{-with} \end{array} \right\} \left\{ \begin{array}{ll} \text{a.} & \text{ò} \\ & \text{I} \\ \text{b.} & \text{mùɨʔtsʰì \ mɛ̀} \\ & \text{we.DuM SAP} \end{array} \right\} \left. \begin{array}{l} p^h\acute{\varepsilon}\text{ː-ʔì} \\ \text{go-}\langle\text{t}\rangle \end{array} \right.$$

a. 'I go with my brother.'
b. 'With my brother, he and I go.'

There are two instances of -ma 'with' in 725. The first (in the subordinate clause) marks the co-subject of 'work'; the second (in the main clause) marks the co-subject of 'go'.[17]

(725) Dííbyema wákímeííbyema péjúcoóbe.

[tí-ːpʲɛ̀$_j$-mà   kpákʰímɛ̀í-]-ːpʲɛ̀$_k$-mà   pʰɛ́-húɨkʰòːpɛ̀$_i$
that-⟨SgM⟩-with work-   -⟨SgM⟩-with go-now-⟨SgM⟩

'He$_i$ went with the one$_k$ who works with him$_j$.'

In 726 tsʰíːɲɛ́ ìːɲúɨhɨ̀tʰùɨ tsʰáːpèmà 'with the one (SgM) who came from another country' is in apposition to tsʰíˣpʰìmà 'with the other (SgM)'.

(726) Tsíjpima tsííñé iiñújɨtu tsáábema íhjyúvaábe.

tsʰíˣpʰì-mà Ⓐ [tsʰíː-ɲɛ́   ìːɲúɨ-hɨ̀-tʰùɨ   tsʰá   ]-ːpɛ̀-mà
other-with   other-⟨ø⟩ dirt-⟨disk⟩-sou come -⟨SgM⟩-with

íʔhʲúɨβàːpɛ̀   'He is talking with the one
talk-⟨SgM⟩   who came from another country.'

---

[17] Compare 725 with the following, in which i 'self' is the subject of the subordinate clause:

Dííbyema iwákímeííbyema péjúcoóbe.

[tí-ːpʲɛ̀$_k$-mà   ì$_i$ kpákʰímɛ̀í-]-ːpʲɛ̀$_k$-mà   pʰɛ́-húɨkʰòːpɛ̀$_i$
that-⟨SgM⟩-with self work-   -⟨SgM⟩-with go-now-⟨SgM⟩

'He$_i$ went with the one$_k$ he$_i$ works with ø$_k$.'

10.6.2 Circumstance

A subordinate clause bearing -ma 'with' may mark a phrase indicating a circumstance. In 727 it follows a subordinate clause and is interpreted temporally:

(727) Aane imájchónema péjúcoóbe.
```
à:-nè      [ì    máˣʧʰó ]-nè-mà      pʰɛ́-húíkʰò-:pè
thm-⟨ø⟩    self  eat     -⟨ø⟩-with   go-now-⟨SgM⟩
```
'Then, after eating, he went.'

See also example 662, page 277.

10.6.3 Instrument

Instruments are normally marked by -ɾi 'inanimate obliques'. However there are some cases where -mà 'with' seems to indicate an instrument.

In the following three examples, the sentence-initial connective of the second sentence bears -mà 'with', and the connective seems to refer to an object in the context, one that is used as an instrument in the sentence that the connective initiates. (The object referred to is virtually always mentioned explicitly in the preceding sentence.) In the second sentence of 728 it appears to refer to the aforementioned gun.

(728) Íícúiváa ávyéjuube ujcú íañúju. Áánemáváa oohííbyeke áñuube cuwájá pañétu.

```
í:kʰúɪ̀-βa-a̋       áβʲɛ́hùɪ-:pè    ùˣkʰúɪ-ʔ í   a̋ɲúɪ-hùɪ
quickly-rpt-rem    reign-⟨SgM⟩    get-⟨t⟩      self shoot-⟨gun⟩

á:-nè-má-βa̋-a̋      ò:ʔí-:pʲè-kʰè         áɲùɪ-:pè
thm-⟨ø⟩-with-rpt-rem jaguar-⟨SgM⟩-objAn  shoot-⟨SgM⟩

kʰúɪ̋kpá-há  ⓖ  pʰa̋ɲɛ́-tʰùɪ
sleep-⟨net⟩    inside-sou
```
'Quickly the chief got his gun. Then with it he shot the jaguar from inside the sleeping net.'

In the second sentence of 729 it appears to refer to the aforementioned skins:

(729) Mííhenéváa ávyéjuube tsajtyé cóómívuú. Áánemáváa wájyamu újcuúbe.

mí:ʔɛ̀-né-βa-a̋ áβʲɛ́hùɪ-:pɛ̀ tsʰà˟tʲʰɛ́-ˀ kʰó:mí-βùɪ:
skin-pl-rpt-rem reign-⟨SgM⟩ take-⟨t⟩ town-goal

á:-nɛ̀-má-βa̋-a̋ kpáhʲàmùɪ úɪ˟kʰùɪ-:pɛ̀
thm-⟨ø⟩-with-rpt-rem cloth get-⟨SgM⟩

'The chief took the skins to town. With them, he got cloth.'

In the second sentence of 730 it appears to refer to the aforementioned water. (tʰɯ 'cook' means to cook by boiling in water.)

(730) Aané boonévaa nújpacyo újcuúbe. Áánemáváa nééjpicyóke tuube cúújúwá hallúvu.

[à:-né ⓖ pò:né]-βa̋-a̋ núɪ˟pʰàkʲʰò úɪ˟kʰùɪ-:pɛ̀
 thm-⟨ø⟩   after -rpt-rem water get-⟨SgM⟩

á:-nɛ̀-má-βa̋-a̋ né:pʰìkʲʰó-kʰɛ̀ tʰùɪ-:pɛ̀
thm-⟨ø⟩-with-rpt-rem squirrel-objAn cook-⟨SgM⟩

[kʰúɪ:húɪkpá ⓖ ˀa̋tʃúɪ]-βùɪ
 fire top -goal

'After that he got water. With that (the water) he cooked the squirrel on top of the fire.'

Despite appearances, the connectives in 728–730 may simply indicate *circumstance*, with -ma used as in the previous section (10.6.2).

10.6.4 Beneficiary

The suffix -ma (-ma) may be used on a noun phrase that indicates the beneficiary of the event indicated by the clause, as in 731 and 732. (These should be compared with similar cases in section 10.7.1.)

(731) Táwajyámú óóma dsíjcolle.

tʰá kpáhʲámúɪ ó:-mà tsíˣkʰò-tʃɛ̀   'She sewed
my clothes   I-with sew-⟨SgF⟩ my clothes for me.'

(732) Téhdure úúma díwajyámú ó tsiváhi.

tʰɛ́-ˀtùɪ-ɾɛ̀ úɪ:-mà tí kpáhʲámúɪ ó tsʰìβá-ʔì
that-⟨like⟩-only you-with your cloth I bring-⟨t⟩
'I also brought your cloth for you.'

10.7 -hlliíhye ~ -llii 'motive'

The suffix -ˀʧi:ʔʲɛ (-hlliihye) 'motive' is used in two ways: to indicate a beneficiary (10.7.1; cf. section 10.6.4) and to indicate a reason or motive (10.7.2). As to form, -⁽ˀ⁾ʧi:ʔʲɛ is used at the end of a sentence and the shorter form -⁽ˀ⁾ʧii is used sentence medially.

10.7.1 Beneficiary

The suffix -⁽ˀ⁾ʧi(:ʔʲɛ) (-lliihye) indicates that its host's referent is the person benefited by the event indicated by the clause. Examples follow:

(733) Óhllii teene méénuúbe.
  ó-ˀʧì: tʰɛ̀:-nɛ̀   mɛ́:nɯ̀-:pɛ̀   'He made it for me.'
  I-motive that-⟨ø⟩   make-⟨SgM⟩

(734) Teene ó meenú táiiñújɨ múnáálliíhye.
  tʰɛ̀:-nɛ̀ ó mɛ̀:nɯ́-ˀ [[tʰá i̥:ɲɯ́-hɨ̥] mɯ́má:]-ʧì:ʔʲɛ̀
  that-⟨ø⟩ I make-⟨t⟩   my dirt-⟨disk⟩ people   -motive
  'I made that for the people of my country.'

10.7.2 Reason

When a clause subordinated with -nɛ ⟨event⟩ is followed by -⁽ˀ⁾ʧi(:ʔʲɛ) (-lliihye) 'motive', it is interpreted as the reason or motive for the event of the main clause. For example, the reason for not going indicated in 735 is that I am sick:

(735) Tsá o pééityú o chéménélliíhye.
  tsʰáᴴˀ ò pʰɛ́:-ì-tʲʰɯ́ɯ̀ [ò ʧʰɛ̌ᵐmɛ́]-nɛ́-ʧì:ʔʲɛ̀
  not I go-fut-neg I be.ill -⟨event⟩-motive
  'I will not go because I am sick.'

Other examples follow. See also example 668, page 280.

(736) Pááa májchoobe iájyábáávaténélliíhye
  pʰá:à máˣʧʰò-:pɛ̀ [ì̥   áhʲápá:-βà-tʰɛ́-nɛ́-ʧì:ʔʲɛ̀
  bread eat-⟨SgM⟩   self hunger-become-go.do-⟨event⟩-motive
  'He ate the bread because he became hungry.'

(737) Tsɨ́ɨ́mene táánéllii tsɨɨju ihbúcúhi.
[tsʰɨ́ːmènè tʰáː]-né-tʃìː   tsʰɨ̀ːhùɪ ì́ʔpúɪkʰúɨ-ʔì
child   cry -⟨event⟩-motive mother pick.up-⟨t⟩
'Because the child cried, the mother picked it up.'

-nè-tʃi (-⟨ø⟩-motive) is also used this way in sentence-initial connectives referring to the preceding sentence, as in 738:

(738) Áánéllii o péjucóóhi.
áː-né-tʃìː   ò pʰɛ́-hùɪkʰóː-ʔì   'For that reason,
that-⟨event⟩-motive I   go-now-⟨t⟩   I am now going.'

Another possibility is to use -⁽ʔ⁾tʃi(:ʔʲɛ) 'motive' with a nonfinite verb. In this case it does not bear -nɛ ⟨ø⟩ and may "possess" its direct object:

(739) Ávyéjuube pítyácójcatsí mɨ́amúnáama éhjácóbá ímibájchóllɨ́hye.
áβʲéhùɪ-ːpè   pʰítʲʰákʰó-ˣkʰàtsʰɨ́-ʔì mɨ́amúmáà-mà
reign-⟨SgM⟩ discuss-recip-⟨t⟩   people-with

[ɛ́ʔ-há-kʰópá   ⓖ ímìpáˣtʃʰó]-tʃìː ʔʲɛ̀
that-⟨shelter⟩-big fixing   -motive
'The chief coordinated with the people about fixing the big house.'

10.8 -hdu 'comparative'

As to form, -ⓛ◯ʔtɯ (-hdu) 'comparative (like)' occurs after monosyllabic roots and -ⓛ◯tɯ (-du) occurs elsewhere.

-ⓛ◯⁽ʔ⁾tɯ is different from the other case markers in that sometimes it behaves like a classifier (glossed as ⟨like⟩) and sometimes like a case marker (glossed 'like'). As a case marker it indicates similarity to its host's referent; as a classifier it refers to the nature or characteristics of its host's referent or, particularly when it heads a relative clause, to the manner of an event. -ⓛ◯tɯ can occur as a case marker following a pronoun or a name, where a classifier cannot occur. For example, a classifier may not occur after o 'I', but -ʔtɯ 'like' may do so, as in 740:

(740) ó-ʔtɯ̀ nè-ːpè   (Óhdu neébe.) 'He is like me.'
I-like   say-⟨SgM⟩

Likewise a classifier may not follow pʰáːβòɾò 'Paul', but -ʔtɯ may, as in example 741:

(741)
- a. hóáà pʰá:βòró-tùɪ̱   (Jóáa Páávoródu.)
   John Paul-like
- b. pʰá:βòró-tùɪ̱ hóáà:¹⁸   (Páávoródu Jóáaá.)
   Paul-like   John-emph

a,b. 'John is like Paul.'

(742) a. Táñahbédú dííbye.
b. Táñahbe dííbyedu.

   a. tʰá ⓖ ɲa̋-ʔpé-tűɪ̱   tì-:pʲè   'He is like
      my   sib-⟨SgM⟩-like that-⟨SgM⟩   my brother.'

   b. tʰá ⓖ ɲa̋-ʔpè   tí-:pʲè-tùɪ̱   'My brother
      my   sib-⟨SgM⟩   that-⟨SgM⟩-like   is like him.'

(743) Tsá dííbyedu o néétune.

   tsʰa̋ʔ tí-:pʲè-tùɪ̱   ò né:-tʰùɪ-nè
   not that-⟨SgM⟩-like I   say-neg-⟨n⟩
   'I am not like him.' (lit. 'I do not say like him.')

-ⓛ◯tɯ 'comparative' may also be used to compare two actions. For example, 744 compares "how the others do it" to how "he does it." In this case -tɯ is a classifier and heads the relative clause that is the direct object of the main clause. (More is said about such cases below.)

(744) Tsá tsijtye dibye méénudu méénutúne.

   tsʰa̋ʔ tsʰì-ˣtʲʰè   [tì-pʲè   mé̋:nùɪ]-tùɪ̱   mé:nùɪ-tʰűɪ-nè
   not other-⟨AnPl⟩   that-⟨SgM⟩ do   -⟨like⟩ do-neg-⟨n⟩
   'The others do not do like he does.'

In 745 -ⓛ◯tɯ heads a postpositional phrase (tí-:pʲè-tùɪ̱) that complements iˣkʲʰa 'be'; the predicate-complement sentence is the object complement of ìmìtʃé 'want':

(745) Ó imillé dííbyedu o íjcyane.

   ó ìmìtʃé-ʔ [tí-:pʲè-tùɪ̱   ò íˣkʲʰà]-nè   'I want to be
   I want-⟨t⟩ that-⟨SgM⟩-like I be   -⟨ø⟩   like him.'

In 746 -ʔtɯ heads a postpositional phrase that is a predicate complement within a relative clause:

(746) Ó imíllé tsawa úméhewa íwahdu nééwaá.

   ó ìmítʃé-ʔ   tsʰa̋-kpà   ⓐ űmé-ʔè-kpà
   I want-⟨t⟩ one-⟨slab⟩   tree-⟨tree⟩-⟨slab⟩

---

¹⁸The final low vowel has undergone FLTS.

10.8. -HDU 'COMPARATIVE'

(A) [í-kpà-ʔtùɪ̰   ø$_i$ nɛ̰:]-kpà:$_i$
    this-⟨slab⟩-like   say -⟨slab⟩
    'I want a plank like this one.'

In 747 -tɯ heads a relative clause:

(747) O íjcyadu tsá dibye íjcyatúne.

[ò ḭˣkʲʰà]-tùɪ   tsʰá̰ʰʔ tì-pʲɛ̀   i̋ˣkʲʰà-tʰɯ́-nɛ̀
 I be   ⟨like⟩ not that-⟨SgM⟩ be-neg-⟨n⟩
'He does not live like I live.'

Let us now return to cases where -ʔtɯ behaves like a classifier. There are various reasons for considering it to be a classifier. First, it can be followed by a case marker. (We know of no other case where a case marker is followed by another case marker.) For example, in 748 -ʔtɯ ⟨like⟩ is followed by -tʰɯ 'source':

(748) ¡Múhdutúráami ó péétsáméiíj!

mɯ́-ʔtɯ̀-tʰɯ́-rá-àmì   ó pʰɛ́:-tsʰá-mɛ̂ì-í-ˣ
WH-⟨like⟩-sou-frs-wonder I go-cause-r/p-fut-voc
'...How in the world can I make it disappear?!'

Second, $^{(?)}$tɯ ⟨like⟩ frequently follows bound pronominal roots, which *must* be followed by a classifier. These are tʰɛ- 'that', a- 'thematic', ɛ- 'that', mɯ- 'who, which', and pʰa- 'all'.

Third, $^{(?)}$tɯ ⟨like⟩ can head a relative clause, as in 744 and 747 above and in 749:

(749) Áronéváa ipyéhdú pehíjcyáhi.

á-rò-nɛ́-β̰a-a̰   [ì pʲʰɛ̰ʰˢ]-ʔtɯ́   pʰɛ̀-ʔ i̋ˣkʲʰá-ʔì
thm-frs-⟨ø⟩-rpt-rem self go   -⟨like⟩ go-sub be-⟨t⟩
'It kept on happening like it was happening.'

Fourth, a classifier never follows a case marker but, as we have seen many times, a classifier may follow another classifier. -kpa ⟨slab⟩ is unquestionably a classifier, but in example 750 it follows -ʔtɯ, showing that in this case it is a classifier.[19]

(750) éhduwáre

ɛ́-ʔtɯ̀-kpá-rɛ̀   'a slab (plank,...) just like that one'
that-⟨like⟩-⟨slab⟩-only

---

[19]The structure of 750 is as follows, where both -ʔtɯ and -kpa head phrases:

10.9 Vocative

The vocative differs from other case markers in that it does not indicate the grammatical relation of a noun phrase to a verb. Rather, a vocative indicates speech directed toward an interlocutor. The Bora vocative may occur on a noun phrase (such as a name, a kinship term, or a nominalized clause).

When a phrase (usually a name) is used to address a particular person (or persons) it bears -^{x} (-j) 'vocative'. Examples follow:[20]

(751) Llihíyoj, ¡dúcaáve!
  tʃîʔíjò-^{x} , t-úɨkʰà-ːβɛ̀
  father-voc youImp-enter-sIn
  'Father, come in!'

(752) Ámuúha táñahbémuj, méucááve.
  ámùːʔà tʰá Ⓖ ɲà-ʔpé-mùɨ-^{x} , mɛ́ ùɨkʰá-ːβɛ̀
  you.pl my   sib-⟨SgM⟩-plAn-voc SAP enter-sIn
  'You, my brothers, enter!'

(753) Ámúhakye o wájyumej, méucááve.
  ámúɨʔà-k^{jh}ɛ̀ ò kpáh^{j}ùɨ-mɛ̀-^{x} , mɛ́ ùɨkʰá-ːβɛ̀
  you.pl-objAn I esteem-⟨AnPl⟩-voc SAP enter-sIn
  'Esteemed ones, enter!'

(754) Méucááve, táwajyújtej.
  mɛ́ ùɨkʰá-ːβɛ̀ , tʰá kpáh^{j}úɨ-^{x}tʰɛ̀-^{x}
  SAP enter-sIn my esteem-⟨AnPl⟩-voc
  'Enter, my esteemed ones!'

When a vocative phrase involves the reduplication of a word or phrase, the first of the reduplicated parts is shortened and does not bear -^{x} 'vocative':

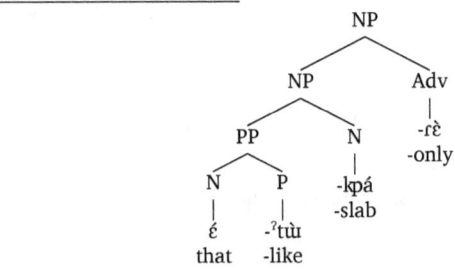

---

[20] The comma indicates a break/pause.

10.9. VOCATIVE

(755) Péédo, Péédoroj, ¡dichájuj!
pʰɛ́:tò , pʰɛ́:tòrò-ˣ , tì-tʃʰá-hùɪ-ˣ
Peter   Peter-voc   youImp-come-quick-voc
'Peter, Peter, come quickly!'

Some conventional vocatives are listed in 756:

(756) a. ɲàˣ   (ñaj)   'sibling'
      b. nɛ́ʔnìˣ   (néhnij)   'ugly (one)'
      c. kʰɛ́mɛ̀ˣ   (kémej)   'old one'
      d. ⎰ tʃìʔíjòˣ (llihíyoj) ⎱
         ⎨ tʃìʔíùɪˣ (llihíuj) ⎬ 'father, son'
         ⎱ tʃíʔìˣ   (llíhij)   ⎰

Proper names are also frequently shortened. For example, whereas 757a would be used to refer to someone named Mary, 757b is how one would call someone so named:

(757) a. márímùɪtʃɛ̀ (Márímulle)
      b. májìˣ   (Máyij)

-ˣ 'vocative' may occur at the end of reported speech that was directed to an interlocutor. In this use it often follows a verb, as in 758 and 759. (See also examples 755 above and 667, page 280.)

(758) Aanéváa neébe: "Llíhij, májo memájchokij".

à:-né-βa-a̋   nè-:pɛ̀   tʃíʔì-ˣ ,
thm-⟨ø⟩-rpt-rem   say-⟨SgM⟩   son-voc

máhò mɛ̀   mã̌ˣtʃʰò-kʰì-ˣ
let's SAP   eat-pur-voc
'Then he said, "Son let's eat".'

(759) óβìì , ò tʃɛ́:nɛ̀-ˣ (Óvíi, o lléénej.) 'Wait, I'll eat it.'
       wait   I eat-voc

This use of -ˣ is also found in self-directed quotes, that is thoughts represented as direct quotes, as in 748 above.

Chapter 11

Clitics

Enclitics (which we generally refer to simply as "clitics") have syntactic or semantic "scope" over an entire phrase. They attach themselves phonologically to the last word of a phrase.[1] Bora uses the following types of clitics (among others, e.g., the personal pronominal subject proclitics of table 10.1, page 270):

1. SECOND POSITION clitics occur only following a clause's first constituent; these include:
   (a) TEMPORAL, i.e., ones that indicate tense (the time of an event relative to the time of speaking) are -pʰɛ ~ -⒣ó̍ 'remote past', -⁽ˀ⁾nɛ 'recent past', and -ììkʲʰɛ̀ ~ -ì 'future'. These are discussed in section 5.9.3. They are also included in figure 11.1; note that they do not all occupy the same position relative to the other clitics.
   (b) EVIDENTIAL, i.e., ones that indicate how the speaker came to know what she or he is reporting; see section 11.1.
   (c) The verb 'to be' iˣkʲʰa has become a second-position clitic in a type of predicate complement structure; see section 5.10.2.
2. ADVERBIAL clitics follow various classes of sentence constituent; see section 11.2.
3. A NEGATIVE clitic is discussed in section 13.3, page 13.3.

The clitics occur in the order given in table 11.1:

---

[1] We do NOT intend a strong claim that the morphemes discussed here are strictly *clitics* as opposed to *suffixes*. Examples like 790, in which -rò 'frs' precedes -ːpɛ̀ -⟨SgM⟩, suggest that -rò is a suffix rather than a clitic.

Table 11.1 The order of clitics

ONLY	MODAL	FUT[a]	FRS[b]	PROB[c]	REALIZE	REP[d]	NWIT[e]	TENSE
-ɾɛ	-huɯkʰo	-i(ɨkʲʰɛ)	-ɾo	-ɯpa	-ʔa(ákʰa)	-βa	-ʔha	-pʰɛ ~ -Ⓗσ̇
	-hɨː(βa)				-kʰa			-ne
	-ʔiˣkʲʰa							
	-ʔtɛ							

[a] future
[b] frustrative, contraexpectation
[c] probable
[d] reportative
[e] nonwitnessed

The clitics combine quite freely, but some combinations are semantically incompatible. It is not infrequent to find four clitics on a single word, e.g.:

(760) Ááneréjucóhjáa
    á:-nè-ɾɛ́-hùɯkʰó-ʔhá-à   'After that only now'
    that-⟨ø⟩-only-now-nwit-rem

11.1 Evidential clitics

The evidential clitics are -ʔha 'nonwitnessed' and -βa 'reportative'.

There is no clitic indicating direct, first hand information, but the absence of an evidential clitic (in a declarative sentence) implies first hand infomation. If a speaker fails to include an evidential clitic when reporting an event he or she did not witness, they may be challenged by the hearer.

11.1.1 -hja 'nonwitnessed'

The evidential -ʔha (-hja) 'nonwitnessed' indicates that the speaker did not see, hear, smell, or have tactile experience regarding what she or he is saying. It always co-occurs with either -pʰɛ ~ -Ⓗσ̇ 'remote past' or -⁽ʔ⁾nɛ 'recent past'. The effect of -ʔha 'nonwitnessed' in 761 is to indicate that, although we saw what you made, we did not see you make it:

(761) Muha muurá máájtyumɨ́jucóó éhnéhjáa u méénune.
    mùʔà mùːrá   má   áˣtʲʰùmɨ́-hùɯkʰóː-ʔ
    we   confirm SAP see-now-⟨t⟩

11.1. EVIDENTIAL CLITICS

[ɛ́ʔ-né-ʔha̋-à̀   ùɨ   mɛ̂ːnùɨ]-nɛ̀
that-⟨ø⟩-nwit-rem you make   -⟨ø⟩
'We (ex.) have already seen what you made.'

Other examples follow:

(762) Oohííbyéhjá $\begin{Bmatrix} \text{-pe} \\ \text{-a} \end{Bmatrix}$ úmɨváhi.

ò̗ːʔí-ːpʲɛ́-ʔha̋ $\begin{Bmatrix} \text{-p}^h\grave{\epsilon} \\ \text{-à} \\ \text{rem} \end{Bmatrix}$ úmɨ̀β́á-ʔɨ̀   'The dog escaped
dog-⟨SgM⟩-nwit   escaped-⟨t⟩   some time ago.'
                                                        (I did not see it.)

(763) Oohííbyéhjáne úmɨváhi.

ò̗ːʔí-ːpʲɛ́-ʔhá-nɛ̀   úmɨ̀β́á-ʔɨ̀   'The dog escaped recently.'
dog-⟨SgM⟩-nwit-rec escaped-⟨t⟩   (I did not see it.)

Example 764 implies that the speaker saw the burned house, but the effect of adding -ʔha (-hja) 'nonwitnessed' is to indicate that he did not see it while it was burning, only some considerable time after it burned:

(764) Ó ájtyumɨ́ tsajáhjáa jaa aíívyeja.

ó áˣtʲʰùmɨ́-ʔ tsʰà-há-ʔha̋-à̀
I see-⟨t⟩   that-⟨shelter⟩-nwit-rem

Ⓐ [hà: aí-ːβʲɛ̀²]-hà
   shelter burn-sIn -⟨shelter⟩
'I saw a house that had burned (but I did not see it happen).'

11.1.2 -va 'reportative'

-βa (-va) 'reportative' indicates that the speaker is reporting something said by another person. It is used both like a reportative evidential and as a marker of indirect quotation. It is used in folktales and legends. -βa may follow the first constituent of either a main clause, as in 765, or a subordinate clause as in 766b:

(765) Diibyévá peé úúmaá.

tì-ːpʲɛ́-β́á   pʰɛ̀-ɛ́-ʔ   úː-mà: 'Someone says that he
that-⟨SgM⟩-rpt go-fut-⟨t⟩ you-with   will go with you.'

---

[2]Note the nonfinite tone in 764; if it were high tone this would be a relative clause, implying that the house was seen at the time it was burning. This is not acceptable because it would contradict the implication of the nonwitnessed suffix.

(766) a. Áánerá táñáálleke neebe ipyééityúne.

b. Áánerá táñáálleke neebe iiva ipyééityúne
á:-nè-ɾá   tʰá ⓖ ɲá:-tʃɛ̀-kʰɛ̀   nɛ̀-ːpɛ̀
that-⟨event⟩-frs my   sib-⟨SgF⟩-objAn say-⟨SgM⟩

{ a. ì   pʲʰɛ́ː-ì-tʲʰɯ́ɯ̀-nɛ̀
      self go-fut-neg-⟨n⟩
  b. ì:-βà   ì   pʲʰɛ́ː-ì-tʲʰɯ́ɯ̀-nɛ̀
      self-rpt self go-fut-neg-⟨n⟩ }

'On the contrary, he$_i$ told my sister that (someone said) he$_i$ would not go.'

Example 766a (without the reportative) means simply that he told my sister that he was not going. By contrast, 766b—with the reportative in the subordinate clause—means that he told my sister that someone reported that he was not going.

(767) Oke táñahbe úúballé ávyéjuubéváa íiiñúj+vu pééneé.

ò-kʰɛ̀   tʰá ⓖ ɲá-ˀpɛ̀   ɯ́ːpàtʃɛ́-ˀ [áβʲɛ́hɯ̀ː-ːpɛ́-βa̱-a̱]
I-objAn my   sib-⟨SgM⟩ tell-⟨t⟩   reign-⟨SgM⟩-rpt-rem

í   ǐːɲɯ́ɯ̀-hɨ̀-βɯ̀   pʰɛ́ː]-nɛ̀ː
self dirt-⟨disk⟩-goal go   -⟨ø⟩

'My brother told me that the chief went to his country ...so my brother was told.'

(768) a. Tsá ova o pééityúne.

b. Tsáhava o pééityúne.

a. tsʰá̰ˀ ò-βà   'Someone said that
    not I-rpt   } ò pʰɛ́ː-ì-tʲʰɯ́ɯ̀-nɛ̀   I am not going.'
b. tsʰá̰ˀà-βà   I go-fut-neg-⟨n⟩
    not-rpt

Compare the sentences in 769: 769a is a direct quote, 769b is an indirect quote, and 769c reports the content of what someone else said. Examples 769a and b would be used by the person to whom "he" said "Tomorrow I am going...". By contrast, 769c would be used if this information had been passed through a number of speakers.

(769) a. Oke neébe, "Péjcore ó peé táiiñúj+vu".

b. Oke neebe péjcore íiiñúj+vu ipyééiñe.

c. Péjcorévá pééiibye íiiñúj+vu.

a. ò-kʰὲ   nè-ːpὲ   ,³ "pʰɛ́ˣkʰòrὲ ó pʰὲ-ɛ́-ˀ
   I-objAn say-⟨SgM⟩   tomorrow I go-fut-⟨t⟩

   tʰá ịɲɯ́ɨ-hɨ-βɨ̀ɨ"
        ᴳ
   my dirt-⟨disk⟩-goal

b. ò-kʰὲ   nè-ːpὲ   pʰɛ́ˣkʰòrὲ í   ịɲɯ́ɨ-hɨ-βɨ̀ɨ
                                        ᴳ
   I-objAn say-⟨SgM⟩ tomorrow self dirt-⟨disk⟩-goal

   ì   pʲʰɛ́ː-ì-ɲὲ
   self go-fut-⟨ø⟩

c. pʰɛ́ˣkʰòrɛ́-βá pʰɛ́ː-ì-ːpʲὲ   í   ịɲɯ́ɨ-hɨ-βɨ̀ɨ
                                     ᴳ
   tomorrow-rpt go-fut-⟨SgM⟩ self dirt-⟨disk⟩-goal

a. "He said to me, "Tomorrow I will go to my country."
b. 'He said to me that he would go to his country tomorrow.'
c. 'He will go to his country tomorrow (so I was told).'

The clitic -βa 'reportative' may be used in questions, as in 770:

(770) a. à   ɨ̀ɨ-βà
          ques you-rpt   ɯ́ɨ pʰὲ-ɛ́-ˀì   { a. ¿A uva ú peéhi?
       b. à-βà   you go-fut-⟨t⟩   { b. ¿Ava ú peéhi?
          ques-rpt

a,b. 'Are you going (as I was told)?'

In 771 the evidential refers to the implicit subject; ímɨ̀áːnὲ is a predicate complement to an implicit copula:

(771) ¿Ava ímɨááne?
                    ᴸ
      à-βà   ímɨ́áː-nὲ   'Is what he said true?'
      ques-rpt true-⟨ø⟩

The two evidential clitics, -βa 'reportative' and -ˀha 'nonwitnessed', may co-occur:

(772) Jotséeváhjápe úmɨvá.
                 ᴴ   ᴸ
      hòtsʰɛ́ὲ-βá-ˀha-pʰɛ́   úmɨβá-ˀ   'Joseph escaped
      Joseph-rpt-nwit-rem escape-⟨t⟩   (some time ago).'

---

³In 769a PLTS applies to nè-ːpὲ where it is phrase final (as indicated by the comma), so it is pronounced nɛ̀ὲpὲ (written neébe). By contrast, in 769b PLTS does not apply because it is not phrase final, so nè-ːpὲ is pronounced nὲːpὲ (written neebe).

Here, -βa 'reportative' indicates that someone informed the speaker that Joseph had escaped; -ʔha 'nonwitnessed' indicates that the person who reported this to the speaker had not seen (nor otherwise experienced) him escaping. Example 773 is similar:

(773) Táñáhbé ocájikyéváhjáa oohííbye dsɨ́jɨ́vetsó bájú pañe.

tʰá ⓖ ɲá-ʔpɛ́   ok̬ʰáhì-kʲʰɛ́-βá-ʔh̬a-a̬   o̬ːʔí-ːpʲɛ̀
my   sib-⟨SgM⟩ cow-objAn-rpt-nwit-rem jaguar-⟨SgM⟩

tsíhíβɛ̀-tsʰó-ʔ [páhɯ́ ⓖ pʰa̬ɲɛ̀]
die-caus-⟨t⟩   jungle   inside

'A jaguar killed my brother's cow in the jungle.'

Whoever said 773 heard it from someone who had not observed the event, but who had deduced it based on the evidence (the tracks, the dead cow,...).

11.2 Adverbial clitics

The adverbial clitics are: -rɛ 'only' (11.2.1), -hɯkʰo 'focus' (11.2.2), -hɨː(βa) 'deny' (13.3), -ɯpa 'probable' (11.2.3), -ʔa(aːkʰa) 'realize' (11.2.4), -ra -ro 'frustrative, contraexpectation' (11.2.5), -kʰà 'doubt' (11.2.6), -ʔa(ha) 'challenge veracity' (11.2.7), -ami 'disgust' (11.2.8), -ʔtɛ 'able' (11.2.9), -mɛi 'pity' (11.2.10), -ˣtʰanɛ 'exclude' (11.2.11), -βɛ́hɨɯ 'similar to' (11.2.12), and -ijo 'contrary' (11.2.13).

-ra ~ -ro 'frustrative, contraexpectation' may follow any constituent in a clause; see section 5.12.1.2. The others may follow any major constituent except the verb (although some occur only in the main clause).

11.2.1 -re ~ -ye 'only'

-rɛ (-re) ~ -jɛ (-ye) 'only' indicates the host's referent to the exclusion of others. Examples follow:

(774) Dííllere cheméhi.

tíː-tʃɛ̀-rɛ̀   tʃʰɛmɛ́-ʔì   'Only she is sick' or
that-⟨SgF⟩-only sick-⟨t⟩   'She alone is sick.'

(775) Ó imíllé táñáhbekéré o tsájtyene.

ó ìmítʃɛ́-ʔ tʰá ⓖ ɲá-ʔpɛ̀-kʰɛ́-rɛ́   ò tsʰáˣtʲʰɛ̀-nɛ̀
I want-⟨t⟩ my   sib-⟨SgM⟩-objAn-only I take-⟨ø⟩

'I want to take just my brother (no one else).'

(776) íkʲʰᴸo:kʰá-ɾɛ̀ (ícyoocáre) 'right now'
now-only

(777) Tsáápiye teene meenúhi.
tsʰá:-pʰì-jɛ̀   tʰɛ̀:-nɛ̀   mɛ̀:núɨ-ʔì   'Only one guy did that.'
one-⟨SgM⟩-only that-⟨ø⟩ did-⟨t⟩

(778) a. Tsá múúhaye wákimyévu mepééityúne.
 b. Tsá múúhaye mewákímyeítyéityú(ne).

tsʰá?ᴴ mɨ́ɨ:ʔà-jɛ̀   { a. kpákʰìmʲɛ́-βɨ̀ɨ mɛ̀ pʰɛ́:-ì-tʲʰɨ́ɨ-nɛ̀
not we-only   work-goal   SAP go-fut-neg-⟨n⟩
                     b. mɛ̀ kpákʰímʲèí-tʲʰɛ́-ì-tʲʰɨ́ɨ-(nɛ̀)
                        SAP work-go.do-fut-neg-⟨n⟩

'We (ex.) are not the only ones { a. going to the job (work).'
                                  b. going to work.'

(779) Ó wáhdáhɨ́númeí tátyájkíityu tánɨ̵tsúwaríye.
ó kpáʔtáʔɨ́-núɨ-mèí-ʔ tʰá Ⓖ tʲʰáˣkʰîi-tʲʰɨ̀ɨ
I cut-mTr-ɾ/p-⟨t⟩   my   leg-sou

tʰá Ⓖ nɨ̀:tsʰɨ́ɨ-kpà-ɾí-jɛ̀
my machete-⟨slab⟩-oblIn-only
'I cut my leg with my very own machete.'

11.2.2 -juco 'focus'

The second-position clitic -ⒹⒸhɨ̀ɨkʰo (-juco) 'focus' is obviously related to the verbal suffix -ⒹⒸhɨ̀ɨkʰo: 'now' discussed in section 5.12.1.1. The difference is that the clitic marks information as focal whereas the verbal suffix is a temporal pointer.

-ⒹⒸhɨ̀ɨkʰo 'focus' occurs on various types of constituents to mark them as focal, as in 780 and 781:

(780) a. tì-:pʲɛ́-hɨ̀ɨkʰò   (Diibyéjuco.) '(It was) HE.'
        that-⟨SgM⟩-focus
    b. tí-:pʲɛ̀-ɾɛ́-hɨ̀ɨkʰò   (Dííbyeréjuco.) '(It was) ONLY he.'
        that-⟨SgM⟩-only-focus

(781) Íñeríyéjuco tsahróbari nujpáñu.⁴
 í-ɲè-ɾí-jé-hɨ̀ɨkʰò   tsʰà̰ɾópà-ɾì   nɨ̀ɨˣpʰá-ɲɨ̀ɨ
 this-⟨ø⟩-oblIn-only-focus basket-oblIn water-do
 'Now get water with THIS, with this basket.'

In 782 the focus is on the situation—the villain's being attached to a line to cross the river in pursuit of the heroine:

(782) Ahdújucóváa ékéévéébeke dityétsí píjyúcuróné vúdoové pɨ́ɨ́née-móvúre.
 à-ˀtɨ́ɨ-hɨ̀ɨkʰó-βá-à   [ɛ̀kʰɛ́-ːβɛ́-ːpɛ̀-kʰɛ̀   tì-tʲʰɛ́tsʰɨ́
 thm-⟨like⟩-focus-rpt-rem grab-sIn-⟨SgM⟩-objAn that-⟨DuM⟩

 pʰɨ́hʲɨ́ɨkʰɨ̀ɨ-ɾó]-nɛ́   βɨ́ɨtò-ːβɛ́-ʔì
 hook-frs   -⟨ø⟩   break-sIn-⟨t⟩

 pʰɨ́ːnɛ́-è-mó-βɨ́ɨ-ɾɛ̀
 middle-per-⟨big.river⟩-goal-only
 'It was THUS that the line to which he was attached broke as they approached the middle of the big river.'

-hɨ̀ɨkʰo 'focus' is used in the formation of a sort of CLEFT sentence. This is formed by placing -hɨɨkʰo 'focus' on the focal constituent and subordinating the main clause, by virtue of which the verb bears high tone on the first syllable and ends with -nɛ̀ ⟨ø⟩ on the main verb. For example, in 783 the focus is on the trail and the verb is pʰɛ́ː-nɛ̀ (go-⟨ø⟩):

(783) Aallévа́a juuvа́yiyéjuco pééne ijyééúwuúmuma.
 à:-tʃé-βá-à   hɨ̀ɨːβá-jì-jé-hɨ̀ɨkʰò   pʰɛ́ː-nɛ̀
 thm-⟨SgF⟩-rpt-rem trail-oblIn-only-focus go-⟨ø⟩
 í   hʲɛ́-ɨ́ɨ-kpɨ́ɨɨ́-mɨ̀ɨ-mà.
 self   pet-sg-dim-plAn-with
 'Thus it was ON THAT TRAIL that she went with her pets.'

11.2.3 -uba 'probable'

-ⓛ○ɨ́pa (-uba) 'probable' indicates that the referent of the phrase to which it is cliticized probably was (or did) what is asserted of it. Examples

---

⁴In 781 nɨ̀ɨˣpʰáɲɨ̀ɨ 'get water' is derived from nɨɨˣpʰa 'water' by the addition of the verbalizer -ⓛ○nɨɨ 'do' (discussed in section 4.3.2.2, 110). Presumably because this suffix imposes its low tone on the noun's initial syllable, the verb does not get the expected imperative low tone on the second syllable (as discussed in section 14.1.1), since the two low tones would violate the *LLX constraint.

follow:

(784) a. tì-ːpʲɛ́-ǜpá̄   (Diibyéubá.)
         that-⟨SgM⟩-prob
     b. tí-ːpʲɛ̀-ɾɛ́-hù̀kʰó-ǜpà   (Dííbyeréjucóuba.)
         that-⟨SgM⟩-only-focus-prob

     a. 'It is probably he.'
     b. 'It was probably ONLY he.'

(785) ¿Aca ú ɨjtsúcunú u pééiñe? Tsáháuba u pééityú(ne).
     à-kʰà   ú̄   ɨ̄ˣtsʰɨ́-kʰɨ̀mɨ́-ʔ [ù̀   pʰɛ́ː-ì]-ɲɛ̀
     ques-doubt you think-sSt-⟨t⟩   you go-fut -⟨ø⟩

     tsʰá̄ʔá-ǜpà ù̀ pʰɛ́ː-ì-tʲʰɨ́-(nɛ̀)
     not-prob   you go-fut-neg-⟨n⟩
     'Do you think you are going? It is doubtful that you will go.'

11.2.4 -háaáca ~ -ha 'realize'

-ʔaːkʰa ~ -ʔa (-haaca ~ -ha) 'realize' indicates recognition that the referent of the phrase to which it is cliticized was (or did) what is said about it.[5] -ʔaːkʰa is used sentence medially if another clitic follows, as in 786, and sentence finally, as in 787:

(786) Jotséeváhaacáa úmɨváhi.
     hòtsʰɛ́ɛ̀-βá-ʔàːkʰá-à   úmɨ̀βá-ʔì   'Oh, they say that Joseph
     Joseph-rpt-realize-rem flee-⟨t⟩   fled some time ago!'

(787) tì-ːpʲɛ́-ʔàːkʰà   (¡Diibyéhaáca!) 'It is he.' (I realize
     that-⟨SgM⟩-realize   that he was the one.)

Otherwise the form is -ʔa, as in 788:

(788) òːʔíː-pʲɛ́-ʔà   úmɨ̀βá-ʔ (¡Oohííbyéha úmɨvá!)
     dog-⟨SgM⟩-realize escape-⟨t⟩
     'The dog escaped.' (I realize that it was the dog that escaped.)

11.2.5 -ra ~ -ro 'frustrative, contraexpectation'

-ɾa (-ra) ~ -ɾo (-ro) 'frustrative, contraexpectation' indicates, contrary to what the hearer might think, that the referent of the host of -ɾa is prop-

---

[5] -ʔaːkʰa ~ -ʔa, here glossed as 'realize', might be more technically glossed 'mirative'.

erly identified as the one of whom the sentence is predicated.[6] Examples follow:

(789) Diibyéjúcoóro
tì-ːpʲɛ́-húɨkʰòː-ɾò̱   'But it is HE (although it does not
that-⟨SgM⟩-focus-frs   appear to be).'

(790) ɨ́hnáhó chémeébe. Ároobe wákímyeítyéhi.
íʔnáʔóʔ   ʧʰɛ́mɛ̀-ːpɛ̀ á-ɾò̱-ːpɛ̀   ƙpákʰímʲɛ̀í-tʲʰɛ́-ʔì
very.much sick-⟨SgM⟩ thm-frs-⟨SgM⟩ work-go.do-⟨t⟩
'He was very sick. However, he went to work.'

See section 5.12.1.2, page 158, for a discussion of -ɾa ~ -ɾo 'frustrative, contraexpectation' as used on verbs. In particular, compare example 790 with 306.

11.2.6 -ca 'affirm'

-kʰa (-ca) 'affirm' either affirms or requests affirmation for the proposition asserted by the clause:

(791) ¿Aca ú májchoóhi?
à-kʰa̱   úɨ má˟ʧʰò-ó-ʔì   'Are you sure you will eat it?'
thm-affirm you eat-fut-⟨t⟩

(792) ó-kʰa̱   ó má˟ʧʰò-ó-ʔì (Óca ó májchoóhi.)   'Yes, I will eat it.'
I-affirm I eat-fut-⟨t⟩

(793) Dihñétúcá oke daácu.
tìʔ-ɲɛ́-tʰúɨ-kʰá   ò-kʰɛ̀   t-àːkʰùɨ   'Give me something
your-⟨ø⟩-sou-affirm I-objAn youImp-give   that is really yours.'

(794) Óréiikyéca ó májchoóhi.
ó-ɾɛ́-ìːkʲʰɛ́-kʰa̱   ó má˟ʧʰò-ó-ʔì   'I affirm that only
I-only-PT-affirm I eat-fut-⟨t⟩   I will eat (it).'

11.2.7 -haja ~ -ha 'challenge veracity'

-ʔa(ha) (-haja ~ -ha) 'challenge veracity, verify' occurs only in questions.[7] It challenges the hearer to demonstrate the veracity of a previous claim.

---

[6]Although -ɾa ~ -ɾo 'frustrative, contraexpectation' is treated in this section, we withhold judgement as to whether it is, strictly speaking, a *clitic* or a *suffix*. Note that in example 789 it follows -ːpʲɛ́-húɨkʰòː, suggesting that it is a clitic. In the second clause of example 790, however, it precedes -ːpɛ̀ ⟨SgM⟩, suggesting that -ɾa ~ -ɾo is a suffix.

[7]The final syllable of -ʔa(ha) may be cognate with -ˣ 'vocative' discussed in section 10.9.

For example, if someone points out a bird to a person who has trouble seeing it, then that person might challenge the first with 795, which is as though to say "Where in the world is it; I don't see anything!"

(795)
mɨ́ɨ-ʔtsʰí-ʔàhà   (¿Múhtsíhaja?)
WH-⟨place⟩-verify
kʰíá-ʔàhà   (¿Kíáhaja?)
where-verify
} 'Where?! (incredulous)'

If someone says (pointing to a group) "He did it." someone who cannot identify the referent could respond with 796:

(796) kʰà-ːpʲɛ́-ʔàhà   (¿Caabyéhaja?) 'Which one?'
     which-⟨SgM⟩-verify

In response to something incredible one can respond with 797:

(797) mɨ̀ɨ-ʔtɨ́ɨ-rá-ʔàhà   (¡Muhdúráhaja!) 'How could that be!'
     WH-⟨like⟩-frs-verify

Other examples:

(798) mɨ̀ɨ-ːpá-ʔàhà   (¿Muubáhaja?) 'Who could it be?'
     WH-⟨SgM⟩-verify

(799) ¿Muubáha tsááhií?
     mɨ̀ɨ-ːpá-ʔà   tsʰáː-ʔìː   'Who (SgM) could be coming?'
     WH-⟨SgM⟩-verify come-⟨t⟩

11.2.8 -ami 'disgust'

-àmì 'disgust' expresses disgust. It is only used in rhetorical questions.

(800) ɨ̀ː-ná-àmì   (¿Ɨ̈náami?) 'What? (when provoked
     what-⟨ø⟩-disgust   by something)'

(801) mɨ́ɨ-ʔtɨ́ɨ-àmì   tʰɛ̀ː-nɛ̀   (¡¿Múhdúami teéne?!) 'How can
     WH-⟨like⟩-disgust that-⟨ø⟩   that be!'

(802) ¡Ɨ́veekíami ehdu méénuúbe!
     íβɛ̀ː-kʰí-àmì   è-ʔtùɨ   méːnùɨ-ːpè   'What did he do
     what-pur-disgust that-⟨like⟩ do-⟨SgM⟩   THAT for?!'

11.2.9 -hde 'be able'

-ʔtɛ 'be able' indicates that its host's referent is able to do the action indicated by the verb:

(803) ó-ʔtɛ̀   ó máˣt͡ʃʰò-ó-ʔì (Óhde ó májchoóhi.) 'I can eat it.'
      I-able I eat-fut-⟨t⟩

(804) Óréhdéiikyéca ó méénuúhi.
      ó-ɾέ-ʔtέ-ì:kʲʰέ-kʰà   ó mɛ́:nù̵-ú̵-ʔì   'I can do it, and
      I-only-able-be-affirm I do-fut-⟨t⟩   do it I will!'

It can also be used to indicate permission, as in 805:

(805) Anéhde waáca dipye.
      àné-ʔtɛ̀   kpà:-kʰà   tì-pʲʰɛ̀   'O.K., then,
      concede-able permit-affirm youImp-go   you may go.'

11.2.10 -mei 'pity'

-mɛi (-mei) 'pity' indicates compassion or pity. For example:

(806) tí-:pʲɛ̀-mɛ́ì   (dííbyeméi) 'poor thing (SgM)!'
      that-⟨SgM⟩-pity

(807) Tsɨ́ɨ́méneméi áákityé íyé íjcyaábe.
      tsʰɨ́:ménɛ̀-mɛ́ì á:kʰìtʲʰέ-ʔ Ⓐ [í-jέ   ˢìˣkʲʰà]-:pɛ̀
      child-pity   fall-⟨t⟩   self-only be   -⟨SgM⟩
      'The poor child fell, being alone.'

11.2.11 -jtane 'exclude'

-ˣtʰanɛ (-jtane) 'exclude' indicates that an action is done without taking into consideration another person or thing. For example:

(808) Diityéjtane dsɨ́ɨ́neébe.
      tì:-tʲʰέ-ˣtʰànɛ̀   tsí:nɛ̀-:pɛ̀   'He ran leaving
      that-⟨AnPl⟩-exclude run-⟨SgM⟩   them behind.'

(809) Áámye majchó ájyújtane.
      á:mʲɛ̀   màˣt͡ʃʰó-ʔ áhʲú̵-ˣtʰà̱nɛ̀ᴸ
      she.prox eat-⟨t⟩   husband-exclude
      'This one (SgF) ate without including her husband.'

11.2.12 -véjɨu 'similar to'

-βɛ́hɨ̀ɯ̀ (-véjɨu) 'similar to' indicates similarity or likeness. For example:

(810) kpàʔáɾó-βɛ́hɨ̀ɯ̀ òó (Wahárovéjɨu oó.) 'I am like my mother.'
    mother-similar I

11.2.13 The combination -i-ɾo 'contrary'

The combination of -i 'projected time' and -ɾo ~ -jo 'frustrative, contra-expectation' is cliticized to noun phrases to indicate that some situation is contrary to what one expects, what one might want, what is likely to happen, and so forth. For example, 811 runs contrary to the expectation that a singular masculine being would be present:

(811) kʰà-ːpʲɛ́-ì-jò   (¿Caabyéiyo?) 'Which one (SgM)?'
    which-⟨SgM⟩-PT-frs

Examples 812–817 run contrary to the expectation that the person or object in question would be present:

(812) kʰàː-tʲʰɛ́-ì-jò   (¿Caatyéiyo?) 'Which ones (AnPl)?'
    which-⟨AnPl⟩-PT-frs

(813) ɨ̀ː-nɛ́-ì-jò   (¿Ɨ̀ɨnéiyo?) 'Which one (In)?'
    which-⟨ø⟩-PT-frs

(814) kʰɛ̀ː-kpá-ì-jò   (keewáiyo) 'Which plank (table,
    which-⟨slab⟩-PT-frs   machete,…)?'

(815) tʰà²-ɲɛ́-ì-jò   (Tahñéiyo.) 'I wish it were mine (but it isn't).'
    my-⟨ø⟩-PT-frs

(816) Wajpíiyo pééneé.

    kpàˣpʰí-ì-jò pʰɛ̌ː-nɛ̀ː   'A MAN should have gone
    man-PT-frs go-⟨ø⟩   (not a woman or child).'

(817) Wajpi pééiyóne.

    kpàˣpʰì pʰɛ̌ː-ì-jó-nɛ̀   'A man SHOULD go.'
    man   go-PT-frs-⟨ø⟩

Chapter 12

Some Minor Categories

The minor categories include: conjunctions, interjections, particles, and onomatopoeic expressions.

12.1 Conjunctions

Bora has no word like English *and*. The conjunction of nominals is achieved by means of suffixes or by a "summation" word as discussed in section 7.6.

There are two disjunctive morphemes, àmí 'or' and mìt^{jh}á 'or', which to our knowledge are entirely interchangable. They are used to ask which of two alternatives is correct, occurring between the clauses that express the alternatives, as in the following examples:

(818) ¿A ú májchoó mityá tsá u májchóityúne?
 à ú má^{x}tʃ^{h}ò-ó-$^{\textrm{?}}$ mìt^{jh}á ts^{h_H}a$^{\textrm{?}}$ ù má^{x}tʃ^{h}ó-ì-t^{jh}ú-nè
 y/n you eat-fut-⟨t⟩ or not you eat-fut-neg-⟨n⟩a
 'Will you eat or not?'

(819) ¿A óma ú peéhi mityá ú cóévaáhi díñáállema?
 à ó-mà ú p^{h}è-έ-ʔì mìt^{jh}á ú k^{h}óέβà-á-ʔì
 y/n I-with you go-fut-⟨t⟩ or you stay-fut-⟨t⟩

 tí Ⓖ ɲá:-tʃὲ-mà
 your sib-⟨SgF⟩-with
 'Will you go with me or stay with your sister?'

Examples 820 and 821 show that much of the second clause may be ellipsed:

(820) ¿A ú peéhi amí tsáhaá?
 à ɯ́ pʰɛ̀-ɛ́-ʔì , àmí tsʰá?àá 'Will you go or not?'
 y/n you go-fut-⟨t⟩ or not

(821) ¿A ú peéhi mityá áánuú?
 à ɯ́ pʰɛ̀-ɛ́-ʔì , mìtʲʰá á:nɯ̀ɯ́ 'Will you go or will
 y/n you go-fut-⟨t⟩ or this.SgM this one (go)?'

12.2 Interjections

The interjections listed below express the speaker's emotions or attitude. They are never part of a sentence.[1]

ɯ́ˣ (új) ~ hɯ̀ʔɯ́:: (juhúú) expresses surprise
tʃʰɨ́ˣ (chíj) ~ tʃʰɨ́:: (chíí) expresses surprise or admiration
ɲó:ò: (ñóóoo) expresses happiness

Many other interjections are used in the interaction between people: to get another's attention, to answer, or to indicate a reaction. A few of the more common follow:

ɛ́hɛ̀ (éje) calls attention to look at something (like English 'Look!')
áhɯ̀ (áju) calls attention to receive something given (like English 'Here! Take it!')
áàˣ (áaj) answers a call or indicates a question (like English 'Yes, what do you want?')
hɯ̀ɯ́hɯ̀ˣ (juújuj) ~ hɯ̀ɯ́ (juú) ~ ɯ̀ɯ́ (uú) indicates agreement (like English OK.)
màáʔɯ̀ɯ́ˣ (maáhuúj) indicates that one does not know (like English 'I don't know!')
hɯ̀:ɯ̀ (juuu) indicates incredulity (like English 'I can't believe it!')

12.3 Particles

The PARTICLES listed below call attention, express surprise, ask permission, and so forth. In contrast to the interjections discussed in section 12.2, the particles are sentence constituents.

---
[1] However, they might be used at the margin of a sentence, much like we might say in English "OK. I'll go."

12.3. PARTICLES

a(:) (a) 'yes/no' is used to ask questions that can be answered with 'yes' or 'no'.

(822) à   ɯ́   pʰɛ̀-ɛ́-ʔì   (¿A ú peéhi?) 'Are you going?'
      y/n you go-fut-⟨t⟩

a-kʰa (aca) (y/n-doubt aca) is used to ask regarding something that the speaker heard, asking for confirmation and simultaneously indicating disapproval or incredulity, as in 823. (See also example 785, page 313.)

(823) ¿Aca ú peéhi?
      à-kʰà   ɯ́   pʰɛ̀-ɛ́-ʔì   'You are going?!
      y/n-doubt you go-fut-⟨t⟩   (I don't want that!)'

a-βa (ava) (y/n-rpt ava) is used to ask regarding something reported by another person (not the person to whom the question is addressed):

(824) ¿Ava ú peéhi?
      à-βà   ɯ́   pʰɛ̀-ɛ́-ʔì   'Is it true (as someone told me)
      y/n-rpt you go-fut-⟨t⟩   that you will go?'

(825) ¿Acává ú peéhi?
      à-kʰá-βá   ɯ́   pʰɛ̀-ɛ́-ʔì   'Has somebody said
      y/n-doubt-rpt you go-fut-⟨t⟩   you are going.'

pò[2] (bo) 'well'; see example 828.

kʰána (cána) ~ kʰa ca requests or grants permission to do something.

(826) Cána uke ó úúbállej.
      kʰánà   ɯ̀-kʰɛ̀   ó   ɯ́ːpátʃɛ̀-ˣ   'Allow me to tell you.'
      permit   you-objAn I   tell-voc

(827) a. Cána né cóóvaíñú úmɨhétu u tsáábeé.
      b. Cóóvaíñú ca úmɨhétu u tsáábeé.

    ⎧ a. kʰánà   nɛ́ʔ(ì)   kʰóː-βà-íɲɯ́   ⎫
    ⎪   permit implore firewood-have-do.go   ⎪
    ⎨   ⎬
    ⎪ b. kʰóː-βà-íɲɯ́   kʰà   ⎪
    ⎩   firewood-have-do.go   permit   ⎭

      [ɯ́mɨ̀ʔɛ́-tʰɯ̀ ɯ̀ᵢ   tsʰá   ]-ːpɛ̀ɛ́ᵢ
      field-sou   you come   -⟨SgM⟩

      a,b. 'I suggest that you gather firewood when you come from the field.'

---
[2]The full form, used in isolation, is pòʔò.

(828) a. Cána bo né dicha.
　　　b. Cá bo né dicha.
　　　　a. kʰánà　　　⎫
　　　　b. kʰá　　　　⎬　pòʔ　nɛ́ʔ(ì)　tì-tʃʰà
　　　　　　permit　　⎭　well implore youImp-come
　　　　'I suggest that you come.'

mùːɾá (muurá) indicates confirmation, as in 829:

(829) Ááné boone muurá peebe íiñújɨvu.
　　　á:-nɛ́　ⓖ　pòːnɛ̀　mùːɾá?　pʰɛ̀-ːpɛ̀　í　íːɲɯ́-hɨ̀-βɯ̀
　　　that-⟨ø⟩　　　after　confirm　go-⟨SgM⟩　self　dirt-⟨disk⟩-goal
　　　'Afterwards he went to his country.'

nɛ́ʔ (né) 'implore'; see examples 827a and 828.
kpáì (wái) indicates permission, as in 830:

(830) kpáì　mɛ̀　pʰɛ̀-ˣ　(Wái mepej.) 'Well, go (plural)!'
　　　permit　SAP　go-voc

12.4 Onomatopoeia

Onomatopoeic expressions (ideophones) generally imitate their referent; for example, kʰàʔó-kʰáʔò imitates the sound of chewing something hard. In 831 áβɨˣ imitates the sound of a tree's leaves moving. (By virtue of not being reduplicated, this indicates a single action.)

(831) Daallí áákityé 'ávɨj'.
　　　tàːtʃì　áːkʰìtʲʰɛ́-ʔì　áβɨˣ
　　　sloth　fall-⟨t⟩　　swish
　　　'The sloth fell "swish" (making the sound of movement through the branches).'

Many onomatopoeic expressions are formed by the reduplication of a verb root; see section 2.6. These indicate multiple action. Examples follow:

(832) a. 'Allíhállíʔ ihjyúvaábe.
　　　b. 'Allíhállíʔ néébeé.
　　　c. 'Allíhállíʔ tsíñááveébe.

　　　　　　　　　⎧ a. ìʔhʲɯ́ββ̀à-ːpɛ̀　　　　'He speaks lying.'
　　　　　　　　　⎪　　speak-⟨SgM⟩
àtʃíʔ-átʃí　　　　⎨ b. nɛ́-ːpɛ̀ɛ́　　　　　　'He is a liar.'
lie-lie　　　　　　⎪　　say-⟨SgM⟩
　　　　　　　　　⎪ c. tsʰíɲá-ːβɛ̀-ːpɛ̀　　　'He has become a liar.'
　　　　　　　　　⎩　　turnout-sIn-⟨SgM⟩

12.4. ONOMATOPOEIA

A reduplicated form may be used as a clause's predicate, but it never bears affixes (so is not a verb per se).

Some onomatopoeic expressions are conventional references to a movement, a characteristic, or a sensation. For example, in 833, àkʲʰɛ́ʔ-ákʲʰɛ̀ refers to the movement of a child in its crib when it does not sleep well:

(833) Aabye tsíímene 'akyéhákyéré' cuwáhi.
 à-ːpʲè tsʰíːmènè àkʲʰɛ́ʔ-ákʲʰɛ́-ɾɛ́ kʰùɯkpá-ʔì
 thm-⟨SgM⟩ child wake-wake-only sleep-⟨t⟩
 'That child sleeps, waking up frequently.'

As in 833, for many onomatopoeic words the sound symbolism is not transparent, as illustrated further in 834:

(834) a. kʰàmá-kʰámà (camácáma) 'doing one thing after another'
 b. kʰàtʃúɯ-kʰátʃùɯ (callúcállu) 'digging up the ground'
 c. kʰàɲáʔ-kʰáɲà (cañáhcáña) 'crawling'
 d. kʰùɯmí-kʰúɯmì (cunícúni) 'jumping on one leg'

Onomatopoeic expressions are generally used adverbially as in 832a and 833 but they may also be used in other ways, even as nouns as in 832b and c.

Chapter 13

Negation

This chapter discusses negation with adjectives (13.1), simple negation in finite clauses (13.2), contrastive negation (13.3), prohibitions (13.4), and negation in subordinate clauses (13.5).

13.1 Negation with adjectives

-tʰɯ (-tu) 'neg' may be added to adjectives (of which there are very few) to derive the opposite sense, e.g., iˀtsʰɯtʰɯ 'strong' is derived from iˀtsʰɯ 'weak'. Other examples follow; in 835a and 836 the tone is high on -tʰɯ 'neg' because the adjective is used as a predicate.

(835) a. Ímítyú diíbye.
    b. Ímityúné méénudí(ñe).
    a. ímí-tʲʰɯ́   tì-ːpʲɛ̀   'He is bad.'
       good-neg that-⟨SgM⟩

    b. ímì-tʲʰɯ́-né   mɛːnɯ̀-tí-(ɲɛ̀)   'Do not do bad things.'
       good-neg-⟨ø⟩ do-neg-⟨n⟩

(836) Ímyétú teéne.
    ímʲɛ́-tʰɯ́   tʰɛ̀-ːnɛ̀   'That is insipid (lacking
    savory-neg that-⟨ø⟩   sweetness or saltiness).'

13.2 Simple negation in finite clauses

A finite verb or predicate complement is negated by placing high tone on its first syllable and suffixing -Ⓛtʰɯ-nɛ (-tune) 'negative-⟨n⟩' or simply -Ⓛtʰɯ. (-tu). We will first discuss cases with preverbal subjects and then those with postverbal subjects.

With preverbal subjects, tsʰá?(a) 'not' is added to the beginning of the clause, as in 837–840:

(837) Tsá dibye péétune.

    tsʰá? tì-pʲɛ̀   pʰɛ́:-tʰɯ̀ɪ-nɛ̀   'He did not go.'
    not that-⟨SgM⟩ go-neg-⟨n⟩

(838) Tsá dibye májchotú(ne).

    tsʰá? tì-pʲɛ̀   máˣtʃʰò-tʰɯ́ɪ-(nɛ̀)   'He has not eaten.'
    not that-⟨SgM⟩ eat-neg-⟨n⟩

(839) tsʰá? ò á:ʔíβɛ̀-tʰɯ́ɪ   (Tsá o ááhívetú.)   'I did not go home.'
    not I go.home-neg

(840) Tsá dibye májchóityú(ne).

    tsʰá? tì-pʲɛ̀   máˣtʃʰó-ì-tʲʰɯ́ɪ-(nɛ̀)   'He will not eat.'
    not that-⟨SgM⟩ eat-fut-neg-⟨n⟩

Three features of negatives suggest that negative clauses are structurally subordinate clauses, complements to a higher predicate tsʰá?a 'not':

1. low tone on the proclitic subject pronoun,
2. high tone on the verb's first syllable, and
3. -nɛ ⟨n⟩ at the end of the clause. Although this has been glossed ⟨n⟩, it may be the suffix glossed ⟨ø⟩ that is used in forming subordinate clauses.

The structure of 839 would be as in 841:

(841) [V tsʰá?] [NP [S [NP ò] á:ʔíβɛ̀-tʰɯ̀ɪ   ] -nɛ̀]
    not   I go.home-neg -⟨ø⟩

Further examples with preverbal subjects:

(842) Tsá o chéénetú(ne).

    tsʰá? ò tʃʰɛ́:nɛ̀-tʰɯ́ɪ-(nɛ̀)   'I did not eat (fruit).'
    not I eat-neg-⟨n⟩

(843) Tsá o áwácunútu(ne).

ts<u>ʰá</u>ʔ ò álɓákʰùmúɨ-tʰùɾ-(nὲ)   'I did not yawn.'
not I yawn-neg-⟨n⟩

(844) Tsá o ááji̵vetétú(ne).

ts<u>ʰá</u>ʔ ò á:híβὲ-tʰέ-tʰúɾ-(nὲ)   'I did not go to eat.'
not I eat-go.do-neg-⟨n⟩

tsʰáʔ(a) 'not' may be followed by the clitic -i 'projected time' (PT); in this case the negation applies to the meaning of the clitic. For example, in 845 tsʰáʔáì (not-PT) denies that the event has already happened:[1]

(845) Tsáhái dibye tsáátune.

tsʰáʔá-ì̵ [tì-pʲὲ   ts<u>ʰá</u>:-tʰùɾ]-nὲ   'He has not yet come.'
not-PT   that-⟨SgM⟩   come-neg -⟨n⟩

With postverbal subjects, there is no overt negative word (like tsʰáʔ(a) 'not' in the previous examples) and the classifier subject occupies the place of -nɛ ⟨ø⟩. Thus, two arguments for the claim that these negatives are subordinate are not available; the only available argument is that the first syllable of the verb bears high tone (as characteristic of subordinate clauses). Examples follow. In 846, -Ⓛ:pὲ ⟨SgM⟩ delinks the low tone of -Ⓛtʰɯ 'neg' in order to place its low tone on -tʰùɾ.

(846) má^xtʃʰó-<u>tʰùɾ</u>-:pὲ (Májchótuúbe.) 'He has not eaten (bread).'
      eat-neg-⟨SgM⟩

(847) a. tó:-<u>tʰùɾ</u>-:pὲ   (dóótuúbe)   'He has not eaten (meat).'
      b. á:ʔíβέ-<u>tʰùɾ</u>-:pὲ   (ááhívétuúbe) 'He did not visit.'
      c. má^xtʃʰò-<u>tʰúɾ</u>-mὲ (májchotúme)   'They have not eaten (bread).'

13.3 Contrastive negation with -ji̵i̵va 'deny'

-hi̵:(βa) (-ji̵i̵va) 'deny' indicates contrastive or emphatic negation, denying that the referent of the phrase to which it is cliticized was or did what has been asserted (or assumed) about it. The form -hí:βa is used at the end of a sentence and -hí: is used within a sentence. -hí:(βa) may be cliticized to verbs (13.3.1) or to nominals (13.3.2).

---

[1] This is consistent with the suggestion that tsʰaʔa behaves like a complement-taking verb.

13.3.1 -jɨ́ɨ́va with verbs

With verbs, -hɨ́ː(βa) 'deny' imposes a low tone on its host's final syllable. Further, the host's initial syllable must bear high tone (in the same way as -⑴tʰɯ 'neg'; see section 3.10.) Thus, the form for verbs is: #⑪...-⑴hɨ́ː(βa).

When someone is accused of doing something bad, he can emphatically deny this by saying:

(848) ò mɛ́ːnɯ́-ːpɛ̀-hɨ́ːβà (O méénúúbejɨ́ɨ́va.) 'I did NOT do it!'
 I do-⟨SgM⟩-deny

Note that—contrary to the PREVERBAL SUBJECT CONSTRAINT, page 129)—there seem to be two subjects in 848: the preverbal o 'I' and the postverbal classifier -⑴ːpɛ ⟨SgM⟩. However, this is not the case if its structure is as in 849, where the clause is subordinate:

(849) [ò mɛ́ːnɯ́]-ːpɛ̀ [ᵥ hɨ́ːβà]
 I do -⟨SgM⟩ deny

This structure not only resolves the conflict with the PREVERBAL SUBJECT CONSTRAINT, it also accounts for the verb's initial high tone (since the initial syllable of the verb of a subordinate clause always bears a high tone).

The question in 850a could be answered by either 850b or c. The difference is that 850b is more emphatic than 850c:

(850) a. ¿A tsúúca dítyáábá majchójucóó?
 b. Tsáhái; májchóllejɨ́ɨ́va.
 c. Tsáhái dille májchotúne.

 a. à tsʰɯ́ːkʰà tí ⑥ tʲʰáːpá màˣʧʰó-hɯ̀ːkʰó:
  y/n already your wife eat-now

 b. tsʰáʔá-ì ; máˣʧʰó-ʧɛ̀-hɨ́ːβà
  not-PT eat-⟨SgF⟩-deny

 c. tsʰáʔá-ì tì-ʧɛ̀ máˣʧʰò-tʰɯ́-nɛ̀
  not-PT that-⟨SgF⟩ eat-neg-⟨n⟩

 a. 'Has your wife already eaten?'
 b. 'Not yet; she has not eaten.'
 c. 'She has not yet eaten.'

Likewise, the first sentence in 851 may be followed by either 851a or 851b; the former is more emphatic than the latter:

(851) Tañaalle oomí ihjyávu. $\begin{cases} \text{a. Ímíléllejɨ́ɨ́} \\ \text{b. Tsá dille ímílletú} \end{cases}$ imájchone.

tʰá̰ ɲà:-tʃɛ̀   ò:mí-ˀ   ì   ˀhʲá-βɯ̀ɯ̀
my sib-⟨SgF⟩ return-⟨t⟩ self house-GOAL

$\begin{cases} \text{a.} \qquad\qquad \text{ímítʃé-tʃɛ̀-hɨ́:} \\ \qquad\qquad\qquad \text{want-⟨SgF⟩-deny} \\ \text{b. tsʰá tì-tʃɛ̀} \quad \text{ímítʃɛ̀-tʰɯ́ɯ́} \\ \quad\text{not that-⟨SgF⟩ want-neg} \end{cases}$ ì máˣtʃʰò-nɛ̀
self eat-⟨n⟩

'My sister returned to her house. She did not want to eat.'

A further example is given in 852; see also example 1123, page 432.

(852) ¿Muhdú májchóóbejɨ́ɨ́ ú peéhi?

mɯ̀ɯ̀-ˀtɯ́ɯ́   má̰ˣtʃʰó-:pɛ̀-hɨ́:   ɯ́ɯ́   pʰɛ̀-é-ˀì
WH-⟨like⟩ eat-⟨SgM⟩-deny you go-fut-⟨t⟩

'How is it that you are going without eating?'

13.3.2 -jɨ́ɨ́va with nominals

With pronouns, nouns or noun phrases -hɨ:βa (-jɨ:va) 'deny' imposes a low tone on its hosts antepenult, while itself bearing high tone: -ⓁO͡hɨ́:βa.

-ⓁO͡hɨ́:βa 'deny' follows the constituent that is focally negated, as in the following conversational exchanges. (See also example 1122, page 432.)

(853) a. Áádií; díñahbéuba tsájucóó.
    b. Tsáhaá; diibyéjɨ́ɨ́va. Tsá dibye íhajchíí tsááityúne.

   a. á:tìí   ; tí Ⓖ ɲa̋-ˀpé-ɯ̋pà   tsʰá-hɯ̀ɯ̀kʰó:
      that.one(distal)   your   sib-⟨SgM⟩-prob come-now-⟨t⟩

   b. tsʰá̰ʔàá ; tì-:pʲé-hɨ́:βà
      not   that-⟨SgM⟩-deny

      tsʰá̰ˀ tì-pʲɛ̀   íˀàˣtʃʰí: tsʰá:-ì-tʲʰɯ̀ɯ̀-nɛ̀
      not that-⟨SgM⟩ today come-fut-neg-⟨n⟩

   a. '(Look at) that one over there; your brother must be coming.'
   b. 'No; that is not he. He will not come today.'

(854) a. ¿Ava dínaalle peéhi ámejúvu?
b. Tsáhaá; diilléjɨ́ɨ́va. Óóréjuco.

   a. à-βà tí ⓖ ná̹:-tʃɛ̀ pʰɛ̀-ɛ́-ʔì ámɛ̀hɯ́-βɯ̀
     y/n-rpt your sib-⟨SgM⟩ go-fut-⟨t⟩ downriver-goal

   b. tsʰá̹ʔàá ; tì:-tʃɛ́-hɨ́:βà . ó-ːɾɛ́-hɯ̀kʰò
     not   that-⟨SgF⟩-deny I-only-focus

   a. 'Will your sister go downriver (as they say)?
   b. 'No, not she. Only I (will go).'

(855) a. Díoohííbye tácáracáke lliihánúhi.
b. Tsáhaá; diibyéjɨ́ɨ́va. Díoohííbyére.

   a. tí o̹:ʔí-:pʲɛ̀ tʰá ⓖ kʰáɾa̹kʰá-kʰɛ̀ tʃì:ʔánɯ́-ʔì
     your dog-⟨SgM⟩ my chicken-objAn kill-⟨t⟩

   b. tsʰá̹ʔàá ; tì-:pʲɛ́-hɨ́:βà . tí o̹:ʔí-:pʲɛ́-ɾɛ̀
     not   that-⟨SgM⟩-deny your dog-⟨SgM⟩-only

   a. 'Your dog killed my chickens.'
   b. 'No, not THAT one. YOUR dog (did it).'

13.4 Prohibitions

Imperatives are discussed in chapter 14; this section deals with prohibitions, i.e., negative imperatives.

-ⓛ⁽ˀ⁾ti 'prohibit' indicates that the action of the host verb should not be done, forming a PROHIBITION or NEGATIVE IMPERATIVE. -ⓛˀti (-hdi) is used with monosyllabic verbs and -ⓛti (-di) with polysyllabic ones. As with ⓛtʰɯ 'neg', -ɲɛ ⟨n⟩ may follow -⁽ˀ⁾ti. These points are illustrated in the following examples:

(856) pʰɛ̀-ˀtí-(ɲɛ̀)   (¡Pehdíñe! ~ ¡Pehdí!) 'Don't go!'
     go-prohibit-⟨n⟩

(857) mɛ́:nɯ̀-tí-(ɲɛ̀) (¡Méénudíñe! ~ ¡Méénudí!) 'Don't do it!'
     do-prohibit-⟨n⟩

(858) a. Dohdíñe! ~ Dohdí!
   b. Májchodíñe ~ Májchodí!
   c. Tomájcodíñe! ~ Tomájcodí!

   a. tò-ʔtí-(ɲɛ̀)   'Do not eat (meat)! (sg)'
   b. máˣʧʰò-tí-(ɲɛ̀)   'Do not eat (bread)! (sg)'
   c. tʰòmáˣkʰò-tí-(ɲɛ̀) 'Do not touch it!   (sg)'

(859) Memájchodíñe! ~ Memájchodí!
   mɛ̀ máˣʧʰò-tí-(ɲɛ̀)   'Do not eat (bread)! (pl)'
   SAP eat-neg-⟨n⟩

Generally a prohibition will end ((...σ̇)σ̈)σ̇-tí-(ɲɛ̀)#. However, the Ⓛ of -Ⓛ⁽ˀ⁾ti may be blocked by another low tone, as in 860 with -Ⓛtʰɛ 'go to do':

(860) máˣʧʰȯ-tʰɛ́-tí-(ɲɛ̀) (¡Májchotédí(ñe)!) 'Do not go to eat (bread)!'
   eat-go.do-neg-⟨n⟩

13.5 Negation in subordinate clauses

Subordinate clauses are negated with -Ⓛtʰɯ 'neg' but they never have tsʰáʔ(a) 'not' as in main clauses. In 861 negation occurs in a relative clause and in 862 and 863 it occurs in a case-marked subordinate clause used as an adverb:

(861) Diibye májchótuube dsíjɨvéhi.

   tì-ːpʲɛ̀   Ⓐ [máˣʧʰó-tʰɯ̀ː]-ːpɛ̀   tsíhɨ̀βɛ́-ʔì
   that-⟨SgM⟩   eat-neg   -⟨SgM⟩   die-⟨t⟩
   'The one who did not eat died.'

(862) Diibye imájchótúneri dsíjɨvéhi.

   tì-ːpʲɛ̀²   [ì   máˣʧʰó-tʰɯ́ː]-nɛ̀-rì   tsíhɨ̀βɛ́-ʔì
   that-⟨SgM⟩ self eat-neg   -⟨event⟩-oblIn die-⟨t⟩
   'Because he did not eat, he died.'

(863) Imájchótúneri dsíjɨveébe.

   [ì   máˣʧʰó-tʰɯ́ː]-nɛ̀-rì   tsíhɨ́βɛ̀-ːpɛ̀
   self eat-neg   -⟨event⟩-oblIn die-⟨SgM⟩
   'Because he did not eat, he died.'

---

[2]In 862 the first word has a long vowel, even though it is the subject. This is because a subordinate clause intervenes between the subject and the verb; see the discussion that accompanies example 635, page 270.

Negation within a complement may be expressed in the main clause (yielding the sort of example that has been used to motivate "neg raising"). For example, 864 is understood to mean 'I want that [he <u>not</u> go]', where either 'he' or 'go' is negated. However, structurally tsʰá⁽ʔ⁾ [...]-tʰɯ́ɾ(nè) has within its scope the main verb ímítʃè 'I want', the object complement of which is extraposed:

(864) Tsá o ímílletú dibye pééneé.

<u>tsʰá</u>ʔ ò ímítʃè-<u>tʰɯ́ɾ</u> [tì-pʲè   pʰɛ̂ː]-nɛ̀ɛ́   'I don't want
not I want-neg   that-⟨SgM⟩ go -⟨ø⟩   him to go.'

Chapter 14

Imperatives

Imperatives are generally used to tell the hearer to do or not to do something. One type of imperative, namely prohibitions, was discussed in section 13.4. In this chapter, the form of imperatives is discussed in section 14.1, various ways to modify imperatives in section 14.2, and degrees of strength of imperatives in 14.3.

Imperative verbs bear the nonfinite low tone as described in section 14.1.1. Throughout this grammar, the nonfinite tone is sometimes represented with N over the vowel of the syllable that bears the nonfinite low tone. In this chapter this nonfinite low tone is represented with I to remind the reader that this is the "imperative" tone.

14.1 The form of imperatives

Imperative clauses are distinguished from indicative ones in the following ways:

1. An imperative never has an overt subject noun phrase. Rather, the subject of an imperative (i.e., the addressee) is indicated by a pronominal proclitic[1] as now described. (Note, syllables are counted before the application of PLTS (section 3.7.1) or FLTS (section 3.7.2).)
   singular subject:
   If the verb is monosyllabic, the pronominal proclitic is ti- 'you (imperative)'.

---

[1] These are the same as some of the pronouns used as possessors in the genitive construction; see section 14.1.2.

(865) tí-tʲo̗-: (¡Dídyoó!) 'Eat (meat)!'
     you-eat-emph

If the verb stem is polysyllabic and begins with a vowel, it is simply t- 'you':

(866) t-ó:-tʰɛ̗-: (¡Dóóteé!)
     you-eat-go.do-emph
     'Go eat (meat, singular emphatic)!'

If the verb stem is polysyllabic and begins with a consonant, the subject is left implicit (with no explicit pronoun):

(867) __máˣtʃʰo̗ (Májcho.) 'Eat!' (singular, bread)
       eat

plural subject: In all cases, the pronoun is mɛ ~ ma 'SAP' (speech act participant):

(868) mɛ́ to̗:-tʰɛ̀ (¡Médoóte!) 'Go eat (pl, meat)!'
     SAP eat-go.do

(869) a. mɛ́ pʰɛ̗é (¡Mépeé!) 'Go! (pl)'
     b. mɛ́ máˣtʃʰò (¡Mémajcho!) 'Eat! (pl, bread)'
     c. {mɛ́ / má} a:púɨkʰừ ({¡Méaabúcu! / ¡Máaabúcu!}) 'Hold up! (pl)'
     d. {mɛ́ / má} ákʰứ:βɛ̀ ({¡Méacúúve! / ¡Máacúúve!}) 'Sit down! (pl)'
     e. mɛ́ ímipáˣtʃʰò (¡Méímibájcho!) 'Fix it! (pl)'

2. There are three suffixes that occur on imperative verbs which do not occur on indicatives; these are discussed in section 14.2.2.
3. The second syllable of the proclitic+stem is Ⓛ if there are no more than three syllables. Otherwise the verb receives nonfinite tone; see section 14.1.1 for details.

14.1.1 Tone in imperatives

Imperative verbs bear the nonfinite low tone, represented below with ɪ (for "imperative") over the vowel, docked according to the following rule:

> Taking the pronoun and verb stem together, the imperative low tone occurs as early as possible but (1) not before the antepenult and (2) not on the initial syllable, which must bear high tone.[2]

---

[2]Example 781, page 311, is exceptional in having a low tone on the initial syllable; for discussion see footnote 4, page 311.

14.1. THE FORM OF IMPERATIVES

This pattern is motivated by the cases in which the imperative consists of a monosyllabic pronoun followed by a nonfinite verb stem, as is true of the singular imperatives of monosyllabic verbs and of all plural imperatives. The pronoun bears high tone and the verb stem bears the nonfinite low tone, which docks "regressive to the antepenult":

$$[_{\text{pronoun}} \overset{H}{\sigma}] + [_{\text{nonfinite verb stem}} ...\overset{N}{\sigma}(\sigma(\sigma))].$$

If that were all that there is to it, the characterization in terms of the nonfinite tone would suffice and it would not be necessary to speak of an "imperative" tone. However, singular imperatives of polysyllabic verbs do not have an additional syllable corresponding to the pronoun. Despite this, the verb's initial syllable bears high tone and the imperative tone follows (but never earlier than on the antepenult). For example, in 867 I docks on the final syllable of ma^{x}tʃʰo 'eat'.

Thus, the tone pattern for imperatives, including the singular imperatives of polysyllabic verbs, consists in placing a high tone on the first syllable (whether or not that actually falls on a pronoun) and docking the imperative low tone regresssive to the the antepenult (but without displacing the high tone on the initial syllable). This justifies speaking of an "imperative" tone, understood as a special case of nonfinite tone. The following table is given for comparison. The imperative forms include the syllable that corresponds to the pronoun (if present).

IMPERATIVE	NONFINITE
$\overset{I}{\sigma}\sigma$	$\overset{N}{\sigma}$
$\overset{I}{\sigma}\sigma\sigma$	$\overset{N}{\sigma\sigma}$
$\sigma\overset{I}{\sigma}\sigma\sigma$	$\overset{N}{\sigma\sigma\sigma}$
$(...\sigma)\sigma\overset{I}{\sigma}\sigma\sigma$	$(...\sigma)\overset{N}{\sigma\sigma\sigma\sigma}$

Figure 14.1 A comparison of imperative and nonfinite tone

We now illustrate the various cases. (Remember that syllables are counted before the application of PLTS and FLTS.)

1. There are no **monosyllabic** imperatives (although the verb stem may be monosyllabic as in 865).
2. If the combination of the pronoun and verb stem have two or three syllables, then the second syllable (of the combination) bears the imperative low tone, as in the following examples.

Bisyllabic:

(870) tí-pʲʰɛ̀-:   (Dípyeé.) 'Go!'
  youImp-go-emph

Trisyllabic:

(871) t-á:pɯ̀kʰɯ̀   (Dáábucu!) 'Endure!'
  youImp-endure

(872) mɛ́ mǎˣtʃʰò (Mémajcho!) 'Eat (pl)!'
  SAP eat

Example 873 is trisyllabic, although it ends up with four syllables due to the application of PLTS:

(873) t-ákʰɯ̀-:βɛ̀   (Dácuúve!) 'Sit down!'
  youImp-sit-sIn

The verb stem may include a derivational suffix:

(874) a. t-ómà-ˣkʰò   (Dómajco!) 'Touch! (sg)'
  youImp-touch-implore

    b. máˣtʃʰò-tʰɛ̀   (Májchote!) 'Go to eat! (sg)'
  eat-go.do

3. If the combination of the pronoun and verb stem have more than three syllables, then the stem bears the imperative low tone on its antepenult. This tone overrides any lexically marked tones. Examples follow:

(875) a. t-ímìpáˣtʃʰò   (Dímibájcho!) 'Fix it! (sg)'

    b. t-álpàkʰɯ́mɯ̀ (Dáwacúnu!)   'Yawn! (sg)'

    c. kʰáβɯ̀ɯ̀ʔhʲákʰò (Cávúihjyáco!) 'Push! (sg)'

(876) mɛ́ ímìpáˣtʃʰò (Méímibájcho!) 'Fix it (plural)!'

When the root is followed by derivational suffixes, the antepenult is determined from the end of the *stem*, as in the following:

(877) t-ímìpáˣtʃʰò   (Dímibájcho!)   'Fix it! (sg)'
  t-ímípàˣtʃʰó-tsʰò   (Dímíbajchótso!)   Cause it to
                                                be fixed!'
  t-ímípáˣtʃʰò-tsʰó-tʰɛ̀ (Dímíbájchotsóte!) 'Go cause it to
                                                        be fixed!'

The imperative tone delinks the tones imposed by suffixes. For example, it delinks the Ⓛ of -Ⓛtʰɛ 'go to do' in 878 and 879:

(878) t-ímíphàˣtʃʰó-tʰɛ̀ (dímípajchóte) 'Go fix it! (sg)'

(879) mɛ́ mǎˣtʃʰó-tʰɛ̀ (Mémajchóte) 'Go eat! (pl, bread)'

14.1.2 Comparison of imperative and genitive pronominal proclitics

The proclitics t(i)- 'you, your' and mɛ 'SAP' occur in both the imperative and genitive constructions. Their tones in these constructions differ because the genitive low tone may dock on the proclitic pronoun whereas the imperative (nonfinite) low tone does not. Compare the following pairs:

(880) GEN: mɛ̰̂ máˣtʃʰò (memájcho)   'our (SAP) food'
    SAP food
    IMP: mɛ́ ma᷆ˣtʃʰò (Mémajcho.)   'Eat (pl)!'
    SAP eat

(881) GEN: mɛ́ Ⓝ ímìpáˣtʃʰò (meímibájcho)   'our fixing/job'
    IMP: mɛ́ ímìpá᷆ˣtʃʰò (¡Méímibájcho!)   'Fix it (pl)!'

(882) GEN: mɛ̰̂ páˣtsʰò (mebájtso)   'our (SAP) planting'
    SAP planting
    IMP: mɛ́ pa᷆ˣtsʰò (Mébajtso.)   'Plant! (pl)'
    SAP plant

(883) GEN: $\begin{Bmatrix} \text{mɛ̰} \\ \text{ma̰} \end{Bmatrix}$ átò $\begin{Bmatrix} \text{meádo} \\ \text{maádo} \end{Bmatrix}$ 'our/your (pl) drink'
    SAP   drink
    IMP: $\begin{Bmatrix} \text{mɛ́} \\ \text{má} \end{Bmatrix}$ a᷆tò $\begin{Bmatrix} \text{Méado!} \\ \text{Maado!} \end{Bmatrix}$ 'Drink (pl)!'
    SAP   drink

However, the proclitics of imperatives may be shortened or deleted with polysyllabic verbs (or verb stems), as illustrated in 884. By contrast, in 885 the verb is monosyllabic so the proclitics do not differ between the genitive and imperative (except for tone):

(884) GEN: tḭ́ átò (diádo)   'your (sg) drink'
    IMP: t-a᷆tò (¡Dádoó!) 'Drink (sg)!'

(885) GEN: tḭ́ tʲò (didyo)   'your (sg) meat'
    IMP: tí t᷆ʲo (¡Dídyoó!) 'Eat your meat!'

14.1.3 Stem changes in imperatives

The singular imperative of some verbs differs slightly from the corresponding nonimperative:

1. Some roots that begin with a light syllable add a glottal stop in the singular imperative, making the initial syllable heavy.³

IMPERATIVE		NONIMPERATIVE		GLOSS
t-á̰ʔkpá:	(dáhwaá)	àkpà	(awa)	'diet'
t-ɨ̰ʔtʃó:	(díhlloó)	ɨ̀tʃò	(illo)	'chop'
t-á̰ʔɲṵ̀ː	(dáhñuú)	àɲṵ̀	(añu)	'shoot'

2. Some roots that begin with a syllable made heavy by vowel length (/V:/) replace this with a glottal stop in the singular imperative. Verbs that show this behavior follow:⁴

IMPERATIVE		NONIMPERATIVE		GLOSS
t-á̰ʔmṵ̀ː	(dáhmuú)	à:mṵ̀	(aámu)	'throw and hit'
t-ɛ̰́ʔβɛ̀:	(déhveé)	ɛ̀:βɛ̀	(eéve)	'read'
t-ɨ̰́ʔnɛ̀	(díhneé)	ɨ̀:nɛ̀	(ɨ́ɨne)	'move over'
t-ɨ̰́ʔtʰɛ̀	(díhteé)	ɨ̀:tʰɛ̀	(ɨ́ɨte)	'look'
t-ó̰ʔmì	(dóhmií)	ò:mì	(oómi)	'return'
t-ṵ̀ʔhɛ́tʰɛ̀	(dúhjete)	ṵ̀:hɛ́tʰɛ̀	(uujéte)	'arrive'

   Consider also the alternation between the singular and plural imperatives in 886:

   (886) a. t-ṵ̀ʔhɛ́-tʰɛ̀ (¡Dúhjete!) 'Go (sg) see.'
   youImp-see-go.do

   b. mɛ́ ṵ̀:hɛ́-tʰɛ̀ (¡Méuujéte!) 'Go (pl) see.'
   SAP see-go.do

3. Some verbs that begin with /Vˣ/ in the nonimperative make this into a long vowel (/V:/) in the singular imperative. Verbs that behave this way are:

IMPERATIVE		NONIMPERATIVE		GLOSS
t-á:kʰṵ̀ː	(dáácuú)	àˣkʰṵ̀	(ajcu)	'give'
t-ɨ́:kʲʰà	(díícya)	ɨ̀ˣkʲʰà	(ijcya)	'be'
t-ṵ́ːkʰṵ̀	(dúúcuú)	ṵ̀ˣkʰṵ̀	(ujcu)	'get'

   For example, note the alternation in 887:

   (887) a. ò-kʰɛ̀ má àˣkʰṵ̀ (¡Oke máajcu!) 'Give (pl)
   I-objAn SAP give   it to me!

   b. ò-kʰɛ̀ t-à:kʰṵ̀ (¡Oke daácu!) 'Give (sg)
   I-objAn youImp-give   it to me!'

---

³Note that the first two imperatives have split final vowels due to FLTS.
⁴PLTS has applied in the penult of many of the nonimperative forms.

14.1. THE FORM OF IMPERATIVES

These changes are summarized in table 14.1; the first line of each cell gives the imperative and the second gives the corresponding nonfinite stem.[5] (The plural imperatives of these verbs involve no change to the stem; they simply add the proclitic mɛ.)

Table 14.1 Singular imperatives: changes in the initial syllable

V^ʔ ⇕ V	V^ʔ ⇕ V:	V: ⇕ V^x
t-á^{ʔ}k͡pàá 'diet!' àk͡pà	t-á^{ʔ}k^{h}ít^{jh}ɛ̀ 'fall down!' à:k^{h}ít^{jh}ɛ̀	t-á:k^{h}ɯ̀ɾɯ́ 'give it!' à^{x}k^{h}ɯ̀ɾ
t-í^{ʔ}tʃòó 'cut it down!' ìtʃò	t-á^{ʔ}mɯ̀ɾɯ́ 'hit it!' àámɯ̀ɾ	t-ì:k^{jh}àá 'stay!' ì^{x}k^{jh}à
t-á^{ʔ}ɲɯ̀ɾɯ́ 'shoot!' àɲɯ̀ɾ	t-í^{ʔ}nɛ̀ɛ́ 'move over!' ìínɛ̀	t-ɯ́:k^{h}ɯ̀ɾɯ́ 'get it!' ɯ̀^{x}k^{h}ɯ̀ɾ

Many verbs undergo neither change:[6]

1. Some have a long vowel in both the singular imperative and the nonimperative: t-ɛ́:pɯ̀ɾ from ɛ̀:pɯ̀ɾ, t-á:pàt^{h}ɛ́ts^{h}ò from á:pàt^{h}ɛ́ts^{h}ò, t-á:pò: from à:pò, t-á:pɯ́k^{h}ɯ̀ɾ from à:pɯ́k^{h}ɯ̀ɾ, t-á:p^{j}ɯ́k^{h}ɯ̀ɾ from à:p^{j}ɯ́k^{h}ɯ̀ɾ, t-á:ʔìβɛ̀, from à:ʔíβɛ̀, t-í:k^{h}ɯ̀ɾ: from ì:k^{h}ɯ̀ɾ, t-ɯ́:pàtʃɛ̀ from ɯ̀:pátʃɛ̀.
2. Some verbs have a glottal stop closing the first syllable in both the singular imperative and the nonimperative: t-í^{ʔ}tɛ̀nɯ̀ɾ from ì^{ʔ}ténɯ̀ɾ, t-í^{ʔ}t^{h}ɛ́ts^{h}ò from ì^{ʔ}t^{h}ɛ́ts^{h}ò, t-í^{ʔ}t^{h}ɯ̀ɾ: from ì^{ʔ}t^{h}ɯ̀ɾ, t-í^{ʔ}βɛ́^{x}ts^{h}ò from ì^{ʔ}βɛ́^{x}ts^{h}ò, t-í^{ʔ}βɛ́t^{h}ɛ̀ from ì^{ʔ}βɛ́t^{h}ɛ̀, t-á^{ʔ}tòts^{h}ò from à^{ʔ}tóts^{h}ò, t-á^{ʔ}tò: from à^{ʔ}tò, t-ít^{j}ò: from tò:, t-í^{ʔ}pɯ̀k^{h}ɯ̀ɾ from ì^{ʔ}pɯ́k^{h}ɯ̀ɾ, t-í^{ʔ}h^{j}ɯ́ɾβà from ì^{ʔ}h^{j}ɯ́ɾβà, t-í^{ʔ}h^{j}ɯ̀ɾβáts^{h}ò from í^{ʔ}h^{j}ɯ̀ɾβáts^{h}ò, t-ó^{ʔ}pàɲɯ̀ɾ from ò^{ʔ}páɲɯ̀ɾ, t-ɯ́ɾ^{ʔ}pà: from ɯ̀ɾ^{ʔ}pà.
3. In some verbs, preaspiration closes the first syllable in both the singular imperative and the nonimperative: t-í^{x}ts^{h}àmɛ́ì from í^{x}ts^{h}àmɛ́ì, t-í^{x}ts^{h}ɯ̀k^{h}ɯ́mɯ̀ɾ from í^{x}ts^{h}ɯ̀k^{h}ɯ́mɯ̀ɾ, t-á^{x}k^{h}à: from à^{x}k^{h}à, t-á^{x}tʃ^{h}ɯ̀k^{h}ɯ́mɯ̀ɾ from à^{x}tʃ^{h}ɯ́k^{h}ɯ̀mɯ̀ɾ, t-á^{x}k^{jh}ɛ̀: from à^{x}k^{jh}ɛ̀, t-í^{x}tʃ^{h}ìβ^{j}ɛ̀ from ì^{x}tʃ^{h}íβ^{j}ɛ̀, t-í^{x}tʃ^{h}ìβ^{j}ɛ́ts^{h}ò from í^{x}tʃ^{h}ìβ^{j}ɛ́ts^{h}ò, t-í^{x}tʃ^{h}ò: from ì^{x}tʃ^{h}ò.
4. Some verbs have a short vowel in both the singular imperative and the nonimperative: t-ípáts^{h}ɯ̀ɾ^{ʔ}hák^{h}ò from ípáts^{h}ɯ̀ɾ^{ʔ}hák^{h}ò, t-ík^{h}ɯ̀ɾpá^{ʔ}rà

---

[5]Other cases of the alternation between V^ʔ and V: are as follows:

imperative	t-í^{ʔ}nɛ̀ts^{h}ò	t-í^{ʔ}t^{h}ɛ̀ɛ́	t-ó^{ʔ}mìí	t-ó^{ʔ}mìtʃ^{h}ò	t-ɯ́ɾ^{ʔ}hɛ̀t^{h}ɛ̀
	'move it over'	'look!'	'return!'	'return it!'	'go see!'
non-imperative	ì:nɛ́ts^{h}ò	ìít^{h}ɛ̀	òómì	ò:mítʃ^{h}ò	ɯ̀:hɛ́t^{h}ɛ̀
	'make move over'	'look'	'return'	'make return'	'go see'

[6]For the meanings of the verbs below, see (Thiesen & Thiesen 1998).

from íkʰùɾpáʔɾà, t-ítà:tsʰótʃɛ̀ from ítà:tsʰótʃɛ̀, t-ítà:tsʰóβɛ̀ from ítà:tsʰóβɛ̀, t-íkpàˣkʰáɾò from íkpàˣkʰáɾò, t-íkpà:βɛ̀ from ìkpá:βɛ̀, t-ɛ́kʰɛ̀:βɛ̀ from ɛ̀kʰɛ́:βɛ̀, t-ákʰùɾ:βɛ̀ from àkʰùɾ:βɛ̀, t-átò: from àtò, t-ámàpúíkʰùɾ from ámàpúíkʰùɾ, t-áβò:βɛ̀ from àβó:βɛ̀, t-áβùɾʔkʰùɾ from àβúɾʔkʰùɾ, t-áβʲɛ́ˣtsʰò from àβʲɛ́ˣtsʰò, t-áβʲɛ̀hú́ɾˣtsʰò from áβʲɛ̀hú́ɾˣtsʰò, t-ákpà: from àkpà, t-áɲùɾˣkʰùɾ from àɲúɾˣkʰùɾ, t-íhʲòkʰúɾ:βɛ̀ from íhʲòkʰúɾ:βɛ̀, t-ítʃà:jò from ítʃà:jò, t-ítʃòˣkʰò from ìtʃóˣkʰò, t-ímìpá:βʲɛ̀ from ímìpá:βʲɛ̀, t-ímìpáˣtʃʰò from ímìpáˣtʃʰò, t-ímìhʲúɾ:βɛ̀ from ímìhʲúɾ:βɛ̀, t-ímìβʲɛ̀ from ìmíβʲɛ̀, t-úɾàkʰò from ùɾákʰò, t-úɾàjò from ùɾájò, t-úɾkʰà:βɛ̀ from ùɾkʰá:βɛ̀, tí-ùɾ: from ùɾ:.

14.2 Modifying imperatives

14.2.1 Emphatic imperatives

An imperative can be made more emphatic by the addition of -Ⓛ:. Compare the unmarked and emphatic imperatives in 888:

(888) a. máˣtʃʰó (Májcho.) 'Eat! (sg, nonemphatic)'
b. máˣtʃʰó-: (Májchoó!) 'Eat! (sg, emphatic)'
   eat-emph

The addition of -Ⓛ: creates the conditions for applying FLTS, wherby the final vowel "splits." This is reflected in the orthographic forms of 888b as well as 889a and b:

(889) a. t-ímìpáˣtʃʰò-: (Dímibájchoó!) 'Fix it! (emphatic)'
  you-fix-emph
b. t-ímìpáˣtʃʰó-tʰɛ̀-: (Dímíbajchóteé!) 'Go fix it! (emphatic)'
  you-fix-go.do-emph

Compare 890a and b:

(890) a. máˣtʃʰò-tʰɛ́-ʔì (májchotéhi) 'goes to eat'
b. máˣtʃʰó-tʰɛ̀ᴸ: (¡Májchóteé!) Go eat! (sg, emphatic)'

We expect the second syllable of 890b to bear low tone for two reasons: (1) it precedes -Ⓛtʰɛ 'go to do', and (2) it should bear the imperative low tone because the word is a trisyllabic imperative. However, it bears high tone. This is evidence that the emphasis morpheme imposes low tone on the host's final syllable and adds a mora: -Ⓛμ. The tone delinks the low tone of the preceding syllable and the conditions for FLTS are met. The tone derivation of máˣtʃʰótʰɛ̀ɛ́ 'Go to eat!' is given in figure 14.2.

14.2. MODIFYING IMPERATIVES

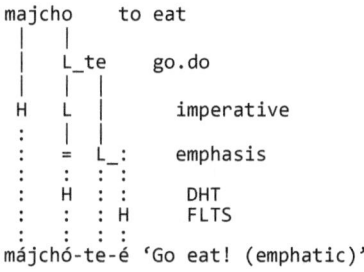

májchó-te-é 'Go eat! (emphatic)'

Figure 14.2 TD: májchóteé

14.2.2 -co 'implore' and -juj 'quick' with imperatives

The suffixes -kʰo (-co) 'implore' and -hɯˣ (-juj) 'quick' can be added to an imperative verb. They occur only on imperatives and they may not co-occur.

The suffix -kʰo 'implore' is added to encourage the hearer to do the action indicated by the verb it follows, as in 891 and 892. Example 892 could be either a plea or an emphatic directive.

(891) máˣtʃʰó-kʰò (¡Májchoco!) 'Please eat!'
  eat-implore

(892) pʰɛ́:-kʰó-: (¡Péécoó!) 'Go immediately!'
  go-implore-emph

The suffix -ⓁHɯ-ˣ (-juj) 'quick-vocative' instructs the hearer to carry out the action indicated by the verb with haste. The preceding verb stem bears the imperative tone (with perhaps some exceptions); because -ⓁHɯ-ˣ 'quick-vocative' is not a derivational suffix, it is not taken into account in locating the nonfinite tone (which is determined from the end of the stem), as illustrated in 893:

(893) a. t-ímípáˣtʃʰó-tʰɛ̀-hɯ̀-ˣ (¡Dímíbajchótejuj!) 'Go (sg) fix it!'
   you-fix-go.do-quick-voc

 b. t-ómáˣkʰò-hɯ̀-ˣ (¡Domájcojuj!) 'Touch (sg) it!'
   you-touch-quick-voc

 c. máˣtʃʰó-βà-hɯ̀-ˣ (majchóvajuj) 'Come (sg) to
   eat-come.do-quick-voc   eat now!'

-ⓁHɯ-ˣ imposes a low tone on its host's final syllable *if possible*; it does not delink the nonfinite tone, as illustrated in 894:

(894) máˣtʃʰó-hɯ̀-ˣ (¡Majchójuj!) 'Eat (sg) quickly!'
       eat-quick-voc

In 895, -ⓁO βa 'come to do' makes the stem trisyllabic. Its Ⓛ docks on the antepenult, in this case the root's first syllable, coinciding with nonfinite low tone. Finally, -Ⓛhɯ-ˣ docks its Ⓛ on its host's final syllable:

(895) mɛ́   máˣtʃʰó-βà-hɯ̀-ˣ   (¡Mémajchóvajuj!) 'Come (pl) eat
       SAP eat-come.do-quick-voc   (bread) now!'

In 896a and b, "quick" modifies "going" rather than "eating".

(896) a. máˣtʃʰó-tʰɛ̀-hɯ̀-ˣ   (¡Majchótejuj!) 'Go (sg) quickly to eat!'
         eat-go.do-quick-voc
      b. tó:-tʰɛ́-hɯ̀-ˣ   (¡Dootéjuj!)   'Go (sg) quickly
         eat-go.do-quick-voc   to eat (meat)!'

Compare 896b with the corresponding plural in 897. The nonfinite tone docks on the proclitic (as stated above for plural imperatives). The allows the Ⓛ of -Ⓛhɯ-ˣ to dock on the host's final syllable, which was not possible in 896b because the nonfinite tone docked on the host's penult.

(897) mɛ̀   tó:-tʰɛ̀-hɯ̀-ˣ   (¡Medóótejuj!) 'Go (pl) quickly
       SAP eat-go.do-quick   to eat (meat)!

14.2.3 The adverb ɨ́ɨcúi 'quickly; hurry'

The adverb ɨ́:kʰɯ́ɯ̀ (ɨ́ɨcúi) 'quickly; hurry' may follow an imperative verb, as in 898 and 899. Note that the verbs bear the tones expected for an imperative verb.

(898) Májchote ɨ́ɨcúií.

       máˣtʃʰó-tʰɛ̀ ɨ́:kʰɯ́ɯ̀-:   'Go quickly to eat.'
       eat-go.do   quickly-emph

(899) Mémajchóté ɨ́ɨcúií.

       mɛ́   máˣtʃʰó-tʰɛ́ ɨ́:kʰɯ́ɯ̀-:   'Go quickly to eat.'
       SAP eat-go.do   quickly-emph

Or ɨ́:kʰɯ́ɯ̀ 'hurry' may precede the verb to express an urgent imperative, as in 900–902. Note that in this case the verb bears the nonfinite low tone.

(900) ɨ́:kʰɯ́ɯ̀ máˣtʃʰò (¡ɨ́ɨcúi majcho!) 'Hurry up, eat!'
       hurry   eat

14.2. MODIFYING IMPERATIVES

(901) ¡ɨ́ɨcúi didyo!
ɨ:kʰúɨ̀ tì-tʲo̊ᴺ   'Hurry up, eat (meat)!'
hurry youImp-eat.meat

(902) ɨ́ɨcúi dipye dihjyávu.
ɨ:kʰúɨ̀ tì-pʲʰɛ̀ᴺ   tɨ̀ᴳ˞   hʲá-βùɨ
hurry youImp-go your house-goal
'Quickly, go to your house.'

Note further that ɨ̋:kʰúɨ̋ 'quickly' ends with a low tone which is immediately followed by a verb that bears an initial low tone. Thus, the "adverb" and the verb do not belong to the same phonological phrase because, if in the same phrase, the adjacent low tones would violate the *LLX constraint. Further note that the verbs in 900–902 do not have high tone on the initial syllable as expected for an imperative verb (as discussed in section 4.1); they have the tones of a nonfinite verb.

In light of these factors, we consider ɨ́:kʰúɨ̀ 'hurry' to be a verb that takes a nonfinite complement. To see the contrast between the simple imperative and ɨ́:kʰúɨ̀ followed by a nonfinite complement, a number of verbs are given in table 14.2, first with the finite imperative (bearing the imperative low tone I), and then the nonfinite verb that would follow ɨ́:kʰúɨ̀. In plural imperatives, the verb is preceded by the proclitic mɛ 'SAP' and, surprisingly, the nonfinite tone (N) can dock on the proclitic if the stem is mono- or bisyllabic. This is illustrated in 903:

(903) mɛ̋ᴺ má˟ʧʰò-hùɨ-˟ (¡Memájchojuj!) 'Eat (sg, bread) now!'
SAP eat-quick-voc

Table 14.2 Simple imperatives and complements to ɨ́cúi 'hurry'

	SINGULAR		PLURAL	
go!	tí-pʲʰɛ̄:	dípyeé	mɛ́ pʰɛ̄:	mépeé
ɨ̄:kʰúɨ̀	tì-pʲʰɛ̀ᴺ	dipye	mɛ̀ᴺ pʰɛ̀	mepe
eat (fruit)!	tʃɛ́:nɛ̄:	llééneé	mɛ́ tʃɛ́:nɛ̀	mélleéne
ɨ̄:kʰúɨ̀	tʃɛ̀:nɛ̀ᴺ	lleéne	mɛ̀ᴺ tʃɛ́:nɛ̀	mellééne
eat (bread)!	má˟tʃʰō:	májchoó	mɛ́ má˟tʃʰò	mémajcho
ɨ̄:kʰúɨ̀	mà˟tʃʰòᴺ	majcho	mɛ̀ᴺ má˟tʃʰò	memájcho
eat (meat)!	tí-tʲō:	dídyoó	mɛ́ tō:	médoó
ɨ̄:kʰúɨ̀	tì-tʲòᴺ	didyo	mɛ̀ᴺ tò	medo
swallow!	mɛ́ʔtō:	méhdoó	mɛ́ mɛ́ʔtò	mémehdo
ɨ̄:kʰúɨ̀	mɛ̀ʔtòᴺ	mehdo	mɛ̀ᴺ mɛ́ʔtò	meméhdo
touch!	tómá˟kʰō	dómajco	mɛ́ tómá˟kʰò	médomájco
ɨ̄:kʰúɨ̀	tòmá˟kʰò	domájco	mɛ́ tòmá˟kʰò	médomájco
stop doing!	tí ʔβɛ́tʰɛ̀	dɨ́hvete	mɛ́ ɨ́ʔβɛ́tʰɛ̀	méɨhvéte
ɨ̄:kʰúɨ̀	t-ɨ̀ᴺʔβɛ́tʰɛ̀	dɨhvéte	mɛ́ ɨ́ʔβɛ́tʰɛ̀	méɨhvéte
fix!	t-ímɨpá˟tʃʰō	dímibájcho	mɛ́ ímɨpá˟tʃʰò	méímibájcho
ɨ̄:kʰúɨ̀	t-ímɨpá˟tʃʰòᴺ	dímibájcho	mɛ̀ ímɨpá˟tʃʰò	meímibájcho
throw out!	kpá:kō:	wáágoo	mɛ́ kpá:kóò	méwaagóo
ɨ̄:kʰúɨ̀	kpà:kóòᴺ	waagóo	mɛ́ kpà:kóò	méwaagóo
yawn![a]	t-ákpakʰúmuɨ̄	dáwacúnu	mɛ́ àkpákʰúmuɨ	méawácunu
ɨ̄:kʰúɨ̀	t-àkpákʰúmuɨ	dawácunu	mɛ́ àkpákʰúmuɨ	méawácunu

---

[a] The lexically marked low tones of àkpakʰúmuɨ 'to yawn' block the docking of the imperative (nonfinite) low tone on the antepenult of the last three of the forms given here. We do not know why the same is not true of the first form.

14.3 Degrees of strength of imperatives

This section describes explanations (14.3.1), exhortations (14.3.2), hortatives (14.3.3), and a way to soften imperatives (14.3.4).

14.3.1 Explanations

Although explanations are not imperatives, we begin with them because they can be interpreted as suggestions, that is, as very weak imperatives. Explanations present the subject with either mɨ́ːnɛ̀ (IndefAnPl) 'indefinite animate plural' or mɨ̀ʔà (IndefAnSg) 'indefinite animate singular'. The verb bears the pronominal proclitic mɛ- (me- ~ ma-) 'SAP' and ends with -ʔì ⟨t⟩. This is illustrated in 904:[7]

(904) a. Íllu múúne núhbake méímíbajchóhi.
     b. Íllu muha núhbake méímíbajchóhi.

$$\text{ítʃùɪ}\atop\text{like.that} \left\{ {\text{a. mɨ́ːnɛ̀}\atop\text{IndefAnPl}} \atop {\text{b. mɨ̀ʔà}\atop\text{we.ex}} \right\} \text{nɨ́ɨʔpà-k}^\text{h}\text{ɛ̀ \ \ mɛ́ \ ímípà}^\text{x}\text{tʃ}^\text{h}\text{ó-ʔì}\atop\text{clock-objAn SAP fix-}\langle\text{t}\rangle$$

a. 'One fixes the clock like this.'
b. 'We (ex.) fix the clock like this.'

14.3.2 Exhortation

To exhort a hearer to some action, the pronoun mɨ́ɨ̀ɨ̀ (múu) 'indefinite animate singular' is used as the preverbal subject. For example, 905a is a declarative and 905b is the corresponding exhortation:

(905) a. Ú ímíbajchó dɨhmɨ́ɨ́ne.
     b. Múu ímíbajchó dɨhmɨ́ɨ́ne.

$$\left\{{\text{a. ɨ́ɨ}\atop\text{you}}\atop{\text{b. mɨ́ɨ̀ɨ̀}\atop\text{IndefAnSg}}\right\}\text{ímípà}^\text{x}\text{tʃ}^\text{h}\text{ó-ʔ}\ \text{tɨ}^\text{G}\text{ʔ}\ \ \text{mɨ́ːnɛ̀}\atop\text{fix-}\langle\text{t}\rangle\ \ \ \ \text{your canoe}\left\{{\text{a. 'You fixed}\atop\text{your canoe.'}}\atop{\text{b. 'You ought}\atop\text{to fix your}\atop\text{canoe.'}}\right.$$

Example 906 is a negative exhortation:[8]

---

[7] The singular declarative corresponding to 904b is:

  ítʃùɪ nɨ́ɨʔpà-kʰɛ̀ ó ímípàˣtʃʰó-ʔì (Íllu núhbake ó ímíbajchóhi)
  thus clock-⟨ø⟩   I   fix-⟨t⟩
  'I fix the clock like this.'

[8] Note that, because 906 is negative, the verb bears -nɛ ⟨n⟩ rather than -ʔi ⟨t⟩, as in the corresponding imperative:

(906) Tsá múu ímityúné méénutúne.

tsʰá⁽ᴴ⁾ʔ múrùɪ⁽ᴴ⁾ ímì-tʲʰɯ́-né mɛ́:nùɪ-tʰɯ́-nɛ̀
not IndefAnSg good-neg-⟨ø⟩ do-neg-⟨n⟩
'One should not do bad things.'

Compare the exhortation of 907a with the explanation in 907b:

(907) a. Íllu múu meenúhi.
      b. Íllu múune mémeenúhi.

a. ítʃùɪ   mú̃rùɪ⁽ᴴ⁾   mɛ̀:nɯ́-ʔì   'You ought to do it
   like.that IndefAnSg   do-⟨t⟩   this way.'
b. ítʃùɪ   múɪ:nɛ̀   mɛ́   mɛ̀:nɯ́-ʔì   'This is how we do it.'
   like.that IndefAnPl SAP   do-⟨t⟩

14.3.3 Hortatives with májo and métsu 'let's go'

The words máhò (májo) 'let's (du.in.)!' and métsʰùɪ (métsu) 'let's (pl in.)!' are inherently imperative verbs (bearing high-low tone). They may be used by themselves, in which case they mean 'Let's go!', or they may have a complement. The verb of the complement verb is preceded by the pronominal proclitic mɛ 'SAP' and may be followed by -Ⓛkʰi 'purpose'. If the complement's verb is clause final, -Ⓛkʰi normally occurs, as in 908 and 909. If, however, it is clause medial, /kʰi/ is normally absent, although its low tone is still docked on the preceding syllable (unless blocked by another low tone), as in 910. The complement's verb always bears high tone on its first syllable because it is subordinate; this tone is not overridden by the low tone of -Ⓛkʰi, as in 908 and 910.

(908) ¡Májo mepéé(kií)!

máhò   [mɛ̀ pʰɛ́:⁽ˢ⁾-(kʰì:)]   'Let's both of us go!'
let's.go SAP go-pur

(909) ¡Métsu memájcho(ki)!

métsʰùɪ [mɛ̀ máˣtʃʰò⁽ˢ⁾-(kʰì)]   'Let's go eat! (plural)'
let's.go SAP eat-pur

ímì-tʲʰɯ́-nɛ́ mɛ́:nùɪ-tì-nɛ̀ (Ímityúné méénudíne.)   'Do not do bad things.'
good-neg-⟨ø⟩ do-neg-⟨n⟩

Moreover, the negative suffix of 906 is -tʰɯ, which is used only with finite verbs; it is not -⁽ʔ⁾ti, as in the corresponding imperative.

14.3. DEGREES OF STRENGTH OF IMPERATIVES

(910) Métsu mepéé cóómívuú!

métsʰùɪ [mɛ̀ pʰɛ̀ː_ kʰóːmí-βùːː]   'Let's go to town!'
let's.go SAP go   town-goal

(911) ¡Májo meááhíve!

máhò mɛ̀ àːʔíβɛ̀   'Let's visit.'
let's.go SAP visit

(912) Métsu meááhíveté.

métsʰùɪ mɛ̀ àːʔíβɛ̀-tʰɛ́-kʰì̀   'Let's go to visit.'
let's.go SAP visit-go.do-pur

(913) Májo íícúi teene wákimyéi meníjkévaki.

máhò íːkʰúìì tʰɛ̀ː-nɛ̀ kpákʰìmʲɛ̂ì mɛ̀ nɨ́ˣkʰɛ́βà-kʰì̀
let's.go quickly that-⟨ø⟩ work SAP finish-pur
'Let's finish the work quickly.'

In 913, kpákʰìmʲɛ̂ì 'work' bears a low tone on the antepenult because it is nonfinite and nɨ́ˣkʰɛ́βà-kʰì̀ 'finish-pur' bears a high tone on the initial syllable because it is the verb of a subordinate clause.

The tone patterns of maho and mɛtsʰuɪ vary, providing three degrees of urgency, as shown in table 14.3:

Table 14.3 Three degrees of urgency with májo and métsu

		DUAL	PLURAL	
NOT URGENT	HL	máhò (májo)	métsʰùɪ (métsu)	'Let's go!'
URGENT	LL	màhò (majo)	mètsʰùɪ (metsu)	'Come on now; let's go!'
VERY URGENT	HL:	máhò: (májoó)	métsʰùɪ: (métsuú)	'Come on, let's get moving!'

With other verbs, degrees of urgency are usually indicated with qualifying adverbs or adverbial suffixes, as discussed in the following section.

14.3.4 Softening imperatives with kpai 'permit'

An imperative (but not a prohibition) may be softened to a suggestion or a statement of permission by putting kpa(i)[9] (wái) 'permit' before it. This

---

[9] The final /i/ of kpáì 'permit' may be dropped, in which case it is like saying: "Alright, go on and do it, but I'm not very happy about it."

is illustrated in the following imperatives. (Note that the final /ˣ/, glossed as 'vocative', reflects the absence of a glottal stop that would ordinarily be present.)

(914) Wái majchoj.
    ƙpáì   màˣʧʰò-ˣ   'You (sg) may eat (bread).'
    permit eat-voc

(915) Wái majchótej.
    ƙpáì   màˣʧʰó-tʰὲ-ˣ   'You (sg) may go eat (bread).'
    permit eat-go.do-voc

(916) Wái tómajcótej.
    ƙpáì   tʰómàˣkʰó-tʰὲ-ˣ   'You (sg) may go touch it.'
    permit touch-go.do-voc

(917) Wái méwaagóoj.
    ƙpáì   mɛ́   ƙpà:kóò-ˣ   'You (pl) may throw it out.'
    permit SAP throw-voc

(918) Wái méímibájchoj.
    ƙpáì   mɛ́   ímìpáˣʧʰò-ˣ   'You (pl) may fix it.'
    permit SAP fix-voc

(919) Wái méwaagóotej.
    ƙpáì   mɛ́   ƙpà:kóò-tʰὲ-ˣ   'You (pl) may throw it out.'
    permit SAP throw-go.do-voc

(920) Wái méímibajchótej.
    ƙpáì   mɛ́   ímìpàˣʧʰó-tʰὲ-ˣ   'You (pl) may go fix it.'
    permit SAP fix-go.do-voc

Note that in all these cases the verb following ƙpáì 'permit' bears nonfinite tone (as discussed in section 4.1). This suggests that, like ɨ́:kʰɨ́rì 'hurry' discussed in section 14.2.3, ƙpáì 'permit' is a verb that takes a nonfinite complement.

Chapter 15

Question Formation

There are two types of question: "yes/no" questions (15.1) and "content" questions (15.2).

Questions are spoken with the same intonation as declaratives, but there may be tone changes.

15.1 Yes/no questions

Yes/no questions are formed from indicative sentences by starting them with a 'yes/no',[1] as in 921 and 922. (See also example 955, page 361.)

(921) ¿A u tsáá ámèjutu?
 à ùɪ tsʰá:-ˀ áméhùɪ-tʰùɪ 'Do you come
 y/n you come-⟨t⟩ downriver-sou from down river?'

(922) ¿A mítyáábécoba diíbye?
 à mítʲʰá-:pέ-kʰòpà tì-:pʲὲ 'Is he a big one (SgM)?'
 y/n big-⟨SgM⟩-aug that-⟨SgM⟩

15.2 Content questions

Content questions always begin with an interrogative phrase. This might

---
[1] In isolation this is áà, as in áà (¿Áa?) 'What?'.

be simply an interrogative pronoun (as described below). For example, 923 is a simple statement and 924 is a question, in which the interrogative pronoun mǘʔà 'who' is used as the subject:

(923) O tsáá áméjutu.
    ò tsʰá:-ʔ   ámɛ́hù-tʰù   'I come from down river.'
    I come-⟨t⟩ down.river-sou

(924) ¿Múha tsáá áméjutu?
    <u>mǘʔà</u> tsʰá:-ʔ   ámɛ́hù-tʰù   'Who comes from
    who come-⟨t⟩ down.river-sou   down river?'

Interrogative phrases are formed from the roots and stems of table 15.1:

Table 15.1 The interrogative roots

mǘʔà^a	(múha)	'who (animate, nominative)'
ɨ̀:-nɛ̀ ~ ɨ̀:-ná^b	(ɨɨne ~ ɨɨná)	'what (inanimates)'
kʰà-^{c}	(ca-)	'which (animate)'
kʰɛ̀:-	(kee-)	'which (inanimate)'
ɨ́βɛ̀:-	(ɨ́vee-)	'why'
mù-	(mu-)	'WH'

^{a}mǘʔà 'who' is never followed by a classifier. It is only used as the subject; ɨ̀:-nɛ̀ ~ ɨ̀:-ná is used in other cases.
^{b}ɨ̀:- 'what' is never followed directly by a classifier other than -nɛ̀ ⟨ø⟩.
^{c}kʰà- and kʰɛ̀:- ask for the identification of an individual (or individuals) from some set of possible candidates, as constrained by the classifier that follows. kʰà- is used for animates and kʰɛ̀:- for inanimate.

The roots mù- 'WH' and ɨ́βɛ̀:- 'why' can be followed by either an animate or an inanimate classifier and, of course, a case marker. This gives them great generality, as illustrated in table 15.2 and the examples that follow.

Table 15.2 Interrogative phrases with mu- 'WH' and ɨ́vee- 'why'

mǘ-ìhʲɯ	(múijyu)	'when'	ɨ́βɛ̀:-kʰi	(ɨ́veeki)	'why'
mù-ʔtɯ	(muhdu)	'how'	ɨ́βɛ̀:-pɛ	(ɨ́veebe)	'why he'
mù:-kʰá	(muucá)	'who' (obj)	ɨ́βɛ̀:-tʃɛ	(ɨ́veelle)	'why she'
mù-ʔtì-(tʲʰɯ)	(muhdityu)	'about whom'	ɨ́βɛ̀:-mɛ	(ɨ́veeme)	'why them'
mǘ-tʃíːʔʲɛ	(múllihye)	'for whom'	ɨ́βɛ̀:-nɛ	(ɨ́veene)	'why that'
mǘ:-màá	(múúmaá)	'with whom'			
mùʔ-ná	(muhná)	'whose'			
mǘ-kʰò:kʰa	(múcooca)	'when'			
mǘ-tsʰìí	(mútsií)	'where'			

15.2. CONTENT QUESTIONS

The interrogative phrase generally ends with a high tone indicated in the gloss by .¿?.

(925) ¿Muhdí(tyú) ihjyúvaábe?
  mṵ̀ɨ-ʔtí-(tʲʰɨ́ɨ)   ìʔhʲɨ́ɨβà-ːpɛ̀   'About whom does he speak?'
  WH-anim-sou.¿? speak-⟨SgM⟩

(926) mṵ̀ɨ-má   ɨ́ɨ   pʰɛ̀-έ-ʔì   (¿Muumá ú peéhi?) 'With whom will
  WH-with.¿? you go-fut-⟨t⟩   you go?'

(927) mɨ́ɨ-ìhʲɨ́ɨ   ɨ́ɨ   pʰɛ̀-έ-ʔì   (¿Múijyú ú peéhi?) 'When are
  WH-⟨time⟩.¿? you go-fut-⟨t⟩   you going?'

iβɛɛ 'why' can be followed by either an animate or an inanimate classifier; see 928:

(928) a. ¿ɨ́véébeke ú tsiváhi?
     b. ¿ɨ́veewa ú tsiváhi?

a. íβέ-ːpɛ̀-kʰɛ̀
   why-⟨SgM⟩-objAn
                        } ɨ́ɨ tsʰìβá-ʔì { a. 'Why did you bring him?'
b. íβὲː-kpà   you bring-⟨t⟩   b. 'Why did you bring
   why-⟨slab⟩   that slab (table, plank,...)?'

Interrogative pronouns may be animate (15.2.1) or inanimate (15.2.2).

15.2.1 Animate interrogative pronouns

Animate interrogative pronouns are masculine, feminine or unspecified for gender. They are third person, and either singular, plural or dual. See table 15.3 and the examples that follow.

Table 15.3 Animate interrogative pronouns formed with mu- 'who'

	SINGULAR	DUAL	PLURAL
masc.	mṵ̀ɨ-ːpɛ̀ (muúbe)	mṵ̀ɨ-tʰέ-tsʰì (muutétsi)	mṵ̀ɨ-tʰɛ̀ (muúte)
fem.	mṵ̀ɨ-tʃɛ̀ (muúlle)	mṵ̀ɨ-tʰέ-pʰɨ̀ (muutépɨ)	
unspec.	mɨ́ɨ-ʔà (múha)		

(929) ¿Múúbécoba tsááhi?
  mɨ́ɨ-ːpέ-kʰòpà tsʰáː-ʔì   'Who is the big guy that came?'
  WH-⟨SgM⟩-aug come-⟨t⟩

In 930 the interrogative pronoun bears -Ⓛkʰɛ 'objAn' because it is an animate direct object:

(930) ¿Múúbeké ú tsiváhi?
  mɯ́ː-ːpè-kʰɛ́   ɯ́ː   tsʰìβá-ʔì   'Whom (SgM)
  WH-⟨SgM⟩-objAn.¿?   you bring-⟨t⟩   do you bring?'

As stated above, the interrogative phrase generally ends with a high tone (glossed ".¿?".) There are two cases where this is not so. First, mɯ́ʔà 'who' never bears a final high tone. Second, in an embedded question (discussed on page 364) the interrogative word ends with a low tone.

When used as the subject of a clause, the forms that end in /e/ change this to a high tone /a/, as shown in 931 and illustrated in 932.

(931) NONSUBJECT   SUBJECT
  mɯ̀ːpè (muúbe)   ⟶   mɯ̀ːpá (muubá) 'who (SgM)'
  mɯ̀ːtʃè (muúlle) ⟶   mɯ̀ːtʃá (muullá) 'who (SgF)'
  mɯ̀ːtʰè (muúte)   ⟶   mɯ̀ːtʰá (muutá) 'who (AnPl)'

(932) ¿Muubá tsááhií?
  mɯ̀ː-ːpá   tsʰá-ːʔìí   'Who (SgM) comes?'
  WH-⟨SgM⟩.¿?   come-⟨t⟩

Likewise, when the interrogative phrase is an object terminated with the animate object suffix, the form is -kʰa rather than -kʰɛ; for example:

(933) ¿Mucá ú tsiváhi?
  mɯ̀-kʰá   ɯ́ː   tsʰìβá-ʔì   'Whom (Sg/Du/Pl) are
  WH-objAn.¿?   you bring-⟨t⟩   you bringing?'

These two facts—the final high tone and the vowel change—are evidence of an interrogative suffix that (1) has a Ⓗ to be docked on its host's final syllable, and (2) causes the change of /e/ to /a/.[2]

The interrogative pronouns of table 15.4 ask for the identification of the person or animal with respect to some group (in the same way that *which* does in English). When used in a question, the final syllable of the interrogative phrase bears high tone but (unlike the forms in table 15.3) do not change /e/ to /a/. (These interrogative pronouns are also used in embedded questions; see examples 960 and 961, page 364.)

Table 15.4 Animate interrogative pronouns formed with *ca-* 'which'

	singular	dual	plural
masc.	kʰàːpè (caábe)	kʰàː-tʲʰétsʰì (caatyétsi)	kʰàː-tʲʰè (caátye)
fem.	kʰàːtʃè (caálle)	kʰàː-tʲʰépʰɨ (caatyépɨ)	

---

[2]This morpheme is likely to have developed historically from a morpheme *ʔa 'verify', reflexes of which are now present in mɯ́ʔà 'who' and -ʔa(ha) 'challenge veracity' (see section 11.2.7). The change of /e/ to /a/ could have arisen by vowel harmony or coalesence.

In 934 the interrogative pronoun is the direct object; because it is animate it bears -①kʰɛ 'objAn':

(934) ¿Caatyétsikyé ú tsiváhi?
  kʰà:-tʲʰɛ́tsʰì-kʲʰɛ́   úɨ   tsʰìβá-ʔì   'Which two (DuM) are
  which-⟨DuM⟩-objAn.¿? you bring-⟨t⟩   you bringing?'

In 935 the interrogative pronoun takes -⁽ˀ⁾ti (-hdi) 'benefactive' because it is animate:

(935) ¿Cáábyedí(tyú) ú ihjyúváhi?
  kʰá-:pʲɛ̀-tí-(tʲʰúɨ)   úɨ   ìˀhʲúɨβá-ʔì
  which-⟨SgM⟩-anim-sou.¿? you speak-⟨t⟩
  'About which one (SgM) of them are you talking?'

15.2.2 Inanimate interrogative pronouns

Inanimate interrogative pronouns are third person and may be singular, dual, or plural. They do not reflect gender. There are two roots. First, ɨ:- 'what' is used to ask for the identity of one or more things. It is always followed by -nɛ̀ ⟨ø⟩, presumably because the one who asks does not know what it is and thus cannot use a more specific classifier.³

(936) a. ɨ̱:-ná   (ɨɨná)   'what (sg)'
         what-⟨ø⟩.¿?
     b. ɨ́-nɛ̀-:kʰúɨ   (ɨneecú) 'what (du)'
         what-⟨ø⟩-du.¿?
     c. ɨ́-nɛ̀-ˀhɨ́   (ɨnehjɨ) 'what' (pl)'
         what-⟨ø⟩-pl.¿?

When used as a subject (as in 937), as direct object (as in 938), or as predicate complement (as in 939), ɨ:nɛ́ changes to ɨ:ná

(937) ɨ:-ná   á:kʰìtʲʰɛ-ʔì (¿Ɨɨná áákityéhi?) 'What fell?'
     what-⟨ø⟩.¿? fall-⟨t⟩

(938) ɨ:-ná   úɨ   tsʰìβá-ʔì (¿Ɨɨná ú tsiváhi?) 'What did you
     what-⟨ø⟩.¿? you bring-⟨t⟩   bring?'

(939) ɨ:-ná   í:-ɲɛ̀ɛ́ (¿Ɨɨná íɨ́ñeé?) 'What is this thing?'
     what-⟨ø⟩.¿? this-⟨ø⟩

The questions in 940 ask for more specific information regarding a tree or means of transportation:

---
³However, another classifier may follow -nɛ̀ ⟨ø⟩, as in 940.

(940) a. ¿ɨ́ɨnehé teéhe?
   b. ¿ɨ́ɨnemɨ teémɨ?
   a. ɨ́:-nè̠-ʔɛ́   tʰɛ̀ɛ́-ʔɛ̀   'What tree is that?'
      what-⟨ø⟩-⟨tree⟩   that-⟨tree⟩
   b. ɨ́:-nè̠-mɨ̀   tʰɛ̀:-mɨ̀   'What canoe (car,…)
      what-⟨ø⟩-⟨canoe⟩   that-⟨canoe⟩   is that?'

Second, pronouns like those of table 15.5 are used to ask for the identity of one thing from among various things. These are formed from kʰɛ(:)- 'which', some classifier, and optionally a pluralizer: -:kʰɯ 'duIn' or -⁽ʔ⁾hɨ 'plural'. The classifiers used in table 15.5 are -nɛ, which refers to things in general (not specified), -mɨ, which refers to canoes, cars, airplanes and other means of transport, and -hɨ, which refers to disk-like things (including coins, pills, buttons, the earth, the sky,…).

Table 15.5 Inanimate interrogative pronouns formed with ke- 'which'

	singular	dual	plural
thing	kʰɛ̀:-nè̠ (keéne)	kʰɛ́-nè̠-:kʰɯ̀ (kéneécu)	kʰɛ́-nè̠-ʔhɨ̀ (kénehjɨ)
transport	kʰɛ̀:-mɨ̀ (keémɨ)	kʰɛ́-mɨ̀-:kʰɯ̀ (kémɨɨ́cu)	kʰɛ́-mɨ̀-ʔhɨ̀ (kémɨhjɨ)
disk-like	kʰɛ̀:-hɨ̀ (keéjɨ)	kʰɛ́-hɨ̀-:kʰɯ̀ (kéjɨɨ́cu)	kʰɛ́-hɨ̀-ʔhɨ̀ (kéjɨhjɨ)
…	…	…	…

kʰɛ̀:-nɛ́ becomes kʰɛ̀:-ná when used as a subject, as a predicate adjective, or as a direct object, as in 941:

(941) kʰɛ̀:-ná   ɯ́ɯ   tsʰɨ́β́á-ʔɨ̀   (¿Keená ú tsiváhi?) 'Which have
      which-⟨ø⟩.¿?   you   bring-⟨t⟩   you brought?'

15.3 Rhetorical questions

Sometimes a point can be made very effectively by using the form of a question, but without really expecting an answer, that is, by a RHETORICAL QUESTION. For example, a speaker could say 942 to make the point that the hearer has come without bringing something for the speaker:

(942) ¿Ɨɨnéubá óhdivu tsívátúroobe u tsááhií?
      ɨ̀:-né-ɯ̀pá   ó-ʔtɨ̀-βɯ̀   tsʰɨ́β́á-tʰɯ́-ɾò-:pɛ̀   ɯ̀
      what-⟨ø⟩-prob   I-anim-goal   bring-neg-frs-⟨SgM⟩   you

      tsʰá:-ʔɨ̀-:
      come-⟨t⟩-emph
      'Did you come without bringing me anything?!'

15.3. RHETORICAL QUESTIONS

Other examples of rhetorical questions are given in 943:

(943) a. ¿Muhdú?
    b. ¿Muhdúrá?
    c. ¡Muhdúráha(ja) teéne!

    a. mù̱ɨ-ʔtúɨ   'How's that?'
        WH-⟨like⟩.¿?
    b. mù̱ɨ-ʔtúɨ-ɾá   'How's that? (I expected
        WH-⟨like⟩-frs.¿?   something different)'
    c. mù̱ɨ-ʔtúɨ-ɾá-ʔà(hà)   tʰὲ:-nὲ   'That's incredible! (Prove it!)'
        WH-⟨like⟩-frs-verify that-⟨ø⟩

Chapter 16

Complementation

16.1 General comments about subordination

Bora subordinate clauses are either adverbial or nominal. If nominal, they may be followed by a case marker. See figure 16.1.

$$[\overset{s}{\sigma}...]_{\text{verb stem}} - \begin{cases} \begin{cases} -k^ho{:}k^ha & \text{'when'} \\ -tɯ & \langle\text{like}\rangle \\ -k^ha & \text{'if'} \\ -ʔa^xʧ^hi{:} & \text{'if'} \\ -ih^jɯ & \text{'time'} \\ -k^hi & \text{'pur'} \end{cases} & \text{ADVERBIAL} \\ \begin{cases} -nɛ\ \langle\varnothing\rangle, \langle\text{event}\rangle \text{ or} \\ \text{OTHER CLASSIFIER} \end{cases} \text{CASE} & \text{NOMINAL} \end{cases}$$

Figure 16.1 STR: subordinate clause verbs

Adverbial subordinate clauses are discussed in chapter 17. There are various types of nominal subordinate clauses. Relative clauses are discussed in chapter 18. Complements are dealt with here in section 16.2: subject complements in section 16.2.1 and object complements in section 16.2.2.

The first syllable of the verb of a subordinate clause bears high tone, represented here by S over the vowel. For example, compare 944a, a subordinate clause headed by a verb with the initial high tone, with 944b,

a nonfinite verb with the low nonfinite tone on the antepenult. Note that the meanings differ in the expected way.

(944) a. Ó ájtyumɨ́ áíívyeja.

b. Ó ájtyumɨ́ aíívyeja.

ó á˟tʲʰùmɨ́-ˀ   {a. áí-:βʲɛ̀ }   'I saw a
I see-⟨t⟩   {b. áí-:βʲɛ̀ } -hà   {a. house burning.'
                 { burn-sIn } ⟨shelter⟩ {b. burned house.'

A subordinate clauses has an overt subject. (There are rare cases in which there is no overt subject.) It must be a preverbal subject. It may be a personal pronoun, such as tì-pʲɛ̀ (that-⟨SgM⟩) in 994. It may be a bound adjectival stem followed by a classifier, such as tsʰà-:tʰɛ̀ (one-AnPl) in 981. It may be a simple noun phrase, such as tsʰɨ́:mɛ̀nɛ̀ (child) 'child' in 737. It may be a genitive phrase, such as í ò:ʔí-:pʲɛ̀ (self dog-⟨SgM⟩) as in 953. It may be a relative clause headed by a classifier, such as ɛ̀ˀ-túɨ-βá-à nɛ́:-tʃɛ̀-rɛ̀ (that-⟨like⟩-rpt-rem say-⟨SgF⟩-only) 'she who said like that' in 688. Most frequently it is a pronominal proclitic: o 'I', ɯ 'you', mɛ 'SAP', or the anaphor i 'self',[1] which generally refers to an element of the superordinate clause, as in 982 in which i refers to the subject of the main clause.[2] Further examples follow:

(945) Ó ájtyumɨ́ u áwácunúne.

ó á˟tʲʰùmɨ́-ˀ   [ùɨ   ákpákʰùɨnúɨ]-nɛ̀   'I saw you yawn.'
I see-⟨t⟩   you yawn   -⟨ø⟩

(946) U ááhɨ́vetéhajchíí ó imíllé uma o pééneé.

[ùɨ   a:ʔíβɛ̀-tʰɛ́   ]-ʔà˟tʃʰɨ́: ó ìmítʃɛ́-ˀ   [ùɨ-mà   ò pʰɛ̀:]-nɛ̀ɛ́
you visit-go.do -if   I want-⟨t⟩ you-with I go   -⟨ø⟩
'If you go visiting, I want to go with you.'

(947) Ó aahɨ́veté u méénújá pañévu

ó à:ʔíβɛ̀-tʰɛ́-ˀ   [[ùɨ   mɛ́:núɨ]-há   Ⓖ pʰáɲɛ́]-βùɨ
I visit-go.do-⟨t⟩   you make   -⟨shelter⟩ inside -goal
'I'm going to visit inside the house you made.'

The structure of 947 is given in figure 16.2:

---

[1] "Anaphor" in the sense that it is generally bound within the domain of the closest accessible subject. See section 8.3 for discussion.
[2] Compare the pronominal tìtʲʰɛ̀ in 229, page 131.

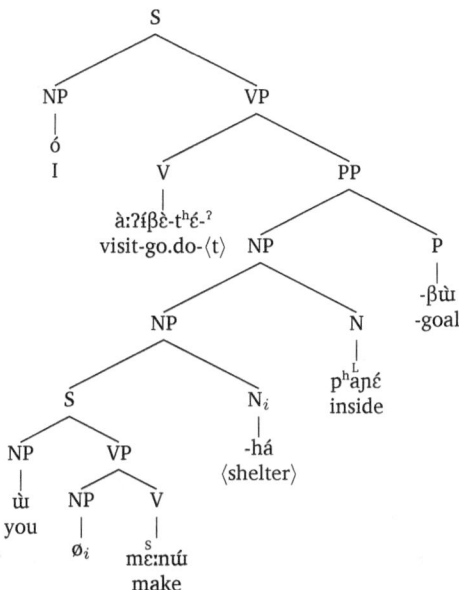

Figure 16.2 STR: Ó aahíveté u méénújá pañévu

16.2 Complements

Generally a classifier following a subordinate verb forms a relative clause referring to a being or object of the type indicated by the classifier; see chapter 18. In this section we consider subordinate clauses in which the classifier following the verb is -nɛ ⟨ø⟩ ('thing'). These are COMPLEMENTS, and may function as the subject of a sentence (16.2.1) or as direct objects (16.2.2).

Some subordinate clauses, such as that in 948, are ambiguous between a complement and a relative clause. This comes about because the maximally unspecified classifier -nɛ ⟨ø⟩ may refer either to a object or to an event, as discussed in section 16.3.

(948) Ó ájtyumɨ́ dibye májchone.

    ó á^xt^{jh}ùmɨ́-ʔ [tì-p^jɛ̀   á^xtʃ^hò]-nɛ̀
    I see-⟨t⟩   that-⟨SgM⟩ eat   ⟨ø⟩

    'I saw that he ate.' (event) or 'I saw that which he ate.' (thing)

16.2.1 Subject complements

The subject of a sentence may be a subordinate clause. For example, in 949 the subject is tì:pʲɛ̀ pʰɛ́:nɛ̀: 'that he goes', f̓tátsʰó⁽ʔ⁾ 'sad' is a predicate adjective, and the copula is implicit:

(949) f̓hdátsó diibye pééneé.

    f̓tátsʰó⁽ʔ⁾ [tì-:pʲɛ̀   pʰɛ̂ˢ:]-nɛ̀:   'It is sad that he goes.'
    sad   that-⟨SgM⟩ go   -⟨ø⟩

16.2.2 Object complements

The following verbs (among many others) take object complements: aˣtʲʰɯmi 'see', ìːtʰɛ 'look', tʃɛːpo 'hear', imitʃɛ 'want', pʰiːβʲɛtʰɛ 'be able', and kpaːhakʰɯ 'know'. The object complement usually follows the complement-taking verb, but it may also precede it.

The verb of the complement always bears a high tone on the first syllable and is always followed by -Ⓛ○nɛ ⟨ø⟩.³ -Ⓛ○nɛ does not impose its Ⓛ on a monosyllabic or bisyllabic verb because the initial syllable must bear high tone. Further, the tones of #̷...-Ⓛ○ne ⟨ø⟩ do not override the tones imposed by, for example, a preceding -Ⓛ○tɯ 'like' or -Ⓛ○iɲɯ 'go after doing'.

We now present various examples. Note that in 950a the subject of the complement, which is coreferential to the subject of the main clause, is a pronoun; it is not—as might be expected—an anaphor. By contrast, in 951, in which the subject of the complement is third person, the anaphor i 'self' is used.

(950) ó ìmítʃé-ʔ [{ a. ò / I / b. ɯ̀ɪ / you } pʰɛ̂ˢ:]-nɛ̀ɛ́ { a. Ó imíllé o pééneé. 'I want to go.' / b. Ó imíllé u pééneé. 'I want you to go.' }
    I want-⟨t⟩   go -⟨ø⟩

(951) Muurá tsá dibye ímílletú ipyééneé.

    mùːrá tsʰáᴴʔ tì-pʲɛ̀   ímítʃè-tʰɯ́ [ì   pʲʰɛ̂ˢ:]-nɛ̀ɛ́
    confirm not   that-⟨SgM⟩ want-neg   self go   -⟨ø⟩
    'Well, he does not want to go.'

The sentence in 952a (which contains a relative clause) is embedded under a sensory verb in 952b:

---

³Relative clauses and some sensory verb complements are followed by a different classifier; for example, see 956 and example 80, page 68.

16.2. COMPLEMENTS

(952) a. Ú méénuja áiivyéhi.

b. Ó ájtyumɨ́ ú méénuja áiivyéne.

a. [ɯ́ mɛ̃́:nɯ̀ɯ̀]-hà áì-:βʲɛ́-ʔì
you build -⟨shelter⟩ burn-sIn-⟨t⟩

b. ó áˣtʲʰɯ̀mɨ́-ʔ [[ɯ́ mɛ̃́:nɯ̀ɯ̀]-hà áì-:βʲɛ́]-nɛ̀
I saw-⟨t⟩ you build -⟨shelter⟩ burn-sIn -⟨ø⟩

a. 'The house [that you built] burned.'

b. 'I saw [[the house that you built] burning].'

Example 953 illustrates a factive complement; 954, an object complement to a sensory verb; and 955, a complement to pʰɨ̀:βʲɛ́tʰɛ́-ʔ 'be able'. Example 367, page 178, has an object complement to a phasal verb.

(953) Jóáa waajácú íoohííbye dsɨ́jɨvéne.

hóáà kpà:hákʰɯ́ɯ̀-ʔ [í ó:ʔí-:pʲɛ̀ tsɨ̀hɨ̀βɛ́]-nɛ̀
John knows-⟨t⟩ self dog-⟨SgM⟩ die -⟨ø⟩
'John knows that his dog died.'

(954) Ó ájtumɨ́ Jóáa wákímyeíñe.

ó áˣtʰɯ̀mɨ́-ʔ [hóáà kpàkʰímʲèí]-ɲɛ̀ 'I saw John working.'
I saw-⟨t⟩ John work -⟨ø⟩

(955) ¿A ú piivyété cújúwajúúha u méénune?

à ɯ́ pʰɨ̀:βʲɛ́tʰɛ́-ʔ [kʰɯ́ɯ̀hɯ́ɯ̀kpà-hɯ́ɯ̀:ʔà ɯ̀ mɛ̃́:nɯ̀ɯ̀]-nɛ̀
y/n you be.able-⟨t⟩ fire-⟨charcoal⟩ you make -⟨ø⟩
'Are you able to make charcoal?'

Example 956 contrasts a sensory verb complement in 956a with relative clauses in 956b and c. In 956b tʰɛ́-tsʰɨ 'that child' is the subject of the subordinate clause, whereas in 956c it is the direct object of the main clause, with the relative clause appositive to it.

(956) a. Ó ájtyumí tetsɨ wájpí hallúrí íjcyane.

b. Ó ájtyumí tétsɨ wájpí hallúri íjcyátsɨke.

c. Ó ájtyumí tétsɨke wájpí hallúri íjcyátsɨke.

ó á^{x}t^{jh}ùmí-$^{\text{?}}$
I see-⟨t⟩

a. [t^{h}è-ts^{h}ɨ   kpá^{x}p^{h}í ⓖ $^{\text{?L}}$atʃúɨ-rí ^{S}ɨ^{x}k^{jh}à]-nè
   that-⟨child⟩ man   on.top-oblIn be-⟨ø⟩
b. [t^{h}έ-ts^{h}ɨ   kpá^{x}p^{h}í ⓖ $^{\text{?L}}$atʃúɨ-rì ^{S}ɨ^{x}k^{jh}á]-ts^{h}ɨ-k^{h}ὲ
   that-⟨child⟩ man   on.top-oblIn be   -⟨child⟩-objAn
c. t^{h}έ-ts^{h}ɨ-k^{h}ὲ   Ⓐ [kpá^{x}p^{h}í ⓖ $^{\text{?L}}$atʃúɨ-rì   ø$_i$ ^{S}ɨ^{x}k^{jh}á]-ts^{h}ɨ$_i$-k^{h}ὲ
   that-⟨child⟩-objAn   man   on.top-oblIn   be   -⟨child⟩-objAn

a. 'I saw that the child was on top of the man.'

b,c. 'I saw the child that was on top of the man.'

Compare the sensory verb complement in 957 to the relative clauses in 999 and 1000, page 382.

(957) Ó ájtyumɨ teja áiivyéne

ó á^{x}t^{jh}ùmí-$^{\text{?}}$ [t^{h}è-hà   aì-:β^{j}έ ^{s}]-nè
I see-⟨t⟩   that-⟨shelter⟩ burn-sIn -⟨ø⟩
'I saw that house burning.' or 'I saw that house was burning.'

Example 958 has a sensory verb complement within which there is a relative clause.

(958) Ó ájtyumɨ oohííbyé oke ɨhdoobe dsɨɨnene bájú pañe.

ó á^{x}t^{jh}ùmí-$^{\text{?}}$ [[[ò:ʔí-:p^{j}έ   ò-k^{h}ὲ ^{S}ɨ$^{\text{?}}$tò]-:pὲ]
I see-⟨t⟩   jaguar-⟨SgM⟩ I-objAn bite   -⟨SgM⟩

tsɨ:nὲ^s]-nὲ páhúɨ ⓖ p^{hL}àɲὲ]
run-⟨ø⟩   jungle   inside
'I saw the jaguar that bit me running in the jungle.' (The jaguar was running in the jungle—not I.)

The structure of the object complement is given in figure 16.3.[4]

---

[4]The phrase páhúɨ p^{h}àɲὲ 'in the jungle' is interpreted as a modifier of tsɨ:nὲnὲ 'run', as indicated by the coindexed null ø$_k$.

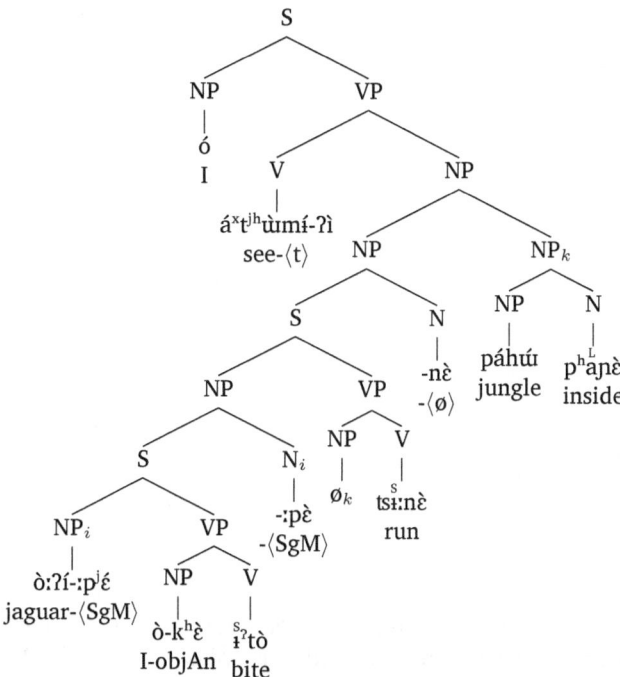

Figure 16.3 STR: ...oohííbyé oke íhdoobe dsíínene bájú pañe.

Example 959 begins "I was gladdend" (not included in 959), followed by an adverbial clause of the sort discussed in section 17.4.2. The verb of this clause is "tell," which has an object complement expressing what was told. (The subject of the complement clause is the noun phrase "those to whom I taught the truth.") The structure of 959 is given in figure 16.4:

(959) ...ímɨáájú o úwaabómé ímí úraavyéné oke ditye úúbálléneri.

[[[ímɨá:hɨ́ɨ ø$_i$ ò ɯ̋kpà:pó]-mɛ́$_i$ ímíˀ ɯ̋rà-:βʲɛ́]-né ò-kʰɛ̀
truth   I teach   -⟨AnPl⟩ good follow-sIn -⟨ø⟩ I-objAn

tì-tʲʰɛ̀   ɯ̋:pátʃɛ́]-nè-ɾì
that-⟨AnPl⟩ tell   -⟨ø⟩-oblIn

'(I was gladdened when) they told me that those to whom I taught the truth are following well.'

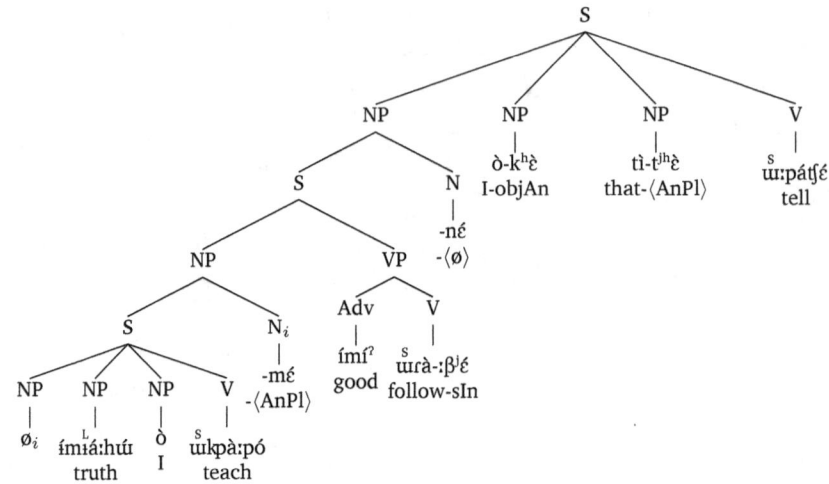

Figure 16.4 STR: ɨmɨáájú o úwaabómé ímí úraavyéné oke ditye úúbállé(neri)

An object complement may be an embedded content question, as in the subordinate clause beginning with múɨ-ːpè-kʰɛ́ 'whom' in 960 and with múɨ-ʔà 'who' in 961. Embedded alternative questions are expressed using a conditional clause, as in 973.

(960) Tsá o wáájácutú múúbeké u tsívane.

tsʰá²ʔ ò kpáːhákʰùɨ-tʰɨ́ɨ [múɨ-ːpè-kʰɛ́   ùɨ   tsʰⁱβà]-nè
not I know-neg   who-⟨SgM⟩-objAn you bring -⟨ø⟩
'I do not know whom (SgM) you are bringing.'

(961) Tsá o wáájácutú múha tsááneé.

tsʰá²ʔ ò kpáːhákʰùɨ-tʰɨ́ɨ [múɨ-ʔà tsʰá:]-nèɛ̀
not I know-neg   WH-Pl come   -⟨ø⟩
'I do not know who (or what animals) come.'

16.3 -ne ⟨ø⟩ versus ⟨event⟩

Three suffixes have the segmental shape /-nɛ/. One, glossed ⟨n⟩, follows -①tʰɯ (-tu) 'negative'; see section 13.2. The other two are glossed ⟨ø⟩ and ⟨event⟩. This section deals with the contrast between these two.

⟨ø⟩ represents a *thing*, that is, an inanimate object that typically persists over time (and can be localized in space). By contrast, an *event* typically

16.3. -NE ⟨∅⟩ VERSUS ⟨EVENT⟩

begins at some time, continues for a while, and then ends; that is, events do not typically have the time stability of objects.[5] Both -⓪◯nɛ ⟨∅⟩ and -nɛ ⟨event⟩ are used following subordinate verbs, so the verb's initial syllable bears high tone. However, the former imposes a low tone on its host's penult while the latter does not:

$$\#\overset{H}{\sigma}...\overset{L}{\sigma}\sigma\text{ne} \quad \langle\emptyset\rangle \text{ (thing)}$$
$$\#\overset{H}{\sigma}...\overset{H}{\sigma}\sigma\text{ne} \quad \langle\text{event}\rangle$$

This difference is visible only on verbs that have three or more syllables,[6] as in 962, in which the tone of the verb's penult (/pa/) correlates with whether the clause bearing -nɛ refers to an object (962a) or an event (962b):

(962) a. Iímíbajchóné tsajtyéébe.

b. Teene iímíbájchóne tsajtyéébe.

a.   ì   ˢimípà̠ˣtʃʰó-nɛ́
            self fix-⟨∅⟩
b. tʰɛ̀:-nɛ̀ ì   ˢimípá̠ˣtʃʰó-nɛ̀
    that-⟨∅⟩ self fix-⟨event⟩

           tsʰáˣtʲʰɛ́-ːpɛ̀
           take-⟨SgM⟩

a. 'He carried off the thing that he fixed.'

b. 'After having fixed it, he carried (it) off.'

Both types of -nɛ are present in mèkʰá⁷kʰúɾˣtsʰónè mèímípà:βʲɛ́nɛ́ in figure 16.5; this is a subordinate clause which has a subordinate adverbial clause within it:[7] The adverbial clause bears -nɛ ⟨event⟩ while the clause in which it is embedded bears -nɛ ⟨∅⟩. (The tone of the proclitics is explained in section 3.12.2, page 93.)

---

[5] The distinction corresponds closely to what Langacker calls *objects* and *interactions*; he writes (Langacker 1991:183):

> Conceptually, objects and interactions present a maximal contrast, having opposite values for such properties as domain of instantiation (space vs. time), essential constituent (substance vs. energy transfer), and the possibility of conceptualizing one independently of the other (autonomous vs. dependent). Physical objects and energetic interactions provide the respective prototypes for the noun and verb categories, which likewise represent a polar opposition among the basic grammatical classes.

[6] The crucial syllable is the host's penult, which must not be the initial syllable because for both suffixes the host's initial syllable bears the subordination high tone.

[7] This example is taken from (Thiesen et al. 1982).

```
me  cáhcújtsó    believe      me  ímíba:vyé      fix
 |    |    :                   |    |  :  |   :
 |    |    :    .-ne  <event>  |    |  :  L___._né   <∅>
 |    H    :    :              |    H  :      :      subordinate
 |    :    :    L              |    :  :      L      FDLT
 |    :    H    H              |    :  H  :   H      DHT
 L    :    :    :              L    :  :  :   :      proclitic tone
 :    :    :    :              :    :  :  :   :
 me  cáhcújtsó-ne              me   ímíba:vyé-né
 SAP believe-<event>           SAP  fix-<∅>
```

'...that you be put right after having believed'

Figure 16.5 TD: mecáhcújtsóne, meímíba:vyéné

To this point we have not discussed -nɛ's tonal properties. -nɛ ⟨event⟩ seems to (1) impose a high tone on the host's initial syllable and (2) delink low tones between itself and the initial syllable, thereby making them high: #⒣...-ʰnɛ. However, it is not necessary to specify that -nɛ imposes the initial high tone provided we recognize that the main verbs of all subordinate clauses bear high tones on their first syllables, as indicated by #⒣...-ʰnɛ 'subordinate' in the tone derivation of ì kpá:hàkʰɯ́-hɯ́ɪkʰó:-nè in figure 16.6. Further, note that the low tone borne by -juco (:) 'now' is delinked but *not* the Ⓛ that it imposes on the host's penult. (Unfortunately, at this point we can not say which low tones -nɛ ⟨event⟩ fails to delink.)

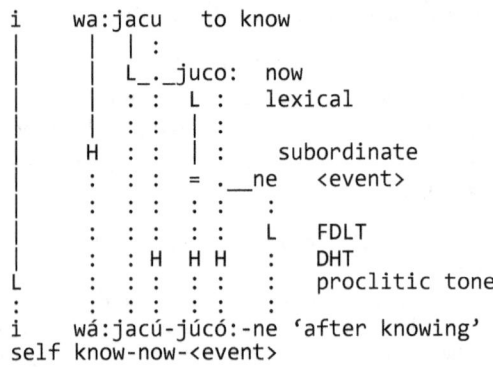

Figure 16.6 TD: delinking by ⟨event⟩: i wá:jacújúcó:ne

To this point we have characterized the difference between ⟨∅⟩ and ⟨event⟩ as semantic. But consider 963:

16.3. -NE ⟨Ø⟩ VERSUS ⟨EVENT⟩

(963) a. O dóóne ú ájtyumɨ́hi.
b. O dóóne o péjucóóhi.
c. Idóóne péjúcoóbe.

a. [ò tó:ˢ]-nɛ̀ ɯ́ á\^xtʲʰɯ̀mí-ʔì. 'You saw me eating (meat).'
   I eat -⟨Ø⟩ you see-⟨t⟩

b. [ò tó:ˢ]-nɛ̀ ò pʰɛ́-hɯ̀kʰó:-ʔì 'Having eaten (meat),
   I eat -⟨event⟩ I go-now-⟨t⟩   I go now.'[8]

c. [ì tó:ˢ]-nɛ̀ pʰɛ́-hɯ́kʰò-:pɛ̀ 'Having eaten (meat),
   self eat -⟨event⟩ go-now-⟨SgM⟩   he goes now.'

Is there any sense in which the sensory verb complement in 963a is less an event than the adverbial clauses in 963b and c? (Here tone does not help because the verb is too short.) The generalization seems to be this: When a subordinate clause is headed by -nɛ and is a direct object, then this -nɛ is -Ⓛ○nɛ ⟨Ø⟩. This—we assume—is the result of subcategorization; that is, verbs like aˣtʲʰumɨ 'see' in 963a subcategorize for a complement headed by -Ⓛ○nɛ ⟨Ø⟩. If this is correct, the tone difference is due to a syntactic condition, not a semantic difference.

Returning now to the -nɛ ⟨n⟩ that follows -Ⓛtʰɯ 'negative' (mentioned at the very start of this section), it may be desirable to identify this with -Ⓛ○nɛ ⟨Ø⟩. There are two reasons. First, the tone is consistent; indeed the Ⓛ imposed by -tʰɯ may actually be the Ⓛ imposed by -Ⓛ○nɛ ⟨Ø⟩. Second, this is consistent with the suggestion that negative clauses are subordinate clauses.

---

[8] The following, in which the first person is indicated by an overt pronoun in the subordinate clause and by a subject classifier in the main clause, is not acceptable:

*[ò tóˢ]-nɛ̀ pʰɛ́-hɯ́kʰò-:pɛ̀ 'Having eaten (meat), I go now.'
  I eat -⟨event⟩ go-now-⟨SgM⟩

Chapter 17

Adverbial Clauses

A subordinate clause may function as an adverb of manner, time, place, condition, purpose, and so forth, just as the adverbs discussed in section 5.12. The first syllable of a verb of an adverbial clause bears high tone; see section 3.12.1.

17.1 Purpose clauses

Adverbial clauses with -Ⓛ(kʰi) 'purpose' indicate the purpose for the event indicated by the main clause. Utterance finally -Ⓛkʰì is used; see examples 964a, 965, and 966. Utterance medially /-kʰi/ is usually omitted, but even when the segments are absent, the host's final syllable bears the low tone imposed by -Ⓛkʰi, and the host's penult bears high tone, as though /-kʰi/ were present;[1] see examples 964b and 967.

(964) a. Peeme ihjyávú icyúwaki.
   b. Peeme icyúwa ihjyávu.

$$\text{pʰɛ̀ː-mɛ̀} \atop \text{go-}\langle\text{AnPl}\rangle \begin{cases} \text{a. ì}^{\text{G}_\text{ʔ}} \quad \text{hʲá-βɯ́ɯ} \quad \text{ì} \quad \text{kʲʰɯ̋kpá-kʰɪ̀} \\ \quad \text{self house-goal self sleep-pur} \\ \text{b. ì} \quad \text{kʲʰɯ̋kpá-}\_\_ \quad \text{ì}^{\text{G}_\text{ʔ}} \quad \text{hʲá-βɯ̀ɯ} \\ \quad \text{self sleep-pur self house-goal} \end{cases}$$

a,b. 'They went to their house to sleep.'

---

[1] If an additional syllable follows the host, the low tones on the host's penultimate and final syllables violate the *LLX constraint.

(965) O péé tahjya o ímíbájchoki.

ò pʰɛ́:-ʔ [tʰá̂ʔ hʲà   ò ímípá༌ˣtʃʰò]-kʰì   'I go to fix
I go-⟨t⟩   my house I fix   -pur my house.'

(966) Mááhóvu oke daacu o májchoki.

má:ʔó-βɯ̀   ò-kʰɛ̀ t-à:kʰɯ̀   [ò máˣtʃʰò]-kʰì
cassava-goal I-objAn youImp-give I eat   -pur
'Give me some cassava so I can eat it.'

(967) Tahjya o ímíbájcho o pééhi.

[tʰá̂ʔ hʲà   ò ímípáˣtʃʰǒ]-_ ò pʰɛ́:-ʔì   'I go to fix my house.'
my house I fix-pur   I go-⟨t⟩

In 968a ì ɲɛ́ʔkʰò-kʰì bears the expected tones: high on the root's initial syllable and low preceding -ⓁkʰI 'purpose'. In 968b the initial syllable of ɲɛ́ʔkʰòtʰɛ́:pɛ̀ is high because of the Ⓛ imposed by -Ⓛtʰɛ̀ 'go to do' on the second syllable. In 968c, the first syllable of nɛ́ʔkʰò-βɯ̀ bears high tone because of the genitive low tone docked on the modifier's final syllable.

(968) a. Peebe úméhecóóné iñéhcoki.

pʰɛ̀-:pɛ̀ [úmɛ́-ʔɛ̀-kʰó:-nɛ́   ì   ɲɛ́ʔkʰò]-kʰì
go-⟨SgM⟩ tree-⟨tree⟩-⟨pole⟩-pl self hunting -pur

b. Úméhecóóne ñéhcotéébe.

[úmɛ́-ʔɛ̀-kʰó-:nɛ́   ɲɛ́ʔkʰò]-tʰɛ́-:pɛ̀
tree-⟨tree⟩-⟨pole⟩-pl hunting -go.do-⟨SgM⟩

c. Peebe úméhecóóne néhcovu.

pʰɛ̀-:pɛ̀ [úmɛ́-ʔɛ̀-kʰó-:nɛ̂   nɛ́ʔkʰò]-βɯ̀
go-⟨SgM⟩ tree-⟨tree⟩-⟨pole⟩-pl hunting -goal

a. 'He went to hunt for poles.'
b. 'He went to hunt poles.'
c. 'He went to the hunting of poles.'

The imperative verbs maho 'Let's (dual) go!' and mɛtsʰɯ 'Let's (plural) go!' take purpose complements. (See section 14.3.3 for further discussion.) For example:

(969) Métsu memájchoté(ki).

mɛ́tsʰɯ̀ [mɛ̀ máˣtʃʰò]-tʰɛ́-(kʰì)   'Let's go eat.'
let's   SAP eat   -go.do-pur

In 969 the high tone preceding -Ⓛkʰi is due to the low tone imposed by -ⓁtʰƐ 'go to do'; it blocks the Ⓛ of -Ⓛkʰì because its docking would violate

the *LLX constraint. Likewise, in 970, the high tone preceding -⒧kʰi is due to the lexically marked low of kpakʰimḛ́i.

(970) Peebe iúmɨhévú iwákímyeíki.

pʰɛ̀-ːpɛ̀   i̍ᴳ   úmɨ̀ʔɛ́-βɯ́ [ì   kpa̋kʰímʲɛ̰́i]-kʰì
go-⟨SgM⟩ self field-goal   self work   -pur
'He is going to his field to work.'

17.2 Conditional adverbial clauses

There are two types of conditional clauses: "normal" conditionals (17.2.1) and counterfactual conditionals (17.2.2).

17.2.1 "Normal" conditional clauses

"Normal" conditional adverbial clauses are formed with -ʔàhtʃʰíː(hʲɯ̀ɯ̀) (-hajchííjyu) 'if'. These indicate that the event of the main clause depends on that of the subordinate clause. Sentence finally -ʔàˣtʃʰíːhʲɯ̀ɯ̀ (-hajchííjyu) is used, as in 971, and sentence medially -ʔàˣtʃʰíː (-hajchíí) is used, as in 972.[2]

(971) Ó peé u ímílléhajchííjyu.

ó pʰɛ̀-ɛ́-ˀ   [ɯ̀   i̍mítʃɛ́ˢ]-ʔàˣtʃʰíːhʲɯ̀ɯ̀   'I will go if you wish.'
I go-fut-⟨t⟩   you want   -if

(972) U ímílléhajchíí úúma ó peéhi.

[ɯ̀   i̍mítʃɛ́ˢ]-ʔàˣtʃʰíː úɾ̀ː-mà   ó pʰɛ̀-ɛ́-ʔì   'If you wish, I will
you want   -if   you-with I go-fut-⟨t⟩   go with you.'

Embedded alternative questions are expressed using -ʔahtʃʰiihʲɯ̀ɯ̀, as in 973:

---

[2] A fuller version of 972 follows:

U ímílléhajchíí úúma ó peé díhjyávú memájchoki.

[ɯ̀   i̍mítʃɛ́ˢ]-ʔàˣtʃʰíː úɾ̀ː-mà   ó pʰɛ̀-ɛ́-ˀ   [tíˀ   ⒢ hʲá]-βɯ́
you want -if   you-with I go-fut-⟨t⟩   your   house -goal

[mɛ̀   ma̋ˣtʃʰò ˢ]-kʰì
SAP eat   -pur

'If you wish, I will go with you to your house to eat.'

(973) Tsá o wáájácutú diibye tsááhajchííjyu.

tsʰá̰ʔ ò kpá:kákʰɯ̀ɾ-tʰɯ́ɾ [tì-:pʲɛ̀   tsʰá̰:   ]-ʔà˟t͡ʃʰí:hʲɯ̀ɾ
not I know-neg   that-⟨SgM⟩ comes -if
'I do not know whether or not he is coming.'

17.2.2 Counterfactual conditional clauses

Counterfactual conditional clauses are formed with -kʰ⁽ʲ⁾a (-ca) 'if (contrary-to-fact)' (CF). Their underlying assumptions are: (1) the truth of the main clause depends crucially[3] on the truth of the conditional clause, (2) the conditional clause is false, and (3) therefore the main clause is false.

The verb of the main clause always bears -i 'future' and -ɾa ∼ -ɾo 'frustrative, contraexpectation'.[4] For example:

(974) U májchoca tsúúca ú tsɨ́jpanúiyáhi.

[ɯ̀ ma̰˟t͡ʃʰò]-kʰà tsʰɯ́ːkʰà ɯ́ tsʰɨ˟pʰànɯ́ɾ-ì-já-ʔì
 you eat   -CF already you be.strong-fut-frs-⟨t⟩
'If you had eaten, you would now be strong.'

(975) Teene u májchótuca tsá u chéméítyuró(ne).

[tʰɛ̰̀:-nɛ̀   ɯ̀ ma̰˟t͡ʃʰó-tʰɯ̀ɾ]-kʰà
 that-⟨ø⟩ you eat-neg   -CF

tsʰá̰ʔ ɯ̀ t͡ʃʰɛ́mɛ́-í-tʲʰɯ̀ɾ-ɾó-(nɛ̀)
not you be.ill-fut-neg-frs-⟨n⟩
'If you had not eaten that, you would not have taken ill.'

(976) ¿Aca ííímútuca meke pɨ́ááboíyóne?

à-kʰà   [ì ḭ́:mɯ́ɾ-tʰɯ̀ɾ   ]-kʰà
ques-doubt self be.savory-neg -CF

mɛ̀-kʰɛ̀   pʰɨ́á:pó-ì-jó-nɛ̀
SAP-objAn help-fut-frs-⟨ø⟩
'If it were not savory, would it help us?'

Note that the order of the main and subordinate clauses is reversed in 977:

---

[3]This is generally a *causal* dependence.
[4]This requirement—that the main verb bear both the future and the frustrative (contraexpectation) suffixes—negates the future possibility of the event of the main clause, thereby giving the counterfactual meaning.

(977) Ámuha muurá tsá oke mecáhcújtsóítyuró méénúráítyúronéhjɨ o méénuhíjcyátuca.

ámùɨʔà mùːɾáʔ tsʰáʰ⁽ᴴ⁾ ò-kʰɛ̀ mɛ̀ kʰáʔkʰúɾˣtsʰó-í-tʲʰùɨ-ɾó
youPl confirm not I-objAn SAP believe-fut-neg-frs

[mɛ̌ːnúɨ-ɾá-í-tʲʰúɨ-ɾò-nɛ́-ʔhɨ́ ò mɛ̌ːnùɨ-ʔ ɨˣkʲʰá-tʰùɨ]-kʰà
do-frs-fut-neg-frs-⟨ø⟩-pl I do-sub be-neg -CF

'If I had not done those unexpected things, you would not have believed me.'

17.3 Temporal adverbial clauses

Temporal adverbial clauses are formed by adding one of the following directly after the verb: -kʰoːkʰa (-cooca) 'when', -naa(ːkʰa) (-naaaca) 'while', -ihʲɯ (-ijyu) ⟨time⟩, -nɛ (-ne) ⟨event⟩.

-kʰoːkʰa 'when' and -ihʲɯ ⟨time⟩ indicate that the time of the main clause must wait for the completion of the event indicated by the subordinate clause. For example, in 978, their going to their house will happen only after they come:

(978) Ditye tsácooca peeímyé ihjyávu.

[tì-tʲʰɛ̀ tsʰáˢ]-kʰòːkʰà pʰɛ̀ː-í-mʲɛ́ ɨʔ⁽ᴳ⁾ hʲá-βùɨ
that-⟨AnPl⟩ come -when go-fut-⟨AnPl⟩ self house-goal

'When they come, they will go to their house.'

(979) Dííbyeke o ájtyúmɨijyu dííbyema ó ihjyúvaáhi.

[tíː-pʲɛ̀-kʰɛ̀ ò áˢˣtʲʰúmɨ́]-ihʲùɨ tíː-pʲɛ̀-mà
that-⟨SgM⟩-objAn I see- -⟨time⟩ that-⟨SgM⟩-with

ó ɨʔhʲúɨβà-á-ʔì
I speak-fut-⟨t⟩

'When I see him, I will speak to him.'

-naǎ(ːkʰa) (-náaáca) 'while' indicates that the event of the main clause happened during the time that the event of the subordinate clause was ongoing. Sentence finally -naǎːkʰa (-náaáca) is used, as in 980, and sentence medially -naǎ is used, as in 981.

(980) Tsaate ɬcú tsijtye ádónáaáca.
  tsʰà-ːtʰɛ̀   ɬːkʰɯ́ɾ-ʔ [tsʰǐ-ˣtʲʰɛ̀   átó   ]-náaákʰà
  one-⟨AnPl⟩ play-⟨t⟩ other-⟨AnPl⟩ drink -while
  'Some play while others drink.'

(981) Tsaate májchónáa tsijtye ɬcúhi.
  [tsʰà-ːtʰɛ̀   máˣt͡ʃʰó]-náá   tsʰì-ˣtʲʰɛ̀   ɬːkʰɯ́ɾ-ʔì
  one-AnPl eat   -while other-⟨AnPl⟩ play-⟨t⟩
  'While some eat, others play.'

-nɛ ⟨event⟩ may refer to time, indicating that the time of the main clause follows that of the subordinate clause. A case marker is not required, as in 982:[5]

(982) ì   máˣt͡ʃʰó-nɛ̀ pʰɛ̀-ːpɛ̀   (Imájchóne peébe.) 'He went after
  self eat-⟨event⟩ go-⟨SgM⟩   he ate.'

A case marker may follow -nɛ ⟨event⟩ to clarify the temporal relation. For example, -ma 'with' is added in 983:

(983) Aane imájchónema péjúcoóbe.
  àː-nɛ̀   [ì   máˣt͡ʃʰó]-nɛ̀-mà   pʰɛ́-hɯ́ɯkʰò-ːpɛ̀
  thm-⟨ø⟩ self eat   -⟨event⟩-with go-now-⟨SgM⟩
  'Then, in the circumstance of having eaten, he went.'

A temporal noun may follow: pòːnɛ 'after', íˑtɛ 'before' or ʔaˣt͡ʃʰotʰa 'duration'.[6] These words head a genitive construction; the modifier is the phrase (with subordinate clause) headed by -nɛ ⟨event⟩.

pòːnɛ 'after' indicates that the event of the main clause follows that of the subordinate clause:

(984) O májchóné boone o péjucóóhi.
  [[ò máˣt͡ʃʰó]-nɛ́[7]   ⓖ pòːnɛ̀] ò pʰɛ́-hɯ̀ɯkʰóː-ʔì
  I eat   -⟨event⟩   after   I go-now-⟨t⟩
  'After having eaten, I go now.'

Although the bracketed clause is *functionally* a time adverb, *structurally* it is a noun phrase headed by pòːnɛ 'after', as represented in figure 17.1.

---

[5] In 982 both syllables of maˣt͡ʃʰo 'eat' bear high tones, which is characteristic of -nɛ̀ ⟨event⟩; see section 16.3.

[6] There is also a classifier -ʔàˣt͡ʃʰótʰà that indicates temporal duration or spatial extension.

[7] The high tone on -nɛ is forced by the lexically marked tone of pòːnɛ, to avoid violating the *LLX constraint.

17.4. ADVERBIAL RELATIVE CLAUSES

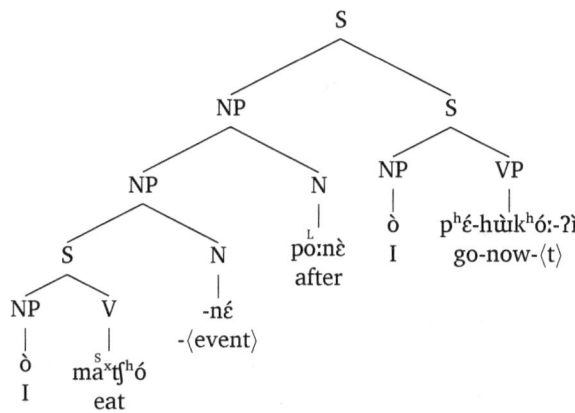

Figure 17.1 STR: O májchóné boone o péjucóóhi.

ɨ́ˀtɛ (ɨhde) 'before' (example 985) indicates that the event of the main clause precedes that of the subordinate clause, while ʔàˣt͡ʃʰóthà (hajchóta) 'duration' (example 986) indicates that the events of the main and subordinate persisted for the same length of time.

(985) O májchóíyóné ɨhde o péjucóóhi.

[[ò máˣt͡ʃʰó-í-jó]-né ⓖ ɨ́ˀtɛ̀] ò pʰɛ́-hùɪkʰó:-ʔì
I eat-fut-frs -⟨event⟩ before I go-now-⟨t⟩
'I go now, before eating.'

(986) O májchóné hajchótá cúwaábe.

[[ò máˣt͡ʃʰó]-né ʔáˣt͡ʃʰóthá] kʰúɪkpà-:pɛ̀
I eat -⟨event⟩ duration sleep-⟨SgM⟩
'He slept the whole time that I was eating.'

17.4 Adverbial relative clauses

What are *functionally* adverbial clauses may *structurally* be relative clauses headed by a classifier such as ⟨event⟩, ⟨place⟩, and so forth, and possibly followed by a case marker.

17.4.1 Place

Relative clauses headed by the locative classifiers -tsʰi(:) (-tsii ~ -tsih ~ -tsi) ⟨place⟩[8] and -ʔɯtʃɛ (-hulle) ⟨yonder⟩ may be used as locative adverbs. Examples follow:

(987) Iímíllétsii íjcyaábe.

[ì imítʃɛ́]-tsʰì: íˣkʲʰà-ːpɛ̀   'He is in the place that
self want -⟨place⟩ be-⟨SgM⟩   he likes.'

(988) Téhulle diibye iímíbáchohíjcyáhulle.

tʰɛ́-ʔɯ̀tʃɛ̀   tìːpʲɛ̀   [ì imípátʃʰòˀ íˣkʲʰá]-ʔɯ̀tʃɛ̀
that-⟨yonder⟩ that-⟨SgM⟩ self fix-sub   be   -⟨yonder⟩
'He is there where he always fixes things.'

Embedded clauses referring to place may indicate the source or goal of some motion using -β⁽ʲ⁾ɯ ~ -ɯ 'goal' or -tʰ⁽ʲ⁾ɯ 'source'. Examples follow:

(989) O péé tahmɨ́ɨ́né o ímíbájchótsihvu.

ò pʰɛ́ː-ˀ   [tʰáˀ mɨ́ːnɛ́ ò imípáˣtʃʰó]-tsʰìˀ-βɯ̀
I go-⟨t⟩ my canoe I fix   -⟨place⟩-goal
'I go to where I fix my canoe.'

(990) O tsáá teene o ímíbájchóhullétu.

ò tsʰáː-ˀ   [tʰɛ̀ː-nɛ̀ ò imípáˣtʃʰó]-ʔɯ̀tʃɛ́-tʰɯ̀
I come-⟨t⟩ this-⟨ø⟩ I fix   -⟨yonder⟩-sou
'I come from where I have fixed this.'

(991) O tsáá tahmɨ́ɨ́né o ímíbájchótsihdyu.

ò tsʰáː-ˀ   [tʰáˀ mɨ́ːnɛ́ ò imípáˣtʃʰó]-tsʰìˀ-tʲɯ̀
I come-⟨t⟩ my canoe I fix   -⟨place⟩-sou
'I come from where I am fixing my canoe.'

17.4.2 Causal adverbial clauses

-ɾi (-ri) 'inanimate oblique' may follow -nɛ ⟨event⟩ to indicate an event (action or state) that caused the event of the main clause, as in 992 and 993:

---

[8]Note that the length of -tsʰi(:) ⟨place⟩ is realized as [ˀ] before -β⁽ʲ⁾ɯ 'goal' and -tʰɯ 'source', as seen in 989 and 991.

17.4. ADVERBIAL RELATIVE CLAUSES

(992) Mítyane iwákímeíñeri táñahbe pávyeenúhi.

[mít^{jh}à-nɛ̀ ì k͡pȧ̊k^{h}ímɛ̋ í]-ɲɛ̀-ɾɩ̀   t^{h}á ⓖ ɲa̋-^{ʔ}pɛ̀
much-⟨ø⟩ self work   -⟨ø⟩-oblIn my   sib-⟨SgM⟩

p^{h}áβ^{j}ɛ̀:nɯ́-ʔɩ̀   'By working a lot, my brother tired.'
tire-⟨t⟩

(993) Mítyane iwákímeíñeri chémeébe.

[mít^{jh}à-nɛ̀ ì k͡pȧ̊k^{h}ímɛ̋ í-ɲɛ̀]-ɾɩ̀   t͡ʃ^{h}ɛ́mɛ̀-ːpɛ̀
much-⟨ø⟩ self work-⟨ø⟩   -oblIn be.ill-⟨SgM⟩

'He got sick by working a lot.'

17.4.3 Comparison and manner

What is structurally a relative clause headed by -tɯ (-du) ⟨like⟩ may be used as an adverbial clause indicating comparison or manner, as in 994–995:

(994) Ó imíllé dibye ímillédú o íjcyane.

ó ìmít͡ʃɛ́-^{ʔ} [[tì-p^{j}ɛ̀   ìmìt͡ʃɛ́]-tɯ́   ò i̊^{x}k^{jh}à]-nɛ̀
I want-⟨t⟩   that-⟨SgM⟩ want -⟨like⟩ I be   -⟨ø⟩

'I want to be like he wants (that I be).'

(995) O íhjyuvádu tsáh dibye íhjyúvatúne.

[ò i̊^{ʔ}h^{j}ɯ̀βá]-tɯ̀   ts^{h}a̋^{ʔ} tì-p^{j}ɛ̀   i̋^{ʔ}h^{j}ɯ̋βà-t^{h}ɯ́-nɛ̀
I talk   ⟨like⟩ not that-⟨SgM⟩ talk-neg-⟨n⟩

'He does not talk like I talk.'

When one thing is compared to another, the object of comparison may be a relative clause headed by the classifier that corresponds to that object, followed by -tɯ. For example, in 996 the relative clause is headed by -ha ⟨shelter⟩, followed by -tɯ. (In this case -tɯ functions more like a case marker than a classifier. See section 10.8 regarding comparatives.)

(996) Dibye méénujádú ó méénúiyáhi.

[tì-p^{j}ɛ̀   ø$_i$ mɛ̋ːnɯ̀]-há$_i$-tɯ́   ó mɛ́ːnɯ́-ì-já-ʔɩ̀
that-⟨SgM⟩ make   -⟨shelter⟩-like I make-fut-frs-⟨t⟩

'I want to make a house (shirt, pants,…) like he made (but I am in some way hindered from doing so).'

Chapter 18

Relative Clauses

Generally, a RELATIVE CLAUSE is a subordinate clause that modifies a noun, usually restricting the referent of that noun to those persons or things of which that clause is true. Bora has relative clauses, both restrictive and nonrestrictive (as in example 1011, page 386). Classifiers, as we shall see, play an important role in their formation.

In Bora, the initial syllable of the verb of a relative clause bears high tone. (This is true for all Bora subordinate clauses, but see the discussion with example 114.) For example, ǘkpá:pòpɛ̀ in the relative clauses in 997a and b bears high tone on the first syllable, as does ǘkpà:pónɛ̀ in the subordinate clause in 997c. By contrast, the nonfinite verb ùkpá:pò-:pɛ̀ in 997d does not bear high tone on its initial syllable; rather, it bears the nonfinite low tone that docks on the stem's antepenult. (See also example 132, page 102, and accompanying discussion.)

(997) a. Jóáake úwááboobe tsááhi.

[ø$_i$ hóáà-k^{h}ɛ̀   ǘkpá:pò]-:pɛ̀ $_i$ ts^{h}á:-ʔì
 John-objAn teach   -⟨SgM⟩ came-⟨t⟩

b. Diibye Jóáa úwááboobe tsááhi.

tì-:p^{j}ɛ̀ $_i$ Ⓐ [ø$_i$ hóáà ǘkpá:pò]-:pɛ̀ $_i$ ts^{h}á:-ʔì
that-⟨SgM⟩ Ⓐ   John teach   -⟨SgM⟩ came-⟨t⟩

c. Ó ájtumɨ́ Jóáa úwaabóne.

ó á^{x}t^{h}ùmɨ́-ʔ [hóáà ǘkpà:pó]-nɛ̀
I see-⟨t⟩   John teach   -⟨ø⟩

d. Diibye uwááboobe Jóáa tsááhi.

tì-ːpʲɛ̀ᵢ Ⓐ ṹkpá:pò-ːpɛ̀ᵢ Ⓐ hóáàᵢ tsʰá:-ʔì
that-⟨SgM⟩   teacher-⟨SgM⟩   John came-⟨t⟩

a. 'The one who$_i$ [ø$_i$ taught John] came.'
b. 'The one whom$_i$ [John taught ø$_i$] came.'
c. 'I see John teaching.'
d. 'He$_i$, the teacher$_i$, John$_i$, came.'

The noun modified by a relative clause must be understandable as having some semantic relation/role with respect to the modifying clause, since this makes it possible to assess the truth of the modifying clause since it pertains to the modified noun. In many cases the modified noun is understood as the subject of the modifying clause, as illustrated in example 997a. Such "subject relatives" are discussed in section 18.2.

In other cases, the modified noun is understood as having some role other than that of the subject of the modifying clause, as illustrated in example 997b above. Such cases are discussed in section 18.3.

Note that the relative clauses of 997a and b differ from complements, like the sensory verb complement in 997c, and from nonfinite verbs as in 997d.

However, before illustrating subject and non subject relative clauses, we will discuss various structural alternatives for relative clauses.

18.1 The structure of relative clauses

Bora relative clauses are always verb final, and always headed by a classifier following the verb. The noun or noun phrase that—in other languages—would head the relative clause, in Bora may stand in various relationships to the modifying clause with the following classifier. Four possibilities are represented in table 18.1. (The gap in the relative clause is represented by ø$_i$. This is coindexed with the classifier head and, if present, an overt coreferential NP. The verb of the subordinate clause bears a high tone on its first syllable, represented here by an s over the verb's initial syllable.)

18.1. THE STRUCTURE OF RELATIVE CLAUSES

Table 18.1 STR: relative clauses

a. basic relative
clause: [$_{NP}$ [$_S$...ø$_i$...[$_V$ ó̇...]]-[$_N$classifier$_i$]]
b. apposition: NP$_i$ Ⓐ [$_{NP}$ [$_S$...ø$_i$...[$_V$ ó̇...]]-[$_N$classifier$_i$]]
c. head-internal or
retained pronoun: [$_{NP}$ [$_S$...NP$_i$...[$_V$ ó̇...]]-[$_N$classifier$_i$]]
d. genitive
construction: [$_{NP}$ [$_S$...ø$_i$...[$_V$ ó̇...]] Ⓖ [$_N$classifier$_i$]]

Consider the noun or noun phrase that in other languages would head the relative clause.

a. In basic relative clauses there simply is no such noun phrase. For example, in 997a above, the relative clause is headed by the classifier -Ⓛ:pɛ ⟨SgM⟩, which is coindexed with a gap that corresponds to the direct object of the modifying clause, but there is no overt coreferential NP.

b. Frequently the noun or noun phrase that in other languages would head the relative clause *precedes* the relative clause. The relative clause is appositive to it. These are discussed in section 18.1.1.

c. Alternatively, the coreferential noun phrase may occur within the relative clause. These are discussed in section 18.1.2.

d. Finally, the relative clause may "possess" the head, employing the genitive construction. These are discussed in section 18.1.3.

18.1.1 Appositive embedded clauses

The relative clause in 998 is appositive to ò:ʔí:pʲɛ́kʰɛ̀ 'dog-objAn':[1]

(998) Ó ájtumɨ́ oohííbyéke oke ɨhdóóbeke.
    ó á^{x}tʰùmɨ́-ʔ [ò:ʔí-:pʲɛ́   ]-kʰɛ̀
    I see-⟨t⟩   dog-⟨SgM⟩ -objAn

    Ⓐ [ø$_i$ ò-kʰɛ̀   ɨ́ʔtó]-:pɛ̀-kʰɛ̀
       I-objAn bite   -⟨SgM⟩-objAn
    'I see the dog that bit me.'

---
[1] Compare 998 with example 1015, page 388, in which -Ⓛkʰɛ 'objAn' does not follow ò:ʔi:pʲɛ 'dog', and thus is the subject of the relative clause.

Compare the basic relative clause in 999 with the appositive relative clause in 1000:

(999) Ó ájtyumɨ́ áíívyeja.

    ó áˣtʲʰùmɨ́-ˀ [ø$_i$ áí-ːβʲɛ̀   ]-hà$_i$
    I see-⟨t⟩   burn-sIn -⟨shelter⟩
    'I saw a house that was burning.'

(1000) Ó ájtyumɨ́ tsaja jaá áiivyéne.

    ó áˣtʲʰùmɨ́-ˀ tsʰà-hà   Ⓐ [hàá áì-ːβʲɛ̀   ]-nɛ̀
    I see-⟨t⟩   one-⟨shelter⟩   house burn-sIn -⟨ø⟩
    'I saw a house burning.' (lit. 'I saw a shelter-like thing, a house that was burning.')

In 1001, the embedded clause ('that bit me') modifies the singular masculine classifier that follows it:[2]

(1001) Oohííbyé oke ɨ́hdoobe tsájucóóhi.

    òːʔí-ːpʲɛ́   ò-kʰɛ̀   ɨ́ʔtò-ːpɛ̀   tsʰá-hùɨkʰóː-ʔì
    dog-⟨SgM⟩ I-objAn bite-⟨SgM⟩ come-now-⟨t⟩
    'The dog that bit me is coming.'

Example 1001 is structurally ambiguous between the following alternatives:

1. òːʔí-ːpʲɛ́ 'dog' is a preverbal subject within the subordinate clause, while the classifier heads the phrase:

(1002) oohííbyé oke ɨ́hdoóbe ...

    [òːʔí-ːpʲɛ́$_i$ ò-kʰɛ̀   ɨ́ʔtò]-ópɛ̀$_i$ 'the dog that
    dog-⟨SgM⟩ I-objAn bite -⟨SgM⟩   bit me...'

Recall that a classifier subject may not co-occur with an overt, preverbal subject. (See page 129.) However, 1002 satisfies this condition because -Ⓛːpɛ ⟨SgM⟩ is not the subject of the subordinate clause, but heads the relative clause, occurring outside of that clause.

2. òːʔí-ːpʲɛ́ 'dog' heads the noun phrase, which is modified by an appositive, postnominal relative clause (itself headed by a classifier):

(1003) oohííbyé oke ɨ́hdoobe ...

    òːʔí-ːpʲɛ́$_i$ Ⓐ [ò-kʰɛ̀   ɨ́ʔtò]-ːpɛ̀$_i$ 'the dog that bit me...'
    dog-⟨SgM⟩   I-objAn bite -⟨SgM⟩

---

[2] The following is given for comparison:
    òːʔí-ːpʲɛ́   ò-kʰɛ̀   ɨ́ʔtó-ʔì   (Oohííbyé oke ɨ́hdóhi.) 'The dog bit me.'
    dog-⟨SgM⟩ I-objAn bite-⟨t⟩

18.1. THE STRUCTURE OF RELATIVE CLAUSES

While for 1001 there seems to be no evidence in favor of one or the other of these analyses, sometimes there is evidence in the form of a second-position clitic. For example, in 1004 the remote past marker follows ò:ʔi:pʲɛ̌ 'dog'. This strongly suggests that this noun is not within the modifying clause, but rather that it and the modifying clause are in apposition. If, however, the second-position clitic follows the clause, as in 1005, this strongly suggest that ò:ʔi:pʲɛ̌ 'dog' is within the modifying clause.

(1004) Oohííbyée oke ɨ́hdoobe cheméhi.

    ò:ʔí-:pʲɛ̌-ɛ̱ $^{H\ L}$ Ⓐ [∅$_i$ ò-kʰɛ̀   ɨ́ʔtò ^{Sʔ}]-:pɛ̀$_i$ ʧʰɛ̀mɛ́-ʔɨ̀
    dog-⟨SgM⟩-rem   I-objAn bite   -⟨SgM⟩ be.ill-⟨t⟩

'The dog that bit me (some time ago[3]) is sick.'

(1005) Oohííbye oke ɨ́hdoobée cheméhi.

    [ò:ʔí-:pʲɛ̀   ò-kʰɛ̀   ɨ́ʔtò ^{Sʔ}]-:pɛ̀-ɛ̱ $^{H\ L}$ ʧʰɛ̀mɛ́-ʔɨ̀
    dog-⟨SgM⟩ I-objAn bite   -⟨SgM⟩-rem be.ill-⟨t⟩

'The dog that bit me (some time ago) is sick.'

In 1006a tsʰɨ́:ménèkʰɛ̀ 'child (object)' is the object of tʰa:po 'cure' and thus within the relative clause, but in 1006b, in which -kʰɛ is absent, tsʰɨ́:ménè is the subject of the main clause:

(1006) a. [[Tsɨ́ɨ́méneke] dibye tááborotsɨ] dsɨ́jɨvéhi.

    b. [Tsɨ́ɨ́méne] [dibye tááborotsɨ] dsɨ́jɨvéhi.

tsʰɨ́:ménè   { a. -kʰɛ̀
child   -objAn
              b. -∅ }

tì-pʲɛ̀   tʰá:pó-ɾò-tsʰɨ̀ ^{S} tsɨ́hɨ̀βɛ́-ʔɨ̀
that-⟨SgM⟩ cure-frs-⟨child⟩ die-⟨t⟩

a,b 'The child that he treated died.'

---

[3] Curiously, the remote past tense marked on the first constituent of 1004 applies to "biting" rather than "being sick."

In 1007 the modified noun is tì:pʲɛ̀ 'he'.[4]

(1007) Ááneri diibye oohííbyeke dsɨ́jɨ́vétsoobe núcójpɨ̈véhi.
á:-nè-rì   tì-:pʲɛ̀$_i$ Ⓐ [ø$_i$ ò:ʔí-:pʲɛ̀-kʰɛ̀
that-⟨ø⟩-oblIn that-⟨SgM⟩   dog-⟨SgM⟩-objAn

tsɨ̆híβɛ́-tsʰò]-:pɛ̀$_i$ nɯ́ɯ̆kʰóˣpʰɨ̈-:βɛ́-ʔì
die-caus   -⟨SgM⟩   be.ashamed-sIn-⟨t⟩
'The one who killed the dog became ashamed.'

Example 1008 is similar, where the indefinite pronoun tsʰà-:pʰì 'one (SgM)' is followed by an appositive relative clause:

(1008) Íjcyaabée tsaapi Jóáa imyéme íjcyaábe.
ɨ́ˣkʲʰà-:pɛ̆$_i$-ɛ̀   Ⓐ [$_{NP}$tsʰà-:pʰì   Ⓐ [$_{NP}$ [$_S$hóáà [ɨ̂ mʲɛ́mɛ̀]
be-⟨SgM⟩-rem   one-⟨SgM⟩   John self name

ɨ̆ˣkʲʰà]-ápɛ̀]
be   -⟨SgM⟩
'There was a man named John.'

Compare 1008 to 1009, in which two noun phrases are in apposition within a noun phrase marked for case by -kʰɛ 'objAn', as represented in figure 18.1.

(1009) Ó ájtumɨ́ tsaapi Jóáa imyéme íjcyáábeke.
ó áˣtʰɯ̀mɨ́-ʔ [tsʰà-:pʰì   Ⓐ [$_{NP}$ [$_S$[hóáà [ɨ̂ mʲɛ́mɛ̀]
I see-⟨t⟩   one-⟨SgM⟩   John self name

ɨ̂ˣkʲʰá]-:pɛ̀   ]-kʰɛ̀
be   -⟨SgM⟩ -objAn
'I saw one (male) whose name is John.'

---
[4]Functionally tì:pʲɛ̀ is a pronoun, but its internal structure is that of a noun phrase: it is a demonstrative adjective that modifies a noun.

18.1. THE STRUCTURE OF RELATIVE CLAUSES

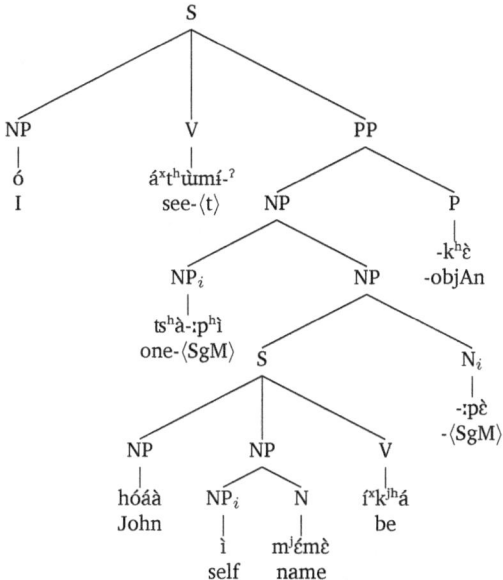

Figure 18.1 STR: Ó ájtumɨ́ tsaapi Jóáa imyéme íjcyáábeke.

In 1010 (below), tì-ːpʲɛ̀ does not bear -Ⓛkʰɛ 'objAn'. This might lead one to feel that it is the subject of the subordinate clause. However, note that tì-ːpʲɛ̀ has long vowel; if it were the subject, this should be shortened, as explained in section 8.1.1. Thus, it is not the subject, but is appositive to the relative clause, but within the scope (c-command domain) of -Ⓛkʰɛ 'objAn':[5]

---

[5]The following example is similar to 1010 but differs in that (1) the case marker on the subordinate clause is different, and (2) the main verb is transitive in 1010 but intransitive in the following:

Árónáa diibye oohííbyeke dsɨ́jɨ́vétsóóbedi ɨ́dáátsovéme.
á-ró-náà [tì-ːpʲɛ̀ Ⓐ [òːʔɨ́-ːpʲɛ̀-kʰɛ̀
thm-frs-while that-⟨SgM⟩ dog-⟨SgM⟩-objAn

tsɨhíβɛ́-tsʰó]-ːpɛ̀]-tì ɨ́táːtsʰò-βɛ́-mɛ̀
die-caus -⟨SgM⟩ -anim.sou pity-sIn-⟨AnPl⟩
'But they pitied the one who killed the dog.'

(1010) Árónáa diibye oohííbyeke dsɨ́jɨ́vétsóóbeke ɨ́daatsólléme.
á-ró-náà   [tì-ːpʲɛ̀   Ⓐ [NP [S ∅ᵢ òːʔí-ːpʲɛ̀-kʰɛ̀
thm-frs-while that-⟨SgM⟩   dog-⟨SgM⟩-objAn

tsɨhíβɛ́-tsʰó]-ːpɛ̀ᵢ]]-kʰɛ̀   ɨ́tàːtsʰó-tʃɛ́-mɛ̀
die-caus   -⟨SgM⟩   -objAn pity-treat.as-⟨AnPl⟩
'But they pitied the one who killed the dog.'

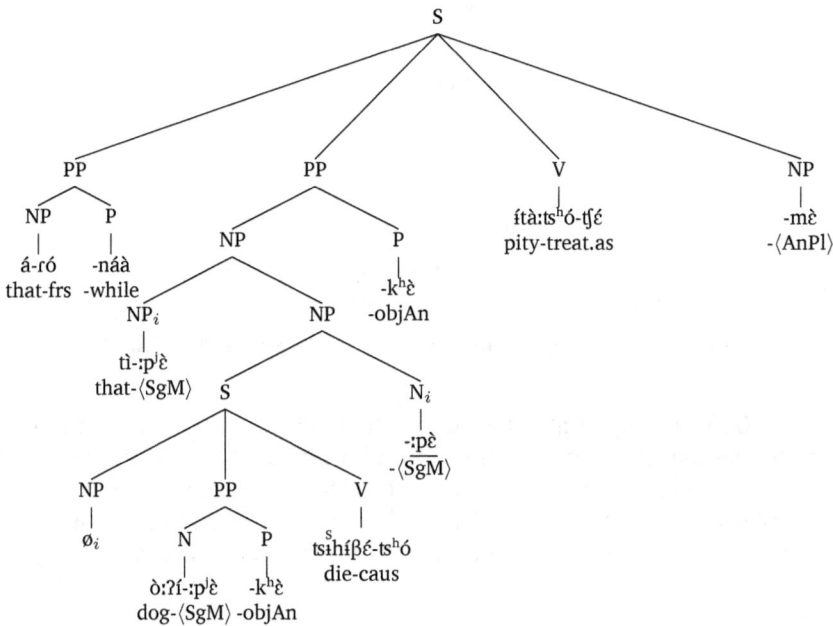

Figure 18.2 STR: Árónáa diibye oohííbyeke dsɨ́jɨ́vétsóóbeke ɨ́daatsólléme.

An appositive relative clause may be nonrestrictive, as in 1011:

(1011) Nɑníyo ávyeta kéémejúcóóroobe paíjyuváré wákímyeíhijcyáhi.
nàníjò Ⓐ [áβʲɛ̀tʰà   kʰɛ̀ːmɛ́-húɪkʰóː-ɾò]-ːpɛ̀
uncle   very.much be.old-now-frs   -⟨SgM⟩

pʰà-íhʲùβá-ɾɛ́ kpákʰímʲèí-ʔ ìˣkʲʰá-ʔì
all-day-only   work-sub   be-⟨t⟩
'My uncle, although he is now very old, works every day.'

18.1. THE STRUCTURE OF RELATIVE CLAUSES

Examples 1012–1014 further illustrate appositive relative clauses in the a. sentences, each case accompanied by a nonappositive alternative in the b. sentences.[6]

(1012) a. Diibye ditye úwááboobe waajácú páneére.
  b. Dííbyeke ditye úwááboobe waajácú páneére.

  a. tì-ːpʲɛ̀$_i$ Ⓐ [ø$_i$ tì-t^{jh}ɛ̀   ɯ̀kpáːpò^S]-ːpɛ̀$_i$
     that-⟨SgM⟩   that-⟨AnPl⟩ teach   -⟨SgM⟩
  b. [tí-ːpʲɛ̀$_i$-k^{h}ɛ̀   tì-t^{jh}ɛ̀   ɯ̀kpáːpò^S]-ːpɛ̀$_i$
     that-⟨SgM⟩-objAn that-⟨AnPl⟩ teach   -⟨SgM⟩

  kpàːhák^{h}ɯ́ɯ̀ p^{h}á-nɛ̀-ːɾɛ̀
  know   much-⟨ø⟩-only
  a,b. 'The one whom they taught knows everything.'

(1013) a. Ímí teene pááa dibye májchone.
  b. Pááa dibye májchone ímí nééneé.

  a. ímí^ʔ t^{h}ɛ̀ː-nɛ̀ Ⓐ [p^{h}áːà$_i$ tì-pʲɛ̀   má^{x}tʃ^{h}ò^S]-nɛ̀$_i$
     good that-⟨ø⟩   bread that-⟨SgM⟩ eat   -⟨ø⟩

  b. [p^{h}áːà$_i$ tì-pʲɛ̀   má^{x}tʃ^{h}ò^S]-nɛ̀$_i$ ímí^ʔ néː-nɛ̀ɛ́
     bread that-⟨SgM⟩ eat   -⟨ø⟩ good say-⟨ø⟩
  a,b. 'The bread that he ate was good.'

(1014) a. Pɨ́pá tétsii dibye pááa májchotsíi.
  b. Pááa di-bye májchotsíi pɨpáhre.
  a. p^{h}ɨ́p^{h}á^ʔ
     wet

  t^{h}ɛ́-ts^{h}ìː   Ⓐ [tì-pʲɛ̀   p^{h}áːà má^{x}tʃ^{h}ò]-ts^{h}îi
  that-⟨place⟩   that-⟨SgM⟩ bread eat   -⟨place⟩

  b. [p^{h}áːà tì-pʲɛ̀   má^{x}tʃ^{h}ò]-ts^{h}îi p^{h}ɨ̀p^{h}á-^{ʔ}ɾɛ̀
     bread that-⟨SgM⟩ eat   -place wet-only
  a,b. 'The place where he ate the bread was wet.'

18.1.2 Relative clauses with an internal coreferent

A noun phrase coreferential with the head may occur within the relative clause. Sometimes this noun phrase is a noun, in which case this is similar

---

[6]Example 327, page 165, corresponds to 1012 but with relativization into the subject rather than object.

to the "internally-headed" relative clauses of other languages, and sometimes it is a pronoun (usually headed by the same classifier that heads the relative clause), in which case this is similar to a "pronoun retention" strategy. We will consider these two possibilities in turn.

In 1015 the clause internal argument coreferential to the head is ò:ʔí:pʲɛ́ 'dog'. (Compare 998, page 381, and the discussion therewith.)

(1015) Ó ájtumɨ́ oohííbyé oke ɨ́hdóóbeke.

ó áˣtʰùmɨ́-ˀ [ò:ʔí-:pʲɛ́ᵢ ò-kʰɛ̀ ɨ̀ˀtó]-:pɛ̀ᵢ-kʰɛ̀
I see-⟨t⟩   dog-⟨SgM⟩ I-objAn bite -⟨SgM⟩-objAn
'I see the dog that bit me.'

In many cases such a clause internal argument is a pronoun, as is the case for ɛ̀:kpà 'that plank' in 1016:

(1016) Oke daacu eewa ééjá lliiñe íjcyawávu.

ò-kʰɛ̀   t-à:kʰɨ̀ɨ̀   [ɛ̀:-kpàᵢ   Ⓐ
I-objAn youImp-give that-⟨slab⟩

[[ɛ́:-há   Ⓖ tʃɨ́:ɲɛ̀] ɨ́ˣkʲʰà]-kpáᵢ]-βɨ̀ɨ̀
  that-⟨shelter⟩   below   be   -⟨slab⟩ -thm
'Give me the plank that is under that house.'

ɛ̀:kpà 'that plank' is a pronoun, and the relative clause of 1016 manifests a pronoun retention strategy. (This is an effective strategy for relativizing into difficult positions; see Keenan & Comrie (1977).) In Bora this is a very effective strategy because the "pronouns" are so specific, being formed from a pronominal root and one of over 300 classifiers.

18.1.3 Relative clauses possessing their head

Consider the noun phrase in 1017, taken from The Creator's Daughter (sentence 51).

(1017) ...ámúhtsikyéne o wáñehjɨ́núíyóné ijtyámú...

[ₙₚ [sámɨ́ɨ̀ˀtsʰɨ̀-kʲʰɛ́-nɛ̀   ò kpáɲɛ̀ʔhɨ́-nɨ́ɨ́-í-jó]-nɛ́]
     you.DuM-objAn-?? I festival-do-fut-frs -⟨∅⟩

ɨ́ˣtʲʰá-mɨ́ɨ́
starch-plAn

'...the starch with which I would have honored you with a festival...'

Here the relative clause "possesses" the following "head" in a genitive construction. This is evident from the tones: the head is trisyllabic (the pluralizer counting as part of the stem) so the genitive tone docks on the head's initial syllable. The semantic relationship between the modifier (possessor) and the head is precisely that seen in the noun phrase [kpàɲɛ́ʔhí ^{G}íˣtʲhá-mùɨ] (festival starch-pl) 'starch for a festival', in which the head's referent is an object (starch) used in the event indicated by the modifier (the festival).

Casting the relative clause as the modifier (possessor) in a genitive construction is reserved for cases where the "head" has an oblique relationship to the modifying clause. That is, it is not used when the "head" is the subject, the direct object, or the theme (possibly the indirect object) of the modifying clause.

18.2 Relativizing into subjects

This section deals with "subject relatives," that is ones for which the modified noun is understood as the subject of the modifying clause. For example, consider the simple clause in 1018:

(1018) Mítyane wákímeííbye.
  mítʲhà-nɛ̀ kpákhímɛ̀í-ːpʲɛ̀   'He works a lot.'
  much-adv work-⟨SgM⟩

Such a clause may be embedded as a noun phrase, referring to its subject, as in 1019–1021. In each case the modified "noun" is the classifier that follows.

(1019) Mítyane wákímeííbye tsájucóóhi.
  [mítʲhà-nɛ̀ ∅$_i$ kpá̊khímɛ̀í]-ːpʲɛ̀$_i$ tshá-hùɨkhóː-ʔì
  much-adv   work   -⟨SgM⟩ come-now-⟨t⟩
  'The one who works a lot comes now.'

(1020) Téhulle wákímyeíhíjcyaabe tsááhií.
  [thɛ́-ʔùɨtʃɛ̀   ∅$_i$ kpá̊khímʲɛ̀í-ˀ íˣkʲhà]-ːpʲɛ̀$_i$ tsháː-ʔìː
  that-⟨yonder⟩   work-sub be- ⟨SgM⟩ come-⟨t⟩-emph
  'The one who always works over there came.'

(1021) Oohííbyeke dsíjívétsoobe tsúúca péjucóó ihjyávu.
  [∅$_i$ òːʔí-ːpʲɛ̀-khɛ̀   tsɨ́híβɛ́-tshò]-ːpɛ̀$_i$
    dog-⟨SgM⟩-objAn die-caus   -⟨SgM⟩

tsʰúː:kʰà pʰɛ́-hùɾkʰóː-ʔì ǐ⁽ᴳ⁾ hʲá-βùɾ
already go-now-⟨t⟩   self house-goal
'The one who killed the dog has now gone to his house.'

In both 1022 and 1023 the relative clause is the direct object of the main clause (but nonetheless relativizes into the subject):

(1022) Mítyane wákímeííbyeke ó ahdóhi.

[ø$_i$ mítʲʰà-nɛ̀ kpa̋kʰímɛ̀í]-:pʲ$_i$ɛ̀-kʰɛ̀   ó à'tó-ʔì
    much-adv work   -⟨SgM⟩-objAn I pay-⟨t⟩

'I paid the man who worked a lot.'

(1023) Oohííbyeke dsɨ́jɨ́vɛ́tsóóbeke ó uhbáhi.

[ø$_i$ ò:ʔí-:pʲɛ̀-kʰɛ̀   tsɨ̋híβɛ́-tsʰó]-:pɛ̀$_i$-kʰɛ̀   ó ùɾ'pá-ʔì
    dog-⟨SgM⟩-objAn die-cause   -⟨SgM⟩-objAn I upbraid-⟨t⟩

'I upbraided the one who killed the dog.'

In 1024, the embedded clause is the benefactee (in a rather extended sense) of the main clause. (Compare 1023.)

(1024) Oohííbyeke dsɨ́jɨ́vɛ́tsóóbedítyú tsijtye ihjyúváhi.

[ø$_i$ ò:ʔí-:pʲɛ̀-kʰɛ̀   tsɨ̋híβɛ́-tsʰó]-:pɛ̀$_i$-tí-tʲʰúɾ
    dog-⟨SgM⟩-objAn die-cause   -⟨SgM⟩-anim-sou

tsʰì-ˣtʲʰɛ̀   ì'hʲúɾβá-ʔì
other-⟨AnPl⟩ speak-⟨t⟩

'Others spoke about the one who killed the dog.'

In 1025, the embedded clause is a "co-subject" of the main clause. Note that the full pronoun in the relative clause is coreferential with the sentence's subject.[7]

(1025) Dííbyema wákímeíbyema péjúcoóbe.

[ø$_i$ tí-:pʲɛ̀$_k$-mà   kpa̋kʰímɛ̀í]-:pʲɛ̀$_i$-mà   pʰɛ́-hùɾkʰò-:pɛ̀$_k$
    that-⟨SgM⟩-with work   -⟨SgM⟩-with go-now-⟨SgM⟩

'He$_k$ went with the one$_i$ who works with him$_k$.'

---

[7]There are sufficient structural barriers between the subject and the pronoun (both indexed k) so that the former may bind the latter without violating the principle that a pronoun must be free in its governing category.

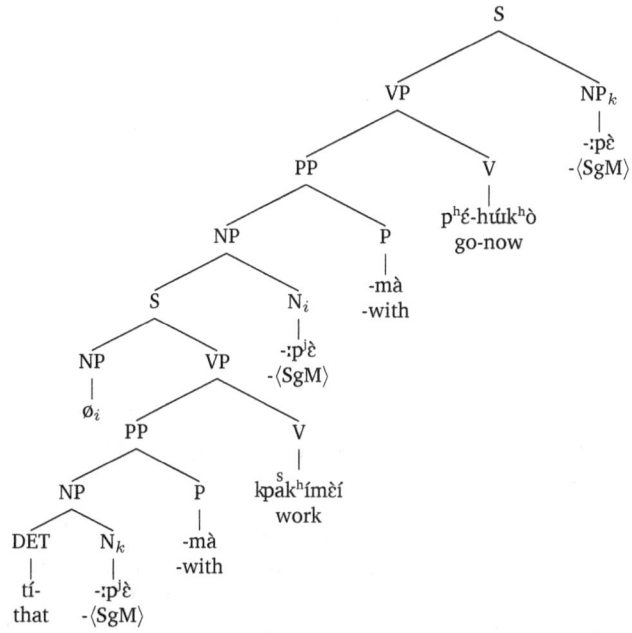

Figure 18.3 STR: Dííbyema wákímeíbyema péjúcoóbe.

Other examples of relativization into the subject follow.

(1026) Diibye pááa májchoobe péjucóó.

tì-ːpʲɛ̀ Ⓐ [∅ᵢ pʰáːà ma̋ˣʧʰò]-ːpɛ̀ᵢ pʰɛ́-hɯ̀ɯ̀kʰóː-ʔì
that-⟨SgM⟩ bread eat -⟨SgM⟩ go-now-⟨t⟩

'He that ate the bread has gone.'

(1027) Tsíímeke muha meúwaabómé tsá tsíñéhjɨri meíjcyatúne.

[tsʰɨ́ːmɛ̀-kʰɛ̀ mɯ̀ʔà mɛ̀ ɯ́kpàːpó]-mɛ́ tsʰa̋ʔ
children-objAn we SAP teach -⟨AnPl⟩ not

tsʰɨ́-ɲɛ́-ˀhɨ́-rì mɛ̀ íˣkʲʰà-tʰɯ́ɯ̀-nɛ̀
other-⟨ø⟩-pl-oblIn SAP be-neg-⟨n⟩

'We who teach children do not get involved in other things.'

18.3 Relativizing into nonsubject positions

The relative clauses above have been "into" the subject position, that is, the head is understood to be coreferential with the subject of the modifying clause. However, relativization is not limited to such cases. In 1028

relativization is into the direct object. Compare this to 1029, in which relativization is into the subject.

(1028) Táñahbe májchótsoobe péjucóóhi.

[tʰá ⓖ ɲá-ʔpɛ̀ ⓛ ø$_i$ mã^{sx}tʃʰó-tsʰò]-ːpɛ̀$_i$ pʰɛ́-hɯ̀kʰóː-ʔì
my sib-⟨SgM⟩ eat-caus -⟨SgM⟩ go-now-⟨t⟩

'The one (SgM) that my brother fed has now gone.'

(1029) Táñáhbeke májchótsoobe péjucóóhi.

[ø$_i$ tʰá ⓖ ɲá-ʔpɛ̀-kʰɛ̀ mã^{sx}tʃʰó-tsʰò]-ːpɛ̀$_i$
my sib-⟨SgM⟩-objAn eat-caus -⟨SgM⟩

pʰɛ́-hɯ̀kʰóː-ʔì
go-now-⟨t⟩

'The one (SgM) that fed my brother has now gone.'

Example 1030 also illustrates relativization into the direct object. The relative clause in 1030a is headed by -ːpɛ ⟨SgM⟩, coreferential to the dog. Because it is animate -ti 'animate' must follow, and the internal coreferent bears -ⓛkʰɛ 'objAn'. By contrast, the relative clause in 1030b is headed by -nɛ ⟨ø⟩ (presumably because there is no more-specific classifier for bread), satisfying the structural requirements for a classifier head, and the internal coreferent, being inanimate, does not bear the object marker.

(1030) a. Táñahbe oohííbyeke iájtyúmɨ́ɨbedívú oke ajcúhi.
 b. Táñahbe pááa iájtyúmɨnévú oke ajcúhi.

tʰá ⓖ ɲá-ʔpɛ̀$_k$ { a. [òːʔíːpʲɛ̀$_i$-kʰɛ̀
my sib-⟨SgM⟩   dog-⟨SgM⟩-objAn
                      b. [pʰáːà$_i$
                         bread

ì$_k$ ã^{sx}tʲʰɯ́mí]-ːpɛ̀$_i$-tí-βɯ́ɯ̀
self find   -⟨SgM⟩-anim-thm   } òkʰɛ̀ à^{x}kʰɯ́ɯ̀-ʔì
ì$_k$ ã^{sx}tʲʰɯ́mì]-nɛ́$_i$-βɯ́ɯ̀   I-objAn give-⟨t⟩
self find   -⟨ø⟩-thm

'My brother$_k$ gave me { a. the dog he$_k$ found },
                         b. the bread he$_k$ found

Further examples of relativization into the direct object follow. (See also 366, page 178.)

18.3. RELATIVIZING INTO NONSUBJECT POSITIONS

(1031) Óóma u dsɨ́jcójama ó peé wañéhjɨvu.
[ó:-mà ùɨ ø$_i$ tsɨ́^{x}k^{h}ó]-<u>hà</u>$_i$-mà^8
I-with you   sew   -⟨shelter⟩-with

ó p^{h}ɛ̀-ɛ́-$^?$ kpàɲɛ́$^?$hɨ̀-βùɨ
I go-fut-⟨t⟩ festival-goal
'I will go to the festival with the clothes (shirt, pants,...) you sewed for me.'

(1032) Táwajyámúu o dsɨ́jcoja tsúúca nójcanúhi.
[t^{h}á Ⓖ kpȁh^{j}ámǜ-ɨ̀]$_i$ Ⓐ [ò ø$_i$ tsɨ́^{x}k^{h}ò]-<u>hà</u>$_i$
my   clothes-rem   I   sew   -⟨shelter⟩

ts^{h}ɨ́ːk^{h}à nó^{x}k^{h}ànɨ́-ʔì
already deteriorate-⟨t⟩
'The clothes that I sewed are now deteriorated.'

Recall that we claimed in section 10.3.2 that a^{x}k^{h}ɯ 'give' obligatorily undergoes inversion, the recipient being marked as a direct object and the theme (what is given) being marked with -βɯ 'goal'. After inversion, it is possible to relativize into the direct object (the recipient); if the theme (what is given) is expressed, it is marked with -βɯ 'goal', as in 391, page 190. Likewise, it is possible to relativize into the direct object (theme, what is given); if expressed, the recipient is marked as a direct object. This is illustrated in examples 1033–1035:[9]

(1033) Okée u ájcúwari ó wákímyeíhi.
[ò-k^{h}ɛ̀-ɛ́   ùɨ   ø$_i$ a^{x}k^{h}ɨ́ɨ]-kpà$_i$-rì   ó kpák^{h}ím^{j}èí-ʔì
I-objAn-rem you give   -⟨slab⟩-oblIn I work-⟨t⟩
'I am working with the machete (plank,...) that you gave me (some time ago).'

(1034) Okée u ájcúwatu ó meenú llééhowa.
[ò-k^{h}ɛ̀-ɛ́   ùɨ   ø$_i$ a^{x}k^{h}ɨ́ɨ]-kpà$_i$-t^{h}ùɨ ó mɛ̀ːnɨ́-ʔì
I-objAn-rem you give   -⟨slab⟩-sou I make-⟨t⟩

tʃɛ́ːʔò-kpà
door-⟨slab⟩
'I made a door with the plank you gave me (some time ago).'

---

[8]In 1031 -ma 'with' is used rather than -ri 'inanimate oblique', probably because one would not ordinarily put on his new clothes until arriving at the festival; that is, he would go—as it were—in the company of his new clothes. (This observation was made by Eva Thiesen, personal communication.)

[9]See also example 438, 203.

(1035) Cáraca táñáhbeke o ájcuube dsíjɨvéhi.

kʰáràkʰà Ⓐ [[tʰá Ⓖ ɲá-ˀpɛ̀   ]-kʰɛ̀   ∅ᵢ ò ǎˣkʰɯ̀]-ːpɛ̀ᵢ
chicken   my   sib-⟨SgM⟩ -objAn   I give   -⟨SgM⟩

tsɨ́hɨ̀βɛ́-ʔɨ̀
die-⟨t⟩
'The chicken that I gave my brother died.'

Chapter 19

Some Comments on Discourse

In this chapter we discuss the form and use of the the thematic connectives (19.1), make an observation on defining context (19.2), and comment on ellipsis (19.3).

19.1 The thematic connective

In connected discourse, each sentence except the first usually begins with a connective that indicates the relevance of that sentence to the context. The connective is the sentence's thematic link to the preceding discourse, particularly to the preceding sentence.

19.1.1 The form of connectives

The connectives are formed with a(:)- (*aa-*) 'thematic' and at least one following morpheme. When a(:)- is followed by a classifier the connective functions as a pronominal, and may serve as an argument of the verb of the main clause. The formation of pronominal connectives is discussed in section 19.1.1.1. When a(:)- is followed by a classifier referring to time, place, (and so forth) the connective functions as an adverb; these are discussed in section 19.1.1.2.

19.1.1.1 Pronominal connectives

(Pro)nominal connectives refer to some participant in the preceding context. There are two types: animate and inanimate. The animate pronominal connectives are given in table 19.1.

Table 19.1 Animate thematic pronouns (connectives)

	singular	dual	plural
masculine	à:-pɛ̀ (aábe) 'he'	à:-mútsʰɨ̀ (aamútsi) 'those two (masc.)'	à:-mɛ̀ (aáme) 'they'
feminine	à:-tʃɛ̀ (aálle) 'she'	à:-mútpʰɨ̀ (aamúpɨ) 'those two (fem.)'	

The inanimate connectives are formed with a(:)- 'thematic' and an inanimate classifier.[1] The classifier may be followed by -:kʰɯ 'duIn' or -⁽ˀ⁾hɨ 'plural'. Examples follow.

(1036) a. à:-ʔɛ̀   (aahe)   'that tree'
         thm-⟨tree⟩
    b. á-ʔɛ̀:-kʰɯ̀   (áheécu) 'those two trees'
         thm-⟨tree⟩-du
    c. á-ʔɛ̀-ˀhɨ   (áhehjɨ) 'those trees'
         thm-⟨tree⟩-pl

(1037) a. à:-kpà   (aawa)   'that slab (plank, bench,
         thm-⟨slab⟩   machete,...)'
    b. á-kpà-:kʰɯ̀   (áwaacu) 'those two slabs (planks,
         thm-⟨slab⟩-du   tables, machetes,...)'
    c. á-kpà-ˀhɨ   (áwahjɨ) 'those slabs (planks,
         thm-⟨slab⟩-pl   benches, machetes,...)'

(1038) a. á-ʔà:mɨ̀   (áhaámɨ)   'that leaf (paper, book,...)'
         thm-⟨leaf⟩
    b. á-ʔà:mɨ́-kʰɯ̀   (áhaamɨ́cu) 'those two leaves (paper,
         thm-⟨leaf⟩-du   book,...)'
    c. á-ʔà:mɨ́-hɨ   (áhaamɨ́jɨ) 'those leaves (papers,
         thm-⟨leaf⟩-pl   books,...)'

---

[1] Because these are inanimate, they never bear -⟨L⟩kʰɛ 'objAn' nor -⁽ˀ⁾ti 'benefactive'.

19.1.1.2 Adverbial connectives

Adverbial connectives refer to the preceding event or to the situation or circumstance resulting from it. Within the clause initiated by the connective, it functions as an adverb, referring to manner, time, place, duration, distance, degree, reason, and so forth. (Note, although these *function* as adverbs, *structurally* they are nominals.) Table 19.2 lists some of the more common adverbial connectives:

Table 19.2 Common adverbial connectives

à-ʔtùù thm-⟨like⟩	(ahdu)	'in that way'
á-ìhʲùù thm-⟨time⟩	(áijyu)	'at that time'
áː-nɛ́-tʃìː thm-⟨ø⟩-motive	(áánéllii)	'for that reason'
àː-nɛ̀ thm-⟨event⟩/-⟨ø⟩	(aane)	'then'
á-ɾó-náà thm-frs-while	(áɾónáa)	'but'
á-tsʰìʔtʲùù thm-⟨place⟩-sou	(átsihdyu)	'from that place'
áː-náà thm-while	(áánáa)	'meanwhile'
á-ʔàˣtʃʰó-tʰà thm-⟨duration⟩-relating.to	(áhajchóta)	'for that time/distance'

19.1.2 The use of thematic connectives

To introduce a referent into the universe of discourse, it must be clearly identified. This can be accomplished with a sentence having a noun phrase subject, as in 1039, or—if the context is sufficiently rich—with a pronoun, as in 1040:

(1039) òːíː-pʲɛ́   tsɨːnɛ́-ʔì (Ooííbyé dsɨɨnéhi.) 'The dog runs.'
   dog-⟨SgM⟩ run-⟨t⟩

(1040) áːnùù tʃʰɛ̀mɛ́-ʔì (Áánu cheméhi.) 'This one (SgM) is sick.'
   this be.ill-⟨t⟩

A sentence that continues a discourse usually begins with a connective that ties the sentence to the context, almost always to the immediately preceding sentence. The connective is always the first phrase in the sentence.

It may refer to the situation created by the preceding events, to the time of the most recently-mentioned event, or to the most thematic element of the preceding sentence. The connective may have a grammatical relation within the sentence it initiates (subject, direct object,...) or function adverbially (place, time, reason,...).

For example, the story "A woman becomes a toucan" starts as in 1041. A woman is introduced in the first sentence with a noun phrase (which are actually two appositive phrases). In the second sentence she is referred to by the thematic connective à:tʃéβáà.[2]

(1041) Tsáápilléváa bádsɨ́jcaja awáhi.

Aalléváa paíjyuváré pehíjcyá úmɨhévú íhmaahóma.

tsʰá:-pʰìtʃɛ́-βa-a̋   pátsɨ́ˣkʰà-hà   àkpá-ʔ
one-⟨SgF⟩-rpt-rem adolescentF-sg diet-⟨t⟩a

à:-tʃɛ́-βa-a̋   pʰà-íhʲùɨ-βá-ɾɛ́   pʰɛ̀-ʔ   ɨ́ˣkʲʰá-ʔì
thm-⟨SgF⟩-rpt-rem all-⟨time⟩-pl-only go-sub be-⟨t⟩

úmɨ̀ʔɛ́-βúɨ í ʔ   ma̋:ʔó-mà
field-goal self cassava-pl

'A young girl was dieting. She would go every day to the field with her cassava.'

Likewise, in 1042 the first sentence introduces the shelter while the second uses it both as the thematic link to the context and as the goal of putting, by virtue of which it has the case marker -βɯ 'goal':

(1042) ...meenú íñuujúwa. Ááwavúváa pícyoíñuube...

...mè:núɨ-ʔ í   ɲűɨ:húɨ-kpà
make-⟨t⟩ self shelter-⟨slab⟩

á:-kpà-βúɨ-βa-a̋   pʰíkʲʰò-íɲùɨ-:pɛ̀...
thm-⟨slab⟩-goal-rpt-rem put-do.go-⟨SgM⟩

'...he made himself a little shelter. Into that shelter he put...'

In example 1043, taken from "A chief goes to the jungles" there are three sentences. The connective of the second refers to the skins mentioned in the first, while the connective of the third refers to the cloth mentioned in the second.

---

[2] The connective that begins the second sentence of 1041 is the subject of the second sentence. Thus the main verb bears -ʔì ⟨t⟩ because there is a preverbal subject.

19.1. THE THEMATIC CONNECTIVE

(1043) Mííhenéváa ávyéjuube tsajtyé cóómívuú.
Áánemáváa wájyamu újcuúbe. Aajáváa tsajtyéébé ihjyávu.

mí:?è-né-βá-á   áβʲéhùɨ-:pè   tsʰáˣtʲʰɛ́-ˀ kʰó:mí-βùɨ́ɨ́
skin-pl-rpt-rem reign-⟨SgM⟩ take-⟨t⟩ town-goal

á:-nè-má-βá-à   kpáhʲàmùɨ ɨ́ˣkʰùɨ-:pè
thm-⟨ø⟩-with-rpt-rem cloth   get-⟨SgM⟩

à:-há-βá-à   tsʰáˣtʲʰɛ́-:pɛ́ íˀ   hʲá-βùɨ
thm-⟨cloth⟩-rpt-rem take-⟨SgM⟩ self house-goal

'The chief took the skins to town. With those he got cloth. He took that cloth to his house.'

As seen in the examples above, nominal connectives bear whatever case marker is appropriate for the grammatical relation they bear in their clause: an animate direct object bears -⓵kʰɛ 'objAn'; a goal bears -βɨ 'goal', and so forth. Further examples follow. The mini-discourse in 1044–1047 is followed by some explanatory comments.[3]

(1044) Tsáijyúi ó peé táiiñújɨvu.

tsʰá-ìhʲɨ́ɨ-ì   ó pʰè-ɛ́-ˀ   tʰá ì:ɲɨ́-hì-βùɨ
one-⟨time⟩-PT I go-fut-⟨t⟩ my dirt-⟨disk⟩-goal

'At some time I will go to my country.'

(1045) Aabe ó wáyééévéehi.[4]

à-:pè   ó kpájɛ́ɛ́-:βè-ɛ́-ʔì
thm-⟨SgM⟩ I rest-sIn-fut-⟨t⟩

'Then I will rest.'

(1046) Áábeke táátsíɨju ɨ́ɨ́cúveéhi.

á-:pè-kʰɛ̀   tʰá: Ⓖ tsʰɨ́:hùɨ ɨ:kʰɨ́ɨ-βè-ɛ́-ʔì
thm-⟨SgM⟩-objAn my   mother serve-sIn-fut-⟨t⟩

'My mother will serve me (food).'

---

[3]Note that the tone on à:- in 1045 is low. However, in 1046 and 1047, it must become high to avoid violating the *LLX constraint.

[4]The sequence ééé is orthographically ambiguous between /éé:/ and /é:é/. Evidence that it is the former is that, in the present-past tense, in which the two instances of /ɛ/ bear different tones, the length is associated with the second vowel. Thus, the éee sequence of ó wáyéeevéhi 'I rest' is /éɛ̀:/. This is as expected because morphophonemically the sequence is /éɛ̀-:/, with the length contributed by -:βɛ '-sIn'.

(1047) Áábedi óhdi tsijtye ídáátsóveéhi.
a-:pè-tì   ó-ʔtì
thm-⟨SgM⟩-anim.sou I-anim.sou

tsʰì-ˣtʲʰɛ̀   ítá:tsʰó-βɛ̀-ɛ́-ʔì
other-⟨AnPl⟩   pity-sIn-fut-⟨t⟩
'And others will have compassion for me.'

Example 1044 does not begin with a connective because it initiates the discourse. In 1045, à:pɛ̀ refers to the subject of 1044. In 1046, á:pɛ̀kʰɛ̀ refers to the subject of 1045, bearing -Ⓛkʰɛ 'objAn' because it is the direct object of 1046. In 1047, á:-pè-tì refers to the direct object of 1046, bearing -ti 'animate (source)' because it is the "source" for pity within the main clause of 1047. Significantly, the first person has been maintained as discourse theme/topic by means of the connectives.

The inanimate connectives are illustrated in the following examples.

(1048) Éijyúpe ó bajtsó tsahe mútsíítsɨhe táhjyá úníutu.
Aahe tsúúca neeváhi.

ɛ́-ìhʲúɨ-pʰɛ̀   ó pàˣtsʰó-ʔ tsʰà-ʔɛ̀   múɨtsʰɨ́:tsʰɨ̀-ʔɛ̀
that-⟨time⟩-rem I plant-⟨t⟩ one-⟨tree⟩ pear.apple-⟨tree⟩

[[tʰá? Ⓖ hʲá]   Ⓖ ǘmíùɨ]-tʰùɨ à:-ʔɛ̀   tsʰúɨ:kʰà nɛ̀:βá-ʔì
    my   house   beside   -sou   thm-⟨tree⟩ already   fruit-⟨t⟩.
'Some time ago I planted one pear apple tree beside my house. That tree is already bearing fruit.'

(1049) Úméhewááné ó nahjɨheenúhi.
Ááwáhjɨtu ó méénuú ácúvewááne.

úmɛ́-ʔɛ̀-kpá:-né   ó nàʔhɨ́ʔɛ̀-:núɨ-ʔì
tree-⟨tree⟩-⟨slab⟩-pl I buy-sTr-⟨t⟩

á:-kpá-ʔhɨ̀-tʰùɨ   ó mɛ́:nùɨ-úɨ-ʔ   àkʰúɨβɛ̀-kpá-:nɛ̀
thm-⟨slab⟩-pl-sou   I make-fut-⟨t⟩ sit-⟨slab⟩-pl
'I bought some boards. With those boards I will make benches.'

(1050) Juuváríyée ó ájtyumɨ́ waajácúhaamɨ́cu.
Áhaamɨ́cúu ó tsajté ááhɨvu.

hùɨ:βá-rí-jɛ̃̀-ɛ̀   ó áˣtʲʰùmɨ́-ʔ kpà:hákʰúɨ-ʔà:mɨ́-kʰùɨ
trail-oblIn-only-rem I see-⟨t⟩   know-⟨leaf⟩-du

19.1. THE THEMATIC CONNECTIVE

á-ʔà:mí-kʰűɨf-ɯ̀   ó tsʰàˣtʰɛ́-ʔ á:ʔɨ̀-βɯ̀ɨ
thm-⟨leaf⟩-du-rem I take-⟨t⟩ home-goal
'I found two books on the trail. I took those books home.'

We now illustrate the use of adverbial connectives. In the second sentence of 1051, á:nétʃì: indicates that the first sentence is the reason or motive for the second:

(1051) Ihjyúijyu ó cheméhi. Áánéllii tsáhái o májchotú(ne).
ì ʔhʲɯ́ɨ-ìhʲɯ̀ɨ   ó tʃʰɛmɛ́-ʔì
yesterday-⟨time⟩ I be.ill-⟨t⟩

á:-nɛ́-tʃì: tsʰáʔá-ì ò máˣtʃʰò-tʰɯ́ɨ-(nɛ̀)
thm-⟨ø⟩-motive neg-PT I eat-neg-(⟨n⟩)
'I was sick yesterday. For that reason I have not yet eaten.'

In the second sentence of 1052, áɾónáà indicates 'in spite of that', referring to the event indicated by the preceding sentence:

(1052) Áijyúu táñaalle tsivá cahgúnuco.

Áɾónáaacáa tsá o ímílletú o ádone.

á-ìhʲɯ̀ɨ-ɯ̀   tʰá Ⓖ ɲà:-tʃɛ̀   tsʰìβá-ʔ
thm-⟨time⟩-rem my   sib-⟨SgF⟩ bring-⟨t⟩

kʰàʔkúmɯ̀ɨ-kʰò
manioc.drink-⟨InSg⟩

á-ɾó-náà:kʰá-à   tsʰáʔ ò ímítʃɛ̀-tʰɯ́ɨ [ò àtò   ]-nɛ̀
thm-frs-while-rem not I want-neg I drink -⟨ø⟩
'On that day my sister brought manioc drink. But I did not want to drink.'

Now let us illustrate more broadly with the mini-text in 1053–1058, following which there is discussion.

(1053) Ópée o péé táiiñújɨvu.

ó-pʰɛ́ɛ̀ ò̱ pʰɛ́:-ʔ [tʰá ì:ɲɯ́ɨ-hì   ]-βɯ̀ɨ   'I went to
I-rem I go-⟨t⟩ my dirt-⟨disk⟩ -goal my country.'

(1054) Áábekée táñahbe ímí waatsúcúpejtsóhi.

á-:pɛ̀-kʰɛ́-ɛ̀   [tʰá Ⓖ ɲà-ʔpɛ̀]
thm-⟨SgM⟩-objAn-rem my   brother

ímíʔ   kpà:tsʰúɨ-kʰúɨ-pʰèˣtsʰó-ʔì
good receive-sTr-find-⟨t⟩
'My brother received me well.'

(1055) Áijyúu mítyane muhtsi méihjyúvájcatsíhi.
    á-ìhʲúɨ-ùɨ   mítʲʰà-nè mùɨʔtsʰì mé ìʔhʲúɨβá-ˣkʰàtsʰí-ʔì
    thm-⟨time⟩-rem many-⟨ø⟩ we.du SAP speak-recip-⟨t⟩
    'At that time we talked about many things.'

(1056) Áhduŕee táñaalle tsáá tétsihvu.
    á-ʔtùɨ-ɾɛ́-ɛ̀   [tʰá ⓒ ɲà:-tʃɛ̀] tsʰá:-ʔ
    thm-⟨like⟩-only-rem my sib-⟨SgF⟩ come-⟨t⟩

    tʰɛ́-tsʰì-ʔβùɨ
    that-⟨place⟩-goal
    'My sister also came there.'

(1057) Aallée múhtsima majcho meenúhi.
    à:-tʃɛ́-ɛ̀   mùɨʔtsʰì-mà màˣtʃʰò mè:núɨ-ʔì
    thm-⟨SgF⟩-rem we.du-with food prepare-⟨t⟩
    'And she prepared the food for us.'

(1058) Aanée muhtsi mémajchóhi.
    à:-nɛ́-ɛ̀   mùɨʔtsʰì mé màˣtʃʰó-ʔì
    thm-⟨ø⟩-rem we.du SAP eat-⟨t⟩
    'And we ate it.'

In 1054, á:pèkʰɛ́ɛ̀ refers to the subject of 1053, and it is the direct object of 1054. In 1055, áìhʲúɨùɨ refers to the time of 1054, and functions as a time adverbial in 1055. In 1056, á-ʔtùɾɛ́ɛ̀ refers to something that also happened at that time. In 1057, à:tʃɛ́ɛ̀ refers to the subject of 1056, and is the subject of 1057. In 1058, à:nɛ́ɛ̀ refers to the time after 1057, and functions as a time adverbial in 1057.

19.1.3 Thematic connectives and subordinate clauses

In examples 1059 and 1060, the first sentence establishes John as a topic. Then, in the second sentence, the thematic connective refers to that topic, i.e., to John. This connective is the subject of the main clause. The subject of the subordinate clause is the anaphoric pronoun i 'self'; it refers to the subject of the main clause, i.e., to the connective à-:pè (that-⟨SgM⟩):

19.1. THE THEMATIC CONNECTIVE

(1059) Jóáa péé cóómívuú. Aabe ichéménéllii tsá íícúi tsáátune.

hóáà pʰɛ́:-ˀ kʰóːmí-βùɾúɨ · à-ːpɛ̀$_i$
John go-⟨t⟩ town-goal   that-⟨SgM⟩

[ì$_i$ tʃʰɛ́mɛ́]-nɛ́-tʃì: tsʰáˀ íːkʰúɨì tsʰáː-tʰùɨ-nɛ̀
self sick- ⟨ø⟩-because not hurry come-neg-⟨n⟩

'John went to town. Because he was sick, he did not come quickly.'

A more remarkable case is seen in the three synonymous mini-texts represented in 1060a–c. The thematic connective of the second sentence, á-ɾò-ːpɛ̀ (that-frs-⟨SgM⟩), is understood as the subject of the subordinate clause.

(1060) a. Jóáa wajtsɨ́hi. Ároobe ó imíllé dibye pééneé.

b,c. Jóáa wajtsɨ́hi. Ároobe pééne ó imílléhi.

hóáà$_i$ kpàˣtsʰɨ́-ʔì
John arrive-⟨t⟩

⎧ a. á-ɾò-ːpɛ̀$_i$ ó ìmítʃɛ́-ʔì [tì-pʲɛ̀$_i$ pʰɛ́:]-nɛ̀ɛ́
⎪   that-frs-⟨SgM⟩ I want-⟨t⟩ that-⟨SgM⟩ go   -⟨ø⟩
⎨ b. [á-ɾò-ːpɛ̀   pʰɛ́:]-nɛ̀ ó ìmítʃɛ́-ʔì
⎪   that-frs-⟨SgM⟩ go   -⟨ø⟩ I want-⟨t⟩
⎪ c. á-ɾò-ːpɛ̀$_i$ [ø$_i$ pʰɛ́:]-nɛ̀ ó ìmítʃɛ́-ʔì
⎩   that-frs-⟨SgM⟩   go   -⟨ø⟩ I want-⟨t⟩

a–c. 'John arrived. However, I want him to leave / that he leave.'

In 1060a the referential tie is made by having the pronoun ti-pʲɛ as the subject of pʰɛ́: 'go' in the subordinate clause. In 1060b the thematic connective simply *is* the subject of the subordinate clause. As might be expected, this is more natural than 1060a.

If a second position clitics were to occurr in either a. or b., it would directly follow the thematic connective. This is unproblematic in 1060a but for 1060b, it would locates a second position clitic within a subordinate clause. This motivates the alternate structure in 1060c, in which, like in 1060a, the thematic connective is a constituent of the main clause. 1060c is also like 1060a in that the subject of the subordinate clause is a pronoun that refers to the thematic connective, but this is achieved by positing a silent pronoun.

Obviously, which analysis is preferred will depend on theoretical assumptions. We will not attempt to settle the matter here.

19.1.4 Topic decay and reestablishment

Consider the following text fragment taken from "A woman becomes a toucan." This is a story about a woman, so not surprisingly she is the most topical participant throughout.

...(1) Aaméváa péé dííllé kemúellére. (2) Aaméváa ííténáa teene cátuujɨ ityábáhcyóné lléhdolléré pééhií. (3) Aanévá diityéké iájtyúmíne tsane ɨdɨbéévéne wááménelle cáámevújuco, tsúúca núlledívú píívyetélleréjuco. (4) Aanévá diitye úúballévá...

...(1) à:-mɛ́-β́á-à pʰɛ́:-ˀ tí:-tʃɛ́ kʰèmɯ́-ɛ̀tʃɛ́-ɾɛ̀. (2) à:-mɛ́-β́á-à ɨ́:tʰɛ́-náà tʰɛ̀:-nɛ̀ kʰátʰɯ̀:hɨ̀ ɨ̀-tʲʰápá-ˀkʲʰó-nɛ́ tʃɛ́ˀtò-tʃɛ́-ɾɛ́ pʰɛ́:-ʔíí. (3) à:-nɛ́-β́á-à tɨ̀:-tʲʰɛ́-kʰɛ́ ɨ̀-áˣtʲʰúmí-nɛ̀ tsʰà-nɛ̀ ɨ̀-típɛ́-:βɛ́-nɛ̀ kpá:mɛ́nɛ̀-tʃɛ̀ kʰá:mɛ̀-βɯ̀-hɯ̀ɾkʰò, tsʰɯ́:kʰà nɯ́ɾtʃɛ̀-tí-βɯ́ pʰí:βʲɛ̀-tʰɛ́-tʃɛ̀-ɾɛ́-hɯ̀ɾkʰò. (4) à:-nɛ́-β́á-à tɨ̀:-tʲʰɛ̀ ɯ́:pàtʃɛ́-β́á-ˀ...

...(1) Then they went after her at a distance. (2) While they were looking she pulled up some *ñejilla* palm fruit and went eating it. (3) Then seeing them, she put one between her lips and flew up high becoming a toucan. (4) Then they came and told...

The topic of sentences preceding this fragment is the people who observed the woman. In the first and second sentences of this fragment, they are referred to by the connective à:-mɛ́-β̂á-à (thm-⟨AnPl⟩-rpt-rem) 'they'. The second and third sentences also refers to the woman with the classifier -tʃɛ ⟨SgF⟩ 'she' and the anaphoric pronoun ì 'self'. This is possible because she is the main participant of the text as a whole, so the topicality of the observers does not displace her as a readily-available topic. (In the third and fourth sentences the connective à:-nɛ́-β́á-à simply means 'then'.) In the fourth sentence, the people are reestablished as topic by means of the pronoun tì:-tʲʰɛ̀ (that-⟨AnPl⟩) 'they'. This illustrates part of the following generalization: Thematic connectives and classifier subjects maintain topics, whereas other pronouns establish or reestablish them.

19.2 Co-text or context

In virtually all cases, if the thematic connective refers to a person or thing (as opposed to a time, place, manner, circumstance, and such), it will have been mentioned explicitly in the previous sentence. Thus it is tempting to claim that the connective must be coreferential to some element of the

preceding sentence, to an adjacent portion of the CO-TEXT. However, it is more accurate to say that the connective refers to an element of the CONTEXT (what the speaker assumes the hearer has in mind at the point of uttering a sentence) and that this is usually—but not always—explicit in the co-text.

For example, in 1061 (taken from "The Creator's Daughter") the first sentence refers to digging in the ashes of the fireplace. The thematic connective of the second sentence refers to *the hole*, which has not been explicitly mentioned. Of course, *digging* brings a hole very much to mind, i.e., *digging* brings a hole into the context, so the hole can be referred to by the thematic connective.

(1061) Ehdúváa nééllere tsehdí įjcyujúwá llíjyutu.

Áhejúriváa dityépɨ péjúcóóronáa óómille...

ɛ̂ʔ-túɨ-βa̋-a̋   nɛ̏ː-tʃɛ̏-ɾɛ̏   tsʰɛ̂ʔtí-ʔì í   ˣkʲʰɯ̋húɨkpá
that-⟨like⟩-rpt-rem say-⟨SgF⟩-only dig-⟨t⟩ self fire

tʃíhʲɯ̀-tʰɯ̀ á-ʔɛ̀hɯ́-ɾì-βa̋-a̋   tì-tʲʰɛ́pʰɨ
ashes-sou thm-⟨hole⟩-oblIn-rpt-rem that-⟨DuF⟩

pʰɛ̋-hɯ́kʰóː-ɾó-náà óːmì-tʃɛ̀...
go-now-frs-while return-⟨SgF⟩

'Thus saying she dug up some ashes from her fireplace. While they were going into that hole she returned...'

In the light of such examples, we must say that the connective must link to some element of the *context*, not necessarily to one that is explicit in the preceding *co-text*.

19.3 Ellipsis and gapping

In a sufficiently rich context much of a sentence may be ellipsed, even the verb. For example, in answer to the question in 1062, one could answer with 1063. (See also examples 277 and 278, page 152.)

(1062) à ɯ̀ pʰɛ́-hɯ̀kʰóː-ʔì (¿A u péjucóó?) 'Are you going now?'
y/n you go-now-⟨t⟩

(1063) tsʰá̋ʔá-ìɨ́kʲʰɛ̀ (Tsáháiíkye.) 'Not yet (but soon).'
not-PT

In 1064, the verb of the second clause is ellipsed:

(1064) Aane tsaíjyú ménijtyú teene ítsɨtsɨ́ɨ́ne; téhdure tsaíjyú óónováne.

à:-nɛ̀ tsʰà-íhʲɯ́ɯ mɛ́ nɯ̀ˣtʲʰɯ́ɯ-ˀ tʰɛ̀:-nɛ̀ Ⓐ í tsʰɨ̌tsʰɨ́:-nɛ̀
thm-⟨ø⟩ one-⟨time⟩ SAP wash-⟨t⟩ that-⟨ø⟩ self white-⟨ø⟩

tʰɛ́-ˀtɯ̀-ɾɛ̀ tsʰà-íhʲɯ́ɯ ____ ó:nòβá-nɛ̀
that-⟨like⟩-only one-⟨time⟩ colored-⟨ø⟩

'At one time we wash the white ones (from among them); in the same way, at another time ___ the colored ones.'

Appendix A

Dialect Differences

There are several Bora dialects, each spoken by a different clan. They differ mainly in terms of palatalization. The following words are given for three clans.

GLOSS	Íñeje	Báácoje	Llívamu
1 to put	pʰìkʲʰò	pʰìkʰò	pʰìkʰò
2 my watch	tʰàɲɯ́ʔpà	tʰànɯ́ʔpà	tʰànɯ́ʔpà
3 hammock	kpàápʲà	kpàápà	kpàápà
4 rope	kpá:pʲàɯ̀	kpá:pàɯ̀	kpá:pàjɯ̀
5 needle	ánɛ̀ɛ́tʰò	ánɛ̀ˣtʰò	ánɛ̀ˣtʰò
6 needles	ánɛ̀tʰó:nɛ̀	ánɛ̀ˣtʰónɛ̀	ánɛ̀ˣtʰónɛ̀
7 to clean	pʰà:hʲɯ́kʰɯ̀	pʰà:hʲɯ́kʰɯ̀	pʰà:hɯ́kʰɯ̀
8 to hurt	àβʲéβɛ̀	àβʲéβɛ̀	àβéβɛ̀
9 to be exchanged	kʰápʰàjó:βɛ̀	kʰápʰàjó:βɛ̀	kʰápʰàó:βɛ̀
10 to exchange	kʰápʰájòákʰò	kʰápʰájòákʰò	kʰápʰáòákʰò
11 chief	áβʲéhɯ̀ɯ́pɛ̀	áβʲéhɯ̀ɯ́pɛ̀	áβéhɯ̀ɯ́pɛ̀
12 water	nɯ́ˣpʰàkʲʰò	nɯ́ˣpʰàkʲʰò	nɯ́ˣpʰàkʰò
13 to burn	àí:βʲɛ̀	àí:βʲɛ̀	àí:βɛ̀
14 to fall	à:kʰítʲʰɛ̀	à:kʰítʲʰɛ̀	à:kʰítʰɛ̀
15 to bring	tsʰìβà	tʃʰìβà	tsʰìβà
16 me	òkʰɛ̀	òkʲʰɛ̀	òkʰɛ̀
17 I come	ò tsʰáhɯ̀kʰó:	ò tsʰáhàkʰó:	—
18 we	mɯ̀ɾʔtsʰì	mɯ̀ɾʔtʃʰì	mɯ̀ɾʔtsʰì
19 to be burned	àˣtʲʰɛ̀	àˣtʰɛ̀	àˣtʰɛ̀
20 porcupine	áɲí:ɲìpà	áɲí:nìpà	—
21 nail	àɲɯ́í:ʔʲò	àɲɯ́hí:ʔò	—
22 tarantula	à:ɾíkʲʰò	à:ɾíkʰò	à:ɾíkʰò

APPENDIX A. DIALECT DIFFERENCES

GLOSS	Íñeje	Báácoje	Llívamu
23 liquor	áβʲèˣpʰákʲʰò	áβʲèˣpʰákʲʰò	áβèˣpʰákʰò
24 to yawn	ákpàkʰɯ́mɯ̀ɹ	ákpàkʲʰɯ́mɯ̀ɹ	ákpàkʰɯ́mɯ̀ɹ
25 to stir	pòɾíˣkʲʰò	pòɾíˣkʰò	pòɾíˣkʰò
26 who	kʰà:pʲɛ́	kʰà:pɛ́	kʰà:pɛ́
27 flood	nɯ́ˣpʰàpʲà	nɯ́ˣpʰàpà	nɯ́ˣpʰàpà
28 to heat	kʰàɾɯ́ʔkʰò	kʰàɾíʔkʰò	—
29 cup	kʰànɛ́kʰò	kʰànɯ́ɹkpà	—
30 to jump	kʰátsʰɪ̀ɲí:βʲɛ̀	kʰátʃʰɪ̀ní:βɛ̀	—
31 my leg	tʰàˣkʲʰɯ́ɹpà	tʰàˣkʰɯ́ɹpà	tʰàˣkʰɯ́ɹpà
32 pineapple plant	kʰɯ́ɹtʃîkʲʰò	kʰɯ́ɹtʃîkʰò	kʰɯ́ɹtʃîkʰò
33 to chew coca	tèíˣkʲʰɯ̀ɹ	tèíˣkʰɯ̀ɹ	tèíˣkʰɯ̀ɹ
34 spoon	tèíhɯ̀ɹkpà	tèíhʲɯ̀ɹkpà	tèíhɯ̀ɹkpà
35 guava	tʰɯ́ɹ:tsʰìhʲɯ̀ɹ	tʰɯ́ɹ:tʃʰìhɯ̀ɹ	—
36 lamp	tɯ́ɹ:ɾɯ́ɹpàíʔkʲʰɯ̀ɹ	tɯ́ɹ:ɾɯ́ɹpàíʔkʰɯ̀ɹ	tɯ́ɹ:ɾɯ́ɹpàíʔkʰɯ̀ɹ
37 yes	ɛ́:ɛ̀	hɛ́:ɛ̀	—
38 beads	íkʲʰá:βɛ̀ʔɪ̀	íkʰá:βɛ̀ʔɪ̀	—
39 now	íkʲʰòókʰà	íkʰòókʰà	íkʰòókʰà
40 to be	ɪ̀ˣkʲʰà	ɪ̀ˣkʰà	ɪ̀ˣkʰà
41 to stand	ìhʲókʰɯ̀mɯ̀ɹ	ìhókʰɯ̀mɯ̀ɹ	ìhókʰɯ̀mɯ̀ɹ
42 to leave	ɪ̀ˣtʃʰíβʲɛ̀	ɪ̀ˣtʃʰíβɛ̀	ɪ̀ˣtʃʰíβɛ̀
43 this day	íˣkʲʰòóhɪ̀	íˣkʰòóhɪ̀	íˣkʰòóhɪ̀
44 yesterday	ìíhʲɯ̀ɹ	ìíhɯ̀ɹ	ìíhɯ̀ɹ
45 his name	ìmʲɛ́mɛ̀	ìmɛ́mɛ̀	ìmɛ́mɛ̀
46 aunt	í:mʲɛ̀ɛ́	í:mɛ̀ɛ́	í:mɛ̀ɛ́
47 to finish	ìmíβʲɛ̀	ìmíβɛ̀	ìmíβɛ̀
48 to dance	kʰɪ̀ˣkʲʰò	kʰɪ̀ˣkʰò	kʰɪ̀ˣkʰò
49 to sweep	tʃìhʲà	tʃìhà	tʃìhà
50 broom	tʃìhʲákʰó:ʔà	tʃíhákʰó:ʔà	tʃìhákʰó:ʔà
51 to get drunk	tʃíjì:kʲʰáβɛ̀	tʃíjì:kʰáβɛ̀	tʃíjì:kʰáβɛ̀
52 bowl	tʃíjìʔtʃò	tʃíɾìʔtʃò	—
53 cooking pot	tʃíjìíʔʲò	tʃíɾìíʔò	—
54 to knot a lasso	tʃóʔpʰìkʲʰáɾò	tʃóʔpʰìkʰáɾò	—
55 to joke	máˣtʃʰíhʲɯ̀ɾɯ́	máˣtʃʰíhɯ̀ɾɯ́	—
56 song	màˣtsʰɪ̀	màˣtʃʰɪ̀	màˣtsʰɪ̀
57 to sing	màˣtsʰíβà	màˣtʃʰíβà	màˣtsʰíβà
58 ghost	má:tsʰɪ̀í	má:tʃʰɪ̀í	—
59 he is big	mítʲʰàápɛ̀	mítʲʰàápɛ̀	mítʰàápɛ̀
60 two people	mí:tʲʰɛ́tsʰɪ̀í	mí:tʰɛ́tʃʰɪ̀í	mí:tʰɛ́tsʰɪ̀í
61 to be sad	nɛ̀ʔníβʲɛ̀	nɛ̀ʔníβɛ̀	nɛ̀ʔníβɛ̀
62 squirrel	nɛ́:pʰìkʲʰò	nɛ́:pʰìkʰò	nɛ́:pʰìkʰò
63 to climb	nɛ̀ɾí:βʲɛ̀	nɛ̀ɾí:βɛ̀	nɛ̀ɾí:βɛ̀

GLOSS	Íñeje	Báácoje	Llívamu
64 frog	níʔhʲàkpà	níʔhàkpà	níʔhàkpà
65 to mold	nìˣkʲʰò	nìˣkʰò	nìˣkʰò
66 chigger	ní:kʲʰɨ̀rɨ́	ní:kʰɨ̀rɨ́	ní:kʰɨ̀rɨ́
67 sky	níˣkʲʰɛ̀hɨ̀	níˣkʰɛ̀hɨ̀	níˣkʰɛ̀hɨ̀
68 to wash	nìˣtʲʰɨ̀ɾ	nìˣtʰɨ̀ɾ	nìˣtʰɨ̀ɾ
69 soap	nìˣtʲʰɨ́ɾkpà	nìˣtʰɨ́ɾkpà	nìˣtʰɨ́ɾkpà
70 porcupine	nì:hʲáɨ̀	nì:háɨ̀	nì:háɨ̀
71 to molest	pʰátsʰàɾíˣkʲʰò	pʰátsʰàɾíˣkʰò	pʰátsʰàɾíˣkʰò
72 to gather together	pʰɨ̀ʔkʲʰá:βɛ̀	pʰɨ̀ʔkʰá:βɛ̀	pʰɨ̀ʔkʰá:βɛ̀
73 to thunder	ɾòɾíʔkʲʰò	ɾòɾíʔkʰò	ɾòɾíʔkʰò
74 to dig	tsʰɛ̀ʔtíkʲʰɨ̀ɾ	tsʰɛ̀ʔtíkʰɨ̀ɾ	tsʰɛ̀ʔtíkʰɨ̀ɾ
75 another	tsʰɨ̀íɲɛ̀	tʃʰíɲɛ̀	tsʰɨ̀íɲɛ̀
76 another (male)	tsʰɨ̀ˣpʰɨ̀	tʃʰɨ̀ˣpʰɨ̀	tsʰɨ̀ˣpʰɨ̀
77 something	tsʰíɛ̀mɛ́nɛ̀	tʃʰíɛ̀mɛ́nɛ̀	tsʰíɛ̀mɛ́nɛ̀
78 cold weather	tsʰíʔkʲʰòʔò	tʃʰíʔkʲʰòʔò	tsʰíʔkʰòʔò
79 different	tsʰíʔtʲɨ̀ɾɛ̀	tʃʰíʔtɨ̀ɾɛ̀	tsʰíʔtɨ̀ɾɛ̀
80 far	tsʰíʔɨ̀ɾtʃɛ̀	tʃʰíɨ̀ɾtʃʰɛ̀	—
81 to untie	tsʰíɲàájò	tʃʰínàájò	tsʰínàáɾò
82 mouse	tsʰɨ̀ɲíɨ̀	tʃʰɨ̀ɲíɨ̀	tsʰɨ̀níɨ̀
83 cold place	tsʰɨ́ɾ:kʰòtsʰíî	tsʰɨ́ɾ:kʰòtʃʰíî	tsʰɨ́ɾ:kʰòtsʰíî
84 to become skinny	ɨ̀ɾˣtsʰítʲʰɛ̀	ɨ̀ɾˣtʃʰítʰɛ̀	ɨ̀ɾˣtsʰítʰɛ̀
85 basket	ɨ́ɾβɛ̀ɾɨ́ɾˣtsʰɨ̀	ɨ́ɾβɛ̀ɾɨ́ɾˣtʃʰɨ̀	ɨ́ɾβɛ̀ɾɨ́ɾˣtsʰɨ̀
86 to whip	kpàʔtsʰíʔkʲʰɨ̀ɾ	kpàʔtʃʰíʔkʰɨ̀ɾ	kpàʔtsʰíʔkʰɨ̀ɾ
87 hole	kpáʔʲɛ̀hɨ̀ɾ	kpájɛ̀hɨ̀ɾ	kpáʔɛ̀hɨ̀ɾ
88 piece of log	kpáʔʲòóɨ̀ɾ	kpájòóɨ̀ɾ	kpáʔòóɨ̀ɾ
89 cloth	kpáhʲàmɨ̀ɾ	kpájhàmɨ̀ɾ	—
90 to prune	kpáβìjíˣkʲʰò	kpáβìɾíˣkʰò	—
91 to come	tsʰàá	tʃʰàá	tsʰàá

Appendix B

Speculations on Diachronic Processes

The following are speculations about how some forms may have developed from earlier stages of the language:

1. Two suffixes have the form -:β⁽ʲ⁾ε. One is glossed as 'become' (as in 137); the other is glossed as 'singular intransitive (sIn)' (as in 242). These are at least cognate; perhaps they are a single morpheme with two uses.
2. ímìpáˣʧʰò 'fix' may derive from *imì-pa-ʧʰo (good-verbalizer-caus). Likewise, ḭ̀hʲɯ̀ɾβà 'talk' may derive from *ḭ̀hɯ-βa mouth-verbalizer and ɯ̀ˣkʰáβà 'become fat' from *ɯˣkʰa-βa- fat-verbalizer.
3. ímíhʲɯ̀ 'happy' may derive from *imi-hʲɯ (good-speech); e.g., ímíhʲɯ̀-:βέ-mè 'they became very happy'.
4. ímìβʲέ- 'finish' may derive from ímì-βʲέ- (good-verbalizer). (However ímìβʲέ- is a transitive verb, whereas -:β⁽ʲ⁾ε generally derives intransitive verbs.)
5. í kpàhʲámɯ̀ 'his clothes' may derive from i kpa-ha-mɯ (self ⟨slab⟩-⟨shelter⟩-pl), perhaps because the body is perceived as roughly slab-shaped (like a plank).
6. Perhaps the /pa/ of -kʰopa 'augment' is cognate with pʰa- 'all, big'.
7. maˣʧʰo 'eat (bread)' may derive from *mai-tsʰo- (bread-cause), with the /*i/ palatalizing the /ts/. Support for this is found in the word ma̰ʔo 'cassava bread'.
8. pʰɪ́:βʲɛ̀ 'grow' may derive from pʰi-:βε. The *pʰi would have been either 'body' or 'big'; the *-:βε would have been either the verbalizer

'become' or 'sIn' (which, as suggested above, may have been the same morpheme).

9. -naːák̚ʰa 'meanwhile' may derive from *-nɛ-áːkʰa (⟨ø⟩-realize). This may be due to either a historical or a morphophonemic process.

10. -⁽ʔ⁾ iˣkʲʰa¹ 'be' forms a compound tense indicating imperfective aspect. It is frequently interpreted as habitual. It is now bound but was undoubtedly free at some prior stage of the language.

11. -tsʰi (not palatalized) ~ -tʃʰi (palatalized) ⟨place⟩ and -ʔɯtʃɛ ⟨yonder⟩ ~ ᴴɛ́tʃɛ (root) 'yonder, over there' are probably cognate.

12. Consider the requirement that, when -βɯ 'goal' follows an animate phrase, the phrase must bear the suffix -⁽ʔ⁾ti 'animate', as in example 656, page 276. This suffix, which now appears to mark animacy, may have arisen from the pronoun ti 'that' in locational uses of the genitive construction along the lines of ɛtʃɛ in example 660, page 276.

13. tsʰɨːmɛ 'children' may derive from tsʰɨ́ː-mɛ (baby-ANPL) where tsʰɨ́ː- is cognate with the classifier -tsʰɨ ⟨baby⟩.

14. The /hɯ/ of -Ⓛ◯húrkʰo: 'now, already; focus' may be cognate with the /hɯ/ of -Ⓛhɯ-ˣ 'quick-vocative'.

15. -ʔi ⟨t⟩, the trace left when a subject is moved to before the verb, may be cognate with i 'self'.

16. miː 'two' may be cognate with -mɯ 'dual' as in -mɯtsʰi ⟨DuM⟩ and -mɯpʰɨ ⟨DuF⟩.

17. -naá(ːkʰa) 'while' (discussed in section 17.3 may be derived from -nɛ ⟨event⟩ and the adverbial clitic -ha(ːca) 'realize' (listed in 11.2).

18. The pronoun mɯ́ɯ 'indefinite animate singular' discussed in section 14.3.2 may be cognate with -mɯ 'plAn'.

19. The suffix -Ⓛ◯tsʰa 'each' is probably cognate with the root tsʰà- 'one'.

20. See footnote 11, page 106, regarding probable source of certain verbs often used in compounds.

21. See chapter 15, footnote 2, regarding the possible historical development of an interrogative suffix that docks a high tone on the host's final syllable and causes the final vowel to change from /e/ to /a/.

---

[1]This verb means 'be (at a place)'. The English progressive as in *He is working* arose from *He is at working*. The Bora imperfective (or habitual) may have arisen from such a construction.

Appendix C

A List of Bound Adjectival Stems

The bound adjectival stems below are alphabetized according to the practical alphabet. In example words, a label between square brackets indicates its grammatical category.[1]

Many bound adjectival stems end with a vowel followed by /e/. This is the suffix -ɛ- 'pertain to' (discussed in section 6.2.11). For example, the bound adjectival atérée- is atʰɛrɛ 'worthless' followed by -ɛ- 'pertain to'.

aa- ~ a-   a(:)- 'that' (thematic connective), e.g.,
    á?ùːtʃɛ̀ (áhulle) [adverbial thematic connective] 'that place',
    áìhʲùː (áijyu) [adverbial thematic connective] 'that time',
    àːtʃɛ̀ (aalle) [pronominal thematic connective] 'that one (SgF)',
    àːmɛ̀ (aame) [pronominal thematic connective] 'those (AnPl)',
    àːkpà (aawa) [pronominal thematic connective] 'that slab-like thing'
    -rò ~ -jò 'frs' may be added as in árò?áːmɨ̀ (árohááamɨ) [pronominal thematic connective] 'that leaf-like thing, although it does not seem to be',
    árónáà (árónáa) [adverbial thematic connective] 'but, however, by contrast'

apaa- ~ apa-   ápʰà(:)᷆ 'only' (-rɛ always follows.) For example, àpʰáːmʲɛ́rɛ̀ (apáámyére) [adjective] 'the only ones (AnPl)',
    àpʰá?àːmɨ́rɛ̀ (apáhaamɨ́re) [adjective] 'the only leaf-like thing'

---

[1] In this list, the category of a bound adjectival stem followed by a classifier is generally given as [adjective]. Strictly speaking such phrases are nouns (or noun phrases); these phrases are referred to as "adjectives" because they frequently stand in apposition to another noun (phrase) that they modify ("qualify").

413

414   APPENDIX C. A LIST OF BOUND ADJECTIVAL STEMS

atérée- àtʰɛ́ɾɛ̀ɛ̀- 'worthless, despicable', e.g.,
   àtʰɛ́ɾɛ̀ɛ̀kpà (atéréewa) [adjective] 'worthless slab-like thing'
bee- ~ be- ~ beh-   pɛ̀:- ~ pɛ̀- ~ pɛ̀ʔ- 'new, recent', e.g.,
   pɛ́:pɛ̀ɛ́ ~ [pɛ́:pɛ̀] (béébeé ~ [béébe]) [adjective] 'the one (SgM) that just arrived',
   pɛ̀ˣtʰɛ̀ (bejte) [adjective] 'the new ones (AnPl)',
   pɛ̀ʔhà (behja) [adjective] 'the new shelter-like thing'
bɨwa- pɨ̀kpà- 'the same as before', e.g.,
   pɨ̀kpáhà (bɨwája) [adjective] 'the same slab-like thing',
   pɨ̀kpáʔùɾtʃɛ̀ (bɨwáhulle) [adjective] 'the same place'
bóónée- pó:nɛ́-ɛ̀- 'the following, after a time', e.g.,
   pó:nɛ́ɛ̀ʔá:mɨ̀ (bóónéeháámɨ) [adjective] 'the next leaf-like thing'
bóónétúe- pó:nɛ́-tʰɯ́-ɛ̀- 'following, behind', e.g.,
   pó:nɛ́tʰɯ́ɛ̀mɨ̀ (bóónétúemɨ) [adjective] 'the next vehicle of transportation'
cóee- ~ cóe-   kʰóɛ̀:- ~ kʰóɛ̀- 'extra, excess', e.g.,
   kʰóɛ̀:mɨ̀ (cóeémɨ) [adjective] 'the extra vehicle of transportation',
   kʰóɛ̀pʰátʃì (cóepálli) [adjective] 'the extra field'
ee- ~ e-   ɛ̀:- ~ ɛ̀- 'that (medial)', e.g.,
   ɛ̀:mɨ̀ (eémɨ) [demonstrative pronoun] 'that (medial) vehicle of transportation',
   ɛ́ʔà:mɨ̀ (éhaámɨ) [demonstrative pronoun] 'that (medial) leaf-like thing'
eh- ɛ̀ʔ- 'that (distal)', e.g.,
   ɛ́ʔhɨ̀ɨ ~ ɛ́ʔhɨ̀ (éhjɨɨ ~ éhjɨ) [demonstrative pronoun] 'that disk-like thing'
ehdícya- ɛ̀ʔtíkʲʰà- 'like that', e.g.,
   ɛ̀ʔtíkʲʰà:pɛ̀ (ehdícyaábe) [indefinite pronoun] 'that one (SgM) like this'
éhdɨ́ɨva- ɛ́ʔ-tɨ́:βà- 'of that quality, that kind of', e.g.,
   ɛ́ʔ-tɨ́:βà-pʰá:hɨ̀ (éhdɨ́ɨvapáájɨ) [adjective] 'shoe (can,...) like that one'
ehdu- ɛ̀-ʔtɯ̀- 'like that (in quality, size, quantity)', e.g.,
   ɛ́-ʔtɯ̀-pà (éhduba) [adjective] 'drum (trunk,...) like that one',
   ɛ́-ʔtɯ́-pà-βà (éhdúbava) [quantifier] 'that many drums (trunks,...)'
éhnéjcúe- ɛ́-ʔnɛ́ˣkʰɯ́-ɛ̀- 'that side', e.g.,
   ɛ́-ʔnɛ́ˣkʰɯ́-ɛ̀-ʔì (éhnéjcúehi) [adjective] 'that side of the river'
hajcho- ʔaˣtʃʰo- 'the same size, the same height, the same distance', e.g.,
   ʔàˣtʃʰó-:pɛ̀ (hajchóóbe) 'one (SgM) who is the same height', as in example 495, page 224;
   ʔàˣtʃʰó-hà (hajchója) [comparative adjective] 'one ⟨shelter⟩ the same size as', as in 496, page 224.
hállúe- ʔátʃɯ́-ɛ̀- 'pertain to the upper part', e.g.,
   ʔátʃɯ́-ɛ̀-kpà (hállúewa) [adjective] 'the slab-like thing on top'

hállúvúe- ʔátʃɨ́-βɨ́-ɛ̀- (upper-goal-per) 'pertain to that which is on top or next in sequence',[2] e.g.,
    ʔátʃɨ́-βɨ́-ɛ̀-ʔá:mɨ̀ (hállúvúeháámɨ) [adjective] 'the leaf-like thing that follows (or is on top of) another',
    ʔátʃɨ́-βɨ́-ɛ̀-ˣpʰɨ̀ (hállúvúejpi) [adjective] 'the next one (SgM)'

i- ~ ɨ- ì- ~ ɨ̀- 'this (proximate)', e.g.,
    íhʲɨ̀rɨ́ ~ íhʲɨ̀ɾ (íjyuú ~ íjyu) [demonstrative] 'this (proximate) long thin thing (road, shotgun,...)'

íeve- íɛ́βɛ̀- 'empty, not in use, available, free', e.g.,
    ìɛ́βɛ̀ʔá:mɨ̀ (íveháámɨ) [adjective] 'the available leaf-like thing',
    íɛ́βɛ̀ʔɛ́-hɨ̀ɾ (ívehéju) [adjective] 'empty hole',
    íɛ́βɛ̀-mɨ̀ (ívemɨ) [adjective] 'the empty vehicle of transportation',
    íɛ́βɛ̀-:pɛ̀ (íveébe) [adjective] 'the naked one (SgM)'

ihdícya- ì́ʔtíkʲʰà- 'like this', e.g.,
    ì́ʔtíkʲʰà-mɛ̀ (ihdícyame) [indefinite pronoun] 'like these (AnPl)',
    ì́ʔtíkʲʰá-ìhʲɨ̀ɾ-ɾɛ̀ (ihdícyáijyúre) [indefinite adverb] 'whenever',
    ì́ʔtíkʲʰá-ʔɨ̀ɾtʃɛ̀ (ihdícyá-hulle) [indefinite adverb] 'wherever'

íhdyúe- íʔtʲɨ́ɾɛ̀- 'separate', e.g.,
    íʔtʲɨ́ɾɛ̀-mɨ́:ʔò (íhdyúemɨ́ɨho) [adjective] 'the separated hide (sheet of metal, etc.)'

illu- ìtʃɨ̀ɾ- 'like this', e.g.,
    ítʃɨ̀ɾ-ɾò (ílluro) [demonstrative pronoun] 'like this bottle',
    ítʃɨ́ɾ-ɾò-βà (íllúrova) [quantifier] 'this quantity of bottles'

ímihɨva- ímɨ̀ʔɨ́βà- 'pretty, good', e.g.,
    ímɨ̀ʔɨ́βà-hɨ̀ɾ (ímihɨvaju) [adjective] 'the pretty path (road, shotgun,...)'

íñejcúe- íɲɛ̀ˣkʰɨ́ɾɛ̀- 'pertain to this side', e.g.,
    íɲɛ̀ˣkʰɨ́ɾɛ̀-ʔóˣtsʰɨ̀ (íñejcúehójtsɨ) [demonstrative pronoun] 'the hand of this side'

ɨdsɨhɨva- ɨ́tsɨ̀ʔɨ́βà- 'worthless', e.g.,
    ɨ́tsɨ̀ʔɨ́βà-ɨ́ʔkʲʰɨ̀ɾ (ɨdsɨhɨvaɨhcyu) [adjective] 'worthless frame'

ɨhdée- ɨ́ʔtɛ́-ɛ̀- 'old, pertaining to former time', e.g.,
    ɨ́ʔtɛ́-ɛ̀-ˣpʰɨ̀ (ɨhdéejpi) [adjective] 'the old one (SgM)',
    ɨ́ʔtɛ́-ɛ̀-pʰátʃì (ɨhdéepálli) [adjective] 'the old field'

ɨmɨáá- ɨ́mɨ̀á:- 'generous, proper, just, saintly, valuable', e.g.,
    ɨ́mɨ̀á:-tʃɛ̀ (ɨmɨáálle) [adjective] 'the saint (SgF)',
    ɨ́mɨ̀á:-mɨ̀ (ɨmɨáámɨ) [adjective] 'a good vehicle of transportation'

ɨvee- ɨ́βɛ̀:- 'why', e.g.,
    ɨ́βɛ̀:-kʰɨ́ (ɨveekɨ́) [interrogative advereb o pronoun] 'for what reason',
    ɨ́βɛ̀-:pɛ̀ (ɨveebe) [interrogative pronoun] 'why (SgM)',

---

[2] The presence of -βɨ̀ (-vu) 'goal, theme' in this construction is very interesting.

íβè:-kpà (ɨveewa) [interrogative pronoun] 'why ⟨slab⟩'
kee- ~ ke-   kʰè:- ~ kʰè- 'which', e.g.,
    kʰè:-ʔè (keéhe) [interrogative pronoun] 'which tree',
    kʰɛ́ʔà:-mì (kéhaámɨ) [interrogative pronoun] 'which leaf-like thing'
mi- ~ mii- ~ mɨ- ~ mɨɨ   mì(:)- ~ mɨ̀(:) 'two' (-:kʰɯ 'dual' follows inanimate classifiers.) Examples:
    mí:-ɲɛ́-kʰɯ̀nɯ́ ~ mí:-ɲɛ́-kʰɯ̀ (mííɲécuú ~ mííɲécu) [quantifier] 'two things',
    mí-ˣkʲʰò:hɨ́-kʰɯ̀ (míjcyoojɨcu) [quantifier] 'two days',
    mí:-hɨ́-kʰɯ̀nɯ́ ~ mí:-hɨ́-kʰɯ̀ (mɨ́ɨjɨcuú ~ mɨ́ɨjɨcu) [quantifier] 'two disk-like things',
    mí:-tʲʰɛ́tsʰìí ~ mí:-tʲʰɛ́tsʰì (míítyétsií ~ míítyétsi) [quantifier] 'two (DuM)'
muhdɨ́ɨva-   mɯ̀ʔ-tɨ́:βà- 'how it is, what form it has, what type it is, how it behaves',
    mɯ̀ʔtɨ́:-βà-kʰò (muhdɨ́ɨvaco) [adjective] 'what form (of a long thing thing)'
muhdú-   mɯ̀ʔtɯ́ɨ- 'how it is, how big it is, how many there are', e.g.,
    mɯ́ʔtɯ̀-:pè (múhduúbe) [adjective] 'what size (SgM)',
    mɯ́ʔtɯ́ɨ-pʰɛ̀ˣkʰóβà (múhdúpejcóva) [quantifier] 'how many nights'
néhnɨhɨ́va-   nɛ́ʔnɨ̀ʔíβà- 'bad, perverse, ugly, horrible', e.g.,
    nɛ́ʔnɨ̀ʔíβà-:pè (néhnɨhɨ́vaábe) [adjective] 'the bad one (SgM)',
    nɛ́ʔnɨ̀ʔíβà-kpà (néhnɨhɨ́vawa) [adjective] 'the bad slab-like thing'
nihñée-   nì̀ʔɲɛ́-ɛ̀- 'pertaning to the last', e.g.,
    nì̀ʔɲɛ́-ɛ̀-nɛ̀ (nihñéene) [adjective] 'the last thing',
    nì̀ʔɲɛ́-ɛ̀-ˣpʰì̀ (nihñéejpi) [adjective] 'the last (SgM)',
    nì̀ʔɲɛ́-ɛ̀-ˣpʰákʲʰò (nihñéejpácyo) [adjective] 'the last liquid'
óehɨva-   óɛ̀ʔíβà- 'ugly, horrible, repulsive, despicable', e.g.,
    óɛ̀ʔíβà-pʰá:hì̀ (óehɨvapááji) [adjective] 'the ugly (ring, shoe,...)',
    óɛ̀ʔíβà-tʃɛ̀ (óehɨvalle) [adjective] 'the repulsive (SgF)'
pa- ~ paá-   pʰà- ~ pʰàá- 'all, complete, whole', e.g.,
    pʰà-kpà (pawa) [adjective] 'whole slab-like thing',
    pʰá-ʔà:mì (páhaámɨ) [adjective] 'whole leaf-like thing',
    pʰá-mɛ̀-:ɾɛ̀ (pámeére) [indefinite pronoun] 'all (AnPl)'
páñétú-e-   pʰáɲɛ́tʰɯ́-ɛ̀- 'crucial, most important', e.g.,
    pʰáɲɛ̀tʰɯ́-ɛ̀-ʔáˣkʰɯ̀ (páñetúehájcu) [adjective] 'the most important pillar',
    pʰáɲɛ́tʰɯ́-ɛ̀-ˣpʰì̀ (páñétúejpi) [adjective] 'the most important (SgM), the main authority (SgM)'

pápihchúu- pʰápʰìˀʧʰúɾùɾ- 'three', e.g.,
    pʰápʰìˀʧʰúɾ:ùɾβà (pápihchúúuva) [quantifier] 'three small spherical things',
    pʰápʰìˀʧʰúɾ:ì:ʔʲóβà (pápihchúúiihyóva) [quantifier] 'three pencils (or similar things)'
peve- pʰèβè- 'empty, not in use, ordinary, incomplete', e.g.,
    pʰèβé-tsʰíì (pevétsíi) [adjective] 'empty place',
    pʰèβé-ˣtʰè (pevéjte) [adjective] 'the unemployed (AnPl); the ordinary ones (AnPl)',
    pʰèβé-βì:ùɾ (pevéviíu) [adjective] 'the available pieces of cassava'
pié- ~ piéé- pʰìé(:)- 'same as before', e.g.,
    pʰìé-tsʰìˀβùɾ (piétsihvu) [adjective] 'the same place'
piva- pʰìβà- 'many, numerous', e.g.,
    pʰìβáì:ʔʲóβà (piváiihyóva) [quantifier] 'many pencils (or similar things)'
píínée- pʰí:né-è- 'pertain to the center, central', e.g.,
    pʰí:né-è-ʔè (píínéehe) [adjective] 'the central tree',
    pʰí:né-è-ì (píínéei) [adjective] 'the central river'
pííné-e-hójtsɨ- pʰí:né-è-ʔóˣtsʰɨ- 'four (lit. half a hand)', e.g.,
    pʰí:né-è-ʔóˣtsʰɨ-mè-βà (píínéehójtsɨmeva) [quantifier] 'four (AnPl)'
píínévú-e- pʰí:néβúɨ-è- 'corresponding to the center or middle', e.g.,
    pʰí:néβúɨ-è-kpà (píínévúewa) [adjective] 'the slab-like thing in the middle'
tee- ~ te- tʰè(:)- 'that (aforementioned)', e.g.,
    tʰé-ìhʲùɾ (téijyu) [adverb] 'the aforementioned time',
    tʰè:-nè (teéne) [definite pronoun] 'that aforementioned thing',
    tʰè:-kpà (teéwa) [definite pronoun] 'that aforementioned slab-like thing'
tehdííva- tʰèˀ-tíːβà- 'like the aforementioned', e.g.,
    tʰèˀ-tíːβà-kpà (tehdíívawa) [adjective] 'like the aforementioned slab-like thing'
téhdu- tʰéˀtùɾ- 'similar to the aforementioned in size or quantity', e.g.,
    tʰéˀtùɾ: (téhduu) [adjective] 'the size of the aforementioned ball'
ténejcúe- tʰé-nèˣkʰúɨ-è- 'pertain to the aforementioned side', e.g.,
    tʰé-nèˣkʰúɨ-è-ì (ténejcúei) [definite pronoun] 'that aforementioned side of the river'
tújkénúe- tʰúɾˣkʰénúɨ-è- 'pertain to the beginning', e.g.,
    tʰúɾˣkʰénúɨ-è-ˣpʰì (tújkénúejpi) [adjective] 'the first (SgM)',
    tʰúɾˣkʰénúɨ-è-tsʰíì (tújkenúetsíi) [adjective] 'the first place'
tsaa- ~ tsa- tsʰà(:) 'one', e.g.,
    tsʰà:pʰì (tsaápi) [quantifier] 'one (SgM)',
    tsʰàmɨ (tsamɨ) [quantifier] 'one vehicle of transportation'

tsáhojtsɨ- tsʰá-ʔòˣtsʰɨ̀- 'five (lit. one hand)',
   tsʰá-ʔòˣtsʰɨ́-hɨ̀ˣtʰó-βà (**tsáhojtsɨ́jɨjtóva**) [quantifier] 'five lines'
tsanéemé- tsʰànɛ́-ɛ̀mɛ́- 'the same size as', e.g.,
   tsʰànɛ́-ɛ̀mɛ́-nɛ̀ (**tsanéeméne**) [adjective] 'thing of the same type',
   tsʰànɛ́-ɛ̀mɛ́-mɨ̀ (**tsanéemémɨ**) [adjective] 'vehicle of transportation of the same type'
tsánejcúe- tsʰá-nɛ̀ˣkʰɯ́ɯ-ɛ̀- 'one side of', e.g.,
   tsʰánɛ̀ˣkʰɯ́ɯ̀ɛ̀kpà (**tsánejcúewa**) [adjective] 'one side of the slab-like thing'
tsii- ~ **tsi-** ~ **tsɨɨ-** ~ **tsɨ-**   tsʰɨ̀(ː)- ~ tsʰɨ̀(ː)- 'other', e.g.,
   tsʰɨ̀ː-ɲɛ̀ (**tsiíñe**) [indefinite pronoun] 'other thing',
   tsʰɨ́-ʔàːmɨ̀ (**tsíhaámɨ**) [indefinite pronoun] 'other leaf-like thing',
   tsʰɨ̀ː-mɨ̀ (**tsɨɨ́mɨ**) [indefinite pronoun] 'other vehicle of transportation'
tsíemé- tsʰɨ́-ɛ̀mɛ́- 'some, whichever', e.g.,
   tsʰɨ́-ɛ̀mɛ́-ˣpʰɨ̀ (**tsíeméjpi**) [indefinite pronoun] 'someone (SgM)',
   tsʰɨ́-ɛ̀mɛ́-ˣpʰà (**tsíeméjpa**) [indefinite pronoun] 'whichever soup'
tsííñejcúe- tsʰɨ́ː-ɲɛ̀ˣkʰɯ́ɯ-ɛ̀- 'other side of', e.g.,
   tsʰɨ́ː-ɲɛ̀ˣkʰɯ́ɯ-ɛ̀-mɨ́ːʔɛ̀ (**tsííñejcúemɨ́ɨhe**) [indefinite pronoun] 'pertain to the other side of the skin'
tsí-ñé-emé- tsʰɨ́-ɲɛ́-ɛ̀mɛ́- 'other type of', e.g.,
   tsʰɨ́-ɲɛ́-ɛ̀mɛ́-pápʲà (**tsíñeemébábya**) [adjective] 'other kind of sack'
tsúúcáa- tsʰɯ́ːkʰá-à- 'pertain to the past', e.g.,
   tsʰɯ́ːkʰá-à-ˣpʰɨ̀ (**tsúúcáajpi**) [adjective] 'the one (SgM) of old',
   tsʰɯ́ːkʰá-à-nɛ̀ (**tsúúcáane**) [adjective] 'the thing out of the past',
   tsʰɯ́ːkʰá-à-ˣpʰákʲʰò (**tsúúcáajpácyo**) [adjective] 'the soup that is past its time'
wáhdíe- kpáʔtí-ɛ̀- 'ordinary, common', e.g.,
   kpáʔtíà-hà (**wáhdíaja**) [adjective] 'an ordinary house'
wahdɨ́ɨva- kpàʔ-tɨ́ːβà- 'insignificant', e.g.,
   kpàʔ-tɨ́ːβà-nɛ̀ (**wahdɨ́ɨvane**) [adjective] 'insignificant thing'

Appendix D

A Partial List of Affixes

This appendix lists many of the principle affixes; it is by no means a complete list of affixes. Some classifiers are also included; many more are listed in appendix E.

Section D.1 lists affixes that are primarily suprasegmental. Section D.2 lists suffixes that include segmental material, possibly with suprasegmental effects. These are listed alphabetically by their spelling as written in Bora (i.e., in the "practical orthography").

Within each entry, the information is given in roughly the following order:

1. The affix written according to the Bora writing system (with the possible exception of optional h, j or the added duration a suffix might contribute to the preceding syllable).
2. The affix written with the International Phonetic Alphabet, its tonal properties, and its variants (with mention of the environments where these occur).
3. In single quote marks, a rough characterization of the meaning of the affix. At the end, in parentheses, is the gloss used in examples.
4. In brackets, the affix's morphotactic properties. Notation X/Y indicates that
   (1) the suffix attaches to something of category X, and
   (2) the combination of the host and affix is of category Y.
   For example, N/V means that the suffix attaches to a noun and the result of adding it is a verb.
5. Examples and further comments.

D.1 Affixes without segments

The affixes listed in this section are primarily suprasegmental, that is, indicated by tone (pitch) and vowel length (duration). Some also have segmental variants.

#ό... (that is, a high tone on the first syllable) '**subordinate clause** (indicated by s over the vowel)' [V/N, V/V$_{subordinate}$]

$$\# \; [_V \quad\quad\quad \sigma ... $$
$$\Updownarrow$$
$$\# \; [_{V[+subordinate]} \quad \overset{H}{\sigma}... $$

-Ⓛμ '**emphasis** (emph)'. This always results in -σ̄σ̄ ^{LH} with adjacent, homorganic vowels.[1] It only occurs at the end of an utterance-final verb. For an example, see figure 14.2, page 341.

[-Ⓛ:] '**future**'. See -i ∼ -Ⓛ:, page 429.

-Ⓛ○μ̇ ∼ -Ⓛ○pʰė '**remote past** (rem)'. [V/V, N/N, Adj/Adj, Adv/Adv (second position clitic)] There are two forms:

1. The most frequent form is -Ⓗσ̇, that is, a high tone imposed on the host's final syllable, followed by a copy of the final vowel with low tone.[2]

    (1065) Aanée úmívaábe.
    à:-nɛ̂-ɛ̀   úmíβà-:pɛ̀   'So he fled (long ago).'
    thm-⟨ø⟩-rem flee-⟨SgM⟩

    (1066) a. Mítyamée tsááhi.
            b. Mítyamévάa tsááhi.

    a. mítʲʰà-mɛ̂-ɛ̀   tsʰá:-ʔì   'Many came long ago.'
    many-⟨AnPl⟩-rem come

    b. mítʲʰà-mé-βâ-à   tsʰá:-ʔì   'Many came long ago
    many-⟨AnPl⟩-rpt-rem come   (it is said).'

2. The other form of the future is -Ⓛ○pʰɛ, as in 1067 (which is similar to 1110):

---

[1]One could argue that the form of this suffix is simply -: (or -μ) and that -σ̄σ̄ ^{LH} is the result of FLTS.

[2]This form of the remote past suffix may be simply -Ⓛ○σ, that is, a low tone is imposed on the host's penult, thereby causing the host's final syllable to bear high tone; however, there are possible counter-examples which make us think that this may be one of the rare cases where a suffix imposes a high tone.

(1067) Aanépe úmɨ́vaábe.

a̖ː-nɛ̋-pʰɛ̀   úmíβà-ːpɛ̀   'So he escaped (long ago).'
thm-⟨ø⟩-rem escape-⟨SgM⟩

Examples 1068 (like 277) is a one-word response that adds -ː 'emphasis'; FLTS applies to yield the final split vowel.

(1068) /ő:-pʰɛ̀-ː/ [óːpʰɛ̀ɛ̀] (Óópeé.) 'I (long ago).'
I-rem-emph

Compare 1068 to 366, 1053, and 278. Other examples are found in 1048 and 772.

D.2 Suffixes with segments

The suffixes listed in this section add phonological segments. Many also contribute tone (pitch) and/or vowel length (duration).

-ami   -Ⓛ○ā̖mi 'incredulity' [V/V, N/N, Adj/Adj, Adv/Adv]

(1069) kʰà-ːpʲɛ́-àmì   (¿Caabyéami?) 'Which?! (I can't
       which-⟨SgM⟩-incredulity   believe it!)'

-ba   #σ̄...-Ⓛ○pa³ 'multiple action, intransitive (mIn)' [V/V]. See the tone derivation of ó kʰàːjó-pá-ʔì in figure D.1 as well as those of figure 4.3 (page 120).

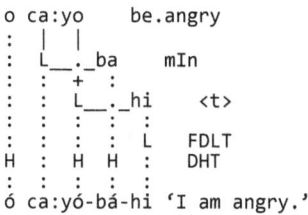

```
o ca:yo       be.angry
: | |
:  L__._ba    mIn
:    +  :
:    :  L__._hi   ⟨t⟩
:    :    :   :
:    :    :   :   L    FDLT
H :  H    H   :        DHT
:    :    :   :
ó ca:yó-bá-hi  'I am angry.'
```

Figure D.1 TD: ó caːyóbáhi

-ːbe ~ -ːbye   -Ⓛːpe 'singular masculine ⟨SgM⟩' [classifier] This suffix may delink conflicting tones except those of a relocation suffix.

-ca   -kʰa 'counterfactual conditional (if)' [V_subordinate/Adv]

(1070) U pééca muurá úúma ó pééiyáhi.

ù̖   pʰɛ̋ː-kʰà̖ mùːɾá ú̖ː-mà   ó pʰɛ́ː-ì-já-ʔì
you go-CF   confirm you-with I go-fut-frs-⟨t⟩

'If you had gone, I would have gone with you.'

---
³This suffix makes its host's initial syllable heavy; see section 5.7.3.

-ca(:) -ⓁOkʰa 'bid for affirmation (affirm)' [V/V, N/N, Adj/Adj, Adv/Adv]

(1071) ¿A úca ú májchoó?
    à úɨ-kʰà̰ úɨ máˣʧʰò-ó-ʔḭ̀ 'Are you going to eat it?'
    y/n you-affirm you eat-fut-⟨t⟩

In 1072 -ⓁOkʰàá comes about by the addition of -: 'emphasis' and the application of FLTS.

(1072) ò:-kʰà̰á (Oócaá.) 'I!'
    I-affirm-emph

-co -kʰo 'implore (implore)' [V_imperative/V (used only with imperatives)]

(1073) ɨ́:kʰúɾḭ̀ tsʰà̰:-kʰò (Ɨ́ɨ́cúi tsaáco.) 'Hurry up and come!'
    quick come-implore

-coba ~ -cyoba -kʰö̌pa 'big (aug)' [N/N, Adj/Adj]

(1074) kpáˣpʰíː-kʲʰò̰pà̰ (wájpíícyoba) 'big man'
    man-aug

(1075) mítʲʰámɛ́-kʰò̰pà̰ (mítyámécoba) 'a great many'
    many-aug

```
llo:ra       parrot
 L   :       lexical
 :   ._coba  augment
 :   : L |   lexical
 :   : : +
 :   : : L_mu  plAn
 :   : : :  :
 :   : : :  L    FDLT
 :   H : H  :    DHT
 :   : : :  :
llo:rá-cobá-mu 'big parrots'
```
Figure D.2 TD: llo:rácobámu

-cooca -kʰǒ:kʰa 'when (when)' [V_subordinate/Adv]

(1076) O tsáácooca úúma ó ihjyúvaáhi.
    ò tsʰá:-kʰò:kʰà̰ úɨ:-mà ó ḭ̀ʔhʲúɨ-βà-á-ʔḭ̀
    I come-when you-with I mouth-have-fut-⟨t⟩
    'When I come, I will speak with you.'

-cu -ⓁOkʰɯ 'singular transitive (sTr)' [V/V]

Example 1077a implies multiple acts of swallowing because mɛʔto 'swallow' is inherently multiple transitive. By contrast, in 1077b the addition of -ⓁOkʰɯ 'sTr' makes the verb singular transitive, so indicates a single act of swallowing.

D.2. SUFFIXES WITH SEGMENTS

(1077) a. Tsúúca taabójɨ́ɨ́ne ó mehdóhi.
    b. Tsúúca taabójɨ́ ó mehdúcúhi.
    a. tsʰɨ́ɨːkʰà tʰàːpó-hɨ́ː-nɛ̀ ó mɛ̀ʔtó-ʔì   'I've already swal-
       already cure-⟨disk⟩-pl I swallow-⟨t⟩   lowed the pills'

    b. tsʰɨ́ɨːkʰà tʰàːpó-hɨ́   ó mɛ̀ʔtɨ́ɨ-kʰɨ́ɨ-ʔì   'I've already swal-
       already cure-⟨disk⟩ I swallow-sTr-⟨t⟩   lowed the pill.'

-ːcu ∼ -ːcuu ∼ -ːcyu   -k⁽ʲ⁾ʰɨɨ 'dual (du)' [N_{inanimate}/N, Adj/Adj]

ɨ́mɛ̀-ʔɛ́-ːkʰɨ̀ɨ	(úmehéécu)	'two trees'
tree-⟨tree⟩-du		
tʰɛ́-nɛ̀-ːkʰɨ̀ɨ	(téneécu)	'these two things'
this-⟨ø⟩-du		
mí-ɲɛ́-ːkʰɨ̀ɨɨ́	(míñéécuú)	'two things'
two-⟨ø⟩-du		
kʰómì-kʲʰɨ̀ɨ	(cómicyu)	'two towns'
town-du		
ɨ́mɨ́á-kpá-ːkʰɨ̀ɨ	(ɨ́mɨ́áwáácu)	'two good slab-like things'
good-⟨slab⟩-InDu		

-cunu ∼ -cyunu   -k⁽ʲ⁾ʰɨ́mɨ 'multiple action (mIn or mTr)' [V/V]

(1078) Píívámeva dsɨ̀ɨnécunú dííbye déjuvu téhullévu.
    pʰíːβá-mɛ̀-βà   tsɨ̀ːnɛ́-kʰɨ̀ɨnɨ́ɨ-ʔ
    numerous-⟨AnPl⟩-rpt run-mIn-⟨t⟩

    tí-ːpʲɛ̀   téhɨ̀ɨ-βɨ̀ɨ   tʰɛ́-ʔɨ̀ɨtʃɛ́-βɨ̀ɨ
    that-⟨SgM⟩ behind-goal that-⟨yonder⟩-goal
    'Many ran behind him to that place.'

-di ∼ -hdi   -Ⓛ⁽ʔ⁾ti 'negative imperative (neg)' [V/V] For examples see section 13.4 and 237, page 132.

-di ∼ -hdi   -Ⓛ⁽ʔ⁾ti 'animate (anim)' [N/N, N/N_{case}] See example 14, page 31. In figure D.3, note that in the derivation of kʰáːní-tì-βɨ̀ɨ the Ⓛ of -ti is delinked by the Ⓛ of -βɨɨ 'goal' whereas in the derivation of ámánà-tí-tʲʰɨ̀ɨ it blocks the Ⓛ of -tʲʰɨɨ 'source':

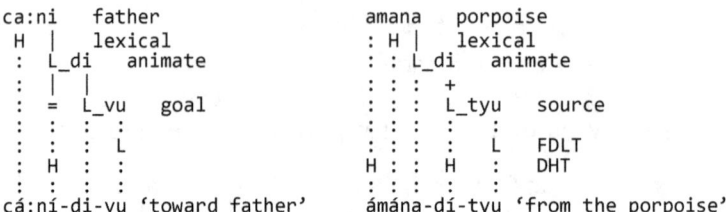

Figure D.3 TD: cá:nídivu, ámánadítyu

-dɨ́ɨva -tɨɨβa 'type of ⟨type⟩' [classifier] (or possibly [N/N]).

(1079) ¿ɨ́nevú ú tsivá ehdɨ́ɨvane?
ɨ́-nè-βɨ́ɨ   ɨ́ɨ   tshìβá-ˀ   èˀ-tɨ́:βà-nè
what-⟨ø⟩-goal you bring-⟨t⟩ that-⟨type⟩-⟨ø⟩
'To where are you bringing that kind of thing?'

-du ~ -dyu ~ -hdu There are two cases. Both mean 'likeness, similarity, comparative' but they differ in their tonal properties and distribuion. (1) -Ⓛ⁽ˀ⁾t⁽ʲ⁾ɯ is a case marker, glossed 'like'; (2) -Ⓛ○⁽ˀ⁾t⁽ʲ⁾ɯ is a classifier, glossed ⟨like⟩. We illustrate each in turn.

1. -Ⓛ⁽ˀ⁾t⁽ʲ⁾ɯ 'likeness, similarity, comparative (like)' [N/N_case].

    (1080) kʰɛ́:mè-tɨ̀ɨ   (kéémedu)   'like an old man'
    tí-:pʲè-tɨ̀ɨ   (dííbyedu)   'like him'
    kʰáná:mà-tɨ̀ɨ   (cánáámadu) 'like salt'

    (1081) tɨ́:   ⓖ tsʰɨ́:hɨ̀ɨ-tɨ̀ɨ   (dɨ́ɨtsɨ́ɨjudu) 'like your mother'
    your   mother-like

    (1082) ò-ˀtɨ̀ɨ tì-:pʲè   (Ohdu dííbye.) 'He is like me.'
    I-like that-⟨SgM⟩

    When -Ⓛt⁽ʲ⁾ɯ follows a monosyllabic classifier, it does not ordinarily delink the low imposed by that classifier on the preceding noun, e.g., ɨ́mɛ́ˀɛ̀-kpá-tɨ̀ɨ (tree-⟨slab⟩-like) 'like a slab-like thing'. Even if that monosyllabic classifier's Ⓛ is blocked, the Ⓛ of -Ⓛtɯ may fail to dock, as though that classifier's Ⓛ were present: kpáᴸkʰó-ˀɛ́-tɨ̀ɨ (flower-⟨tree⟩-like) 'like a flowering tree'.

2. -Ⓛ○⁽ˀ⁾t⁽ʲ⁾ɯ 'likeness, similarity, comparative ⟨like⟩' [V_subordinate/N_case, V_subordinate/V_adverb]. This suffix may delink conflicting tones; for example, figure 3.27, page 85, shows that -Ⓛ○tɯ (-du) 'like' can delink the Ⓛ of -Ⓛɯβɯ (-uvu) 'maximal'.

The tones of the host depend on the number of syllables. The initial tone is always high because the verb is subordinate (indicated σ̇). Hosts with more than two syllables bear the suffix-imposed Ⓛ on the penult.

D.2. SUFFIXES WITH SEGMENTS

However, bisyllabic hosts unexpectedly bear a low tone on their final syllable. (It is as though the suffix's Ⓛ, having been blocked by the subordination tone, docks on the host's final syllable.) See the following chart and the examples that follow it.

HOST	TONES
1 syllable	σ̄-tɨɨ (S)
2 syllables	σσ̀-tɨɨ (S L)
3 syllables	σσσ́-tɨɨ (S L)
4 syllables	σσ́σσ́-tɨɨ (S L)

(1083) nɛ́-ʔtɨ̀ɨ (néhdu) 'like saying'

(1084) íˣkʲʰa̠-tɨ̀ɨ (íjcyadu) 'like being…'
   tóˣkʰo̠-tɨ̀ɨ (dójcodu) 'as when (small things) fall (one after the other)'

(1085) Dibye méénudu tsá o méénutúne.
   [tɨ̀-pʲɛ̀ mɛ:nɨ̀ɨ]-tɨ̀ɨ   tsʰá̋ʔ ò mɛ́:nɨ̀ɨ-tʰɨ́ɨ-nɛ̀
   that-⟨SgM⟩ do   -⟨like⟩ not I do-neg-⟨n⟩
   'I do not do what he does.'

(1086) kʰó-βa̠-ˣtsʰó-tɨ̀ɨ   (cóvajtsódu) 'like burning it'
   firewood-have-caus-like

(1087) iwáájácutsódu
   ì kpá:hákʰɨ̀ɨ-tsʰó-tɨ̀ɨ   ' having informed (someone)'
   self know-caus-like

Figure 3.27, page 85, shows that -ⒺⓄtɨɨ 'like' can delink the Ⓛ of -Ⓛɯβɯ 'maximal'.

-e -è̠ (L) 'pertain to (per)' [N_bound/N Adj/Adj, must be followed by a classifier]

(1088) Diityéejpi áánuú.
   tɨ̀:-tʲʰɛ́-è̠-ˣpʰì   á:nɨ̀ɨ́ɨ́
   that-⟨AnPl⟩-per-⟨SgM⟩ this.SgM
   'This one (SgM) is one of them.'

(1089) ímíbájchóewa
   ímípáˣt͡ʃʰó-è̠-kpà
   fix-per-⟨slab⟩
   'slab (plank,…) pertaining to those that are fixed (e.g., the planks resting on them)'

(1090) a. Diéllevu tsaálle.
   b. Dííélledívú tsaálle.

   a. tí̬ ɛtʃɛ̀-βừɪ   ⎫
      you place-goal   ⎬ tsʰà:-pɛ̀
   b. tí:-ɛ́-tʃɛ̀-tí-βứɪ   ⎬ come-⟨SgM⟩
      you-per-⟨SgF⟩-goal   ⎭

   a. 'He came to where you were.'
   b. 'He came to your female relative.'

-eme -ême 'similar to (sim)' [N/N, Adj/Adj, must be followed by a classifier]

(1091) tí-:pʲɛ́-èmɛ́-ˣpʰì   (dííbyéeméjpi)   'one like him'
       that-⟨SgM⟩-sim-⟨SgM⟩

(1092) íwáeméwa
       í-kpá-èmɛ́-kpà   'a slab (plank, bench, table,
       self-⟨slab⟩-sim-⟨slab⟩   machete,...) like this one'

-haaca ~ -ha -Ⓛ○ʔá(:kʰa) 'realize (realize)' [V/V, N/N, Adj/Adj, Adv/Adv]

(1093) Diibyéha tsáájucóóhi.
       tì-:pʲɛ́-ʔà   tsʰá:-hừkʰó:-ʔì   'He, I see,
       that-⟨SgM⟩-realize come-now-⟨t⟩   is now coming.'

(1094) tì-:pʲɛ́-ʔàkʰà   (Diibyéhaáca.)   'It is HE.'
       that-⟨SgM⟩-realize

The tone derivations of tʰɛ̀:ʔí-ừpá-ʔà and kpàˣpʰí-ừpá-ʔákʰà follow:

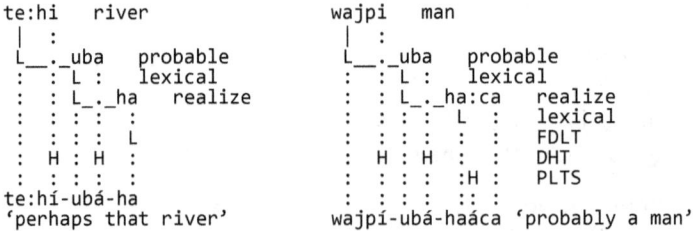

Figure D.4 TD: te:híubáha, wajpíubáhaáca

-ha(ja) -Ⓛ○ʔa(ha) 'challenge veracity, curiosity, perplexity (verify)' [V/V, N/N, Adj/Adj, Adv/Adv, only used with questions] See section 11.2.7.

D.2. SUFFIXES WITH SEGMENTS

(1095) $\begin{Bmatrix} \text{mùːpá-ʔàh̀à} \\ \text{mùːpá-ʔà} \\ \text{WH-verify} \end{Bmatrix}$ $\begin{Bmatrix} \text{¿Muubáhaja?} \\ \text{¿Muubáha?} \end{Bmatrix}$ 'Who might it be?'

-hajchíɨ́jyu ~ -hajchiː -ʔáˣtʃʰiː(hʲɯ) 'if, conditional (if)' [V$_{\text{subordinate}}$/Adv]

(1096) U ímílléhajchíí úúma ó peéhi.
  ɯ̀ ímítʃé-ʔáˣtʃʰí: úːː-mà ó pʰɛ̀-ɛ́-ʔɩ̀
  you want-if   you-with I go-fut-⟨t⟩
  'If you want, I (will) go with you.'

(1097) Májo u ímílléhajchíɨ́jyu.
  máhò ɯ̀ ímítʃé-ʔáˣtʃʰíːhʲɯ̀
  let's.go you want-if
  'Let's go, if you want.'

-hañe -ʔaɲe 'various, collection, set (var)'

1. [N/N, Adj/Adj]

  (1098) ìjámɛ̀-ʔáɲɛ̀ (iyámeháñe) 'various kinds of animals'
      mɨ́amɯ́ɴáá-ʔáɲɛ̀ (mɨamúnáaháñe) 'types of people'
      pʰíːmʲɛ̀-ʔáɲɛ̀ (píímyeháñe) 'type of ants'
      nɯ̀ʔné-ʔàɲɛ̀ (núhnéhañe) 'caterpillars (various types)'

  (1099) háː-ʔàɲɛ̀ (jááhañe) 'houses (hamlet)'

  (1100) nìːhʲá-ʔàɲɛ̀ (nííjyáhañe) 'various rains' (phrase final)
      kʰòːhɨ́-ʔáɲɛ́ (cóójɨháñé) 'various days' (nonfinal)

2. [V$_{\text{nonfinite}}$/N] óʔaɲe 'collection, set (var)' The genitive tone will dock on the nonfinite verb's final syllable unless blocked by the nonfinite tone. This is clearest when the verb has three or four syllables:

  (1101) pʰíʔkʲʰáː-ːβɛ̀ ʔáɲɛ̀ (pihcyáávehañe) 'gatherings'
      gather-sIn var

When the verb is bisyllabic, the nonfinite tone occurs on the first syllable, which blocks the genitive tone from docking on its first syllable. However, the first syllable of ʔaɲɛ will bear tone as though the genitive low tone were present:

  (1102) kpáˣkʰó Ⓖ ʔáɲɛ̀ (wajcóháñe) 'various kinds of flowers'
      tʃʰɛmɛ́ Ⓖ ʔáɲɛ̀ (cheméháñe) 'various sicknesses'
      ató Ⓖ ʔáɲɛ́ (adóháñé) 'beverages'

The noun phrase headed by ʔaɲɛ 'set' may be possessed, as in 1103 and 1104:

(1103) ímyéénujcátsiháñé

í ⓖ [mʲɛ́:nɯ̈-ˣkʰátsʰí ⓖ ʔáɲɛ́] 'their battles'
self   do-recip   var

(1104) méimítyuháñe

mɛ́ ⓖ [ímí-tʲʰɯ̈ ⓖ ʔáɲɛ̀] 'our evil deeds'
SAP   good-neg   var

-hde ~ -hdye -ⓛ◯ʔt⁽ʲ⁾e 'concede (concede)' [V/V, N/N, Adj/Adj, Adv/Adv] See section 11.2.9.

(1105) Anéhde waáca dipye.

à-nɛ́-ʔtɛ̀   kpàá-kʰà   tì-pʲʰɛ̀   'OK, then, you
thm-⟨ø⟩-concede permit-affirm youImp-go   may go.'

-hnécu -ⓛʔnekʰɯ 'immediate result (result)' [V_active/Adv]

(1106) Íñehi ó wátsahjyúcú baavu callájahnécu.

íɲɛ̀-ʔì   ó kpátsʰà-ʔhʲɯ́ɾkʰɯ́-ʔ pà:-βɯ̀
aguaje-⟨cluster⟩ I cut-sTr-⟨t⟩   below-goal

kʰàtʃáhà-ʔnɛ́kʰɯ̀.
scattered-result

'I cut the cluster of *aguaje* palm fruit down with the result that it scattered all over.'

-hi -ⓛ◯ʔ(i) ⟨t⟩ [classifier] (This occurs on main clause verbs when the subject is not a classifier.) Utterance medial the form is -ⓛ◯ʔ while utterance final it is -ⓛ◯ʔi. -hi is generally written sentence finally. Sentence medially the glottal stop is pronounced but not written; the final high tone adequately indicates its presence.

(1107) a. Táñaalle dsɨjcó íwajyámu.

b. Táñaalle íwajyámú dsɨjcóhi.

a. [tʰá ⓖ ɲá:-tʃɛ̀] tsɨˣkʰó-ʔ [í ⓖ kpahʲámɯ̀ɾ]
my   sib-⟨SgF⟩ sew-⟨t⟩ self clothes

b. [tʰá ⓖ ɲá:-tʃɛ̀] [í ⓖ kpahʲámɯ́ɾ] tsɨˣkʰó-ʔì
my   sib-⟨SgF⟩ self clothes sew-⟨t⟩

a,b. 'My sister sews her clothes.'

-hijcya   -ʔiˣkʲʰa
This is an affixal form of the verb 'be'; see section 5.10.

1. [V/V]   -Ⓛʔiˣkʲʰa 'habitual (be)' In 1108 the Ⓛ is blocked by the host's lexically marked low tone:

   (1108) Paíjyuváré wakímyeíhíjcyaábe.

   pʰà-íhʲùɪ-βá-ɾɛ́   kpàkʰímʲɛ́í-ʔ íˣkʲʰà-ːpɛ̀   'He works
   all-⟨day⟩-rpt-only   work-sub   be-⟨SgM⟩   every day.'

   Note that in 1151, page 436, -ʔiˣkʲʰa- does not seem to indicate 'habitual' specifically, but a more general imperfective aspect.

2. [N/V] -ʔiˣkʲʰa 'characteristic (be)'

   (1109) Diibyéhijcya ávyeta ímí.

   tì-ːpʲɛ́-ʔíˣkʲʰà   áβʲɛ̀tʰà ímíʔ   'He is always very good.'
   that-⟨SgM⟩-be   very   good

-hja   -ⓁO̜ʔha 'not witnessed (nwit)' [V/V, N/N, Adj/Adj, Adv/Adv]

(1110) Aanéhjápe peebe ihjyávu.

à:-nɛ́-ʔhá-pʰɛ̀   pʰɛ̀-ːpɛ̀   [iˀ hʲá]-βùɪ
thm-⟨event⟩-nwit-rem   go-⟨SgM⟩   self house -goal
'So he went to his house (but I did not see it).'

-i ~ -Ⓛ: (or equivalently, -Ⓛμ)   'future (fut)' [V/V] There are two forms of this suffix.

1. When followed by a suffix other than -ⓁO̜ʔi ⟨t⟩, the form is simply -ì, as illustrated in figure D.5a and b.
2. When followed by -ⓁO̜ʔi ⟨t⟩, the future suffix is indicated by (1) a low tone on the host's final syllable (delinking any conflicting low tone that might be present, as in 271b), and (2) lengthening the host's final vowel; the verb so formed almost always occurs phrase finally so the lengthened vowel undergoes PLTS and thus the host-future-⟨t⟩ sequence ends with V̂V̀ʔì. Compare the tone derivations of páˣtsʰó-ì-tʃɛ̀, máˣtʃʰò-í-mɛ̀, and máˣtʃʰò-ó-ʔì in figure D.5c.

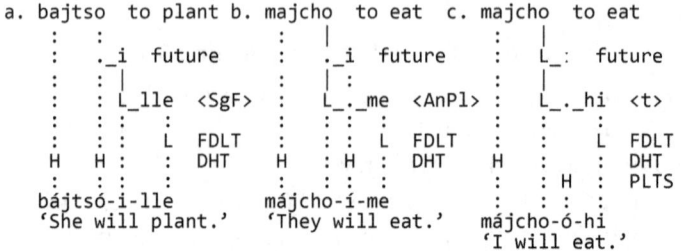

Figure D.5 TD: bájtsóille, májchoíme, májchoóhi

We now consider further this second form of the future suffix. First, one might think that this form of the future suffix does not need to specify Ⓛ (the low tone of the host's final syllable) because it is imposed by the following -Ⓛ◯ʔi ⟨t⟩. However, -Ⓛ◯ʔi does not delink a conflicting low tone, as can be seen, for example, in D.1, page 421. Thus, the delinking seen in examples like 271b must be the result of a low tone imposed by the future suffix.

Second, generally suffixes that bear tones that dock on their hosts are blind to whether the host's vowels are short or long: the tones dock on *syllables*, not *moras*. However, in the case of the long vowel created by this form of the future tense, the addition of -Ⓛ◯ʔi counts the length as a syllable, docking its low tone on the host's final syllable rather than on its penult.

This exception—to what is otherwise a very robust generalization—undoubtedly reflects the full syllabicity of -i, 'future' (perhaps simply by analogy but more likely as a reflex of a shared origin).

Third, given that -Ⓛ◯ʔi counts the length added by the future suffix as a syllable, it is tempting to suppose that this variant of the future is Ⓛσ, that is, the low tone to be docked on the host's final syllable and the addition of a syllable. If we assume—as seems quite reasonable—that the syllable is realized in the most minimal way, that is, as a vowel, and that this vowel would draw its (place and manner) features from the preceding vowel, then this second form of the future is accounted for without using PLTS.

However, compare 1111a. and b. The first treats the verb as phrase final, thus undergoing PLTS, as described above, whereas the second treats the verb as phrase internal, thus failing to undergo PLTS. Thus, to account for this we assume that the future suffix adds length (a mora) and not a syllable.

D.2. SUFFIXES WITH SEGMENTS

(1111) a. Ó májchóteé tahjyávu.
b. Ó májchótee tahjyávu.

$$
\begin{array}{l}
\acute{o} \\
I
\end{array}
\left\{
\begin{array}{l}
\text{a. má}^x\text{tʃʰó-tʰè̠-ɛ́-}^{\text{ʔ}} \\
\text{má}^x\text{tʃʰó-tʰè̠-}ː\text{-ʔì} \\
\text{eat-go.do-fut-}\langle\text{t}\rangle
\end{array}
\right\}
\begin{array}{l}
\text{tʰá}^G \text{ʔhʲá-βùɪ} \\
\text{my house-goal}
\end{array}
$$
'I will go to eat at my house.'

-i ~ -iíkye -i^L ~ -(Ⓛ)◯i:kʲʰe^L 'projected time (PT)' [V/V, N/N, Adj/Adj, Adv/Adv] (See section 5.9.3.3.) The full form (-i̠:kʲʰè) is used utterance finally or if another clitic follows; otherwise (i.e., utterance medially with no following clitic) the short form (-i) is used.

(1112) tsʰá̠ʔá-i̠:kʲʰè (tsáháiíkye)   'not yet'
not-PT

(1113) Tsáhái dibye tsáátune.
tsʰá̠ʔá-i̠^{L} tì-pʲè̠   tsʰá:-tʰùɪ-nè̠   'He has not yet come.'
not-PT that-⟨SgM⟩ come-neg-⟨n⟩

See also 794, page 314.

-icho -itʃʰó$^{H\ Hʔ}$ 'sort of, a little bit (ish)' [Adj/Adj] See section 7.8.5.2.

-ijyu -ihʲɯ^L 'at that time ⟨time⟩' [V$_{\text{subordinate}}$/NP]

(1114) Taabóóbé oke tááboó cóómívu o pééijyu.
tʰà:pó-:pɛ́ ò-kʰè̠   tʰá:pò-ó-^{ʔ} [kʰó:mí-βùɪ ò pʰè̠:^{S}]-ìhʲùɪ
cure-⟨SgM⟩ I-objAn cure-fut-⟨t⟩ town-goal I go   -⟨time⟩
'The doctor will treat me when I go to town.'

-iñu -(Ⓛ)◯iɲɯ 'go after doing (do.go)' [V/V]

(1115) Íllure oke pajtyéíñuúbe.
ítʃùɪ-ɾè̠   ò-kʰè̠   pʰá^{x}tʲʰɛ́-íɲùɪ-:pè̠   'He passed in front
like.that-only I-objAn pass-do.go-⟨SgM⟩   of me, leaving me.'

-iyo ~ -iya -(Ⓛ)◯i-yo^L ~ -i-ya^L (fut-frs) 'should, would' [N/N, follows a classifier if present] (See example 1070.)

-j -Ⓛ^{x} 'vocative (voc)' [N/N$_{\text{case}}$, V/V]

(1116) tʃí:ʔì-^{x} , tí-tʃʰàá   (Llííhij, díchaá.)   'Son, come!'
son-voc youImp-come

-jcatsi -ˣkʰát̄sʰi 'reciprocal (recip)' [V/V]

(1117) Úhbájcatsímútsí méwá hallútu.

úɨʔpá-ˣkʰàtsʰí-múɨtsʰí mɛ́kpá ⓖ ʔatʃúɨ-tʰùɨ
argue-recip-⟨DuM⟩ wife   top-sou
'They argued about the wife.'

-je -Ⓛhe 'come after doing (do.come)' [V/V] Contrary to the generalization that the low tones imposed by pronominal classifiers are blocked by the low tones of relocation suffixes, in example 104, page 84, the Ⓛ of -Ⓛ:pɛ ⟨SgM⟩ delinks the Ⓛ of -Ⓛhɛ 'come after doing'.

-jɨ ~ -hjɨ -Ⓛ◯⁽ʔ⁾hɨ 'plural (pl)' [N_inanimate/N, Adj/Adj]

(1118) ɛ̀:-né-ʔhɨ̀   (eenéhjɨ) 'those (things)'
       that-⟨ø⟩-pl

(1119) ímí-tʲʰùɨ-né-ʔhɨ̀ (ímítyunéhjɨ) 'bad (things)'
       good-neg-⟨ø⟩-pl

(1120) ímí-ʔà:-mí-hɨ̀   (ímíhaamɨ́jɨ) 'good (books, papers,
       good-⟨tree⟩-⟨leaf⟩-pl   bills,...)'

(1121) a. Mítyame tsááhi.
       b. Mítyaméhjɨ tsááhi.

a. mítʲʰà-mè   ⎫   ⎧ a.   'Many are coming.'
   many-⟨AnPl⟩   ⎬ tsʰá:-ʔì   ⎨ b.   'Many big ones are
b. mítʲʰà-mé-ʔhɨ́   ⎭ come   ⎩ ws'coming.'
   many-⟨AnPl⟩-pl

-jɨɨva ~ -jɨɨ -Ⓛ◯hɨ:(βa) 'deny (deny)' [V_subordinate/V, N/N, Adj/Adj, Adv/Adv] The final syllable (βa) only occurs sentence finally.

The tones for nouns and verbs are different.

1. Following a noun the form is -Ⓛ◯hɨ:(βa).

   (1122) tì-:pʲé-hɨ́:βà   (Diibyéjɨ́ɨva.) 'It is not he.'
          that-⟨SgM⟩-deny

2. Following a verb (after the classifier subject) the form is #Ⓗ... -Ⓛhɨ:(βa). This may delink conflicting tones, particularly those of a preceding pronominal classifier, as illustrated in 1123.

   (1123) Májchóóbejɨ́ɨ mítyane.
          máˣtʃʰó-:pè-hɨ́:   mítʲʰà-nè 'He did not eat much.'
          eat-⟨SgM⟩-deny much-⟨ø⟩

D.2. SUFFIXES WITH SEGMENTS

-jkimei -ˣkiʰmḛ̄i 'behave like, to act like (act.like)' [N/V]

(1124) ó tsʰíːmɛ́nɛ́-ˣkʰímɛ̀í-ʔ(ì) (Ó tsíímɛ́néjkímeí.)
I child-act.like-⟨t⟩
'I act like a child.'

-jtane -ˣtʰāne 'exclude, without regard for (exclude)'
[V/V, N/N, Adj/Adj, Adv/Adv]

(1125) Díítyéjtāne dsííneébe.
tíː-tʲʰɛ́-ˣtʰānɛ̀   tsíːnɛ̀-ːpɛ̀   'He ran without giving
that-⟨AnPl⟩-exclude run-⟨SgM⟩   them a thought.'

See also 809, page 316.

-juco(ː) ∼ **-co**: We list here two closely related morphemes, the verbal suffix -Ⓛ◯huk̄ʰo: 'now' discussed in section 5.12.1.1 and the second-position clitic -Ⓛ◯huk̄ʰo 'focus' discussed in section 11.2.2.

1. [V/V] -Ⓛ◯huk̄ʰo: 'now, already (now)'
   (1126) ò pʰɛ́-hùkʰóː-ʔ(ì) (O péjucóó.) 'I go now.'
   I go-now-⟨t⟩
   This shortens to -kʰò: (-coo) in certain (rare) cases, as in 1127:
   (1127) ìˣkʲʰá-kʰóː-tʃɛ̀-híː   (Ijcyácóóllejíí.) 'She is no
   be-now-⟨SgF⟩-deny   longer here.'

2. [N/N, Adj/Adj, Adv/Adv] -Ⓛ◯huk̄ʰo 'focus (focus)'
   (1128) tì-ːpʲɛ́-hùkʰò   (Diibyéjuco.) 'It is HE.'
   that-⟨SgM⟩-focus
   For examples, see the tone derivations in figure 3.10, page 67.

-juj -Ⓛhɯ-ˣ 'quick (quick-voc)' [V_{imperative}/V] The host bears nonfinite tone (with perhaps some exceptions) and -Ⓛhɯˣ cannot delink this. Therefore the Ⓛ does not dock unless the stem is at least three syllables long. For examples see section 14.2.2.

-ke ∼ **-kye**   -Ⓛk⁽ʲ⁾ʰe 'animate object (objAn)' [N/N_{case}] This suffix delinks conflicting tones.

(1129) Oohííbyeke ó aamú.
òːʔí-pʲɛ̀-kʰɛ̀   ó àːmɯ́-ʔ(ì)   'I shot the jaguar/dog.'
jaguar-⟨SgM⟩-objAn I shoot-⟨t⟩

-ki   -⓪kʰi 'purpose (pur)' This suffix delinks conflicting tones.
1. [V_subordinate/Adv]
   (1130) O péé tahjyávú o májchoki.
   ò pʰɛ́:-ˀ [[tʰáˀ hʲá]-βúɪ
   I go-⟨t⟩   my house -goal
   ò máˣtʃʰò]-kʰì
   I eat   -pur
   'I go to my house to eat.'
2. [V_relocation/V] This is also used on the main verb following a relocation suffix, for example:
   (1131) ó máˣtʃʰò-tʰɛ́-kʰì⁴ (Ó májchotéki.)   'I go to eat.'
   I eat-go.do-pur

-lle   -⓪◯tʃe 'treat like (treat)' [N/V]
(1132) Dííbyeke ó tsɨ́ɨ́menélléhi.
   tí-:pʲɛ̀-kʰɛ̀   ó tsʰɨ́:mɛ̀né-tʃɛ́-ˀì   'I treat him
   that-⟨SgM⟩-objAn I child-treat-⟨t⟩   like a child.'

-lle   -⓪tʃe 'try (try)' [V/V]
(1133) ¿Ɨ́veekí oke ú méénulléhi?
   íβɛ̀:kʰí ò-kʰɛ̀   úɪ   mɛ́:nùɪ-tʃɛ́-ˀì   'Why are you trying
   why   I-objAn you hit-try-⟨t⟩   to hit me?'

(1134) ò-kʰɛ̀   mɛ́:núɪ-tʃɛ̀-:pɛ̀ (Oke méénúlleébe.) 'He tried
   I-objAn hit-try-⟨SgM⟩   to hit me.'

-lle   -⓪tʃe 'singular feminine ⟨SgF⟩' [classifier] This suffix may delink conflicting tones except those of a relocation suffix.
(1135) máˣtʃʰò-tʃɛ̀ (Májcholle.) 'She eats.'
   eat-⟨SgF⟩

-lliíhye ~ -hlliíhye ~ -llii ~ -hllii   -⁽ˀ⁾tʃ́i:(ˀʲe) 'reason, motive, purpose (motive)' [N/N_case V_subordinate/Adv]
(1136) Ehdu méénuube tsɨ́ɨ́júlliíhye.
   ɛ̀ˀ-tùɪ   mɛ́:nùɪ-:pɛ̀   tsʰɨ́:húɪ-tʃ́ɨ:ˀʲɛ̀   'He made it like that
   that-⟨like⟩ make-⟨SgM⟩   mother-for   for his mother.'

In 738, page 299, -tʃ́ìi 'motive' forms part of a sentence-initial connective.

---
⁴In 1131 the low tone of -⓪kʰì 'purpose' is blocked by that of -⓪tʰɛ 'go to do'.

Section 10.7.2 presents examples where -tʃĩ̀ 'motive' follows a subordinate clause (always preceded by -nɛ ⟨event⟩).

-ma   -Ⓛma 'instrument, accompaniment (with)' [N/N$_{case}$] This suffix delinks conflicting tones.

(1137) Táñáhbema ó táávátééhi.
  [tʰá Ⓖ ɲá-ʔpɛ̀]-mà ó tʰá:βá-tʰɛ̀-ɛ́-ʔì
  my   sib-⟨SgM⟩ -with I hunt-go.do-fut-⟨t⟩
  'I go with my brother to hunt.'

(1138) Táñaalle óóma dsɨjcó táwajyámu.
  [tʰá Ⓖ ɲà:̌-tʃɛ̀] ó:-mà tsɨˣkʰó-ʔ tʰá k͡pȁh^{j}ámùɪ
  my   sib-⟨SgF⟩ I-with sew-⟨t⟩ my clothes
  'My sister sewed my clothes.'

-me ~ -mye 'animate plural'

1. [V/V$_{complete}$] -Ⓛ○m$^{(j)}$e ⟨AnPl⟩ This suffix may delink conflicting tones except those of a relocation suffix.

   (1139) màˣtʃʰó-mɛ̀ (Majchóme.) 'They are eating.'
     eat-⟨AnPl⟩

2. [N$_{animate}$/N$_{plural}$] -Ⓛm$^{(j)}$e ⟨AnPl⟩ -mɛ (-me) ⟨AnPl⟩ may form the plural of certain nouns:

   (1140) ò:ʔí-:p^{j}ɛ̀ (jaguar-⟨SgM⟩ oohííbye) 'jaguar'
     ò:ʔí-m^{j}ɛ̀ (jaguar-⟨AnPl⟩ oohímye) 'jaguars'

   (1141) /pʰá-mɛ̀-:rɛ̀/ (pámeére) 'all of them (animate)'
     all-⟨AnPl⟩-only

See also the tone derivation in figure 3.33, page 90.

-mei -Ⓛmei 'expression of compassion or pity (poor)' [V/V, N/N, Adj/Adj, Adv/Adv]

(1142) ¡Áyúú, ɨ́dátsó áádiméi!
  ájúɪ: ɨ́tátsʰó á:tì-mɛ́ì   'Oh! Poor him!'
  oh   sad   that.SgM-poor

(1143) ¡Éje, áádiméi; ú úvañú!
  ɛ́hɛ̀ , á:tì-mɛ́ì ; úɪ ú̀βàɲú̀ɪ-ʔì
  Look that.one-poor you make.suffer-⟨ø⟩
  'Look at that poor man! You really made him suffer!'

-mei -m$^{(j)}$ěi 'reflexive, passive (r/p)' [V/V (valence reducing)]

(1144) k͡páʔtàɨ-nú̀ɪ-mɛ̀ì-:p^{j}ɛ̀ (Wáhdaɨnúmeííbye.) 'He cut himself.'
  cut-mTr-r/p-⟨SgM⟩

Although the verb of 1144 bears -nɯ 'multiple transitive (mTr)', it generally refers to a single cut, not to many cuts nor to cutting repeatedly.

-mu -Ⓛm⁽ʲ⁾ɯ 'plural (for animate nouns) (plAn)' [N$_{animate}$/N, Adj/Adj]

(1145) mɛ́:nì-<u>mɯ̀ɯ̀</u>   (méénimu) 'peccary'
peccary-plAn

(1146) ní:βɯ́ɨkpà-<u>mʲɯ̀ɯ̀</u> (níívúwamyu) 'deer (plural)'
deer-plAn

-mutsi -Ⓛmɯtsʰi 'dual masculine ⟨DuM⟩' [classifier N/N][5] This suffix may delink conflicting tones except those of a relocation suffix.

(1147) ímípá^{x}ʧʰò-<u>mɯ́tsʰɨ̀</u> (ímíbájchomútsi)) 'the two (DuM) fixed (it)'
fix-⟨DuM⟩

(1148) Ihjyúvájcatsímútsi.

ì^{ʔ}hʲɯ́ɨβá-^{x}kʰátsʰí-<u>mɯ́tsʰɨ̀</u>[6]   'Those two (males) are talking'.
talk-recip-⟨DuM⟩

-mupɨ -Ⓛmɯpʰɨ 'dual feminine ⟨DuF⟩' [classifier N/N][7] This suffix may delink conflicting tones except those of a relocation suffix.

(1149) ímípá^{x}ʧʰò-<u>mɯ́pʰɨ̀</u> (ímíbájchomúpɨ) 'the two (DuF) fixed (it)'
fix-⟨DuF⟩

(1150) Úmɨhé pañe wákímyeímúpɨ.

úmɨ̀ʔɛ́ Ⓖ pʰáɲɛ̀ kpákʰímʲɛ́í-<u>mɯ́pʰɨ̀</u>[8]   'Those two (females)
field   inside work-⟨DuF⟩   work in the field.'

-naaaca ~ -naa -naá(:kʰa) 'while' [V$_{subordinate}$/Adv] There are two forms:
Sentence finally the form is -naá:kʰa. By PLTS, this becomes #Ⓗ...-náàákʰà.

(1151) Tsɨɨju goocó tsɨ́ɨ́mene tahíjcyánáaáca.

tsʰɨ́:hɯ̀ kò:kʰó-$^?$ [tsʰɨ́:mɛ̀nɛ̀ tʰà-$^?$ i^{Sx}kʲʰá]-<u>náàákʰà</u>
mother laugh-⟨t⟩ child   cry-sub be   -while
'The mother laughs while the baby is crying.'

Sentence medially the form is simply #Ⓗ...-naá.

---

[5] -Ⓛmɯtsʰi may be the combination of -Ⓛmɯ 'plAn' and -tsʰi ⟨DuM⟩.
[6] The Ⓛ of -mɯtsʰi ⟨DuM⟩ is blocked by the lexically marked Ⓛ of the reciprocal suffix.
[7] -Ⓛmɯpʰɨ may be the combination of -Ⓛmɯ 'plAn' and -pʰɨ ⟨DuF⟩.
[8] The Ⓛ of -mɯpʰɨ ⟨DuF⟩ is blocked by the root's lexically marked Ⓛ.

D.2. SUFFIXES WITH SEGMENTS

-ne ∼ -ñe   -ⓁOnɛ̀ 'singular (sg)' [Adj_{inanimate}/Adj] Adj_{inanimate} includes adjectival, numeral and qualifier phrases.

-(:)ne ∼ -(:)ñe   -ⓁO(:)nɛ 'plural (plIn)' [N_{inanimate}/N]; for example, kʰómì-ɲɛ̀ (cómiñe) 'towns' and úmɛ̌ʔɛ́-ːnɛ̀ (úmehééne) 'trees'. The tone derivation of úmɨ̀ʔɛ́-kpùɾɨ́-nɛ̀ 'little fields' follows:

```
                umɨhe      field
                : L :
                : : ._wuu    dim
                : :   L:     lexical
                : :   |:
                : :   L._ne  plIn
                : :   :: 
                : :   ::  L  FDLT
                H : H :H  :   DHT
                : :   ::  :
                úmɨhé-wuú-ne    'little fields'
```
Figure D.6 TD: úmɨhéwuúne

See also [úmɛ́-ʔɛ̀-kpá-ːnɛ̀] (tree-⟨tree⟩-⟨slab⟩-plIn úméhewááanetu) 'clothes pins' in 703, and [úmɛ̀ʔɛ́-ːnɛ̀-ʔáɲɛ̀] (tree-plIn-var úmehéénehéñe) 'many diverse trees' in figure 3.6.

-ne   -nɛ ⟨ø⟩ is the minimally meaningful inanimate classifier. It may be used to refer to a thing, circumstance, event, time, place,.... It is used in various morphosyntactic contexts, with some differences in the tone it imposes on its host. We will consider three cases:

1. [N_{bound}/N, Adj_{bound}/N]   -Ⓛne ⟨ø⟩ may follow a noun or adjective. In this case it docks a low tone on the host's final syllable. This is normal for a monosyllabic classifier as stated in section 6.1.4. The tone derivations of kʰóʔpʰɛ̀-nɛ̀ 'hard thing' and kʰóʔpʰɛ́-nɛ̀-ɨ́βɨ̀ 'really hard thing' follow:

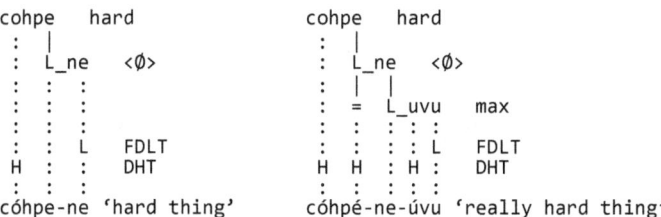

Figure D.7 TD: cóhpene, cóhpéneúvu

2. [V/V_{complete}]   -ⓁOne ⟨ø⟩ may follow a verb as a classifier subject, as discussed in section 6.2.1. Note that in this case -ne ⟨ø⟩ docks a low tone on the host's penultimate syllable, as in 1152, for which the tone derivation is given in figure D.8:

438 APPENDIX D. AFFIXES

(1152) tʰúɨtʰáβà -ːβɛ́-<u>nɛ̀</u> (Tútávaavéne.) 'It soured.'
sour-sIn-⟨ø⟩

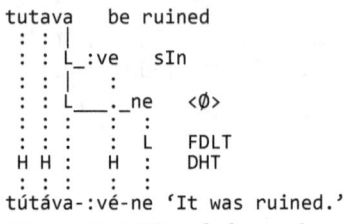

Figure D.8 TD: tútávaavéne.

3. [V_{subordinate}/N,⁹ V_{subordinate}/AdvCl] -Ⓛ◯nɛ may follow a subordinate verb. (Recall that the verb of a subordinate clause bears a high tone on its first syllable, as discussed in section 3.12.1.)
The subordinate clause may be a COMPLEMENT, as discussed in chapter 16: a subject complement, as in example 949, page 360, or an object complement, as in example 950, page 360.
A case marker may follow -nɛ ⟨event⟩ to indicate the relationship of the subordinate clause to the higher verb, as in example 983. However, if the subordinate clause is a direct object, a case marker does not follow.
The subordinate clause may be a a RELATIVE CLAUSE, , as discussed in chapter 18. See, for example, 1013, page 387.
Or the subordinate clause may be an ADVERBIAL CLAUSE, in which case -nɛ may refer to an event, a circumstance, a state of affairs, or such; these are glossed as ⟨event⟩ rather than as ⟨ø⟩. The main and subordinate clauses may be temporally related, as in 1153, in which the event of the main clause is understood as occurring after the event indicated by the subordinate clause.

(1153) Imájchóne péjúcoóbe.
ì   máˢˣʧʰó-<u>nɛ̀</u>   pʰɛ́-húkʰò-ːpɛ̀   'After eating, he left.'
self eat-⟨event⟩ go-now-⟨SgM⟩

-ne ~ -hne   -Ⓛ◯⁽ˀ⁾ne 'recent (rec)' [V/V, N/N, Adj/Adj, Adv/Adv, second position clitic]

(1154) Ohné ó meenú.
ò-ˀ<u>nɛ́</u> ó mɛ̀ːnɨ́-ʔ(ì)   'I did it recently.'
I-rec I do-⟨t⟩

(1155) tì-ːpʲɛ́-<u>nɛ̀</u>   mɛ̀ːnɨ́-ʔ(ì) (Diibyéne meenú.) 'He did it
that-⟨SgM⟩-rec do-⟨t⟩   recently.'

---
⁹When the subordinate clause is a relative clause, what results is really a noun *phrase* headed by -ne ⟨ø⟩.

D.2. SUFFIXES WITH SEGMENTS

-nu -ⓁОnɯ 'do, become, cause to be, cause to have (do)' [N/V]

(1156) Dííbyeke ó dsɨɨdsɨ́nuhi.

    tí-ːpʲɛ̀-kʰɛ̀   ó tsɨ̀ːtsɨ́-nɯ́-ʔɪ̀   'I helped him have money.'
    that-⟨SgM⟩-objAn I money-do-⟨t⟩

The tone derivations of kpáɲɛ̀ʔhɨ́-nɯ́-ɨ̀-já-ʔɪ̀ and kpáɲɛ̀ʔhɨ́-nɯ́-ɨ́-jó-tʃɛ̀-kʰɛ̀ follow:

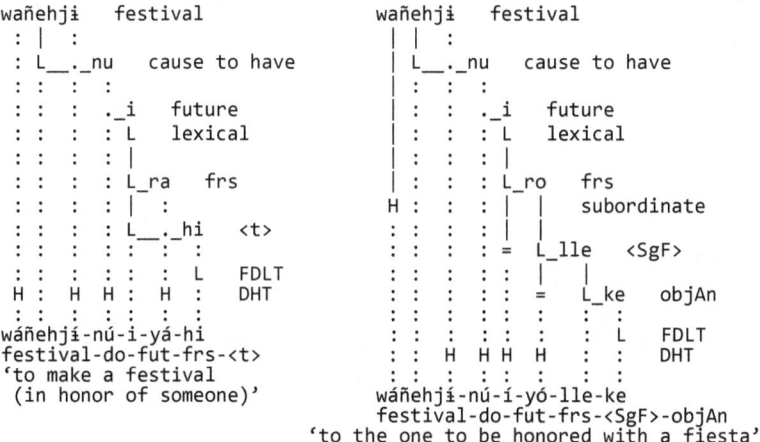

Figure D.9 TD: wáñehjɨ́núiyáhi, wáñehjɨ́núíyólleke

-pe -ⓁОpʰé̤ ~ -ⓁОμ̤ See **remote past**, page 420.

-pejtso -pʰéˣtsʰo 'upon encountering (meet)' [V/V]

(1157) Ihjyávu óómííbyeke ó úhbápejtsóhi.

    [[[ɪ̂ᴳ_i ʔhʲá]-βɯ̀ː
    self house -goal

    òːmíˢ]-ːpʲɛ̀_i]-kʰɛ̀   ó ɯ́ʔpá-pʰɛ̀ˣtsʰó-ʔɪ̀.
    arrive -⟨SgM⟩ -objAn I upbraid-meet-⟨ø⟩
    'I bawled him$_i$ out when he$_i$ returned to his$_i$ house.'

Example 531 is similar.

-pi -ⓁОpʰi 'excessively, habitually (excess)' [V/V]

(1158) Tájtsɨɨméné cuwápíhi.

    tʰáˣtsʰɨ̀ːméné kʰɯ̀kpá-pʰɨ́-ʔɪ̀   'My baby always sleeps.'
    child   sleep-excess-⟨t⟩

In 1159 the host's penult is not low (as expected) because this word is a predicate adjective:

(1159) kʰɨ́ɾkpá-pʰɨ́-ʔ   ùɾɨ́ɨ (Cúwápí uú.) 'You sleep too much.'
    sleep-excess-⟨t⟩ you

-ra   See -ro ~ -ra ~-yo ~ -ya 'frustrative, contraexpectation (frs)'

-re ~ -ye   -(ː)ɾɛ ~ -(ː)ɾɛ 'only'
[N/N, Adj/Adj, Adv/Adv, V_{nonfinite}/V_{nonfinite}]
 -(ː)ɾɛ ~ -(ː)jɛ 'only' does not bear any inherent tones but, by adding a syllable, could cause a violation of the *LLX constraint. This is avoided in the following ways:

1. If the word to which -ɾɛ ~ -jɛ is added would have ended LL#, then—whether it is verbal or nominal—the tones become LH-ɾɛ.
2. If the word to which -ɾɛ is added would have ended HL#, then those tones remain: HL-ɾɛ.

With some exceptions, -(ː)ɾɛ ~ -(ː)jɛ lengthens the preceding vowel only if the word does not have a heavy syllable earlier in the word. Compare, for example, kpáˣpʰɨ̀-jɛ̀ 'man only', in which there are no long vowels before -(ː)jɛ and it does lengthen the preceding syllable, with the following words in which there are earlier long vowels and -(ː)jɛ does not lengthen the preceding vowel: hɨ̀ːβá-ɾɛ̀ 'trail only', íkʲʰòːkʰá-ɾɛ̀ 'only now', tɨ̀ː-tʲʰɛ́-ɾɛ̀ 'they only', tíː-tʃɛ̀-ɾɛ̀ 'she only'.

-ri ~ -yi   -ⓁɾI ~ -Ⓛji 'inanimate oblique (oblIn)' [N/N_{case}]

(1160) Ínɨ̈ːtsúwari wákímyeííbye.
    ínɨ̀ːtsʰɨ́ɨ-kpà-ɾɨ̀   kpákʰímʲèí-ːpʲɛ̀   'He works with his
    machete-⟨slab⟩-oblIn work-⟨SgM⟩   machete.'

(1161) Mítyane imájchóneri chémeébe.
    [mítʲʰà-nɛ̀ ì   máˣtʃʰó]-nɛ̀-ɾɨ̀   tʃʰɛ́mɛ̀-ːpɛ̀
    much-⟨ø⟩ self eat   -⟨ø⟩-oblIn sick-⟨SgM⟩
    'He got sick because he ate too much.'

-rívaco   #óː....-ɾìβakʰo 'resulting position (result.posit)'
[V_{nonfinite root}/Adv] See 180, page 114.

-ro ~ -ra ~-yo ~ -ya   -Ⓛɾo ~ -Ⓛɾa 'frustrative, contraexpectation (frs)'
[V/V, N/N, Adj/Adj] Note that in 1162 and 1163 the syllables preceding -ɾo and -ja 'frustrative' bear low tone:

(1162) Mítyane ó májchorá. Áároobe tsá o újcávatú.
    mítʲʰànɛ̀ ó máˣtʃʰò-ɾá-ʔì   áː-ɾò̀-ːpɛ̀   tsʰàʔ
    much I eat-frs-⟨t⟩   thm-frs-⟨SgM⟩ not

ò úrˣkʰáβà-tʰɯ́(nὲ)
I become.fat-neg
'I eat a lot. However, I do not get fat.'

(1163) Ó májchóiyáhi.
ó máˣʧʰó-ì-já-ʔì   'I want to eat (but there is nothing).'
I eat-fut-frs-⟨t⟩

-ⓁɾO ~ -Ⓛɾa 'frustrative' delinks conflicting tones; see figures 3.30 and 3.31, page 87 and example 1164, in which -ɾo 'frustrative' delinks the Ⓛ from the penult of -Ⓛ◯húɯ̋kʰo 'focus':

(1164) tì-ːpʲέ-húɯkʰò:-ɾò¹⁰   (Diibyéjúcoóro.)
that-⟨SgM⟩-focus-frs
'It is HE (but that does not matter).'

However, apparently -ɾo ~ -ɾa 'frustrative' does not delink a root's lexically marked tone, as shown by the tone derivations of íʔβètʰέ-ɾá-ʔì and íʔβètʰέ-ɾó-nὲ in figure D.10:

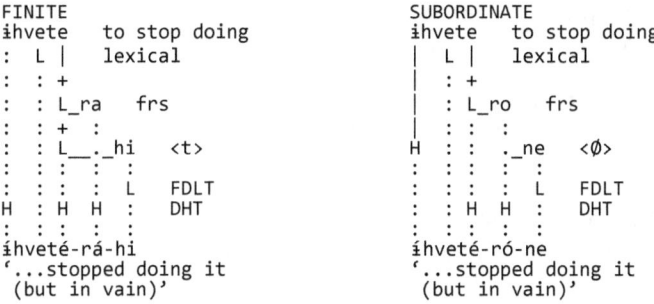

Figure D.10 TD: íhvetéɾáhi, íhvetéɾóne

-te   -Ⓛtʰe 'go to do (go.do)' [V/V] This suffix delinks conflicting tones.

(1165) Májchotééb́é ihjyávu.
máˣʧʰò-tʰέ-ːpé [íʔ ʰʲá   ]-βɯ̀   'He went home to eat.'
eat-go.do-⟨SgM⟩ self house -goal

-te ~ -jte -Ⓛ⁽ˣ⁾tʰe ~ -Ⓛ:tʰe 'animate plural ⟨AnPl⟩' [N/N]
(1166) tsʰà-ːtʰὲ   (tsaáte) 'some (AnPl)'
one-⟨AnPl⟩

---

¹⁰We do not know why the penultimate vowel is long in this word.

(1167) tì-:tʲʰɛ̀ (diitye) 'those (AnPl)'
tsʰà-:tʰɛ̀ (tsaáte) 'some (AnPl)'
tsʰì-ˣtʲʰɛ̀ (tsijtye) 'others (AnPl)'

In table D.1, note that the low tone of -Ⓛkʰɛ̀ 'objAn' delinks the Ⓛ imposed by -Ⓛ:pɛ ⟨SgM⟩ but not that of -Ⓛˣtʰɛ ⟨AnPl⟩:

Table D.1 Tone resistance by -jte ⟨AnPl⟩

	peccary	peccary + objAn
singular	mínè-:pè míneébe	míné-:pè-kʰɛ̀ mínéébeke
plural	mínè-ˣtʰɛ̀ mínejte	mínè-ˣtʰɛ́-kʰɛ̀ mínejtéke

-tsa -Ⓛ◯tsʰa 'each' [Adj_numeral/Adj (only on numeral phrases), follows the classifier]

(1168) a. tsápiítsa
tsʰápʰìː-tsʰà   'each one'
one-each

b. míítyetsítsa
míː-tʲʰɛ̀tsʰí-tsʰà   'two each'
two-⟨AnM⟩-each

c. píínéehójtsɨmevátsa
pʰɨ́ːnɛ́-ɛ̀-ʔóˣtsʰɨ́-mɛ̀-βá-tsʰà   'each four'
half-per-⟨hand⟩-⟨AnPl⟩-pl-each

-tso ~ -tsa -Ⓛtsʰo ~ -Ⓛtsʰa 'causative (caus)' [V/V (valence increasing)]

(1169) Mehéró májchotsó ɨ́jtsɨɨméneke.
mè?ɛ́ɾó máˣt͡ʃʰò-tsʰó-ʔ [ɨ́ ˣtsʰɨ́ːménè]-kʰɛ̀
aunt eat-caus-⟨t⟩ self child -objAn
'My aunt fed her child.'

-tsʰò becomes -tsʰà before -mɛi 'r/p':

(1170) tsɨ́hɨ́βɛ́-tsʰá-mɛ́ɨ-:pʲɛ̀ (Dsɨ́jɨ́vétsámeííbye.) 'He caused his
die-caus-r/p-⟨SgM⟩   own death.'

D.2. SUFFIXES WITH SEGMENTS

-tu ~ -tyu -t⁽ʲ⁾ʰɯ ~ -t⁽ʲ⁾ɯ 'source (sou)' [N/N_case]

(1171) Ávyéjuube tsáá ihjyátu.

áβʲéhɯ̀-ːpè tsʰáː-ˀ [íG ˀhʲá]-tʰɯ̀ 'The chief comes
reign-⟨SgM⟩ come-⟨t⟩ self house -sou from his house.'

-tu(ne) ~ -tyu(ne) 'negative (neg)'

1. [V_stem/V] #ó̋...-Ⓛt⁽ʲ⁾ʰɯ(ne)
2. [V/V_stem] #ó̋...-t⁽ʲ⁾ʰɯ̖(ne)
3. [Adj/Adj]
   (1172) ìmí-tʲʰɯ̀ (imítyu) 'bad'
   good-neg

The optional final syllable nè of -tʰɯ(nɛ) ~ -tʲʰɯ(nɛ) only occurs sentence finally, as in 1173:

(1173) Tsá dibye múijyú tsíjtyeke píáábotú.

tsʰa̋ˀ tì-pʲɛ̀ mɯ́-ìhʲɯ́ tsʰí-ˣtʲʰɛ̀-kʰɛ̀
not that-⟨SgM⟩ WH-time other-⟨AnPl⟩-objAn

pʰíáːpò-tʰɯ́-(nè)
help-neg-⟨n⟩
'He never helps others.'

The tone derivations of íˀβètʰέ-tʰɯ̀-ɾó-nè and áːʔíβè-tʰέ-tʰɯ̀-ɯ́pè follow:

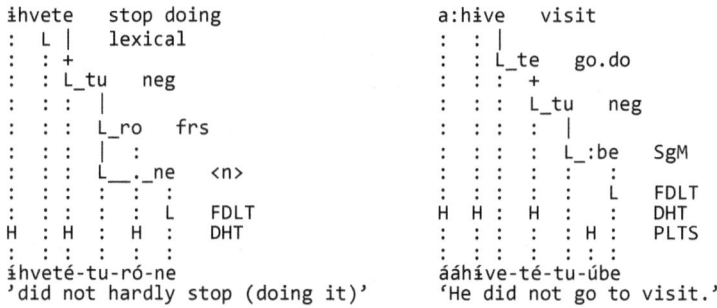

Figure D.11 TD: íhvetéturóne, ááhívetétuúbe

-u. See -vu.

-uba   -ⓁO̊úpa 'probable (prob)' [V/V, N/N, Adj/Adj, Adv/Adv]

(1174) Diibyéubá tsááhi.
    tì-ːpʲɛ́-ùɨpá   tsʰáː-ʔì   'He probably comes.'
    that-⟨SgM⟩-prob come-⟨t⟩

See also figure D.4, page 426.

When a word ending with -ⓁO̊ɨ̀pɨ 'max' is used as the modifier (possessor) in a genitive construction the lexically marked low tone of the /u/ is overridden This is as expected with genitives; see section 9.1, page 252.

-ucunu   -Ⓛɨkʰɨ̊mɨ 'singular stative (sSt)' [V/V]

-uvu   -Ⓛɨβɨ 'to the maximum extent (max)' [N/N, Adj/Adj, V$_{nonfinite}$/N]
Generally -Ⓛɨβɨ docks a low tone on its host's final syllable; however, after some lexically-marked high tones, -Ⓛɨβɨ becomes -ɨ̊βɨ.

The tone derivations of ɨ́hɨ́kʰò-ɨ̀βɨ̀ and à^{x}tʃʰɨ́ʔóːɨ̀-ɨ̀βɨ̀-ɾɛ́-hɨ̀ɨkʰò follow:

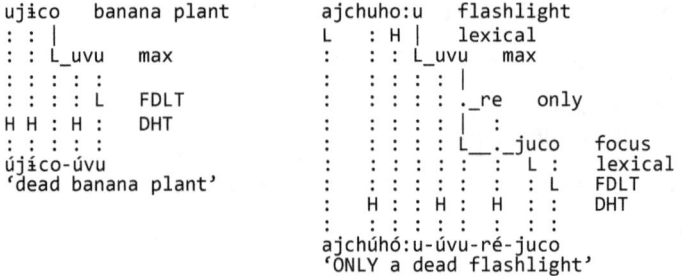

Figure D.12 TD: újɨcoúvu, ajchúhóːuúvuréjuco

(1175) tʰá: Ⓖ kʰáːní-ɨ̀βɨ̀ (táácááníuvu) 'my deceased father'
    my   father-max

(1176) ¿Kiátú áánúuvu tsááhi?
    kʰìá-tʰɨ́   áːnɨ́-ɨ̀βɨ̀   tsʰáː-ʔì   'Where does THIS (SgM)
    where-sou this.SgM-max come-⟨t⟩   come from?'

-ɨ̀βɨ̀ (-uvu) is also used as a superlative following -nɛ ⟨ø⟩:

(1177) à^{x}tʲʰɨ́βá-nɛ̀-ɨ̀βɨ̀ (ajtyúváneúvu)   'the brightest green/blue'
    green-⟨ø⟩-max

(1178) Ímíñeúvú méénuco.
    ímí-ɲɛ̀-ɨ̀βɨ́   mɛ́ːnɨ̀-kʰò   'Do it the best you can.'
    good-⟨ø⟩-max do-implore

D.2. SUFFIXES WITH SEGMENTS

-va -βa 'plural (pl)' [Adj$_{numeral}$/Adj (only used with numerals)]

(1179) tsʰá-ʔòˣtsʰɨ́-mɛ̀-β̱à (tsáhojtsɨ́meva) 'five live beings'
one-⟨hand⟩-⟨AnPl⟩-pl

-(:)va -Ⓛ○(:)βa 'have' [N/V]

(1180) àhʲá-β̱à (ajyáva) 'to have a son-in-law'
ì:ɲɨ́-β̱à (iiñúva) 'to be dirty'
tɨ̀:tsɨ́-β̱à (dɨ+dsɨ́va) 'to have money'

The tone derivation of kpáɲɛ̀ʔhɨ́-β̱à-tʰɛ́-nɛ̀-βʉ̀ follows:

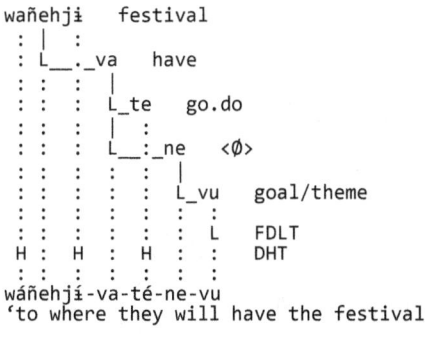

Figure D.13 TD: wáñehjɨ́vaténevu

In 1181 -Ⓛ○βa should dock its low tone on the last syllable of kʰaráᴸkʰa but this is blocked by the root's lexically marked low tone:

(1181) Mítyane cáracámúvalle.

[mítʲʰà-nɛ̀ kʰaráᴸkʰá]-mɨ́-β̱à-tʃɛ̀ 'She has many
many-pl chicken -⟨AnPl⟩-have-⟨SgF⟩ chickens.'

-va -Ⓛ○βa 'learned by hearsay, reportative (rpt)' [V/V, N/N, Adj/Adj, Adv/Adv]

(1182) Diibyévá peé úúmaá.

tì-:pʲɛ́-β̱á pʰɛ̀-ɛ́-ʔ ʉ́:-màá[11] 'He will go with you
that-⟨SgM⟩-rpt go-fut-⟨∅⟩ you-with (it is said).'

(1183) a. Mítyámeva tsááhi.
b. Mítyamévá tsááhi.

---

[11]When the pronoun becomes long, the final vowel of the suffix splits by FLTS.

a. mítʲʰá-mɛ̀-βà
many-⟨AnPl⟩-plQ

b. mítʲʰá̠-mɛ́-βá
many-⟨AnPl⟩-rpt

} tsʰá:-ʔì come {
a. 'Many are coming.'
b. 'Many are coming (they say).'
}

The tone derivation of màˣʧʰó-βà-:pɛ́-βàˣ follows:

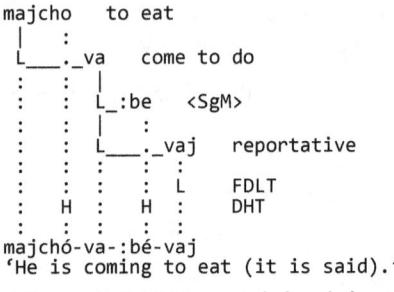

Figure D.14 TD: majchóva:bévaj

-va -Ⓛ◯βa 'come to do (come.do)' [V/V]

(1184) Ó cuwává dihjyá pañévu.

ó kʰùɨkpá-βá-ˀ   [[tìˡ̠ˀ   hʲá]   Ⓖ pʰa̠ɲɛ́]-βùɨ
I sleep-come.do-⟨t⟩ your house   inside -goal
'I come to sleep in your house.'

-:ve ~ -:vye -Ⓛ:β⁽ʲ⁾e 'singular intransitive (sIn)' or 'become' [N/V] Examples follow. The tone derivation for 1187 is given in figure 3.18, page 75. This suffix may delink conflicting tones, as seen in example 1188 and the corresponding tone derivation in figure D.15.

(1185) póʔɛ́hùɨ-:βɛ̀ (bóhéjuuve)   'to have a hole'
       póʔókpà-:βɛ̀ (bóhówaave)   'become visible, appear'
       kʰáˀpʰì-:βʲɛ̀ (cáhpiivye)   'to be poured out'

(1186) o̠:ʔí-:pʲɛ́-:βɛ̀-:pɛ̀   (oohííbyééveébe) 'He lives like a dog
       dog-⟨SgM⟩-sIn-⟨SgM⟩   (lit. became a dog).'

(1187) mɛ́:ní-:βʲɛ̀-:pɛ̀ (Mééníívyeébe.) 'He became a pig.'
       pig-sIn-⟨SgM⟩

(1188) Mí̠amúnáájpíívyeébe.

       mí̠amúmá-:ˣpʰí:-βʲɛ̀-:pɛ̀   'He became a human.'
       person-⟨SgM⟩-sIn-⟨SgM⟩

D.2. SUFFIXES WITH SEGMENTS

The tone derivation of míàmúmá:-ˣpʰí-:βʲè-:pè follows:

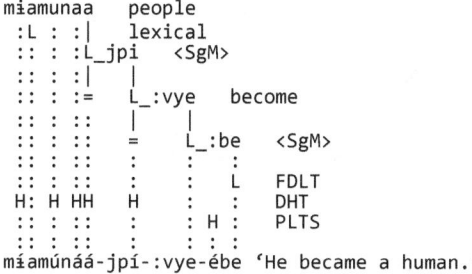

Figure D.15 TD: mɨamúnáájpí:vyeébe

-véjɨu -βéhɨɯ 'similar to (similar)' [V/V, N/N, Adj/Adj, Adv/Adv] This suffix has very limited use. It seems to mean exactly the same as -Ⓛ○⁽ˀ⁾tɯ 'like'. See example 810, page 317

-vu ~ -vyu ~ -u -Ⓛβ⁽ʲ⁾ɯ ~ -Ⓛɯ 'goal, theme (goal, thm)' [N/N$_{case}$] See 1110, page 429.

(1189) Ávyéjulle péé ihjyávu.

áβʲéhùɨ-tʃè pʰέ:-ˀ [ǐˀ hʲá]-βùɨ   'The chieftess goes
reign-⟨SgF⟩ go-⟨t⟩ self house -goal   to her house.'

-wu(u) -kpǔɨ(ɯ) 'diminutive, very (dim)' [N/N, Adj/Adj]. Word medially, i.e., when some suffix or clitic follows, the form is -kpúɨɯ. Word finally the form is -Ⓗkpǔɨ.¹² Further, the tone patterns are different for nouns and adjectives:

1. When -kpǔɨ follows a noun, all preceding tones are high except for any lexically marked low tones, as in the examples that follow:

(1190) kpáˣpʰí-kpǔɨ (wájpíwu) 'small man'
man-dim

(1191) ájá-nέ-kpǔɨ (áyánéwu) 'few things'
few-frs-⟨ø⟩-dim

The tone derivations of ájá-nέ-kpùɨ and ámáná-kpùɨú-mùɨ are given in figure D.16 and that of óˀtsʰárɨ́hɨ́-kpùɨú-mùɨ-ɾέ-hùɨkʰò is given in figure D.17.

---

¹²Even though, as here, a second /ɯ/ is not present, the syllable preceding -kpǔɨ must bear high tone; i.e., it behaves as though the extra syllable were present.

```
aya      few                amana
 | :                         : H :    lexical
 L_._ne          <∅>         : : ._wuu    dim
 | :  :                      : : :  L|   lexical
 = :  ._wu    dim            : : :  :+
 : :  :  L    lexical        : : :  :L_mu   plAn
 H H  H  :    DHT            : : :  ::   |
 : :  :  :                   : : :  ::   L   FDLT
 áyá-né-wu                   H : H  ::   :   DHT
 'few things'                : : :  ::   :
                             ámáná-wuú-mu   'little porpoises'
```

Figure D.16 TD: ámánáwuúmu, áyánéwu

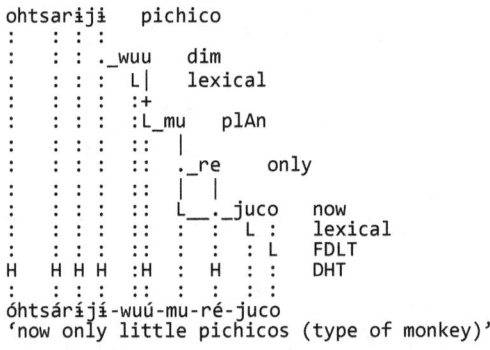

Figure D.17 TD: óhtsárɨ́jɨwuúmuréjuco

2. When -kpʉ̈ follows an adjective, it imposes a low tone on the adjective's first syllable, as seen in 1192 and 1193: (L)...-kpʉ̈(ɯ). It is used to enhance adjectives, as in 1192:

(1192) ìmí-kpʉ̀ɯ tìː-tʃɛ̀ (Imíwu diílle.) 'She is very pretty.'
    good-dim that-⟨SgF⟩

(1193) kʰájópá-kpʉ̈ (cayóbáwu) 'very angry'
    kpákʰímʲéípʰí-kpʉ̈ (wakímyéípíwu) 'very good worker'

-ya See entry -ro ~ -ra ~-yo ~ -ya 'frustrative, contraexpectation'.

-ye. See entry -re ~ -ye 'only'.

-yi. See entry -ri ~ -yi 'inanimate oblique'.

-yo See entry -ro ~ -ra ~-yo ~ -ya 'frustrative, contraexpectation'.

Appendix E

The Bora Classifiers

E.1 Explanation and disclaimers

This section presents a list of Bora classifiers.[1] The list is organized alphabetically by the spelling in the practical orthography. (Note: long vowels are alphabetized as though they were short.) It was translated from a draft of (Thiesen & Thiesen 1998). A committee of Iñeja Bora speakers reviewed this list and, for inclusion in (Thiesen & Thiesen 1998), removed those that are flagged with ∘. They did so for various reasons, among them: (1) certain forms are characteristic of dialects other than Iñeje, (2) certain forms would be used very infrequently (possibly because the younger generation of Bora speakers is using a smaller set of classifiers than the older generation). Thiesen identified about 150 classifiers as those that are more commonly used. These are identified with • as an aid to anyone learning the Bora language.

The descriptions of the classifiers given here are not intended as exhaustive, but as illustrative of many other facts that could be mentioned. A category is included with each classifier: shape (e.g., smashed very flat), botanical (e.g., plant or tree with one root but a number of trunks), being (e.g., person or animal with a solid, well built body), spatial (path through space that leads to some place), substance (e.g., very curved and flexible at the tip, like a fishing rod), time (e.g., late in the day), liquid (e.g., sap of a tree), object (e.g., ridge-pole of a house), action (e.g., turning sideways to pass through a narrow place), sound (e.g., disagreeable, bothersome

---

[1] A diagnostic test for classifiers is the following: only classifiers may follow the bound demonstrative roots discussed in section 8.4.

sound), condition (e.g., leaning over about to fall), figurative (e.g., speech or teachings < long and narrow like a trail), object (e.g., the sediment left in the bottom in the preparation of some drink), position (e.g., out of place, misaligned). *These categories are intended as suggestive, not as an absolute taxonomy of Bora classifiers.*

E.2 Classifiers

-aacóroho /-áːkʰoɾoʔo/ *shape:* resembling a blown-up bag or a dress without a waist

-acúúu /-ákʰɯːɯ/ *position:* seated (or setting)

-aalláco /-áːtʃakʰo/ *shape:* resembling a tube with a bulge in the middle

-allúrou /-átʃɯɾoɯ/ *shape:* large bulging eyes of people or animals

-aamái /-áːmai/ *shape:* a column of people or animals one after another

-aapárou /-áːpʰaɾoɯ/ *shape:* a circular stain

-aráára /-áɾaːɾa/ *shape:* having many small holes in it (e.g., a hide with holes made by a shotgun)

-aráárau /-áɾaːɾaɯ/ *shape:* a small stain

-atyóhrajɨ /-átʲʰoʔɾahɨ/ *shape:* loose, not rolled up (e.g., a pile of clothes tossed in a heap)

-avóhoóu /-áβoʔoːɯ/ *position:* turned face down

•-ba, -bya or -hba /-Ⓛpa ~ -Ⓛpʲa ~ -Ⓛʔpa/

1. *shape:* thick, long and round, e.g., a log
2. *shape:* any kind of package, carton or box
3. *shape:* a musical instrument like a drum or a guitar
4. *liquid:* thick drinks such as those made from palm fruit, pineapple, plantains, and so forth
5. *substance:* soft fruits that can be broken open with the hand to be eaten
6. *time:* year
7. many other things, e.g., ɯ́nìpà (úniba) 'lip', nɨ́ˣtʲʰɯ̀pà (níjtyuba) 'strainer', tòʔhɨ́pà (dohjɨ́ba) 'sling for carrying a baby on the shoulder', ɯ́kʰɛ̀ːpà (úkeéba) 'swampy area', kpàːpʲà (waábya) 'hammock', tsɯ̀tsápà (dsudsába) 'type of palm called *huicungo*', ɯ́tʃɛ̀pà (úlleba) 'frying pan', tsʰàʔɾópà (tsahróba) 'tightly woven basket'

•-babya or -Ⓛhbabya /-Ⓛpapʲa ~ -Ⓛʔpapʲa/ *shape:* a container the shape of a bag

•-bajcu /-Ⓛpaˣkʰɯ/ *shape:* any type of bone

•-baju or -hbaju /-Ⓛpahɯ ~ -Ⓛʔpahɯ/ *botanical:* stand of trees

-banúúnui /-pánɯːnɯi/ *shape:* long, narrow ridge like those made by a plow

•-bau or -hbau /-Ⓛpaɯ ~ -Ⓛʔpaɯ/ *shape:* mound, hill or round protuberance

- •-:be /-Ⓛːpɛ/ *being:* male person or animal (singular masculine ⟨SgM⟩)
- -beeróba or -beeróu /-pɛ̄ːropa ~ -pɛ̄ːroɯ/ *shape:* a bald dome (e.g., a head without hair)
- •-bewa /-Ⓛpɛkpa/ *shape:* a stack of things
- -bɨhjɨ /-Ⓛpɨʔhɨ/ *shape:* a stain
- -bojɨ /-Ⓛpohɨ/ *liquid:* a stationary bubble or pool of some liquid (e.g., a drop of water on the table, a pool of water)
- -buhtsa /-Ⓛpɯʔtsʰa/ *shape:* a small mound of dirt (e.g., at the foot of an upturned tree)
- -cadóóu /-kʰā̄toːɯ/ *substance:* having two colors, each end being a different color
- -cadúhdáu /-kʰātɯʔtāɯ/² *shape:* hung suspended from both ends (e.g., a hammock)
- -cadsúdsuúu /-kʰā̄tsɯtsɯːɯ/ *shape:* having shrunk in size
- -cahdádau /-kʰāʔtataɯ/ *position:* with the head bowed down, showing sadness, embarrassment, or disgust
- -cahmái /-kʰā̄ʔmai/ *shape:* a pile up of people, plates, boxes, or other things
- -cahmátajɨ /-kʰā̄ʔmatʰahɨ/ *condition:* things stuck together
- -cahjói or -cahjyói /-kʰā̄ʔhoi ~ -kʰā̄ʔhʲoi/ *shape:* having a wavy edge, e.g., the rim of a hat, the edge of a canoe
- •-caája /-Ⓛkʰaːha/ *spatial:* place like a gully or swamp
- -caji /-Ⓛkʰahi/ *being:* a cow or tapir
- -callájaáu /-kʰā̄tʃahaːɯ/ *shape:* a disorganized group of things, people, or animals
- -calléjuwa /-kʰā̄tʃɛhɯkpa/ *shape:* having raised edges, but lacking much depth
- -callóu /-kʰā̄tʃoɯ/ *position:* person or animal with the head down
- -callúrɨ́jɨ /-kʰā̄tʃɯriːhɨ/ *position:* one edge of an object higher than the opposing edge
- -camáhjába /-kʰāmaʔhā́pa/³ *shape:* broken pieces (of some object)
- ○-camáhllaba /-kʰāmaʔtʃapa/ *object:* the sediment left in the bottom in the preparation of some drink
- ○-camáhtajɨ /-kʰāmaʔtʰahɨ/ *object:* disk-shaped stopper for plugging up holes in wood or openings in the ground
- -camújtyuhi /-kʰāmɯˣtʲʰɯʔi/ *shape:* a short neck of a person or animal
- ○-camúruúi /-kʰāmɯrɯːi/ *position:* an obstruction in something tube-shaped
- -canóóu /-kʰā̄noːɯ/ *position:* bowing the head
- ○-canúnuúi /-kʰā̄nɯnɯːi/ *shape:* very full, e.g., a bag or basket
- -caanúroi /-kʰā̄ːnɯroi/ *shape:* very full, e.g., a bulging bag or basket
- -capátyuúu /-kʰā̄pʰatʲʰɯːɯ/ *shape:* a sharp object pierced through something else
- ○-capújuúu /-kʰā̄pʰɯhɯːɯ/ *position:* someone stooped over to pass under something
- -carááu /-kʰā̄raːɯ/ *shape:* a deep hole

---

²This derives from the verb kʰatɯʔta '(something suspended) to come loose'.

³This may derive from the verb kʰāmaʔha; compare kʰàmá-ːβɛ̀ 'to put together'.

-caríhjyau or -caríjyaáu /-kʰá̠ɾiʔ-hʲaɯ ∼ -kʰá̠ɾihʲaːɯ/ *position:* two poles together at the top with the bottom points apart; a person standing with his legs apart

-caróhjawa /-kʰá̠ɾoʔhakpa/ *shape:* a high riverbank or precipice

-carééju /-kʰá̠ɾoːhɯ/ *shape:* cut at an angle or several objects cut at different heights or lengths

-catóroóu /-kʰá̠tʰoɾoːɯ/ *shape:* a prop (supporting something); a person leaning against something

-catsóói /-kʰá̠tsʰoːi/ *position:* jacked up above the middle (e.g., a pair of pants jacked up above the waist)

-cayáhtyaji /-kʰá̠jaʔtʲʰahi/ *condition:* a ruptured eyed

-cayííji /-kʰá̠jiːhi/ *condition:* a deformed mouth

•-co, -cyo, -coo, or -cyoo /-Ⓛkʰo ∼ -Ⓛkʲʰo ∼ -Ⓛkʰoː ∼ -Ⓛkʲʰoː/
  1. *shape:* a slender pole
  2. *other things of various shapes*, e.g., kʰanékʰò (canéco) 'cup', kʰáʔkɯ́nɯ̀kʰò (cáhgúnuco) 'starch drink', ʔɯ́mɨ̀kʰò húmɨco 'forehead' (formed from ʔɯ̀mɨ̀ᴴ húmɨɨ 'face'), néːpʰɨ̀kʲʰò (néépicyo) 'squirrel', mɯ́ːmɯ̀kʰò (múúmuco) 'wasp nest', nɨ̀ːmɯ́kʰò (niimúco) 'paujil (type of bird)'

•-coóha /-Ⓛkʰoːʔa/ *shape:* a tree with branches but no leaves or other similar things (e.g., a broom)

•-cohna /-Ⓛkʰoʔna/ *shape:* long and narrow (e.g., the legs of people, animals or furniture)

o-cohña /-Ⓛkʰoʔɲa/ *shape:* resembling a bicycle pedal

•-coóho /-Ⓛkʰoːʔo/ *shape:* resembling a fishnet (string knotted together like a fishnet)

•-coja /-Ⓛkʰoha/ *shape:* a rapidly made basket with very loose weave

•-coómi /-Ⓛkʰoːmi/ *spatial:* a place where people live (town or village)

-cotyái /-kʰotʲʰai/ *shape:* long narrow supports (e.g., the legs of a table)

o-cubáu /-kʰɯ́paɯ/ *shape:* unnaturally short (e.g., cut-off pants, an amputated limb)

-cuhco /-Ⓛkʰɯʔkʰo/ *condition:* very thin (person or animal)

-cuhllu /-Ⓛkʰɯʔtʃɯ/ *shape:* curved or twisted, e.g., a pole or a road

o-cuhtsíu /-kʰɯ́ʔtsʰiɯ/ *shape:* deformed, twisted, e.g., a person standing on one leg, a person who has a twisted hip causing the leg to be short

•-cuhvi /-Ⓛkʰɯʔβi/ *shape:* a shriveled hand

-cujúúu /-kʰɯ́hɯːɯ/ *position:* a log that does not reach across to the other side

-cujúroba /-kʰɯ́hɯɾopa/ *shape:* underdeveloped or severed (e.g., a leg, an arm, a pole cut too short)

-cuumúruji /-kʰɯ́ːmɯɾɯhi/ *shape:* a hump-backed person or animal

-cuníiu /-kʰɯ́niːɯ/
  1. *shape:* resembling a foot without toes
  2. *figurative:* a person who does not walk normally because of pain in the toes

o-cunɨ́ɨ́rɨu /-kʰɯ́nɨːɾɨɯ/ *condition:* having a dull edge or tip (an instrument such as a machete, axe, arrowhead,...)

-chaácha /-Ⓛtʃʰa:tʃʰa/ condition: soft and mushy (e.g., muddy ground or fruit that has been trampled)
-chachóóho /-tʃʰatʃʰo:ʔo/ shape: the legs of a bowlegged person, table legs bent inwards
-chahpi /-Ⓛtʃʰaʔpʰi/ shape: fluffed out (e.g., ruffled hair or feathers)
o-chaája /-Ⓛtʃʰa:ha/ condition: rotten or decomposed
-chehmúwa /-tʃʰɛʔmɯkpa/ shape: resembling a protruding jaw (e.g., that of a person lacking teeth)
-cheíji /-tʃʰɛihi/ shape: fine lines (e.g., scratches)
•-cheére /-Ⓛtʃʰɛ:ɾɛ/ shape: a split in a board or a canoe
•-chi or -tsi /-Ⓛtʃʰi ~ -Ⓛtsʰi/ spatial: a place (⟨place⟩)
-chihyo /-Ⓛtʃʰiʔʲo/ shape: the frayed end of a rope
-chohra /-Ⓛtʃʰoʔra/ shape: hanging over (e.g., a cock's comb hanging off to one side, a rope hanging over something)
-chuhchu /-Ⓛtʃʰɯʔtʃʰɯ/ shape: a short stump of a limb left on a tree that was not cut close to the trunk
-dajca /-Ⓛtaˣkʰa/ condition: trampled (grass or weeds)
-dɨbééu /-tɨpɛːɯ/ position: held between opposing objects, e.g., something held between the lips or teeth, or held in a vise
o-dɨmúmuúu /-tɨmɯmɯːɯ/ shape: opposing objects (one above, the other below) misaligned, e.g., the upper teeth biting the lower lip
-dɨhríjɨ /-tɨʔrihɨ/ shape: round and wider than high (e.g., a tuna can)

o-dobééu /-tópɛːɯ/ shape: pulled together (e.g., as when one closes the top of a sack)[4]
-dochóhoóu /-totʃʰoʔoːɯ/ shape: two poles leaning towards each other, or the legs of a table pointing inward
o-doódi /-Ⓛto:ti/ shape: a crack in a wall, a pole or, the ground
-dodo /-Ⓛtoto/ shape: very full and bulging
-doríhjyau /-tóriʔhʲaɯ/ shape: two poles leaning away from each other, the legs of a table spread apart
o-doríɨu /-tóriːɯ/ condition: having a very dull point (e.g., a nail lacking a sharp point)
-dootóroji /-toːtʰorohɨ/ shape: hump-backed or curved
-dovíyiíu /-toβijiːɯ/ shape: rolled up in leaves (paper, blanket,...)
-dujca /-Ⓛtɯˣkʰa/ shape: a cove in the river, a bay in the ocean
-dujúúu /-tɯhɯːɯ/ shape: upright and leaning forward
-dsaádsa /-Ⓛtsaːtsa/ shape: the point of something that is fibrous and splintery
-dsaára /-Ⓛtsaːra/ shape: uncombed hair, stiff bristles, a porcupine's needles
o-dseédse /-Ⓛtsɛːtsɛ/ sound: a disagreeable, bothersome sound
•-dseére /-Ⓛtsɛːɾɛ/ sound: a very high pitched sound, e.g., that of a cicada
o-dsɨhdsɨu /-tsɨʔtsɨɯ/ shape: a very short object
-dsɨríɨu /-tsɨriːɯ/ shape: a big round-bellied clay pot
-dsujgúruu /-tsɯˣkɯrɯː/ shape:

---

[4]Compare tòpɛ́-ːβɛ̀ (gather-sIn dobééve) 'to be gathered together'.

short and chubby
o-ejdéu /-êˣtɯ/ *shape:* a thick board or disc
o-eréreéi /-ɛ́rɛrɛːi/ *shape:* a stick-like thing with a sharp point
o-eróvaáu /-ɛ́roβaːɯ/ *shape:* liquid-filled blister
-eténiíu /-ɛ́tʰeniːɯ/
  1. *shape:* the face made by someone not wanting to cough
  2. *shape:* the face made by someone having difficulty in defecating
-geréreéi /-kɛ́rɛrɛːi/ *shape:* protruding (about to come out)
-goñɨ́ɨjɨ /-kóɲiːhɨ/ *shape:* an open mouth so you can see the teeth
-guhña /-Ⓛkɯˀɲa/ *shape:* S-shaped
o-gurúrujɨ /-kɯ́rɯrɯhɨ/ *shape:* a paddle with a rounded point
•-ha or -haá /-Ⓛʔa(ː)/
  1. *shape:* a big grouping of animals, birds, fish, or people
  2. *shape:* a pineapple
•-hadsɨ /-Ⓛʔatsɨ/ *shape:* a small grouping of people, (of animals, of trees,...)
•-hajca /-Ⓛʔaˣkʰa/ *shape:*
  1. a hand of bananas
  2. a big pile-up of something
•-hajcu /-Ⓛʔaˣkʰɯ/
  1. *shape:* a stump, house pole, post, and such
  2. *sound:* a big loud noise
•-hajɨ /-Ⓛʔahɨ/ *shape:* wrapped in leaves or paper and tied at the top
•-haámɨ /-Ⓛʔaːmɨ/ *shape:* very thin (e.g., a leaf or a piece of paper)
•-hajtsɨ /-Ⓛʔaˣtsʰɨ/ *spatial:* a clearing (e.g., a yard around the house)
•-hajchóta /-²âˣtʃʰotʰa/
  1. *time:* duration
  2. *spatial:* distance

•-hbahya /-Ⓛˀpaˀʲa/ *shape:* a pile of things
o-hbɨjɨ /-Ⓛˀpihɨ/ *shape:* wrapped up
•-he or -heé /-Ⓛʔɛ(ː)/ *botanical:* a tree or a tree-like plant
o-heéba /-Ⓛʔɛːpa/ *shape:* having a thin middle (e.g., a girl with a narrow waist)
•-hejte /-Ⓛʔɛˣtʰɛ/
  1. *shape:* e.g., the fibers of cotton
  2. *shape:* the spines of certain trees
•-heju /-Ⓛʔɛhɯ/ *shape:* a hole
•-hi /-Ⓛʔi/ *shape:* a stalk of bananas (a bunch of grapes,...)
•-hiíba /-Ⓛʔiːpa/ *shape:* a blade of grass or a stalk of grain
•-hiícyo /-Ⓛʔiːkʲʰo/ *shape:* a cactus or pineapple plant
-hijyáwa /-²ˡihʲakpa/ *shape:* a square
o-hɨjpɨ /-Ⓛʔɨˣpʰɨ/ *spatial:* a place to sit on a fallen log
o-hiíñe /-Ⓛʔiːɲɛ/ *spatial:* the sleeping platform that each family has in a multiple family round house
•-hɨíwa /-Ⓛʔɨːkpa/ *shape:* a big open, clear place in a wall or in the jungle that resembles a doorway
-hɨjpɨ /-Ⓛʔɨˣpʰɨ/ See -ɨjpɨ.
-hllahi /-Ⓛˀtʃaʔi/ *shape:* a bundle of herbs or flowers that can be held in the hand
-hllalla /-Ⓛˀtʃatʃa/ *shape:* resembling the bristles of a brush
-hllohi /-Ⓛˀtʃoʔi/ *shape:* resembling small bunches of grapes
•-ho or -hoó /-Ⓛʔo(ː)/
  1. *shape:* oval-shaped (e.g., cacao fruit)
  2. *spatial:* a room in a house
-hoóba /-Ⓛʔoːpa/ *spatial:* gable end of a house
•-hoóha /-Ⓛʔoːʔa/ *shape:* a group of people, animals or things

- -hoója /-Ⓛʔoːha/ *shape:* a cylindrical hole, either in the ground or the cavity of an empty tin can
- -hojtsɨ /-Ⓛʔoˣtsʰɨ/ *shape:* hand-shaped
- -hoóu /-Ⓛʔoːɯ/ *shape:* long and cylindrical (e.g., a log)
- -hoówa /-Ⓛʔoːkpa/ *shape:* an open space
- -hulle /-Ⓛʔɯʧɛ/ *spatial:* some place away from the speaker (⟨yonder⟩)
- -i or -ii /-Ⓛi ∼ -Ⓛiː/ *shape:* a long, slender thing (e.g., a stick, a river)
- -ibíiu /-ɨ̄piiɯ/ *shape:* cheeks puffed out when the mouth is filled with coca powder
- -ihbáu /-ɨ̄ʔpaɯ/ *shape:* things that are bulged out in the middle (e.g., a man with a big stomach)
- -ihbúcuúu /-ɨ̄ʔpɯkʰɯːɯ/ *shape:* things in uneven lengths
- -ihcyu /-Ⓛiʔkʲʰɯ/ *shape:* some sort of framework
- -ihllo /-Ⓛiʔʧo/ *shape:* resembling a water or cooking pot
- -iíhyo or -ihyo /-Ⓛiːʔʲo ∼ -Ⓛiʔʲo/ *shape:* things round and long (e.g., a pencil)
- -ijyócuúu /-īhʲokʰɯːɯ/ *position:* things standing up
- -ijyu /-Ⓛihʲɯ/ *time:* a reference to time
- -imíjyau /-īmihʲaɯ/ *substance:* good, beautiful and appreciated things
o -ityóroóu /-ītʲʰoroːɯ/ *position:* not parallel to the rest
- -ivórowa /-ɨ̄βorokpa/ *shape:* twisted and bent (e.g., a board laid out in the sun)
- -ɨɨbɨ́bɨho /-ɨ̄ːpɨpɨʔo/ *condition:* a very full mouth, an overfull container
- -ɨhdsɨ /-Ⓛɨʔtsɨ/
  1. *shape:* fibers (e.g., those that remain after manioc has been grated)
  2. *condition:* hair that is bushy and not combed
- -ɨɨjɨ /-Ⓛɨːhɨ/ *shape:* an elevated platform or floor
- -ɨjpɨ ∼ -hɨjpɨ /-Ⓛɨˣpʰɨ ∼ -Ⓛʔɨˣpʰɨ/
  1. *spatial:* the point from which something develops, e.g., the roots of a plant
  2. *figurative:* something's creator or originator
o -ɨtótoói /-ɨ̄tʰotʰoːi/ *shape:* bumps caused by many points of things in a bag
- -ɨtsɨ́ɨu /-ɨ̄tsʰɨːɯ/ *position:* leaning forward
- -ɨvóhoóu /-ɨ̄βoʔoːɯ/ *position:* lying face down
- -ja /-Ⓛha/ *shape:* a covering (e.g., a house, a pair of pants, a shirt)
- -jaába /-Ⓛha:pa/ *botanical:* a clump of trees left standing in a field that has been cut down
- -jaáu /-Ⓛhaːɯ/ *botanical:* a branch with leaves only at the tip
- -jcaáha /-Ⓛˣkʰaːʔa/ *botanical:* plants with runners (e.g., vines)
- -jcaáhya /-Ⓛˣkʰaːʔʲa/ *condition:* very thin (person or animal)
- -jcaámɨ /-Ⓛˣkʰaːmɨ/ *spatial:* a place full of mud (e.g., a mud hole)
- -jcoójɨ /-Ⓛˣkʰoːhɨ/ *time:* day or daytime
- -jcuúve /-Ⓛˣkʰɯːβɛ/ *time:* late in the day
- -jɨ /-Ⓛhɨ/ *shape:* a flat, round thing, disk-like
- -jɨɨco /-Ⓛhɨːkʰo/ *shape:* resembling a funnel
- -jɨha /-Ⓛhɨʔa/ *spatial:* an abandoned field or garden
- -jɨho /-Ⓛhɨʔo/ *shape:* things put one

- -jɨhto /-Ⓛhɨʔtʰo/ *shape:* an emptied container (e.g., an empty sack)
- -jɨjto /-Ⓛhɨˣtʰo/
  1. *spatial:* a path through space that leads to some place
  2. *figurative:* a line of teaching and beliefs
- -jke /-Ⓛˣkʰɛ/ *botanical:* climbing vines
o -jkejɨ /-Ⓛˣkʰɛhɨ/ *spatial:* a place in the jungle where there are a lot of vines used for tying up things
- -jkeéme /-Ⓛˣkʰɛːmɛ/ *being:* an old man
  -jkeéwa /-Ⓛˣkʰɛːkpa/ *shape:* a notch chopped into a tree
- -joóro /-Ⓛhoːɾo/ *shape:* a gully or a canal bed
- -jpa /-Ⓛˣpʰa/ *liquid:* a soup or broth
- -jpacyo /-Ⓛˣpʰakʲʰo/ *liquid:* all liquids
- -jpayu /-Ⓛˣpʰajɯ/ *liquid:* small pockets of water on any surface
- -jpi /-Ⓛˣpʰi/ See -pi.
- -jpille /-Ⓛˣpʰitʃɛ/ See -pille.
  -jtatááwa /-ˣtʰaL tʰaːkpa/ *shape:* a piled up tangle of vines and leaves forming a shelter
- -jte, -jtye, or -te /-Ⓛˣtʰɛ ~ -Ⓛˣtʲʰɛ ~ -Ⓛtʰɛ/ *being:* three or more people or animals (animate plural ⟨AnPl⟩)
- -jtepɨ or -tepɨ /-Ⓛˣtʰɛpʰɨ ~ -Ⓛtʰɛpʰɨ/ *being:* two women or female animals (dual feminine ⟨DuF⟩)
- -jtetsi or -tetsi /-Ⓛˣtʰɛtsʰi ~ -Ⓛtʰɛtsʰi/ *being:* two men or male animals (dual masculine ⟨DuM⟩)
- -jto /-Ⓛˣtʰo/ *shape:* having a point, e.g., a needle, a cow's horn
o -jtoha /-Ⓛˣtʰoʔa/ *shape:* wrapped up in leaves and tied at one end
- -jtoi /-Ⓛˣtʰoi/
  1. *shape:* a curve in the river or on a trail
  2. *shape:* the curve on the front of a bald head
o -jtu /-Ⓛˣtʰɯ/ *liquid:* the sap of a tree
- -jtuha /-Ⓛˣtʰɯʔa/ *shape:* resembling a foot
- -jtsuúho /-Ⓛˣtsʰɯːʔo/
  1. *shape:* rolled up
  2. *figurative:* a sickly person who has no energy
  3. *figurative:* a person shivering from the cold
- -ju /-Ⓛhɯ/
  1. *shape:* long and narrow, e.g., a trail, a river, a road
  2. *figurative:* speech or teachings
- -juúho /-Ⓛhɯːʔo/ *botanical:* a palm leaf
  -jumi /-Ⓛhɯmi/ *object:* the ridgepole of a house
- -juúva /-Ⓛhɯːβa/ *shape:* a trail left by tracks made by man or animal
  -juwa /-Ⓛhɯkpa/ *shape:* missing a piece
  -kehgórai /-kʰɛL ʔkoɾai/ *shape:* thin in the middle and thicker at each end, e.g., a long neck
o -kejtúhi /-kʰɛL tʰɯʔi/ *shape:* having a long, thin neck
  -kejtsétsei /-kʰɛL tsʰɛtsʰei/ *position:* stretching to see something (i.e., craning the neck to get the eyes into a position from which they can see something)
o -kihdyáhɨɨu /-kʰɨL ʔtʲaʔiːɯ/ *shape:* of a very staight cut board
  -kihvújɨ /-kʰɨL ʔβɯhɨ/ *shape:* a lady's short haircut
  -kiíjye /-Ⓛkʰiːhʲɛ/ *botanical:* the cap of a tree including all the branches and leaves
o -kiityúu /-kʰɨL ːtʲʰɯɯ/ *shape:* a notched cut around the circumference of a cylindrical object (e.g., a

tree)

o-kiityúrujɨ /-kʰɨ:tʲʰɯɾɯhɨ/ *shape:* a flat cut around the circumference of a cylindrical object

-llaáhi /-ⓁtʃaːʔI/ *shape:* an old deformed basket

-llahlláɾɨjɨ /-tʃa̰ʔtʃaɾihɨ/ *shape:* flapping, e.g., a bit of torn cloth on a shirt that flaps

o-llahpɨ́ɾɨco or -llapɨ́ɾɨco /-tʃa̰ᴸʔpʰiɾikʰo ~ -tʃa̰ᴸpʰiɾikʰo/ *being:* a short, pot-bellied person

o-llajvávau /-tʃa̰ᴸˣβaβaɯ/ *shape:* a person, animal or thing with a bulge in the middle

•-llaára /-Ⓛtʃaːɾa/
1. *condition:* old torn clothes
2. *figurative:* a person dressed in rags

-llavájriwa /-tʃa̰ᴸβaˣɾikpa/ *shape:* a hole made in something by violence, e.g., an opening made in a palm leave roof by a strong wind

•-lle /-Ⓛtʃɛ/ *being:* a woman or female animal (singular feminine ⟨SgF⟩)

-lle /-Ⓛtʃɛ/ *spatial:* yonder, over there

-llevéhrou /-tʃẽᴸβɛʔɾoɯ/ *shape:* cirlcular

o-lli /-Ⓛtʃi/ *shape:* a bunch of fibers tied together at one end

•-lliíhyo /-Ⓛtʃiːʔʲo/ *shape:* palm heart

o-lliihyójɨ /-tʃĩːᴸʔʲohɨ/ *shape:* rays of light, e.g., those made by the sun or a flashlight

•-llijyu /-Ⓛtʃihʲɯ/ *shape:* any kind of powder

o-llovái /-tʃõᴸβai/ *shape:* conical, long and cylindrical with a gradually diminishing thickness toward the end

-lloívojɨ /-tʃõᴸiβohɨ/ *shape:* things twisted and spiral

-lloóllo /-Ⓛtʃoːtʃo/ *shape:* things wrinkled

o-llumɨ́ba or -llumɨ́:ho /-tʃũᴸmɨpa ~ -tʃũᴸmɨːʔo/ *shape:* thick and prominent eyelids

-maacyájɨ /-ma̰ᴸːkʲʰahɨ/ *condition:* a color streak that can appear on a shiny surface, e.g., a streak of oil in water

o-mahtájɨ /-ma̰ᴸʔtʰahɨ/ *shape:* a dark blotch on a surface

o-mapóhewa /-ma̰ᴸpʰoʔɛkpa/ *shape:* a large dark blotch on a surface

-mavíyoóho /-ma̰ᴸβijoːʔo/ *shape:* things that are curled up, e.g., dry leaves or hair

•-me
1. with nouns: /-Ⓛmɛ/ *being:* three or more people or animals (animate plural with a few animate nouns ⟨AnPl⟩)
2. with verbs: /-Ⓛ○mɛ/ *being:* three or more people or animals (animate plural ⟨AnPl⟩)

o-mibyééu /-mipʲɛ̃ːᴸɯ/ *shape:* wrapped up

-mihñíu /-mḭʔɲiɯ/ *shape:* a pile of things aligned lengthwise

-mivíyiíu /-mḭᴸβijiːɯ/ *shape:* coiled up, e.g., a coiled up rope

•-mɨ or -mɨ́ /-Ⓛmɨ(ː)/ *shape:* a canoe or other vehicles of transportation

•-mɨ́he /-Ⓛmɨːʔɛ/ *shape:* a skin of an animal, a sheet of metal

•-mɨ́ho /-Ⓛmɨːʔo/ *shape:* flat thin sheet, e.g., bark of tree, a sheet of metal, fingernail

•-mɨjco /-Ⓛmɨˣkʰo/
1. *shape:* a fenced enclosure
2. *shape:* a circle of people

-mɨ́mɨ /-Ⓛmɨːmɨ/ *shape:* a dent or indentation

•-mɨ́ro /-Ⓛmɨːɾo/ *shape:* a shallow

cavity
- -mɨróójɨ /-mɨ̄ro:hɨ/ *shape:* a concavity in a surface
- •-mo /-ⓁmØ/ *shape:* a large body of water, e.g., a big river, the ocean
- -mocódsɨ́ɨu /-mo̅kʰotsɨ:ɯ/ *shape:* an angry facial expresion
- •-motsííu /-mo̅tsʰi:ɯ/ *condition:* turning dark before it starts to rain
- •-mu /-Ⓛmɯ/
  1. *shape:* umarí fruit
  2. *shape:* signal drum
- o-muhmúu /-mɯ̄ʔmɯɯ/ *object:* a termite nest
- •-mupɨ /-Ⓛmɯpʰɨ/ *being:* two women or female animals (dual feminine ⟨DuF⟩)
- •-mutsi /-Ⓛmɯtsʰi/ *being:* two men or male animals (dual masculine ⟨DuM⟩)
- •-naatsóu /-na̅:tsʰoɯ/ *shape:* thing with a sharp point
- •-ne or -ñe /-nɛ ~ -ɲɛ/ the default classifier (maximally unspecified) There are two (or more) cases which differ in tonal effect and meaning:
  1. /-Ⓛ○nɛ/ thing
  2. /#Ⓗ...ʰnɛ/ event
- •-nehníjyau /-nɛ̅ʔnihʲaɯ/ *condition:* bad things or bad actions
- •-nejcu /-Ⓛnɯˣkʰɯ/ *spatial:* the side of something, e.g., the side of a house
- -nejcúu /-nɛ̅ˣkʰɯɯ/ *shape:* strong muscles
- •-niíhyo /-Ⓛni:ʔʲo/ *being:* woman who has children, animal with young
- •-nijkye /-Ⓛniˣkʲʰɛ/ *spatial:* a burial place, grave
- o-niíñe /-Ⓛni:ɲɛ/ *spatial:* a place beyond
- o-nipájchau /-nīpʰaˣtʃʰaɯ/ *shape:* a full bladder or other things of that shape, e.g., a blown up balloon
- -nɨhcórou /-nɨ̅ʔkʰoroɯ/ *shape:* things resembling a big ladle or dipper (used in the kitchen)
- -nocóriwa /-no̅kʰorikpa/ *shape:* things resembling the downward curve of a hawks beak
- -nohcórou /-no̅ʔkʰoroɯ/ *shape:* things curved, e.g., a rainbow
- •-noóra /-Ⓛno:ra/ *shape:* holes made by breaking through to a cavity below the surface
- •-nuhba /-Ⓛnɯʔpa/ *time:* used to number months (in relation to the moon)
- o-nuuhéju /-nɯ̅:ʔɛhɯ/
  1. *condition:* a rebellious person, one who does not listen to advice
  2. *condition:* people, animals or things that do not move in a straight line
- o-nuhmɨrajɨ or -numɨhrau /-nɯ̅ʔmɨrahɨ ~ -nɯ̅:miʔraɯ/ *shape:* big ears
- •-nuhtsɨ /-Ⓛnɯʔtsʰɨ/ *shape:* a mound formed at the foot of a fallen tree
- o-nuumɨ́ho /-nɯ̄:mɨʔo/ *being:* a person or animal with big ears
- o-nuhmɨu /-nɯ̅ʔmɨɯ/ *shape:* cups and pots with handles ("ears").[5]
- •-ñaáhi /-Ⓛɲaʔi/ *shape:* things that have dents in them
- -ñohco /-Ⓛɲoʔkʰo/ *shape:* a curved

---

[5] Compare -nɯ̀ʔmɨrahɨ ~ -nɯ̀:miʔraɯ 'ears', -nɯ̀:mɨʔo 'person or animal with big ears', and -nɯ̀ʔmɨɯ 'cups and pots with handles ("ears")'. The common semantic component "ear" obviously corresponds to the recurring partial nɯ̀ʔmɨ.

[6] Compare nòʔkʰo 'stork'.

handle on a pot⁶

-ñuhííu /-ɲɯ̃ʔiːɯ/ *shape:* a face with a frown

-oobɨ́rau /-òːpiɾaɯ/ *shape:* a solid sphere of some substance, e.g., a ball of dough or mud

-oodsɨ́jyau /-òːtsɨhʲaɯ/ *shape:* a bulky place around a pole, tree or vine

o-ohcu /-Ⓛoˀkʰɯ/ *shape:* broken pieces of pottery on which to place a pot above the fire

-ohcúu /-òˀkʰɯɯ/ *shape:* a swelling

•-oóhi /-Ⓛoːʔi/ *being:* jaguar, dog

-ohtóu /-òˀtʰoɯ/ *shape:* a round hole in a shirt, board or wall

o-omóniíu /-òmoniːɯ/ *shape:* deformed (e.g., an animal that has been burned by a fire)

•-oonái /-òːnai/ *shape:* rolled up (e.g., a piece of paper or a pancake)

o-ootsɨ́rɨho /-òːtsʰiɾiʔo/ *shape:* a bulge about the perimeter of something cylindrical (with both ends being narrower), e.g., a bulge in the middle of a tree trunk

•-pachíchaáu /-pʰat̠ʃʰit̠ʃʰaːɯ/ *shape:* things that are criss-crossed

•-paáji /-Ⓛpʰaːhɨ/
  1. *shape:* a tubular hole (e.g., a pipe, a hollow tree trunk)
  2. *shape:* shoe

•-pajtsɨ /-Ⓛpʰaˣtsʰi/ *shape:* circular, e.g., ring, roll of wire

•-palli /-Ⓛpʰat̠ʃi/ *botanical:* a planted field

•-patúúu /-pʰátʰɯːɯ/ *shape:* stretched out, e.g., a rubber band pulled taut

o-patúruúi /-pʰátʰɯɾɯːi/ *position:* a person or animal stetched out

o-patúruúu /-pʰátʰɯɾɯːɯ/ *position:* a rope or vine sretched out between two trees

-patsááho /-pʰátsʰaːʔo/ *botanical:* trees left standing in a field that has been cut down

•-pejco /-Ⓛpʰɛˣkʰo/ *time:* darkness or night

o-peróówa or -peyóówa /-pʰɛ́ɾoːkpa ~ -pʰɛ́joːkpa/ *position:* thing not in its place

•-pi or -jpi /-Ⓛpʰi ~ -Ⓛˣpʰi/ *being:* a man or a male animal (singular masculine ⟨SgM⟩)

•-pille or -jpille /-Ⓛpʰit̠ʃɛ ~ -Ⓛˣpʰit̠ʃɛ/ *being:* a woman or a female animal (singular feminine ⟨SgF⟩)

o-pihchúu /-pʰíˀt̠ʃʰɯɯ/
  1. *being:* two people or animals on top of each other
  2. *figurative:* used to form the number three

-pihllárɨjɨ /-pʰíˀt̠ʃaɾihɨ/ *shape:* curled under (e.g., the lower lip curled down)

-piijyúu /-pʰíːhʲɯɯ/ *shape:* having an end curled back sharply, e.g., a fishhook

o-pinónowa /-pʰínonokpa/ *shape:* having a twisted point

-piúmiíu /-pʰíɯmiːɯ/ *shape:* doubled back and flattened, e.g., the crimped edge of a sheet of tin

•-pɨ /-Ⓛpʰɨ/ *botanical:* bitter cassava root (manioc)

o-pɨ́ha /-Ⓛpʰɨːʔa/ *substance:* very limp or flexible

-pɨhra /-Ⓛpʰɨʔra/ *shape:* flexible and hanging down, e.g., the ears of some dogs

-pɨ́ɨjɨ /-Ⓛpʰɨːhɨ/ *substance:* having the consistency of mashed potatoes

-pɨóójɨ /-pʰɨ́oːhɨ/ *action:* a duck walk (a gait like a duck)

-pɨúdɨ́ɨjɨ /-pʰɨɯtɨːhɨ/ *shape:* a con-

vexity in a surface, e.g., an upward bulge in the floor of a canoe

o-pohrɨ /-Ⓛpʰoʔɾɨ/ *shape:* wrapped up (e.g., a lump of dough)

o-puhpúwa /-pʰɯ̃ʔpʰɯkpa/ *shape:* a haircut in the form of a bowl

o-raáhe /-Ⓛɾaːʔɛ/ *being:* a chicken

•-rahja /-Ⓛɾaʔha/ *shape:* a break in an enclosure caused by missing poles

•-raáho or -yaáho /-Ⓛɾaːʔo ~ -Ⓛjaːʔo/
  1. *spatial:* the distance or space between two points
  2. *time:* a span or period of time

•-raára /-Ⓛɾaːɾa/ *shape:* punched full of holes; rotted

-ravájchau /-ɾaβaˣtʃʰaɯ/ *shape:* resembling a bloated stomach

-rehmíjɨ /-ɾɛʔmɨhɨ/ *being:* having very short legs or arms

-reére /-Ⓛɾɛːɾɛ/ *substance:* things glutinous and transparent, e.g., clear gelatine

-reróóu /-ɾɛ̃ɾoːɯ/ *condition:* leaning to one side

•-revóóu /-ɾɛβoːɯ/ *shape:* a person, animal or thing twisted toward the back, e.g., a person looking over his shoulder

-rihjyáwa /-ɾĩʔhʲakpa/ *shape:* things having the form of an arch (e.g., a pair of pliers)

o-rihji /-Ⓛɾiʔhi/ *shape:* bad and missing teeth

o-rihpájɨ /-ɾĩʔpʰahɨ/ *being:* a bowlegged person or animal

-rijyááu /-ɾihʲaːɯ/ *position:* legs extended as when taking a step

-rɨjpáyu /-ɾɨ̃ˣpʰajɯ/ *being:* a short person with a big stomach

-rɨ́rɨ /-Ⓛɾɨːɾɨ/ *condition:* a runny sore or infected, drippy eyes

•-ro or -yo /-Ⓛɾo ~ -Ⓛjo/ *shape:* a bottle

o-rohcájɨ /-ɾõʔkʰahɨ/ *shape:* crescent, half-moon

-rohllo /-Ⓛɾoʔtʃo/ *shape:* long, thin and curved, e.g., a car's leaf spring

-rohpéwa /-ɾõʔpʰɛkpa/ *shape:* a deformed fruit

o-rootímyeho /-ɾõːtʰimʲɛʔo/ *being:* a person or animal with a solid, well built body

-rootóho /-ɾõːtʰoʔo/ *shape:* having a thick middle

-rovíícyo /-ɾõβiːkʲʰo/ *shape:* concave, e.g., the cavity of an ear

o-ruhjɨ /-Ⓛɾɯʔhɨ/ *shape:* long, thin and wavy (not straight)

-ruhllo /-Ⓛɾɯʔtʃɯ/ *shape:* permanently bent joint, e.g., a leg that can not be extended

-ruhrái /-ɾɯʔɾai/ *shape:* long and cylindrical

•-rujtsi /-Ⓛɾɯˣtsʰi/ *object:* a woven basket

o-ta /-Ⓛtʰa/ *shape:* a portion of something

-tahcárajɨ /-tʰaʔkʰaɾahɨ/ *position:* sprawled out

-tajɨwa /-tʰãhikpa/ *shape:* smashed very flat

o-tajkíiu or -tajkíba /-tʰãˣkʰiiɯ ~ -tʰãˣkʰipa/ *shape:* a person or animal with very thick legs

-tallíyiíu /-tʰatʃiji:ɯ/ *shape:* twisted, e.g., a propeller

-tamɨduúu /-tʰamiɯːɯ/ *shape:* a low place in a flat surface

-tarɨ́jyaáu /-tʰaɾihʲaːɯ/ *action:* standing with the legs apart

-tarójɨɨu /-tʰaɾohiːɯ/ *shape:* long and curved (e.g., a tree, branch, or bar)

-taáta /-Ⓛtʰaːtʰa/ *shape:* small

fibers in disarray, e.g., uncombed hair

-tyaátya /-Ⓛtʲʰaːtʲʰa/ *shape:* having collapsed sides, e.g., an empty soft-sided suitcase

-tehkéreu /-tʰɛ̕ʔkʰɛɾɛɯ/ *shape:* round and smooth, e.g., the surface of a bald head

•-tojco /-Ⓛtʰoˣkʰo/ *spatial:* a corner in a room (in a box,...)

-tyohkéyeu /-tʲʰo̕ʔkʰejɛɯ/ *shape:* a swelling on the body

-tohra /-Ⓛtʰoʔɾa/ *shape:* suspended empty bag-like thing, e.g., an empty bag hung on a hook

-tuátsaáji /-tʰɯ̕atsʰaːhɨ/ *shape:* having the legs upward (e.g., a table turned up side down, an animal with its legs up in the air)

-tuhra /-Ⓛtʰɯʔɾa/ *shape:* a hanging flexible object that flaps in the wind

o-tuhtsáji /-tʰɯ̕ʔtsʰahɨ/ *shape:* the snout of a pig

•-tujke /-Ⓛtʰɯˣkʰɛ/ *botanical:* the stem of a leaf or a fruit

o-tujkéba /-tʰɯ̕ˣkʰɛpa/ *botanical:* a thick stem of a fruit

-tujúi /-tʰɯ̕hɯi/ *shape:* having a sharp point, e.g., the pointed nose of a tapir or anteater

•-tujúwa /-tʰɯ̕hɯkpa/ *shape:* having a dull point, e.g., a very prominent nose

-turúúu /-tʰɯ̕ɾɯːɯ/ *condition:* leaning over about to fall

o-turúruúji /-tʰɯ̕ɾɯɾɯːhɨ/ *condition:* standing upright but very flexible, e.g., a rush stalk

-tsaáhe /-Ⓛtsʰaːʔɛ/ *shape:* a handful of long, thin cylindrical objects (small rods)

o-tsahtsáwa /-tsʰá̕ʔtsʰakpa/ *shape:* resembling a large lock of hair

-tsañúúi /-tsʰá̕ɲɯːi/ *shape:* spool of thread and similar things

-tsaára /-Ⓛtsʰaːɾa/ *shape:* needle-like

-tseróóji /-tsʰɛ̕ɾoːhɨ/ *shape:* cross-eyed

•-tsii or -chii /-Ⓛtsʰiː ~ -Ⓛtʃʰiː/ *spatial:* a place in general

•-tsiíba /-Ⓛtsʰiːpa/ *spatial:* peninsula

•-tsijtyo /-Ⓛtsʰiˣtʲʰo/ *shape:* a line around an object's circumference

-tsipáraáu /-tsʰi̕pʰaɾaːɯ/ *shape:* tear or rupture

-tsipóóu /-tsʰi̕pʰoːɯ/ *shape:* a big bend made in something (e.g., a pole bent without breaking)

•-tsɨ /-Ⓛtsʰɨ/ *being:* a baby

o-tso /-Ⓛtsʰo/ *shape:* long things that gradually taper toward the tip

-tsoodónoho /-tsʰó̕ːtonoʔo/ *being:* a person or animal with a large chest

•-tsohna /-Ⓛtsʰoʔna/ *shape:* a pyramid or upright cone

•-tsoóho /-Ⓛtsʰoːʔo/ *botanical:* plants or trees with one root but a number of trunks

•-tsoója /-Ⓛtsʰoːha/ *shape:* hollow cone, funnel-shaped

-tsovúúruho /-tsʰó̕βɯːɾɯʔo/ *shape:* a person, animal or thing with missing limb-like parts, e.g., tree trunk with the branches cut off, a carcass with the limbs removed

•-tsuúho /-Ⓛtsʰɯːʔo/ *being:* a person or animal with short bent arms or legs

•-tsujɨ /-Ⓛtsʰɯhɨ/ *shape:* the flat, thin "ribs" that grow along the trunks of some trees

-tsuúri /-Ⓛtsʰɯːɾi/ *shape:* long narrow stip

•-tsuútsu /-Ⓛtsʰɯːtsʰɯ/ *shape:* a fragment (of something)

- •-u /-Ⓛɯ/ *shape:* spherical, e.g., a ball, a marble
- o-ubáu /-ɯ̋paɯ/ *being:* a person missing an arm or a leg
- -uubóu /-ɯ̋ːpoɯ/ *shape:* a small swelling on the surface
- •-uúha /-Ⓛɯːʔa/ *shape:* a single kernel or chip (e.g., a kernel of wheat, a grain of sand)
- -uúho /-Ⓛɯːʔo/ *spatial:* place where many vines hang from the trees
- -uhro /-Ⓛɯʔɾo/ *shape:* a tall pot or jar
- -uhtsárau /-ɯ̋ʔtsʰaɾaɯ/ *shape:* hair standing on end, e.g., that of a porcupine
- •-újcucu /-ɯˣkʰɯkʰɯ/[7] *spatial:* the place where two trails meet
- -ujéého /-ɯ̋hɛːʔo/ *action:* turning sideways to pass through a narrow place
- -umɨ́cou or -humɨ́cou /-ɯ̋mɨkʰoɯ ~ -ʔɯ̋mɨkʰoɯ/ *shape:* a very prominent forehead on man or animal (This is formed from ʔɯmɨkʰo -húmɨco 'forehead', which is formed from ʔɯ̋mɨ̋ 'face'.)
- -umúúu /-ɯ̋mɯːɯ/ *shape:* lips held together very tightly
- -unɨ́bau /-ɯ̋nɨpaɯ/ *shape:* very big lips
- o-uutsíyojɨ /-ɯ̋ːtsʰijohɨ/ *shape:* lying on its side
- o-utsúcuúu /-ɯ̋tsʰɯkʰɯːɯ/ *shape:* tight fitting (e.g., a small shirt on a big man)
- -vaája /-Ⓛβaːha/ *shape:* rip in a cloth
- o-vaáre /-Ⓛβaːɾɛ/ *being:* a person controlled by a demon
- -vaári /-Ⓛβaːɾi/ *shape:* tattered, e.g., clothing
- o-vechíhcyo /-β̋ɛt͡ʃʰiʔkʲʰo / *substance:* very curved and flexible at the tip, e.g., a fishing rod
- o-vehrátsai /-β̋ɛʔɾatsʰai/ *shape:* oval
- -vihcya /-Ⓛβiʔkʲʰa/ *shape:* sharply curved, e.g., a fishhook
- o-vihcyo /-Ⓛβiʔkʲʰo/ *shape:* a thing that has a hook on the end
- -vijvíi /-β̋iˣβii/ *shape:* a thing that has the shape of a large claw or fingernail
- o-viívi /-Ⓛβiːβi/ *shape:* elongated openings (e.g., the eye of an oriental person)
- •-viíu /-Ⓛβiːɯ/ *shape:* a piece of something
- •-vɨɨa /-Ⓛβɨːa/ *shape:* a puncture made by a needle
- o-vɨójtsoco /-β̋ioˣtsʰokʰo/ *shape:* a very round hole (e.g., the hole made by rounding the lips)
- -vɨɨtso /-Ⓛβɨːtsʰo/ *shape:* tubular with both ends open (e.g., a pipe)
- -vuúdo /-Ⓛβɯːto/ *shape:* a short, broken piece of a vine
- -vuúru /-Ⓛβɯːɾɯ/ *shape:* short and thick
- •-wa /-Ⓛk͡pa/ *shape:* long, flat and roughly rectangular, e.g., plank, door, bench, table, machete
- -wachájaáu /-k͡pat͡ʃʰahaːɯ/ *shape:* things in total disarray
- •-wachéke /-k͡pat͡ʃʰɛkʰɛ/ *shape:* two things crossed, e.g., a cross
- -wadáriíu /-k͡pataɾiːɯ/ *shape:* lodged between other things
- -wadéke /-k͡patɛkʰɛ/ *spatial:* the place at which something divides (e.g., a branch on a tree or a trail leads off in another direction)
- o-waádi /-Ⓛk͡paːti/ *shape:* a long split or crack (as there might be in a board or in a wall)

---

[7] Note that the first syllable bears high tone, unlike the other trisyllabic classifiers.

- -wadsɨrooho /-ƙpatsɨɾo:ʔo/ shape: bulged out due to internal pressure, e.g., cheeks bulging with coca powder
- •-waáhye /-Ⓛƙpa:ʔʲɛ/ object: crumbs
- •-waáhyo /-Ⓛƙpa:ʔʲo/ shape: things lying side by side, e.g., a log raft
- •-wajca /-Ⓛƙpaˣkʰa/ botanical: branch of a tree (or perhaps other rigid limb-like projections)
- •-wajcyo /-Ⓛƙpaˣkʲʰo/ shape: a hook on the end of a pole used to pull down fruit
- •-waju /-Ⓛƙpahɯ/ shape: ground that is not level
- -wallááu /-ƙpatʃa:ɯ/ position: a thing with the open side up, a person on his or her back
- •-waáne /-Ⓛƙpa:nɛ/ shape: end of a hip roof
- o-wanɨ́jrɨwa /-ƙpanɨˣrɨƙpa/
  1. shape: puffed up chest, e.g., that of a strutting turkey
  2. figurative: a man showing his prowess
- •-waanúwa /-ƙpa:nɯƙpa/ shape: a notch made on a pole or tree
- -wapɨ́raáu /-ƙpapʰɨra:ɯ/ position: clothes hung over a line to dry
- -warɨ́jyaáu /-ƙparihʲa:ɯ/ position: out of place, misaligned
- -watyúúu /-ƙpatʲʰɯ:ɯ/ position: not lined up (with the orientation of its background)
- -watsɨ́ɨu /-ƙpatsʰi:ɯ/
  1. condition: a thing not finished
  2. condition: a thing of two colors
- -watsújaáu /-ƙpatsʰɯha:ɯ/ shape: flared out, e.g., a skirt that spreads out at the bottom
- -wayááu /-ƙpaja:ɯ/ shape: turned to one side, e.g., person looking to the side, canoe not going straight
- •-waáwa /-Ⓛƙpa:ƙpa/ shape: a canal or ditch
- -wayóóho /-ƙpajo:ʔo/ shape: a thing twisted at the tip
- -wayóójɨ /-ƙpajo:hɨ/ shape: a thing out of its right shape, e.g., a twisted mouth
- o-weéwe or -wyeéwye /-Ⓛƙpɛ:ƙpɛ ~ -Ⓛƙpjɛ:ƙpjɛ/ shape: a very short crack
- •-yojke /-Ⓛjoˣkʰɛ/ shape: a long straight stretch

Appendix F

Bora Kinship Terminology

Bora kinship terminology reflects the traditional social structure of this polity/ethnic group.[1]

The Bora people refer to themselves as mɨ́ámúmàà (mɨamúnaa) 'the people' and all others as tsʰɨ́ˣtʲʰɛ̀ múmàà (tsíjtye múnaa) 'other people'.

The Bora were organized into clans. Each clan includes all those descended from a common ancestor through the male line. Each clan had a chief (áβʲɛ́hɯ̀ɯ́pɛ̀ ávyéjuúbe) who was in full control of those in his clan íàβʲɛ́hɯ̀ː (íavyéju).

Each clan traced its ancestry back to a totem (ìhʲɛ́ɛ̀nɛ̀ ijyéene), either animate or inanimate; this was revered and not eaten by the clan members. The clan totem was the name (ítʲʰòˀhípà ítyohjɨ́ba) of the clan members. Each clan had its own design (íòːnóβà íoonóva) for painting the body or some personal object.

Originally each clan lived in a large communal house, the rear of which was occupied by the chief. Each married couple with their children had a platform on which they slept and under which they prepared their food. Each male member of the clan brought his bride to live with his close relatives (i.e., the traditional residence pattern was patrilocal).

Today the picture is changing, although much of the original social structure can still be seen. The big house is smaller. It is seldom used for sleeping quarters except by the chief and his immediate family. Others now sleep in individual family houses with raised floors. However, the

---

[1] See (Thiesen 1975b), an earlier description of Bora kinship terminology, on which this chapter is based.

big house is still used for the preparation of food and for social activities.

The system of Bora kinship terms is summarized in two diagrams. The terms of REFERENCE are diagrammed in figure F.1, followed by the corresponding terms. The terms for ADDRESSING a kinsman are diagrammed in figure F.2, followed by the corresponding terms.

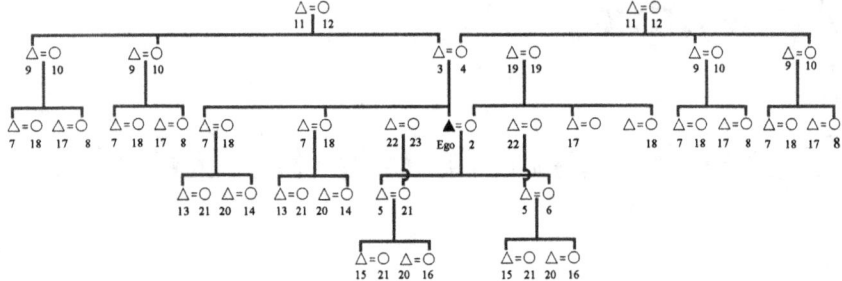

Figure F.1 Terms of reference for kinsmen

The following terms—corresponding to figure F.1—are used to refer to someone in terms of kinship relationship:

1. át^{jh}á:hɨ́ (átyáájɨ́ɨ́) 'my husband'
2. át^{jh}á:pàá (átyáábaá) 'my wife'
3. tʃì?íjò (llihíyo) 'father', t^{h}á:k^{h}á:nìí (táácáánií) 'my father'
4. kpà?áɾò (waháro) 'mother', t^{h}á:ts^{h}ɨ́:hùɾɨ́ (táátsɨ́ɨ́juú) 'my mother'
5. à^{x}tʃ^{h}ì (ajchi) 'my son'[2]
6. àh^{j}ɨ́ɨ̀kpà (ajyúwa) 'my daughter'[3]
7. t^{h}áɲà?pè (táñahbe) 'my brother (or male first cousins)'
8. t^{h}áɲà:tʃè (táñaálle) 'my sister (or female first cousins)'
9. nànìjò (naníyo) 'uncle', t^{h}á:ɲá?nìí (tááñáhnií) 'my uncle'
10. mè?éɾò (mehéro) 'aunt', t^{h}áì:m^{j}è (táíímye) 'my aunt'
11. t^{h}à?tíjò (tahdíyo) 'grandfather', t^{h}á:t^{jh}á?tìí (táátyáhdií) 'my grandfather'
12. t^{h}à:tʃéɾò (taalléro) 'grandmother', t^{h}á:t^{jh}á:tʃèé (táátyáálleé) 'my grandmother'
13. tòmíkpɨ̀ (domíwu) 'nephew', t^{h}áp^{j}è:pè (tábyeébe) 'my nephew'
14. tò?íkpɨ̀ (dohɨ́wu) 'niece', t^{h}áp^{j}è?tʃè (tábyehlle) 'my niece'
15. à?tʃ^{h}íkpɨ̀ (ahchíwu) 'grandson', t^{h}áìà:tʃ^{h}ì (táiááchi) 'my grandson'
16. à?k^{jh}ɨ́ɨ̀kpà (ahcyúwa) 'granddaughter', t^{h}áìà:k^{jh}ɨ̀ɨ̀kpà (táiáácyuwa) 'my granddaughter'
17. át^{jh}ónɨ̀:pè (átyónuúbe) 'my brother-in-law'

---

[2] t^{h}á^{x}ts^{h}ɨ̀:ménè (tájtsɨ́ɨméne) 'my child' is also used.
[3] t^{h}á^{x}ts^{h}ɨ̀:ménè (tájtsɨ́ɨméne) 'my child' is also used.

18. átʲʰónùːtʃè (átyónulle) 'my sister-in-law'
19. ápáːpèé (ábáábeé) 'my father-in-law or mother-in-law'
20. áːhʲàá (áájyaá) 'my son-in-law'
21. tʰáìàːhà (táiáája) 'my daughter-in-law'
22. tʰánìɨ́ːpè (tániúúbe) 'my son's or daughter's father-in-law'
23. tʰánìɨ́ːtʃè (tániúúlle) 'my son's or daughter's mother-in-law'

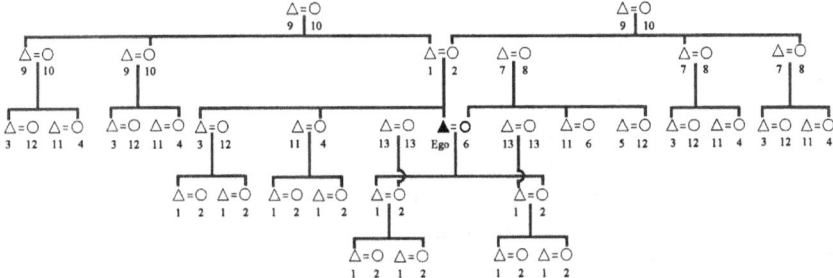

Figure F.2 Terms for addressing another person

The following terms—corresponding to figure F.2—are used to address someone in terms of their kinship relation to the speaker:

1. tʃíʔìˣ (llíhij) 'father, son, nephew, grandson, son-in-law'
2. kpáʔàˣ (wáhaj) 'mother, daughter, niece, granddaughter, daughter-in-law'
3. pʰéɲùɾˣ (péñuj) 'brother, male first cousin, nephew'
4. tóʔmìˣ (dóhmij) 'sister, female first cousin, niece'
5. mùːpèˣ (muúbej) 'husband'
6. mùːtʃèˣ (muúllej) 'wife'
7. nánìˣ (nánij) 'uncle, father-in-law'
8. mɛ́ʔɛ̀ˣ (méhej) 'aunt, mother-in-law'
9. tʰáʔtìˣ (táhdij) 'grandfather'
10. tʰàːtʃèˣ (taállej) 'grandmother'
11. átʲʰòˣ (átyoj) 'brother-in-law'
12. pɨ́ɾʔhìˣ (búhjɨj) 'sister-in-law'
13. tʰánìˣ (tánij) 'child's father-in-law or mother-in-law'

Commentary:
- There are kinship terms for five generations: ego's, parents', grandparents', children's, and grandchildren's. Great-grandparents are referred to as grandparents, which term also refers to one's immediate ancestors. Great-grandchildren are referred to as grandchildren.
- The system does not make a distinction between siblings and cousins; both are called "brothers" or "sisters".

- Bora does not distinguish cross-cousins[4] and parallel cousins.[5]
- The terms of address for father/son and mother/daughter are reciprocal.
- There are terms of reference and address for one's child's in-laws, that is, the parents of one's child's spouse.

We will now present the Bora kinship system in terms of the following eight basic relationships:

1. husband ↔ wife,
2. sibling ↔ sibling,
3. parent ↔ child,
4. grandparent ↔ grandchild,
5. uncle/aunt ↔ nephew/niece,
6. brother-in-law ↔ sister-in-law,
7. parents-in-law ↔ son-/daughter-in-law, and
8. fathers-in-law ↔ mothers-in-law
9. not related by kinship

F.1 Husband — wife relationship

A person may only marry someone outside of his or her lineage as indicated by the kinship terms. Anyone not related (as indicated by the kinship terms) is a potential partner.

After marriage the wife joins the clan of her husband although she never loses identity with her own clan. If her husband dies she returns to live with her own clan. Children belong to the father's clan and stay with him if a separation occurs.

The husband refers to his wife as át^{jh}á:pàá (átyáábaá) 'my wife' and addresses her as mùː:tʃɛ̀^{x} (muúllej).[6] Other persons refer to his wife as ít^{jh}á:pàá (ítyáábaá) 'his wife' or mɛ̀kpà (mewa) (before child-bearing) and mɛ́kpàɲíː:ʔ^{j}ò (méwañííhyo) (after child-bearing).

The wife refers to her husband as át^{jh}á:hɨ̀ (átyáájɨ̵) 'my husband' and addresses him as mùː:pɛ̀^{x} (muúbej).[7] Other persons refer to her husband as ít^{jh}á:hɨ̀ (ítyáájɨ̵) 'her husband' or áh^{j}ùɾú (ájyuú).

---

[4]That is, mother's brother's children and father's sister's children.

[5]That is, mother's sister's children and father's brother's children.

[6]This is mɯː:-tʃɛ-^{x} Muú-lle-j (age.mate-<SgF>-voc). (Thiesen & Thiesen 1998:190) gives its meaning as 'sister (vocative)', used to address a sister, a female cousin, or another woman about the same age.

[7]This is mɯː:-pɛ-^{x} muú-be-j (age.mate-<SgM>-voc), used to address a man about the same age who is a brother or friend.

An older man may address his wife—as a term of endearment—with nɛ́ʔnìˣ (néhnij) 'ugly'.

F.2 Sibling — sibling relationship

The sibling relationship extends to any who have the same grandfather and grandmother. Thus siblings and first cousins refer to each other as tʰáɲàʔpɛ̀ (táñahbe) 'my brother' or tʰáɲàːʧɛ̀ (táñaálle) 'my sister'. Other persons refer to them as íɲàʔpɛ̀ (íñahbe) 'his or her brother' or íɲàːʧɛ̀ (íñaálle) 'his or her sister'.

A brother addresses his sister or a female cousin as tóʔmìˣ (dóhmij). A sister addresses her brother or a male cousin as pʰɛ́ɲùˣ (péñuj).

Second cousins are not "siblings," so are eligible as marriage partners. There is no term for second cousins.

F.3 Parent — child relationship

Parents refer to their children as átsʰɨ̀ːmɛ̀ (átsɨ́ɨ́me) 'my children' or tʰáˣtsʰɨ̀ːmɛ́nɛ̀ (tájtsɨ́ɨ́méne) 'my child'. A son is referred to as àˣʧʰì (ajchi) or àˣʧʰíkpùɾ (ajchíwu) and is addressed as either ʧíʔìˣ (llíhij), ʧìʔíjòˣ (llihíyoj) or ʧìʔíùɾˣ (llihíuj). A daughter is referred to as àhʲúɨ̀kpà (ajyúwa). She is addressed as either kpáʔàˣ (wáhaj), kpàʔáɾòˣ (wahároj) or kpàʔáùɾˣ (waháuj). Others refer to the son as íʧíí (íllií) 'his or her son' and to the daughter as ítsɨ̀í (ídsɨ́ɨ́) 'his or her daughter'.

Children refer to their father as ʧìʔíjò (llihíyo), ʧìʔíùɾ (llihíu) or tʰáːkʰáːnìí (táácáánií) 'my father' and address him the same as a parent addresses a son: ʧíʔìˣ (llíhij), ʧìʔíjòˣ (llihíyoj) or ʧìʔíùɾˣ (llihíuj).

Children refer to their mother either as kpàʔáɾò (waháro), kpàʔáùɾ (waháu) or tʰáːtsʰɨ̀ːhùɾú (táátsɨ́ɨ́juú) 'my mother' and address her the same as a parent addresses a daughter: kpáʔàˣ (wáhaj), kpàʔáɾòˣ (wahároj) or kpàʔáùɾˣ (waháuj). Thus parents and children use reciprocal terms af-dress.

Others refer to their father as íːkʲʰáːnìí (íícyáánií) 'his or her father' and to their mother as íːtsʰɨ̀ːhùɾú (ɨ́ɨ́tsɨ́ɨ́juú) 'his or her mother'.

F.4 Grandparent — grandchild relationship

Grandparents refer to a grandson or a sibling's grandson as à$^{\textrm{ʔ}}$tʃʰíkpùɨ (ahchíwu) or tʰáìá:tʃʰì (táiááchi) 'my grandson' and address him as tʃíʔìˣ (llíhij), tʃìʔíjòˣ (llihíyoj) or tʃìʔíùɨˣ (llihíuj). A granddaughter or a sibling's granddaughter is referred to as à$^{\textrm{ʔ}}$kʲʰúɨkpà (ahcyúwa) or tʰáìá:kʲʰúɨkpà (táiáácyuwa) 'my grandaughter', and addressed as kpáʔàˣ (wáhaj), kpàʔáɾòˣ (wahároj) or kpàʔáùɨˣ (waháuj). Others refer to them as ííá:tʃʰì (íiááchi) 'his or her grandson' and ííá:kʲʰúɨkpà (íiáácyuwa) 'his or her granddaughter'.

Grandchildren refer to a grandfather as tʰàʔtíjò (tahdíyo), tʰàʔtíùɨ (tahdíu) or tʰá:tʲʰáʔtìí (táátyáhdií) 'my grandfather' and address him tʰáʔtìˣ (táhdij), tʰàʔtíjòˣ (tahdíyoj) or tʰàʔtíùɨˣ (tahdíuj).

A grandmother is referred to as tʰà:tʃɛ́ɾò (taalléro), tʰà:tʃɛ́ùɨ (taalléu) or tʰá:tʲʰá:tʃɛ̀ɛ́ (táátyáálleé) 'my grandmother', and addressed as tʰà:tʃɛ̀ˣ (taállej), tʰà:tʃɛ́ɾòˣ (taalléroj) or tʰà:tʃɛ́ùɨˣ (taalléuj).

Others refer to them as í:tʲáʔtìí (íídyáhdií) 'his or her grandfather' and í:tʲʰá:tʃɛ̀ɛ́ (íítyáálleé) 'his or her grandmother'. The same terminology is used for maternal as well as paternal grandparents. tʰáʔtìˣ (táhdij) and tʰà:tʃɛ̀ˣ (taállej) are also used when addressing a man or woman old enough to be one's grandparent, even though they are unrelated.

F.5 Uncle/aunt — nephew/niece relationship

An uncle or aunt refers to a son of any whom they address as tʰájnàʔpɛ̀ (táñahbe) 'my brother' or tʰájnà:tʃɛ̀ (táñaálle) 'my sister' with the term tòmíkpùɨ (domíwu) or tʰápʲɛ̀:pɛ̀ (tábyeébe) 'my nephew' and address him either as tʃíʔìˣ (llíhij) or pʰɛ́ɲùɨˣ (péñuj).

They refer to a daughter of any whom they address as tʰájnàʔpɛ̀ (táñahbe) 'my brother' or tʰájnà:tʃɛ̀ (táñaálle) 'my sister' with the term tò:ʔíkpùɨ (doohɨ́wu) or tʰápʲɛ̀ʔtʃɛ̀ (tábyehlle) 'my niece' and address her as kpáʔàˣ (wáhaj) or tóʔmìˣ (dóhmij). Others refer to them as ípʲɛ̀:pɛ̀ (íbyeébe) 'his or her nephew' and ípʲɛ̀ʔtʃɛ̀ (íbyehlle) 'his or her niece'. Thus all one's cousins' children are included as nephews and nieces.

A nephew or niece refers to a brother of his or her father or mother as nàníjò (naníyo), nàníùɨ (naníu) or tʰá:ɲáʔnìí (tááñáhnií) 'my uncle' and address him as nà:nìˣ (naánij), nà:níjòˣ (naaníyoj) or nà:níùɨˣ (naaníuj). The sister of a parent is referred to as mɛ̀ʔɛ́ɾò (mehéro), mɛ̀ʔɛ́ùɨ (mehéu) or tʰáì:mʲɛ̀ (táiímye) 'my aunt' and addressed as mɛ́ʔɛ̀ˣ (méhej), mɛ̀ʔɛ́ɾòˣ (mehéroj) or mɛ̀ʔɛ́ùɨˣ (mehéuj). Others refer to them as íɲáʔnìí (íñáhnií)

'his or her uncle' and íːmʲèé (íímyeé) 'his or her aunt'. Wives and husbands of father's or mother's brothers or sisters are included. nàːnì˟ (naánij) 'uncle' and mɛ́ʔɛ̀˟ (méhej) 'aunt' are also used to politely address people of that age group, even though they are unrelated.

F.6 Brother-in-law — sister-in-law relationship

A husband refers to his wife's brother or a husband of any whom he calls tʰáɲàːtʃè (táñaálle) 'my sister' as átʲʰónùːpè (átyónuúbe) 'my brother-in-law', and addresses him as átʲʰò˟ (átyoj).

A wife refers to her husband's brother or a husband of any whom she calls tʰáɲàːtʃè (táñaálle) 'my sister' also as átʲʰónùːpè (átyónuúbe) 'my brother-in-law' and addresses him átʲʰò˟ (átyoj) as well. Others refer to him as ítʲʰónùːpè (ítyónuúbe) 'his or her brother-in-law'.

A husband refers to his wife's sister or a wife of any whom he calls tʰáɲàʔpè (táñahbe) 'my brother' as átʲʰónùtʃè (átyónulle), and addresses her púɾʔhɨ˟ (búhjɨj).

A wife refers to a sister of his brother or a wife of any whom she calls tʰáɲàʔpè (táñahbe) 'my brother' also as átʲʰónùtʃè (átyónulle) and addresses her as púɾʔhɨ˟ (búhjɨj) as well. Others refer to her as ítʲʰónùtʃè (ítyónulle) 'his or her sister-in-law'.

F.7 Parents-in-law — son-/daughter-in-law relationship

A son-in-law, the husband of any addressed as tʰápʲɛ̀ʔtʃè (tábyehlle) 'my niece', and the husband of any addressed as tʰáìàːkʲʰùkpà (táiáácyuwa) 'my granddaughter' are referred to as áːhʲàá (áájyaá) 'my son-in-law'. He is addressed by the parents-in-law as tʃíʔì˟ (llíhij) 'son'. Others refer to him as ìáhʲàá (iájyaá) 'his or her son-in-law'.

A husband's parents refer to their daughter-in-law, the wife of any whom they call tʰápʲɛ̀ːpè (tábyeébe) 'my nephew' and the wife of any whom they call tʰáìàːtʃʰì (táiááchi) 'my grandson' as tʰáìàːhà (táiáája) 'my daughter-in-law' and address her as kpáʔà˟ (wáhaj) 'daughter'. Others refer to her as îàːhà (íiáája) 'his or her daughter-in-law'.

A husband refers to his wife's father and mother, her uncles and aunts and her grandfather and grandmother as ápáːpɛ̀ɛ́ (ábáábeé) 'my in-law'

and addresses the father and uncles as nánì^x (nánij) 'uncle', and the mother and aunts as mɛ́ʔɛ̀^{x} (méhej) 'aunt'. He addresses the grandfather as t^{h}á^{ʔ}tì^x (táhdij) and the grandmother as t^{h}à:tʃɛ̀^{x} (taállej). Others refer to them as ípá:pɛ̀ɛ́ (íbáábeé) 'his in-law'.

A wife, in the same way, refers to her husband's father and mother, his uncles and aunts and his grandfather and grandmother as ápá:pɛ̀ɛ́ (ábáábeé) 'my in-law' and addresses the father and uncles nánì^{x}n (nánij) 'uncle' and the mother and aunts mɛ́ʔɛ̀^{x} (méhej) 'aunt'. She addresses the grandfather t^{h}á^{ʔ}tì^x (táhdij) and the grandmother t^{h}à:tʃɛ̀^{x} (taállej). Others refer to them as ípá:pɛ̀ɛ́ (íbáábeé) 'her in-law'.

F.8 Fathers-in-law — mothers-in-law relationship

Parents refer to their child's father-in-law as t^{h}ánìɯ́:pè (tániúúbe) 'my child's father-in-law' and address him t^{h}ánì^x (tánij) and to their child's mother-in-law as t^{h}ánìɯ́:tʃè (tániúúlle) 'my child's mother-in-law' and address her t^{h}ánì^x (tánij) also. These are reciprocal terms used between the husband's and wife's parents. Others refer to them as íɲìɯ́:pè (íñiúúbe) 'his or her father-in-law' and íɲìɯ́:tʃè (íñiúúlle) 'his or her mother-in-law'.

F.9 Addessing persons not related by kinship

In polite speech one uses the following terms of address with persons who are not related by kinship:

1. one's own generation
   male: mɯ̀:pì^x (muúbij)
   female: mɯ̀:tʃɛ̀^{x} (muúllej)
2. member of one's parent's generation
   male: nánì^x (nánij) 'uncle'
   female: mɛ́ʔɛ̀^{x} (méhej) 'aunt'
3. member of one's grandparent's generation
   male: t^{h}átì^x (tádij) 'grandfather'
   female: t^{h}à:tʃɛ̀^{x} (taállej) 'grandmother'
4. member of one's child's or grandchild's generation
   male: tʃí^{ʔ}ì^x (llíhij) 'son'
   female: kpá^{ʔ}ɛ̀^{x} (wáhej) 'daughter'

Appendix G

Bora Texts

Included below are six native-authored texts, written as the Bora people write the Bora language.[1] The first four were written in the late 1950s and early 1960s by school children ranging in age from 12–16.[2] Texts 1, 2, and 4 are folktales. Text 5 is an imagined drama; the sixth an explanation.

1. Walle Píívyeté Núlledívu 'A woman becomes a toucan' (Mibeco N. *et al.* 1975:92–93).
2. Tsáníhyoke Bɨɨrúmujɨ Tsájtyene 'An aguoti takes a wife' (Mibeco N. *et al.* 1975:38–39).
3. Ávyéjuubéváa Péé Bájú Pañévu 'A chief goes to the jungles'.
4. Píívyéébé Ajyúwá Uubálle 'The Creator's Daughter' (Mibeco N. *et al.* 1975:6–19). This story is important to the Bora people. It has the moral that sexual relation with a close relative brings drastic consequences.[3]
5. Ajcyómé Úmɨhe 'They cultivate the field'. This is an imagined drama. Note that the dialog is interrupted only three times by the narrator.
6. Íllu Múúne Méwákímyeí 'This is how we work' was written by Julia Mibeco based on her experience helping with the household chores in the Thiesen home. An appropriate subtitle might be: "The curious ways of the foreigners." It is included because of its accessibility to those familiar with western culture (setting table and such things).

---

[1] Eduardo Soria translated the texts into Spanish. Wes Thiesen translated them into English and added the glosses. David Weber added the analysis in the footnotes.

[2] Julia Mibeco, one of the authors, corrected the spelling and made editorial changes. Two of these stories were included in (Mibeco N. *et al.* 1975).

[3] Marriage is prohibited between first cousins since they are regarded as siblings, as reflected in the kinship terminology; see appendix F.

At the foot of each page of text is given a tentative analysis of each sentence. These are very schematic, abstracting only the major structural and functional characteristic of each sentence.

Abbreviations

The following abbreviations and conventions are used in these analyses, in addition to some from pages xxix–xxxiii.

| apposition (between two appositive constituents)
‖ cleft (contrastive focus)
≀ juncture between the modifier and head in a genitive construction
(BE) implicit 'be'
Ø$_i$ coindexed null pronoun
Adj adjective
Adv adverb or adverbial clause
    Adv$_D$ adverbial clause with a different subject
    Adv$_S$ adverbial clause with the same subject
    AdvDeg adverb of degree
Aux auxiliary
    Aux-s auxiliary verb with a classifier subject
(BE) implicit copula
Cir circumstance or circumstantial adverbial clause,
    Cir$_d$ circumstantial adverbial clause with a different subject,
    Cir$_s$ circumstantial adverbial clause with a same subject,
    Cir$_s^n$ the n-th circumstantial adverbial clause with a same subject
ComplOfKnow complement of the verb "know"
Cond conditional
CoS co-subject
Dem demonstrative
DO direct object
    DO$_{recip}$ direct object indicating the recipient of "give"
F feminine
frs frustrative, contraexpectation
Goal NP with "goal" case marking
    Goal$_{theme}$ goal-marked noun phrase indicating the thematic argument of "give"
impl implore
Instr NP with "instrument" (oblIn) case marking
Interj interjection
-KI implicit /-ki/ 'purpose'
Link sentence-initial connector, usually an anaphoric pronoun
Loc NP with "location" case marking
Man NP indicating manner
N noun
Neg negative
NP noun phrase
O object of a verb of saying, telling,...
oblIn oblique (case marker) for inanimate noun phrases
PostPos pospositional phrase
PredCmpl predicate complement
ProSent pro-sentence
pur purpose
Pur purpose clause, noun phrase indicating purpose,
    Pur$_d$ purpose clause with a different subject,
    Pur$_s$ purpose clause with a same subject
Q interrogative pronoun. This may be followed by the function:

QS questioned subject,
QDO questioned direct object,
QGoal questioned goal,
and so forth for QCoS, QInstr,
QLoc, QManSou, QPur, QSim,
and QTime
$Q_{y/n}$ yes/no question
Quan quantifier
rec recent past
S subject, $S_{partitive}$ partitive subject
Sim similarity, comparison
Site site of attachment
Sou source
sub subordinator (followed by an auxiliar verb)
Sum list terminator
s-V verb with a pronominal proclitic subject
TempN temporal noun like (boone) 'after'
TempP temporal phrase headed by a TempN
Th theme
Time time
V verb
V-s verb with a classifier subject (cliticized)
Voc vocative

Conventions

X_i, X_j, X_k The subscripted indices indicate coreference, e.g., <**Goal**$_i$> to indicate that this Goal is coreferential to another constituent bearing a subscripted i.

X* X will be further described in the same note, e.g., **DO*** indicates that this direct object will be further described.

X_s The subject of X is *coreferential* to the subject of the superordinate clause, e.g., **Adv**$_s$ is an adverbial clause with same subject as the higher clause.

X_d The subject of X is *not coreferential* to the subject of the superordinate clause, e.g., **Cir**$_d$ indicates that the subject of this circumstantial clause is not coreferential to the subject of the higher clause.

X^1, X^2 Superscripted digits distinguish constituents to be further described in the annotation, e.g., to distinguish Cir_s^1 and Cir_s^2.

<X> The wedges indicate that the enclosed is a sentence-initial thematic link.

Early Attachment. The analyses (given at the foot of the page) generally favor **early attachment**. For example, the sentence in 1194a could be analyzed either as in 1194b or as in 1194c:

(1194) a. ... baajúrí me íhtune mé nijtyúhi
b. ...[[manioc we peel]   we wash]
c. ... [manioc [we peel]   we wash]

b. 'after having peeled the manioc, we wash it'
c. 'after having peeled it, we wash the manioc'

In 1194b, the direct object 'manioc' is attached to the verb 'we peel' and then this phrase is attached to 'we wash'. ; hence [[DO s-V] s-V]. In 1194c, on the other hand, the attachment of 'manioc' is deferred until 'we peel (it)' has been attached to 'we wash'; hence [DO [s-V s-V]].

Walle Píívyeté Núlledívu

A Woman Becomes a Toucan

¹Tsáá-pillé-vá-a   bádsɨ́jca-ja   awá-hi.
one-<SgF>-rpt-rem   adolescentF-sg   diet-<t>

²Aa-llé-vá-a   pa-íjyu-vá-ré   pe-h   íjcyá-h
thm-<SgF>-rpt-rem   all-day-pl-only   go-sub   be-<t>

úmɨhé-vú   íh   maahó-ma.   ³Ih-dyú-vá-hacá-a
field-goal   self   cassava-pl   this-<like>-rpt-realize-rem

[cátúújɨ   behjɨbáá-né]   i   lléhdo-KI   tsatyé-h
ñejilla   shoot-pl   self   eat-pur   take-sub

íjcya-lle.   ⁴Aa-né-vá-a   tsaa-te   néé-hií:
be-<SgF>   thm-<ø>-rpt-rem   one-<AnPl>   say-<t>

"¿ɨ́vee-kí-ami   aa-lle   pa-íjyu-vá-ré
why-pur-wonder   that-<SgF>   all-day-pl-only

tsatyé-h   ijcyá-h   íh   maaho   [úmɨhé
take-sub   be-<t>   self   cassava   field

pañé-vu]?"   ⁵Eh-dú-vá-a   i   ñéé-ne
inside-goal   that-<like>-rpt-rem   self   say-<event>

úra-avyé-mé   tsá-jcoojɨ   díí-lle-ke.
follow-sIn-<AnPl>   one-day   that-<SgF>-objAn

⁶Aa-mé-vá-a   péé-h   [díí-llé   kemú-ellé-re].
thm-<AnPl>-rpt-rem   go-<t>   that-<SgF>   far-<place>-only

⁷Aa-mé-vá-a   ɨ́ɨ́té-náa   [[tee-ne   cátuujɨ]   i
thm-<AnPl>-rpt-rem   look-while   that-<ø>   ñejilla   self

tyábá-hcyó-né]   lléhdo-llé-ré   péé-hií.
pull.up-mTr-<event>   eat-<SgF>-only   go-<t>

¹A young girl was dieting. ²She went every day to the field with her cassava. ³Thus, she always takes *ñejilla* palm shoots to eat (with meat). ⁴Then some said, "Why does she always take cassava with her to the field?" ⁵After saying that they followed her one day. ⁶They went after her at a distance. ⁷While they were looking she pulled up some *ñejilla* and went along eating it.

---

¹S | S V   ²S Time V Aux Goal DO   ³<Man$_i$> Cir$_s$ DO Pur$_s$ V Aux-s (where Cir$_s$ = [ø$_i$ V-s] and Pur$_s$ = [s-V]). The DO could be within the Purpose clause   ⁴Link S V "QPur S Time V Aux DO Goal"   ⁵<O$_i$> Cir$_s$ V-s Time DO (where Cir$_s$ = [ø$_i$ V-s])   ⁶S V Loc   ⁷<S$_i$> Time$_d$ Cir$_s$ V V (where Time$_d$ = [ø$_i$ V]); Cir$_s$ = [DO s-V] The final verbs are conjoined "go and eat"

⁸Then she seeing them, put one between her lips and flew up high becoming a toucan. ⁹Then they came and told, "She always takes *ñejilla* to eat together with her cassava. ¹⁰After seeing us she flew up and became a toucan." ¹¹That is how she became a toucan.

⁸Aa-né-vá-a   [dii-tyé-ké   i
   thm-<ø>-rpt-rem   that-<AnPl>-objAn   self

ájtyúmɨ́-ne]   [tsa-ne   ɨ   dɨ́bé-évé-ne]
see-<event>   one-<ø>   self put.between.lips-sIn-<event>

wááméne-lle   cááme-vú-juco,   [tsúúca   núlle-dí-vú
fly-<SgF>   high-goal-focus   already   toucan-anim-goal

pí-ívye-té-lle-ré-juco].   ⁹Aa-né-vá-a
body-sIn-go.do-<SgF>-only-focus   thm-<ø>-rpt-rem

dii-tye   úúballé-vá-hi: "[Cátuujɨ́-haca   i
that-<AnPl>   tell-come.do-<t>   ñejilla-realize   self

lléhdo-KI]   tsatyé-h   íjcya-lle   íh   maáho".
eat-pur   carry-sub   be-<SgF>   self cassava

¹⁰Aa-ne   [múúha-kye   i   ájtyúmɨ́-ne]
thm-<ø>   we.ex-objAn   self   see-<event>

wááméne-lle   [tsúúca   núlle-dí-vu-ré-juco
fly-<SgF>   already   toucan-anim-goal-only-focus

íjcya-lle].   ¹¹Eh-dú-vá-a   pí-ívye-té-llé
be-<SgF>   that-<like>-rpt-rem   body-sIn-go.do-<SgF>

núlle-dí-vu.
toucan-anim-goal

---

⁸Link Cir_s Cir_s V Goal Result_s (where Cir_s = [DO s-V]; Cir_s = [DO s-V]; Result_s = [Adv Goal V-s])   ⁹Link S V "Pur_s V Aux-s DO" (where Pur_s = [DO s-V])   ¹⁰Link Cir_s V-s Result_s (where Cir_s = [DO s-V]; Result_s = [Adv V-s])   ¹¹Man V-s Goal.

Tsáníhyoke Bɨɨrúmujɨ Tsájtyene
An Agouti Takes a Wife

¹Tsaa-pí-vá-a   péé-h   méwá-nííhyo-ma
one-<SgM>-rpt-rem   go-<t>   wife-<childbearer>-with

[bájú   pañé-vu].   ²Aa-mé-vá-a   i
jungle   inside-goal   thm-<AnPl>-rpt-rem   self

úúje-té-dú   meenú-h   í-ñuujú-wa.
arrive-go.do-<like> make-<t>   their-woven-<slab>

³Áá-wa-vú-vá-a   pícyo-íñu-ube
thm-<slab>-goal-rpt-rem   put-do.go-<SgM>

[té-niihyo   méwá-nííhyo]-ke   [i
that-<childbearer>   wife-<childbearer>-objAn self

úúje-té-KI   i   dyáhpé-i-tsíi].   ⁴[Áá-né
arrive-go.do-pur   self trap-fut-<place>   thm-<ø>

hallú]-ri-vá-a   [me-hdu   mía-múnaá-dú
top-oblIn-rpt-rem   SAP-<like>   Bora-people-<like>

i   ípíyé-évé-ne]   Bɨɨrúmu-jɨ   tsajtyé-h
self   become-sIn-<event>   agouti-sg   take-<t>

té-nííhyo-ke.   ⁵[Áá-né   boonéj-vá-a
that-<childbearer>-objAn   thm-<ø>   after-rpt-rem

wajtsɨ́-ɨ́bé   iévé-tsih-vú-ré-juco.
arrive.here-<SgM>   empty-<place>-goal-only-focus

⁶Tsáhá-jucó-vá-a   té-niihyo   íjcya-tú-ne.
no-focus-rpt-rem   that-<childbearer>   be-neg-<n>

⁷Áá-né-lliihyé-vá-a   [di-bye   kééva-ró]-né
thm-<ø>-motive-rpt-rem   that-<SgM>   call-frs-<ø>

tsá(h)   té-nihyo   áñújcu-tú-ne.
no   that-<childbearer>   answer-neg-<n>

¹A man went with his wife into the jungle. ²Upon arrival they made a little shelter. ³He put his wife into the shelter and left to go to where he would set his trap. ⁴Meanwhile, becoming like a human being, an agouti took the wife. ⁵Then he (the man) arrived to an empty place. ⁶That wife was not there. ⁷For that reason his wife did not answer his calling.

---

¹S V CoS Goal   ²S Cir_s V DO (where Cir_s = [s-V])   ³Goal V-s DO | DO Pur_s (where Pur_s = [s-V Goal*] and Goal* = [[s-V]-head])   ⁴Time Cir_s S V DO (where Cir_s = [Sim | Sim s-V])   ⁵TempP V-s Goal   ⁶Neg ∥ S V   ⁷Reason DO Neg S V; DO = [[S V]-head]

⁸Then he, the agouti, caused her to arrive to a festival, to where there was an animal festival. ⁹ᵃThat wife kept looking at all the different animals that were at the festival. ⁹ᵇA deer was there. ⁹ᶜA tapir was there. ⁹ᵈA snake was there. ⁹ᵉThey were all animals, that many.

¹⁰Then the wife looked at everything that was in the big house. ¹¹However, that place was empty. ¹²And while they were dancing she

⁸Aa-né-vá-a   [dii-bye   bɨɨrúmu-jɨ]
thm-<ø>-rpt-rem   that-<SgM>   agouti-sg

úúje-té-tsó-h   wañéhjɨ-vu, | [[iyá-mé
arrive.go.do.caus-<t> festival-goal   animal-<AnPl>

wañéhjɨ] íjcya-né]-vu.   ⁹ᵃÁ-niihyó-vá-a
festival be-<ø>-goal   thm-<childbearer>-rpt-rem

ɨ́ɨte-h   íjcyá-h   [[[pá-ábé   ɨhdé-e-jpi]
look-sub   be-<t>   all-<SgM>   before-per-<SgM>

iyá-ábé]   úúbámye-nú-ne].   ⁹ᵇNíívuwá-vá-a
animal-<SgM>   invited.ones.do-<ø>   deer-rpt-rem

uubámye-nú-hi.   ⁹ᶜócáji-vá-a uubámye-nú-hi.
invited.ones.do-<t>   tapir-rpt-rem invited.ones.do-<t>

⁹ᵈííñimyé-vá-a uubámye-nú-hi.   ⁹ᵉ[pá-me-ere
snake-rpt-rem   invited.ones.do-<t>   all-<AnPl>-only

mú-hdu-mé   iyá-mé]   íjcya-me.
WH-<like>-<AnPl> animal-<AnPl>   be-<AnPl>

¹⁰Aa-né-vá-a   ɨ́ɨte-nííhyó
thm-<ø>-rpt-rem   look-<childbearer>

[[[tsá-já-hcóbá   pañe   i   íjcya]-ne.
one-<shelter>-aug   inside self   be]-<ø>

¹¹Á-ró-náacá-vá-a   [ih-dyu   pevé-tsíí-ye-ro]
thm-frs-while-rpt-rem   that-<like> clear-<place>-only-frs

té-tsii.   ¹²Aa-né-vá-a   [di-tye
that-<place>   thm-<ø>-rpt-rem   that-<AnPl>

kíjcyó-náa]   tsá(h) di-lle   ímílle-tú
dance-while   no   that-<SgF>   want-neg

---

⁸Link S | S V Goal | Goal* (where Goal* = [S V])   ⁹ᵃS V Aux DO (where DO = [[[Quan Adj] N] V])   ⁹ᵇS V   ⁹ᶜS V   ⁹ᵈS V   ⁹ᵉS (BE) (where S = [S PredCmpl]; S = [Quan N]; Note: íjcya-me is nominalized.)

¹⁰Link V-s DO (where DO = [[Loc s-V]-head]); Loc = [N loc]
¹¹Time PredCmpl S (where PredCmpl = [Sim N]). The link signals background?   ¹²Time Cir_d Neg S V DO (where DO = [s-V]-s)   ¹³Man

[i   wáhtsɨ]-ne.   ¹³Í-llu-ré-vá-a   did not want to
self   dance-<ø>   this-<like>-only-rpt-rem   dance. ¹³Thus
cúwa-lle.   ¹⁴Aa-né-vá-a   me   tsɨ́tsɨ-ɨvé-dú   she just slept.
sleep-<SgF>   thm-<ø>-rpt-rem   SAP white-go.do-<like> ¹⁴Then, waking at dawn she
ajkyé-va-nííhyó   [[bájú-j pɨɨne]   i   was in the middle of the jungle. ¹⁵No one
awake-come.do-<childbearer>   jungle-x middle   self
íjcya]-ne.   ¹⁵Tsáhá-jucó-vá-a   mú-ubá-rá   was there.
be-<ø>   no-focus-rpt-rem   WH-<SgM>-frs
íjcyá-júcoo-tú-ne
be-now-neg-<n>

V   ¹⁴Link Time V-s Result$_s$ (where Time = [s-V]-sim; Result$_s$ = [Loc s-V]-<ø>)   ¹⁵Neg ∥ S V.

Ávyéjuubéváa Péé Bájú Pañévu
A Chief Goes to the Jungle

¹A chief went into the jungle to hunt for animals. ²His son also went. ³The chief got his gun. ⁴He gave his gun to his son. ⁵His son took the gun. ⁶Also he took a lot of food.

¹Ávyéju-ubé-vá-a   péé-h   [bájú pañé-vú]
 reign-<SgM>-rpt-rem go-<t>   jungle inside-goal

[iyá-me-ke   i   ñéhco-ki].   ²Í-lli-vá-a
 animal-<AnPl>-objAn self hunt-pur   self-son-rpt-rem

péé-h   té-hdu-re.   ³Ávyéju-ubé-vá-a   ujcú-h
go-<t>   that-<like>-only   reign-<SgM>-rpt-rem   get-<t>

í   añú-ju.   ⁴Í-llí-kye-vá-a   ájcu-ube
self shoot-<channel>   self-son-objAn-rpt-rem   give-<SgM>

í   añú-ju-vu.   ⁵Aa-né-vá-a   í-lli
self shoot-<channel>-goal   thm-<ø>-rpt-rem   self-son

tsajtyé-h   añú-ju.   ⁶Mítya-né-vá-a   majcho
take-<t>   shoot-<channel>   much-<ø>-rpt-rem   food

tsajtyé-ébé té-hdu-re.
take-<SgM>   that-<like>-only

⁷The chief wants to get cloth. ⁸Therefore he went to the jungle to get skins. ⁹They also took a sleeping net into the jun-

⁷Ávyéju-ubé-vá-a   imíllé-h   [wájyamu
 reign-<SgM>-rpt-rem   want-<t>   cloth

i   újcu]-ne.   ⁸Áá-né-lliihyé-vá-a
self get-<ø>   thm-<ø>-motive-rpt-rem

pee-be   bájú   pañé-vú   mífhe-ne   i
go-<SgM>   jungle inside-goal   skin-pl   self

újcu-ki.   ⁹Té-hdu-ré-vá-a   cuwá-já
get-pur   that-<like>-only-rpt-rem   sleep-<shelter>

---

¹S V Goal Pur$_s$ (where Pur$_s$ = [DO s-V])   ²S V Adv   ³S V DO
⁴DO$_{recip}$ V Goal$_{theme}$ ⁵Link S V DO   ⁶<DO$_i$> [ø$_i$|DO] V-s Adv (Because of clitics we cannot regard the first two nouns as NP = [Quant N].)
⁷S V DO (where DO = [DO s-V-<Ø>])   ⁸Reason V Goal Pur$_s$ (where Pur$_s$ = [DO s-V])   ⁹Link DO V Goal   ¹⁰S | S V Loc

Ávyéjuubévááa Péé Bájú Pañévu

tsajtyé-mútsi [bájú pañé-vu]. ^{10}Mítya-né-vá-a
take-<DuM>   jungle inside-goal   much-<ø>-rpt-rem

waa-myu   ijcyá-h [bájú pañe].
mosquito-<AnPl> be-<t> jungle inside

^{11}Áá-né-lliihyé-vá-a   ávyéju-ube   tsajtyé-h
thm-<ø>-motive-rpt-rem   reign-<SgM>   take-<t>

cuwá-ja. ^{12}Té-hdu-ré-vá-a   cánááma
sleep-<shelter>   that-<like>-only-rpt-rem   salt

tsajtyé-ébe.
take-<SgM>

^{13}Tsí-hullé-vá-a   pee-mútsi [bájú
other-<yonder>-rpt-rem   go-<DuM>   jungle

pañé-vu.] ^{14}Ávyéju-ubé-vá-a   ájtyumí-h
inside-goal   reign-<SgM>-rpt-rem   see-<t>

tojpá-u-ke. ^{15}i Ilí-kye-vá-a   neé-be:
partridge-sg-objAn   self son-objAn-rpt-rem say-<SgM>

"Ɨ́cúi tojpáu-ke   d-ahñu   me dóó-kií".
quickly partridge-objAn youImp-shoot SAP eat-pur

^{16}Í-lli-vá-a   neé-hi: "Juújuj. ^{17}Ɨ́cúi
self-son-rpt-rem   said-<t>   ok   quickly

tsiva   añú-ju." ^{18}Áá-né-lliihyé-vá-a
bringImp shoot-<channel>   thm-<ø>-motive-rpt-rem

ávyéju-ube   dsɨɨné-h [í   añú-ju   élle-vu].
reign-<SgM>   run-<t>   self shoot-<channel> place-goal

^{19}Ɨ́cúi-vá-a   tsíva-abe   í   añú-ju   [í-llí
quickly-rpt-rem   bring-<SgM>   self shoot-<channel> self-son

---

gle. ^{10}There were many mosquitos in the jungle. ^{11}Therefore the chief took a sleeping net. ^{12}Also he took salt.

^{13}They went a long way into the jungle. ^{14}The chief saw a partridge. ^{15}He said to his son, "Quickly shoot the partridge so we can eat." ^{16}His son said, "OK. ^{17}Quickly bring the gun." ^{18}Therefore the chief ran to where the gun was. ^{19}He quickly brought

---

^{11}Reason S V DO ^{12}Sim DO V (The final tones of *tsajtyé-ébe* do not split because the root's first syllable is a lexically marked low tone.) ^{13}Loc V Goal ^{14}S V DO ^{15}O V "Adv V Pur$_d$" (where Pur$_d$ = [s-V]) ^{16}S V "ProSent" ^{17}Adv V DO ^{18}Reason S V Goal ^{19}Adv V-s DO Goal ^{20}DO V-s ^{21}DO Neg S V ^{22}S V ^{23}Link DO V-s

his gun to his son. ²⁰He hunted for a partridge. ²¹He did not see one. ²²The partridge fled. ²³However he saw a squirrel. ²⁴The son got the squirrel the chief shot. ²⁵He took it to eat.

²⁶"OK let's go," said the chief.
²⁷They went a long way into the jungle. ²⁸There the chief's son made a shelter. ²⁹He made the shelter well. ³⁰He also made a floor. ³¹He did not make steps. ³²He made a

élle-vu].
place-goal

²⁰Tojpá-u-ké-vá-a néhco-óbe.
partridge-sg-objAn-rpt-rem hunt-\<SgM\>

²¹Áá-be-ké-vá-a tsá(h) di-bye
thm-\<SgM\>-objAn-rpt-rem no that-\<SgM\>

ájtyúmɨ-tú.
see-neg

²²Tojpá-u-vá-a úmɨvá-hi.
partridge-sg-rpt-rem flee-\<t\>

²³Á-ró-náacá-vá-a néépicyó-ke ájtyúmɨ-íbe.
thm-frs-while-rpt-rem squirrel-objAn see-\<SgM\>

²⁴Néépicyó-ke-vá-a | [ávyéju-ube áñú-úbe-ke]
squirrel-objAn-rpt-rem reign-\<SgM\> shoot-\<SgM\>-objAn

í-lli ujcú-hi.
self-son get-\<t\>

²⁵Áá-be-ké-vá-a
thm-\<SgM\>-objAn-rpt-rem

tsajtyé-ébé i dyóó-kií.
take-\<SgM\> self eat-pur

²⁶"Ayúwa majo" ávyéju-ubé-vá-a néé-hi.
ready let's.go reign-\<SgM\>-rpt-rem say-\<t\>

²⁷Tsí-hullé-u-vá-a | [bájú pañé-vu]
other-\<yonder\>-goal-rpt-rem jungle inside-goal

pee-mútsi.
go-\<DuM\>

²⁸Té-hullé-vu-vá-a [ávyéjú-úbé
that-\<yonder\>-goal-rpt-rem reign-\<SgM\>

ájchi] núújuwa meenú-hi.
son shelter made-\<t\>

²⁹Ímíh-ye-vá-a
good-only-rpt-rem

núújuwa méénu-úbe.
shelter made-\<SgM\>

³⁰Té-hdu-ré-vá-a
that-\<like\>-only-rpt-rem

wáɨjɨ méénu-úbe.
floor made-\<SgM\>

³¹Niityé-wááhyo-vá-a tsá(h)
go.down-\<steps\>-rpt-rem no

---

²⁴DO$_i$|DO S V (where second DO = [S ø$_i$ V])   ²⁵DO V-s Pur$_s$ (where Pur$_s$ = [s-V])

²⁶"ProSent Adv V" S V (Note: the second-position clitic follows the subject of the quote margin.)

²⁷Goal | Goal V-s   ²⁸Loc S Do V   ²⁹Adv DO V-s   ³⁰Sim DO

Ávyéjuubéváa Péé Bájú Pañévu

di-bye	méénu-tú.	³²Llijyá-cóóha-vá-a		
that-\<SgM\>	make-neg	sweep-\<fork\>-rpt-rem		

méénu-úbe.	³³Aa-bé-vá-a		[núújúwá	pañe]
made-\<SgM\>	thm-\<SgM\>-rpt-rem		shelter	inside

llijyáá-hi.	³⁴[Aa-né	booné]-vá-a	cuwá-ja
sweep-\<t\>	thm-\<ø\>	after-rpt-rem	sleep-\<shelter\>

pícyo-obe	[wáɨjɨ	hallú-vu].	³⁵ᵃ"Áyu	llíhi-j"
put-\<SgM\>	floor	top-goal	ready	papa-voc

nee-bé-vá-a.	³⁵ᵇ"Tsúúca	ó	ímivyé-hi.	³⁶Ovíi
say-\<SgM\>-rpt-rem	already	I	finish-\<t\>	wait

mé	cúwa-j."			
SAP	sleep-voc			

	³⁷Ávyéju-ubé-vá-a	cóó-va-té-h	
	reign-\<SgM\>-rpt-rem	firewood-have-go.do-\<t\>	

[cúújuwa	i	myéénu-kií].	³⁸Ímíh-ye-vá-a	
fire	self	make-pur	good-only-rpt-rem	

cúújuwa	méénu-úbe.	³⁹[Aa-né	
fire	made-\<SgM\>	thm-\<ø\>	

booné]-vá-a	nú-jpacyo	újcu-úbe.	
after-rpt-rem	water-\<liquid\>	get-\<SgM\>	

⁴⁰Áá-ne-má-vá-a	néépicyó-ke	tu-ube	
thm-\<ø\>-with-rpt-rem	squirrel-objAn	cook-\<SgM\>	

cúújúwá	hallú-vu.	⁴¹Áá-ne-vá-a	
fire	top-goal	thm-\<ø\>-rpt-rem	

cánaamá-nu-úbe.	⁴²Ímíh-ye-vá-a	majcho	
salt-do-\<SgM\>	good-only-rpt-rem	food	

ávyéju-ube	túú-hi.	⁴³Mááho-vá-a	i
reign-\<SgM\>	cook-\<t\>	cassava-rpt-rem	self

broom. ³³He swept the inside of the shelter. ³⁴After that he put the net on the floor. ³⁵ᵃ"Papa," he said. ³⁵ᵇ"I have already finished. ³⁶Wait and we will sleep."

³⁷The chief went to get firewood to make a fire. ³⁸He made a fire well. ³⁹After that he got water. ⁴⁰With that (the water) he cooked the squirrel on top of the fire. ⁴¹Then he salted it. ⁴²The chief cooked the food superbly. ⁴³After

---

V-s   ³¹DO Neg S V   ³²DO V-s   ³³S DO V   ³⁴TempP DO V-s Goal
³⁵ᵃ["Adv Voc" V-s   ³⁵ᵇ"Adv S V.   ³⁶ProSent s-V

³⁷S V Pur$_s$ (where Pur$_s$ = [DO s-V])   ³⁸Adv DO V-s   ³⁹TempP DO V-s   ⁴⁰Cir DO V-s Goal (Note: Cir with -*ma* 'with'.)   ⁴¹Link V-s
⁴²Adv DO S V   ⁴³\<DO$_i$\> Time$_s$ O V-s "Adv V Pur$_s$" (where Time$_s$ =

getting cassava, he said to his son, "Ready, let's eat."

újcú-ne í-llí-kye ne-ébe: "Áyúwa, májo me dóó-KI".
get-<event> self-son-objAn say-<SgM> ready let's SAP eat-pur

⁴⁴His son said, "OK." ⁴⁵"Give me some cassava so I can eat it."

⁴⁴"Juúju", í-lli-vá-a néé-hi. ⁴⁵"Mááhó-vu o-ke d-aacu [o májcho-ki]".
ok self-son-rpt-rem say-<t> cassava-goal I-objAn youImp-give I eat-pur

⁴⁵They ate real well. ⁴⁶Then the chief said to his son, "OK, son, that's enough." ⁴⁷"Thanks." ⁴⁸"Wash the dishes." ⁴⁹He said, "OK."

⁴⁵Ímíh-ye-vá-a májcho-mútsi.
good-only-rpt-rem eat-<DuM>

⁴⁶Aa-né-vá-a ávyéju-ube néé-h
thm-<ø>-rpt-rem reign-<SgM> say-<t>

í-llí-kyeé: "Áyu(h) llíhi-j, éh-du-né-re".
self-son-objAn ok son-voc that-<like>-<ø>-only

⁴⁷"Te-hdú-juco". ⁴⁸"Níjtyu bohtá-mu".
that-<like>-focus washImp dish-pl

⁴⁹"Juúju", ne-ebé-vá-a.
ok say-<SgM>-rpt-rem

⁵⁰Then he went to the river to wash the dishes. ⁵¹He washed the dishes with the soap he had taken along. ⁵²Then he took them to the

⁵⁰Aa-né-vá-a pe-ebe téé-hi-vu
thm-<ø>-rpt-rem go-<SgM> river-<stick>-goal

[bohtá-mu i níjtyu-ki]. ⁵¹Nijtyú-wa-vá-a
dish-pl self wash-pur wash-<slab>-rpt-rem

[i tsájtyé]-wa-ri níjtyu-ube bohtá-mu.
self take-<slab>-oblIn wash-<SgM> dish-pl

[ø$_i$ s-V])
⁴⁴"ProSent" S V ⁴⁵Goal$_{theme,i}$ DO$_{recip}$ s-V Pur$_d$ (where Pur$_d$ = [S ø$_i$ V])
⁴⁵Adv V-s ⁴⁶Link S V O "ProSent Voc PredCmpl (BE)"
⁴⁷PredCmpl (BE) ⁴⁸s-V DO ⁴⁹"ProSent" V-s
⁵⁰Link V-s Goal Pur$_s$ (where Pur$_s$ = [DO s-V]) ⁵¹<DO$_i$> Instr$_s$ V DO; Instr$_s$ = [ø$_i$ s-V]-head ⁵²Link V-s Goal

Ávyéjuubéváa Péé Bájú Pañévu

⁵²Aa-né-vá-a   tsajtyé-ébé núújúwa-vu.
thm-<ø>-rpt-rem take-<SgM>   shelter-goal

⁵²′Ávyéju-ubé-vá-a   néé-h   í-llí-kye:
reign-<SgM>-rpt-rem   say-<t> self-son-objAn

"Tsiva   tá-chiiyóro o llíjchu-ki".
bringImp my-flute   I blow-pur

⁵³"Juúju", ne-ebé-vá-a   í-llií.   ⁵⁴"¿A
ok   say-<SgM>-rpt-rem self-son   y/n

ú-pé   ú   tsivá-h   dí-chiiyóro?   ⁵⁵¿Kiá(h)
you-rem you bring-<t>   your-flute   where

teé-ne?   ⁵⁶Tsá(h) o ájtyúmɨ-tú-ne."
that-<ø> no   I see-neg-<n>

⁵⁷[Ávyéjú-úbé   ajchí]-vá-a   nehcó-h   chiiyóro.
reign-<SgM>   son-rpt-rem   hunt-<t>   flute

⁵⁸Aa-bé-vá-a   [[núújúwá pañé-tú]   i
thm-<SgM>-rpt-rem   shelter   inside-sou self

ájtyúmɨ]-né-vú ajcú-h   cáání-kye   [di-bye   i
see-<ø>-goal   give-<t>   father-objAn that-<SgM>   self

llíjchu-ki].
blow-pur

⁵⁹[Ávyéjú-úbé   ajchí]-vá-a   té-hdu-re
reign-<SgM>   son-rpt-rem   that-<like>-only

piivyété-h [chiiyóro i   llíjchu]-ne.
able-<t>   flute   self blow-<ø>

⁶⁰Ávyéju-ubé-vá-a   ihjyúvá-h   í-llí-maá.
reign-<SgM>-rpt-rem talk-<t>   self-son-with

⁵²′ The chief said to his son, "Bring my flute so I can play it." ⁵³"OK," said his son. ⁵⁴"Did you bring your flute? ⁵⁵Where is it? ⁵⁶I do not see it." ⁵⁷The chief's son hunted for the flute. ⁵⁸He found it in the shelter and gave it to his father to play.

⁵⁹The chief's son also could play the flute.

⁶⁰The chief talked with his son. ⁶¹He said to him, "To-

---

⁵²′S V O "s-V DOø$_i$ Pur$_d$" (where Pur$_d$ = [S ø$_i$ V])
⁵³"ProSent" V-s | S   ⁵⁴"Q$_{y/n}$ S | S V DO"   ⁵⁵QLoc PredCmpl (BE)
⁵⁶Neg S V   ⁵⁷S V DO   ⁵⁸S$_i$ Cir$_s$ Goal$_{theme,k}$ ø$_i$ V DO$_{recip}$ Pur$_d$ (where Goal = [Loc ø$_k$ s-V] and Pur$_d$ = [S ø$_k$ s-V])
⁵⁹S Sim V DO (where DO = [DO s-V])
⁶⁰S V CoS   ⁶¹V-s O "Time s-V DO"   ⁶²S V DO (where DO = [DO

morrow we will go hunt animals. ⁶²I want to shoot peccaries. ⁶³I want to shoot peccaries also. ⁶⁴Son, there are many mosquitos. ⁶⁵Hurry, let's go to sleep." ⁶⁶"OK," said his son.

⁶⁷The chief woke up. ⁶⁸Then he said, "Son let's eat. ⁶⁹Already the sun is shining. ⁷⁰I want that we go quickly."

⁷¹Eating quickly they went to hunt for animals ⁷²They went far. ⁷³Already the chief saw

⁶¹Ne-ebé-vá-a   dí-íbye-ke: "Péjco-re mé
say-<SgM>-rpt-rem that-<SgM>-objAn   night-only SAP

néhcó-te-é-h   iyá-me-ke.   ⁶²Ó imíllé-h
hunt-go.do-fut-<t> animal-<AnPl>-objAn   I want-<t>

[mééní-mu-ke o áñu]-ne.   ⁶³Mίne-jté-ké
 peccary-pl-objAn I shoot-<ø>   peccary-<AnPl>-objAn

té-hdu-re   o imíllé-h   [o áñu]-ne.   ⁶⁴Áyu(h)
that-<like>-only I want-<t>   I shoot-<ø>   ready

llíhi-j, mítya-ne waá-myu.   ⁶⁵Majó-jú-j   me
son-voc much-<ø> mosquito-pl   let's-quick-voc SAP

cúwa-ki-j."   ⁶⁶"Juúju", í-lli-vá-a   néé-hi.
sleep-pur-voc   ok   self-son-rpt-rem say-<t>

⁶⁷Ávyéju-ubé-vá-a   ajkyé-hi.
 reign-<SgM>-rpt-rem   wake.up-<t>

⁶⁸Aa-né-vá-a   ne-ébe: "Llíhi-j, májo me
 thm-<ø>-rpt-rem   say-<SgM>   son-voc   let's SAP

májcho-ki-j.   ⁶⁹Tsúúca nuhba ajchú-hi.   ⁷⁰Ifcúi
eat-pur-voc   already   sun   shine-<t>   quickly

ó imíllé-h   [me péé]-neé."
I want-<t>   SAP go-<ø>

⁷¹[Ífcúi-vá-a   i   májchó-ne]
  quickly-rpt-rem   self eat-<event>

pee-mútsí [iyá-me-ke   i   ñéhco-ki].
go-<DuM>   animal-<AnPl>-objAn self hunt-pur

⁷²Tsí-hullé-u-vá-a   pee-mútsi.
  other-<yonder>-goal-rpt-rem   go-<DuM>

⁷³Tsúúcajá-vá-a   ávyéju-ube   ájtyumí-h
  already-rpt-rem   reign-<SgM>   see-<t>

S V]) ⁶³<DO> Sim S V DO (where DO = [S x V]). ⁶⁴ProSent Voc S (BE) (where S = [N | N]) ⁶⁵V Pur_s ⁶⁶"ProSent" S V ⁶⁷S V ⁶⁸Link V-s "Voc V Pur_s" (where Pur_s = [s-V]) ⁶⁹Adv S V ⁷⁰Adv S V DO (where DO = [s-V])

⁷¹Cir_s V Pur_s (where Cir_s = [Adv s-V] and Pur_s = [DO s-V])

Ávyéjuubéváa Péé Bájú Pañévu

mɨ́ne-jté-ke.
peccary-<AnPl>-objAn

⁷⁴[Áá-me élle-vú-vá-a]
thm-<AnPl> place-goal-rpt-rem

dsɨ́ɨ́ne-ébe.
run-<SgM>

⁷⁵Í-lli-vá-a dsɨɨné-h
self-son-rpt-rem run-<t>

té-hdu-re.
that-<like>-only

⁷⁶Mítyá-me-ké-vá-a
much-<AnPl>-objAn-rpt-rem

áñu-mútsi.
shoot-<DuM>

⁷⁷Áá-me-ké-vá-a
thm-<AnPl>-objAn-rpt-rem

tsájtye-mútsi núújúwa-vu.
take-<DuM> shelter-goal

⁷⁸Ávyéju-ubé-vá-a
reign-<SgM>-rpt-rem

waagóó-h té-bajcú-jɨ [téé-hí pañé-vu].
throw-<t> that-<bone>-pl river-<stick> inside-goal

⁷⁹Áá-ne-má-vá-a cánaamá-nu-ube téé-heecó-jɨ.
thm-<ø>-with-rpt-rem salt-do-<SgM> that-<meat>-pl

⁸⁰Í-lli-vá-a cátóro-hcó-h té-mɨɨhé-jɨ.
self-son-rpt-rem stretch-mTr-<t> that-<skin>-pl

⁸¹Ávyéju-ubé-vá-a ɨtojtsó-h téé-heecó-jɨ.
reign-<SgM>-rpt-rem roast-<t> that-<meat>-pl

⁸²Mɨ́ɨhe-né-vá-a dárɨ́-jtso-obe [núhba ájchu-vu].
skin-pl-rpt-rem dry-caus-<SgM> sun shine-goal

⁸³"Cuuvéh-ré-juco teé-ne", ne-ebé-vá-peé.
dark-only-focus that-<ø> say-<SgM>-rpt-rem

"Májo í-llu-ré-juco me májcho-KI o cúwa-ki."
let's this-<like>-only-focus SAP eat-pur I sleep-pur

some peccaries. ⁷⁴He ran to them. ⁷⁵His son ran also. ⁷⁶They shot many. ⁷⁷They took them to the shelter. ⁷⁸The chief threw the bones into the river. ⁷⁹Then he salted the meat. ⁸⁰His son stretched out the skins. ⁸¹The chief roasted the meat. ⁸²The skins he dried (by placing them) in the sun.

⁸³"It's getting dark" he said, "Let's eat so I can sleep."

---

⁷²Goal V-s ⁷³Adv S V DO ⁷⁴Goal V-s ⁷⁵S V Sim ⁷⁶DO V-s ⁷⁷DO V-s Goal ⁷⁸S V DO Goal ⁷⁹Cir V DO (Cir with -*ma* 'with' ⁸⁰S V DO ⁸¹S V DO ⁸²DO V-s Goal (Note that the Goal implies an implicit verb "place.")

⁸³"PredCmpl ‖ S (BE)" V-s "V Sim s-V Pur$_d$ (where Pur$_d$ = [S V])

⁸⁴Thus it was that after eating they went to sleep.

⁸⁴A-hdú-jucó-vá-a   i   májchó-ne
thm-<like>-focus-rpt-rem   self   eat-<event>

di-tyétsí   í-llu-ré-juco   cúwa-ne.
that-<DuM>   this-<like>-only-focus   sleep-<Ø>

⁸⁵At night the chief heard an animal come to the shelter. ⁸⁶For that reason he looked and saw a big jaguar coming. ⁸⁷He was always eating peccaries. ⁸⁸Quickly the chief got his gun. ⁸⁹With it, he shot the jaguar from inside the sleeping net. ⁹⁰The chief's son heard him shoot the jaguar. ⁹¹Therefore getting up he quickly went to see the jaguar. ⁹²The chief threw the

⁸⁵Pejcó-vá-a ávyéju-ube lleebó-h [iyá-ábé
night-rpt-rem reign-<SgM> hear-<t> animal-<SgM>

tsáá-ne   núújúwa-vu].   ⁸⁶Áá-né-lliihyé-vá-a
come-<ø>   shelter-goal   thm-<ø>-motive-rpt-rem

ííte-ebe   ájtyumí-h   [oohí-íbyé-coba   tsáá]-neé.
look-<SgM> see-<t>   jaguar-<SgM>-aug   come-<ø>

⁸⁷Míne-jté-ke-vá-a   do-h   íjcya-ábe.
peccary-<AnPl>-objAn-rpt-rem eat-sub be-<SgM>

⁸⁸Ifcúi-vá-a   ávyéju-ube ujcú-h   í   añú-ju.
quickly-rpt-rem reign-<SgM> get-<t> self shoot-<channel>

⁸⁹Áá-ne-má-vá-a   oohí-íbye-ke   áñu-ube
thm-<ø>-with-rpt-rem jaguar-<SgM>-objAn shoot-<SgM>

[cuwá-já   pañé-tu].   ⁹⁰[Ávyéjú-úbé
sleep-<shelter> inside-sou   reign-<SgM>

ajchí]-vá-a lleebó-h [oohí-íbye-ke
son-rpt-rem hear-<t> jaguar-<SgM>-objAn

dii-bye   áñu-]ne.   ⁹¹Áá-né-lliihyé-vá-a
that-<SgM>   shoot-<ø>   thm-<ø>-motive-rpt-rem

i   ájkyé-ne   ífcúi   pe-ebe   í   ííte-KI
self get.up-<event>   quickly go-<SgM>   self look-pur

oohí-íbye-ke.   ⁹²[Oohí-íbye   hééco]-vá-a
jaguar-<SgM>-objAn   jaguar-<SgM>   meat-rpt-rem

---

⁸⁴Sim ‖ Cir_s S V (where PredCmpl = [Sim V] with a nominalized verb)

⁸⁵Time S V DO (where DO = [S V Goal])   ⁸⁶Reason S V DO (where S is a nominalized verb; DO = [S V])   ⁸⁷DO V Aux-s   ⁸⁸Adv S V DO   ⁸⁹Cir DO V Source (Note: -ma 'with' for circumstance.)   ⁹⁰S V DO (where DO = [DO S V])   ⁹¹Reason Cir_s Adv V-s Pur (where Cir_s

Ávyéjuubévááa Péé Bájú Pañévu

ávyéju-ube   waagóó-h   [téé-hí   pañé-vu].
reign-\<SgM\> throw-\<t\>   river-\<stick\> inside-goal

⁹³Áá-ne-má-vá-a   té-mɨɨhe   pícyo-obe   [cújúwá
thm-\<ø\>-with-rpt-rem   that-\<skin\> put-\<SgM\> fire

hallú-vu].   ⁹⁴Aa-né-vá-a   ne-ébe: "Áyu(h),
top-goal   thm-\<ø\>-rpt-rem   say-\<SgM\>   ready

tsúúca   mítya-ne   mé   hmɨɨhé-ne.   ⁹⁵Májo
already   much-\<ø\>   SAP skin-pl   let's.go

ááhɨ-vú-ré-juco."
home-goal-only-focus

⁹⁶[Áá-né   booné]-vá-a   ávyéju-ube
thm-\<ø\>   after-rpt-rem   reign-\<SgM\>

tsajtyé-h   mɨ́ɨhe-ne.   ⁹⁷Í-lli-vá-a   tsajtyé-h
take-\<t\>   skin-pl   self-son-rpt-rem   took-\<t\>

téé-heecó-jɨ.   ⁹⁸Juuvá-yi-vá-a   ávyéju-ube
that-\<meat\>-pl   trail-oblIn-rpt-rem   reign-\<SgM\>

[mééni-kye   i   ájtyúmɨ́]-ɨbe-ke   añú-hi.
collared.peccary-objAn self see-\<SgM\>-objAn shoot-\<t\>

⁹⁹[Cuuvé   pañé]-vá-a   wajtsɨ́-mútsí   ih
dark   inside-rpt-rem   arrive.here-\<DuM\>   self

jyá-vu.   ¹⁰⁰[Héeco-nee,   mɨ́ɨhe-nee,
house-goal   meat-pl   skin-pl

éh-dú-ne-má]-vá-a   wajtsɨ́-mútsí   ih
that-\<like\>-\<ø\>-with-rpt-rem arrive.here-\<DuM\>   self

jyá-vu.
house-goal

jaguar meat into the river. ⁹³In that circumstance, he put the skin on top of the fire. ⁹⁴Then he said, "Already we have lots of skins. ⁹⁵Let's go home."

⁹⁶After that the chief took the skins. ⁹⁷His son took the meat. ⁹⁸The chief shot a collared peccary he saw on the trail. ⁹⁹When it was dark they arrived to their house. ¹⁰⁰They arrived to their house with meat and skins and such.

= [s-V]; Pur = [V DO])   ⁹²DO S V Goal   ⁹³Cir DO V-s Goal   ⁹⁴Link V-s "ProSent Adv S | S (BE)"   ⁹⁵V Goal   ⁹⁶TempP S V DO   ⁹⁷S V DO   ⁹⁸\<Loc$_i$\> S DO V; DO = [[ø$_i$ DO$_k$ V]-head$_k$]   ⁹⁹Time V Goal   ¹⁰⁰CoS V-s Goal; where CoS = [[N N Sum]-case-clitics]; because CoS is oblique, there must be another subject

[101] "We are coming now," the chief said. [102] We have brought a lot of meat to eat. [103] Also we brought a lot of skins so we can get cloth."

[101] "Muhtsi me tsá-jucóó-hi" nee-bé-vá-a
we.DuM SAP come-now-<t> say-<SgM>-rpt-rem

ávyéju-úbe. [102] "[Mítya-ne hééco-ne] muhtsi mé
reign-<SgM> much-<ø> meat-pl we.DuM SAP

tsivá-h me dóó-kií. [103] Té-hdu-re [mítya-ne
bring-<t> SAP eat-pur that-<like>-only much-<ø>

mɨ́ɨhe-ne] muhtsi mé tsivá-h wájyamu me
skin-pl we.DuM SAP bring-<t> cloth SAP

újcu-ki."
get-pur

[104] The chief took the skins to town. [105] With them, he got cloth. [106] Those pieces of cloth he took to his house. [107] Then he said, "Daughter, I brought it so you can sew my clothes. [108] I also brought your cloth for you."

[104] Mɨ́ɨhe-né-vá-a ávyéju-ube tsajtyé-h
skin-pl-rpt-rem reign-<SgM> take-<t>

cóómí-vuú. [105] Áá-ne-má-vá-a wájyamu
town-goal thm-<ø>-with-rpt-rem cloth

újcu-úbe. [106] Aa-já-vá-a tsajtyé-ébé
get-<SgM> thm-<shelter>-rpt-rem take-<SgM>

ih jyá-vu. [107] Aa-né-vá-a neé-be:
self house-goal thm-<ø>-rpt-rem say-<SgM>

"Wáha-j, ó tsivá-h tá-wajyámú u dsɨ́jco-ki.
daughter-voc I bring-<t> my-clothes you sew-pur

[108] Té-hdu-re úú-ma dí-wajyámú ó tsivá-hi."
that-<like>-only you-with your-cloth I bring-<t>

[101] "S V" V-s | S [102] DO S s-V Pur$_d$ (where Pur$_d$ = [s-V]) [103] Sim DO S s-V Pur$_d$ (where Pur$_d$ = [DO s-V])

[104] DO S V Goal [105] Cir DO V-s (Note: -ma 'with' for "by that circumstance.") [106] DO V-s Goal [107] Link V-s "Voc S V Pur$_d$ (where Pur = [DO S V]) [108] Sim Benefactee DO S V (Note: -ma 'with' for benefactee)

Píívyéébé Ajyúwá Uubálle
Story of the Creator's Daughter

¹Pí-ívyé-ébe-vá-a   wáñehjɨ́-nú-i-yá-h
body-sIn-<SgM>-rpt-rem   festival-do-fut-frs-<t>

í-llí-mútsi-kye.   ²Á-ró-náacá-vá-a
self-son-<DuM>-objAn   thm-frs-while-rpt-rem

díí-lle-ma   di-tye   wáñehjɨ́-nú-í-yó-lle-ke
that-<SgF>-with   that-<AnPl>   festival-do-fut-frs-<SgF>-objAn

[dii-bye   í   ñah-bé-ré]   ééva-tsó-hi.
that-<SgM>   self   sibling-<SgM>-only   pregnant-caus-<t>

³Aa-né-vá-a   tsá(h)   cááni-mu   wáájácu-tú-ne.
thm-<ø>-rpt-rem   no   father-pl   know-neg-<n>

⁴Á-ró-náacá-vá-a   [[dii-bye   Pí-ívyé-ébe]
thm-frs-while-rpt-rem   that-<SgM>   body-sIn-<SgM>

hájkí-mú]   téé-ne-ri   ihjyúva-h   íjcyá-hi.
relative-pl   that-<ø>-oblIn   talk-sub   be-<t>

⁵Áá-ne-tú-vá-a   tsúúca   cáání-mutsi
thm-<ø>-sou-rpt-rem   already   father-<DuM>

waajácú-jucóó-hi.
know-now-<t>

⁶Aa-né-vá-a   i   wáájacú-júcóó-ne   íjcya-abe
thm-<ø>-rpt-rem   self   know-now-<event>   be-<SgM>

cááni   néé-hií: "Cána   wa(h)   o-ke   níípájɨ-ke
father   say-<t>   please   daughter   I-objAn   chigoe-objAn

¹The Creator intended to honor his son and daughter with a festival. ²Meanwhile, however, the daughter's very own brother got her pregnant, the daughter whom they intended to honor with a festival. ³The parents did not know it. ⁴However the Creator's relatives were talking about it. ⁵Then the father and mother came to know about it. ⁶The father, now knowing that, said, "Please daughter come see the chi-

---

¹S V DO   ²Link DO S V; DO = [[Benefactee$_i$ S V]-head$_i$]
³Time/DO Neg S V   ⁴Time S About V Aux (where S = [[Dem N] N] and About bears -*ri* 'oblIn')   ⁵About Adv S V (where About = Source)
⁶Link S*|S V "X Voc DO DO s-V" (where S* = [Cir$_s$ V] or it has

goe on me." ⁷Therefore she came covering her breasts with her hands. ⁸She said, "Where on you is it?" ⁹Therefore he said, "Here on my heel." ¹⁰Thus now in order to inspect him she dropped her hands which covered her breasts. ¹¹Then he saw that the nipples of her breasts were dark. ¹²With that he said, "Oh! ¹³Not having a husband, where did you get your child? ¹⁴Tell me. ¹⁵Which one has been with you?" ¹⁶ᵃTherefore

d-uhjé-va-j".
youImp-see-come.do-voc

tsaa-lle [í   í   mujpáñéé-cú hyójtsɨ-vu
come-<SgF> self self breast-du   hand-goal

i   wátá-jcó-ne-ma].
self cover-mTr-<event>-with

néé-hií: "¿Mú-tsih-dyú   Lli(h) u-ke   dií-bye?"
say-<t>   WH-<place>-sou father you-objAn that-<SgM>

⁹Áá-né-lliihyé-vá-a   ne-ébe: "[Í-chih-dyu
thm-<ø>-motive-rpt-rem   say-<SgM> this-<place>-sou

tá   booráyu-tu".
my   heel-sou

[[díí-bye-ke   i   úvanú]-KI   tee-ne   [í
that-<SgM>-objAn   self consider-pur   that-<ø>   self

mujpáñéé-cú í   hyójtsɨ-vu i   wátá-jco-ró]-né
breast-du   self hand-goal   self cover-mTr-frs-<ø>

di-lle   ácádsɨ-jcaáyó-ne.
that-<SgF>   drop-sTr-<Ø>

tsúúca ájtyúmɨ-ɨbe [díí-llé   mujpáñéé-cú nɨjcau
already see-<SgM>   that-<SgF> breasts-du nipple

cúvéh-ré-juco   néé]-neé.
dark-only-focus   say-<ø>

ne-ébe: "¡Új! ¹³Tájɨ-vá-lle-jɨɨ   ¿kiá-tú
say-<SgM>   oh   husband-have-<SgF>-deny   where-sou

tsɨɨméne-ke ú   ujcú-hi?   ¹⁴O-ke   d-uubálle.
child-objAn you get-<t>   I-objAn youImp-tell

¹⁵¿Caa-byé   úú-ma   ícya-h   ɨjcyá-hi?"
which-<SgM>   you-with   be-sub   be-<t>

⁷Áá-né-lliihyé-vá-a
thm-<ø>-motive-rpt-rem

⁸Aa-llé-vá-a
thm-<SgF>-rpt-rem

⁹Áá-né-lliihyé-vá-a
thm-<ø>-motive-rpt-rem

¹⁰A-hdú-jucó-vá-a
thm-<like>-focus-rpt-rem

¹¹Áá-ne-tú-vá-a
thm-<ø>-sou-rpt-rem

¹²Áá-ne-má-vá-a
thm-<ø>-with-rpt-rem

---

a compound tense (past anterior); [DO DO] is not appositive but conjoined).   ⁷Reason V-s Cir_s (where Cir_s = [DO Th V] w/-ma)   ⁸S V "Loc Voc DO S" (where Loc is ablative (source) because it is the "site of attachment." Note further that this sentence has an implicit verb "burrow in.")   ⁹Reason V-s "Loc | Loc" (where Loc = Source, perhaps static theme)   ¹⁰Sim ‖ Pur_s DO | DO* S V; Pur_s = [DO V]; DO* = [[DO Th V]-head   ¹¹Link Adv V-s DO (where DO = [S PredCmpl

¹⁶ᵃÁá-né-lliihyé-vá-a   neé-lle: "Maáhuúj, tsá(h)
thm-<ø>-motive-rpt-rem say-<SgM>   unknown   no

o wáájácu-tú-ne   ¹⁶ᵇPejco ih-dyu   tsa-h
I know-neg-<n>   night this-<like> come-sub

íjcya-ábe".   ¹⁷Áá-né-lliihyé-vá-a   ne-ébe:
be-<SgM>   thm-<ø>-motive-rpt-rem say-<SgM>

"Ané(h),   [[cáátu   d-éhní-ñe]   [di-bye
  so   genipap youImp-soak-<event> that-<SgM>

di-élle-vu   tsáá]-cooca   d-ékééve-co   í
your-place-goal   come-when   youImp-grab-implore   self

úmɨ́-co-tu   me wáájácu-KI   [ca-abyé
face-<forehead>-sou   SAP know-pur   which-<SgM>

íjcya]-ne".   ¹⁸A-hdú-jucó-vá-a   [[di-lle
be-<ø>   thm-<like>-focus-rpt-rem that-<SgF>

cáátu   i   ééní-ñe]   ijcyá-náa]   di-bye
genipap self soak-<event>   be-while   that-<SgM>

tsáá-ne   pejco.   ¹⁹[Aa-bé-vá-a
come-<ø>   night   thm-<SgM>-rpt-rem

díí-lle-dí-vú   wájtsɨ́-ɨ́be]-ke
that-<SgF>-anim-goal   arrive.here-<SgM>-objAn

téé-ne-tu   i   dyóma-úcunú-ne   éké-éve-lle.
that-<ø>-sou   self   touch-sSt-<event>   grab-sIn-<SgF>

²⁰Áá-né-tú-jucó-vá-a   di-bye   pé-jucóó-né
thm-<ø>-sou-focus-rpt-rem   that-<SgM>   go-now-<ø>

[ɨ   mɨjcó-hó   pañé-vu].   ²¹Aa-bé-vá-a
self corral-<room> inside-goal   thm-<SgM>-rpt-rem

cúúvé-ne-tú-ré   i   ájkyé-ne   mɨ́ɨ́cúmɨ-ri
dark-<ø>-sou-only   self awake-<event>   mirror-oblIn

she said, "Unknown, I do not know. ¹⁶ᵇHe comes at night." ¹⁷Therefore he said, "So then make a dye from genipap and then when he comes to you grab his face so we can know who he is." ¹⁸Thus while she was making the dye from genipap, he came at night. ¹⁹She grabbed the one who arrived to her, having been touching the dye. ²⁰After that he went to his room. ²¹Early in the morning having awakened he look at himself in the mir-

V])   ¹²Cir V-s "X..   ¹³V-s. QLoc DO S V   ¹⁴O s-V   ¹⁵QS CoS V Aux   ¹⁶ᵃReason V-s "Interj Neg S V   ¹⁶ᵇReason V-s "Interj Neg S V. Time Man V Aux-s"   ¹⁷Reason V-s "Interj Cir$_d$ Site V Pur (where Cir$_d$ = [[DO s-V] S Goal V]; Site = Source; Pur$_d$ = [s-V [S V]] ComplOfKnow)   ¹⁸Sim ‖ Cir$_d$ S V Time (where Cir$_d$ = [[S DO s-V] V])   ¹⁹<S$_i$> DO Adv$_s$ V-s; DO = [$_i$ Goal V-s]; Adv$_s$ = [Source s-V]   ²⁰Source ‖ S V Goal   ²¹S Adv$_s$ Instr V DO (where Adv$_s$ = [Time s-V] and DO = [S

ror, at the genipap that had gotten dark. ²²Therefore even though wiping himself, it did not go. ²³Being ashamed he did not want to come to eat. ²⁴Then the father knowing about that, said in his heart, "Why not somebody else and not his sister did my son get pregnant?" ²⁵The mother, waiting in vain for him, went to the field. ²⁶On leaving she said to her younger daughter: Give food to your brother as soon as he comes out. ²⁷It

ííté-meí-h [cúúvé-coba tee-ne cáátu bájtu]-ne.
look-r/p-<t> dark-aug that-<ø> genipap darken-<ø>

²²Áá-né-lliihyé-vá-a di-bye páácyú-meí-yó-né
thm-<ø>-motive-rpt-rem that-<SgM> wipe-r/p-frs-<ø>

tsá(h) péé-tu-ne. ²³Áá-ne-rí-vá-a i
no go-neg-<n> thm-<ø>-oblIn-rpt-rem self

ñúcójpɨ́-vé-ne tsáhá-juco di-bye ímílle-tú [i
shame-sIn-<event> no-focus that-<SgM> want-neg self

íjchi-vyé-né i májcho-ki]. ²⁴Áá-ne-tú-vá-a
leave-sIn-<Ø> self eat-pur thm-<ø>-sou-rpt-rem

cááni i wáájácú-ne néé-h [ɨ íɨbúwá pañe]:
father self know-<event> say-<t> self heart inside

"¿ɨ́vee-kí-ami tsí-jpíllé-úba-ké-jɨɨ hájchí-wu
why-pur-wonder other-<SgF>-prob-objAn-deny son-dim

í ñáá-lle-ke ééva-tso-j?"
self sibling-<SgF>-objAn pregnant-caus-voc

²⁵Áá-be-ké-vá-a tsɨɨju i
thm-<SgM>-objAn-rpt-rem mother self

tyéhme-h íjcyá-ró-ne pé-jucóó-h [úmɨhé
wait-sub be-frs-<event> go-now-<t> field

pañé-vu]. ²⁶Aa-llé-vá-a ɨdsɨ́-wúu-ke
inside-goal thm-<SgF>-rpt-rem her.daughter-dim-objAn

bóné-lle-ke ne-íñú-hi: "Dí-ñáh-be-ke
after-<SgF>-objAn say-do.go-<t> your-sibling-<SgM>-objAn

néhi d-aacu majchó-vú di-bye
anticipation youImp-give food-goal that-<SgM>

| S V]) ²²Reason S Neg V (where S = [S V]) ²³Reason Cir_s Neg S V DO (where Reason = Instr; DO = [V-s Pur_s]) ²⁴About S Cir_s V Loc "QPur DO S DO V" (where DO...DO coordinate alternatives) OR <About> [S x s-V] V ... with About fronted

²⁵<DO_i> S [ø_i s-V Aux] V Goal ²⁶S DO | DO V "DO_{recip} adv s-V Goal_{theme} Adv_d" (where Adv_d = [S V] with -du) ²⁷Sim ‖ S V Aux

Píívyéébé Ajyúwá Uubálle

íjchivyé-du". ²⁷A-hdú-jucó-vá-a
leave-<like>   thm-<like>-focus-rpt-rem

dí-llé-wu   téhme-h íjcyá-ne.   ²⁸Áá-náacá-vá-a
that-<SgF>-dim wait-sub be-<ø>   thm-while-rpt-rem

ijchívyé-júco-óbe.   ²⁹Áá-be-ké-vá-a
leave-now-<SgM>   thm-<SgM>-objAn-rpt-rem

neé-lle: "í-ñe-vá-ne   najme   ú
say-<SgF>   this-<ø>-rpt-rec   brother   you

májcho-ó-hi".
eat-fut-<t>

   ³⁰Aa-né-vá-a   i   májcho-íñú-tsih-dyu
   thm-<ø>-rpt-rem self eat-do.go-<place>-sou

pe-ebe   [bájú pañé-vu].   ³¹Aa-bé-vá-a
go-<SgM>   jungle inside-goal thm-<SgM>-rpt-rem

[múútsú-he-tu   [tee-ne   cáátu]]   í
leche.caspi-<tree>-sou that-<ø>   genipap   self

hyúmɨ-ri íjcya-ne] i   nííñú-ne   déhtsi-dí-vú
face-oblIn be-<ø>   self smear-<event>   bees-anim-goal

cáru-uvé-hi.   ³²Áá-be-ké-vá-a
lift.face-sIn-<t> thm-<SgM>-objAn-rpt-rem

do-h   íjcya-ró-mé   pá-raará-wuú-jɨ.
eat-sub be-frs-<AnPl>   all-<spot>-dim-pl

³³Áá-ne-má-vá-a   tsá-ábe
   thm-<ø>-with-rpt-rem   come-<SgM>

ɨɨté-cunú-meí-va-rá-h   [pá-hdu-re
look-sSt-r/p-come.do-frs-<t> all-<like>-only

te-ne   néé]-neé.   ³⁴Á-ró-ne-má-vá-a
that-<ø> say-<ø>   thm-frs-<ø>-with-rpt-rem

was thus that she was waiting. ²⁸While she was waiting he came out. ²⁹She said to him, "This brother is what you are to eat."

³⁰Then, leaving from where he ate, he went into the jungle. ³¹His face, onto which he had smeared the resin from the leche caspi tree, was uplifted to the bees. ³²Even though they ate it, his face was all pocked. ³³In that circumstance, he came and looked at himself, but it was all just the same. ³⁴In that circumstance

---

²⁸Time V-s   ²⁹O V-s "DO Voc S V" (note clitics in quote)
   ³⁰Link Cir_s V-s Goal   ³¹S DO¹|DO² Goal V; DO¹ = [S² Loc V]; S² = [Sou N | N]; DO² = [s-V].   ³²DO V Aux Result (Result = small clause)   ³³Cir S V DO; S = [V-s]; DO = [PredCmpl S V]   ³⁴Cir V-s

he thought to himself, "How in the world can I make it disappear."
³⁵Thinking like that, he put on the decorations they would have put on him for the festival. ³⁶In that circumstance he said to his little sister, "Now I am going away from you." ³⁷Therefore she said, "Where brother are you going?" ³⁸Therefore he said, "I am going to the sun." ³⁹Therefore she said, "I am going with you." ⁴⁰Therefore he said, "Then, sis, put on all

íjtsámeí-jyúco-óbe:
think-now-<SgM>

"¿Mú-hdu-tú-rá-ami   ó
WH-<like>-sou-frs-wonder   I

péé-tsá-méi-í-j?"
go-caus-r/p-fut-voc

³⁵Eh-dú-vá-a   í   íjtsámeí-yó-ne
that-<like>-rpt-rem   self   think-frs-<event>

[díí-bye-ké-vá-a   [[[tee-ne   wañéhjɨ]
that-<SgM>-objAn-rpt-rem   that-<ø>   festival

pañe]   i   ícyá-ávé-tso-KI]   di-tye
inside   self   decorate-sIn-caus-pur   that-<AnPl>

pícyo-h   íjcyá-ro]-né-vú   pícyá-meí-íbye.
put-sub   be-frs-<ø>-goal   put-r/p-<SgM>

³⁶Áá-ne-má-vá-a   nee-be   dii-lle
thm-<ø>-with-rpt-rem   say-<SgM>   that-<SgF>

í   ñáá-llé-wúu-ke: "Í-cyooca   o
self   sibling-<SgF>-dim-objAn   this-when   I

pé-jucóó-h   ú-hdi-tyu".   ³⁷Áá-né-lliihyé-vá-a
go-now-<t>   you-anim-sou   thm-<ø>-motive-rpt-rem

neé-lle: "¿a-ca   kiá-vú   najme   u
say-<SgF>   y/n-doubt   where-goal   brother   you

péé-hií?"   ³⁸Áá-né-lliihyé-vá-a   neé-be:
go-<t>   thm-<ø>-motive-rpt-rem   say-<SgM>

"O   pé-jucóó-h   [áádí   élle]-vu   [núhba
I   go-now-<t>   that.SgM   place-goal   sun

élle]-vu".   ³⁹Áá-né-lliihyé-vá-a   neé-lle:
place-goal   thm-<ø>-motive-rpt-rem   say-<SgF>

"QManSou S V" (Note the multiple case markers.)

³⁵ <Sim$_i$> Cir$_s$ DO V; Cir$_s$ = [ø$_i$ s-V]; DO = [DO Pur$_s$ S V Aux]; Pur$_s$ = [Loc V]; Loc = [[Dem | N] N]; Note the clitics within the indirect quote. ³⁶Cir V-s O "Time S V Source" ³⁷Reason V-s "Q QGoal Voc S V" ³⁸Reason V-s "S V Goal | Goal" (where each Goal = [N N]) ³⁹Reason V-s "CoS Man Voc S V" ⁴⁰Reason V-s "Interj Voc V

Píívyéébé Ajyúwá Uubálle

"Úú-ma   ih-dyu   ñajme   o   péé-hií".
you-with this-<like> brother I go-<t>

⁴⁰Áá-né-lliihyé-vá-a   neé-be: "Ané(h),
thm-<ø>-motive-rpt-rem say-<SgM>   then

wa(h) pícya-meí   dí-pa-mɨ-jɨ-wuú-ne-vu-j".
sis   putImp-r/p your-all-<ornament>-pl-dim-goal-voc

⁴¹ᵃA-hdú-jucó-vá-a   [di-lle   pícyá-meí]-lle-ke
thm-<like>-focus-rpt-rem   that-<SgF>   put-r/p-<SgF>-objAn

neé-be: "Eh-du   néé-lle   me
say-<SgM>   that-<like>   say-<SgF>   SAP

péé-cooca   cóhpe-ne   míhchú-úve-co.
go-when   hard-adv   close.eyesImp-sIn-implore

⁴¹ᵇD-ɨhté-cunú-dí-ñe."   ⁴²Áá-né-liihyé-vá-a
youImp-look-sSt-neg-<n>   thm-<ø>-motive-rpt-rem

neé-lle: "Juújuj".   ⁴³Aa-né-vá-a   tsúúca
say-<SgF>   ok   thm-<ø>-rpt-rem   already

[í   újɨbá   hallú-vú]   i   pícyóó-lle-ma
self   shoulder   top-goal   self   put-<SgF>-with

wáámené-júco-óbe.   ⁴⁴Á-ró-náacá-vá-a   tsúúca
fly.up-now-<SgM>   thm-frs-while-rpt-rem   already

ílli-tyé-júcóó-llé-wu.   ⁴⁵Aa-llé-vá-a
fear-go.do-now-<SgF>-dim   thm-<SgF>-rpt-rem

wáníjcyá-meí-hi: "¡Ó   áákítye-é-h   nájmee!
scream-r/p-<t>   I   fall-fut-<t>   bud

¡Ó   áákítye-é-hií!"   ⁴⁶Néé-lle-ré-vá-a
I   fall-fut-<t>   say-<SgF>-only-rpt-rem

córɨ-ɨ́ve-íñú-h   baa-vú-juco   úwáhllo-jɨ-ré-juco.
unstick-sIn-do.go-<t>   below-goal-focus nightingale-sg-only-focus

your little jewels." ⁴¹ᵃShe put them on and he said to her, "You being like that, when we go, close your eyes tight. ⁴¹ᵇDo not look." ⁴²Therefore she said, "OK." ⁴³Then, already having put her on his shoulder he flew up. ⁴⁴However she already became scared. ⁴⁵She screamed, "I am going to fall bud, I am going to fall." ⁴⁶Saying that she became unstuck and left to go below being a nightingale now. ⁴⁷After that he flew

---

Th" (Note the change of case with reflexive.)   ⁴¹ᵃCir¹ O V-s "Cir2 Adv_d Adv s-V.; O = [[S_i V]-head_i]; Cir² = [Sim V-s_i]; *cóhpe-ne* is a degree adverb; perhaps it bears *-ne* because it refers to the eyes?   ⁴¹ᵇs-V"   ⁴²Reason V-s "X"   ⁴³Link Cir_s V-s (where Cir_s = [Adv Goal V-s])   ⁴⁴Time Adv V-s   ⁴⁵S V* "S V Voc. S V" Note that the quotative verb is "scream," not "say."   ⁴⁶S* V Goal Result (where S* is nominal-

up by himself. ⁴⁸While he was among the clouds, his father's relatives, who were getting jungle salt, on seeing him said, "He is going now because he is ashamed for having caused his sister to be pregnant." ⁴⁹ᵃFather considering him said, "You will be a father of animals. ⁴⁹ᵇYou go with the shame of having caused your sister to be pregnant like animals who cause their sisters to be pregnant." ⁵⁰That is what he said about his going.

⁴⁷[Áá-né booné-vá-a] ii-yé-juco di-bye
thm-<ø> after-rpt-rem self-only-focus that-<SgM>

wáámené-ne. ⁴⁸Aa-bé-vá-a
fly.up-<Ø> thm-<SgM>-rpt-rem

[[tsí-hullé-juco] [ojtsó pañe] íjcyá-náa] [cááni
other-<yonder>-focus clouds inside be-while father

hájkí-mú] [[úmé bajú-ne-ri] íjcya-me] [i
relative-pl jungle.salt jungle-pl-oblIn be-<AnPl> self

ájtyúmɨ́-ne] néé-hií: "Í ñáá-lle-ké-vá-a
see-<event> say-<t> self sibling-<SgF>-objAn-rpt-rem

i éévá-tsó-ne-ri i ñúcójpɨ́-vé-ne
self pregnant-caus-<event>-oblIn self shame-sIn-<event>

pé-júco-óbe". ⁴⁹ᵃÁá-be-ké-vá-a i
go-now-<SgM> thm-<SgM>-objAn-rpt-rem self

úvanú-ne nee-be cááníí: "Néhi
consider-<event> say-<SgM> father so

[iyá-mé-j cááni] u íjcyá-i-íbye,
animal-<AnPl>-x father you be-fut-<SgM>

⁴⁹ᵇ[[Iyá-mé múú-ne í ñáá-lle-ke
animal-<AnPl> WH-<ø> self sibling-<SgF>-objAn

ééva-tsó]-dú [dí-ñáá-lle-ke u
pregnant-caus-<like> your-sibling-<SgF>-objAn you

éévá-tsó-né] nucójpɨ́]-ri u péé-beé".
pregnant-caus-<event> shame-oblIn you go-<SgM>

⁵⁰Eh-dú-vá-a nee-be di-bye
that-<like>-rpt-rem say-<SgM> that-<SgM>

péé-ne-tu.
go-<ø>-sou

---

ized verb)   ⁴⁷TempP Adv* ‖ S V (Note: *i* 'self' is the root; it must be lengthened because it is a single mora. Word formation does not see the clitics.)   ⁴⁸<S_i> Time S Cir_s^1 V "Cir_s^2 Cir_s^3 V-s" (where Time = [$ø_i$ Loc, Loc V]; S = [N N]; Cir_s^1 = [Instr V] 'be at getting'; Cir_s^2 = [DO V]).   ⁴⁹ᵃ<DO_i> Cir_s V-s S "Interj PredCmpl S V-s.   ⁴⁹ᵇReason S V-s; Reason = [Sim DO s-V]; Sim = [S DO V]   ⁵⁰Sim V-s S Sou ('say about')

Píívyéébé Ajyúwá Uubálle   501

⁵¹A̋a-né-vá-a   [[di-bye   pé-júcóó-né]
thm-<ø>-rpt-rem   that-<SgM>   go-now-<event>
boone]   [dii-lle   ɨdsɨ]-ke   neé-be:
after   that-<SgF>   her.daughter-objAn   say-<SgM>
"Nújpa   caañu   [[[ámúhtsi-kyé-ne   o
water   carryImp   you.DuM-objAn-rec   I
wáñehjɨ́-nú-í-yó]-né   ijtyá-mú]   o   gúnújcu-KI
festival-do-fut-frs-<ø>   starch-pl   I   prepare.drink-pur
[ta   hájkí-mu-ma   muha   ma   ádo-ki]]".
my   relative-pl-with   we.ex   SAP   drink-pur
⁵²A-hdú-jucó-vá-a   di-lle   nújpa   cááñu-ne.
thm-<like>-focus-rpt-rem   that-<SgF>   water   carry-<Ø>
⁵³Aa-né-vá-a   [tee-ne   llíyihlló-né   wáhpe-du]
thm-<ø>-rpt-rem   that-<ø>   pot-pl   full-<like>
nee-be   cááníí: "Í-ñe-rí-yé-juco   tsahróba-ri
say-<SgM>   father   this-<ø>-oblIn-only-focus   basket-oblIn
nujpá-ñu".   ⁵⁴A-hdú-jucó-vá-a   di-lle
water-doImp   thm-<like>-focus-rpt-rem   that-<SgF>
péé-neé.   ⁵⁵Aa-llé-vá-a   [téé-hí
go-<Ø>   thm-<SgF>-rpt-rem   river-<stick>
pañé-vú   úúje-té-llé]   téé-ne-ri   tsahróba-ri
inside-goal   arrive-go.do-<SgF>   that-<ø>-oblIn   basket-oblIn
nupá-ñu-h   íjcya-rá-hi.   ⁵⁶Á-ro-né-vá-a   i
water-do-sub   be-frs-<t>   thm-frs-<ø>-rpt-rem   self
pyé-hdú   pe-h   íjcyá-hi.   ⁵⁷Áá-ne-rí-vá-a
go-<like>   go-sub   be-<t>   thm-<ø>-oblIn-rpt-rem
| [[di-lle   íjcyá-né]   hallú-rí]   cááni-mu
       that-<SgF>   be-<event>   top-oblIn   father-pl

⁵¹After he (the son) had left, he (the father) said to his daughter, "Carry water for the festival in which I would have honored you so I can make the starch drink so that we can drink it with my relatives." ⁵²It was thus that she carried water. ⁵³Then when the pots were full of water father said, "Now get water in this basket." ⁵⁴It was thus that she went. ⁵⁵Arriving at the river she got water in the basket in vain. ⁵⁶However it kept on running out. ⁵⁷While she was at that,

---

⁵¹Link TempP O V "DO V Pur$_d^1$" (where TempP = [[S V]@TempN]; O = [N | N]-case; Pur$_d^1$ = [DO S V Pur$_d^2$]; DO = [[DO S V]@N]) ⁵²Sim ‖ S DO V   ⁵³Link Cir$_d$ V-s | S "Instr | Instr s-V" (where Cir$_d$ = [S | S PredCmpl (BE)])   ⁵⁴Sim ‖ S V   ⁵⁵S Cir$_s$ DO | DO V Aux (where Cir$_s$ = [Goal V-s])   ⁵⁶S Cir$_s$ V Aux (where Cir$_s$ = [s-V])   ⁵⁷Time

the parents bathed in starch in order to run away from her. ⁵⁸She did not know that they were going away from her. ⁵⁹Then she came from the port and arrived to an empty house. ⁶⁰She said, "Where could mom and the others be going?"

⁶¹Her pets were these: ants, snakes, paucars (birds), agouti, (animal), that many. ⁶²One of them she asked, the agouti, "My pet, I wonder where my parents could have gone?" ⁶³Therefore he said: "Here

íjtyá-mu-ri   ávuhcú-jucóó-h   [díí-lle-dí-tyú   i
starch-pl-oblIn   bathe-now-<t>   that-<SgF>-anim-sou self

úmɨva-ki].   ⁵⁸Aa-né-vá-a   tsá(h)   di-lle
flee-pur   thm-<ø>-rpt-rem   no   that-<SgF>

wáájácu-tú   [díí-lle-dí-tyú   di-tye
know-neg   that-<SgF>-anim-sou   that-<AnPl>

pé-jucóó]-ne.   ⁵⁹Aa-né-vá-a   [mújcóju-tu
go-now-<ø>   thm-<ø>-rpt-rem   port-sou

tsáá-lle]   wajtsɨ́-h   íáva-já-vu-ré-juco.
come-<SgF> arrive.here-<t>   empty-<shelter>-goal-only-focus

⁶⁰Aa-llé-vá-a   néé-hií: "¿Kiá-vú-amí
thm-<SgF>-rpt-rem   say-<t>   where-goal-wonder

í-ñe   waháró-mú   pe-é-j?"
this-<ø>   mother-pl   go-fut-voc

⁶¹Aa-né-vá-a   [díí-llé   jéé-mú]
thm-<ø>-rpt-rem   that-<SgF> pet-pl

í-lluú-me: úwaajɨ-muu,   ííwacyoo,   ɨjcuu,
that-thus-<AnPl>   type.ant-pl   snake   paucar

úúcume,   ííhyoo,   é-du-mé-vá-a
agouti   (animal)   that-<like>-<AnPl>-rpt-rem

[díí-llé   jéé-mu].   ⁶²Áá-me-dí-tyu-vá-a
that-<SgF>   pet-pl   that-<AnPl>-anim-sou-rpt-rem

díllo-lle   úúcúme-ke: "Tá-jye-j,   ta-jyéé-u-j,
ask-<SgF> agouti-objAn   my-pet-voc   my-pet-sg-voc

¿kiá-vú-amí-ñe   waháró-mú   peé-j?"
where-goal-wonder-rec   mother-pl   go-voc

| Time* S Instr Pur$_s$ (where Time* = [[S V]@N]; Pur$_s$ = [Sou s-V])
⁵⁸Link Neg S V DO (where DO = [Sou S V])   ⁵⁹Link S V Goal (where S = [Sou V-s])   ⁶⁰S V "QGoal S | S V"
⁶¹Link S (BE) PredCmpl: S* (BE) PredCmpl (where S* = [N N N N Sum])   ⁶²S$_{partitive}$ V-s O "Voc Voc QGoal S V"   ⁶³Reason V-s "Loc[1]

Píívyéébé Ajyúwá Uubálle

⁶³Áá-né-lliihyé-vá-a   ne-ébe: "ííllej,
thm-<ø>-motive-rpt-rem   say-<SgM>   here
[úllébá   lliíñe]."   ⁶⁴Eh-dú-vá-a
plate   underneath   that-<like>-rpt-rem
né-ébe-re   dsɨɨ́ne-íñu-h   íjcyá-h   [úllébá
say-<SgM>-only   run.do.go-sub   be-<t>   plate
lliiñé-vu].   ⁶⁵Áá-náacá-vá-a   íí
underneath-goal   thm-while-rpt-rem   self
tyáá-llé-coba   íñiiñé-rí   i
grandparent-<SgF>-aug   place.near-oblIn   self
hwáábyaá-ri.   ⁶⁶Áá-lle-ké-vá-a
hammock-oblIn   thm-<SgF>-objAn-rpt-rem
neé-lle: "Taá-lle-j,   ¿kiá-vú-amí-ñe
say-<SgF>   grandparent-<SgF>-voc   where-goal-wonder-rec
waháró-mú   peé-j?"
mother-pl   go-voc

⁶⁷Áá-né-lliihyé-vá-a   neé-lle: "Cáhawáá
thm-<ø>-motive-rpt-rem   say-<SgF>   suggest
bo(h)   í-ñe   pá-ne-ere | [dɨɨ́-tsɨ́ɨ́ju   bájtso-háñé]
well   this-<ø>   all-<ø>-only   your-mother   planting-pl.
pihjyúcú   o   óóve-ki".   ⁶⁸A-hdú-jucó-vá-a
gather   I   fill.up-pur   thm-<like>-focus-rpt-rem
di-lle   píhjyucú-né   pá-ne-ere   [tsɨ́ɨ́ju
that-<SgF>   gather-<Ø>   all-<ø>-only   mother
bájtso-háñe].   ⁶⁹Aa-né-vá-a   óóve-lle.
planting-pl.   thm-<ø>-rpt-rem   fill.up-<SgF>
⁷⁰[Áá-né   nɨ́jcáu]-tú-vá-a   neé-lle:
thm-<ø>   end-sou-rpt-rem   say-<SgF>

underneath the plate." ⁶⁴Saying that he ran underneath the plate. ⁶⁵Meanwhile her big grandma was nearby in her hammock. ⁶⁶She said to her grandma: "Grandma, where in the world did my parents go?"

⁶⁷Therefore she said: "Well, I suggest you harvest your mother's fields so I can fill up." ⁶⁸Thus it was that she gathered all of her mother's crop. ⁶⁹Then she filled up. ⁷⁰After finishing that she said: "OK now,

---

Loc² "   ⁶⁴<Simᵢ> S V Aux Goal (where S = [ᵢ V-s])   ⁶⁵Time S Loc |
Loc (BE). Note: locatives marked with -ri 'oblIn'.   ⁶⁶S V-s "Voc QGoal
S V"
⁶⁷Reason V-s "ProSent DO | DO | DO V Pur_d (where Pur_d = [S
V])   ⁶⁸Sim ‖ S V DO   ⁶⁹Link V-s   ⁷⁰Time V-s "ProSent s-V Sou"

let's go after your parents." ⁷¹Thus saying she dug up some ashes from her fireplace. ⁷²While they were going into that hole she returned a little distance from her grandmother. ⁷³Thus it was on that trail that she went with her pets. ⁷⁴She arrived to where the bird (*chicua*) was. ⁷⁵She was with him for a long time. ⁷⁶He said to her in order to go: "You stay here. ⁷⁷I will go hunt at my fields. ⁷⁸If the people beat me up, you will know right from the yellowing of my medicine plant

"Áju(h), májo [dɨ́ɨ-tsɨ́ɨjú-mu déju]-tu".
ready let's.go your-mother-pl behind-sou

⁷¹Eh-dú-vá-a néé-lle-re tsehdí-h [í
that-<like>-rpt-rem say-<SgF>-only dig-<t> self

jcyujúwá llíjyu-tu] ⁷²Á-hejú-ri-vá-a
fire ashes-sou thm-<hole>-oblIn-rpt-rem

[di-tyépɨ pé-júcóó-ró-náa] óómi-lle
that-<DuF> go-now-frs-while return-<SgF>

dii-lle íí tyáá-lle-dí-tyú
that-<SgF> self grandparent-<SgF>-anim-sou

wahájchotá-tú-re. ⁷³Aa-llé-vá-a
short.distance-sou-only thm-<SgF>-rpt-rem

juuvá-yi-yé-juco péé-ne i jyéé-ú-wuú-mu-ma.
trail-oblIn-only-focus go-<Ø> self pet-sg-dim-pl-with

⁷⁴Aa-llé-vá-a úúje-té-h
thm-<SgF>-rpt-rem arrive-go.do-<t>

báádsɨ́-di-vu. ⁷⁵Áá-be-má-vá-a íjcya-lle
type.bird-anim-goal thm-<SgM>-with-rpt-rem is-<SgF>

kémú-élléh-ré-juco. ⁷⁶Áá-lle-ké-vá-a
distant-<place>-only-focus thm-<SgF>-objAn-rpt-rem

i úlle-té-KI ne-ébe: "Di-ícya.
self walk-go.do-pur say-<SgM> youImp-be

⁷⁷Ó-i ó llííñájaa-té-h í-chií-yé-i
I-PT I hunt-go.do-<t> this-<place>-only-PT

tá-hjɨ-háñe. ⁷⁸[[Áá-be-ke o-ke múnaa
my-<disk>-pl thm-<SgM>-objAn I-objAn people

méénú-júcóó-hajchíí] í-ñe tá-ñuubúmu-ba
beat-now-if this-<ø> my-med.pl-sg

Note case: Goal with *-tu* 'source' ⁷¹<Sim$_i$> S V Sou (where S = [ø$_i$ V-s]) ⁷²<Instr$_i$> Time V-s | S Sou | Sou (where Time = [ø$_i$ S V]) ⁷³S Instr ‖ V CoS ⁷⁴S V Goal ⁷⁵CoS V-s Time ⁷⁶<O$_i$> Pur$_s$ V-s "s-V" (where Pur$_s$ = [ø$_i$ s-V]) ⁷⁷S | S V Loc | Loc ⁷⁸Sou S V DO (where Sou = [Cond S | S V], Cond = [DO | DO S V]; DO = [DO S

Píívyéébé Ajyúwá Uubálle

llíjcya-nú-ne-tú-ré]	ú	waajácu-ú-h	[tsúúca o-ke
yellow-do-<ø>-sou-only	you	know-fut-<t>	already I-objAn

di-tye	méénu]-ne".	[79]A-hdú-jucó-vá-a
that-<AnPl>	beat-<ø>	thm-<like>-focus-rpt-rem

di-lle	ɨtso-h	íjcyá-ne.	[80]Áá-náacá-vá-a
that-<SgF>	expect-sub	be-<Ø>	thm-while-rpt-rem

áábaúvú-dú-ré	tee-ne	[díí-byé
suddenly-<like>-only	that-<ø>	that-<SgM>

nuubúmu-ba]	llíjcya-nú-hi.	[81]Aa-né-vá-a
med.pl-sg	yellow-do-<t>	thm-<ø>-rpt-rem

i	ájtyúmɨ́-ne	neé-lle:	"Tsúúcajá-ubá
self	see-<event>	say-<SgF>	already-prob

báádsɨ́-ke	múnaa	meenú-jucóó-hi.	[82]Muurá
chicua-objAn	people	beat-now-<t>	for

í-ñe	tsúúca	í-ñuubúmu-ba	llíjcya-nú-hi.
this-<ø>	already	his-med.pl-sg	yellow-do-<t>

[83]¡Ɨ́vee-kí-hyana!	¿Múú-má	o	íjcya-ki...?"
why-pur-wonder	WH-with	I	be-pur

[84]Eh-dú-vá-a	i	ñéé-ne	tá-júcoo-lle
that-<like>-rpt-rem	self	say-<event>	cry-now-<SgF>

mítya-ne.	[85]Á-tsih-dyú-vá-a	idyé
much-adv	thm-<place>-sou-rpt-rem	like.before

neé-lle:	"¡Ɨ́vee-kí-hyana!	¿kiá-vú	o péé-KI
say-<SgF>	why-pur-wonder	where-goal	I go-pur

tsúúca	báádsɨ	dsɨ́jɨvé-hi?"
already	chicua	die-<t>

that they have already beat me up." [79]Thus it was that she was waiting, anticipating his return. [80]While she was waiting suddenly his medicine plant became yellow. [81]Then seeing that she said: "The people must have already beaten up the chicua bird. [82]Because his medicine plant has already become yellow. [83]Why o why! With whom will I be...?" [84]Having said that she cried very much. [85]At that point as before she said: "Why o why! Where will I go now that the chicua bird has died?"

V]; note that -tu 'source' marks the basis for knowing)   [79]Sim ‖ S V Aux   [80]Time Adv S | S V   [81]<DO_i> Cir_s V-s "Adv DO S V" (where Cir_s = [$ø_i$ s-V])   [82]Link S_i Adv S_i V (where the S_i are appositive, although not adjacent)   [83]Interj QCoS S V   [84]<Sim_i> Cir_s V AdvDeg (where Cir_s = [$ø_i$ s-V]) mítya-ne is a degree adverb   [85]Interj Sim V-s "Pur_d Adv S V" (where Pur_d = [QLoc S V])

[86]Saying that she went on the trail he had said the parents had gone on. [87]She arrived to where the hunchback's wife was. [88]She asked her: “Grandma, on which trail did my parents go?” [89]Therefore she informed: “On this trail. [90a]However it is already dark. [90b]Sleep here with me. [91]Go tomorrow.” [92]Thus it was that she slept with her. [93]She told her: “Going from here you will arrive to ‘this trail, that trail’

[86]Eh-dú-vá-a i ñéé-ne pé-júcoo-lle
that-<like>-rpt-rem self say-<event> go-now-<SgF>

[di-byé-vá-a úúbállé-ju-rí-jyuco]
that-<SgM>-rpt-rem tell-<channel>-oblIn-focus

[tsɨ́ɨ́jú-mu déju]-tu. [87]Aa-llé-vá-a
mother-pl behind-sou thm-<SgF>-rpt-rem

pé-h íjcya-lle úúje-té-h [Cállúrɨɨjɨ́-ba
go-sub be-<SgF> arrive-go.do-<t> hunchback-sg

mééwa-dí-vu]. [88]Áá-lle-ké-vá-a díllo-lle:
wife-anim-goal thm-<SgF>-objAn-rpt-rem ask-<SgF>

“Taá-lle-j, ¿kéé-ju-rí-amí-ñe
grandparent-<SgF>-voc which-<channel>-oblIn-wonder-rec

waháró-mú peé-j?” [89]Áá-né-lliihyé-vá-a
mother-pl go-voc thm-<ø>-motive-rpt-rem

úúbálle-lle: “í-jyuu-rí-ñeécu. [90a]Á-ró-náa
tell-<SgF> this-<channel>-oblIn-affirm thm-frs-while

cúvéh-ré-juco teé-ne. [90b]Ɨ́-chií-yé-i
dark-only-focus that-<ø> this-<place>-only-PT

óó-ma cuwa. [91]Péjco-ré-ca di-pye”.
I-with sleepImp night-only-suggest youImp-go

[92]A-hdú-jucó-vá-a díí-lle-má-i di-lle
thm-<like>-focus-rpt-rem that-<SgF>-with-PT that-<SgF>

cúwa-ne. [93]Áá-lle-ké-vá-a úúbálle-lle:
sleep-<Ø> thm-<SgF>-objAn-rpt-rem tell-<SgF>

“[Í-chih-dyu u péé-lle] ú úújé-te-é-h
this-<place>-sou you go-<SgF> you arrive-go.do-fut-<t>

í-jyu né-ju mééwa-dí-vu.
this-<channel> that-<channel> wife-anim-goal

---

[86] <Sim_i> Cir_s V-s Instr Goal (where Cir_s = [$ø_i$ s-V]; Goal = [N | N]-case, where the case is *-tu* ‘source’; note the use of *-va* ‘reportative’) [87]S Cir_s V Goal (where Cir_s = [V Aux-s]) [88]S V “Voc QInstr S V” [89]Reason V-s “Instr” (There is a direct quote without *nee-* ‘say’; *-ñeécu* ‘affirmation’ is archaic.) [90a]Time PredCmpl || S [90b]Loc CoS s-V [91]Time s-V [92]Sim || CoS S V [93]O V-s “S*|s V Goal” (where S*

⁹⁴Aa-lle	múú-ne	me-ke	dóó-hií.
that-\<SgF\>	WH-\<ø\>	SAP-objAn	eat-\<t\>

⁹⁵Áá-lle-dí-vú		u	úúje-té-lle-ke
thm-\<SgF\>-anim-goal		you	arrive-go.do-\<SgF\>-objAn

ú	díllo-ó-hi:	'Taá-lle-j,
you	ask-fut-\<t\>	grandparent-\<SgF\>-voc

¿kéé-ju-rí-amí-i	waháró-mú
which-\<channel\>-oblIn-wonder-rem	mother-pl

peé-j?'	⁹⁶Áá-né-llii	u-ke	úúbállé-i-lle:
go-voc	thm-\<ø\>-motive	you-objAn	tell-fut-\<SgF\>

'í-jyuú'.	⁹⁷Aa-ne	['í-jyuú'
this-\<channel\>	thm-\<ø\>	this-\<channel\>

u-ke	di-lle	néé-ju-rí-jyuco]
you-objAn	that-\<SgF\>	say-\<channel\>-oblIn-focus

íícúi	u	peé-i-ñe.	⁹⁸[Áá-né
quickly	you	go-fut-\<ø\>	thm-\<ø\>

boone]	[['í-jyuú'	u-ke	di-lle
after	this-\<channel\>	you-objAn	that-\<SgF\>

néé-ró-náa]	u	íjyá-cunú-hajchíí]	u-ke
say-frs-while	you	delay-sSt-if	you-objAn

dóó-i-lle."	⁹⁹Eh-dú-vá-a	díí-lle-ke
eat-fut-\<SgF\>	that-\<like\>-rpt-rem	that-\<SgF\>-objAn

úúbálle-lle.	¹⁰⁰A-hdú-jucó-vá-a
tell-\<SgF\>	thm-\<like\>-focus-rpt-rem

pé-h	íjcya-lle	úúje-té-né	[dii-lle
go-sub	be-\<SgF\>	arrive-go.do-\<ø\>	that-\<SgF\>

| ['í-jyu	hé-ju'	mééwa-dí]]-vu.
this-\<channel\>	that-\<channel\>	wife-anim-goal.

wife. ⁹⁴She is one that eats us. ⁹⁵Arriving to her, ask her: 'Grandma, on which trail did my parents go?' ⁹⁶Therefore she will tell you, 'this trail'. ⁹⁷Then go quickly on the trail that she tells you. ⁹⁸After that, if you delay going on the trail on which she told you to go, she will eat you." ⁹⁹That's what she told her. ¹⁰⁰Thus it was that having gone along she arrived to the 'this trail, that trail' wife. ¹⁰¹She asked her: "On which trail did my

---

= [Sou S V-s]) ⁹⁴S DO | DO V ⁹⁵\<Goal$_i$\> O S V 'Voc QInstr S V'; O = [[ø$_i$ S$_k$ V]-head$_k$ ⁹⁶Reason O V-s 'NP' ⁹⁷Link Instr || Adv S V; Instr = [['NP$_i$' S V]-head$_i$] ⁹⁸TempP Cond DO V-s (where Cond = [Time S V] and Time = ['NP' O S V]) ⁹⁹Sim O V-s ¹⁰⁰\<Sim$_i$\> || Cir$_s$ V Goal (where Cir$_s$ = [ø$_i$ V Aux-s]) ¹⁰¹O V-s "Voc QInstr S V" ¹⁰²Reason V-s "NP" ¹⁰³Instr || S V ¹⁰⁴TempP V-s "..." ¹⁰⁵Time

parents go?"
[102]Therefore she told her: "This trail."
[103]It was on that trail that she went.
[104]After that she (the old woman) said: "This trail, that trail. This trail, that trail."
[105]Right when she said that, she (the girl) ran.
[106]She kept going and arrived to where Uminuri was chopping in his field (in which the underbrush had previously been cut).
[107]Upon seeing her: "Where are you going?" saying, leaving what he was getting,

[101] Áá-lle-ké-vá-a   díllo-lle
thm-<SgF>-objAn-rpt-rem   ask-<SgF>

"Taá-lle-j,   ¿kéé-ju-rí-amí-i
Grandparent-<SgF>-voc   which-<channel>-oblIn-wonder-rem

waháró-mú   peé-j?"
mother-pl   go-voc

[102] Áá-né-lliihyé-vá-a   úúbálle-lle: "Í-jyuú".
thm-<ø>-motive-rpt-rem   tell-<SgF>   this-<channel>

[103] Áá-ju-rí-jyucó-vá-a   di-lle
thm-<channel>-oblIn-focus-rpt-rem   that-<SgF>

péé-neé.   [104][Áá-né   booné]-vá-a   neé-lle:
go-<ø>   thm-<ø>   after-rpt-rem   say-<SgF>

"¡Í-jyu   hé-ju,   í-jyu
this-<channel>   that-<channel>   this-<channel>

hé-ju!"   [105] Á-ró-náacá-jucó-vá-a
that-<channel>   thm-frs-while-focus-rpt-rem

di-lle   dsɨɨné-jucóó-ne.   [106] Aa-llé-vá-a
that-<SgF>   run-now-<ø>   thm-<SgF>-rpt-rem

pé-h   íjcya-lle   úúje-té-h   [Úmɨnurɨ
go-sub   be-<SgF>   arrive-go.do-<t>   (name)

í-ñajá-jɨ   íllo-h   íjcyá]-ábe-dí-vu.
his-cut.underbrush-<disk>   chop-sub   be-<SgM>-anim-goal

[107][Áá-lle-ké-vá-a   i   ájtyúmɨ-ne]
thm-<SgF>-objAn-rpt-rem   self   see-<event>

[["¿Kiá-vú   u   peé-hi?"   né-ébe-re]
where-goal   you   go-<t>   say-<SgM>-only

i   újcu-íñú-ne]   ékeevé-hi.
self   get-do.go-<event>   grab-<t>

‖ S V   [106]S | S* V Aux Goal; S* = [V-s]; Goal = [S_i DO V]-head$_i$]
[107]<DO$_i$> Cir$_s^1$ S Cir$_s^2$ V (where Cir$_s^1$ = [ø$_i$ s-V]; S = ["QGoal S V" V-s]; Cir$_s^2$ = [s-V])   [108]<DO$_i$> Goal V-s DO | DO (where Goal = [ø$_i$ Goal s-V]) úmé 'jungle salt' is made from the ashes of certain trees; although here and below the word is only 'salt', it is understood that it refers to the packet in which the salt is stored.   [109]CoS ‖ S V   [110]S

Píívyéébé Ajyúwá Uubálle

[108]Áá-lle-ké-vá-a   [[[úmé   pañé-vú]   i
thm-<SgF>-objAn-rpt-rem   salt   inside-goal self

pícyóó-llé]   hallú-vú]   chíjchu-ube   tee-ne   ume.
put-<SgF>   top-goal   tie-<SgM>   that-<ø> salt

[109]Áá-lle-má-jucó-vá-a   di-bye   tsáá-neé.
thm-<SgF>-with-focus-rpt-rem   that-<SgM>   come-<ø>

[110]Aa-bé-vá-a   méwa-kye   nee-vá-hi:
thm-<SgM>-rpt-rem   wife-objAn say-come.do-<t>

"Muú-lle-j,   bújcájaa-co   [ta-úmé kikííjyeba]
age.mate-<SgF>-voc   bakeImp-urgent   my-salt brains

o lléhdo-ki".   [111]Áá-né-lliihyé-vá-a   áñújcu-lle
I eat-pur   thm-<ø>-motive-rpt-rem   answer-<SgF>

mewa: "Juújuj".   [112]Á-tsih-dyú-vá-a
wife   ok   thm-<place>-sou-rpt-rem

idyé ne-ébe: "Ó-i   muu-lle   ó
after say-<SgM>   I-PT   age.mate-<SgF>   I

cóó-va-té-hi".   [113]Aa-bé-vá-a
firewood-have-go.do-<t>   thm-<SgM>-rpt-rem

pé-jucóó-hi."   [114][Áá-né   boonée]-vá-a   ih-dyu
go-now-<t>   thm-<ø>   after-rpt-rem this-<like>

neé-lle: "¡Behtyúne íjcyá-hi!   ¿Mú-hwúu-ké-jucó
say-<SgF>   be.certain   be-<t>   WH-dim-objAn-focus

i   tsívá-ne   Umínurɨ   ɨɨ-ná: "[Ta-úmé
self bring-<event> (name)   this-<ø>   my-salt

kikííjyeba] o lléhdo-KI bújcájaá-co"   né-h   ijcyá-ne.
brain   I eat-pur   bake-urgent   say-sub be-<ø>

[115]Eh-dú-vá-a   néé-lle-re   tee-ne   [úmé
thm-<like>-rpt-rem   say-<SgF>-only   that-<ø> salt

[108]Having put her into his salt pack, he tied it over where she was. [109]Along with her, he came. [110]He came and said to his wife: "Bake these brains with my salt so I can eat them together." [111]Therefore the wife answered: "OK." [112]At that point he said: "Sister, I'll go get firewood." [113]He went now. [114]After that she said: "For certain! Whom is this Uminuri bringing saying, 'Bake my salt and brains so I can eat them'?" [115]Saying that and untying

---

O V "Voc s-V DO$_i$ Pur$_s$" (where Pur$_s$ = [S ø$_i$ V])   [111]Reason V-s | S "ProSent"   [112]Link Adv V-s "S Voc S V" Note that -tu 'source' is not aspirated in Á-tsih-dyú-vá-a; this may be because of the preceding glottal stop, checking the aspiration of ts?   [113]S V   [114]TempP Sim V "Pred-Cmpl V. <QDO> s-V | S Cir$_s$" (where Cir = ['Pur V' V Aux]; Pur = [DO s-V]   [115]Sim$_i$ Cir$_s$ Cir$_s$ V DO (where Cir$_s$ = [ø$_i$ s-V]; Cir$_s$ = [DO

the salt packet she stared at that grin. ¹¹⁶Thereupon she said, "What are you grinning about? ¹¹⁷He keeps bringing people in order to eat them. ¹¹⁸And what are you doing?" ¹¹⁹ᵃThus saying and untying that, she said: "You may go. ¹¹⁹ᵇWhat in the world! ¹¹⁹ᶜYou whom he brought to eat are grinning! ¹²⁰Your parents went on this trail." ¹²¹Thus it was that she went on that trail.

¹²²Then, after she had left, she exchanged her with a squash. ¹²³In

chíjchu-ta]   i   tsíñaá-yó-ne   ɨɨté-cunú-h
tie-<used>   self untie-sTr-<event> look-sSt-<t>

té-goojú-cunu.   ¹¹⁶Áá-ne-ré-jucó-vá-a
that-grin-sSt   thm-<ø>-only-focus-rpt-rem

di-lle   néé-neé: "¿ɨɨ-ná   ú   goojú-cunú-h
that-<SgF> say-<Ø>   this-<ø> you grin-sSt-sub

ijcyá-hi?   ¹¹⁷Muurá(h) [ee-ne   i   dyóó-KI]
be-<t>   for   that-<ø> self   eat-pur

mɨamúnáa-ke   tsíva-h   íjcya-ábe.   ¹¹⁸Áá-náa
people-objAn bring-sub be-<SgM>   thm-while

¿ɨɨ-ne-rí   uú?"   ¹¹⁹ᵃEh-dú-vá-a
what-<ø>-oblIn you   that-<like>-rpt-rem

néé-lle-re   i   tsíñaá-yó-ne   néé-hií: "Wa
say-<SgF>-only   self   untie-sTr-<event> say-<t>   permission

di-pye-j,   ¹¹⁹ᵇ¡ɨɨ-ná!   ¹¹⁹ᶜ[i   dyóó-KI
youImp-go-voc   this-<ø>   self eat-pur

u-ke   di-bye   tsíva]-lle   ú   goojú-cunú-h
you-objAn   that-<SgM>   bring-<SgF>   you   grin-sSt-sub

ijcyá-hi.   ¹²⁰Í-jyuu-rí-ñe   dɨɨ-tsɨɨju-mu
be-<t>   this-<channel>-oblIn-rec   your-mother-pl

péé-hií."   ¹²¹A-hdú-jucó-vá-a   di-lle
go-<t>   thm-<like>-focus-rpt-rem   that-<SgF>

péé-ne   téé-ju-ri.
go-<Ø>   that-<channel>-oblIn

    ¹²²Aa-né-vá-a   [[di-lle
       thm-<ø>-rpt-rem   that-<SgF>

péé-né]   boone]   cápáyo-áco-lle
go-<event>   after   exchange-sTr-<SgF>

| DO s-V]; DO = [s-V] (an active participle))   ¹¹⁶Link || S V "X S V Aux   ¹¹⁷Link Pur$_s$ DO V Aux (where Pur$_s$ = [DO s-V])   ¹¹⁸Time Instr S   ¹¹⁹ᵃSim$_i$ Cir$_s^1$ Cir$_s^2$ V "Modal s-V. (where Cir$_s^1$ = [ø$_i$ V-s]; Cir$_s^2$ = [ø s-V]   ¹¹⁹ᵇInterj   ¹¹⁹ᶜS¹|S V Aux; S¹ = [Pur$_s$ DO$_i$ V]-head$_i$; Pur$_s$ = [ø$_i$ s-V]   ¹²⁰Instr S V   ¹²¹Sim || S V Instr

¹²²Link TempP V-s Sou (where Time = [Cir$_s$ PostPos]; Cir$_s$ = [S

Píívyéébé Ajyúwá Uubálle			

dóótó-u-tu.
squash-<sphere>-sou

¹²³Áá-ne-má-vá-a
thm-<ø>-with-rpt-rem

chíjchu-lle   di-byé-vá-a   chíjchu-du
tie-<SgF>   that-<SgM>-rpt-rem   tie-<like>

cóhpé-ne-úvu.
hard-adv-max

¹²⁴Á-ró-náacá-jucó-vá-a
thm-frs-while-focus-rpt-rem

di-bye   tsáá-neé.
that-<SgM>   come-<Ø>

¹²⁵Aa-bé-vá-a
thm-<SgM>-rpt-rem

cujúwaa-ñú-vá-hi.
fire-make-come.do-<t>

¹²⁶Aa-né-vá-a
thm-<ø>-rpt-rem

[péété-né   hallú-vú]   wátyu-áco-obe
burn-<event>   top-goal   put.across-sTr-<SgM>

tee-ne   i   úme.
that-<ø>   self   salt

¹²⁷Aa-né-vá-a
thm-<ø>-rpt-rem

áí-ívyé-ne-tu   tee-ne   dóóto-u
burn-sIn-<event>-sou   that-<ø>   squash-<sphere>

neebó-h   "tóó"
pop.open-<t>   "bang".

¹²⁸Áá-né-lliihyé-vá-a
thm-<ø>-motive-rpt-rem

ne-ébe: "¡Úú!   ¿ɨvee-kí-ami   [ta-úmé
say-<SgM>   wow   why-pur-wonder   my-salt

kikííjyeba]   ɨcúbáhrá-meíí?"
brains   ruin-r/p

¹²⁹Eh-dú-vá-a
that-<like>-rpt-rem

né-ébe-re   dóuhá-yo-jé-h
say-<SgM>-only   break-sTr-do.come-<t>

mááhó-jɨ-tu.
cassava-<disk>-sou

¹³⁰Áá-ne-má-vá-a
thm-<ø>-with-rpt-rem

i   chíhchá-có-ne   májchó-ro-obe
self   dunk-sTr-<event>   eat-frs-<SgM>

that circumstance she tied it up like he had, real tight. ¹²⁴However while she was doing that he came. ¹²⁵He came and built a fire. ¹²⁶Then he put his salt packet on top of the fire. ¹²⁷After it heated up, it popped open with a bang. ¹²⁸Therefore he said: "Wow, why I wonder did my salt and brains get ruined?" ¹²⁹Saying that he went and broke off a piece of cassava. ¹³⁰With that (cassava), dunking it (in hot sauce), he ate it, but it was very bit-

---

V]) ¹²³Cir V-s Sim$_d$ Result (where Sim$_d$ = [S V]) *cóhpé-ne-úvu* is a degree adverb. ¹²⁴Time ‖ S V ¹²⁵S V ¹²⁶<S$_i$> Goal V-s DO | DO; Goal = [[ø$_i$ V] @ LOC] ¹²⁷<S$_i$> Cir$_s$ V "..." (where Cir$_s$ = [ø$_i$ V]) ¹²⁸Reason V-s "Interj QPur S V" ¹²⁹Sim S V-s DO$_{partitive}$. (Note partitive with *-tu* 'source'.) ¹³⁰<DO$_i$> Cir$_s$ V-s Result (where Cir$_s$ =

ter. [131]Then being frustrated he said: "Sister, I bet you sent away what I caught on my hunt." [132]After that he said: "What is it that I eat?" [133a]Whereupon again he said: "Instead should I eat you? [133b]Why did you send away what I caught on my hunt?" [134]Thus saying he hit her with a stick resulting in drawing blood. [135]Then getting (her dead body), he ate what he had stirred in the pot.

[136]After that he returned from getting his di-

paapá-wu.   [131]Á-ró-ne-má-vá-a   ne-ébe:
bitter-dim   thm-frs-<ø>-with-rpt-rem   say-<SgM>

"Muú-lle-j,   ú-ubá-hja-né   [tá-lliiñája-j
age.mate-<SgF>-voc you-prob-nwit-rec my-hunt-x

táává] ú   wallóó-hi".   [132][Áá-né   boonél-vá-a
catch   you sent-<t>   thm-<ø>   after-rpt-rem

ne-ébe: "¿íí-ne-ré-juco   o májcho-ró-ne?"
say-<SgM>   what-<ø>-only-focus   I eat-frs-<Ø>

[133a]Á-tsih-dyú-vá-a   idyé   ne-ébe:
thm-<place>-sou-rpt-rem   before say-<SgM>

"¿Mityá   uu-ké-ré   o   dóó-h   íjcya-lle?
instead   you-objAn-only   I   eat-sub be-<SgF>

[133b]ívee-ná [tá-lliiñája-j   táává]   ú   wallóó-hi?"
why-<ø>   my-hunt-x   catch   you send-<t>

[134]E-hdú-vá-a   né-ébe-re   díí-lle-ke
that-<like>-rpt-rem   say-<SgM>-only   that-<SgF>-objAn

íllaá-yó-h   úmé-hé-hi-yi   [apáhajchíí
hit-sTr-<t>   tree-<tree>-<stick>-oblIn   extent

tú-jpacyó]-ré-juco.   [135]Aa-né-vá-a
blood-<liquid>-only-focus   thm-<ø>-rpt-rem

i   újcú-ne   [llíyíhllo-ri   i   bóri-jcyó]-ne
self   get-<event>   pot-oblIn   self stir-mTr-<ø>

do-óbe.
eat-<SgM>

[136][Áá-né   boonê-tu]-vá-a   í   wahdá-hí
thm-<ø>   after-sou-rpt-rem   self   divining-<stick>

újcú-je-ebe   téé-hi-yi   i   wáájácu-KI
get-do.come-<SgM>   that-<stick>-oblIn self know-pur

[ø$_i$ s-V]); -có is an allomorph of -acó 'sTr'   [131]Cir V-s "Voc S DO S V" (where DO = [[s-V] @ N])   [132]TempP V-s "QDO ∥ S V"   [133a]Cir Adv V-s "QDO ∥ S V Aux"   [133b]Reason DO S V   [134]<Sim$_i$> Cir$_s$ DO V Instr Result; Cir$_s$ = [ø$_i$ V-s]; Result = [AdvDeg N]   [135]<DO$_i$> Cir$_s$ Instr DO$_s$ V-s (where Cir$_s^1$ = [ø$_i$ s-V] DO$_s^2$ = [Loc s-V])

[136]TempP DO V-s Pur$_s$ (where Pur$_s$ = [s-V DO]; DO = [QGoal

[kiá-vú   di-lle   péé]-neé.   ¹³⁷Aa-né-vá-a
where-goal that-\<SgF\> go-\<ø\>   thm-\<ø\>-rpt-rem

tsúúca i   wáájácú-ne   úrá-ávye-ebe
already self know-\<event\> follow-sIn-\<SgM\>

díí-lle-ke.   ¹³⁸Í   piijyú-wa-vá-a
that-\<SgF\>-objAn self   hook-\<slab\>-rpt-rem

[di-bye   wááo]-ne   [díí-llé   nííwá-co]-tu
that-\<SgM\>   throw-\<ø\> that-\<SgF\> head-\<hair\>-sou

cápa-avyé-hi.   ¹³⁹Aa-wá-vá-a   i   újcú-ne
hook-sIn-\<t\>   thm-\<slab\>-rpt-rem self get-\<event\>

wájcá-tu   pícyoó-lle.   ¹⁴⁰Aa-né-vá-a
branch-sou put-\<SgF\>   thm-\<ø\>-rpt-rem

tsáá-ro-obe   pevé-tsih-vu   wajtsɨ́-hi.
come-frs-\<SgM\>   empty-\<place\>-goal   arrive.here-\<t\>

¹⁴¹Á-tsih-dyú-vá-a   pé-h   íjcya-lle
  thm-\<place\>-sou-rpt-rem   go-sub be-\<SgF\>

úúje-té-h   móóa-vu.   ¹⁴²Áá-lle-ké-vá-a
arrive-go.do-\<t\> big.river-goal   thm-\<SgF\>-objAn-rpt-rem

tsóvɨráco-mútsí   pajtyé-tsó-hi.   ¹⁴³[Í
alligator-\<DuM\>   pass-caus-\<t\>   self

piijyú-wá   dohjɨ́]-ri-vá-a   pajtyé-tso-mútsi.
hook-\<slab\>   line-oblIn-rpt-rem   pass-caus-\<DuM\>

¹⁴⁴Áá-náacá-vá-a   ee-ne   díí-lle-ke
  thm-while-rpt-rem   that-\<ø\> that-\<SgF\>-objAn

úrá-ávye-h   íjcya-abe   wajtsɨ́-jucóó-h
follow-sIn-sub   be-\<SgM\>   arrive.here-now-\<t\>

S V])   ¹³⁷\<DO$_i$\> Cir$_s$ V-s DO (where Cir$_s$ = [Adv ø$_i$ s-V])
¹³⁸\<S\>|S* Site V (where S* = [[S ø$_i$ S V]-head$_i$]; Note case markers: Site with -*tu* 'source', somewhat like English *by the hair*.)   ¹³⁹\<DO$_i$\> Cir$_s$ Site V-s (where Cir$_s$ = [ø$_i$ s-V])   ¹⁴⁰Link S Goal V
   ¹⁴¹Sou$_i$ S V Aux Goal (where S = [ø$_i$ V-s])   ¹⁴²DO S V   ¹⁴³Instr V-s   ¹⁴⁴Time S | S* V Goal (where S* = [DO V Aux]-s)   ¹⁴⁵ᵃS s-V

was following her arrived there. ¹⁴⁵ᵃHe said, "Take me across. ¹⁴⁵ᵇYou---I am aware---helped my catch across." ¹⁴⁶ᵃTherefore they said: "No, we don't see. ¹⁴⁶ᵇHow can we pass you over? ¹⁴⁷Therefore he said: "Even so, like you did before, cause me to get across, so I can follow my catch." ¹⁴⁸"OK," they said and tied the hook to a very old line. ¹⁴⁹With that they said: "Come on then, grab hold here so that we can pass you across." ¹⁵⁰Thus it was that the line to which the two

té-tsih-vu.
that-<place>-goal

néé-hií: "O-ke mé pajtyé-tso;
say-<t> I-objAn SAP pass-caus

¹⁴⁵ᵇámuhtsí-hjya-né ta-jtyáává mé pajtyé-tsó-hi".
youDuM-aware-rec my-catch SAP pass-caus-<t>

¹⁴⁶ᵃÁá-né-lliihyé-vá-a nee-mútsi: "Tsáhaá.
thm-<ø>-motive-rpt-rem say-<DuM> no

Muhtsí ma ájtyúmɨ-ne-jɨɨ: ¹⁴⁶ᵇ¿Mu-hdú
we.ex SAP see-<ø>-contra.pos WH-<like>

mé pajtyé-tso-ó-hi?" ¹⁴⁷Áá-né-lliihyé-vá-a
SAP pass-caus-fut-<t> thm-<ø>-motive-rpt-rem

ne-ébe: "Ané-hde ih-dyu o-ke mé
say-<SgM> give.in-before this-<like> I-objAn SAP

pajtyé-tsó [o úrá-ávye-KI ta-jtyááva]".
pass-caus I follow-sIn-pur my-catch

¹⁴⁸["Juújuj", néé-mutsí]-yé-jucó-vá-a
ok say-<DuM>-only-focus-rpt-rem

ɨhdé-é-u-úvu-tu í piijyú-wá
earlier-per-<sphere>-max-sou self hook-<slab>

dóhjɨ-nú-ne. ¹⁴⁹Áá-ne-má-vá-a
tie-do-<ø> thm-<ø>-with-rpt-rem

nee-mútsi: "Cána bo(h) í-chih-dyu
say-<DuM> suggest well this-<place>-sou

¹⁴⁵ᵃAa-bé-vá-a
thm-<SgM>-rpt-rem

d-eké-évé u-ke muhtsí me
youImp-grab-sIn you-objAn we.DuM SAP

pájtyé-tso-ki". ¹⁵⁰A-hdú-jucó-vá-a
pass-caus-pur thm-<like>-focus-rpt-rem

"DO s-V ¹⁴⁵ᵇS DO s-V ¹⁴⁶ᵃReason V-s "ProSent S s-V. (The -ne of the final verb nominalizes the verb. This may be a case of <Ø> but without -juco.) ¹⁴⁶ᵇQSim S s-V ¹⁴⁷Reason V-s "Link Sim DO s-V Pur_d (where Pur_d = [S V DO]) ¹⁴⁸S Site DO V; S = [["ProSent" V]-head] ¹⁴⁹Cir V-s "Modal Site s-V Pur_d" (where Pur_d = [DO S s-V]) ¹⁵⁰Sim ||

[éké-évé-ébe-ke   di-tyétsí   píjyúcu-ró]-né
grab-sIn-<SgM>-objAn that-<DuM> hook-frs-<ø>

vúdo-ové-h   pííné-e-mó-vú-re.
break-sIn-<t>   middle-per-<big.river>-goal-only

[151]Áá-be-ké-vá-a   tsuuca mehdóbá
thm-<SgM>-objAn-rpt-rem already crocodile

dóó-hií.
eat-<t>

[152]Á-tsih-dyú-vá-a   pé-h íjcya-lle
thm-<place>-sou-rpt-rem go-sub be-<SgF>

úúje-té-h   [tsii-ñe   móóa]-vu.
arrive-go.do-<t> again-<ø> big.river-goal

[153]Aa-llé-vá-a   néé-h i jyéé-ú-wuú-mu-ke:
thm-<SgF>-rpt-rem say-<t> self pet-sg-dim-pl-objAn

"Tá-jye, ta-jyéé-mu-j, í-ñe   mooa mé
my-pets, my-pet-pl-voc this-<ø> big.river SAPImp

tsotsó-jcó te-ne i ará-áve-KI me pájtye-ki".
empty-mTr that-<ø> self dry.up-sIn-pur SAP pass-pur

[154]A-hdú-jucó-vá-a   dii-tyé-wuú-jí ádo-h
thm-<like>-focus-rpt-rem that-pl-dim-pl. drink-sub

íjcya-ró-ne.   [155]Aa-né-vá-a   [té-tsii
be-frs-<Ø>   thm-<ø>-rpt-rem that-<place>

di-lle   ícya-h íjcyá-náa] nihba tsáá-hií.
that-<SgF> be-sub be-while alligator come-<t>

[156]Áá-be-ké-vá-a   neé-lle: "Táhdi-j,
thm-<SgM>-objAn-rpt-rem say-<SgF> grandpa-voc

o-ke pajtyé-tso".   [157]Áá-né-lliihyé-vá-a
I-objAn passImp-caus   thm-<ø>-motive-rpt-rem

hooked the one that grabbed on, broke in the middle of the big river. [151]Immediately a crocodile ate him.

[152]From that place going and going she arrived again to a big river. [153]She said to her pets: "My pet my pets, empty this big river so it dries up and we can cross over. [154]Thus it was that the wee ones were drinking, but in vain. [155]Then while she was there, an alligator came. [156]She said to him: "Grandpa, take me over to

---

S V Loc; S = [DO S V]-head   [151]DO Adv S V
[152]<Sou$_i$> Cir$_s$ V Goal (where Cir$_s$ = [ø$_i$ V Aux-s])   [153]S V O
"Voc Voc DO | DO s-V Pur$_d$ Pur$_s$ (where Pur$_d$ = [S V] and Pur$_s$ = [s-V])   [154]Sim || S V Aux   [155]Link Time S V (where Time = [Loc S V Aux])   [156]O V-s "Voc DO V"   [157]Reason V-s "ProSent Goal s-V Goal (The two goals are appositive, but also general ... specific.)   [158]Sim ||

the other side. ¹⁵⁷Therefore he said: "OK, sit down here on my nose." ¹⁵⁸Thus he took her across.

¹⁵⁹From there she went to her mother, but the mother's two sons ate up that one who arrived. ¹⁶⁰After that her mother took that dead woman's child. ¹⁶¹When he grew up he also killed them.

ne-ébe: "Juújuj, í-chih-vu d-acú-úvé
say-<SgM> ok this-<place>-goal youImp-sit.down-sIn

[tá-tyújú-hó hallú-vu]". ¹⁵⁸A-hdú-jucó-vá-a
my-nose-sg top-goal thm-<like>-focus-rpt-rem

péé-lle-ke di-bye pájtye-tsó-ne.
go-<SgF>-objAn that-<SgM> pass-caus-<ø>

¹⁵⁹Á-tsih-dyú-vá-a [péé-lle
thm-<place>-sou-rpt-rem go-<SgF>

tsɨ́ɨ́jú-mu-dí-vú úúje-té-ró]-lle-ke [tsɨ́ɨ́jú
mother-pl-anim-goal arrive-go.do-frs-<SgF>-objAn mother

hájchi-mútsí] dó-pejtsó-hi. ¹⁶⁰Áá-ne-tú-vá-a
son-<DuM> eat-contact-<t> thm-<ø>-sou-rpt-rem

[díí-lle-úvú-j tsɨɨméne]-ke tsɨɨju ujcú-hi.
that-<SgF>-max-x child-objAn mother get-<t>

¹⁶¹Áá-bé-wuú-vá-a i kyéémé-ne
thm-<SgM>-dim-rpt-rem self grow.up-<event>

té-hdu-re dii-tyétsi-kye dsɨ́jɨ́ve-tsó-hi.
that-<like>-only that-<DuM>-objAn die-caus-<t>

DO S V (where DO = [V-s])

¹⁵⁹Sou DO S V; DO = [[S Goal V]-head], S = [V-s])   ¹⁶⁰Time DO S V (where Time bears -*tu* 'source')   ¹⁶¹S | S* Sim DO V (where S* = [s-V])

Ajcyómé Úmɨhe

They Cultivate the Field

¹Father: Wáha-j, majo [úmɨhe ma
 daughter-voc let's.go.Du field SAP

ájcyo-té-ki]. ²Daughter: Juúju. ³Father:
cultivate.go.do-pur ok

"¿Múha tsáá-hií?" ⁴Daughter: Mehéro
 who come-<t> aunt

tsá-jucóó-hi. ⁵Méhe-j, ¿á u tsá-jucóó-hi?
come-now-<t> aunty-voc y/n you come-focus-<t>

⁶Aunt: Ée, o tsá-jucóó-hi. ⁷Majchó-va-j.
 yes I come-focus-<t> eatImp-come.do-voc

⁸Daughter: Juújuj. ⁹Áyu(h) méhe-j,
 ok fine aunty-voc

éh-du-né-re. ¹⁰Ó oové-jucóó-hi. ¹¹Ayúwa
that-<like>-<ø>-only I full-now-<t> ready

metsu úmɨhé-vu. ¹²Father: Llíhi-j, muha me
let's.go.Pl field-goal son-voc we.ex SAP

pé-jucóó-hi. ¹³Son: Juújuj." ¹⁴¿Mú-cooca
go-now-<t> ok WH-when

ámuha mé óómi-í-hi? ¹⁵Father: Cuúve.
you.Pl SAP do.come-fut-<t> dark

¹⁶Son: Muú-lle-j, [u tsá-cooca] cúdsɨ-tu
 age.mate-<SgF>-voc you come-when pineapples-sou

¹Father: Daughter, let's go cultivate the field. ²Daughter: OK. ³Father: Who is coming? ⁴Daughter: My aunt is coming. ⁵Aunty, are you coming? ⁶Aunt: Yes I am coming. ⁷Come eat! ⁸Daughter: OK. ⁹OK aunty, that is enough. ¹⁰I'm full now. ¹¹OK let's go to the field. ¹²Father: Son, we are going now. ¹³Son: OK. ¹⁴When will you return? ¹⁵Father: Late. ¹⁶Son: Sister, when you come, bring some pineapple so I can eat

---

¹Voc V Pur$_s$ (where Pur = [DO s-V]) ²ProSent ³QS V ⁴S V ⁵Voc Q$_{y/n}$ S V ⁶ProSent S V ⁷s-V ⁸ProSent ⁹ProSent Voc PredCmpl (BE) ¹⁰S PredCmpl (BE) ¹¹Adv V Goal ¹²Voc S s-V ¹³ProSent ¹⁴QTime S V ¹⁵PredCmpl (BE) ¹⁶Voc S Cir$_s$ V DO$_{partitive}$ s-V Pur$_d$ (where Cir$_s$ = [S V]; Pur$_d$ = [S V]) ¹⁷Sim DO s-

it. ¹⁷Also bring manioc for me to eat. ¹⁸I will go hunting so we can eat meat. ¹⁹Father: Let's go by trail. ²⁰Daughter: No, the trail is bad. ²¹Let's go by canoe. ²²Father: OK let's go. ²³Daughter, carry the basket.

²⁴Narrator: Then they went to cultivate the field. ²⁵Then when they arrived at the field, one of the women said, "Is this where I cultivate?" ²⁶Father: Yes, cultivate that place. ²⁷Aunt or Daughter: I will cultivate here. ²⁸Daughter:

tsíva-co	[o lléene-ki].	¹⁷Té-hdu-re baajúrí
bringImp-impl	I eat-pur	that-<like>-only manioc

tsíva-co	[o májcho-ki].	¹⁸Ó llííñájáá-te-é-h
bringImp-impl	I eat-pur	I hunt-go.do-fut-<t>

me dóó-kií."		¹⁹Father: Métsu juuvá-rí-ye."
SAP eat(meat)-pur		let's.go trail-oblIn-only

²⁰Daughter: Tsáhaá, néhní(h) juúva.   ²¹Métsu
no   bad   trail   let's.go

mííne-rí-yé me péé-kií.	²²Father: Juúju, métsu.
canoe-oblIn-only SAP go-pur	ok let's.go

²³Wáha-j, úverújtsí piíchu.
daughter-voc basket carryImp

²⁴Narrator: Aa-né-vá-a   péé-me   [úmɨhe
thm-<ø>-rpt-rem go-<AnPl> field

i ájcyo-ki].   ²⁵Aa-mé-vá-a   [té-pallí-vú
self cultivate-pur   thm-<AnPl>-rpt-rem that-<disk>-goal

úje-té-náa]   tsáá-pille néé-hi: "¿A í-chi
arrive-go.do-while one-<SgF> say-<t>   y/n this-<place>

ó ájcyo-ó-hi?"   ²⁶Father: Éee, é-tsií
I cultivate-fut-<t>   yes that-<place>

d-ájcyo.   ²⁷Aunt or Daughter: Í-chi   ó
youImp-cultivate   this-<place> I

ájcyo-ó-hi.   ²⁸Daughter: Méhe-j, úvérujtsí-vú
cultivate-fut-<t>   aunty-voc basket-goal

V Pur$_d$ (where Pur$_d$ = [S V])   ¹⁸S V Pur$_d$ (where Pur$_d$ = [s-V])   ¹⁹V Instr (where Instr = "the trail")   ²⁰Neg PredCmpl (BE) S   ²¹V Instr Pur   ²²ProSent V   ²³Voc DO s-V

²⁴Link V-s Pur$_s$ (where Pur$_s$ = [DO V])   ²⁵<S$_i$> Cir$_d$ S V: "Q$_{y/n}$ Goal DO S V" (where Cir$_d$ = [ø$_i$ Goal V])   ²⁶ProSent Loc s-V   ²⁷Loc S V   ²⁸Voc Goal$_{theme}$ DO$_{recip}$ s-V Pur$_d$ (where Pur$_d$ = [DO S

Ajcyómé Úmɨhe

o-ke	d-aacu	[baajúrí	o	újcu-ki].
I-objAn	youImp-give	manioc	I	get-pur

²⁹Father:

Juúju,	áyu(h)	éh-du-né-re	muha	má
ok	already	that-<like>-<ø>-only	we	SAP

ajcyó-hi.	³⁰Daughter: Cudsɨ ó újcu-té-h
cultivate-<t>	pineapple I get-go.do-<t>

me	tsájtye-ki."	³¹Father: Ovíi	péjco-re
SAP	take-pur	wait	night-only

mé	cáája-á-h	[mátsájca	me bájtso-ki].
SAP	make.hills-fut-<t>	peanuts	SAP plant-pur

³²Daughter:	Áyu(h),	metsu meh	já-vu.
	ready	let's.go SAP	house-goal

³³Tsúúca	nííjya-ba	tsáá-hií.
already	rain-<liquid>	come-<t>

³⁴Cuuvéh-ré-juco	
dark-only-focus	

teé-ne.	³⁵Father: Wáha-j,	úverújtsí tsiva
that-<ø>	daughter-voc	basket bringImp

me	péé-kií.	³⁶Daughter: Ovíi mútsɨ́ɨtsɨ-ba
SAP	go-pur	wait caimito-<liquid>

o	llééne-ki.	³⁷Father: Métsu. ³⁸Nííjya-ba
I	eat-pur	let's rain-<liquid>

tsá-jucóó-hi.
come-now-<t>

³⁹Narrator:	Aa-mé-vá-a	pé-jucóó-h
	thm-<AnPl>-rpt-rem	go-now-<t>

Aunty, give me a basket so I can get manioc. ²⁹Father: OK, that's all we will cultivate now. ³⁰Daughter: I'm going to get pineapple so we can take them. ³¹Father: Wait and we will make hills tomorrow so we can plant peanuts. ³²OK, let's go to our house. ³³Already rain is coming. ³⁴It is getting dark. ³⁵Father: Daughter, bring the basket so we can go. ³⁶Wait so I can eat a caimito fruit. ³⁷Father: Let's go. ³⁸Rain is coming. ³⁹Narrator: Then they went to their house.

V]) ²⁹ProSent Adv Sim S s-V   ³⁰DO S V Pur$_d$ (where Pur$_d$ = [s-V])
³¹ProSent Time s-V Pur$_s$ (where Pur$_s$ = [DO s-V])   ³²ProSent V Goal
³³Adv S V   ³⁴PredCmpl ‖ S   ³⁵Voc DO V Pur$_d$ (where Pur$_d$ = [s-V])
³⁶ProSent DO S V   ³⁷V   ³⁸S V (Note contrast: *tsá-jucóóh* versus *tsáá-hií* in 33.)

⁴⁰The chief said to them, "Are you coming now?" ⁴¹Group: Yes we are coming now. ⁴²Father: Son, we brought a pineapple for you to eat. ⁴³Son: OK. ⁴⁴ᵃWait I'll eat it. ⁴⁴ᵇI shot a partridge and a spotted cavy for us to eat. ⁴⁵Sis, did you bring manioc? ⁴⁶Yes, wait we eat it. ⁴⁷Father: Daughter have you already cooked the manioc? ⁴⁸Sister: Yes, hurry come eat. ⁴⁹Uncle, hurry come eat. ⁵⁰Uncle: OK. Give me a manioc to eat. ⁵¹Uncle: Also give me a piece

ih jyá-vu.	⁴⁰Áa-me-ké-vá-a
self house-goal	thm-\<AnPl\>-objAn-rpt-rem
ávyéju-ube néé-hi:	"¿A ámuha me
reign-\<SgM\> say-\<t\>	y/n you.Pl) SAP
tsá-jucóó-hi?"	⁴¹Group: Éee, muha me
come-now-\<t\>	yes we.ex SAP
tsá-jucóó-hi.	⁴²Father: Llíhi-j, muha mé tsivá-h
come-now-\<t\>	son-voc we.ex SAP bring-\<t\>
cúdsɨ-ha	[u lléene-ki]. ⁴³Son:
pineapples-\<pineapple\>	you eat-pur
Juújuj. ⁴⁴ᵃÓvíi, o lléene-j. ⁴⁴ᵇÓ añú-h
ok wait I eat-voc I shoot-\<t\>
[tojpá-u-kee, tájcu-kee] [éh-du-me
partridge-sg-objAn cavy-objAn that-\<like\>-\<AnPl\>
me dóó-kií]. ⁴⁵Muú-lle-j, ʔa ú
SAP eat-pur age.mate-\<SgF\>-voc y/n you
tsivá-h baajúri? ⁴⁶Daughter: Éee, óvii me
bring-\<t\> manioc yes wait SAP
májcho-j. ⁴⁷Father: Wáha-j, ¿a tsúúca
eat-voc daughter-voc y/n already
baajúri u tú-jucóó-hi? ⁴⁸Sister: Éee, mé
manioc you cook-now-\<t\> yes SAP
majchó-va-ju-j." ⁴⁹Naáni-j, majchó-va-ju-j.
eat-come.do-quick-voc uncle-voc eatImp-come.do-quick-voc
⁵⁰Uncle: Juújuj. O-ke d-aacu tsá-u-vu
ok I-objAn youImp-give one-\<sphere\>-goal

---

³⁹S V Goal ⁴⁰O S V: "Q$_{y/n}$ S V" ⁴¹ProSent S s-V ⁴²Voc S s-V DO Pur$_d$ (where Pur$_d$ = [S V]) ⁴³ProSent ⁴⁴ᵃProSent S V ⁴⁴ᵇS V DO (where DO = [N N]; Cir$_d$ = [Sim s-V]; the DO is the conjunction of two nouns; *me dóó-kií* is an example of final L becoming L.H) ⁴⁵Voc Q$_{y/n}$ S V DO ⁴⁶ProSent ProSent s-V ⁴⁷Voc Q$_{y/n}$ Adv DO S V ⁴⁸ProSent s-V ⁴⁹Voc s-V ⁵⁰ProSent DO$_{recip}$ V Goal$_{theme}$ Pur$_d$ (where

Ajcyómé Úmɨhe

[o májcho-ki]. ⁵¹Té-hdu-re [tojpá-u
I eat-pur   that-<like>-only partridge-sg

éh-ne]-vu o-ke d-aacu [baajúri-ú-vú
that-<ø>-goal I-objAn youImp-give manioc-<sphere>-goal

o lléhdo-ki]. ⁵²Daughter: Juúju. ⁵³Uncle:
I eat.together-pur   ok

Áyu(h), é-hdu-né-re.   ⁵⁴Te-hdú-juco.
ready   that-<like>-<ø>-only   that-<like>-focus

⁵⁵Uncle and Aunt: Muhtsi me pé-jucóó-hi.
                  we.DuM SAP go-now-<t>

⁵⁶Chief: Juújuj, wá-i mé cuwá-te-j.   ⁵⁷Ovíi
         ok   may-PT SAP sleep-go.do-voc wait

péjco-re mé caajá-hi.   ⁵⁸Uncle and Aunt:
night-only SAP make.hills-<t>

Juújuj, wá-i me íjcya.
ok   may-PT SAP is

⁵⁹Narrator: Aa-né-vá-a   tsúúca
            thm-<ø>-rpt-rem already

pé-jucóó-me ih jyá-vu.
go-now-<AnPl> self house-goal

521

of the partridge so I can eat it together with the manioc. ⁵²Daughter: OK. ⁵³Uncle: OK that's enough. ⁵⁴Thanks. ⁵⁵Uncle and Aunt: We are going now. ⁵⁶Chief: OK you may go to go to sleep. ⁵⁷Wait, tomorrow we will make hills. ⁵⁸Uncle and Aunt: OK, you may stay.

⁵⁹Narrator: Then they went to their house.

Pur$_d$ = [S V]) ⁵¹Sim Goal$_{theme}$ DO$_{recip}$ s-V Pur$_d$ (where Pur$_d$ = [Th S V]) ⁵²ProSent ⁵³ProSent PredCmpl (BE) ⁵⁴PredCmpl (BE) ⁵⁵S s-V ⁵⁶ProSent Modal s-V ⁵⁷ProSent Time s-V ⁵⁸ProSent Modal s-V

⁵⁹Link Adv V Goal

Íllu Múúne Méwákímyeí
This Is How We Work

[1] We first wash real dirty clothes in plain water without any soap. [2] After that, finally we put them through the next thing (with water that is soapy). [3] We repeat that, putting them through three batches of water. [4] We put the white clothes in one place; by contrast we (put) the colored clothes in another place. [5] We wash the white ones at one time; likewise, and the colored ones at another time.

[1] Wájyamúú-né | [[ávyétá ɨhnáhó(h)]
clothes-pl   very   strong

ííñu-vá]-né   tujkénú mé   nijtyú-h
earth-come.do-<ø>   first   SAP wash-<t>

iévé-jpácyo-rí-yé-i   [nijtyú-wa-tu
free-<liquid>-oblIn-only-PT   wash-<slab>-sou

pícyoo-tú-ne].   [2] [Áá-né   boone]   botsíi
put-neg-<n>   thm-<ø>   after   finally

mé   picyóó-h   hállú-vú-é-ne-ri.   [3] Aa-ne
SAP   put-<t>   top-goal-per-<ø>-oblIn   thm-<ø>

mé   waúmi-ivyé-h   pápihchúú-ijyú-vá
SAP   repeat-sIn-<t>   three-<day>-pl

bɨwáá-ne-rí-ye.   [4] Aa-ne   mé   picyóó-h
again-<ø>-oblIn-only   thm-<ø> SAP   put-<t>

tsa-tsíh-vú   ɨ   tsɨtsɨ́-já-hjɨ;   áá-ne-tu
one-<place>-goal   self white-<shelter>-pl   thm-<ø>-sou

... tsa-tsí-ú   óónóva-já-hjɨ.
     one-<place>-goal   colored-<shelter>-pl

[5] Aa-ne   tsa-íjyú   mé   nijtyú-h   tee-ne
    thm-<ø> one-<day>   SAP   wash-<t>   that-<ø>

ɨ   tsɨtsɨ́í-ne;   té-hdu-re   tsa-íjyú
self white-<ø>   that-<like>-only   one-<day>

---

[1] DO | DO* Adv s-V Instr Instr (where DO* = [DO$_{partitive}$ s-V]) [2] TempP Adv s-V Instr*. (Note: Instr* has double case marking.) [3] Link s-V Adv Instr [4] Link s-V Goal DO; Link ... Goal DO. (Note the ellipsis.) [5] Link Time s-V DO | DO; Sim Time ... DO. (Note the ellipsis.) [6a] <DO$_i$> DO^1 V; DO^1 = [[DO^2 V]-head]; DO^2 = [[ø$_i$ s V]-head] [6b] DO | DO Goal* s-V. (Note: Goal* is marked with ablative.)

Íllu Múúne Méwákímyeí

óónová-ne. ⁶ᵃAa-ne [[me dótsu-hcú]-né
colored-<ø>   thm-<ø>   SAP squeeze-mTr-<ø>

me tsíva]-ne mé picyóó-hi. ⁶ᵇPa-ja
SAP bring-<ø> SAP put-<t>   all-<shelter>

néé-ja   pá-ihcyú-tú   mé picyóó-hi.
say-<shelter> all-<frame>-sou SAP put-<t>

⁷ᵃÁá-ne-tu   tsíh-dyu-re   ɨ́ɨva-já-hjɨ́
thm-<ø>-sou other-<like>-only different-<shelter>-pl

mé picyóó-hi. ⁷ᵇMóóhó-u-tu   mé
SAP put-<t>   vine-<sphere>-sou SAP

ɨhdo-tsó-h   úmé-he-wáá-ne-tu.   ⁸[Aa-ne
bite-caus-<t> tree-<tree>-<slab>-pl-sou thm-<ø>

dáárɨ-té-cooca] me újcu-ne mé bewá-nú-hi.
dry-go.do-when   SAP get-<ø> SAP fold-do-<t>

⁹[Aa-ne   me béwá-nú-cooca] tsa-tsíh-vú
thm-<ø>   SAP fold-do-when   one-<place>-goal

tsa-né-e-já-hjɨ́   mé picyóó-hi.
one-<ø>-per-<shelter>-pl SAP put-<t>

¹⁰Áá-ne-tu   íh-dyú-e-né-ré   í
thm-<ø>-sou this-<like>-per-<ø>-only self

vahjá-ba-já-hjɨ́   mé picyóó-hi. ¹¹Aa-ne
torn-mIn-<shelter>-pl SAP put-<t>   thm-<ø>

[tsáávaná-háñé me béwá-nú-cooca] tsá(h) me
blanket-pl   SAP fold-do-when   no   SAP

pícyoo-tú í   úniu páñe-vu.
put-neg self side inside-goal

⁶ᵃWe squeeze them, bringing them, then hang them. ⁶ᵇWe put all the one-piece clothes onto hangers. ⁷ᵃBy contrast, the other kinds of clothes we hang on the clothes line. ⁷ᵇWe pin them to a line with clothespins. ⁸When they are dry, getting them, we fold them. ⁹When we fold them, we put the same kind of clothes in one place. ¹⁰We put the torn clothes by themselves. ¹¹When we fold the blankets we do not put the sides to the inside.

---

⁷ᵃLink DO | DO s-V.   ⁷ᵇSou s-V Sou; The use of -tu 'source' for clothespins is strange; it may be because the clothes hang from them as well as from the clothesline.   ⁸Time Cir$_s$ s-V (where Time = [S V] and Cir$_s$ = [s-V])   ⁹Time Goal DO s-V (where Time = [DO s-V])   ¹⁰Link DO$_{partitive}$ Adv DO s-V (The DO may be appositive to DO$_{partitive}$; the meaning would be "from the clothes, those that are torn.")   ¹¹Link Cir$_s$ Neg s-V DO Goal (where Cir$_s$ = [DO s-V])

¹²Now, when we set the table, we first put on the dishes. ¹³After that, we put the cups on the right side. ¹⁴Also we put a fork on the left side. ¹⁵By contrast, we put a knife and a spoon on the right side. ¹⁶Then we put the food in the middle. ¹⁷Then, after the meal, we clear the dishes. ¹⁸Then after that we gather the crumbs left from the food and put it in the garbage. ¹⁹Then finally after that

¹²Áá-ne-tu   [bohtá-mú méétsá-vu me
  thm-<ø>-sou   dish-pl table-goal SAP

pícyóó-cooca] mé picyóó-h tujkénú bohtá-mu.
put-when   SAP put-<t> first   dish-pl

¹³[Áá-né   booné-tú] mé picyóó-h cané-cóó-né
  thm-<ø>   after-sou SAP put-<t> cup-<cup>-pl

[ɨmɨá nejcú-vu].   ¹⁴Té-hdu-re   mé picyóó-h
 right side-goal   that-<like>-only SAP put-<t>

deíjyú-wa-cóóhá   [nání ñejcú-vu].   ¹⁵Áá-ne-tu
spoon-<slab>-<fork> left side-goal   thm-<ø>-sou

[ɨmɨá nejcú-vú] mé picyóó-h nɨɨtsú-wá-wuu,
 right side-goal SAP put-<t> cut-<slab>-dim

deíjyu-waa   éh-du-ne.   ¹⁶Aa-ne   pɨɨné-vu
spoon-<slab>   that-<like>-<ø>   thm-<ø>   middle-goal

mé picyóó-h majchó-háñe. ¹⁷Aa-ne   [majchó
SAP put-<t> food-pl   thm-<ø>   food

boone] bohtá-mú mé ujcú-hi.   ¹⁸[Áá-né   boone]
after dish-pl SAP get-<t>   thm-<ø>   after

[[[tee-ne   majchó] waahyé-né] cóevá-né   me
   that-<ø> food   pieces-pl be.leftover-<ø>   SAP

píhjyú-cú-ne]   mé picyóó-h [ujpá pañé-vu].
gather-mTr-<event>   SAP put-<t>   garbage inside-goal

---

¹²Link Time s-V Adv DO (where Time = [DO Goal s-V])
¹³TempP s-V DO Goal   ¹⁴Sim s-V DO Goal   ¹⁵Link Goal s-V DO (where DO = [N N Sum])   ¹⁶Link Goal s-V DO   ¹⁷Link TempP DO s-V. (Time is literally "after the food"; it is understood as "after having eaten the food.")   ¹⁸TempP Cir$_s$ s-V Goal   cóevá-né 'leftover-<ø>' is the direct object of me píhjyúcú-ne 'we gather'. If cóevá-né 'leftover-<ø>' is taken as a noun, it is in either an appositive or in genitive construction with the preceding NP, so either Cir$_s$ = [DO | DO s-V] or Cir$_s$ = [[N @ N] s-V]. Another possibility is that tee-ne majchó waahyé-né is the subject of cóevá- 'be left over', so Cir$_s$ = [DO s-V] where DO

Íllu Múúne Méwákímyeí

¹⁹Áá-né   boone   botsíi mé paacyú-h ímí-ñe-úvu.
thm-<ø> after finally SAP wipe-<t> good-adv-max

²⁰Áá-ne-tu   [tee-ne   bohtá-mú   me
thm-<ø>-sou   that-<ø>   dish-pl   SAP

nɨ́jtyú-cooca]   tujkénú   mé   picyóó-h [badééjá
wash-when   first   SAP put-<t>   pan

pañé-vú]   állóóco-jpácyo.   ²¹[Á-jpacyó
inside-goal   hot-<liquid>   thm-<liquid>

pañé-vú]   tsii-ñe   mé cahpíó-h   tsúúco-jpácyó
inside-goal other-<ø> SAP pour.out-<t> cold-<liquid>

[té-jpacyo   áyá-né-wu   i   dyáɨhco-ki].
that-<liquid> little-<ø>-dim   self cool-pur

²²Á-jpacyó-rí   botsíi   mé   nijtyú-hi.
thm-<liquid>-oblIn   finally SAP   wash-<t>

²³Tujkénú   í   imí-ñé-hjɨ   pá-ne-ere   mé
first   self   good-<ø>-pl   all-<ø>-only   SAP

nijtyú-hi.   ²⁴Aa-ne   [[tsɨɨ-jɨ   pañé-vú]
wash-<t>   thm-<ø>   other-<disk> inside-goal

me ɨ́ɨné-tsó-ne]   mé nijtyú-h   tútácó-ihlló-né
SAP move-caus-<event>   SAP wash-<t> cook-<pot>-pl

[mú-hdu-ná   í   ñehní-ñé-hjɨ   íjcya-ne].
how-<like>-<ø>   self bad-<ø>-pl   be-<ø>

²⁵Tsá(h)   múú-ne   néhní-jpácyo-ri   me   nɨ́jtyu-tú
no   WH-<ø>   bad-<liquid>-oblIn   SAP wash-neg

í   imí-ñé-hjɨ.   ²⁶Aa-ne   [pá-ne-ere
self good-<ø>-pl   thm-<ø>   all-<ø>-only

we wipe it thoroughly. ²⁰Then when we wash the dishes we first put hot water in the pan. ²¹We pour in some cold water to cool it off a bit. ²²In that water we finally wash. ²³First we wash all the good things. ²⁴Then after moving those into another pan we wash the cooking pots, however many dirty ones there are. ²⁵Nobody washes the good ones in dirty water. ²⁶Then finally

= [S V].   ¹⁹TempP Adv s-V Adv; *ímí-ñe-úvu* is a degree adverb.
    ²⁰Link Cir_s Adv s-V Goal DO (where Cir_s = [DO s-V])   ²¹Goal DO_i s-V DO_i Pur_d (where Pur_d = [S AdvDeg V]; note that the S of the purpose clause refers to the hot water of the preceding sentence, not to the cold water of the main clause. The two DOs in the main clause are appositive (despite not being adjacent).   ²²Instr Adv s-V   ²³Time DO | DO s-V   ²⁴Link Cir_s s-V DO | DO* (where Cir_s = [Goal s-V]; DO* =

we put them away after we have finished putting them all into another pan with boiling water and scalded them. ²⁷Then we put them away, big dishes in one place and the little dishes in another. ²⁸The cups we put in one place. ²⁹Also we put the spoons, knives, forks and whatever else there is, each in it's place.

³⁰Then, when we sweep, we sweep thoroughly, even the crumbs in

me ímivyé-dú]   [[tsíí-jɨ   pañé-vú]   me
SAP finish-<like> other-<disk> inside-goal SAP

pícyóó-ne] [[wááné-jpacyó-tu   tee-ne   ma
put-<event> boil-<liquid>-sou   that-<ø> SAP

áñú-ne]   me   íjchí-vye-tsó-dú]   botsíi
scald-<event> SAP leave-sIn-caus-<like>   finally

me   páácyu-ne mé   picyóó-hi.   ²⁷Aa-ne
SAP wipe-<ø>   SAP put-<t>   thm-<ø>

tsa-tsíh-vú   tsa-né-e-ne   mé   picyóó-h,
one-<place>-goal   one-<ø>-per-<ø>   SAP put-<t>

bohtá-mú: tsa-tsíh-vú   í   mityá-jɨ-hjɨ,
dish-pl   one-<place>-goal self much-<disk>-pl

té-hdu-re   í   ayá-jɨ-hjɨ   tsa-tsíh-vu.
that-<like>-only self small-<disk>-pl   one-<place>-goal

²⁸Cané-cóó-né   tsa-tsíh-vú   mé   picyóó-hi.
cup-<cup>-pl   one-<place>-goal   SAP put-<t>

²⁹Té-hdu-re   [deíjyu-wáá-ne,   nɨɨtsú-wá-wuú-ne,
that-<like>-only   spoon-<slab>-pl   cut-<slab>-dim-pl

deíjyú-wá-coohá-ñe,   [[ɨɨ-ná   tsa-né-e-ne]
spoon-<slab>-<fork>-pl what-<ø>   one-<ø>-per-<ø>

íjcya]-ne]   tsa-tsɨ́-hjɨ-vu   mé   picyóó-hi.
be-<ø>   one-<place>-pl-goal SAP put-<t>

³⁰Áá-ne-tu   me   llíjyáá-cooca   múú-ne
thm-<ø>-sou   SAP sweep-when   WH-pl

mé   llijyáá-h   pɨrú-ne-úvú   [wááhye-ne
SAP sweep-<t>   complete-adv-max   crumb-pl

[S(quantifier) PredCmpl V])   ²⁵Neg S Instr s-V DO   ²⁶Link Cir$_s^1$ Cir² Adv Cir$_s^3$ s-V (where Cir$_s^1$ = [DO s-V]; Cir$_s^2$ = [Goal ø s-V]; Cir$_s^3$ = [DO s-V], DO = [Sou DO s-V]). Note the use of -*du* 'upon completion' at the end of Cir$_s^3$.   ²⁷Link Goal DO$_i$ s-V DO$_i$: Goal DO, Sim Goal DO. *tsa-né-e-ne* and *bohtá-mú* are appositive, meaning 'each dish.'   ²⁸DO Goal s-V   ²⁹Sim DO Goal s-V (where DO = [N N N [PredCmpl V]])

³⁰Link Cir$_s$ S s-V AdvDeg DO (where Cir$_s$ = [s-V]; DO = [S Loc

Íllu Múúne Méwákímyeí

té-tojcó-jɨ́   pañe].   ³¹Tsá(h) tsa-ne   me
that-<corner>-pl inside   no   one-<ø>   SAP

cóévá-tso-tú.   ³²Aa-ne   tsa-tsíh-vú   bɨɨva   me
remain-caus-neg   thm-<ø>   one-<place>-goal   trash   SAP

píhjyu-cú-né   mé   picyóó-h   ráátá-hóójá   pañé-vú
gather-mTr-<ø> SAP put-<t>   can-<can>   inside-goal

me   wáágóo-ki.
SAP throw.out-pur

³³Áá-ne-tu   tsɨ́ɨ́méne-ke   me   téhmé-cooca
  thm-<ø>-sou   child-objAn   SAP watch-when

mé   tehmé-h   ímí-ñe-úvu.   ³⁴Tsá(h)   me
SAP watch-<t>   good-adv-max   no   SAP

táá-tso-tú.   ³⁵Tsá(h)   me   wápáá-jco-tú.
cry-caus-neg   no   SAP   hit-mTr-neg

³⁶Tsá(h)   néhní-ñé-hjɨ-vu   ma   ájcu-tú   tsɨ́ɨ́méne-ke.
  no   bad-<ø>-pl-goal   SAP   give-neg   child-objAn

³⁷Í-llu-re   mé   ɨ́ɨ́cu-tsó-h   ímí-ñe-úvú-re.
 This-<like>-only   SAP   play-caus-<t>   good-adv-max-only

³⁸Áá-ne-tu   [majcho   me   méénú-cooca]
  thm-<ø>-sou   food   SAP   make-when

[tsí-emé-né   [cúdsɨ-há   dɨ́ɨ́va-ne]
 other-similar-<ø>   pineapple-<pineapple>   likeness-pl

me   ɨhtú-í-cyooca]   tujkénú   mé   nijtyú-h.
SAP   peel-fut-when   first   SAP   wash-<t>

the corners. ³¹We don't allow any to remain. ³²Then we gather together the trash and put it in a can to throw out.

³³When we watch a child, we watch him very well. ³⁴We do not make him cry. ³⁵We do not hit him. ³⁶We do not give the child anything dirty. ³⁷We just help him to play very nicely.

³⁸When we make food and when we are going to peel something like a pineapple we first wash it in cold water. ³⁹Then fi-

---

(BE)]; *pírú-ne-úvú* is a degree adverb.   ³¹Neg DO s-V   ³²Link DO$_i$ s-V Goal Pur$_s$ (where DO = [Goal DO$_i$ s-V]; Pur$_s$ = [ø$_i$ s-V])
  ³³Link Cir$_s$ s-V AdvDeg (where Cir$_s$ = [DO s-V]) *ímí-ñe-úvu* is a manner adverb   ³⁴Neg s-V   ³⁵Neg s-V   ³⁶Neg Goal$_{theme}$ s-V DO$_{recip}$ ³⁷Sim s-V Adv; *ímí-ñe-úvú-re* is a manner adverb.
  ³⁸Link Time^1_s Time^2_s Adv s-V Instr (where Time^1_s = [DO s-V]; Time^2_s = [DO | DO s-V])   ³⁹Link Adv s-V   ⁴⁰Link Adv s-V DO (where DO = [s-V]). Note *-juco*: the Bora peel the pineapple before dividing it so

nally we divide it. ⁴⁰Then finally we peel it after we have divided it. ⁴¹Then after putting it in a dish we finally put it on the table.

⁴²Then after having peeled, divided and washed taro we cook it. ⁴³Then when that is done we take it off the fire, we throw out the water, grind up the other in the grinder and, putting it in a dish, we put it on the table. ⁴⁴Whenever we are going to make something, we first

nú-jpácyo-ri.
water-<liquid>-oblIn

pɨtséu-hcú-hi.
divide-sTr-<t>

pɨtséu-hcú-ne-ré-juco.
divide-sTr-<ø>-only-focus

pañé-vú me pícyoo]-ne
inside-goal SAP put-<ø>

méétsá-vuú.
table-goal.

³⁹Áá-ne botsíi mé
thm-<ø> finally SAP

⁴⁰Aa-ne botsíi mé ɨhtú-h me
thm-<ø> finally SAP peel-<t> SAP

⁴¹[Aa-ne bohtá-jɨ
thm-<ø> dish-<disk>

botsíi mé picyóó-h
finally SAP put-<t>

⁴²Áá-ne-tu [[oona me ɨhtu]-ne me
thm-<ø>-sou taro SAP peel-<ø> SAP

wáwá-jcó-ne me níjtyu]-ne me túú-hi.
divide-sTr-<event> SAP wash-<ø> SAP cook-<t>

⁴³Aa-ne [[[te-ne báábá-cooca] me píñaó]-né
thm-<ø> that-<ø> done-when SAP remove-<ø>

té-jpacyo me wáágóó-ne] [[té-né-hjɨ
that-<liquid> SAP throw.out-<event> that-<ø>-pl

tálliyíjcyo-ri pá-llijyu me tállíyi-jcyó]-né
grinder-oblIn all-<powder> SAP grind-mTr-<ø>

[bohtá-jɨ pañé-vú] me pícyoo]-ne botsíi
dish-<disk> inside-goal SAP put-<ø> finally

méétsá-vu mé picyóó-hi. ⁴⁴Pá-ne-ere
table-goal SAP put-<t> all-<ø>-only

tsí-emé-né me méénú-í-cyooca tujkénú
other-similar-<ø> SAP make-fut-when first

---

this is surprising information. ⁴¹Link Cir_s Adv s-V Goal (where Cir_s = [Goal s-V]; this could also be regarded as the direct object of the main clause)
⁴²Link Cir$_s^1$ Cir$_s^2$ Cir$_s^3$ s-V (where Cir$_s^1$ = [DO$_i$ s-V]; Cir$_s^2$ = [ø$_i$ s-V], Cir$_s^3$ = [ø$_i$ s-V]) ⁴³Link Time Cir$_s^1$ Cir$_s^2$ Cir$_s^3$ Cir$_s^4$ Adv Goal V (where Time = [S$_i$ V]; Cir$_s^1$ = [ø$_i$ s-V]; Cir$_s^2$ = [DO s-V]; Cir$_s^3$ = [DO$_i$ DO Result s-V]; Cir$_s^4$ = [Goal ø$_i$ s-V]) ⁴⁴Cir$_s$ Adv s-V (where Cir$_s$ = [DO

mé nijtyú-hi. ⁴⁵[Té-hdu-re baajúrí me
SAP wash-<t>   that-<like>-only manioc SAP

ɨhtu]-ne mé nijtyú-hi. ⁴⁶[Aa-ne me
peel-<ø> SAP wash-<t>   thm-<ø> SAP

wáwa-jcó]-né me túú-hi. ⁴⁷[[Hééco me
cut.up-mTr-<ø> SAP cook-<t>   meat SAP

wárɨ-hcó-cooca] [aríína-tu tujkénú me pícyoo]-ne]
fry-mTr-when   flour-sou first   SAP put-<ø>

mé wárɨhcó-hi.
SAP fry-<t>

⁴⁸Áá-ne-tu [ado me méénú-cooca] mé
thm-<ø>-sou drink SAP make-when   SAP

ujcú-h nú-jpacyo eevé-ri. ⁴⁹[Á-jpacyó
get-<t> water-<liquid> measure-oblIn thm-<liquid>

pañé-vú] mé picyóó-h tee-ne [ɨɨ-ná me
inside-goal SAP put-<t> that-<ø> what-<ø> SAP

pícyoo-í]-ñe. ⁵⁰[Aa-ne me bóri-jcyó]-né mé
put-fut-<ø>   thm-<ø> SAP stir-mTr-<ø> SAP

ímu-jtsó-hi. ⁵¹Aa-ne botsíi mé picyóó-h
sweet-caus-<t>   thm-<ø> finally SAP put-<t>

méétsá-vuú.
table-goal

wash it. ⁴⁵Also after peeling the manioc we wash it. ⁴⁶Then after cutting it up we cook it. ⁴⁷When we fry meat, we fry it after first putting flour on it.

⁴⁸When we make a drink we get a measured amount of water. ⁴⁹We put into that water whatever we are going to put in. ⁵⁰Then we stir it and sweeten it. ⁵¹Then we set it on the table.

| DO s-V]) ⁴⁵Sim [DO s-V] s-V ⁴⁶DO V; DO = [[DO s-V]-head]
⁴⁷Time DO s-V (where Time = [DO* s-V], DO = [DO$_{partitive}$ Adv s-V])
⁴⁸Link Time s-V DO Instr (where Time = [DO s-V]) ⁴⁹Goal s-V DO | DO*; DO* = [[DO s-V]-head] ⁵⁰Link DO s-V (where DO = [s-V]) ⁵¹Link Adv s-V Goal

Bibliography

Allin, Trevor. 1976. *A grammar of Resígaro*. Horsleys Green: Summer Institute of Linguistics.

Aschmann, Richard. 1993. *Proto Witotoan*. The Summer Institute of Linguistics and the University of Texas at Arlington Publications in Linguistics, no. 114. Dallas: Summer Institute of Linguistics.

Baker, Mark C. 1988. *Incorporation: A theory of grammatical function changing*. Chicago: The University of Chicago Press.

Brack Egg, Antonio, & Yáñez, Carlos (coordinators). 1997. *Amazonía peruana: Comunidades indígenas, conocimientos y tierras tituladas*. Lima: GEF (Fondo Mundial del Ambiente)/Programa de las Naciones Unidas para el Desarrollo) Proyectos RLA/92/G31,32,33.

Chirif, Alberto, & Mora, Carlos. 1977. *Atlas de Comunidades Nativas*. Lima: Dirección General de Organizaciones Rurales, Sistema Nacional de Apoyo a la Movilización Social.

Costales, Piedad, & Costales, Alfredo. 1983. *Amazonía – Ecuador, Peru, Bolivia*. Quito, Ecuador: Mundo Shuar. Pages 86–87.

Dixon, R. M. W. 1982. *Where have all the adjectives gone? and other essays in semantics and syntax*. Berlin: Mouton.

Girard, Rafael. 1958. *Indios selváticos de la Amazonía Peruana*. Ciudad de Mexico: Libro Mex Editores. Pages 85–124.

Jackendoff, Ray. 1991. *Semantic structures*. Cambridge, MA: The MIT Press.

Keenan, Edward L., & Comrie, Bernard. 1977. Noun phrase accessibility and universal grammar. *Linguistic Inquiry*, **8**, 63–99.

Kenstowicz, Michael. 1994. *Phonology in Generative Grammar*. Cambridge, MA: Blackwell.

Kew, Jonathan, & McConnel, Stephen R. 1990. *Formatting interlinear text*. Occasional Publications in Academic Computing, vol. 17. Dallas: Summer Institute of Linguistics.

Langacker, Ronald L. 1991. *Descriptive applications*. Foundations of Cognitive Grammar, vol. 2. Stanford: Stanford University Press.

Marlett, Stephen. 1993. Goals and indirect objects in Seri. *Work Papers of the Summer Institute of Linguistics, University of North Dakota session*, **37**, 1–20.

McCarty, John C. 1988. Is palatalization a mora? *Phonetica*, **43**, 84ff.

McCarty, John C., & Prince, A. S. 1990. Foot and word in prosodic morphology: The Arabic broken plural. *Natural Language and Linguistic Theory*, **8**, 209–283.

Mibeco N., Julia, & Thiesen, Eva. 1974. *Méíhdémúnáaúvú uubállehañe I, (Los cuentos de nuestros antepasados I)*. Colección Literaria Bora N°· 1. Yarinacocha, Perú: Ministerio de Educación.

Mibeco N., Julia, Soria P., Eduardo, & Anderson de Thiesen, Eva. 1975. *Textos folklóricos de los bora: Los cuentos de nuestros antepasados II*. Comunidades y Culturas Peruanas, vol. 2. Yarinacocha, Perú: Instituto Lingüístico de Verano.

Parker, Steve. 2001. The acoustic qualities of Bora vowels. *Phonetica*, **58**, 179–195.

Payne, Doris. 1987. Noun classification in the western amazon. *Language Sciences*, **9**, 21–44.

Ravines, Rogger, & Avalos de Matos, Rosalía. 1988. *Atlas Etnolingüístico del Perú*. Lima: Instituto Andino de Artes Populares. Page 50.

Ribeiro, Darcy, & Wise, Mary Ruth. 1978. *Los grupos étnicos de la Amazonía Peruana*. Comunidades y Culturas Peruanas, vol. 13. Yarinacocha, Perú: Instituto Lingüístico de Verano.

Seifart, Frank. 2002. *El sistema de clasificación nominal del Miraña*. Lenguas Aborígenes de Colombia, Descripciones 13. Bogotá, Colombia: Universidad de los Andes, CCELA.

Steward, Julian. 1948. The Witotoan tribes. *Pages 749–762 of:* Steward, Julian (ed), *Handbook of South American Indians*, vol. 3. Washington, D.C.: Smithsonian Institution, U.S. Government Printing Office.

Thiesen, Wesley. 1957. *The Bora (Witoto) number system*. Vol. 1. Grand Forks: Summer Institute of Linguistics.

Thiesen, Wesley. 1969. The Bora signal drums. *Lore*, **19**(3), 34–42. (also in *Speech Surrogates: Drum and whistle systems,* Part 2 (1976)).

Thiesen, Wesley. 1970. Bora tone modification. Información de Campo, no. 39b. Lima: Instituto Lingüístico de Verano. (field notes, 23 pages of a 29 page microfiche).

Thiesen, Wesley. 1975a. El sistema numérico del bora (huitoto). *Datos Etno-Lingüísticos*, **1**. (14 pages of a 90 page microfiche).

Thiesen, Wesley. 1975b. Terminología bora de parentesco. *Datos Etno-Lingüísticos*, **1**. (12 pages of a 40 page microfiche).

Thiesen, Wesley. 1975c. Un informe breve de la morfología bora. *Datos Etno-Lingüísticos*, **18**. This was written in 1953. (20 pages of a 34 page

microfiche).

Thiesen, Wesley. 1976. Bora. *Pages 7–24 of:* Loos, Eugene (ed), *Materiales para estudios fonológicos I.* Documento de Trabajo, vol. 9. Yarinacocha, Perú: Instituto Lingüístico de Verano.

Thiesen, Wesley. 1989. *El manguaré facilita la escritura del bora.* Colección Literaria y Cultural: Bora N°· 3. Pucallpa, Perú: Ministerio de Educación.

Thiesen, Wesley. 1996. *Gramática del idioma bora.* Serie Lingüística Peruana, vol. 38. Lima: Instituto Lingüístico de Verano.

Thiesen, Wesley, & Anderson de Thiesen, Eva. 1975. Fonemas del bora. *Datos Etno-Lingüísticos,* 1. This was written in 1955. (12 pages of a 40 page microfiche).

Thiesen, Wesley, & Thiesen, Eva. 1985. *El manguaré facilita la lectura del bora.* Colección Literaria y Cultural: Bora N°· 2. Pucallpa, Perú: Ministerio de Educación.

Thiesen, Wesley, & Thiesen, Eva. 1998. *Diccionario bora—castellano castellano—bora.* Serie Lingüística Peruana, vol. 46. Lima: Instituto Lingüístico de Verano.

Thiesen, Wesley, & Weber, David. 1994. *Tone in Bora Possessives.* Presented at the 1994 ELCON.

Thiesen, Wesley, Soria P., Eduardo, & Mibeco, Zacarías (translators). 1982. *Piívyéébé ihjyu Jetsocríjtodítyú cáátúnuháámî.* The Bible League.

Thiesen, Wesley (translator). 1988. *Muhdú pámeere páné iiñújiri ijcyáné miamúnaa meíjcyáiyóne, Homenaje a la Declaración Universal de Derechos Humanos en su 40°· Aniversario 1948–1988.* Lima: Ministerio de Educación.

Weber, David. 2006. *The structural status of Bora classifiers.* unpublished.

Weber, David, & Thiesen, Wesley. 2003. Una sinopsis del tono bora. *Pages 197–228 of:* Solís Fonseca, Gustavo (ed), *Cuestiones de Lingüística Amerindia: Tercer Congreso Nacional de Investigaciones Lingüístico-Filológicas.* Lima: Universidad Nacional Agraria, PROEIB ANDES, GTZ, y Universidad Nacional Mayor San Marcos. (Available in English in the 2001 Work Papers of the Summer Institute of Linguistics, University of North Dakota session. Vol. 45, at www.und.edu/dept/linguistics/2001WeberThiesen.PDF).

Index

A

/a/ for animate objects 354
aa ~ a 'yes/no' 321, 349
a(:)- 'thematic' 177
aa- 'medial or distal pronoun' 240
aábe that-⟨SgM⟩ 396
aáhɨ 'at home' 199
áaj 'Yes, what do you want?' 320
aálle that-⟨SgF⟩ 396
aáme that-⟨AnPl⟩ 396
aamúpɨ that-⟨DuF⟩ 396
aamútsi that-⟨DuM⟩ 396
aanaa 'meanwhile' 397
aane 'then' 397
áá-néllii 'for that reason' 397
abbreviations xxix
able (clitic) 316
about 286
abstract nouns 197
aca 'incredulity' or 'disapproval 321
accusative case 273
active verbs 137
addressee 274
adjective 198, 219
    bound adjectival roots 413
    combined with classifier 223
    derived from verb 113, 198
    enhancing an adjective 226
    negative 325
    suffixes for 226
    used as adverb 226
adverb 157, 198
    adjectives used adverbially 226
    clitics 310
    connective 397
    degree 160, 206, 226
    derived from verb 198
    distance 160
    duration 159
    interrogative 160
    lexical 159
    manner 159
    morphological 157
    place 159
    quantity 160
    reason 160
    time 159
    with imperative 340
adverbial clause 369
    causal 376
    comparative 377
    conditional 371
    counterfactual conditional 372
    locative 376
    manner 377
    motive 298
    purpose 369
    reason 298
    relative clause used adverbially 375
    temporal 373
adverbial clitic
    -ami 'disgust' 315
    -ca 'affirm' 314

clitic
-mei 316
-háaáca ~ -ha 'realize' 313
-haja ~ -ha 'challenge veracity, curiosity, perplexity' 314
-hde 'be able' 316
-i-yo 'contrary' 317
-jtane 'exclude, without regard for' 316
-juco 'focus' 311
-re ~ -ye 'only' 310
-ro ~ -ra ~ -yo ~ -ya 'frustrative, contraexpectation' (frs) 313
-uba 'probable' 312
-véji̧u 'similar to' 317
adverbial clitics 305
affirm (adverbial clitic) 314
affixes
   suffixes with segments 421
   without segments 420
after 289
agreement with numeral phrases 218
ahajchota 'for that time or distance' 397
ahdu 'in that way' 397
áijyu 'at that time' 397
áju 'Here
   Take it
   ' 320
allophonic variation
   of consonants 33
   of vowels 30
alternative questions
   embedded 371
-ami 'disgust' 315
-ami 'incredulity' 421
ami 'or' 319
amuu- 'second person nonsingular pronoun' 231

anaphora 360
anaphoric pronouns
   i 'self' 237
   inanimate 236
animacy 193, 194, 218
   with accusative case 273
animate
   classifiers 163
   concrete nouns 193
   demonstrative pronoun 240
   indefinite pronouns 242
   pronominal connective 396
   qualifier phrases 223
apocope 42
apposition 225, 270, 273
   embedded clauses 381
argument
   of a nonfinite verb 261
árónáa 'but' 397
aspect 154
   habitual 154
   imperfective 154
   with single versus multiple action 154
assimilation of /e/ to /a/ 31
átérée- 'worthless, despicable' 414
átsihdyu 'from that place' 397
ava request for confirmation of reported information 321
avyeta 'very (much)' 160

B

-ba 'multiple action' 139
baa 'below' 199
bases of numeral phrases 212
basic sentence structure 125
-:be ~ -:bye ⟨SgM⟩ 128, 164, 421
beneficiary 298
   with -lliíhye ~ -hlli 298
   with -ma 297
benefit 284
blocking 57, 80

boone 'after' 374
Bora language
    endangerment 5
Bora people
    animal husbandry 16
    bilingual education 4
    bilingualism 5
    burial 21
    clans 465
    dress 18
    drum communication 21
    fishing 15
    food 12
        preparation 13
    history 3
        patronage system 11
    homeland 1
    house construction 16
    hunting 15
    land rights 4
    location 1
    music 21
    population 1
    religion 19
    work 12
bound adjectival roots 413
bound noun
    classifer with 175
bound stem
    followed by classifier 175
bound verbs 116

C

-ca 'affirm' 314
-ca(:) 'bid for affirmation' 422
-ca ~ -cya counterfactual conditional 372, 421
-ca 'animate object interrogative' 352
caa- 'which' 352
caáme 'above' 199
cána (request for permission) 321

case 267
    ablative 282
    about 286
    contrast 290
    partitive 285
    site of attachment 287
    source 283
    time after 289
    about 286
    accusative 273
    beneficiary 297, 298
    causee 275
    circumstance 296
    co-subject 294
    comitative 294
    comparative 299
    contrast 290
    direct object 273
    goal 276
    inanimate oblique 290
        cause or reason 291
        instrument 290
        location 292
        medium 293
        topic of conversation 294
    instrument 296
    location 292
    medium 293
    motive 298
    nominative 268
    object
        of a causativized transitive verb 280
    partitive 285
    reason 298
    site of attachment 287
    source 282, 283
    theme 276
    time after 289
    topic of conversation 294
    vocative 302
    with 294

beneficiary 297
circumstance 296
co-subject 294
comitative 294
instrument 296
causal adverbial clause 376
causative 144
causee 147, 275
of transitive verbs 280
cause 291
causee 275
certainty 161
challenge veracity (adverbial clitic) 314
characteristic 264
chij ~ chii 'surprise or admiration' 320
circumstance 296
clans 465
classifers
explanation and disclaimers 449
list of 450
classifier 128, 163
as a nominalizer 178
classifier subject 127
cognate with derived nouns 170
cognate with incorporated instruments 170
cognate with root 182
derived from verb root 168
following -eme 'similar to' 180
following -e 'pertain to' 180
form 163
forming connective 177
forming participle 168
head of relative clause 178
in qualifier phrases 223
interrogative 175
morphosyntactic features 163
multiple 179

objects as cliticized as 274
structural status of 182
⟨t⟩ and ⟨n⟩ 131
to form qualifier phrase 175
to indicate the subject 173
to make reference specific 179
tone of 94, 171
uses of 173
with adjectives 174, 223
with bound nouns 175
with bound stems 175
with collective nouns 179
with demonstrative 175
with indefinite 175
with nonfinite verbs 177
with numeral 176
with possessive pronoun 179
with quantifier 176
clefts 312
clitic 305
adverbial 310–317
evidential 306–310
nonwitnessed 306
reportative 307
-jɨ́ɨ́va 'deny' 327
with nouns 329
with verbs 328
second-position 305
temporal 151
-co 'implore' 341, 422
co-subject 294
-coba ~ -cyoba 'big, augment' 206, 422
collective
inanimate nouns 196
noun 194, 200
comitative case 294
comparative 299
adverbial clause 377
complement 359
embedded question 364
factive 361

    object 274, 360
    sensory verb 361
    subject 360
complementation 359
compound
    noun 103
        headed by classifier 103
        headed by noun 103
    verb 106
    with bound verb 116
concrete *see* nouns
conditional
    adverbial clause 371
    counterfactual 372
conjunction 319
    list and summation 209
connective 395
    classifier in 177
    form 395
    pronominal 395, 396
    thematic 397
consonant
    inventory 33
content questions 349
context 148
contraexpectation 158
contrary (adverbial clitic) 317
contrast 290
contrastive negation 327
conventional expressions
    onomatopoeic 323
    vocatives 303
conventions xxxii
    citation forms xxxii
    examples xxxii
    index xxxii
    tone xxxiii
    tone derivations xxxiii
    trees xxxiii
-cooca 'when' 373, 422
(-)(j)coojį́-ve 'be tardy (by day), spend the day' 107

counterfactual conditional 372
-:cu 'dual' for inanimates (duIn) 115, 128, 195, 213, 223, 236, 241, 245, 248, 354, 423
-cu 'single action, transitive' 139, 422
-cunu ~ -cyunu 'multiple action' 140, 423

D

degree adverb 160, 206, 226
delinking 57, 82
demonstrative
    modifier 175
    pronoun 240
        animate 240
        inanimate 241
demonstrative pronouns *see* pronouns
deny (adverbial clitic) 327
derivation 99
    by suffixation 108
    by tone change 100
    classifier derived from verb root 168
    verb from noun 109
    verb from verbs 108
    verbal 106
description 264
detransitivization 147, 148
DHT 62
-di ~ -hdi 'animate' 276, 282, 423
-di ~ -hdi 'negative imperative' 330, 423
di- ~ d- 'you, your' 247
    in imperatives 334
di- 'that' in personal pronouns 231
dihñe 'yours' 247
diminutive 207
direct object 273
discourse 395

use of connective 397
disgust (clitic) 315
disjunction 319
distal animate demonstrative pronoun 240
distance adverb 160
-díɨva 'type of' 424
doubt (adverbial clitic) 313
drum communication 21
-du ~ -dyu ~ -hdu 'likeness, similarity, comparative' 299, 377, 424
duration adverb 159

E

-e 'pertain to' 180, 425
ee- ~ eh- 'that' (demonstrative nonproximate) 241
ehdu 'that many' in conjunction 209
éje 'Look' 320
ellipsis 405
embedded questions 364
-eme 'similar to' 180, 426
emphasis 420
   tone with imperatives 340
emphatic negation 327
encounter 117
evidential
   clitic 305, 306
   co-occurrence of 309
   nonwitnessed 306
   reportative 307
excessively 117
exclude (adverbial clitic) 316
exhorbitant see -uvu 'maximal'
exhortation 345
existential presentatives 129
explanation 345

F

factive complement 361

FDLT 60
festivals 7
finalized see -uvu 'maximal'
FLTS 73
focus (adverbial clitic) 311
foot structure 53
free verbs 106
frustrative 158
future tense 149, 429, see projected time
   with negative 150

G

geminate
   glottal stops 36
   vowels 31
gender 193, 218
   in conjoined noun phrases 209
genitive
   construction 251
   proclitics
      comparison with imperative proclitics 337
   tone 252
   uses of 260–266
glottal stop 35
goal 276
   -vu ~ -vyu ~ -u 275
grammatical relations
   in causatives 147
   inversion 278, 280
grammatical tone 65, 88

H

-háaáca ~ -ha 'realize' 313, 426
habitual aspect 154
-haja ~ -ha 'challenge veracity, curiosity, perplexity' 314, 426
-hajchíɨjyu ~ -hajchíɨ 'if' 371, 427
hajchóta 'duration' 375
-hañe 'various, collection, set' 197, 427

-hde ~ -hdye
   'be able' 316
   'concede' 428
-hdi *see* -di ~ -hdi 'negative imperative'
headedness 218
heavy syllables 28, 48
-hi ~ -h ~ ø ⟨t⟩ 43, 131, 225, 428
(-)hijcya 'be' used as 'habitual, characteristic' 154, 429
-hja 'not witnessed' evidential 306, 429
-hjɨ *see* -jɨ ~ -hjɨ 'plural'
-hnécu 'immediate result' 113, 428
-hulle 'yonder' 376

I

-i ~ -iikye 'projected time' 153, 431
-i ~ -ⓛ: 'future' 149, 429
-i 'future'
   in counterfactual conditionals 372
i 'self' 237, 247
í- 'this' (demonstrative proximate) 240, 241
-icho 'somewhat, sort of, a little bit' 227, 431
ideophone 43, 322
if
   conditional adverbial clause 371
   counterfactual conditional 372
-ihde 'before' 375
ihñe 'self's (his, hers, theirs)' 237, 247
(-)iijyéve 'be bothersome' 107
iíjyu 'yesterday' 149
-iikye *see* -i ~ -iikye 'projected time'
ijcya 'be' in conjunction 209
-ijyu ⟨time⟩ 373, 431
imminent *see* projected time

imperative 333
   degrees of strength 344
   emphatic 340
   exhortation 345
   form of 333
   modifying 340
      -co 'implore' 341
      juj 'quick" 341
   negative 330
   plural 334
   proclitics
      comparison with genitive proclitics 337
   softening 347
   tone of 334
imperfective aspect 154
impersonal subject 127
implicit direct objects 136
inanimate
   classifier 167
   concrete nouns 195
   indefinite pronouns 245
   obliques 290
   pronominal connective 396
   pronouns 236
   qualifier phrase 223
inchoative with -nu 107
incorporated instruments 123
   cognate with classifiers and nouns 170
incorporation
   of object 105
incredulity 421
indefinite *see* múúne 'indefinite animate plural'
   modifier 175
   pronouns 242
indefinite pronoun
   animate 242
   inanimate 245
inflection 99
   contrasts in nouns 193

instrument 290, 296
    incorporated 123
interactionals 320
interjections 320
interrogative *see* question
    adverb 160
    modifier 175
    phrase 349–351
    pronoun 351
        animate 351
        inanimate 353
intransitive verbs 136
inversion
    and reflexivization 280
    with 'cover' 278
    with 'give' 278
    with the addressee 274
íñejcúehójtsitu 'from the hand on this side' 215
íñejcúejtúhatyu 'from the foot on this side' 217
-iñu 'go after doing' 118, 431
ɨɨ- 'inanimate interrogative' 353
ɨɨcui 'quickly' 342
-i-yo 'contrary' 317
-iyo ~ -iya 'should, would' 431

J

-j 'vocative' 302, 431
-ja ⟨shelter⟩ (house, clothing,...) 108
-jcátsi 'reciprocal' 146, 148, 432
-je 'come after doing' 118, 432
-jɨ ~ -hjɨ 'plural' 115, 128, 223, 236, 241, 245, 248, 354, 432
-jɨɨva ~ -jɨɨ 'deny' 327, 432
-jkímei 'behave like' 112, 433
-jpi ⟨SgM⟩ 164, 195, 243
-jtane 'exclude, without regard for' 316, 433

-jte ~ -te ⟨AnPl⟩ 200, 231, 243, 441
    versus -me 177
-jtélle ⟨SgF⟩ 164
-jtépɨ ⟨DuF⟩ 164, 195
-jtétsi ⟨DuM⟩ 164, 195
-juco 'focus' 161, 311, 433
-juco(:) ~ -coo 'now' 157, 433
juhúú ~ új (surprise) 320
juj 'quick (vocative)' 341, 433
juújuj ~ juú ~ uú 'Yes!' 320
juuu 'I can't believe it!' 320

K

-ke ~ -kye 'objAn' 233, 273, 433
    with interrogative -ca 352
kee- ~ ke- 'which' 354
-ki 'purpose' 369, 434
kinship 261, 465
    terms for referring *see* figure F.1
    terms of address *see* figure F.2
        brother-in-law–sister-in-law 471
        fathers-in-law–mothers-in-law 472
        grandparent–grandchild 470
        husband–wife 468
        not related by kinship 472
        parent–child 469
        parents-in-law–son-/daughter-in-law 471
        sibling–sibling 469
        uncle/aunt–nephew/niece 470

L

labial-velar obstruent 34
length *see* vowel length
let's go...346
lexical adverbs 159

lexically marked tone 64, 78, 255
light syllables 28
-lle ⟨SgF⟩ 128, 164, 195, 243, 434
-lle 'treat like' 109, 434
-lle 'try to' 117, 434
-(h)lliíhye ~ -(h)llii 'motive'
    beneficiary 298
    reason, motive 298
-lliíhye ~ -hlliíhye ~ -llii ~ -hllii
    'motive' 298–299, 434
lliiñe 'lower part' 199
*LLX constraint 69
Loayza family 4
location 262, 292
locative adverbial clause 376
locative nouns 198
low tone sequences 69

M

-ma 'with' 294, 295, 374, 435
    beneficiary 297
    circumstance 296
    co-subject 294
    instrument 296
    to conjoin noun phrases 208
maáhuúj 'I don't know!' 320
main clauses 125
majo 'Let's (dual) go!' 346, 370
manner
    adverb 159
    adverbial clause 377
maximal see -uvu 'maximal'
-me ~ -mye ⟨AnPl⟩ 77, 128, 164, 435
    for nouns 435
    versus -jte 177
me- ~ ma- 'SAP' 126, 232, 247, 345, 346
    imperative 334
me- ~ ma- 'SAP' 232
medial animate demonstrative pronoun 240

medium 293
meet 117
mehne 'ours (in.)' 247
-mei
    'compassion, pity' 316, 435
    'reflexive, passive' 145, 147, 435
méjtúhatyu 'from our foot' 216
metsu 'Let's (plural) go!' 346, 370
mii- ~ mi- 'two' 213
minimal word 48
minor categories 319
mirative see realize
Miraña 1
mitya 'or' 319
mítyane 'many, much' 222
modifiers
    adjectives used as adverbs 226
    predicate adjectives 225
    prenominal 219
    qualifier phrases 223
mood
    imperative 333
morphology
    derivational 99
morphophonemic 411
motive 298
    adverbial clause 298
-mu 'plural' for animate nouns (plAn) 59, 99, 193, 436
mu 'of whom' 247
muha 'indefinite animate singular' 345
muha 'who' (animate interrogative) 350
~ mu- 351
muhne 'whose?' 247
multiple action
    -ba 139
    inherent 139
    marking intransitive verbs 140
    participle 114

versus single action 137
multiple classifiers 179
-múpɨ ⟨DuF⟩ 128, 193, 194, 196, 436
-mútsi ⟨DuM⟩ 128, 193, 194, 196, 436
muu- 'first person nonsingular pronoun' 231
múúne 'indefinite animate plural' 345
muurá 'confirm' 322

N

-náaáca ~ -náa 'while' 373, 436
name
    shortening of 303
-(:)ne ~ -(:)ñe 'plural' for inanimates (duIn) 195, 437
-ne ~ -hne 'recent past' 152, 438
-ne ~ -ñe 'singular' for inanimate adjectival, numeral and qualifier phrases 437
-ne ⟨ø⟩ 437
    as a classifier subect 437
    event 374
    with adverbial clauses 438
    with an adjective 437
    with complements 438
    with events or circumstances 438
    with relative clauses 438
-ne ⟨n⟩ with negative 131, 132, 330
negation 325
    contrastive or emphatic 327
    future tense 150
    imperative 330
    in finite clauses 326
    postverbal subject 327
    preverbal subject 326
    raising 332
    subordinate clause 326, 331
    with adjective 325
nominal
    inflectional contrasts 193
    suffix 206
nominalization 197
    classifier used for 178
nominative
    case 268
    personal pronoun 232
    with te(:)- 236
nonfinite verb 100
    argument of 261
    tone of 68
nonrestrictive relative clauses 386
nonwitnessed (evidential) 306
noun 193
    cognate with classifier 170, 182
    compound 103
    concrete 193
        animate 193
        inanimate 195
    phrase 189, 225
    pluralizers 200
-nu 'do, become, cause to be, cause to have (do)' 108, 110, 439
number 218
    agreement 126
    in conjoined noun phrases 209
    on noun 200
numeral
    borrowing numeral phrases from Spanish 218
    classifiers with 176
    larger than twenty 218
    paraphrase 214
    phrase 210, *see* -(:)ne ~ -(:)ñe
    with overt nouns 191
ñóóoo expressing happiness 320

O

o 'I' 231

object
  as cliticized classifiers 274
  complement 360
  direct 273
  incorporation 105
  of a causativized transitive verb 280
object complement 274
only (adverbial clitic) 310
onomastic 265
onomatopoeia 161, 322
order of suffixes 206, 207
orthography 27
ownership 260

P

-pa 'multiple action, intransitive' 421
pa- 'all, completely' 115, 176
palatalization 37
pañe 'interior, inside' 199
pápihchúu- 'three' 213
part-whole 261
participle 113, 137
  derived with a classifier 176
  with deverbal classifier 168
particle 320
partitive
  -tu ~ -tyu 'source' 285
passives 147
past tense 420
  recent 152
  remote 152
-pe 'remote past' 152, 420
pejcóve 'be tardy (by night), spend the night' 107
-pejtso 'upon encountering' 117, 439
personal pronoun 231
  form of 231
  use of 234
phrase-final tone changes 70

-pi 'excessively, habitually' 117, 439
pitch of tone sequences 60
pity (adverbial clitic) 316
pivye ~ pivyénu 'desire' 107
-pɨ ⟨DuF⟩ 243
pɨ́ɨ́néehójtsɨ- 'four' 213
place adverb 159
PLTS 70
plural
  for numeral 205
  for quantifier 205
  imperative 334
  of noun 194, 200
population 1
possessed 251
possessive
  genitive construction 251
  pronoun 179, 247
possessor 251
postverbal subject 268, 272
preadjective 160
preaspiration 40, 251
predicate 125
  adjective 130, 225, 268
  complement 129
  locative 130
  nominal 268
present-past tense 149
preverbal subject 268, 358
  constraint 129
probable (adverbial clitic) 312
proclitics
  tone of 93
prohibition 330, *see* iperative, negative535
projected time 153
pronominal connectives 396
pronoun 231, *see* pronominal connectives
  anaphoric 237
  demonstrative 240

animate 240
   distal animate 240
   inanimate 241
   medial animate 240
   proximate animate 240
distal animate demonstrative 240
doubling 271
inanimate
   anaphoric 236
indefinite 242
   animate 242
   inanimate 245
interrogative
   animate 351
   inanimate 353
medial animate demonstrative 240
modified by a relative clause 384
personal 231
   form of 231
   proclitic 270
   use of 234
possessive 247
pronominal connectives 395
proximate animate demonstrative 240
proximate animate demonstrative pronoun 240
purpose clauses 369

Q

qualifier phrases 223
   classifiers to form 175
   form 223
   use 224
quantifier
   classifier with 176
   pluralizer for 205
quantity *see* vowel length
   with monosyllabic roots 49

quantity adverb 160
question 349, *see* interrogative phrase
   answers with -iíkye 154
   content 349
   embedded 364
   embedded alternative question 371
   interrogative pronoun 351
   rhetorical 354
   yes/no 349

R

-ra *see* -ro ~ -ra ~ -yo ~ -ya
-re ~ -ye 'only' 310, 440
realize (adverbial clitic) 313
reason 291, 298
   adverb 160
   adverbial clause 298
recent past tense 152
reciprocal 148
reduplication 43, 161, 322
   with vocative 302
referent tracking 400, 402
reflexives 147
relative clause 379
   genitive 266
   nonrestrictive 386
   relativization into nonsubject positions 391
   relativization into the subject position 389
   restrictive 178
   structure of 380
   used as adverbial clause 375
relocation suffixes 118–120
remote past tense 152, 420
reportative (evidential) 307
resultant
   immediate 113
resulting
   position 114

rhetorical questions 354
-ri ~ -yi 'inanimate oblique' (oblIn) 290, 376, 440
-rɨvaco 'resulting position' 114, 440
-ro ~ -ra ~ -yo ~ -ya 'frustrative, contraexpectation' (frs) 158, 313, 441
    in counterfactual conditionals 372

S

second-position clitic 305
    tense 151
sensory verb complement 361
set membership 265
shortening
    of names 303
    of reduplicated vocatives 302
similar (adverbial clitic) 317
single action
    inherent 140
    small degree 139
    -uve 139
    versus multiple action 137
singular *see* singular action
    by adding a suffix 194
    inanimate noun 195
    noun 194
    of collective noun 200
singular versus multiple
    aspect 154
site of attachment 287
social structure 6
sound symbolism 322
source 283
spatial relators *see* locative nouns
sphere of existence 265
stative verbs 137
stem changes in imperatives 337
stem-forming suffixes 254
subject 125, 268

classifier subject 127
complement 360
marking 333
shortening vowels of personal pronouns 232
subordinate clause
    adverbial 369
    embedded alternative questions 371
    general comments 357
    negation as 326
    negation in 331
    relative 379
    tone 89, 420
suffix
    added to imperative 341
    derivational 108
    order 206, 207
    that modifies noun 206
    used with subordinate clause verb 91
syllable
    heavy 48
    re-syllabification 251
    structure 28
    syllabification and tone 56
    weight 24, 28, 42, 47, 50, 130, 169, 232, 236, 241, 244, 245, 270, 337, 339, 440
    added by -rɨvaco 114
    alternations 50

T

-ta 'corresponding to' 113
ta 'my' 247
tahñe 'mine' 247
-te *see* -jte ~ -te ⟨AnPl⟩
    'become like' 111
    'go to do' 77, 118, 441
te- 'participle' 137
tee- 'previously mentioned' 236
temporal

adverbial clause 373
clitic 151, 305
tense 149, 151
    future 149
    imminent future *see* projected time
    present-past tense 149
    projected time 153
    recent past 152
    remote past 152, 420
    second-position clitic 151
text
    glossed 473
thematic connective 395, 397
thematicity 395
theme 276
    -vu ~ -vyu ~ -u 275
time 264
    adverb 159
    after 289
tone 55
    and grammar 55
    and syllabification 56
    animate classifier 164
    areas for further study 96
    blocking 80
    bumping 88
    changed by suffixation 258
    citation form 76
    conflicts 79
    default high tone (DHT) 62
    default tone of classifiers 94
    delinking 82
      by -jɨɨva 85
      -Ⓛo 'future' 86
      -Ⓛro 'frustrative' 87
      by the person markers 83
      by various suffixes 84
    derivations 62
    emphatic imperative 340
    final default low tone (FDLT) 60
    final low tone split (FLTS) 73
    finite versus nonfinite 102
    future tense 150, 429
    genitive 251, 252
    grammatical 65, 88
    imposed by suffix 76
    in imperatives 334
    in negative preverbal clause 79
    in subordinate clause 358
    interaction of tone and vowel length 75
    lexically marked
      high tones 66
      low tones 65
    making a verb nonfinite 100
    marking the subject 232
    negation 326
    of proclitics 93
    on subordinate clause verbs 89
    overview of basic facts 56
    penultimate low tone split (PLTs) 70
    phrase-final changes 70
    pitch of tone sequences 60
    remote past tense 152
    subordinate clause 102, 420
    the cyclical nature of 63
    the rule of three and boundary marking 95
    to change category 198
    to make nonfinite verbs 68
    tonal elements 60
    with *wai* 'permit' 347
    with classifier 94, 171
    with interrogative pronoun 352
    with noun 171
    writing 27
topic
    decay and reestablishment 404
    establishing 397
    of conversation 294

INDEX 549

toward 288
trace of preposed subject 131
transitive verbs 136
transitivity 136
tsa 'not' 326
-(:)tsa 'one, each (indefinite)' 244, 246, 442
tsa(:)- 'one' 212, 213, 218, 243, 245
-tsi ⟨DuM⟩ 243
tsi(:)- 'other' 243, 245
tsíemé- 'something similar' 245
-tsii ~ -tsih ~ -tsi ⟨place⟩ 283, 376
tsi╪me 'children' 196
-tso ~ -tsa 'causative' 144, 442
-ri 'inanimate oblique'
    cause, reason 291
    instrument 290
    location 292
    medium 293
    topic of conversation 294
-tu ~ -tyu 'source' 282, 283, 376, 443
    about, concerning 286
    contrast 290
    form 282
    partitive 285
    site of attachment 287
    time after 289
(-)tujkénu 'begin' 106
-tu(ne) ~ -tyu(ne) 'negative' 79, 116, 326, 443
typological characteristics xxvii

U

-(:)u derives classifiers from verb roots 115, 168
-u *see* -vu ~ -vyu ~ -u 'goal' or 'theme'
-u ⟨singular⟩ 194
u 'you' 231
-uba 'probable' 312, 444

-úcunu 'singular stative' 444
uj ~ juhuu (surprise) 320
úniu 'along side of, beside' 199
uú ~ juújuj ~ juú 'Yes!' 320
-uve 'single action' 139
-uvu 'maximal' 207, 444

V

-(:)va 'have' 108, 111, 445
-va 'come to do' 118, 446
-va 'plural' for numerals 205, 445
-va 'reportative' 307, 445
valence
    decreasing 147, 148
    increasing 144
    reduction 144
-:ve ~ -:vye 'singular imperative' 446
-:ve 'become' 108, 111
-véj╪u 'similar to' 317, 447
verb
    active 137
    adjective derived from 198
    bound 116
    categories 136
    classifier derived from 168
    derived from noun 109
    derived from verbs 108
    intransitive 136
    made nonfinite by tone 100
    multiple action
        marking intransitive verbs as 140
    nonfinite derived by tone 68
    participle 113
    stative 137
    stem changes in imperatives 337
    structure of 135
    transitive verb 136
vocative *see* addressee, 302
    conventional expressions 303

vowel
    allophones 30
    inventory 29
vowel length 24, 31, *see* quantity
    suppressed by -:cu 'duIn' or -:ne 'plIn' 50
    with anaphoric pronouns as objects 233
    with deverbal classifier 169
-vu ~ -vyu ~ -u 'goal' or 'theme' 275, 376, 447

W

wáábyuta 'benefit' 284
wái 'permit' 322, 347
with 294
word
    flexible order of 126
    formation of 99
    minimal 48
writing system 27
-wuu ~ -wu 'diminutive, very' 59, 77, 207, 226, 227, 447

Y

-ya *see* -ro ~ -ra ~ -yo ~ -ya
-ye *see* -re ~ -ye
yes/no questions 349
-yi *see* -ri ~ -yi 'inanimate oblique' (oblIn)
-yo *see* -ro ~ -ra ~ -yo ~ -ya

www.ingramcontent.com/pod-product-compliance
Lightning Source LLC
Chambersburg PA
CBHW071231300426
44116CB00008B/988